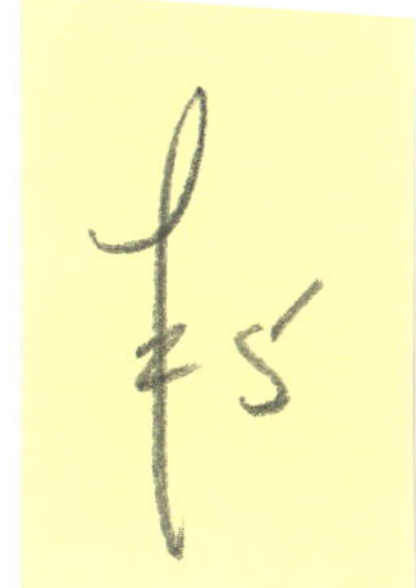

Paul Sandby

PICTURING BRITAIN

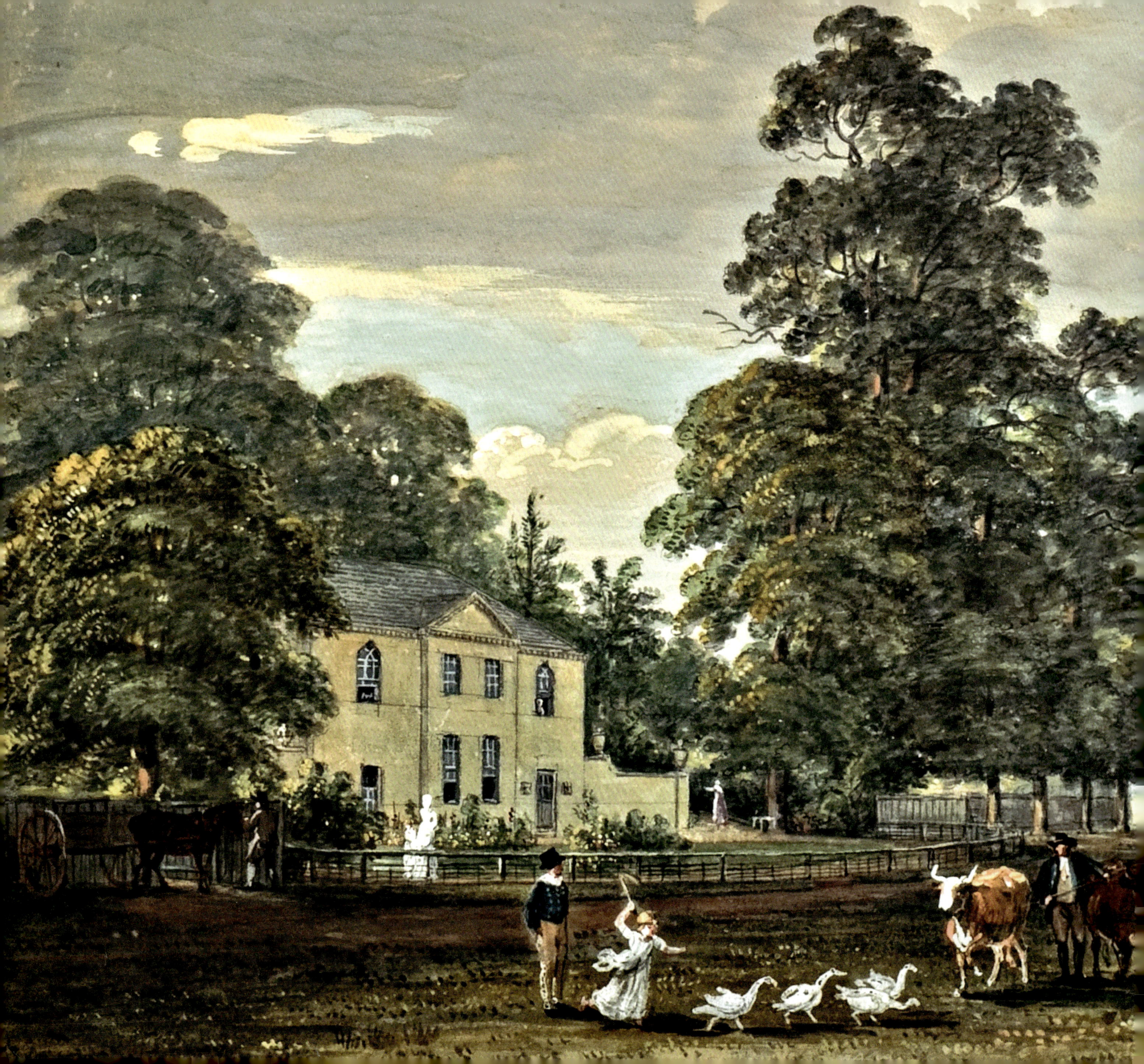

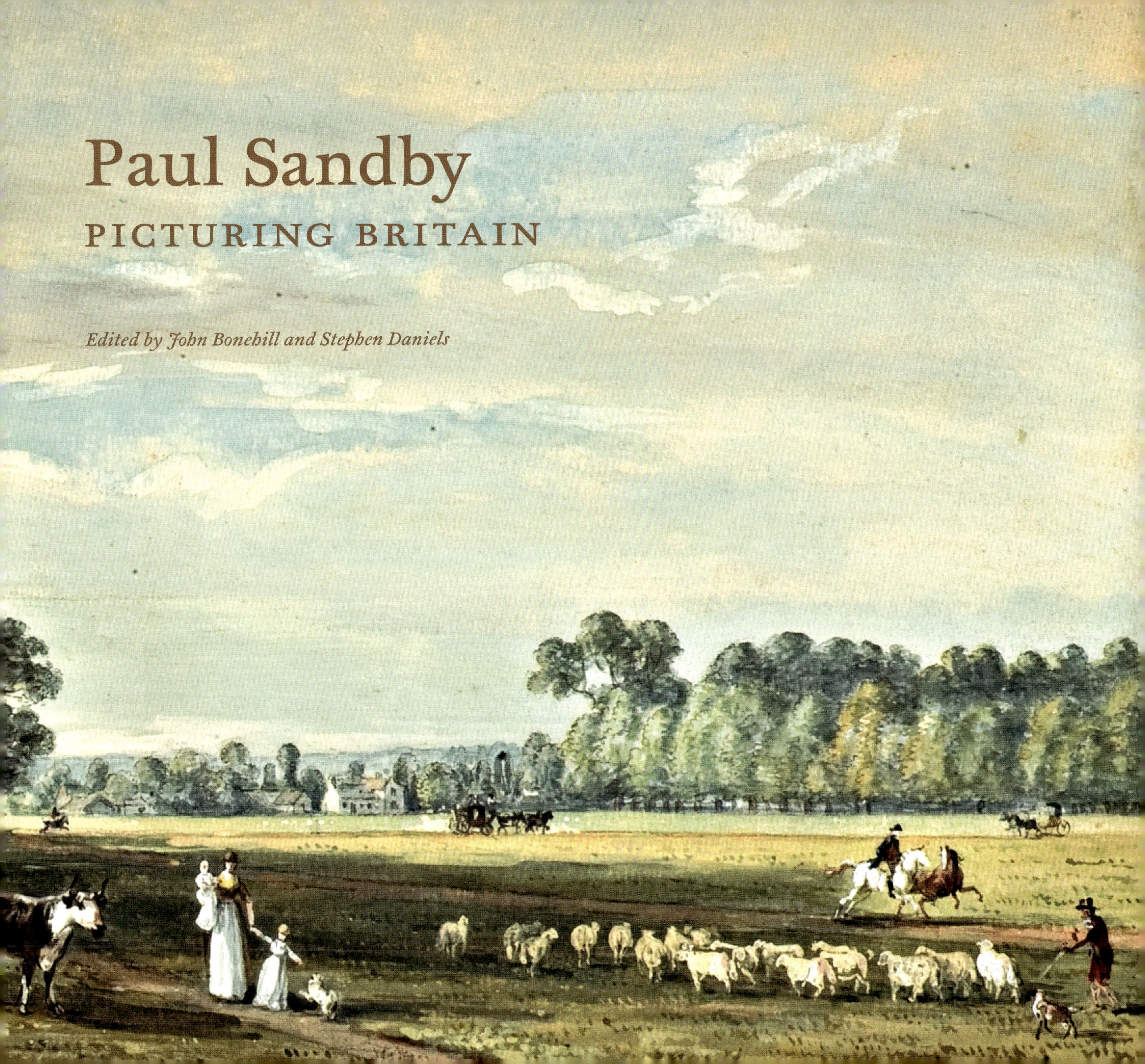

Paul Sandby

PICTURING BRITAIN

Edited by John Bonehill and Stephen Daniels

First published on the occasion of

Paul Sandby (1731–1809): Picturing Britain, A Bicentenary Exhibition

Nottingham Castle Museum and Art Gallery
25 July–18 October 2009

National Gallery of Scotland, Edinburgh
7 November 2009–7 February 2010

Royal Academy of Arts, London
13 March–13 June 2010

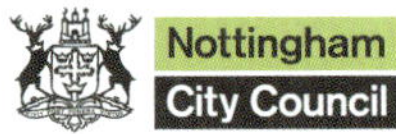

The research for this exhibition and its catalogue was generously funded by the Paul Mellon Centre *for Studies in British Art*

Royal Academy of Arts
2009–2013 Season supported by

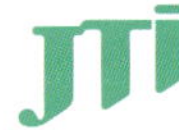

Nottingham City Museums and Galleries, the National Gallery of Scotland and the Royal Academy of Arts are grateful to Her Majesty's Government for agreeing to indemnify this exhibition under the National Heritage Act 1980, and to the Museums, Archives and Libraries Council, for its help in arranging the indemnity.

EXHIBITION CURATOR
John Bonehill

EXHIBITION ADVISOR
Stephen Daniels

EXHIBITION ORGANISER
Sarah Skinner

NATIONAL GALLERY OF SCOTLAND
Christopher Baker, *Curator*
Rosalyn Clancey, *Organiser*

ROYAL ACADEMY OF ARTS
MaryAnne Stevens, *Curator*
Lucy Adams, *Organiser*

PHOTOGRAPHIC AND COPYRIGHT CO-ORDINATION
Lucy Bennett
Miranda Bennion
Sarah Skinner

CATALOGUE
Royal Academy Publications
Lucy Bennett
David Breuer
Carola Krueger
Sophie Oliver
Peter Sawbridge
Nick Tite

British Library Cataloguing-in-Publication Data
A catalogue record for this book is available from the British Library

ISBN 978-1-905711-49-9 (paperback)
ISBN 978-1-905711-48-2 (hardback)

Distributed outside the United States and Canada by Thames & Hudson Ltd, London

Distributed in the United States and Canada by Harry N. Abrams, Inc., New York

Design Philip Lewis
Colour origination Conti Tipocolor

Printed in Italy by Conti Tipocolor

EDITORS' NOTE

All works are by Paul Sandby (1731–1809) unless otherwise stated.

All catalogue entries are by John Bonehill unless otherwise stated.

Titles of works of art are those used at their original exhibition; or those inscribed on the works themselves; or those assigned by various collections.

Dimensions of works of art are given in millimetres, height before width.

The support for all works is paper unless otherwise stated.

Beneath the heading 'Selected Exhibitions' within the catalogue entries, the initials 'RA' followed by a date indicate that a work was exhibited in one of the Annual Exhibitions of the Royal Academy of Arts, London, which have taken place since 1769. The initials 'SA' followed by a date indicate that a work was exhibited in one of the Annual Exhibitions of the Society of Artists, London, which took place from 1760 to 1791. All other exhibitions of works are indicated by an abbreviation that combines the name of the city in which the exhibition first opened with the date of its inauguration. Full details of all exhibition catalogues appear in the Bibliography on pages 238–41, using the same system of abbreviation.

ILLUSTRATIONS

Pages 2–3: detail of cat. 96; pages 10–11: detail of cat. 74; page 12: detail of cat. 50; page 28: detail of fig. 13; page 38: detail of cat. 24; page 48: detail of cat. 60; page 56: detail of cat. 74; page 64: detail of cat. 88; pages 72–3: detail of cat. 3; pages 120–1: detail of cat. 34; pages 152–3: detail of cat. 57; pages 188–9: detail of cat. 84.

Contents

Foreword

Paul Sandby was baptised in Nottingham in January 1731 and died in London in November 1809. Marking the bicentenary of his death, this is the first exhibition to bring together works by this important, if neglected, artist from throughout his long career and from all the major public collections of his work.

Sandby pictured the rapidly changing Britain of his time, its rich variety of people and places, and created a remarkable and innovative range of works. Although he was well versed in continental artistic traditions, Sandby's early employment as a map-maker and draughtsman shaped his innovative approach to landscape. Pictures addressing the contemporary British scene, whether destined for the London exhibition rooms or his patrons' folios and walls, played an important role in cultivating the taste for a new imagery of the nation. Sandby's pictures reward close viewing for they are richly detailed, with social as well as topographical observation. They reveal a world in transition, in which work, leisure and social encounters take place against a backdrop of antiquities and natural wonders, landscape parks and forests, roadside inns, forges and gallows. His pleasure in the process of picture-making enlivens all his work, whether he was producing new scenes or revisiting old ones.

The exhibition was proposed to Nottingham City Museums and Galleries in 2005 by Stephen Daniels, Professor of Cultural Geography at Nottingham University. His direction and support throughout, together with his close involvement with the exhibition and its catalogue, which he has co-edited, are gratefully acknowledged here. Generous funding from The Paul Mellon Centre for Studies in British Art allowed Nottingham City Museums and Galleries to commission Dr John Bonehill to research and select the exhibition and to write its catalogue. The provision of a visiting fellowship at the Yale Center for British Art, New Haven, enabled him to research their rich holdings of Sandby's work. We extend our thanks to these funders and to Dr Bonehill for his conscientious curatorship and his co-editorship and extensive contribution to the catalogue. We thank too the catalogue's other contributors: Nicholas Alfrey, Matthew Craske, Felicity Myrone, Martin Postle, Geoff Quilley and Sarah Skinner.

The works selected for this exhibition have come from both public and private lenders, and include important examples of Sandby's art that are being exhibited for the first time. We record our deep gratitude to all those whose generosity has made possible such a comprehensive and significant review of Sandby's artistic achievement, with particular thanks to Brian Allen, Peter Barber, Amy Meyers, the Hon. Lady Roberts and Scott Wilcox.

The Royal Academy is grateful to JTI, its season supporter of exhibitions in the Sackler Wing of Galleries, and to Lowell Libson for his additional support.

Nottingham City Museums and Galleries are delighted that the exhibition has been supported by such prestigious – and appropriate – touring partners: The National Gallery of Scotland in Edinburgh, the capital city in which Sandby was first employed, mapping the surrounding landscape and sketching the city's street life in his spare time; and the Royal Academy of Arts, London, where Paul and his brother Thomas were foundation members.

PETER MILTON
Head of Cultural Services, Nottingham City Council

MICHAEL CLARKE
Director, The National Gallery of Scotland, Edinburgh

SIR NICHOLAS GRIMSHAW CBE
President, Royal Academy of Arts, London

Acknowledgements

In addition to those listed on the imprint page and in the Foreword, we would like to thank the following people who have assisted us with this exhibition and its catalogue:

Carolyn Anderson
Tristram Aver
Mavis Batey
Nicholas Burnett
Katherine Coombs
Deborah Dean
Anne Dulau
Christopher Fleet
Julian Gascoigne
Andy Graves
Anthony Griffiths
Nicholas Grindle
Kate Heard
Paul Hearnon
Luke Herrmann
Jean Jackson
Russell Jenkins
Paul Joyner
Adrian Locke
Andrew McLean
Elinor McMonagle
Francis Marshall
Lorna Mason
Lynsey Nairn
Katia Pisvin
Kate Retford
Nicholas Savage
Desmond Shawe-Taylor
Tessa Sidey
Robin Simon
Charlotte Topsfield
Clare Walcot
Charles Watkins
Charles Withers
Richard Wrigley

Editors' Preface

JOHN BONEHILL AND STEPHEN DANIELS

Paul Sandby (1731–1809) is a familiar artist whose achievement is yet to be fully recognised. This exhibition, originating in the artist's birthplace, in the year of the bicentenary of his death, explores the range and influence of his output in relation to the cultural world in which he lived and worked. Despite, or perhaps because of, being acknowledged as the 'father of modern landscape painting in water-colours' (a description first used by his obituarists), Sandby is taken for granted, known, yet unknown, often cited, but seldom studied. Examples of his work appear in most key texts on eighteenth-century art and landscape, but authors rarely give them critical attention. Works from his prolific output are found in almost every public collection in Britain (and some abroad), but are rarely seen together. There have been important yet partial exhibitions in his name, drawing largely on one or two major collections, most notably, perhaps, in recent years, Jane Roberts's *Views of Windsor* (1995). However, in contrast to such contemporaries as Richard Wilson, Joseph Wright of Derby or William Hogarth, Sandby has been given no significant retrospective, drawing on all the major collections of his work.

This catalogue accompanies the first exhibition to explore the full range of the artist's practice over the length of his career, and it includes maps, graphic satire and decorative designs, as well as paintings and prints, treating of various subjects, executed in all manner of often innovative techniques and considered in the light of the considerable changes that affected culture and society in the period. Indeed, the bicentenary of Sandby's death provides a convenient moment to re-evaluate his significance to an understanding of the art and culture of the second half of the eighteenth century, not least in terms of recent scholarly concerns with the emergence of art institutions and the expansion of the market for culture in the period, or contemporary attempts to distinguish public and private practice, as well as ongoing assessments of the role of the visual arts in the articulation of an emergent national identity and burgeoning empire. With Sandby's career covering the best part of sixty years, spanning perhaps the most critical phase in the rise of a modern art world in Britain, the anniversary provides an excellent opportunity to take stock of recent art-historical preoccupations and to question why a figure of such major importance has been marginalised.

In addressing these issues and Sandby's vast and versatile body of work, in its figurative as well as topographical aspects, we explore how the artist portrayed the character of the landscape throughout Britain, and indeed contributed to envisioning the country as a nation state from the cementing of the Act of Union with Scotland, after the failure of the 1745 Jacobite Rebellion, to the wars with Revolutionary and Napoleonic France at the century's end. Through extensive tours, initially as a military draughtsman and then as a professional artist, Sandby pioneered the artistic depiction of landscape in Scotland and Wales, and searched out new sites throughout England. His art is arguably unrivalled among that of his contemporaries in its portrayal of the appearance and meaning of a range of subjects, rural and urban, modern and historical, in a country that was experiencing rapid social and commercial development, and engaging with the way business and official interests, including trade, tourism and militarism, opened up new spaces for development and mobilised their resources. This is perhaps best illustrated by reference to the 108 views, all drawn by Sandby, that were published as a set of prints entitled *The Virtuosi's Museum* (1778–81; cat. 76). These ranged over a variety of sites, at considerable geographical remove from each other, surveying antiquities and modern improvements, country seats and prosperous towns, agrarian land and parks, roads, rivers and coastline in areas both familiar and less well known to the principally London-based purchasers of the series. Agriculture and industry feature prominently, as does the movement of materials, goods and peoples. The views portray the British Isles as steeped in history but also undergoing rapid change, and thriving by their 'improvement'. Initially connected with the practice of agriculture, the traditional centre of the nation's economic and social order, the improving impulse had come to extend beyond the land to other areas and activities, promoted both by individuals and government, embracing the personal acquisition of knowledge through drawing or reading, as well as ambitious local and national schemes. If Sandby's art was keenly attentive to the idea of improvement as a gauge of societal progress, and of a stable, well-ordered state, the work he produced towards the end of his career also shows him to have been attuned to the ever more complex and contentious associations that improvement had come to generate by the 1790s and early 1800s.

We have presented the works in four sections, highlighting a number of recurrent thematic concerns in Sandby's art throughout his long career. 'Picture-making' focuses on his early years, both as a military draughtsman and as an independent artist beginning to make a name for himself in London, and introduces the range of Sandby's work in terms of style, subject-matter, media and technique. 'Roads and Street Life' considers the importance of routes, whether as subject-matter or as viewpoint, to a travelling artist like Sandby. 'Antiquities' explores how Sandby addressed the place of the past in a rapidly modernising nation, particularly through architectural studies of its ancient castles and ruined abbeys. The final section considers Sandby's portrayal of estates, in all their cultural variety: from extensive royal and aristocratic parkland to small domestic and commercial gardens, taking in sites of agriculture and industry, raw, mountainous scenery and ancient woodland, as well as views of the surrounding landscape. These four, interrelated sections illustrate the geographical extent and diversity of Sandby's practice as an artist, how his art of travel encompassed the still-novel representation of the Scottish highlands and lowlands, as well as north and south Wales, familiar and less familiar English landscapes and activities. Focused on the complex connections of land and life and their development in various scenes and locations, Sandby's art enlarged and enriched the process of picturing Britain.

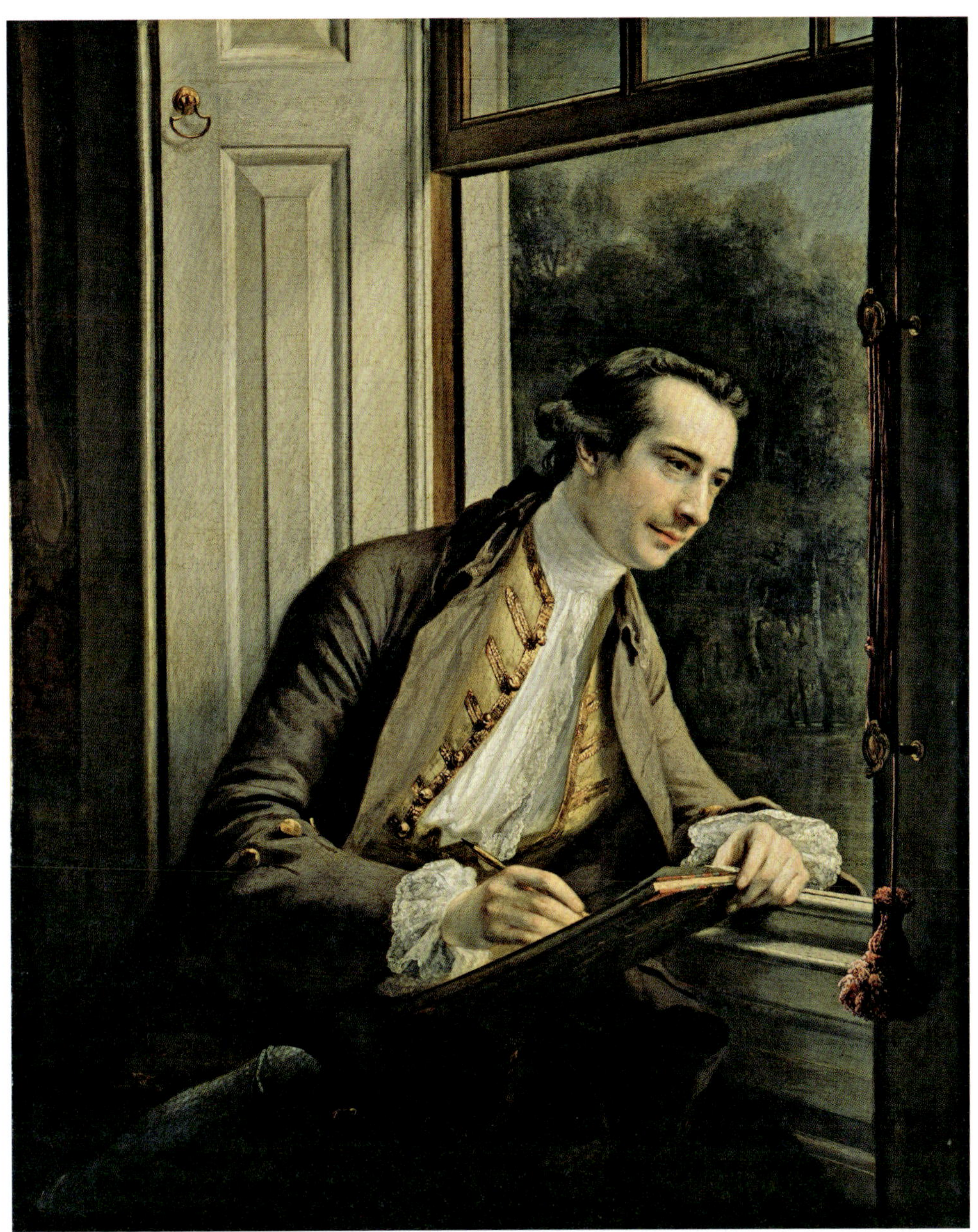

Francis Cotes (1726–1770), *Paul Sandby*, 1761. Oil on canvas, 1251 × 1003 mm. Tate, London

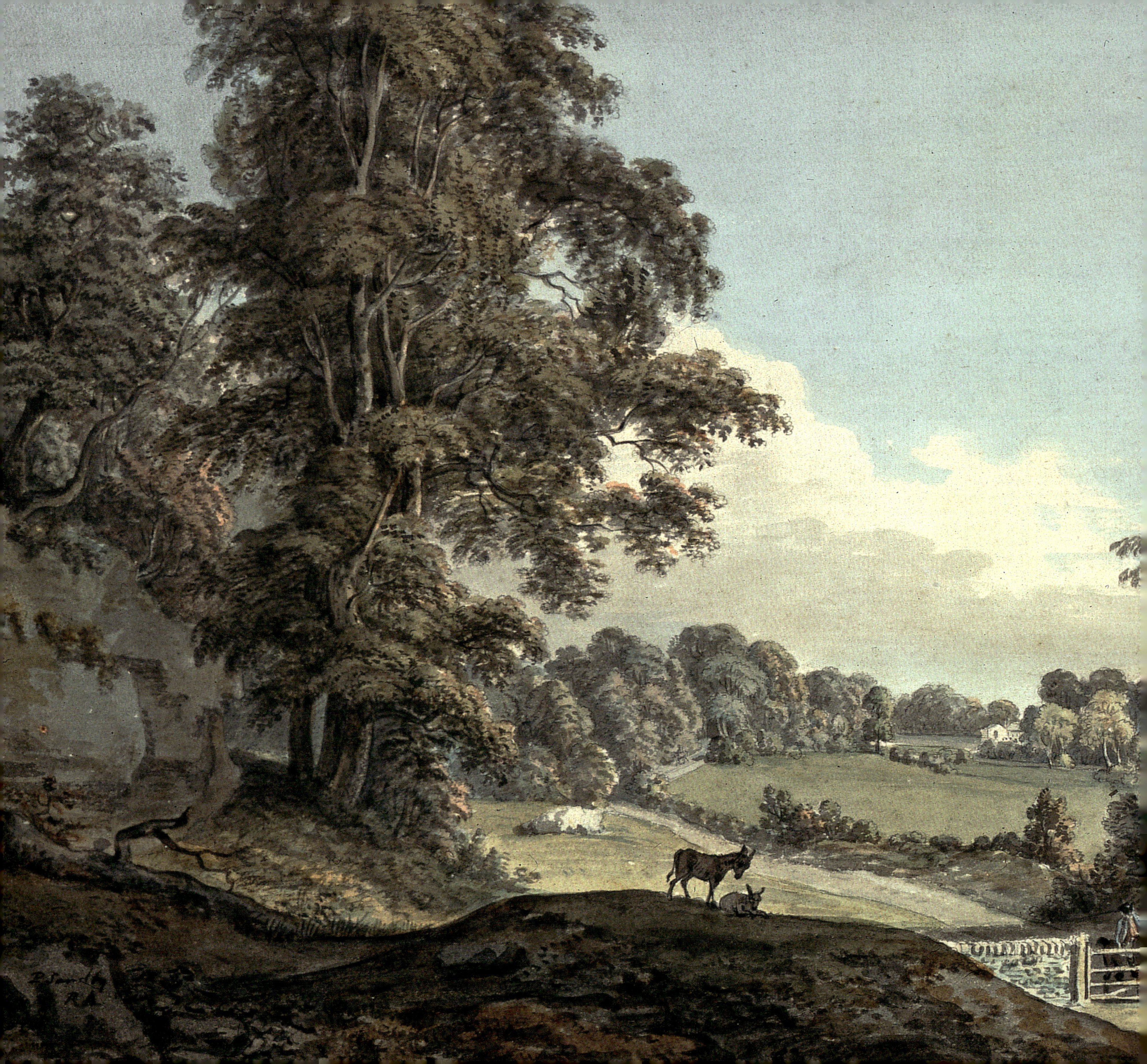

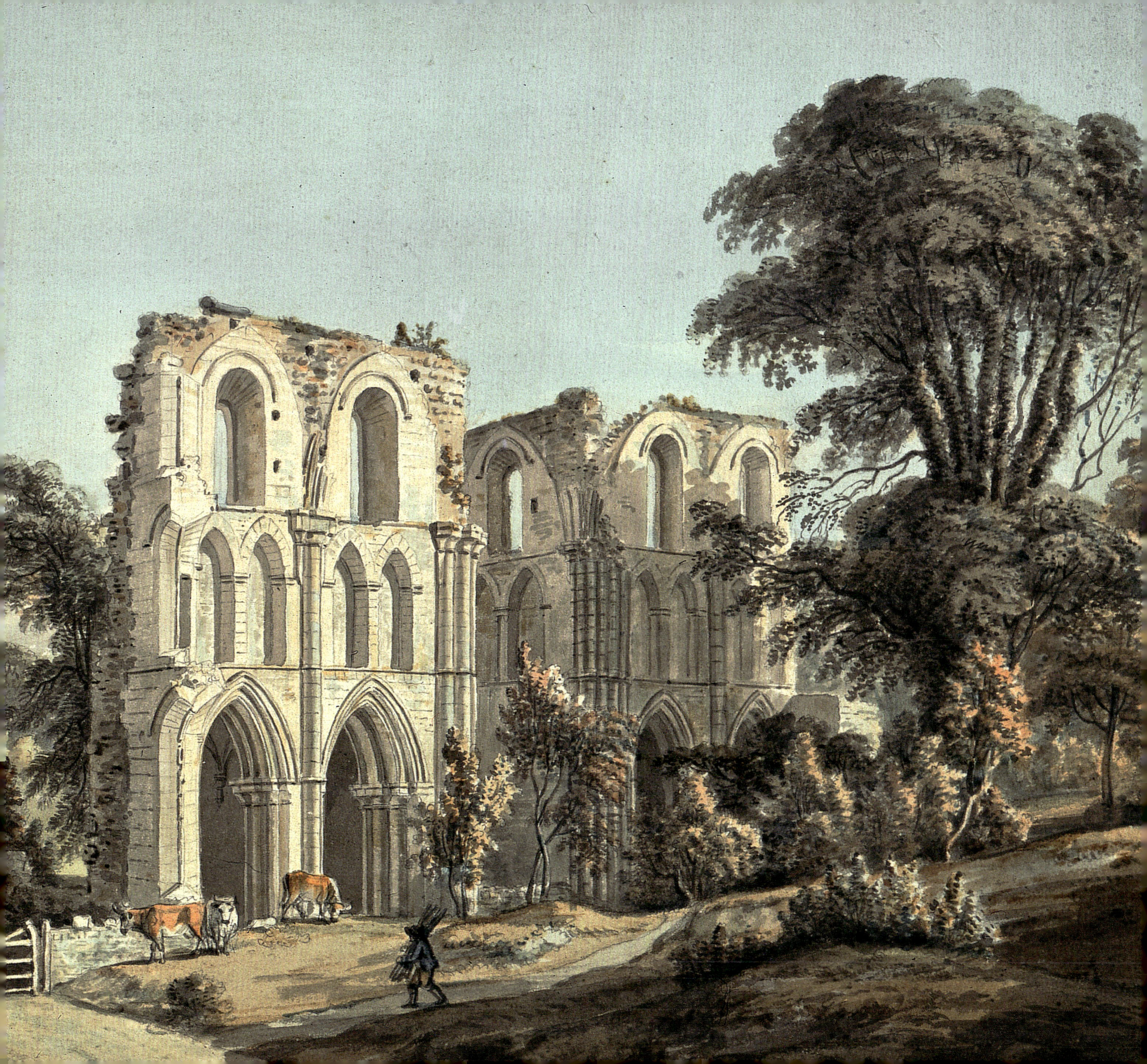

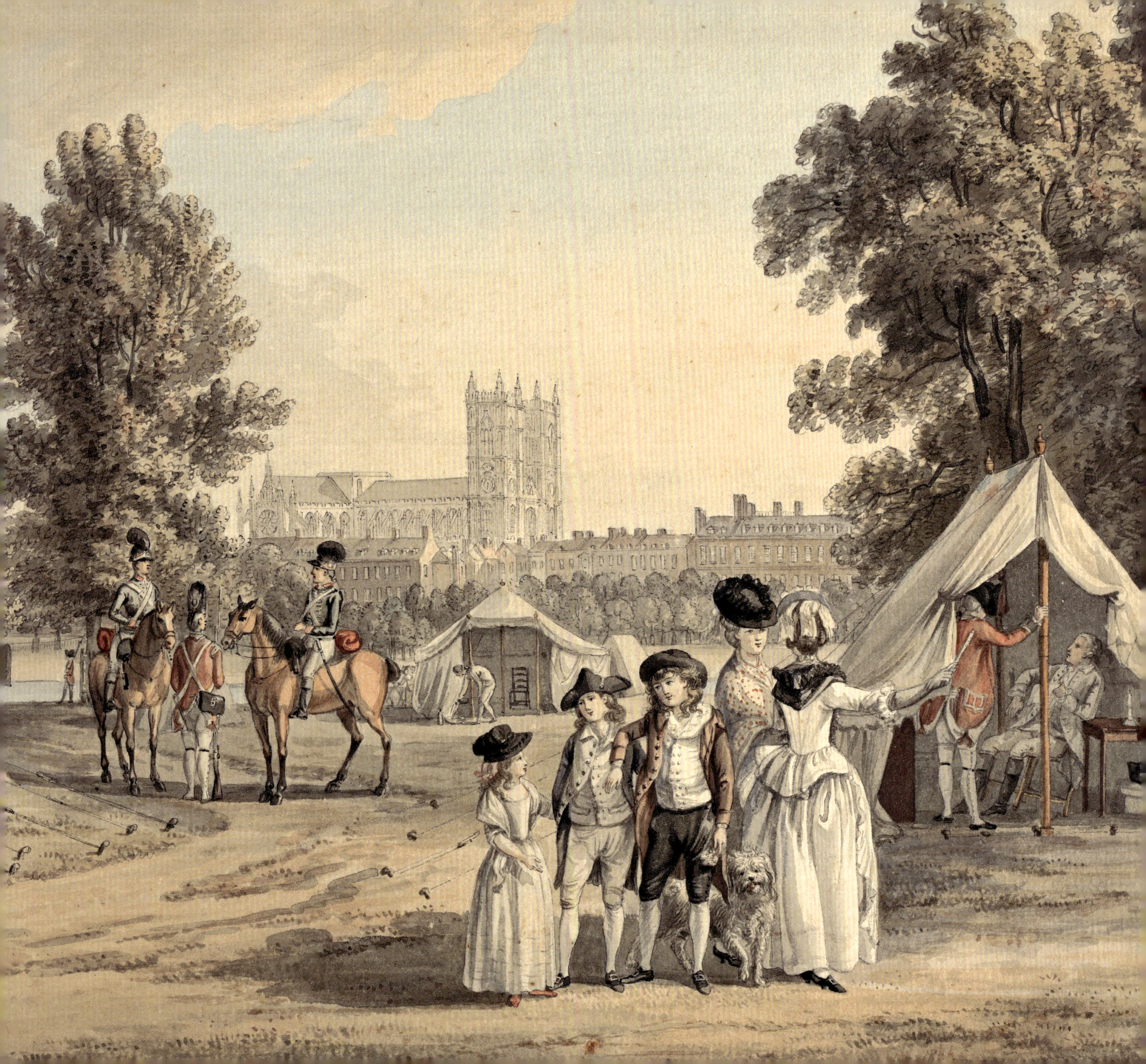

Paul Sandby: Picturing Britain

JOHN BONEHILL, STEPHEN DANIELS
AND NICHOLAS ALFREY

Reviewing the annual Royal Academy exhibition of 1792, the critic of the *Morning Chronicle* was particularly struck by a now untraced picture, entitled simply 'Landscape'. It was the work of Paul Sandby. A prominent figure in the London art world since the 1750s and a foundation member of the Academy, Sandby was deemed by the reviewer 'one of the first English Artists that thought for himself'. Instead of looking to Dutch painters for 'ideas of beautiful scenery and picturesque nature he considered the prospects that are presented in our provinces – took them in the most happy points of view; and, has, by his long practice and taste, formed a style perfectly original and English'.[1] A biographical notice published at the close of the century quoted the poet Thomas Gray to show the cultural range of Sandby's art:

> whose studies have embraced the whole circle of picturesque nature, from the shrub that blossoms in the hedge-row to the poplar that glitters in the glade, 'from the nodding beech, *that wreathes its old fantastic roots so high*, to the majestic oak that towers on the summit of the mountain,' from the cultured vale, waving with yellow grain, to the tremendous rock,
>
> ___ 'Whose lofty brow,
> Frowns o'er the foaming flood below.'
>
> From the frequent contemplation of this variety of scenery, a variety with which Great Britain abounds, he has formed a style peculiarly his own, and peculiarly English, and, among the artists and amateurs of this country, deservedly holds a high character for taste and talent.[2]

For writers on art in the years around 1800, Sandby was esteemed as an artist 'who, by his works, familiarised us with our own scenery', who realised the scenic potential of the national territory, opening up the landscapes of Scotland and Wales for artistic portrayal, searching out the unfamiliar throughout England and portraying the conventional with a fresh eye.[3] He did so as the country was being reshaped, in places transformed, by agricultural, industrial and urban change, and remade, through warfare and trade, as a leading imperial nation state. Sandby's 'peculiarly English' art was particularly attentive to the making and meaning of landscape, and alert to the interaction of people and environment, to the role of skill, technology, communications and social organisation, notably regimes of landed, commercial and military power. This essay examines Sandby's life, work and posthumous standing in terms of the changing geography of Georgian Britain. It considers his career in terms of the places where he lived, drew, taught and travelled, or with which he was closely associated, at the time or in retrospect: Edinburgh and the Scottish highlands and lowlands, north and south Wales, London and its environs, as well as the artist's birthplace, Nottingham. Of particular concern is how Sandby's work was shaped by these places, and how he, in turn, shaped views of them.

In and around Edinburgh

The beginnings of Sandby's career coincide with events and personalities that reinforced the Union of England and Scotland and secured the Hanoverian succession.[4] Following the failure of the Jacobite Rebellion of 1745, the army's Board of Ordnance, the body with responsibility for military infrastructure and mapping, was charged with making 'a compleat and accurate Survey of Scotland',[5] as part of a pacification strategy, 'that a country, so very inaccessible by nature, should be thoroughly explored and laid open'.[6] As well as map-making, this strategy also saw the design and planning of fortifications and buildings, and the construction of roads and bridges. In 1747, the year the resulting Military Survey began, Paul Sandby travelled north to work as 'the chief Draftsman of the fair Plan', in a post almost certainly secured for him by his elder brother Thomas, by then part of the retinue of William Augustus, Duke of Cumberland, Captain-General of forces in North Britain.[7]

In addition to work in the Ordnance Drawing Room at Edinburgh Castle, Sandby accompanied survey teams in a terrain that had recently been a war zone, but he also observed places that had, since the 1707 Act of Union, undergone striking commercial progress in the name of 'improvement', with peasant holdings and common land being replaced by a network of large, powerful estates.[8] The politically influential Andrew Fletcher, Lord Milton, argued that the remedy for the highlanders' support for the Pretender's claims to the throne lay in 'civilising them by introducing Agriculture, Fisherys, and Manufactures, and thereby by degrees extirpateing [*sic*] their barbarity, with their chief marks of distinction, their language and dress, and preventing their idleness, the present source of their poverty, Theift and Rebellion'.[9]

Despite its geographical proximity Scotland was seen – as late as the mid-eighteenth century – as uncharted territory, inhabited by a foreign and 'primitive' people, with its own customs and myths. This sense of a culture at once connected with and different from metropolitan society is

FIG. 1
Paul Sandby, *South Prospect of Leith*, 1747. Pen, ink and watercolour over graphite, 219 × 391 mm. Ashmolean Museum, University of Oxford, WA.C.II.V.219

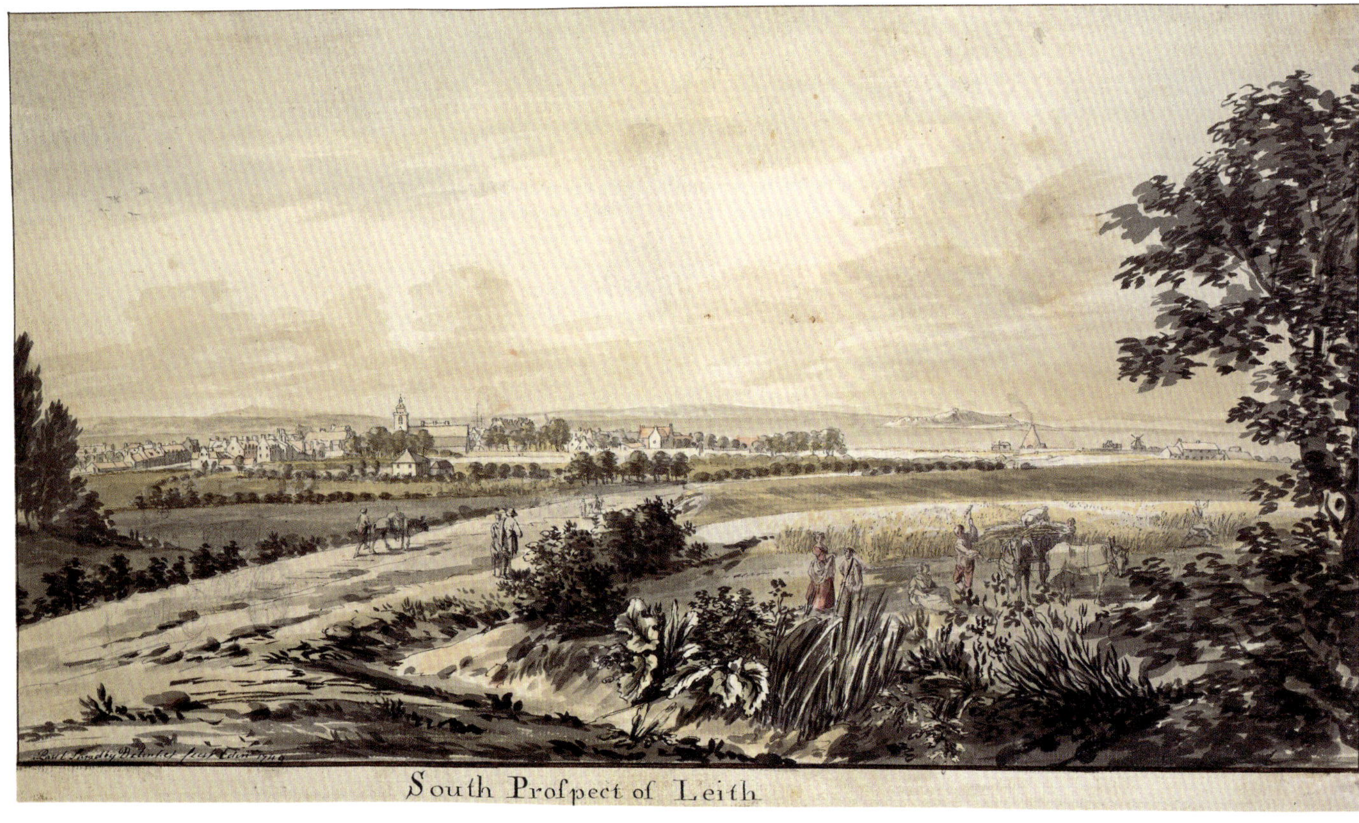

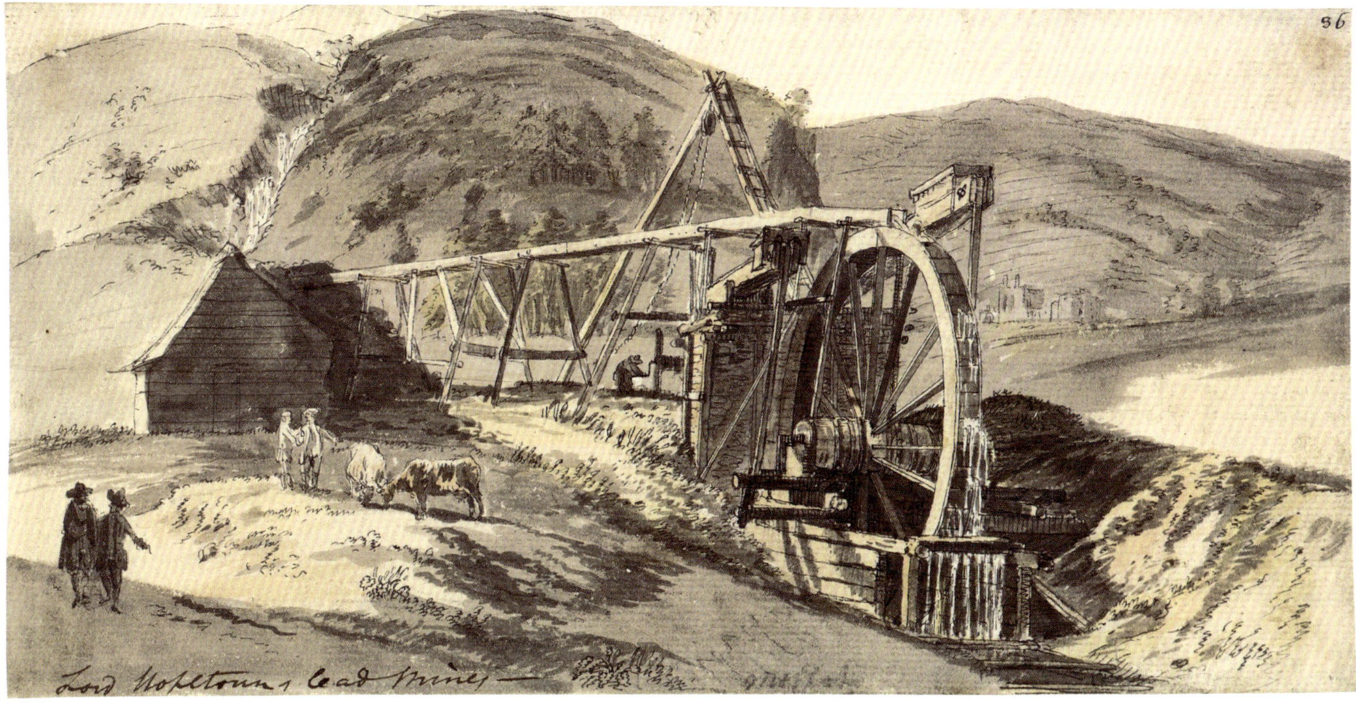

FIG. 2
Paul Sandby, *Lord Hopetoun's lead mine*, 1751. Pen, ink and watercolour over graphite, 123 × 237 mm. Yale Center for British Art, New Haven, Paul Mellon Fund, B1978.39.3

evident in Sandby's remarkable off-duty studies of Edinburgh and Leith street life, which depict a range of ranks and occupations: beggars, lawyers, traders, stallholders, washer-women, criminals, sailors, soldiers and Jacobite prisoners (cats 31–32). Descriptions would often note the chaotic, grubby and dangerous character of Edinburgh's Old Town, a congested area hemmed in by ancient walls, steep, narrow, collapsing and dirty. *Proposals for carrying on certain Public Works in the City of Edinburgh*, a pamphlet published in 1752, complained that 'Confined by the small compass of the walls' there was 'a great want of free air, light, cleanliness, and every other accommodation'. According to the author, Gilbert Elliot, Lord Minto, a local judge and politician, 'few people of rank reside in this city', and it 'is rarely visited by strangers', leaving Edinburgh a place of 'many local prejudices, and narrow notions, inconsistent with polished manners and growing wealth'. A fervent supporter of the recently cemented Union, Elliot saw the commercial prosperity and spirit of improvement evident in the transformation of the lowlands as the spur to 'a project for enlarging and beautifying this city', arguing: 'The improvement of the capital must necessarily bear some proportion to the improvement of the country.'[10]

Many of Sandby's off-duty studies of the landscapes encountered in the surrounding areas record the changes welcomed by improving commentators. *South Prospect of Leith* (fig. 1) details the varied, productive use of the landscape to the north of Edinburgh, from the harvesting of the foreground cornfield to the distant windmill and smoking kiln of the shoreline, and attends closely to the flow of people and produce. If such a view celebrates the benefits of trade and agriculture, other studies record industrialisation, in a Fife fulling mill or a Lanarkshire lead mine on the estate of John Hope, 2nd Earl of Hopetoun (cat. 15, fig. 2). The industrious rustic figures peopling these views of lowland estates stand in stark contrast to the abject, destitute and ragged Jacobites, slumped by a decrepit draw-well, who appear in an etching of 1750 (cat. 18).

The view of Lord Hopetoun's lead mine was probably executed in the spring of 1751, while Sandby was at work on his only recorded private commission of the period, on the nearby estate of Francis Scott, 2nd Duke of Buccleuch at Drumlanrig (cat. 14). A print of the castle and grounds at Drumlanrig published in 1778 has an accompanying letter-press which links the georgic plenitude depicted with the advantages of a modernising estate management:

> ...his Grace is in all respects a warm friend to his country, and by praemia promotes the manufacture of woollen stuffs, and a very strong sort of woollen stockings, and by these methods will preserve on his lands an useful and industrious population, that will be enabled to eat their own bread, and not oppress their brethren, or be forced into exile, as is the case in many parts of North-Britain.[11]

The author of this text, the Welsh antiquarian, naturalist and travel writer Thomas Pennant, had come to know the region and its people to an extent through Sandby's work. Pennant's *Tours of Scotland*, undertaken in 1769 and 1772 and published in 1771 and 1774–76 respectively, did much to publicise the landscape; engravings after Sandby's works featured alongside illustrations by Pennant's servant and personal draughtsman, Moses Griffiths.[12] Pennant was a keen supporter of the Union; indeed, he arguably looked to Scotland as potentially redemptive of a British moral, martial and political life that he considered to have been corrupted by commercial expansion.[13] Accordingly, he assigned to North Britain a key role in defending the achievements of the Glorious Revolution and settlement of 1688, seeing the final defeat of the Jacobite threat and the destruction of highland culture as extreme but necessary measures in removing the remnants of feudalism. On surveying Culloden Moor, Pennant considered it 'the place that *North Britain* owes its present prosperity to, by the victory of *April* 16, 1746', observing elsewhere, 'The rebellion was a disorder violent in its operation, but salutary in its effects.'[14]

These remarks, along with Sandby's studies of the Scottish landscape, should be understood in the context of contemporary attitudes towards travel and its recording. Travel, travel writing and, by extension, pictorial records of the landscapes travelled were political activities. Travel was itself facilitated by progress, by the improvement of roads and means of transport. Features of the landscapes traversed, in turn, prompted political reflection, as the traveller deliberated on visual indications of corruption or improvement, decay or regeneration. Views of the recently contested landscapes of North Britain, ancient or modern, temporarily occupied or settled, populous or desolate, Sandby's drawings provided a pictorial survey of historic sites that had been formative in the securing of the Union. In recording a country in transition, his work responded to the politics that were shaping the terrain and in doing so he also claimed new territory for landscape art.

Windsor and Woolwich

After his return south in 1751, Sandby shared lodgings with his brother in London and stayed with him at Sandpit Gate Lodge, Windsor, where he was now employed. Here the brothers established their near career-long collaboration, in a landscape with which they were to become closely associated. Serving there first under the Rangership of the Duke of Cumberland, Thomas Sandby had a long connection with Windsor Great Park. He was eventually promoted, firstly, to the role of Steward, and, then, in 1765, to Deputy Ranger, a position which appears to have been created for him.[15] His duties extended to estate management, as well as a series of landscape design and engineering projects linked to the park and its embellishment. Although the extent of his involvement in the remodelling of the park during the 1750s is unclear, he was certainly active in the promotion of these activities, publishing a set of eight engravings of the estate in late 1754 (cats 77–80). This lavish series is also significant for establishing the nature of the Sandbys' collaborative enterprise, whereby Thomas's meticulously realised depiction of the topographical features of the landscape is enlivened by Paul's figures. They record Cumberland's recent remodelling of the estate, its improved woodland and plantations, as well as buildings, monuments and striking vistas.[16] Shown in the pictures directing improvements or guiding members of the royal family, Cumberland is represented as a Cincinnatus-like figure, retired from the intrigues of political life. While the obelisk commemorating his quashing of the Jacobite Rebellion looms large, the landscaping celebrated the arts of peace rather than the arts of war, assuaging popular anxieties of a prospective military government.

Views in and around Windsor Castle form an important series of pictures in the mid- to late 1760s (cats 55–62).[17] These surveyed the buildings and their setting from a range of vantage points, close to and at a distance, including close-ups of gardens and gateways as well as expansive prospects of the Thames valley. Variants of these views were to become a mainstay of the works that Paul Sandby displayed in London's then new exhibition rooms, alongside estate and country-house portraits commissioned by some of the most prominent families in the land. This period also saw him acting as drawing master to various members of the royal household, as well as virtual painter-in-residence to the family of Cumberland's aide, George Simon, 1st Earl of Harcourt.[18] It is more than likely that royal favour played its part in securing Thomas Sandby the position of first Professor of Architecture at the newly founded Royal Academy of Arts in 1768, as well as the titles of Grand Architect of the Order of Freemasons in 1775 and joint Architect of the King's Works in 1777, with James Adam. Patronage of this kind had been similarly instrumental in securing Paul Sandby's appointment to the Royal Military Academy at Woolwich a few months earlier.

On assuming the role of Chief Drawing Master at the Woolwich Academy in August 1768, on a salary of £150, Sandby re-entered the employ of the Board of Ordnance. He remained on the staff until late 1796, teaching two days a week, taking lodgings in the nearby village of Old Charlton. While there he took the opportunity of sketching locally in Kent and cultivating the patronage of local estate owners.[19] Established in 1741 for the training of engineers and artillery officers, the Royal Military Academy at Woolwich trained only a minority of officers, but did much to establish the importance of the graphic arts to military culture. Under Sandby's overall tuition officers took daily morning classes in 'Landscapes and Perspective', alongside lessons in French, Latin, mathematics and geography, in a curriculum reflecting refined aspirations.[20] Surviving sketchbooks by Sandby's cadet pupils show them making use of the local landscape, and more especially the buildings and grounds of the Academy itself, to develop perspectival skills. They were encouraged to understand the landscape spatially, as a network of limited prominent landmarks and features, with Woolwich remade as a terrain of prospects and refuges, vantage points and lines of fire. Drawing the landscape was seen as useful, according to the Academy's *Rules and Orders*, in that taking views 'about Woolwich and other places' taught students 'at the same time to break ground, and forms the eye to the knowledge of it'.[21]

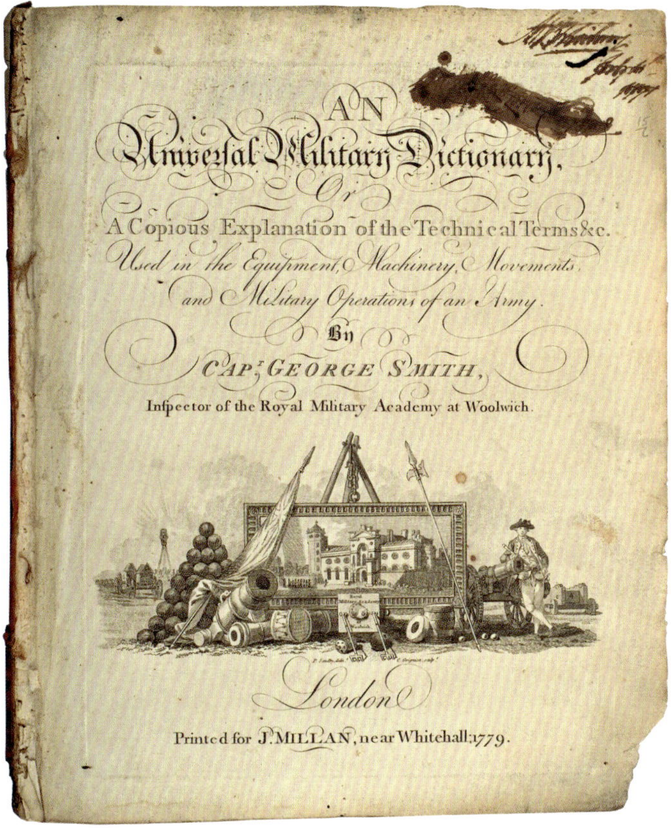

AN
Universal Military Dictionary,
Or
A Copious Explanation of the Technical Terms &c.
Used in the Equipment, Machinery, Movements
and Military Operations of an Army.
By
CAP.T GEORGE SMITH,
Inspector of the Royal Military Academy at Woolwich.
London
Printed for J. MILLAN, near Whitehall, 1779.

FIG. 3
Charles Grignion (1753–1804), after Paul Sandby, Frontispiece to George Smith, *An Universal Military Dictionary*, London, 1779. University of Glasgow Library

An Universal Military Dictionary, published in 1779 by one of Sandby's Woolwich colleagues, Captain George Smith, promoted these skills under the banner of what the author termed 'military science'. Its concerns were demonstrated most eloquently by the elaborate frontispiece, engraved by Charles Grignion after a Sandby design (fig. 3): drum and standard, cannon and shot are arranged around a collection of engineering and surveying instruments illustrative of the arts and science of war, while the gentlemanly status of the cadets trained at the Academy is indicated by the elegantly posed young officer with a telescope. Although the volume places a good deal of emphasis on instrumentation and various aids to military science, the text is also at pains to emphasise the value of practical application and experience: 'Of learning of every kind, theory is the completion,' the author observes, but 'in the study of the military science, it is only the introduction'.[22] This was the guiding principle of Sandby's lessons. While students were encouraged to read 'made-easy' guides on perspective, it was the experience of drawing itself, being brought to bear on a variety of topographies, that formed 'the eye to the knowledge of it'.

Woolwich lessons describing potential battlefields and places of strategic importance, and those learnt in other classes, were disseminated widely, being applied to a kaleidoscopic range of unfamiliar landscapes. The ready adaptability of the pictograms developed by Sandby to the landscapes of Britain's ever-expanding network of territories is striking. Former students like James Pattison Cockburn (1779–1847) and George Heriot (1759–1839) in North America, or William Gravatt (fl. 1790–1867) in the West Indies, ensured Sandby's methods were deployed in a variety of overseas locations.[23] Sandby maintained his links with former students, overseeing the publication of engraved versions of their work, as well as drawings by commanders like Hervey Smith (active 1760) and the colonial administrator and author Thomas Pownall (1722–1805). The artist was instrumental in the publishing of *Scenographia Americana: Or, a Collection of views of North America and the West Indies* (1768), compiled from drawings made by naval officers trained largely at Portsmouth and artillery officers who had studied at Woolwich, and which offered a visual history of the Seven Years War (1756–63), stretching across the east coast of North America, from Montreal to Guadeloupe, then shifting its theatre from the mainland to the Caribbean, following the war's progress.

On the road in north and south Wales

Sandby's first Welsh landscape was a literary one, created before he had visited the principality: *An Historical Landskip, representing the Welch bard, in the opening of Mr Gray's celebrated ode*. For the topography, artist and poet probably both relied on views of Snowdon published by Samuel and Nathaniel Buck or John Boydell in the 1740s. Writing to a friend in October 1761, Gray reported that Sandby and the poet William Mason 'have cook'd up a great picture of Mt. Snowden, in which the Bard & Edward the first made their appearance'.[24] 'Such a picture!' enthused Mason, 'such a bard! such a headlong flood! such a Snowdon! such giant oaks! such desert caves! if this is not the best picture that has been painted this century in any country I'll give up all my taste to the bench of Bishops'.[25] This evidently spectacular but now sadly untraced painting was displayed at the Society of Artists the following year, an exercise in that ambitious form of historical landscape painting practised in the 1760s by Sandby's friend and rival Richard Wilson (1713–1782), a consciously British image, drawing on the contemporary cult of Ancient Britain.[26]

Following his tours of the principality made over three summers in the early 1770s, Sandby made the scenery of Wales a mainstay of his exhibiting and publishing portfolio, represented now from first-hand observation, but also rich in cultural associations, including those of British antiquity. The artist's travels across this landscape came as part of what was, by this period, a well-established working routine, whereby he divided his year between summer travel, generally to the houses and estates of wealthy patrons, and winter teaching and making up pictures for exhibition in London and Woolwich. With little by way of established pictorial precedent, the mountainous landscapes of north Wales, in particular, presented Sandby with a number of challenges, requiring him to improvise a range of compositional strategies. The means by which these works were diffused to a wider public was equally novel. The newly discovered medium of aquatint, named and developed by Sandby, enabled the reproduction of watercolour wash drawings complete with distinctive atmospheric effects.

Those who valued the fidelity of Sandby's views, and their apparent lack of stylistic mannerism, included the country's most fervent promoter of scientific exploration and survey, Joseph Banks (1743–1820), who purchased upwards of seventy of the artist's Windsor views. '*Accuracy* of drawing seems to be a principal reccommendation [*sic*] to Sir Joseph,' the diarist Joseph Farington was later to note.[27] In 1773 Banks employed Sandby on a botanical expedition to south Wales, to retrace the journeys of John Ray (1622–1705), often known as the father of English natural history, accompanied by the naturalists Daniel Solander and the Revd John Lightfoot, with whom Pennant had travelled on his 1772 tour of Scotland. This expedition was to result in a pioneering set of aquatints entitled *XII Views in South-Wales* (1775), 'taken on the spot' and dedicated to Banks and another of Sandby's most enthusiastic patrons, Charles Greville. Lightfoot's journal survives, tracing a tour concentrated on southern coastal areas and then into north Wales via Hereford and Shrewsbury.[28] Directed by botanical interests in the main, the itinerary also appears to have been designed to encompass the ancient monuments that formed the principal focus of Sandby's published views: the ruins of the episcopal palace of St David's or the castles of Chepstow, Cardiff and St Donat's (cat. 71). Sandby's study and recording of such sites in pictorial form might here be seen as analogous to the botanists' collection of specimens of natural history: both activities were part of a desire to know the peculiarities of the region. This extended to the contemporary use of these sites, with Sandby's prints showing scenes of pastoralism, harvesting and quarrying, placing smoking kilns and commercial river traffic alongside architectural reminders of a now distant past. This landscape and its plants, peoples and structures were to be read or appreciated in various ways: as objects of aesthetic apprehension; as a terrain of scientific investigation; and as a repository of history.

Antiquities also featured prominently in a second series of Welsh prints that was published the following year. These were linked to a landscape of income-generating property, and demonstrated an expanded conception of topographic art. As its title page states, *XII Views in North Wales* records 'part of a tour through that fertile and romantick country under the patronage of The Honourable Sir Watkin Williams Wynn' (cat. 93). One of the wealthiest landowners in the country, Wynn had first employed Sandby as a drawing master at his grand ancestral seat of Wynnstay in 1770, paying him handsomely.[29] On his return the following summer, Sandby painted scenes for the house's theatre and accompanied Wynn on a six-week tour of his estate, in a party of fourteen, including nine servants.[30] Conceived as a means to allow Wynn to 'meet his tenants upon coming of age', this survey of his extensive properties was convivial but had a sound practical purpose, not least in securing the political allegiance of neighbours.[31] Surveying the extensive variety of Wynn's pastoral, industrial, natural and historical possessions, the series reconstructs the routes taken and views from them, scenes in contrasting weather and at different times of day, from varied vantage points, by turns fragmentary, compressed and panoramic. The spectator is taken through the territory, with major features like Snowdon both terminating a vista and anticipating the next stage of the tour.

In their shifting, mobile viewpoints and conjunction of contrasting scenes, Sandby's *XII Views in North Wales* conformed to his elder brother's conception of landscape as 'a continual moving Picture', offering an ever-changing 'succession of new and entertaining objects'. The fourth discourse of Thomas Sandby's lectures to Royal Academy architectural students, first delivered in 1770, and given over principally to matters of 'Situation' (the relation of built structures to the surrounding natural scenery), argues that:

> The more cultivated the face of the Country, the more cheerful it will appear; and the different hues of Verdure, produced from the Vernal blossoms to the Autumnal Harvest, gives that endless variety, in shape & colour, which every Eye can perceive, but no pen describe: and if the opening occurs between the rising Hills to a Navigable River, or a High Road, at a distance, they will greatly diversify the Landskip, produce a continual moving Picture and increase our delight by constant succession of new and entertaining objects. The great articles in a prospect, are variety and extent: and altho' there may be something plac'd and composed in a limited View, it will generally be found that the Mind of Man, ever on the search for new matter, either of speculation or Amusement, will naturally tire by the reflection of the same object.[32]

Sandby's views of Wales were eventually to run to four sets and prove particularly influential, establishing codes for picturing the Welsh landscape that were to be imitated by amateur and professional artists alike for the remainder of the century. Such was their success that they came to shape prospective touristic encounters with these landscapes. 'Those that wish to anticipate the views in the intended progress', ran the introduction to Pennant's *Tour of Wales* (1778), 'may satisfy themselves by the purchase of the late publications of the admirable Mr PAUL SANDBY, in whose labours fidelity and elegance are united.'[33]

The appeal to sensation in the Welsh views was developed further in Sandby's spectacular decoration in 1793 of the dining room at Drakelow Hall, Derbyshire, for Sir Nigel Gresley, which was centred on a view of Dolbadern Castle on Llyn Peris, with Snowdon beyond (fig. 4). On visiting Drakelow a year after its completion, the poet Anna Seward found it a room of 'singular happiness':

> It is large, one side painted with forest scenery whose majestic trees arch over the coved ceiling. Through them we see glades, tufted banks, and ascending walks in perspective. The opposite side exhibits a Peak valley, the front shows a prospect of more distant country, vieing with the beauties of the real one, admitted through a crystal wall of window. Its chimney piece, formed of spars and ores and shells, represents a grotto. Real pales, painted green, and breast high, are placed a few inches from the wall and increase the deception. In these are little wicket gates that, half open, invite us to ascend the seeming forest banks. The perspective is so well preserved as to produce a landscape deception little inferior to the watery delusion of the celebrated panorama.[34]

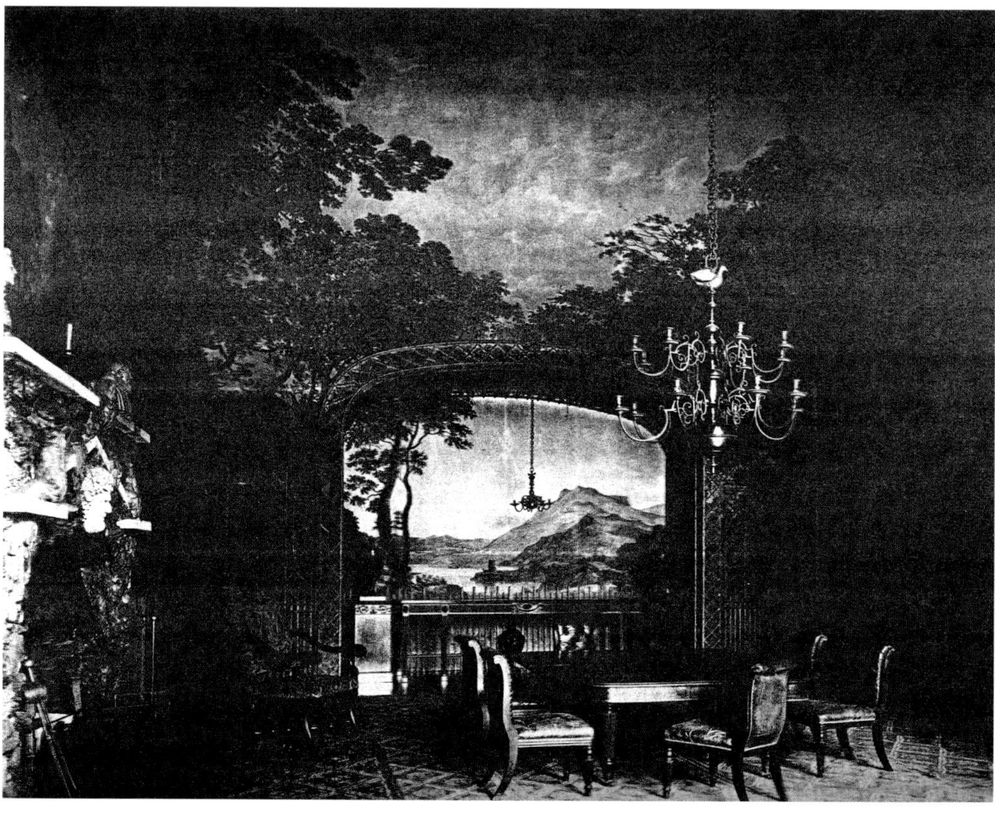

FIG. 4
Paul Sandby, 'Painted Room' at Drakelow Hall, Derbyshire, 1793, as it appeared before its demolition in 1934. Distemper on plaster, H. 6.7 m. Nottingham City Museums and Galleries. A wall is now preserved at the Victoria and Albert Museum, London

In and around London

Throughout his professional career, London was Sandby's place of permanent residence. As the centre of a developing British art world and the pivot of an improving national transport system, London made the stylistic and geographical range of his work possible. Sandby defined his art within the capital's rich and varied world of visual culture and picture-making, commercial drawing, painting and printing in various forms, including maps and trade cards, and popular forms of spectacle and showbusiness, including peep shows, pantomimes and panoramas.[35] No less than the poor street vendors he drew, or the wealthy citizens who purchased his pictures, Sandby was part of the semi-migrant population of the capital, undertaking, as noted above, seasonal sketching tours throughout Britain, sojourning with family, friends and patrons in their villas and country houses, and returning home to London to make and exhibit pictures, teach pupils and socialise. As well as touring Britain in search of subjects, Sandby also journeyed in and around London, in a city which expanded and transformed itself over the course of his career more rapidly than any other, until, by his death in 1809, it had become the world's major metropolis and its most powerful imperial city.

For twenty years or so, from around 1752, Sandby lived in Soho, at the centre of the art world, with its exhibition rooms, art classes, coffee houses, taverns and the houses and studios of painters, engravers, sculptors, architects and framers and gilders. He lodged with his brother for a few years in Poultney Street, where they ran an evening life class followed by a night's eating and drinking, then moved a short distance away to Dufours Court upon his marriage to Anne Stogden in 1757, before settling in Poland Street in 1766.[36] The developing London art world was highly factional, with shifting alliances, and Sandby made his mark early, launching a series of hostile satires against London's leading artist William Hogarth (cats 21–28).[37]

Sandby produced his own distinctive view of the capital in *Six London Views* and *Twelve London Cries*. The published *Cries* (1760) are one of several sets projected by Sandby, comprising over seventy extant drawings of an extensive array of street-sellers (see cats 35, 40–49). If many of the *Cries* figures had a long ancestry in European popular art, others are novel, including the discharged sailor hawking stockings at Charing Cross (cat. 45). The entire series is given a sharp contemporary significance in the urban imagination of the time by the unappealing look and demeanour of the characters, some sullen, others confrontational, a rogues' gallery of vagabonds and outcasts of the kind who provoked campaigns to reform and replan the streets of London in order to create a more stately civic landscape.[38]

Engraved by Edward Rooker, *Six London Views* (1766) is a collaborative project by the Sandby brothers; it depicts the city as both a living entity and an architectural model. Thomas Sandby's Academy discourses, delivered while he was Professor of Architecture at the Royal Academy (1768–98), contrasted the dual claims that inform the writings of many cultural observers of the day, including John Gwynn's *London and Westminster Improved* (1766): public, civic virtue on the one hand, private, metropolitan enterprise on the other, the new world of commerce versus the eternal verities of taste.[39] 'As London is the centre of pleasure and magnificence,' stated Sandby's fourth lecture, 'so it should seem, undoubtedly, the proper stage for action in every scene of life, for men of talents to perform their parts, and to receive the applause due to their merit.'[40] A version of Thomas Sandby's imaginative scheme for a Bridge of Magnificence across the Thames by Somerset House – an image of London *as it should be* – forms the advertisement for *Six London Views*, which are images of London *as it is*, focused on existing examples of architectural magnificence within a more piecemeal urban fabric, including a variety of figures going about their work and leisure. These scenes encompassed buildings by Inigo Jones, among them a view of the Banqueting House (fig. 5) from a yard in Whitehall animated by figures, with two men discussing a copy of Jonathan's Swift's verse 'Van's House' (1701), which lampooned the small dwelling erected by the playwright-architect Sir John Vanbrugh in the yard, and a group of watermen, heading for the public landing stage known as Whitehall Steps, gesticulating to a serving maid at a window on the far side of the yard.[41]

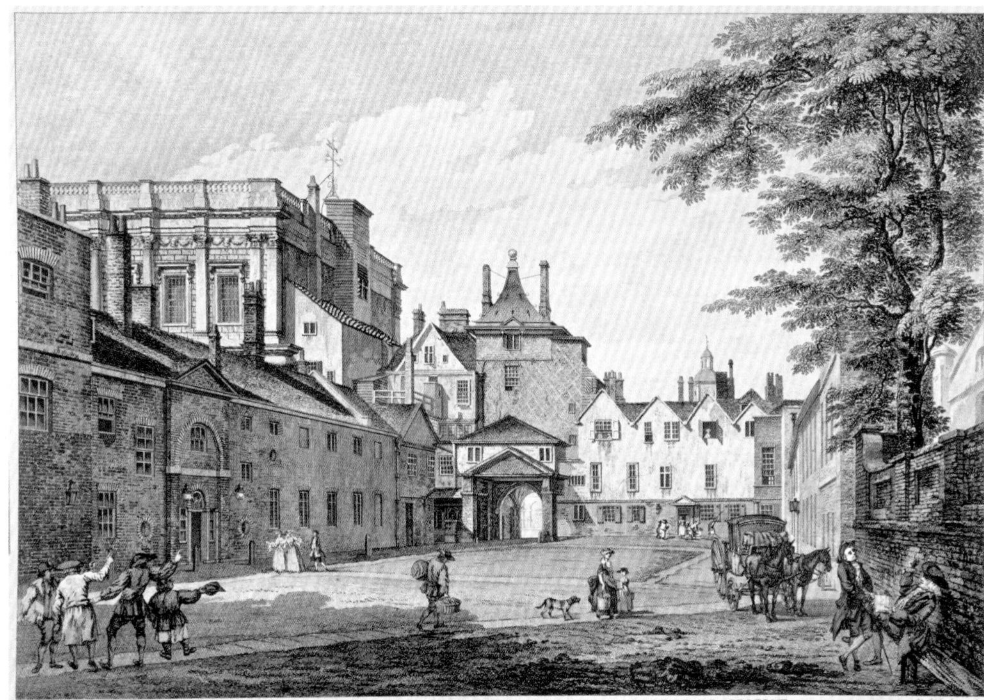

FIG. 5
Edward Rooker (1724–1774), after Paul and Thomas Sandby, *Scotland Yard with part of the Banqueting-House,* from *Six London Views*, published by Edward Rooker, 31 December 1766. Etching, 413 × 552 mm. Guildhall Library, City of London

In 1772 Sandby moved with his wife and three children, Paul, Thomas Paul and Nancy, out of central London, beyond the main area of the West End to 4 St George's Row, a three-storey house overlooking Hyde Park. Sandby lived there for 37 years until his death in 1809. St George's Row was built on the verge of a plot that had been sold to

St George's Church, Hanover Square, for a new burial ground and chapel; the church recouped its outlay by selling 99-year leases to a speculative builder who erected two terraces of seven houses flanking the chapel with a raised, paved footway above the road in front and generously sized gardens at the back. Sandby's move was part of an established progression in the development of the West End, and may be seen as a choice one for an artist who could afford neither a grand townhouse nor a detached villa. St George's Row was a modest version of the grand, loyalist visions of the western entrance to the capital, passing the royal landscape of Hyde Park, that were proposed by a number of architects. It offered practical, suburban gentrification rather than schematic civic virtue.[42]

Sandby's trade card (fig. 6) presents a polite view of his home neighbourhood. We look west from the corner of Oxford Street, past the tollbooth, through the open gates, down the turnpike towards the trees of Kensington Gardens, with the frontage of St George's Row to the right and the wall of Hyde Park to the left. The tollbooth was built on the site of the triangular gallows at Tyburn, which was removed in 1759 (the capital's main execution ground, with a stand for spectators, was maintained just out of view of Sandby's illustration, beyond the gate to Edgware Road, until protests from polite residents at the rough crowds on execution day resulted in its removal to a site outside Newgate Gaol in 1783).[43] In contrast to Thomas Rowlandson's boisterous, crowded and socially mixed image of the tollgate looking towards the city, to Oxford Street (fig. 7), Sandby's view appears like a gateway to an aristocratic estate in the country than an approach to a great city. Sandby produced scores of views of Hyde Park, notably a series of the encampment during the Gordon Riots of 1781, and others of its various lodges, pathways, drives, ponds, ditches, groves and avenues, pasture and livestock. As well as making panoramic views from his house, showing polite society on the move on paths and carriageway, and patrolling and parading soldiers, he also showed St George's Row from across the park as an elegant development, flanking the new chapel, framed by the army encampment in one view (cat. 51) and by trees and cattle in another, as if, no less than the lodges within, it was a constituent element of the royal landscape.

The architect James Gandon (1742–1823) recalled that at St George's Row, Sandby was 'indefatigable in cultivating his power as an artist. He commenced painting in watercolour very early in the morning; the pencil and frequently the pen seldom quitted his hand until evening.' His mealtimes were often spent with friends 'delighted with his wit, conversation and manners'.[44] In his reminiscences, Henry Angelo claimed that when he called on Sandby he saw him 'seated at his window, when nearly four-score years, with all the enthusiasm of a youthful artist, sketching some incidental effect of light and shadow from the opposite scene of Hyde Park' but willing to put down his pencil and go for a walk to see the landscape painter George Barret 'who resided in a most delightful spot, at the upper end of a field, adjacent to old Paddington church'.[45] In Sandby's obituary, his son Thomas Paul noted that his father was working on pictures days before his death and, just a few weeks before, had completed his largest ever oil, but was never too busy to welcome friends, including one of his oldest, and poorest, the engraver Charles Grignion, who walked over one day from Kentish Town.[46] On spring and summer Sundays, after evening service at St George's, Sandby ran informal cultural gatherings at his house which attracted patrons, politicians and writers, and professional and amateur artists, including pupils like the Russian Princess Dashkova (who unusually for a woman took up engraving as well as drawing); Gandon recalled that she once took up a world map on the table and declared her astonishment when she looked at 'dis speck, called England, and do see its large possessions'.[47]

Sandby amassed a large and varied art collection at his house: drawings, paintings and prints by Old Masters as well as contemporaries, and an extensive archive, including many hundreds of works, of his own sketches and finished drawings.[48] Sandby's practice of bodycolour (the addition of Chinese white to render watercolour wash opaque) drew on works by such masters of the medium as Joseph Goupy (1689–1769) and Marco Ricci (1676–1730) that were no doubt familiar to the artist from the Royal Collection or his own rich holdings. He also purchased drawings directly from his contemporary Richard Wilson above the market price, when his friend was reduced to selling them to dealers for a few shillings. His many views of shipping by Willem

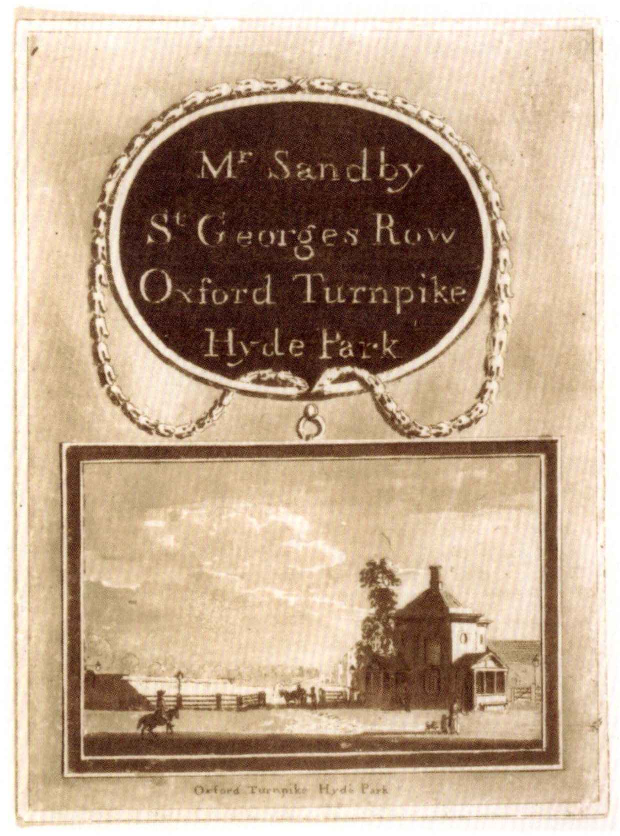

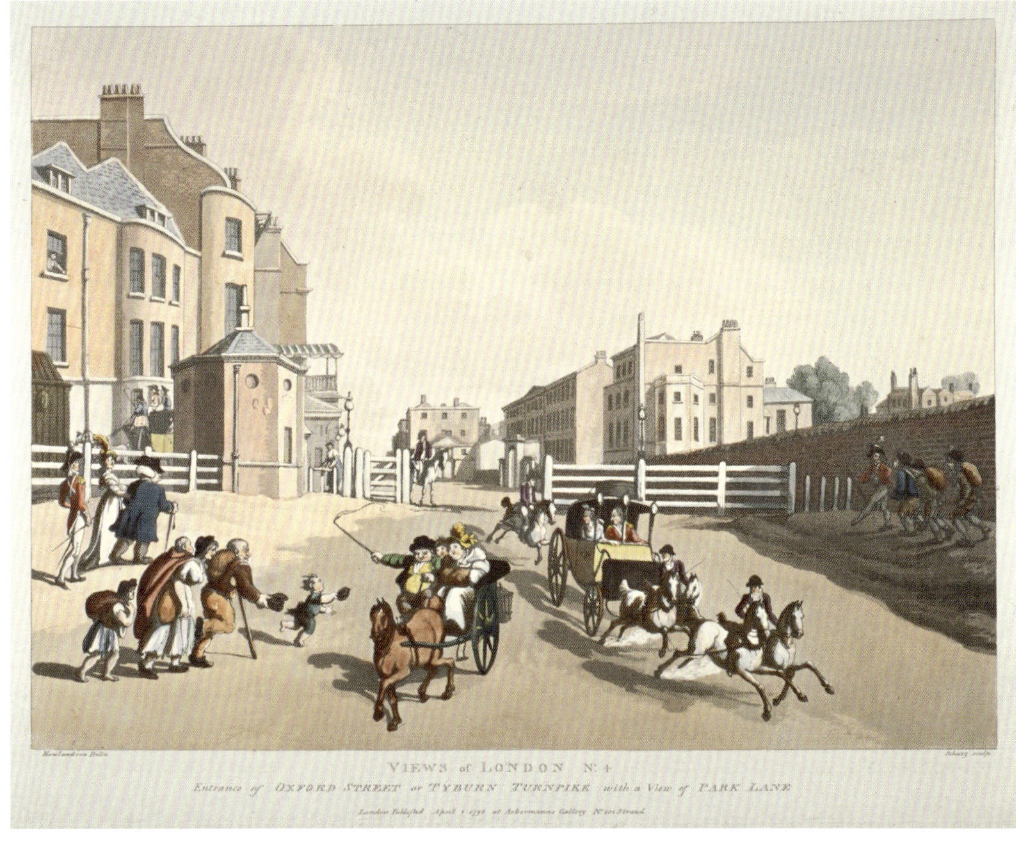

Van der Velde were probably purchased or donated from the collection of his next-door neighbour Dominic Serres, 'the Vanderveld of Modern Days' according to Sandby.[49] Some of his architectural studies by Thomas Sandby he purchased in his brother's posthumous sale of 1799, along with terracotta models and a *camera obscura*. The collection formed a rich resource for his own work as well as his teaching and socialising.

Drawings by Sandby from the back of his house show his studio built at the bottom of his garden, an elegant, neoclassical building at the end of a paved courtyard with busts, urns, pots and bas-reliefs, in the style of the Italian villa scenes by Marco Ricci (cat. 94 and fig. 8). In one view a servant descends with a tray from the steps of the studio, a scullery maid deals with the carpets and laundry, and a cat on the fence observes the scene next door of a whole family gardening, somewhat frenetically watering and hoeing flower beds on a blustery day. Although the picture might be documentary, it is possible that it also represents an architectural or landscape design, possibly by Thomas Sandby, since the contrasting gardens seem to exemplify improved and unimproved styles, as well as satirising the restricted sites of middle-class suburban life in which different versions of cultural aspiration (here classical taste and modern domesticity) were pursued. The studio is itself a garden building, a gazebo-like structure, its large windows taking advantage of the northern light and views over St George's burial ground across the fields and new houses of Paddington towards the northern heights of London.[50]

FIG. 6
Paul Sandby's trade card, *c.* 1770. British Museum, London

FIG. 7
Heinrich Joseph Schutz (1760–1822), after Thomas Rowlandson (1756–1827), *Views of London, no. 4: Entrance of Oxford Street or Tyburn Turnpike with a view of Park Lane*, published by Rudolph Ackermann, 1798. Aquatint, 328 × 410 mm. Guildhall Library, City of London

St George's Row attracted a number of residents from the art world, including Sandby's dealer, the printseller Antonio Poggi, and the watercolourist Thomas Girtin (1775–1802), the engravers Jonathan Spilsbury and Thomas Vivares and Sandby's next-door neighbour and close friend Dominic Serres, a fellow foundation member of the Royal Academy and a marine painter famous for his patriotic battle scenes. Not all was neighbourly on the Row. For some years the landscape artist John 'Warwick' Smith lived three doors from Sandby, in Poggi's house. Farington reported in October 1798 that 'Sandby declined 6 or 7 years ago going near him on acct. of his having abused his works in an illiberal manner', which did not stop Smith, 'moved by jealousy', calling to complain about Sandby's friend, the royal portraitist William Beechey, being knighted.[51]

At St George's Row Sandby was well placed to observe the transformations in an emergent zone on the urban periphery, the so called 'environs of London', which featured in a broad field of written and visual material, including guidebooks, travel writing, satires, garden designs and maps. These works explored the variety and rapid turnover of scenes and subjects, the mixture of public and private developments for visitors and residents, including turnpike gates, pleasure gardens, taverns and spas, the conjunctions of contrasting ranks of people and properties, and pockets of older, rustic-looking developments such as parks, farmsteads, meadows and cottages.[52]

Sandby frequently sauntered down the road to Bayswater, sometimes to call on Beechey at his villa on Craven Hill. A hamlet had developed where the Westbourne stream flowed under the road into Kensington Gardens. The place was renowned for its water, in streams, springs and reservoirs, for drinking, washing, angling and watercress fields. It supplied drinking water in roadside troughs for animals, especially horses (hence its original name Bayswatering). Sandby sketched the stone-built conduit house on Craven Hill that supplied water to properties near Oxford Street, as well as St George's Row; standing by its pond in a grove of elms, the conduit house was a part of the recreational round in this place of resort, above the tea gardens near the roadside. Satirised in stock fashion in *Eccentric Excursions* (1796) as a pretentious venue where hopeless waiters spilled hot kettles on vulgar city visitors, the Bayswater gardens appear in a series of Sandby's sketches, from various vantage points, as an orderly place. Men drink quietly on benches in the beer garden at the back; in the front, by the stuccoed façade and flower beds, two well-dressed women walk, watched by an officer; a boy carries a tray on the path by the stream. In another scene the gardens appear as part of a wider prospect from over the field behind, to the plantations of Kensington Gardens over the road, a complex suburban topography of ploughed fields, grazing paddocks, tree groves and ornamental plantations, articulated by brick walls, wooden palings and wicker fences.[53]

By the roadside is the development which articulated Bayswater as a social arena, the turnpike gate adjacent to the coaching inn, the Old Swan, the subject of a number of scenes by Sandby, including two pairs of exhibits shown at the Royal Academy, one pair in 1791 and the other in 1800, the former looking west and east along the road at the morning and evening rush hour (cat. 48, fig. 40). The scenes are animated by scores of figures, including serving maids, soldiers, farmworkers, builders and laundresses, as well as many types of vehicles, from lumbering carts and wagons to speeding gigs and stage coaches, and a range of equestrians and pedestrians making their way to and from London. These scenes show Sandby's longstanding interest in urban gateways as social arenas, as well as developing a popular genre of turnpike-gate subjects.[54]

In his later life, scenes in London and within easy reach of the capital comprised a growing proportion of Sandby's exhibits, understandably so in view of the physical and financial demands that travel made on an ageing, infirm and latterly impecunious artist, but also perhaps reflecting the popularity of comforting southern 'home' scenes during the Napoleonic Wars. Sandby's last works to be exhibited at the Royal Academy in his lifetime (in the spring of 1809) include *A View on Kilburn Road* and *A View from the Back of No. 4 in St George's Row*. He died in November of that year, and was buried in St George's burial ground at the back of his studio, next to his wife, who had predeceased him in 1797.

Afterlife: Windsor and Nottingham

Sandby was acknowledged by one of his obituarists as 'the father of modern landscape painting in water-colours'.[55]

FIG. 8
Paul Sandby, *The Artist's Studio, 4 St George's Row, Bayswater*, *c.* 1772. Bodycolour, 238 × 280 mm. British Museum, London

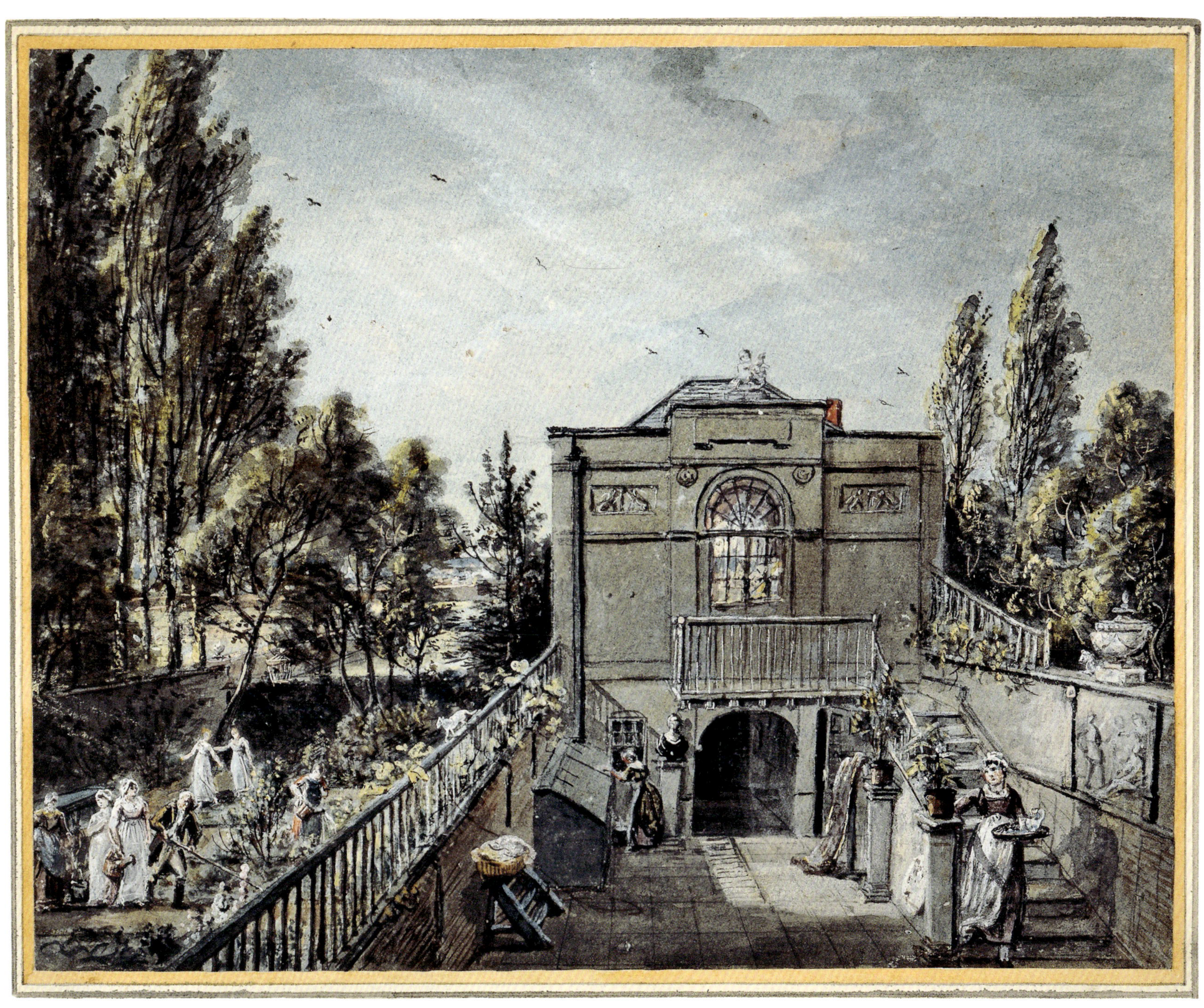

The phrase has been repeated too often, for it over-simplifies his relationship to the traditions of landscape drawing within which his career began and limits consideration of his work as an artist in his own right.[56] He died at a time when there was a heightened interest in the progress of the 'new' art of watercolour, but this only made his work seem all the more distant from the current mode. Farington's negative remarks on 'the great difference between His works & those of Artists who now practice in Water Colours', made on the occasion of the sale of Sandby's estate in May 1811, have invariably been cited in this context.[57] Turner, the leading figure among the artists to whom Farington refers, probably attended the sale, although his interest, significantly, was in Sandby's collection of Old Master drawings rather than those by the artist himself.[58] Later writers have made much of the idea of a reputation eclipsed by the performances of a younger generation, and even Sandby's most enthusiastic advocates have concentrated on the early phases of his career. Given that he continued to attract serious notices throughout the 1790s, however, if rather fewer sales, the extent of the decline in his critical fortunes in his late years has arguably been exaggerated.[59]

In the memoir of his father that appeared in the *Monthly Magazine* of June 1811, presumably timed to help promote the sale he had organised, Thomas Paul Sandby unsurprisingly defended the old values, complaining of those who affected to doubt the importance of adhering to a just representation of nature in favour of 'an undefined wild rumble tumble (or anything else you please) of pencilling'.[60] The vivid, disparaging phrase refers specifically to the approach of amateurs, but the pursuit of ever broader and bolder effect was already a firmly established aspect of modern professional practice. In the years following Sandby's death, the basis of an account of the development of English watercolour in terms of a progression from 'drawing' to 'painting' was being developed by the artist and critic W. H. Pyne. According to Pyne, Sandby established the foundation for a later generation's triumph.[61] This was to prove an influential model of explanation.

There was one area, however, in which Sandby's stock proved exceptional: as Paul Oppé noted, he and his brother Thomas 'are the only artists to have been consistently acquired for the Royal Collection from the dates of their death'.[62] No work was commissioned rather than purchased from either brother by George III, but the Prince Regent made extensive purchases from the 1811 sale of Paul's estate, including several views of Windsor, and went on to acquire further works through the art-dealer Colnaghi.[63] The Royal Collection eventually grew to comprise around 550 drawings by the brothers, and gave rise to what is generally agreed to be the first serious art-historical study of their work: Paul Oppé's *The Drawings of Paul and Thomas Sandby in the Collection of His Majesty The King at Windsor Castle* (1947). Oppé organised the landscape drawings topographically, starting with the castle itself and going on to the Great Park and its vicinity, Richmond, Kew and London, before dealing with figures, interiors, coaches, horses and dogs. The plates showed Windsor as rendered by Paul as a homely, even makeshift, agglomeration of buildings, thoroughfares, courtyards and terraces, very different in character from the appearance of the remodelled royal residence at the time of publication. In the 1940s, threatened by bombs, Windsor had re-emerged as a locus of patriotic feeling, and Kenneth Clark, then Surveyor of the Royal Collection, was instrumental in commissioning a modern artist, John Piper, to produce a new series of watercolour views of the castle. In a letter to John Betjeman, Piper wrote, with a hint of mock-sincerity: 'I follow unworthily in the footsteps of Paul Sandby, who did 200 watercolours for George III which I am instructed to look at earnestly before starting.'[64] Piper made no mention of Sandby in his book *British Romantic Artists* (1942), which was published in the same year that he showed a group of his own Windsor drawings at the National Gallery, and Sandby's idiom evidently still lay outside the terms of the revived interest in topography associated with the neoromanticism of mid-century. But Oppé's catalogue established the idea of the Windsor views as the best of Sandby.[65]

Nottingham Castle played a decisive role in reviving a public audience for the Sandbys. This mansion of the Dukes of Newcastle had proved a significant site for the Sandby brothers in their lifetime. Thomas launched his career with a spectacular prospect view of his native town, in which the castle is a prominent landmark, in 1742 (fig. 45). On returning to Nottingham, as part of a 1774 tour through the midlands, Thomas commemorated the historical geography of the castle and its rock, comparing the terrace views along the Trent Valley with those at Windsor Castle along that of the Thames (cat. 75).[66] Shown in two views, Nottingham Castle is a key site in Paul Sandby's *A Collection of Landscapes* (1777). The west view on the edge of the park shows two visitors making their way up to the castle; the east view shows the castle from the edge of the town, from a horse paddock which also serves as playground for a young family (fig. 23). The accompanying text dilates on the castle's long past, to ancient British settlement, and its extensive prospect reaching over 'the whole of the town' to a view of 'fields, woods and enclosures, as far as the eye can reach'.

After being ruined by fire in the Reform Bill riots of 1832, the restored Nottingham Castle was opened as the first regional art museum in 1878, and in 1884 it presented the first exhibition of Paul and Thomas Sandby: 'Natives of Nottingham'.[67] The initiative for the exhibition came from Nottingham Castle's Director and Curator, G. H. Wallis. Thirty-six drawings were borrowed from the Royal Collection, but the majority of the 276 catalogued items came from the collection of William Arnold Sandby, Thomas's great-grandson and Paul's great-grand-nephew, who wrote the first history of the Royal Academy. His collection was largely the result of his own efforts to put together a memorial to his ancestors, and only a small part of it seems to have descended in the family.

William Sandby produced a more lasting memorial in the form of the monograph on the brothers that he eventually published in 1892, a book that remains the basis for much of our knowledge of the brothers' lives.[68] Sandby opens with an attempt to account for the impression made on an artist by 'the place in which he was born, and the scenery by which he was surrounded in early life'; he goes on to remark that Nottingham might be thought an uncongenial birthplace for a landscape painter, but suggests that the town's picturesque, pre-industrial character must have stimulated Sandby's later interest in old castles, churches and halls.[69] This is in instructive contrast to the kind of claim being advanced by Derby for Joseph Wright in the same period, a claim that accorded with Derby's own self-image as the centre of an enterprising and progressive regional culture.

William Sandby's advocacy of his forebears was continued in 1904 through the terms of his will, by which he bequeathed works from his collection to a wide range of public collections in Britain and abroad. His most substantial bequest, making its collection of their work the largest after the Royal Collection, was to the British Museum.[70] William Sandby's bequest of eight works by Paul to Nottingham did not particularly favour his native town, and, following some earlier independent purchases just after the publication of the monograph, the city's collection was significantly enhanced in the mid-1940s by the important donation of mainly late gouaches by Lady Rich, the widow of another of Sandby's descendants.

A century after staging the first Sandby exhibition, Nottingham Castle Museum's 'The Painters' Progress: The Life and Times of Thomas and Paul Sandby' (1986) attempted to show the social, political and economic contexts of their art, including their early life in Nottingham, and to demonstrate what an artistic career entailed in their period. As there was no accompanying publication,[71] Bruce Robertson's catalogue for the exhibition at the Yale Center for British Art, New Haven, of the previous year, which drew on the most representative collection of Sandby's work to have been formed in recent times, was the only really significant publication on the artist to date.

Sandby has hardly been a neglected figure in accounts of the development of British art, but it could be argued that the predominant models for evaluation have never rendered him full justice. In surveys of watercolour he has been too readily cast as a mere forerunner: the title of an exhibition such as 'View to Vision: British Watercolours from Sandby to Turner at the Whitworth Art Gallery' is indicative, with Sandby establishing the prosaic view as the foil to Turner's vision.[72] The tendency to treat watercolour and landscape as discrete categories, each with its own exclusive history, has also made it more difficult to grasp the measure of Sandby's artistic practice. This exhibition and its catalogue, the first comprehensive, critical study of the artist, endeavour to do so.

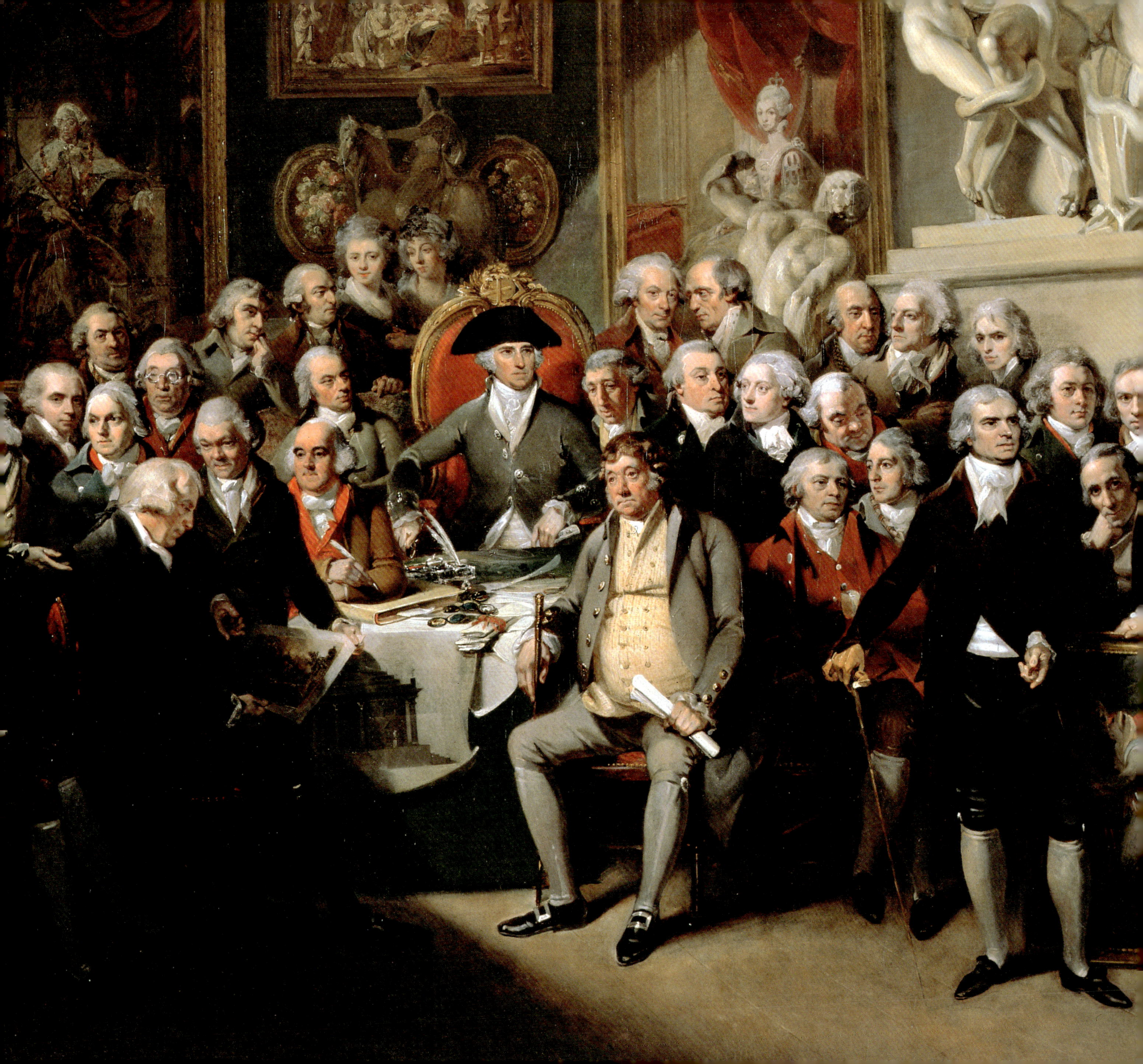

The Sandbys and the Royal Academy

MARTIN POSTLE

In late November 1768, after several years of bitter wrangling within London's artistic community, a group of 22 artists, including Paul Sandby, signed a formal letter to George III requesting his 'gracious assistance, patronage, and protection' in the formation of a new academy which would effectively supplant the existing Society of Artists, formed in 1761. The King assented, and on 10 December he signed a document, known as the Instrument of Foundation, which set out the rules and regulations of the newly formed 'Royal Academy'. A few days later Paul Sandby, together with his brother Thomas, the architect, and their friend, the sculptor William Tyler – who had all been named in the Instrument among the 36 foundation members of the Royal Academy – corresponded with another mutual friend, the painter Sawrey Gilpin, canvassing his membership. They sought to reassure Gilpin, who clearly had serious reservations about the new institution, that the King's patronage would 'entirely silence all envious cabals, all designing manoeuvres, and all intriguing sollicitations [*sic*]'. They also stressed the exclusivity of membership, which, 'by the King's command', could never exceed 40; a regulation which, they claimed, would 'avoid the disagreeable circumstance of that numberless body ever divided in opinion, easily alarmed and easily worked into tumult by the insinuations of artful men'.[1] For whatever reason, Gilpin did not become a foundation member of the Royal Academy. However, within days Paul Sandby had been elected onto the institution's Council (he attended its first meeting on 20 December 1768), and Thomas had been appointed its first Professor of Architecture, a post he was to hold until his death in 1798. From this moment the Sandby brothers were firmly positioned within both the support network and the command structure of the Royal Academy, with all the privileges and responsibilities that this entailed. To understand why the Sandby brothers' affiliation to the Royal Academy was so strong from the outset, we need first to assess their links to previous academic institutions and the nature of their professional relationship with the court.

Paul and Thomas Sandby valued the role of formal academic training. According to a friend of the Sandbys, in their youth the two brothers had 'kept an academy' in Nottingham, before they moved to London in the 1740s.[2] Although the statement has been dismissed on the grounds that Thomas and Paul were then little more than boys, it does not preclude the possibility that they may have had access to some kind of informal drawing class, involving, possibly, the study of living models and plaster casts, or, more likely, making copy-drawings from paintings, prints and illustrations contained in drawing manuals. Evidence that Paul Sandby had undertaken such activities exists in a book of drawings that he made and presented in March 1747 to the Board of Ordnance at the Tower of London as evidence of his competence in draughtsmanship (cats 1–2). All but two are figure drawings; the majority copied from recently published prints after the Dutch artist, Abraham Bloemart.[3] Significantly, the drawing on the title page shows a young artist, seated, drawing from fragments of antique figures, the very cornerstone of European academic pedagogy, affirming surely Sandby's own aspirations as an artist and his allegiance to such lofty ideals.

In 1753, by which time both Sandby brothers were firmly established within London's artistic community, definite proof of their organisational role in drawing activity is provided by a modest watercolour by Paul Sandby, which served to invite the brothers' friend Theodosius Forrest to an evening drawing class at Thomas's house at Poultney Street (fig. 9).[4] The presence in the drawing of a theatrically costumed model on the dais, and the invitation made by accompanying verses to 'attack cold beef and wine' after the evening's study suggest that this was not primarily an academic enterprise but a social occasion conducted in a spirit of conviviality. Paul Sandby, as regular gatherings at his Bayswater home in later life attest, was highly sociable, and had a keen interest in the artistic community as a whole – professional artists, amateurs and connoisseurs alike. It is easy to understand, therefore, how the clubbable Sandbys were attracted to the heady world of artistic debate in the metropolis, centred upon the formation of a professional academy.

The institutional base for the capital's artists in 1753 was the St Martin's Lane Academy. That academy had been reformed in the winter of 1735 under the aegis of William Hogarth, who still maintained a strongly proprietorial interest.[5] He also attempted to shape its ethos, conceiving it as an informal club where subscribers could meet on equal terms – unlike the 'foolish parade of the French academy', which, as a branch of Government, ran on strictly hierarchical lines.[6] Yet, many younger artists were unhappy with the homely atmosphere of Hogarth's academy, and inclined increasingly towards a continental model, viewing an academy as a means to elevate their social as well as their artistic status. Among those who had already expressed their dissatisfaction with the status quo was a friend of the Sandbys, the architect John Gwynn, who in 1749 had published a pamphlet entitled *An Essay on Design; including proposals for Erecting a Public Academy to be supported by Voluntary Subscription (Till a Royal Foundation can be obtain'd) for Educating the British Youth in Drawing and Several Arts thereon.* As the title suggests, Gwynn's ultimate aim was to establish a 'royal' academy (the frontispiece bore the head of George II). A copy of Gwynn's publication in the Beinecke Library, Yale University, is inscribed 'To my ingenious friend Paul Sandby', which suggests that at the very least the dedicatee was sympathetic to Gwynn's views. In October 1753, after almost two decades of vacillation, yet another attempt was made to reform the structure of the

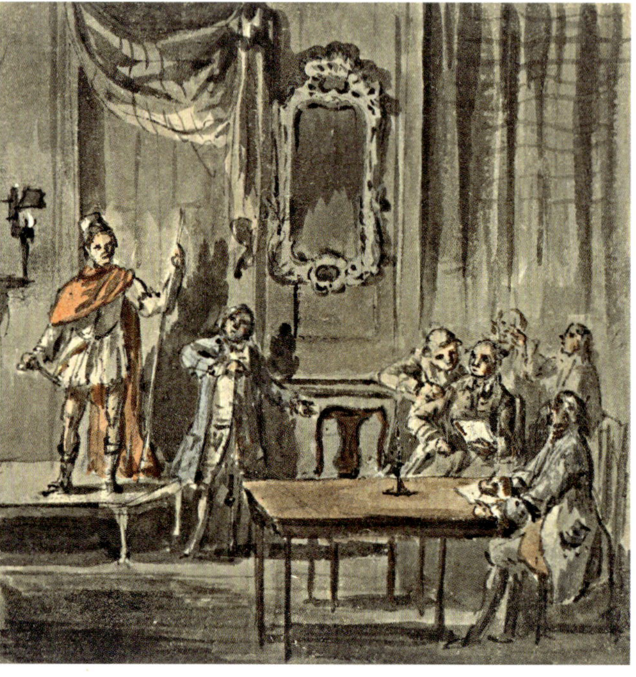

FIG. 9
Paul Sandby, *Invitation to a Sketching Club (36 Poultney Street)*, 1753. Watercolour over graphite, 960 × 910 mm. Museum of London

St Martin's Lane Academy when a circular letter was published inviting artists to attend a meeting the following month at the Thatched House Tavern in order to elect a committee of 'thirteen painters, three sculptors, one chaser, two engravers, and two architects'.[7] Paul Sandby would almost certainly have attended this meeting.[8] At almost the same time, in November 1753, Hogarth published his own highly idiosyncratic academic treatise, *The Analysis of Beauty*. As David Bindman has observed, Hogarth's 'determined empiricism and attempt to reduce the Beau Idéal to an observed method could hardly appeal to those influenced by the classical idealism of Rome'.[9] Nor evidently did it appeal to Paul Sandby who over the ensuing months produced a series of hard-hitting satirical engravings aimed at discrediting Hogarth's artistic theories and undermining his position as the self-appointed leader of the English 'academic' community (cats 21–28). In 1762 Sandby once more attacked Hogarth via a series of satirical prints, motivated this time by Hogarth's support for the unpopular government of John Stuart, 3rd Earl of Bute, and the former's abrupt resignation from the Society of Artists, to which both Sandbys were closely affiliated (cats 31–32).[10] It is nonetheless interesting that during the 1760s, the period in which internecine strife within the Society of Artists was at its most intense, as its directors sought to maintain control and attain royal patronage, the Sandbys kept a low profile. And when the Sandbys were eventually selected as foundation members of the Royal Academy, their royal connections were what guaranteed them their place.

In Johan Zoffany's group portrait entitled *The Academicians of the Royal Academy* (fig. 10) Paul and Thomas Sandby stand to the left of the composition; Paul rests his hand upon Thomas's shoulder, the two brothers deep in conversation. Zoffany, who was acutely aware of the various allegiances and friendships within the Academy, ensures that they are flanked by close friends: to the right of Thomas Sandby, William Tyler, and, to the left of Paul Sandby, Dominic Serres – who was, quite literally, his next-door neighbour in St George's Row. Like Zoffany, whom the King had personally recommended as a foundation member of the Royal Academy, the Sandby brothers were already closely associated with the court and with royal patronage.[11] In the painting Paul Sandby wears a distinctive blue coat with a red collar. This is a form of official dress that may well relate to his recent appointment, in 1768, as Chief Drawing Master

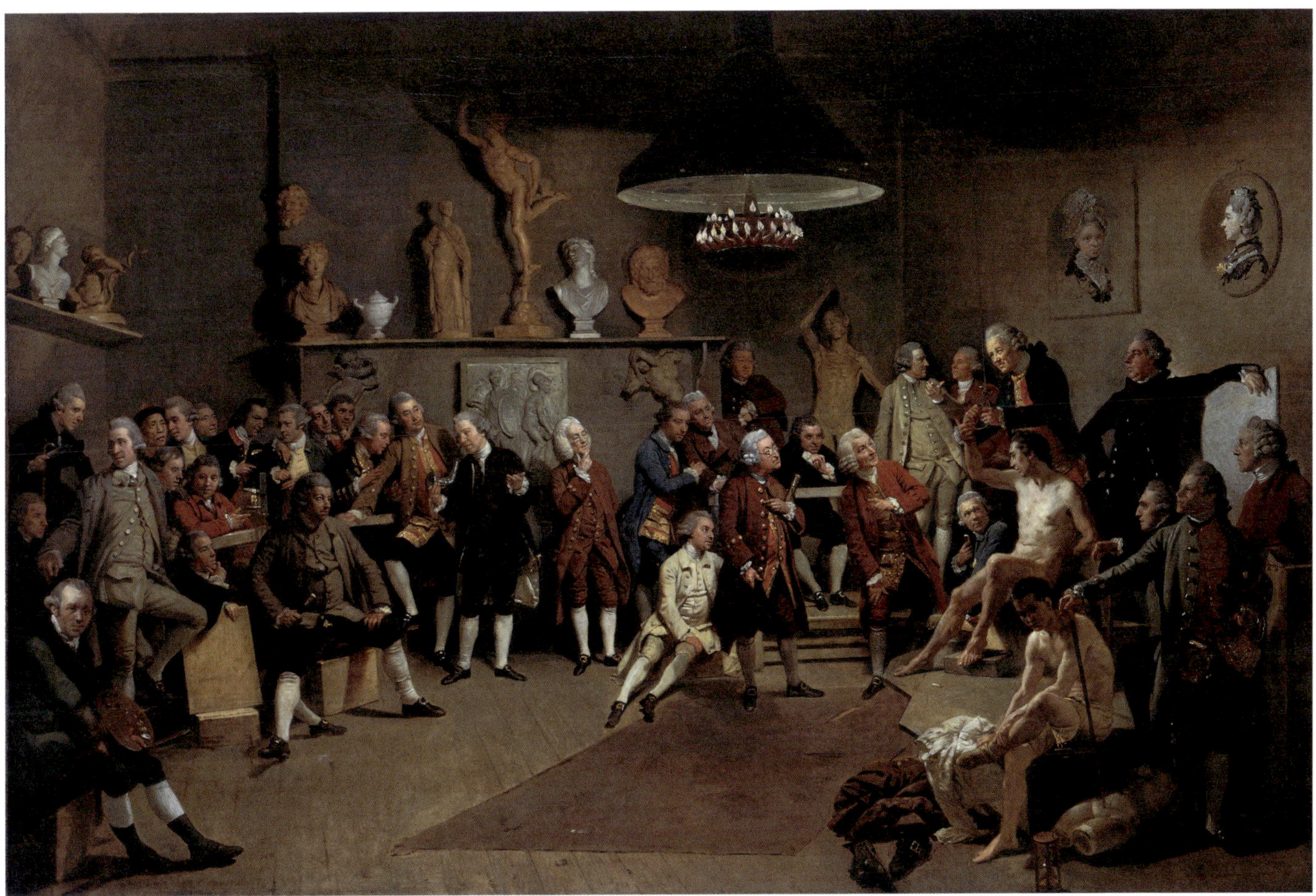

FIG. 10
Johan Zoffany (1733–1810), *The Academicians of the Royal Academy*, 1771–72. Oil on canvas, 1007 × 1473 mm. The Royal Collection

to the Royal Military Academy at Woolwich (with a salary of £150), and which underlines his affiliation to the monarchy.[12] Shortly after the foundation of the Royal Academy, Thomas Sandby's status as a loyal servant of the Crown was apparently to have been recognised by the conferring of a knighthood through the interventions of the Dukes of Cumberland and Gloucester, although for some unknown reason he could not be located at the appropriate time.[13] As Deputy Ranger of Windsor Great Park, in the service of the Duke of Cumberland, Thomas Sandby earned a salary of £400, and in 1777 he was also appointed joint Architect of the King's Works, with James Adam. The Sandbys depended upon the patronage of the court to a greater extent than many of their fellow Royal Academicians, not least the President, Sir Joshua Reynolds, whose relationship with the King was characterised by an atmosphere of barely concealed enmity.

During the 1760s the Sandbys had cultivated close friendships with artists and architects whose careers were aligned with the court. Indeed, Paul Sandby was among an élite band of artists who provided drawing tuition to the royal princes, being described in 1771 as 'Drawing Master to the Prince of Wales'.[14] A close friend of the Sandbys was the portraitist Francis Cotes, who, in addition to painting portraits of Paul Sandby (see page 9) and his wife, was commissioned to paint Queen Charlotte and her children.[15] Another friend influential in royal circles was Sir William Chambers, former architectural tutor to George III. Cotes (who died in July 1770) and Chambers had been instrumental in the foundation of the Royal Academy, the two having been members of a four-man committee designated to draw up a scheme for the new institution and win the King's approval. From the outset, therefore, Chambers, Cotes and the Sandbys were identified as loyalists, individuals who upheld the élitist nature of the new institution in contrast to what has been described as the 'more open trade association' represented by the existing Society of Artists.[16] The Royal Academy was, indeed, far more than an exclusive version of the Society of Artists. Rather, as Holger Hoock has affirmed, it evolved rapidly into a scion of the Hanoverian fiscal-military state, and those artists who made a living by and through it became 'in effect agents of government'. Through the interest and patronage of the King, the Royal Academy was given licence to borrow the state's authority, as a 'national consultative body'.[17] By the end of the century, the tensions that such a situation created, between the desire among artists to promote an aura of cultural patriotism around the Academy and their fear of being regarded as servile courtiers, almost resulted in its destruction. For Thomas Sandby, whose career was more thoroughly aligned to court interests, such tensions remained comparatively remote. Although dedicated to delivering his annual architecture lectures to students at the Royal Academy Schools, he appears to have avoided any direct involvement in Academy politics, and because it was not incumbent upon him to do so, he exhibited comparatively few works there. For Paul, on the other hand, the abiding need to earn a living by selling his art meant that the Annual Exhibition at the Royal Academy provided a highly visible and potentially lucrative shop window in which to promote his work.

Paul Sandby was a prolific exhibitor, showing over 120 works at the Royal Academy between 1769 and his death in 1809. The majority of these exhibits were related to commissioned views of English and Welsh scenery, often with historical features; castles such as Windsor, Warwick, Caernarvon and Rochester; and towns such as Tunbridge, Hereford, Worcester and Shrewsbury. Throughout his career as an exhibitor at the Royal Academy, Sandby presented an image of an inhabited British landscape that was both picturesque and well ordered, a view that accorded with the King's own perspective. And even when Sandby hinted at turbulence beneath the surface, as in his series of encampment pictures of 1781 depicting British soldiers stationed in London's parks in the aftermath of the Gordon Riots, his upbeat patriotic images sought to reassure the public that they remained safe and secure under the protection of the King's well-drilled and disciplined troops (cat. 50).

In 1771 Paul Sandby exhibited a watercolour entitled *A storm, from the Winter's Tale*, which was subsequently engraved and published in 1776. This Shakespearean subject, although atypical of Sandby's *oeuvre* as a whole, was almost certainly painted to demonstrate his allegiance

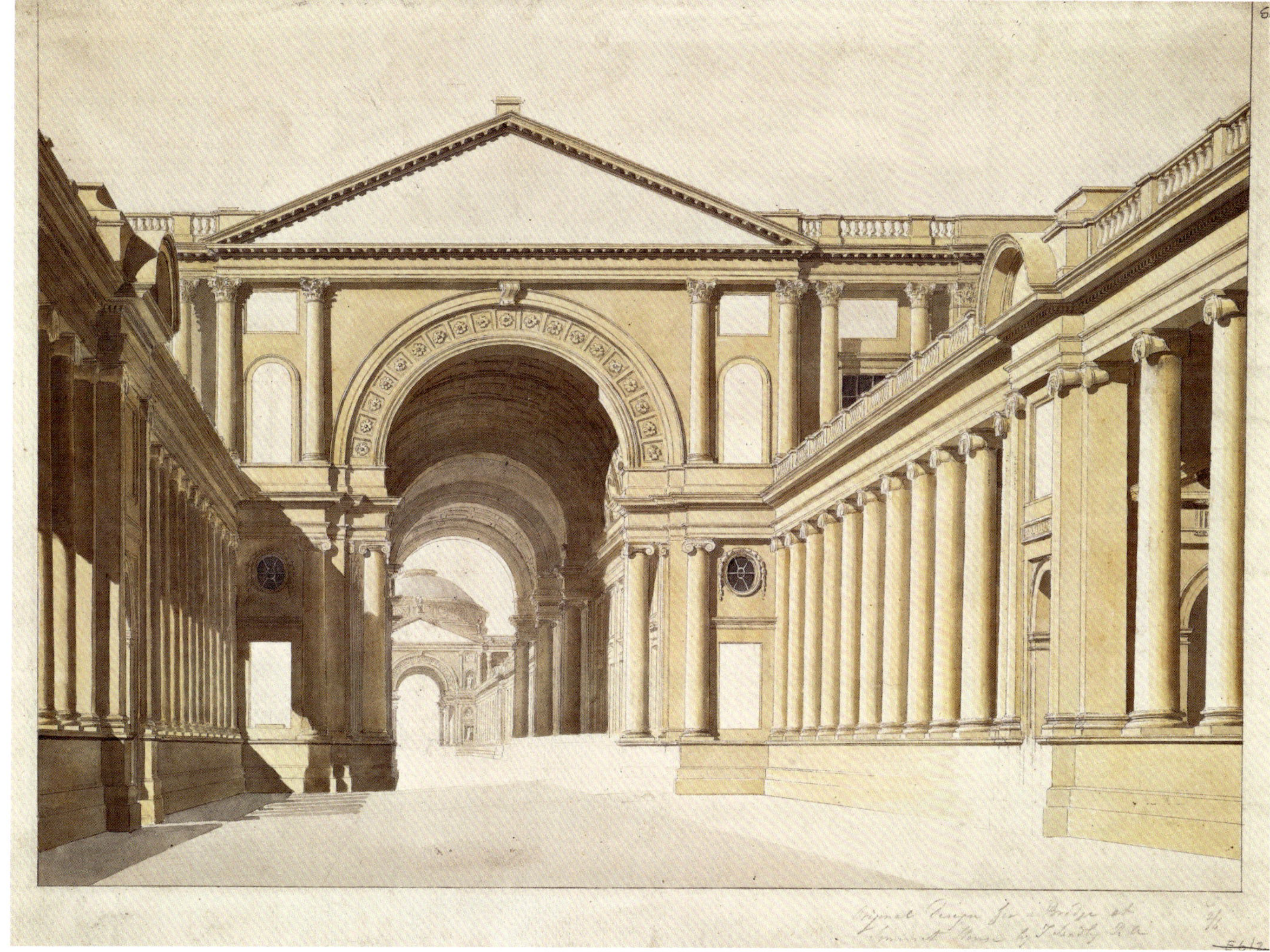

FIG. 11
Thomas Sandby, *A Bridge of Magnificence*, c. 1770s.
Pen, ink and watercolour, 355 × 509 mm. Royal Institute of British Architects, RIBA Library Drawings Collection, SD104/1, London

to the academic ideal of historical and literary landscape painting, which aligned the genre with the aspirations of the new Academy, namely the making of history paintings. Sandby's awareness of the commercial limitations of such paintings perhaps contributed to his decision to exhibit landscapes and genre subjects rather than ambitious Italianate oil paintings in the Wilsonian Grand Manner. And while he continued to draw inspiration from Richard Wilson, particularly in his sensitive handling of light, his own pictorial interests were more closely linked to the local British landscape than to a timeless vision of the classical past.

In 1781 Thomas Sandby exhibited at the Royal Academy a magisterial architectural drawing entitled *A Bridge of Magnificence* (fig. 11), designed as an illustration to his sixth and final series of lectures on architecture at the Royal Academy.[18] As Giles Worsley affirmed, this was a 'radical innovation in British architectural draughtsmanship', made possible by Sandby's experience as a topographer – for among his pedagogical concerns was, as he stated, to teach

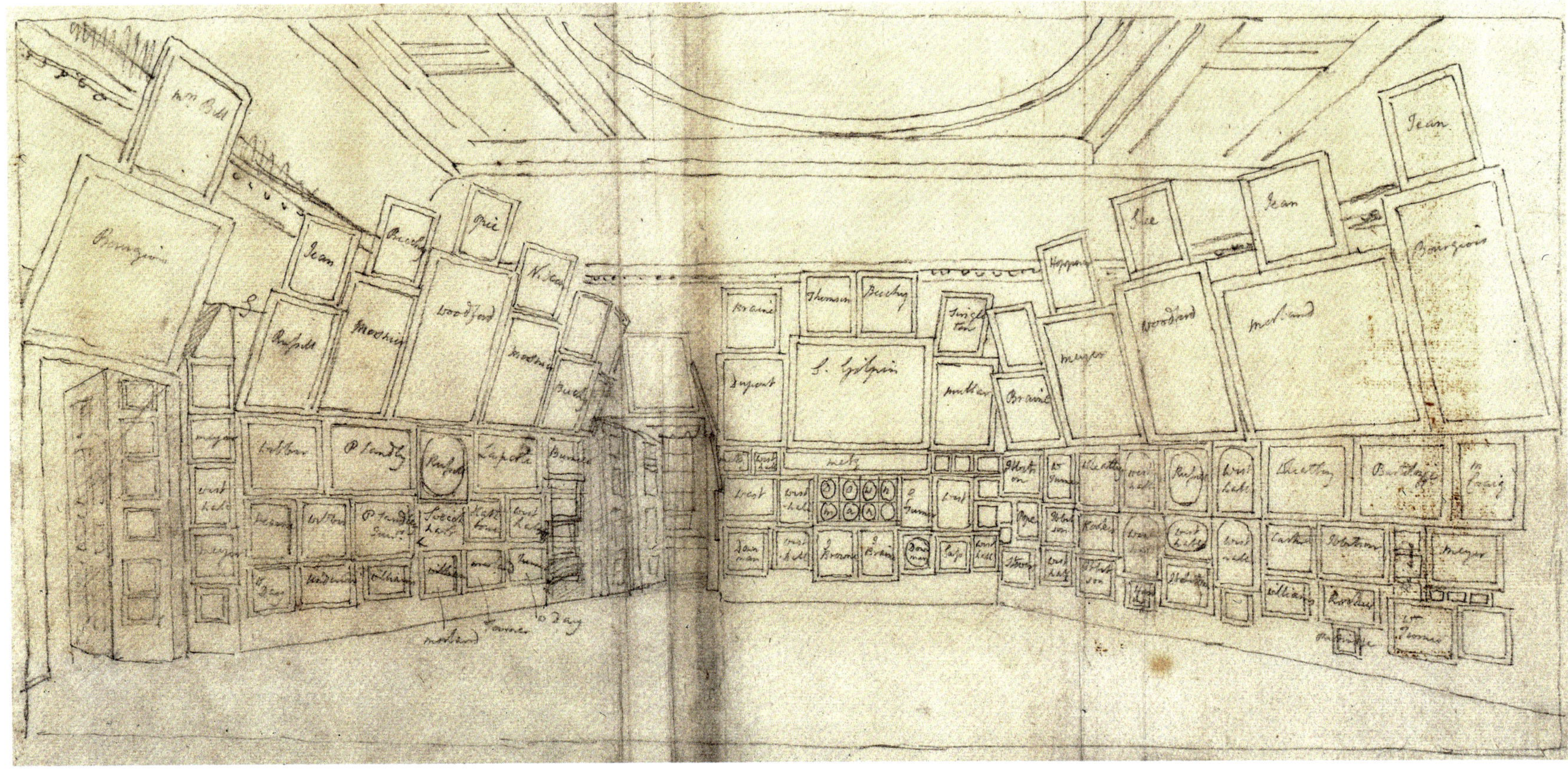

architectural students to 'accustom themselves to draw after real buildings without the use of Rules and Compasses, in the manner of the Landskip Painters'.[19] *A Bridge of Magnificence* met with critical acclaim, being, it has been observed, 'the first, and even perhaps only, time that an architect's design became one of the principal attractions of the exhibition'.[20] Never intended to be built, Sandby's bridge was, as its name suggested, an embodiment of the concept of the Grand Style; the equivalent in architectural terms to High (or Historical) Art. However, its real significance related to Sandby's professorial position in the Royal Academy Schools, where a new generation of young architects, including John Soane, were encouraged to view their discipline in its most elevated form, as a 'civic art' as opposed to a mere trade. Viewed as a whole, the ethos of Thomas Sandby's Royal Academy lectures was aligned closely to the more celebrated *Discourses* of Sir Joshua Reynolds, both works composed in the spirit of philosophical enquiry, with a concern for subjects beyond the strict parameters of their respective disciplines.

Thomas Sandby was officially appointed Professor of Architecture at the Royal Academy on 17 December 1768. He was tasked with presenting a course of six lectures each year at the Royal Academy. He put a great deal of effort into these lectures, not just in terms of the ideas expressed, but in the production of the highly finished drawings that he made to illustrate his lectures. In September 1769, gripped by a violent fever, Thomas Sandby sent Chambers his first lecture, 'which you are pleased to say you will read for me to the Council, if there is any think [*sic*] you wish to add

FIG. 12
Thomas Sandby, *Drawing or tracing of the hang of the Antique Room in the 1792 Royal Academy Annual Exhibition*, 1792. Graphite on tracing paper, 250 × 444 mm. Royal Academy of Arts, London

I hope you will favour me with your thoughts & improvements, in short give it whatever correction you please, there is no one so capable of doing it, or of whom I have so high an Opinion'.[21] The truth was that Chambers coveted the post of Professor of Architecture, and, conscious of Sandby's poor health, was eager to usurp his position.[22] Because Sandby's lectures – unlike Reynolds's *Discourses* – were never published, and his drawings were dispersed after his death, their contribution to eighteenth-century architectural discourse has not been sufficiently acknowledged.[23] More generally, Sandby's views on art and aesthetics as expressed in the lectures are revealing about the conceptual framework that shaped his view of rural and urban landscape, views which are relevant also to the evolution of Paul Sandby's approach to landscape art. Throughout his lectures, Thomas Sandby promoted a Reynoldsian spirit of decorum, which in its respect for established rules and procedures, was coupled with a distaste for the way in which the economic pressures of the market subvert the Ideal.

Thomas Sandby considered London to be 'the essence of pleasure and magnificence'. Yet, he affirms that in 'this overgrown and crowded metropolis every spot of ground is so hardly come at, and so dearly purchased, that in modern houses scarcely anything can be consulted but base convenience', the city being a place where 'business is more considered than pleasure'.[24] It is therefore in a 'cultivated' landscape that the 'gentleman' can best express his good taste, through building and emparkment. Sandby, who was at this time engaged in extensive landscaping projects in Windsor Great Park on behalf of the 2nd Duke of Cumberland, and who now resided there, had a personal stake in the promotion of a 'cultivated' landscape. Thus, in the same lecture, while he states that such a landscape is intended for retirement from 'the bustle of the great city', he concedes that 'retirement is apt to be melancholy'. He concludes, therefore, that the gentleman should 'choose a spot where there is all the retirement and privacy he can wish to enjoy, but still let it be in the reach of company': a situation which then closely matched his own at Windsor, and the landscape art that both he and Paul Sandby made there; cultivated, cheerful, and above all sociable.[25]

Thomas Sandby remained assiduous in his attention to the affairs of the Royal Academy well into the 1790s, providing, for example, detailed pen-and-wash diagrams of the installation of works hung in the 1792 Annual Exhibition (fig. 12), when he sat on the Committee of Arrangement,[26] and continuing to deliver his annual lectures until ill health eventually compelled him to request Edward Edwards to read them on his behalf.[27] On Thomas's death in 1798, Paul encouraged the Royal Academy to purchase his lecture drawings, works which 'had been the employment of his life', and whose sale would benefit his family.[28] Shortly after this attempted sale, Sandby let it be known that he coveted the post of the Academy's Librarian, since he 'had no business now as a teacher & that the income would be an object to him'.[29] Two years later, in 1801, it was rumoured that Sandby would apply directly to the Academy for financial support, 'so much has his fortune been reduced by expenses incurred for his Children'.[30] Although he did not apply to the Royal Academy for funds at that time, Sandby regarded it as a bulwark against penury; a view which reflected one of the founding principles of the Royal Academy, as well as the protection he so badly needed from the vicissitudes of the market-place and the financial uncertainties brought about by old age and familial responsibilities.

In 1795 Paul and Thomas Sandby, as foundation members, occupied prominent positions in Henry Singleton's painting of the Academicians in General Assembly (fig. 13), indicating their advancement through the ranks since Zoffany's 1771 group portrait, in which they had occupied relatively marginal positions. Paul Sandby, in particular, clearly enjoyed the power and privilege that his status as a senior Royal Academician allowed him. In 1794 Sandby was petitioned by James Boswell regarding the appointment of a new Professor of Ancient History at the Academy to succeed Edward Gibbon,[31] while he was constantly asked to exercise his influence on fellow Academicians in the selection of new members. In 1798 he approved the proposed election of J. M. W. Turner as an Associate Academician, although he felt that the sculptor John Flaxman, who was twenty years Turner's senior (and who had been made an Associate the previous year), was still 'yet young in the Academy' to

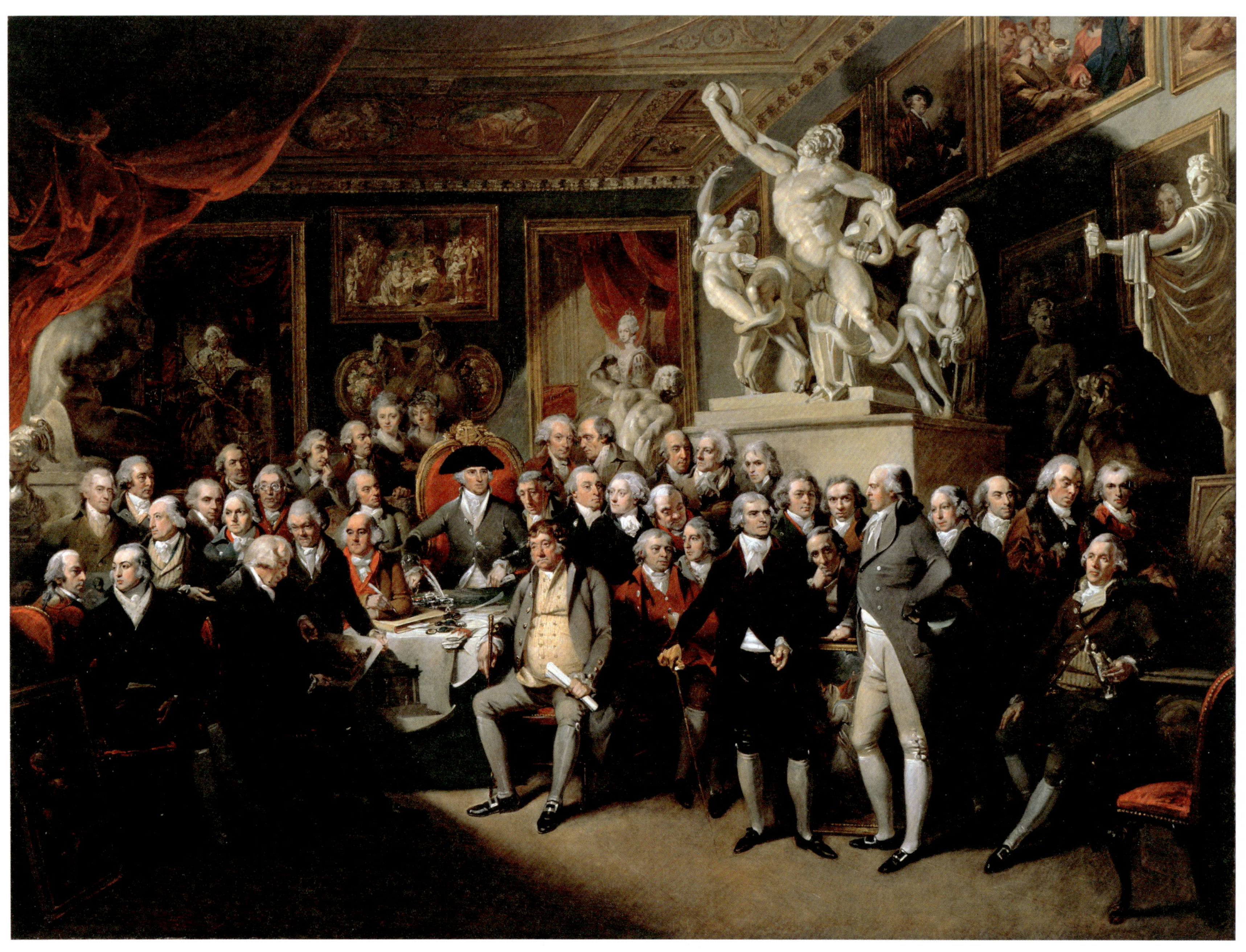

be elected a full Academician. As for the proposal to elect the 59-year-old gem engraver Nathaniel Marchant as an Academician, Sandby simply 'laughed at the Idea'.[32] Even late in life, in 1807, when Sandby himself was in straitened circumstances, his power to influence the selection of new members remained undiminished: the prospective Academician Samuel Woodforde was advised to secure Sandby's vote by arranging a carriage to transport him to the Royal Academy on election night, along with two other elder statesmen, Richard Cosway and Philip de Loutherbourg.[33]

Following the death of Sir Joshua Reynolds, the Academy, under the presidency of Benjamin West, was ostensibly a successful and publicly respected institution. Behind the façade, however, it was increasingly being torn apart by internecine quarrels concerning the power of the Academy's governing Council over the rank and file of its General Assembly, the use (or misuse) of its finances, and its position in the wider political spectrum. In the pages of Joseph Farington's diary Paul Sandby comes across as a man who did not wish to be identified exclusively with any particular clique or cabal. Even so, his allies in the Academy were generally those who moved in court circles, notably the royal portraitist Sir William Beechey, who referred to Sandby affectionately as 'Father Paul', and whose portrait he painted at this time.[34] In the later 1790s, when suspicions over those Academicians who held 'democratical' sympathies were rife, Sandby's loyalist credentials would never have been in doubt.

In 1803 the Royal Academy was virtually torn apart by a rift between the Council and the General Assembly.[35] Without rehearsing the details of the rift here, it is sufficient to note that, as the schism deepened, Sandby was firmly on the side of the 'rebel' court party, who upheld the supremacy of the Council, and whose cause was championed by Beechey, as well as other friends, including J.-F. Rigaud and Henry Tresham. Unhappy with the weak presidency of West, whom they eventually unseated and temporarily replaced with James Wyatt, the rebels asserted the authority of the Council through their overt allegiance to the monarchy and their innate patriotism. In the autumn of 1803 a group of rebel Academicians including Sandby were named in a newspaper advertisement as individual subscribers to the recently established Patriotic Fund, which raised money to support British Forces in the war with France. Although this may appear wholly acceptable for members of an institution which by now had achieved quasi-official status as well as royal patronage, the gesture enraged their opponents, notably Farington, who characterised it as a deliberately divisive ploy intended to 'disgrace the body at large' – since the Academy had not agreed to provide a corporate subscription.[36] Eventually, the breach was healed and the Academy was once more able to present a united front. It was not, however, until some years later, in December 1807, by which time Sandby was 76 years old, that Farington (himself now 60), was able to write in his diary: 'I shook hands with Sandby & had lively conversation with Him, for the first time in many years.'[37] Earlier in the year Benjamin West, now once more in the President's chair, had received a surprise visit from Sandby, who expressed satisfaction on behalf of the former rebel group at West's re-election: '"I told 'em," sd. He "That nothing else would do."' West replied 'that they two were of the small number of original members remaining, & it would be well for them to do whatever they could for the benefit of an Institution which his Majesty had so much favoured'.[38]

Yet, by now, it was Sandby who required material relief from the Academy. His works were failing to find a market, it being noted already in 1804 that 'they are admired but do not sell'.[39] In February 1808 the Council of the Royal Academy reported that Sandby's 'advanced age and infirmities, and a failure of his professional pursuits render it necesary [*sic*] to make an application to the Academy for the Pension by the Laws allowed in that case'. Sandby's application, following a 'proper investigation', was approved and he was duly given an annual pension of £60.[40] While the Academy pension was welcome, Sandby confessed to a friend that he still needed to work, 'so that I must drive on until death drops me in a hole'.[41] In April 1809, Sandby exhibited four works at the Royal Academy's Annual Exhibition, including a view from the back of his house in St George's Row, Bayswater; it was there that he died seven months later.

FIG. 13
Henry Singleton (1766–1839), *The Royal Academicians in General Assembly*, 1795. Oil on canvas, 1981 × 2590 mm. Royal Academy of Arts, London.

Paul Sandby is depicted standing behind and to the right of President Benjamin West's chair. Thomas Sandby features in the left of the foreground, in profile, seated and studying a drawing.

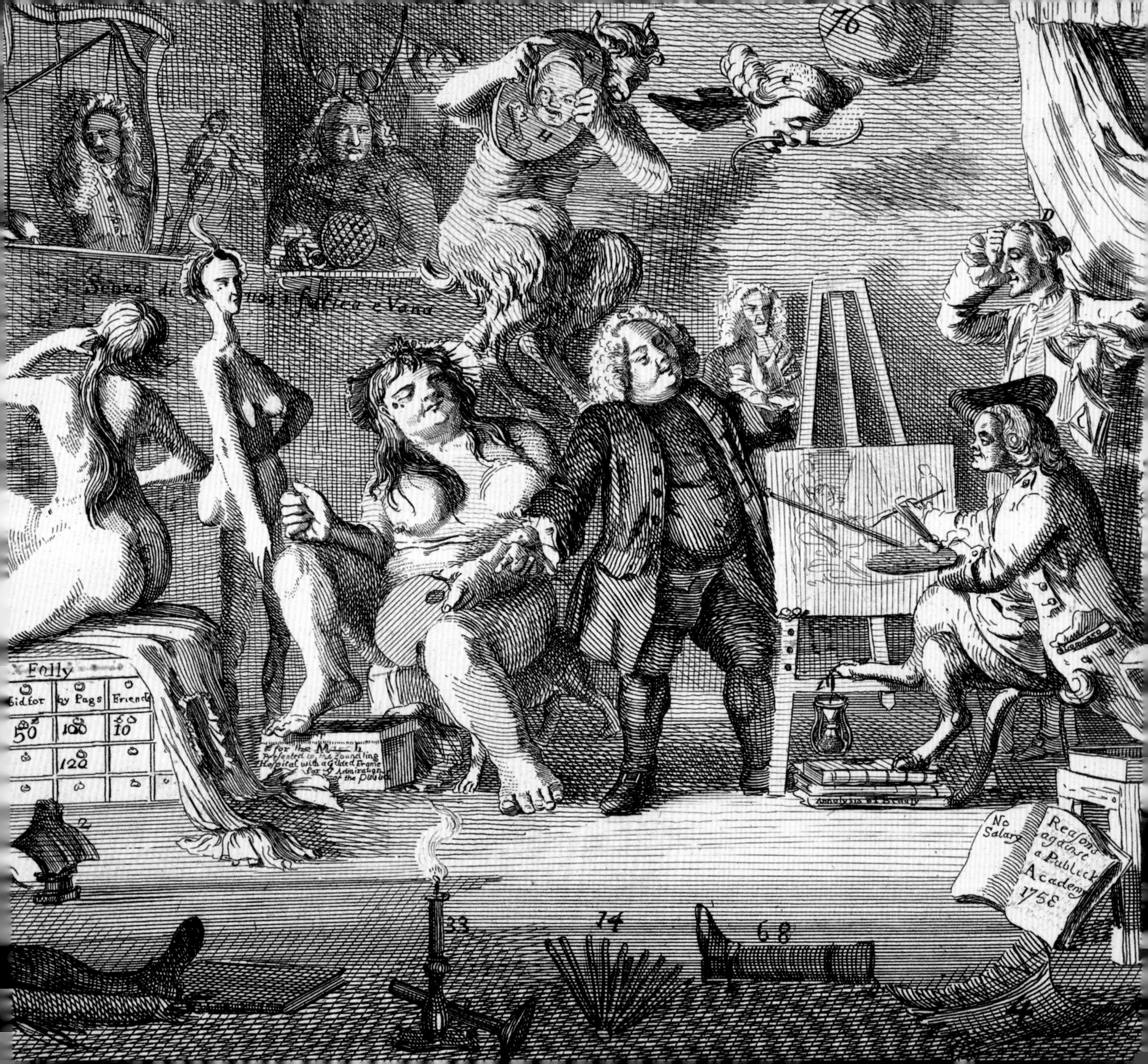

76
Senza di
fabrica e Vana
Folly
Sid for
by Pags
Friends
50
100
10
120
2
For the Ma
Presented to the Foundling
Hospital with a Gilded Frame
for y Admiration
of the Public
Analysis of Beauty
No Salary
Reasons against a Publick Academy 1758
33
14
68

The Analysis of Deceit: Sandby's Satires against Hogarth

GEOFF QUILLEY

William Sandby, author of the first extensive account of the lives of his ancestors Thomas and Paul Sandby, observed that a caricatural or satirical streak and 'indications of a humorous spirit are not wanting in any of the works of Paul Sandby'.[1] This is manifested in a range of guises, from the uncompromisingly unsentimental and bleak treatment of the urban poor in the *Twelve London Cries*, to the mischievous visual pleasure of the title page of *XII Views in Wales* (1777), in which Sandby shows, in typical fashion, a conventional enough view of 'The West Gate of CARDIFF in Glamorgan shire', but undercuts its apparent politeness by including comic, vulgar gestures and attitudes in the figures. He also continued to produce occasional satirical prints throughout his career, such as the 1757 lampoon against the dodgy art-dealer Dr Robert Bragge, or the later topical humour of *An English Balloon* (1784, British Museum, London). However, by far the most extraordinary instance of Sandby's capacity for sardonic visual humour and satire of a particularly sophisticated and pointed kind was the series of caustic prints directed against William Hogarth in the 1750s and early 1760s, which were especially targeted at Hogarth's 1753 publication of *The Analysis of Beauty*.[2] Perhaps the most striking aspects of this group of etchings – of which ten are included here (cats 21–28) – are, firstly, how vitriolic and impassioned they are, almost to the point of pathology; and secondly, how crudely impolite their visual grammar is, particularly when considered alongside the refined propriety of the landscape water-colours for which Sandby has become best known in conventional histories of British art, and which have earned him his reputation as the 'father' of British watercolour painting. In stark contrast, the satires against Hogarth indulge in an undisguised and unapologetic scatological humour that is both disconcerting in its explicitness – which certainly troubled William Sandby and Hogarth's biographer, John Ireland – and also deceptive in the way it diverts attention from the prints' technical sophistication and intellectual vitality.[3] A further remarkable aspect of the 1753–54 satires directed against *The Analysis of Beauty* is the sheer volume of often complex etchings produced over a short period that, however, manage to maintain a consistent focus on their target and an extraordinary energy of splenetic fury.

It is impossible to identify any clear sequence or system of production to the 1753–54 etchings, but the intended opening plate appears to be *A New DUNCIAD* (fig. 14), which loosely adopts the form of a title page, advertising itself as the first of 'eight Compositions' that comprise the 'first Sett' of prints, thus suggesting both that more are to follow and also that the satires were conceived, initially at least, as a coherent and defined group, like the *Twelve London Cries*, rather than being simply a random sequence of crude jibes against England's greatest contemporary artist.[4] *A New DUNCIAD* also presents particular themes and visual devices that recur throughout the other plates in the series, and thus reinforces the sense of unity with the group. So, for example, Hogarth the painter is depicted as an inanely grinning fool in a harlequinade, a characterisation that Sandby develops and varies in many other satires. The principal target, though, is *The Analysis of Beauty*, and Hogarth's supposed plagiarism in it of the sixteenth-century theorist and historian Giovanni Paolo Lomazzo: thus on the floor before Hogarth, set upon a book marked 'Lomazzo', is a fool's cap (implicitly Hogarth's own), which is labelled 'Pyramidal & Serpentine', a reference to the most notorious and disputed feature of Hogarth's treatise, his proposition of the 'line of beauty', which posited the serpentine line as a universal principle of beauty throughout all forms of nature and culture. The visual device that Hogarth invented to represent this aesthetic principle was a serpentine figure contained within an equilateral pyramid, to indicate the harmonisation of beauty with reason, a conceit that Sandby ridicules by proposing the fool's cap as the ideal manifestation of Hogarth's dual principle, since it is in itself both serpentine and pyramidal.

The same motif appears in *A Mountebank Painter* (cat. 27), where it is elaborated as the sign not just of folly but also of deceit and deformity, and thus becomes in Sandby's treatment the principle of the very opposite of beauty. The print shows Hogarth, grotesquely stunted (his torso is shortened: he is almost a 'no-body'), as the leader of a group of fairground tricksters, 'Demonstrating to his Admirers & Subscribers that Crookedness is ye Most Beautifull'. So he points with a serpentine (that is, crooked) stick to his 'Saturnine Analysis', placed on the supine back of his 'Fool' (whose backside is inscribed with a pair of spectacles, as a commentary on the optical impairment implicit in the author and readers of the treatise), before a group of spectators composed of gruesomely deformed characters who comprise the appropriate audience for Hogarth's aesthetic skulduggery. At the centre of this group, as the caption explains, Hogarth's assistant measures the hump of a hunchback with the curved leg of a stool, to demonstrate that 'Crookedness [is] ... according to his Rules, precisely beautifull'. At the back of Hogarth's stage a transparency is illuminated from above by rays of light emanating from the mouth of a head with ass's ears and wearing the same fool's cap as in *A New DUNCIAD* (with the line of beauty inscribed on its triangular peak, again mocking Hogarth's device). The fool's cap here, therefore, assumes a more sinister aspect than denoting Hogarth as a simple clown, for it classifies him also as a knave, and his aesthetic theory as morally fraudulent. This sense is reinforced by the fairground setting, a well-known arena for moral and social transgression which may well allude to Hogarth's own print of *Bartholomew Fair*, a parody of Hogarthian iconography that Sandby uses explicitly in other satires. Thus Hogarth's trumpeter in *A Mountebank Painter* – blowing a serpentine horn, naturally – wears trousers with arrows on them, the garb of a convicted felon. The serious point to the satire, therefore, is that Hogarth's aesthetics are not a rarefied issue of concern only to a small group of artists, but form an act of deception committed on an unsuspecting public, and thus transgress codes of public virtue, morality and politeness, with consequent implications for the maintenance of social order in general. The potential for duplicity in art was clearly a major concern for Sandby at this period: in a slightly later satire, *The Vertù Scavenger & Duper* (fig. 15), he shows the notoriously fraudulent art-dealer Dr Robert Bragge scooping in money from his sale of dodgy 'Old Masters', and comments in the inscription: 'a Man who sells things for what they are not, is a Cheat, and may be prosecuted as such, whether such Sale is in Private or by printed Catalogue with his Name to it.' In the same vein, therefore, we may take Sandby's stance against Hogarth's *Analysis* as a form of 'prosecution' of a 'cheat', whose advocacy of the line of beauty is an attempt to sell something for what it is not, which perhaps explains something of the extraordinary vehemence of Sandby's satires.

This concern with art and deception is explored most fully in *Puggs GRACES Etched from his ORIGINAL Daubing* (cat. 22), a direct parody of plate 1 of Hogarth's *Analysis* (fig. 16), both in its composition, echoing the sculptor's yard of Hogarth's print, and in its absurd numbering system, that mocks the border to Hogarth's plate, with its elaborately obscure and lengthy key. This would seem to be another early image in the set, since the cartouche in the caption includes the words 'to be continued'. It shows Hogarth again seated at his easel, at work on *Moses brought before Pharaoh's Daughter*, a picture that he completed for the Foundling Hospital in 1746. Before him are three grossly distorted and hideous nude 'graces', in a grouping that clearly recalls the iconography of the Judgement of Paris. Hogarth himself is half-man, half-satyr, a hybridisation that is repeated in the inclusion above the three nudes of a diabolical satyr, who holds up a roundel of Hogarth's grinning features before his own face and whose horns ironically take the form of the line of beauty. To the extreme left a bizarre mannequin constructed of straw-filled breeches and bellows (indicating

FIG. 14
Paul Sandby, *A New Dunciad done with a view of [fixing] ye fluctuating Ideas of Taste, without Preface or Introduction*, 1753. Etching, 194 × 231 mm. British Museum, London, 1904,0819.700

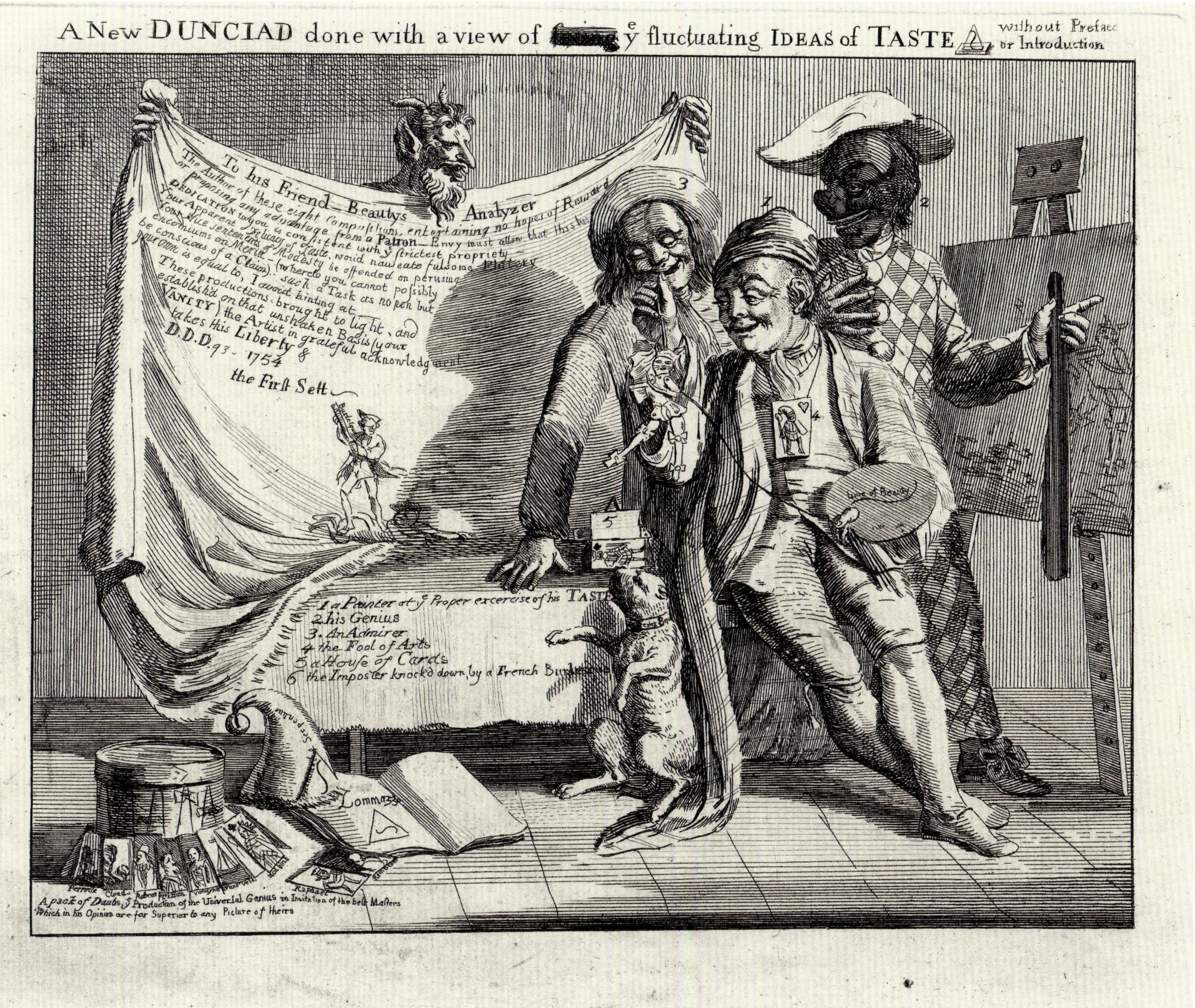
A New DUNCIAD done with a view of ye fluctuating IDEAS of TASTE
without Preface or Introduction
To his Friend – Beautys Analyzer
The Author of these eight Compositions, entertaining no hopes of Reward
or proposing any advantage from a Patron – Envy must allow that this his
DEDICATION to you is consistent with ye strictest propriety –
Your Apparent Delicacy of Taste, would nauseate fulsome Flattery
Your Nice sentements of Modesty be offended on perusing
encomiums on Merit – (whereto you cannot possibly
be conscious of a Claim) – such a Task as no pen but
your own is equal to, I avoid hinting at.
These productions, brought to light, and
establish'd on that unshaken Basis (your
VANITY) the Artist in grateful acknowledgment
takes this Liberty &
D.D.D. 93 – 1754
the First Sett
1 a Painter at ye Proper excercise of his TASTE
2 his Genius
3. An Admirer
4 the Fool of Arts
5 a House of Cards
6 the Imposter knock'd down, by a French
Line of Beauty
Serpentine
Lommazo
Cloud
Rubens
Titian
Vandyke
Raphael
A pack of Daubs, ye Production of the Universal Genius in Imitation of the best Masters
Which in his Opinion are far Superior to any Picture of theirs

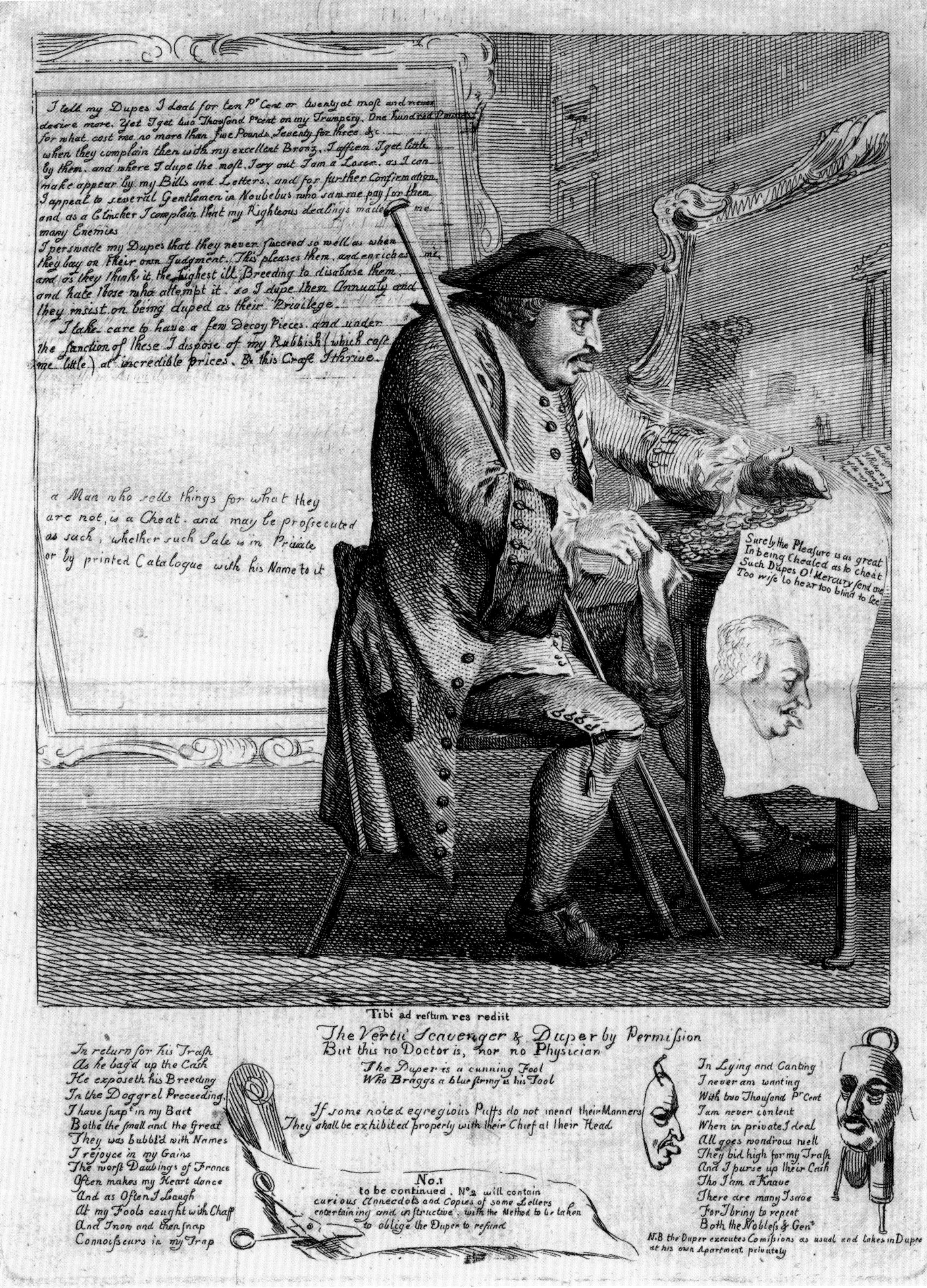

FIG. 15
Paul Sandby, *The Vertù Scavenger & Duper*, 1757. Etching, 279 × 201 mm. British Museum, London, 1868,0808.4092

the vacuity of Hogarth's exercise as a painter) supports a plinth inscribed 'RAPHAEL': on this, however, there is no longer a bust of the Renaissance artist – which now sits decapitated on the floor – but instead a serpentine stick with a wig atop it. The caption explains: '2 a Bust of Raphael Destroyd for pugs Wig.'

The *ad hoc* and incongruous arrangement of the figure clearly picks up on the comical juxtapositions of the statuary in plate 1 of *The Analysis of Beauty*, a burlesque continued in the arbitrary row of objects placed in the foreground, one of which resembles a bunch of sticks, but is explained in the caption as '14 Rays of Light', that is, the same rays of light issuing from the mouth of the fool's head in *A Mountebank Painter* (cat. 27). The implication here, therefore, is that Hogarth's modern artistic practice and aesthetics entail an iconoclastic abandonment of artistic tradition derived from the masters of the Italian Renaissance; a disregard for the rules of art that results in an inability to distinguish beauty from deformity, and to judge what is what. The theme of judgement is pursued in the row of busts on the ledge in the background: a lawyer sporting the crescent of Diana (the goddess of virtue) on his head like cuckold's horns, a judge with a pair of scales whose balance is tipped by a large bag of money, and a parson with a large pair of spectacles upside-down on his head, again in the form of cuckold's horns. The bust of the judge is placed beneath a small gibbet, whose rectilinear frame is distorted into the form of the line of beauty. The larger point that Sandby appears to be making here, then, is that Hogarth's *Analysis* is a subversion of all criteria for aesthetic judgement, and this has dire consequences for other forms of legal, moral and religious judgement. This larger public context is made explicit in the book in the right foreground, open at 'Reasons against a Public Academy 1753', a reference to

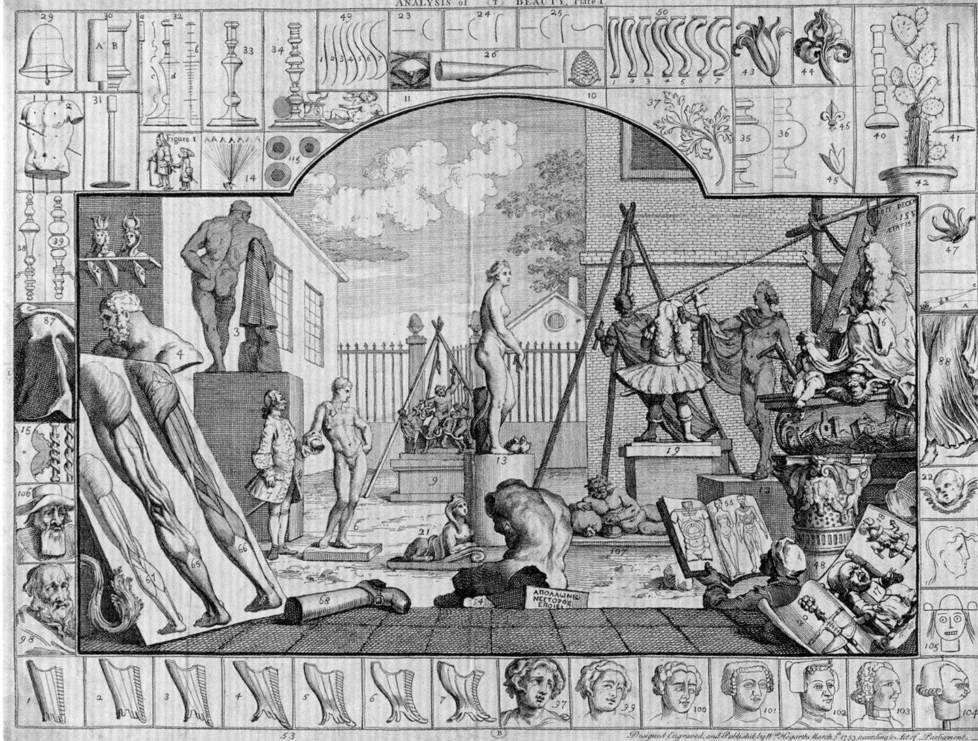

FIG. 16
William Hogarth (1697–1764), *The Analysis of Beauty*, plate 1, 1753. Engraving, 381 × 501 mm. Hunterian Museum and Art Gallery, University of Glasgow

Hogarth's objections, in what Michael Kitson has termed 'the first sustained anti-academic treatise in the history of aesthetics', to proposals for establishing an academy for art in England.[5] Sandby, by contrast, points in this satire to the danger of Hogarth's self-appointed status as arbiter of taste, and the risk of this being no more than an exercise in vanity and delusion, since unlike an academy, it is founded on nothing more than individual taste, with no established rule or tradition to guide it.

The theme of delusion is carried to its logical satirical conclusion in *The Author run Mad* (cat. 28), which shows Hogarth as the insane inmate of Bedlam (no doubt parodying the final plate of Hogarth's *A Rake's Progress*), laughing crazily as he frantically paints every surface of his cell. The picture on the wall before him shows him as 'the Man in ye Moon, painted by himself, the Earth was to Low for his Vanity', beside which he paints a serpentine line: the irony being, however, that the line of beauty, annotated as '4 the precise Line', is now transformed into the line of the chain that shackles his ankle to the floor: the line of beauty is not only delusional, it is also a form of artistic confinement. Meanwhile, beside the caption below the main image, a vignette represents Sandby's sane 'reality' in opposition to Hogarth's delusions satirised in the main image: so Hogarth – again hybridised as half-man, half-satyr – lies on the ground 'By his own Folly Str[u]ck with LUNACY', being beaten by the personification of lunacy holding his attribute, the crescent moon. Behind them is an easel displaying Sandby's satires, denoting the exposure of Hogarth's madness, and again contrasting this with Sandby's satirical sanity and common-sense.

This contrast between delusional folly, shown in the main image, and clear-headed 'real life', represented in the caption below, is employed again in *The Painters March from Finchly* (cat. 26), in which the principal scene, a composite burlesque upon Hogarth's *The March of the Guards to Finchley*, completed again for the Foundling Hospital, and other works, including the *Four Times of Day*, *The Enrag'd Musician* and the *Satire on False Perspective*, is opposed to the vignette below of Hogarth sitting humiliated in the stocks, again represented as no more than a common criminal. This oppositional visual rhetoric is played out at its most sophisticated level, however, in *Burlesque sur le Burlesque* (cat. 21) (also reprinted in English as *The BURLESQUER burlesqued*). Here again Hogarth is shown seated at his easel, upon which stands a half-finished canvas of the 'sacrifice of Isaac' in the 'Dutch' style, as a satirical reference to Hogarth's own treatment of *Paul before Felix* in the manner of Rembrandt: Abraham is shown as a butcher about to fire a gun at Isaac's head, but the angel above intervenes to prevent the sacrifice by urinating on the flintlock. A parrot (known, of course, for blindly copying) seated atop the easel defaecates on the canvas for good measure. The reference to *Paul before Felix* is made explicit in the picture on the wall behind, which in the second (English) edition of the print was explained as '4 his Brains taken out & his Scul serving for a Magic lanthorn, Paul before Felix is reflected from it on ye Wall'.

Meanwhile, the bottom register of the print below the caption is made up of a sequence of street scenes, showing various means of disposing of *The Analysis of Beauty*, including a man carting copies of the book in a barrow to a kitchen to be used as fuel; beside him the treatise is being read by a lowly sweep; next it is sold by the hundredweight for ballast; then an old Frenchwoman offers it at her street stall for the discounted price of four *sous*, with a cartload more being dumped on the ground before her; finally, a hawker, dressed in old rags, has multiple copies slung over his shoulder, suggesting that it is not even fit for him to make a meagre living. All these figures bear a close resemblance to Sandby's studies of street life in Scotland in the 1740s, and the figure of the hawker in particular recalls the similar figure in the *Twelve London Cries*, perhaps suggesting a satirical anti-Hogarthian edge to that series of London street-sellers as well (see cat. 35). In any case, these vignettes of down-to-earth 'real' life are not only intended to undercut the ridiculous pretensions of Hogarth in the main image above, but also to challenge Hogarth's claims, made in the *Analysis* and in his own 'modern moral subjects', to be a painter of modern urban life and the lower classes.

The complex and highly sophisticated inter-referentiality among these prints and between them and other contemporary works by Sandby and Hogarth is epitomised in the picture of the 'Magic lanthorn' on the background wall, which Sandby issued as a separate satire in its own right,

The Magic Lantern (cat. 24). This shows Hogarth seated in profile in a darkened room, with light projecting from his open mouth onto the wall opposite to show a bowdlerised version again of *Paul before Felix*. In the background is a figure pointing to the illumination. The conical form of the projected light is – perhaps subliminally – a variant of Sandby's satirical motif of the fool's cap as the epitome of Hogarth's line of beauty. Perhaps more important here is the sense of Hogarth again as a trickster, a purveyor of empty illusion for a gullible public dazzled by spectacle without substance.

Related to these themes of illusion, madness and fraud is that of Hogarth as iconoclastic anti-Academician, whose aesthetic theory and artistic practice constitute a dangerous subversion of all artistic tradition. This facet of Sandby's satirical denunciation of Hogarth is the principal theme of a highly accomplished print, *The Vile Ephesian* (cat. 25). The carefully and richly organised composition consists of a capriccio of classical structures in a nocturnal landscape, dominated in the right foreground by a monument to the great artists of the past: an elaborate pillar, topped by a flaming urn. At its base crouches Hogarth – again hybridised – whom the inscription on a plaque opposite describes as:

> A self Conceited Arrogant Dauber, groveling in vain to undermin ye ever Sacred Monument of all ye best Painters Sculps Archits &c. in Imitation of the Impious Herostratus who with Sacrilegious Flames Destroyd ye Temple of Diana to perpetuate his Name to Posterity.

Hogarth is portrayed, therefore, as a modern Herostratus, and the temple is accordingly burning in the background. In the distance is a domed building, conspicuously resembling St Peter's or St Paul's, but presumably intended as the dome of a future academy of art, to which Hogarth will next turn his attentions. With doubtless intended irony, the monument to past artists that Hogarth attempts to destroy is formed as a conical pillar wound around by a spiralling snake: thus it is an icon of Hogarth's aesthetic principles, based on the pyramid and the serpentine line, that are illustrated in the caption below, which explains that Hogarth's attempt at sabotage, like that of Herostratus, will be in vain.

All these themes converge in perhaps the most scabrous, vulgar and impolite print of the series, *The Analyst Besh_n in his own Taste* (cat. 23), which centres on the idea of Hogarth being confronted by the ghost of Lomazzo. The extensive caption describes Hogarth as 'an Author Sinking under the weight of his Saturnine Analysis'. He holds a copy of the *Analysis* on a support that buckles into the form of the line of beauty 'by the Mighty Load upon it', and looks up in startled terror at the apparition of Lomazzo, holding aloft the serpentine line as his own, at whose accusations of fraud, misrepresentation and plagiarism Hogarth fills his breeches – his pug is sniffing the odour coming from his backside. Before him, a grossly misshapen, serpentine figure is 'Deformity Weeping at the Condition of her Darling Son', while in the background, to the right, is the triumphal arch of a new 'Public Academy' under construction, and to the left, copies of Hogarth's treatise are being thrown into 'the Cave of Dulness and Oblivion'. The vulgar crudity of this print seems a world apart both from the polite discourse of aesthetics and the contemporary proposals for an academy, and also from Sandby's own polite representations of landscape and country houses. Yet, it alerts us to the rancour with which artistic debates were conducted at this critical period in the development of British art and its institutions, as well as to the uncompromising earthiness of Sandby's other work at this time, particularly the *Twelve London Cries*, which as already suggested may also have a satirical anti-Hogarthian edge. The crudity (and cruelty) of the image of Hogarth also obscures the print's deeper sophistication. For the larger point, when it is taken in context with the other prints of the series, is that Hogarth's *Analysis of Beauty* proposes an aesthetic theory in which any idea of objective critical judgement is undone, so that taste can become its complete opposite: in which the artist must logically end up 'Besh_n'. Such an idea is much closer, of course, to debates on art of our own era, an indication perhaps of the originality and modernity of Sandby's satires, as well as their importance: these were produced several decades before the brilliant lampoons of Rowlandson, Gillray and the Cruikshanks.[6] Yet it also needs to be remembered that, if the vicious and crude visual language employed in these prints is far removed from the refinement of fine art, it is not so from contemporary political satire, which is the genre that Sandby is exploiting here, and which gives a further indication of the larger social and cultural context against which he intended these prints to be read.

The visual rhetoric of political lampoons tended to be much coarser and much more personally vindictive, making it unequivocally clear which individual was the target of the satire.[7] *The Political Vomit for the Ease of Britain* (1742), for example, shows the unpopular and scandal-ridden Prime Minister Robert Walpole vomiting and excreting places and positions that members of the parliamentary opposition are eagerly scooping up (fig. 17). However, this scene of graphic bodily purging by the leader of the nation takes place within the elegant space of a palatial, panelled court interior: the contrast between refinement and coarse vulgarity is stark as a commentary on the discourse and practices of politics. Hogarth's satire, by contrast, operated at a more abstract, philosophical level, maintaining a tradition that placed itself above such vulgarity and name-calling: although specific, identifiable individuals are certainly included in Hogarth's 'modern moral subjects', such as Mother Needham and Colonel Charteris in plate 1 of *A Harlot's Progress*, they are not in themselves presented as the chief butt of the satire; rather it is the values and vices they personify that come under Hogarth's fire.[8] Strikingly, therefore, in his anti-Hogarth prints Sandby was not working within a Hogarthian satirical tradition at all, but in a parallel strain derived from the politics of Parliament and the court. On the contrary, it could further be argued that it was Hogarth, when he later produced plates openly supporting the Prime Minister Lord Bute and denouncing the radical politician John Wilkes, who was following the example of Sandby.

In turn, it was in this latter context that Sandby resumed his anti-Hogarthian stance in 1762, in direct response to Hogarth's two plates of *The Times*, published that year, which were for Hogarth an unusual direct intervention

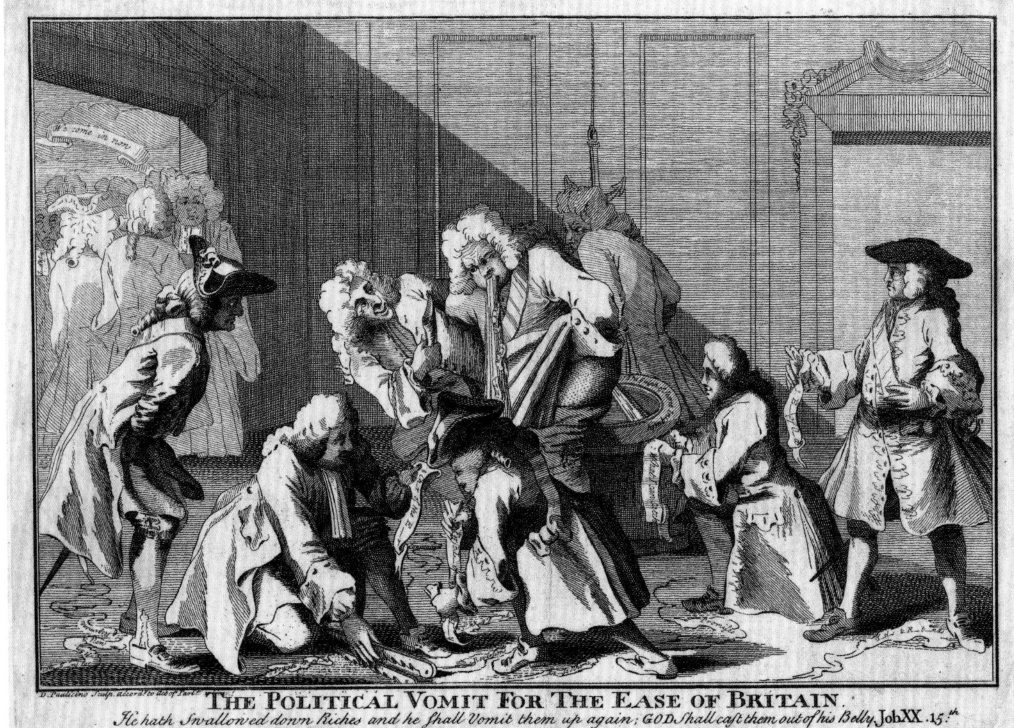

FIG. 17
Anonymous artist, *The Political Vomit for the Ease of Britain*, 1742. Etching, 226 × 314 mm. British Museum, London, 1868,0808.13283

into contemporary politics (fig. 18).[9] In them he publicly announced his support for the contentious and unpopular figure of the Prime Minister, Lord Bute. Sandby's rebuttals, including *The BUTIFYER. A Touch upon The Times Plate I* (cat. 29), and the untitled satire against Hogarth and Bute (cat. 30), thus portray Hogarth as the stooge of Bute and corrupted through being in his pay, showing him – in a parody of Hogarth's own earlier satire against Lord Burlington – as no more than a simple boot-black, painting a large boot (punning on Bute) and 'Bespattering the rest of the Nobility'.[10] It is unclear why the other elaborate and complex print was left untitled and unfinished; perhaps it was simply because the topicality of the subject had passed. These later satires, however, indicate the vehemence with which Sandby pursued his dispute with Hogarth, and its ongoing importance for him over a decade or more. The whole group of satires against Hogarth also affirms the unavoidably political nature of any form of visual art in Britain in the eighteenth century.

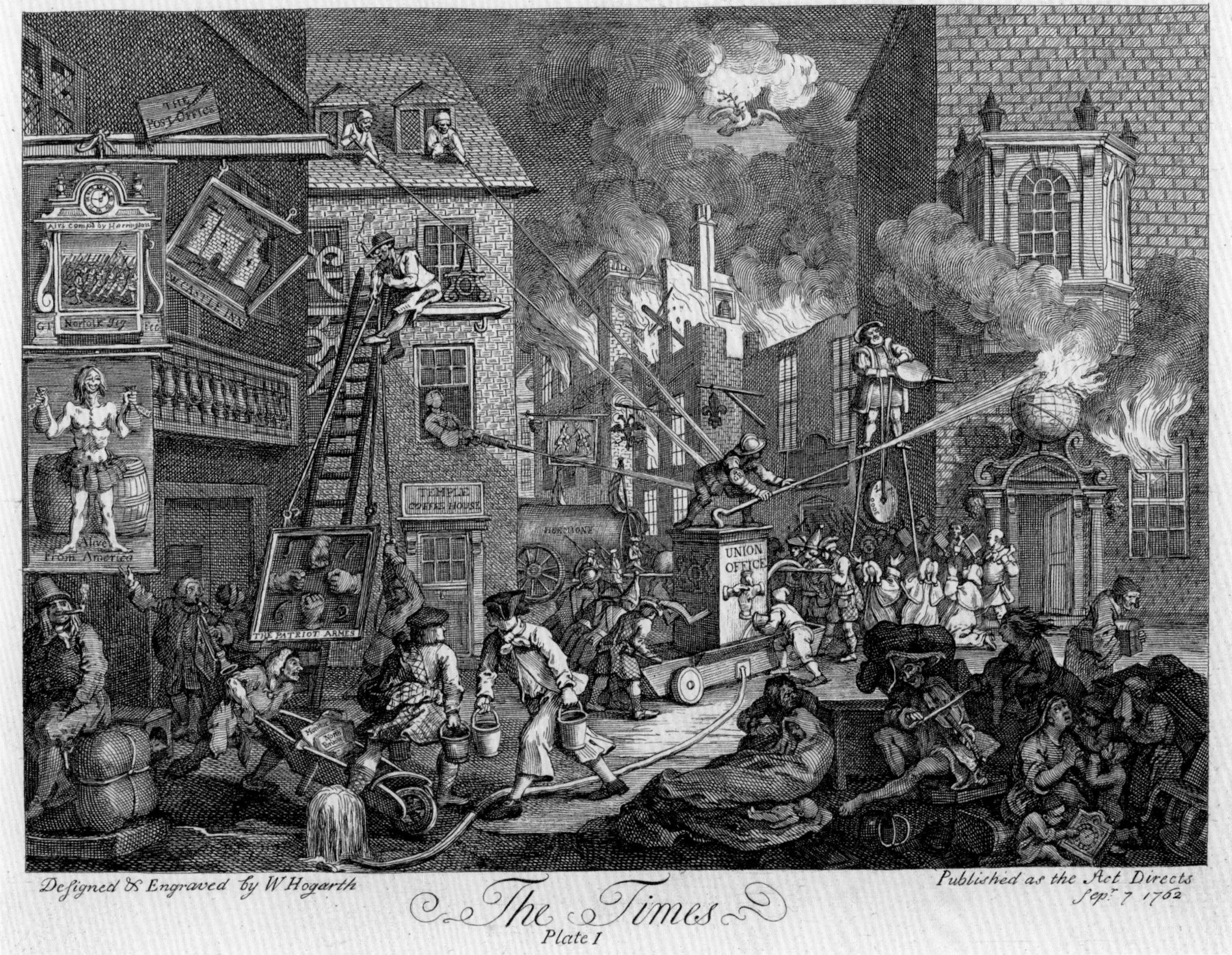

FIG. 18
William Hogarth (1697–1764), *The Times*, plate 1, 1762. Etching and engraving, 246 × 306 mm. British Museum, London, 1825,3 13,34

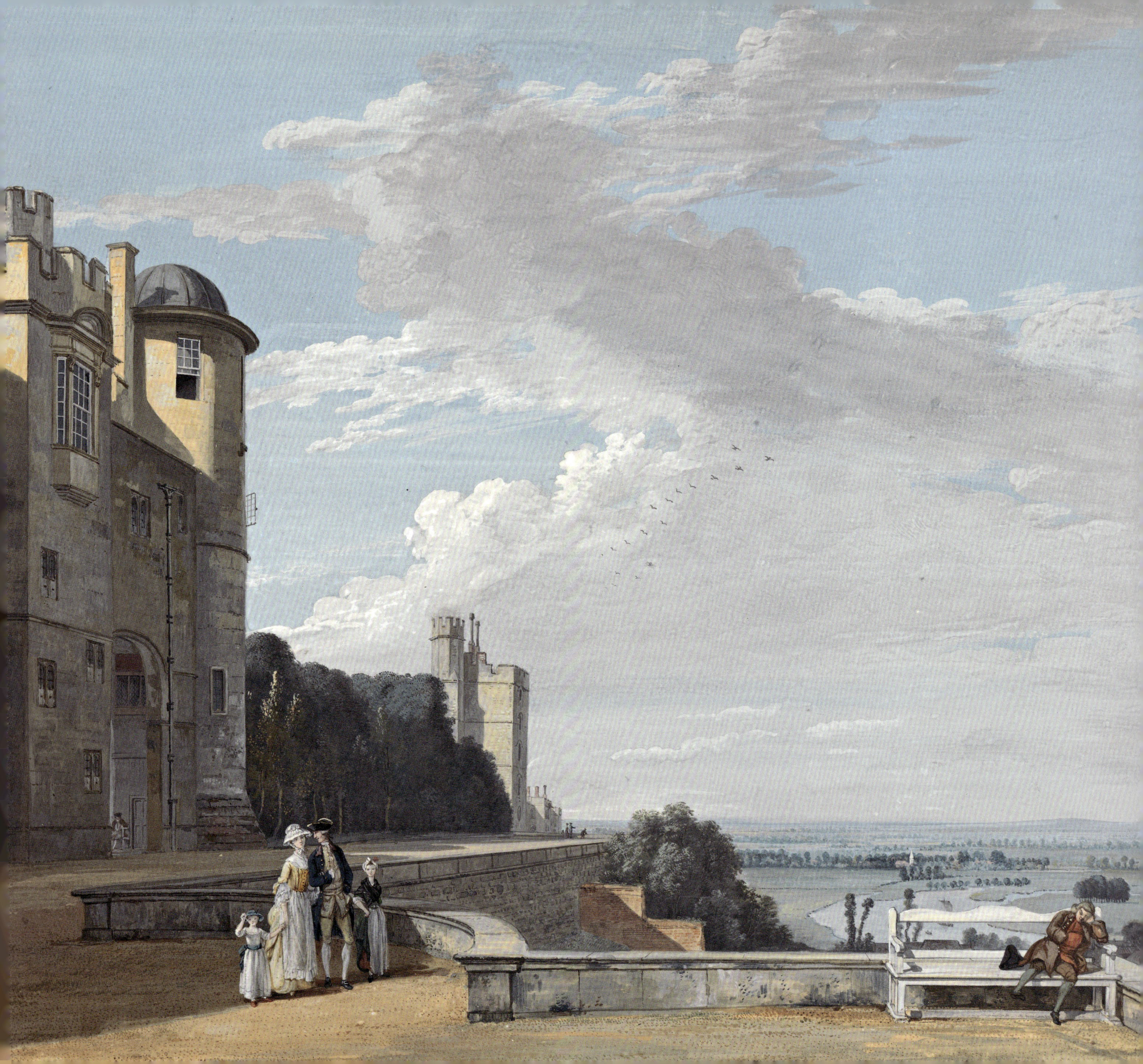

Court Art Reviewed: The Sandbys' Vision of Windsor and Its Environs

MATTHEW CRASKE

Paul Sandby is chiefly remembered as one of the fathers of British landscape painting. That he is overlooked as an important exponent of graphic satire is an impediment to the proper enjoyment of many of his paintings. Classified as landscapes in the topographical tradition, his opus of Windsor scenes are misconstrued if viewed merely as records of the landscape. As I argue below, many are better regarded as entertaining and challenging social commentaries. Numerous Windsor views now in the Royal Collection appear to be the product of fraternal co-operation, Paul's main contribution being the addition of groups of figures who interact to suggest petty social dramas. The most ambitious of these joint ventures relate to the period when Windsor Great Park was the domain of Thomas's first great patron, William Augustus, Duke of Cumberland (1721–1765). Analysis of these shared endeavours reveals that Thomas is likely to be the meticulous hand behind some of the prospects, the presiding expert in matters of perspective and the handling of the *camera obscura*, whereas Paul, although proficient in these matters too, was the better freehand draughtsman and probably added the local colour of foreground figures.

It was partly through the inclusion of comic figures that the Sandbys' views came to reveal facets of Windsor that are not found in printed tourist itineraries. Most publishers of the latter plagiarised Joseph Pote's much promoted guides of the 1740s and 1750s, which were themselves derived from seventeenth-century investigations into the solemn proceedings of the Order of the Garter. Largely produced for private portfolio viewing, many of the Sandbys' accounts of Windsor can be seen to reflect a wry and intimate twist upon these standard perspectives of tour literature.

There is not the scope here for a painstaking account of Windsor's transformation into a tourist destination. It is sufficient to note that at some time between the death of Charles II, who turned the castle into a summer palace, and the appearance of the first cheap guidebooks in the 1750s, Windsor Castle and the Great Park became a prime fixture in the itineraries of those seeking pleasurable days out from London. The last time that the castle had fulfilled its original function as a fortress had been during the Civil War, when it became an important bastion of Parliament. The removal of all evidence of the desecrating rebels was probably a prime stimulus to Charles II to convert the building into an imposing venue for court ritual. After the Restoration, a series of murals celebrating the scope of reinstated monarchical authority was commissioned. Throughout Charles II's reign, the castle was not freely accessible to the public.[1] Indeed, the very purpose of the changes made there was to distance the court from the people; viewing the persons of the King and Queen was architecturally contrived as a distinct privilege. This theatre of state seems to have appealed to William III but not to the first two Hanoverian monarchs, during whose reign the castle, though maintained, became redundant as a royal residence. It remained so until the late 1770s when a middle-aged George III, engulfed by the failing war for America, elected to spend more time there.[2]

The castle's redundancy led to the state rooms slowly becoming the resort of tourists. Charles II's elaborate Guard Chambers lost their military purpose, as there was no monarch in residence to protect. The weapons formerly employed in practical defence were arranged by the master-gunner into elaborate geometric wall decorations to please visitors. For Georgians of the mid-century, the very prospect of the castle became a reminder that they lived in peaceful times and that the tribulations of the Civil War had been firmly consigned to the darker annals of national history. Joseph Pote wrote with pride:

> The present strength of the Castle is considerably abated by the currency of many years and the excellency of our national constitution, whereby fortresses and strongholds are not thought necessary in this Kingdom and a happy union between the Prince and subject is the great security of state.[3]

This sentence appears both in Pote's twelve-shilling guide and a pocket-sized, two-shilling economy version published in the early 1750s. The latter edition was dedicated to the man recently appointed Ranger of Windsor Great Park and Warden of Windsor Forest, the Duke of Cumberland, second son of George II. Cumberland assumed his authority over the Great Park in 1746, as a reward from his father for suppressing the Jacobite Rebellion of 1745. In his dedication, Pote made explicit the perceived link between his patron's transformation of the Park and Forest into a leisure destination, and the suppression of the Rebellion. The inference was that the Duke's military prowess had made possible the pleasures of peace, which his 'improvements' extended to a wider public. Pote described his patron's victory in the highlands as the event through which 'the blessings' of 'our gracious monarch were secured to us and our posterity by your Royal Highness in the day of danger'. It was only after this victory, as Pote reminded his readers, that Cumberland had turned his mind to rendering Windsor 'truly delightful in her Park'. A verse was quoted which praised the Duke in his peaceful endeavours at Windsor for pursuing the cause of 'public liberty' made possible by 'Tyranny's defeat'. Through Cumberland's munificence, the Great Park came more closely to resemble metropolitan royal domains such as Hyde Park, St James's Park and Green Park; becoming the last of the royal pleasure grounds to be converted into a component of the public realm.

Pote's guide did not mention the Sandby brothers but the tenor of its dedication explained the terms of their presence. Thomas, who established a permanent residence at Windsor, arrived there directly from the Duke's campaigns during the War of Austrian Succession, which terminated in early 1749. In the wake of his return from campaign, his patron, the Duke, was immersed in a 'Regency crisis', during which his role as Captain-General of His Majesty's Forces was criticised as being inconsistent with his position as successor to the throne.[4] Amid accusations that he had become a military dictator in waiting, the Duke retired to his role of Ranger. Neutered in public and military life, Cumberland set out to become a hero of the peaceful public realm, gathering around him artists to transform the Great Park into a spectacular pleasure resort. In this respect, Cumberland was probably inspired by Viscount Cobham, the Whig magnate who, twenty years before, had been moved to build a grand public and political garden on his estate at Stowe in Buckinghamshire upon being removed from military office.

Like Cobham, who was into political opposition in the early 1730s, Cumberland regarded enforced retirement as a prompt to a virtuous return to the land, in the manner of the ancient Roman thrust into unjust exile. In retirement the Duke was able to espouse the Low Church, Whig principles for which he had fought in the '45: respect for those who pursued liberty through property and performed unpretentious works of public benefit and improvement. Cumberland inherited, to some extent, the political role of his elder bother, Frederick, Prince of Wales (1707–1751), who frequented a residence at Kew Gardens: a figurehead for an alternative court which functioned in Eden-like isolation from the corruptions of Westminster and St James's.[5] Like his deceased brother, Cumberland discovered the charms of the political wilderness in plants, water and garden buildings. As Cumberland's factotum, Thomas Sandby's role was to make, maintain and record an Eden in which liberty and genteel independence reigned to a more complete extent than in the nation at large. His brother's job was to facilitate the process of record and, through his figure studies, document the effects, or lack of them, on the presiding ideals of the British public.

Cumberland, like Cobham before him, heeded the biblical injunction to 'turn swords into ploughshares', converting the skills of grand military planning, in particular earthworks, to services of gardening and land improvement. As a fine drawing by the Sandbys of the building of Flitcroft's

Grand Palladian Bridge records, Cumberland even employed veterans of his campaigns during the War of Austrian Succession to move the earth (cat. 80).[6] In the opinion of an enthusiastic obituarist, this act of public charity supported Cumberland's claim to have provided a public resort on behalf of his father, George II:

> The greatest part of the large revenues settled on him by his country, as a reward for his services, he returned into her bosom, by constantly employing a great number of hands in adorning Windsor Park, the free access to which renders it as much, in some sort, the property of the subject, as the Monarch.[7]

Central to the Duke's grand scheme of improvements was the opening up of the waterways of the Great Park, which had formerly been unnavigable streams. This process integrated the Park within the itinerary of Thames-side destinations enjoyed by leisure boats on trips from London.[8] Investment in great hydraulic projects had been, at least since the grand improvements visited upon the gardens at Versailles and Marly by Louis XIV, a prime means of communicating metaphorically the power of European royal houses. Cumberland's works contrasted with those of the Sun King and his imitators in so far as they were conspicuously natural. They did not represent the awesome constraint of natural forces to impress, or intimidate, the courtier. Rather, such forces were 'improved', rendered more benign and pleasurable, for the public good. Widened streams and rustic rockworks were preferred to fountains and regimented cascades with sculptural adornments proclaiming political potency with allegorical bluster. No figurative sculpture was erected in Cumberland's Park, no image, allegorical or otherwise, of its presiding royal patron.

When the Duke commissioned Thomas Sandby to make, with the assistance of his brother, a series of eight magnificent engraved views of his improvements at Windsor, the pleasures of waterborne travel, in which the polite public was invited to partake, were the most emphatically celebrated feature (cat. 77). The title page of the series included the image of a conspicuously 'natural' cascade. Two prints celebrated the building of bridges that were designed to allow vistas along the man-made waterways to be fully appreciated. One of the most impressive scenes recorded the ceremonial embarkation of a Chinese barge in which the Duke travelled among the smaller sails of lesser leisure boaters. So important were these engravings to the Duke's sense of what he was trying to achieve at Windsor that he had them glazed and hung in the entrance chambers to his new-built Lodge on the estate.[9]

The *Eight Views of Windsor Great Park* relate overtly to European conventions of court art. They were commissioned in 1754, the same year that Louis XV ordered the production of a series of engravings, after paintings by Claude Vernet, recording improvements to the ports of France. By contrast, the Sandbys' early watercolour studies of the town and castle of Windsor, datable mainly to the 1760s, do not constitute an explicit visual apologia for the effects of royal administrations, these landscapes being beyond the direct control of the Duke. Much as the person, or persons, who made these pictures were drawn to the area by the resources of a court, they too must be seen to relate, albeit as a diversion or subversion, to traditions of court art. In so far as these works generally eschew unambiguous celebration of royal magnificence, they reflect the character of the court which gave rise to them. Pestered by his critics for bringing to England a species of stiff Prussian militarism, Cumberland was particularly keen to run his court with a light, liberal and kindly touch. Thus, his courtiers do not seem to have been expected to perform as subservient, work-to-order flunkies. Although Thomas was entirely financially beholden to Cumberland, the brothers were able to take to their watercolours as independent gentlemen. Residing at Windsor, they were at liberty to form images of the paraphernalia of royalty free of the customary central expectation of 'court art': that it should be conspicuously impressive and explicitly flattering to a commissioning prince.

The freedom to roam, coupled with moneyed leisure time to enjoy it, were prerequisites for the mid-eighteenth-century British tourist in forming his or her view of the world. This spirit of investigation, underscored by a local, candid view of the place, prevails in the Sandbys' early watercolours of Windsor Castle and the town that are now in the Royal Collection. Some of the views of Windsor appear to relate to the patronage of George Brudenell, the

Duke of Montagu, Governor of the Castle.[10] Yet we have no record of them in that patron's possession. Having been encouraged by Montagu to paint these scenes, Sandby proceeded to produce views to no explicit patron's plan or overt commercial purpose, although some were later translated into print, the drawings passing in miscellaneous groups into royal hands or those of subsequent collectors. The modest scale of these views and their benign candour were appropriate to the culture of a court that claimed to rule by mild and jovial consent. The early Hanoverians declined to employ visual artists to create autocratic fictions of the type that had sustained their predecessors, the Stuarts. Accordingly, the Sandby brothers' watercolours of the exterior of the castle formed a stark contrast with the art inside the building that was described by Pote, in particular Verrio's great allegorical murals on the theme of Charles II's imposition of his authority over the state.[11] Intimate, blithe, relaxed and informal, and made to no explicit royal command, the Sandbys' pictures were the opposite of Stuart courtly art.[12] Indeed, the defining atmosphere of many of Paul Sandby's figurative studies of New Windsor is a certain shabby ease, the evidence of crumbling martial authority paying subtle testimony to the comfort with which the security of the modern monarchical state was maintained. On numerous occasions, Sandby took as his subject the open gates to the castle, presenting these portals as locations of informal local sociability. Red-coated foot guards commonly appear in these works, though never as starched functionaries. Rather, they typically lounge, flirt with girls or chat with the townspeople (fig. 20). Emblems of improved times when princes no longer depended upon wary guards and impregnable fortifications, these images exposed as malicious myth allegations that Cumberland had ambitions to transform Britain into a tyrannical state. As Pote suggested, Georgian subjects were privileged to live in easy familiarity with the formerly intimidating paraphernalia of regal authority.

The transformation of Windsor Castle into a tourist destination was nowhere more evident than in the opening up of its terraces to the public. The Sandby brothers communicated their interest in the culture of tourism in their regular employment of these places of promenade as subject-matter (cats 57–58). The famous North Terrace was not, however, simply a setting for fashionable promenade. It was a giant emblem of political liberty, bespeaking circumstances in which the exclusive resort of kings and queens had become a wider forum for public pleasures. As readers of the tourist literature were generally informed, the North Terrace was built, with considerable engineering enterprise, on account of Queen Elizabeth I's predilection for taking the air.[13] The tourist literature also frequently stressed that the original purpose of the North Terrace was to provide visual testimony of the sovereign's power to survey his or her national domain. Pote, who proclaimed this 'the noblest walk in Europe', described it as the product of an 'august' plan to allow the sovereign to 'overlook all adjacent country'. The extension of the monarch's prospect to a wider public was no less than a permit to the citizen to regard his country as his own, assuming a point of view that had formerly been a regal privilege. Paul Sandby was characteristically humorous in reviewing the manner in which his fellow citizens exploited this privilege. In paintings produced throughout his career, the North Terrace is shown as a place where young soldiers flirt, old men ogle pretty girls and drunks doze off the day's indulgences. The tendency of the British public to prefer sex and booze to the awesome view of monarchs appealed to Sandby's Whig sense of humour – in benign sympathy with the ideal of man's improvement but not illiberally insistent upon it.

The development of tourism out of the metropolis and along the Thames valley, concluding with a visit to Windsor, was strongly motivated by the desire to experience extensive views. So hackneyed was the urge to gain a vantage over this part of Britain that in 1775 Henrietta Pye prefaced her guide to Windsor and the Thames valley with a fulsome apology for employing the term 'prospect' with displeasing frequency.[14] Pye understood that touring society's obsession with these prospects had become sufficiently familiar to be legitimately greeted with a certain humorous contempt. In assuming disdain, the feisty Henrietta was being consciously subversive, for many serious men had considered these 'constitutional' views to be no joking matter. Poetic tradition dictated that regarding such landscapes ought to be sobering and instructive.

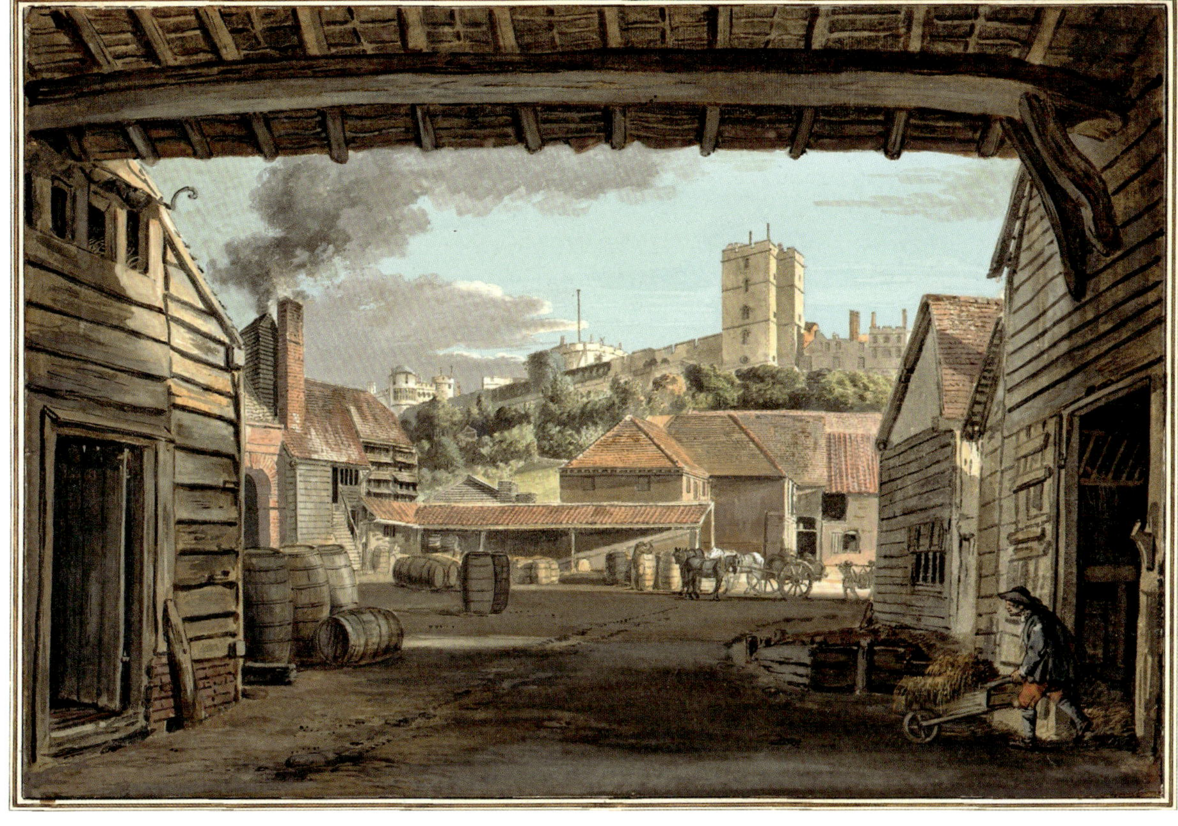

FIG. 19
Paul Sandby, *The north front of the Castle from Isherwood's Brewery in Datchet Lane*, *c.* 1765. Pen, ink and watercolour, 378 × 540 mm.
The Royal Collection, RL 14596

When, in 1743, Thomas Gray elected to make 'a distant prospect' of Eton College the subject of a philosophical *Ode*, he was responding to the area in a conventional manner. Tourist accounts of Windsor and its environs typically paused to quote two famous poems: Sir John Denham's emphatically Royalist 'Cooper's Hill' (1642) and Alexander Pope's 'Windsor Forest' (1713).[15] Of the two, Denham's was perhaps the most treasured point of reference in the mid- and late eighteenth century, as it was clearly the foundation stone of a poetic genre: political prospect poetry. Denham established emphatically the convention of regarding a hill-top as a vantage from which to contemplate constitutional history, specifically the progress of the kingdom towards liberty as exercised within the constraints of wise royal authority. 'Cooper's Hill' was a prime influence upon the tendency to equate the viewing of Thames-side England with taking a dose of enlightening historical medicine. It was probably on account of this convention that the Duke of Cumberland had a viewing tower built at Shrubs Hill in a vaguely gothic manner, a building that was recorded by the Sandbys in their *Eight Views*.[16] The curious design of this tower, in the form of a triangle with semicircular turrets, had its clearest precursor at Stowe, in a Gothic temple dedicated to 'ancestral liberty' and designed by James Gibbs. In both cases, the views afforded by the structure were intended to evoke a progress through history, considered as a Whig journey, as well as geography.

So it was that when the Sandbys came to Windsor and its environs they found there an established landscape forum for gaining insight into the effects of wise rulers upon the

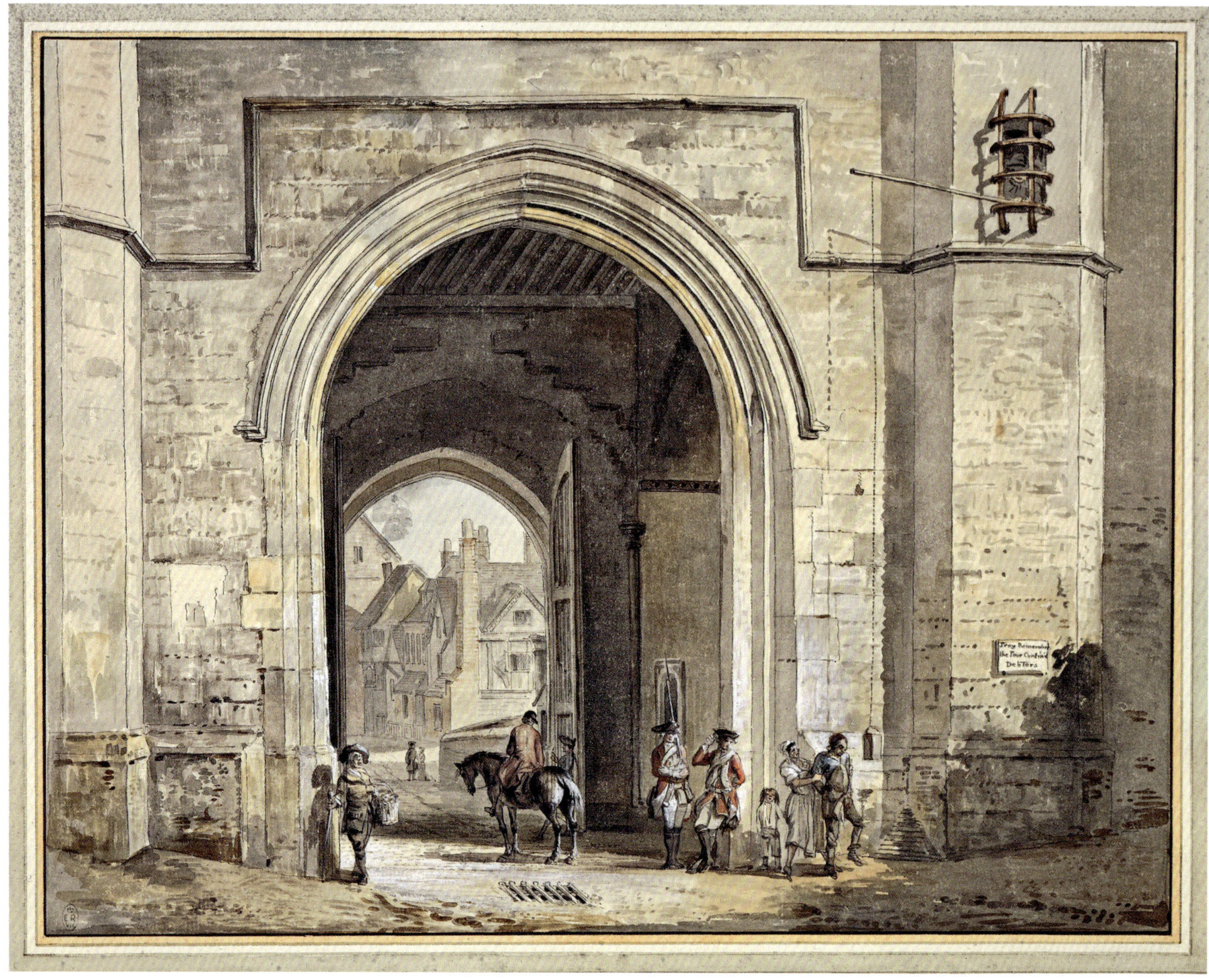

FIG. 20
Paul Sandby, *The Henry VIII Gateway from within the Lower Ward*, *c.* 1770. Pen, ink and watercolour over graphite, 285 × 359 mm. The Royal Collection, RL 14550

nation. The very idea of assuming a 'prospect' of Windsor had a long-term association with the loyal subject's aspiration to emulate the superior vantage of royal eyes. However, although Paul Sandby was much obliged to court patronage through the agency of his brother, he was far from committed to such an elevated stance. Typical in this respect is a view of the castle from the centre of Isherwood's Brewhouse on Datchet Lane (fig. 19). Here the landscape artist assumes a convention associated with the designers of stage sets, by generating a foreground proscenium that acts as a vantage upon a distant scene. Sandby's viewpoint is not just low, it is in the gutter of a rustic courtyard, the closest figure being a man with a wheelbarrow full of straw. The artist makes a witty juxtaposition between the belching chimney of the brewery and the distant tower of the castle which stands against a pure blue sky. In this case, a low viewpoint is as much a social as a spatial construct. Far from paying homage to prospect poetry, and its elevated deferential concerns, this painting is open to interpretation as a satire upon the form. Prospect poetry of a Tory hue, as composed by Denham and Pope, had promoted the wisdom accruing from assuming lofty perspectives on regal order. If the defining Tory vision of the national landscape was, as Isaac Kramnick has argued, 'nostalgic', Sandby can be seen to have devised the antidote.[17]

Popular tourist guides to Windsor and its environs did not recommend, nor indeed did they mention, Isherwood's Brewhouse. Apart from his concern with the North Terrace, Sandby was far from conventional in what he chose to notice about the environs of Windsor Castle. Seeking to cater to respectable folk, Joseph Pote and his many plagiarists stressed that the town surrounding the castle was a civilised place.[18] Sandby seems to have had no special regard for the landmarks that sustained guidebook reassurances of urban respectability, such as the handsome Parish Church and the magnificent Town Hall.[19] Rather it was the dirty and crumbling streets of New Windsor that seem to have fascinated him, along with a range of humble inhabitants who had no place in prosaic record or elegiac strain. Far from reassuring the viewer that the town was elegant and sophisticated, Sandby revelled in the ungainly collisions that he observed between supposedly refined townsfolk and a dirty transient population attracted by their prosperity. His numerous views of the open castle gates typically include witty contrasts between persons of pompous fashion and careless squalor. He seems to have been fascinated by the tendency of such pinches in the street to push together the respectable and the filthy, the prim resident and the vulgar itinerant. The comedy is seldom in unambiguous favour of respectability. Indeed, in one fine painting of Windsor, Sandby delighted in showing a dignified couple stepping out upon the street to be greeted by the dirtiest of vehicles, the slopping cart of the nightsoil man who cleaned their latrines (cat. 60).

Sandby's scenes of the town of Windsor are redolent of a gritty comedic mind which was as unconvinced of the inhabitants' pretensions to respectability as to their virtue. A number of paintings make dark insinuations as to the claims of pillars of the community to Christian charity. In one work a finely attired cleric pointedly refuses to give alms to an invalid of war begging outside the castle, obliging a schoolboy to compensate by reaching for his meagre pocket money (cat. 59). A related painting makes reference to a debtor's prison that was situated within the main gate of the castle. Here a debtor has pitifully lowered a bucket into which, he hopes, townsfolk will place a charitable donation. The only person so to do is a drunken vagrant who is begged by his family not to ruin himself through kindness (fig. 20). Through such revelations, Sandby created a New Windsor where the only indications of civic virtue appeared to come from those who were too poor to aspire to that condition. Careful observation of the largely ignored figures in some of Sandby's Windsor views suggests that there is some irony in his reputation as a graphic champion of the place. By directing dark humour at the town, Sandby may have been catering to sophisticated metropolitan courtiers who were, like him, far from convinced of the claims to refinement of this sleepy byway.

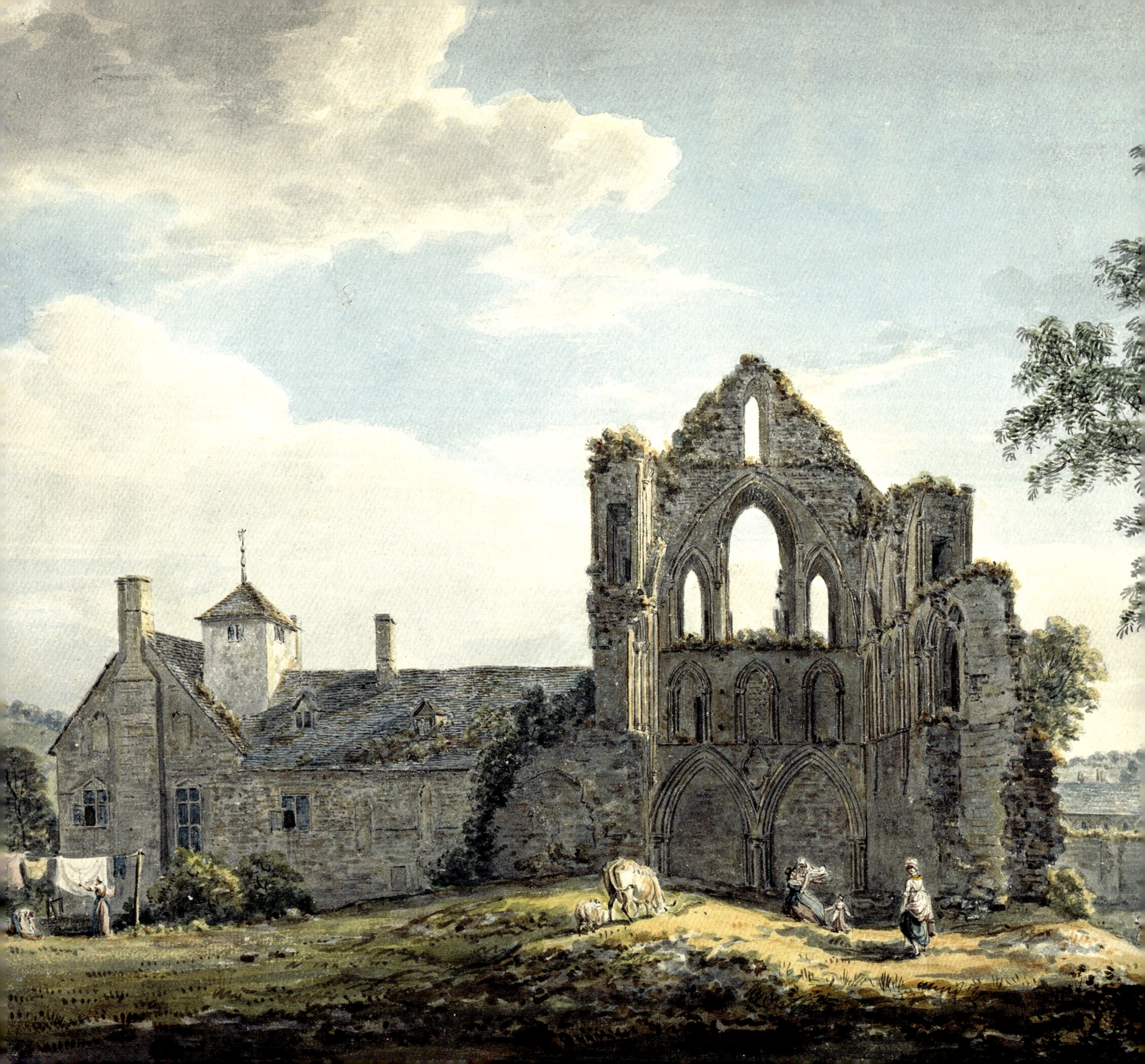

'The Monarch of the Plain': Paul Sandby and Topography

FELICITY MYRONE

Far from being neutrally descriptive, or a stable category of bibliographical classification, the term 'topography' is both value-laden and open to dispute. Definable as a representation of place ('topos') that could be taken as in some sense 'accurate', the term raises considerable questions about the relative value of images and texts, the role of perspective (literal and metaphorical) and material evidence in the creation of historical understanding, and the aesthetics of history itself. Usually commissioned or created in relation to antiquarian projects, but increasingly in the eighteenth century a commercial product that was widely disseminated through the expanding market for prints, topography should be analysed in relation to larger structures of knowledge and value and the changing technologies and communication systems of this nascent consumer society. In these contexts, the meaning of 'topography' is far from simple or self-evident. Yet the word has had a crucial if over-simplified role to play in art-historical narratives of watercolour painting and landscape art in general, and in the career of Paul Sandby in particular.

In this essay I want to review briefly Sandby's reputation as a maker of topographical images and examine the literature on the artist in order to illustrate the art-historical values associated with 'topography'. Taking a cue from the most recent work on eighteenth-century landscape art and antiquarianism, I will then explore Sandby's art in what is proposed here as an expanded field of topographical production. Rather than an artistic genre or a quality within art, topography is here considered as a complex, highly organised field of variegated visual and textual activity, reproduction and categorisation, involving the makers of images (some of whom would consider themselves 'artists' in our modern sense, but many not), antiquarians, collectors and entrepreneurs. Through this discussion, I want to highlight how the major historical collections of topographical materials, such as those of the British Library and the British Museum, have been organised and the challenges that this presents.

Contemporary assessments of Paul Sandby suggest that it was his realistic or 'topographic' style that qualified him as the 'father' of English landscape: Anthony Pasquin described him in 1795 as 'one of those esteemed veterans in the Art, whose reputation has long been stamped with the seal of public approbation'[1] and Alexander Stephens's important biography of Sandby for *Public Characters of 1800–1801* (1801) celebrates his aquatints both for their considerable artistic skill and for their documentary value: 'They unite with a degree of individuality, which renders them mirrors of the places represented, a force, clearness, transparency and picturesque effect, which has been rarely attained by any artist of any period ... their value increases from the bridges, castles, abbeys, and other monuments of ancient days from which they are copied, being mouldering to dust.'[2]

However, topography took on a pejorative meaning early in the nineteenth century, possibly under the influence of Henry Fuseli, who claimed in his fourth Royal Academy lecture on 'Invention' (published in 1810) that many landscapes were no more than a 'tame delineation of a given spot; an enumeration of hill and dale, clumps of trees, shrubs, water, meadows, cottages and houses' and that this amounted to 'little more than topography ... [a] kind of map-work'.[3]

Topography was now seen as an inferior branch of landscape painting, and reinterpretations of Sandby and of his place in art history or the history of watercolour painting started immediately. Joseph Farington wrote in 1811, as a sale of Sandby's works took place after his death, of the 'great difference between His works & those of Artists who now practice in Water Colours. His Drawings so divided in parts – so scattered in effect – detail prevailing over general arrangement.'[4] Sir Richard Colt Hoare, writing in 1822, describes 'the advancement from *drawing* to *painting* in watercolours' as a 'rapid improvement in watercolour painting [which] has taken place within my own memory; for during my younger days Paul Sandby was the monarch of the plain, and esteemed the best artist in this line'.[5]

Sandby's work has continued to be assessed as part of a progressive history of watercolour painting, as marking a transitional point on a path away from 'mere', 'plain' topography towards, but not achieving, a 'finer' art, which was to be exemplified by J. M. W. Turner. This is undoubtedly due to the strong influence of William Henry Pyne, one of the foundation members of the Society of Painters in Water Colours and the author of a series of articles on the 'Rise and Progress of Water-Colour Painting in England'.[6] Articles such as an anonymous review of William Sandby's book on the Sandby brothers display Pyne's influence:

> For the most part the brothers Sandby painted architectural subjects from a topographical point of view; whereas Hearne and Girtin, with Turner in his youth, painted, or tried to paint, architectural subjects from a landscape view. In the one case, the artist was struggling to free himself from tradition, which was topographical; in the other, he had got free, and was turning his wings in the open, which was landscape. But for all this Paul Sandby contributed much to the reputation of English landscape, and paved the way for more illustrious successors.[7]

Richard and Samuel Redgrave published the first serious history of the watercolour movement in Britain in 1866, and took up Pyne's theory of Sandby as a topographer, and of topography as the basis for landscape. Stating that 'The careful delineation of many fine remains of abbeys, cathedrals, churches, castles, and mansions, was … the aim of the early water-colour draughtsman', they include Sandby in a list of 'topographers' and describe his drawings as 'more valuable for their accurate rendering of the various scenes than as works of art'.[8] Topography was now established as the chronological precursor to the heroic phase of landscape painting that lay at the heart of Britain's 'golden age of art'.

Earlier twentieth-century writers tended still to work with this framework, giving Sandby a pivotal or transitional role to play: 'his work … points a way out of topography into picturesque landscape'.[9] Although Sandby 'was one of the first English artists to rob topographical delineation of its abstractness and impersonality. He throws the charms of his genial personality over the scene',[10] 'he never produced a masterpiece … His real gift lay in his ability to record everyday life without pretension and with rare taste. The great school of English watercolour and landscape painting which culminated in Girtin, Turner, Cotman, Bonington and others, owed much to Sandby and his contemporaries.'[11]

Nearer to our own time, Martin Hardie, in his monumental study of watercolour in Britain, argued against 'a continuous tradition of landscape based strictly upon topography, or what may be called the recognisable "view", from Hollar and Place, through Sandby, Dayes, Rooker, and Hearne to a culminating point with Girtin and Turner' but concluded that this is because in fact 'two tempers and systems exist side by side … the one relying for its main interest on a careful and realistic recording of places and buildings; the other depending not so much on topographical interest as on the sentiments aroused by the painter's personal interpretation of some aspect of Nature seen or imagined.'[12] To Hardie, 'Sandby is the last, as he is the greatest, of the topographers … he was not an original artist like Turner or Cozens; he was of his age and gave it what it liked and could understand. The rapid development of watercolour, which began before his death, left no longer any room for such an art as Sandby's. The antiquarian and the connoisseur, topography and landscape art, were cast as opposed and incompatible.'[13]

Even Luke Herrmann, who has been a strong advocate for Paul Sandby and who catalogued the V&A's holdings of his work, discusses Sandby in a slightly embarrassed manner as if conscious of his 'proper place' in art history.

Writing of Sandby's Scottish etchings and known accompanying drawings, Herrmann uses terms such as 'simple topographical view' and concludes that with the exception of one 1747 watercolour of Leith now owned by the Ashmolean Museum, Oxford, the works 'leave a somewhat disappointing impression of Paul Sandby's powers as a landscape artist at this time', and that Sandby must have rejected the 'vivid', 'exciting' path which the Leith view proves he could have taken, for 'with one or two exceptions he rarely again achieved the effect and atmosphere ... He concentrated, rather, on the "accuracy" so strongly emphasised in his son's Memoir. Perhaps his adoption of the more traditional topographical style is an indication that Sandby's was not the character to carry through a revolutionary development, for if he had continued to produce drawings of the quality of [Leith] this is what he would surely have had to do' (fig. 21).[14] Fuseli's division of the descriptive and the ideal remained in play in the 1980s, when Peter Fuller opposed 'pure' watercolours to 'the merely topographical'.[15]

More recent scholars have presented a more complicated view of topographical art and Paul Sandby, looking at aspects of his career, such as his work on the survey of Scotland, his interaction with amateur artists, the motivations behind imagery in *The Virtuosi's Museum*, the political implications of an elevated viewpoint, and the complex working practices of watercolourists in his time.[16] Still, Sandby's art has not, arguably, been placed in the context in which it was originally created and collected, that of the field of topographical text and imagery in its most expansive sense.

Sandby's topographical drawings range from fully worked-up exhibition gouaches or presentation watercolours to slight sketches and illustrations accompanying maps and reports. They, or copies of them, were often collected for portfolios or to be used as extra-illustrations, as Alexander Stephens noted: 'His industry has been as remarkable as his genius; the number of his drawings, disseminated through the cabinets of the amateurs of the arts, has been immense.'[17] They were also reproduced in various publications, such as William Maitland's *The History of Edinburgh, from its foundation to the present time* (1753), or Thomas Pennant's *A Tour in Scotland* (1772). Accordingly, Richard Gough, Director of the Society of Antiquaries of

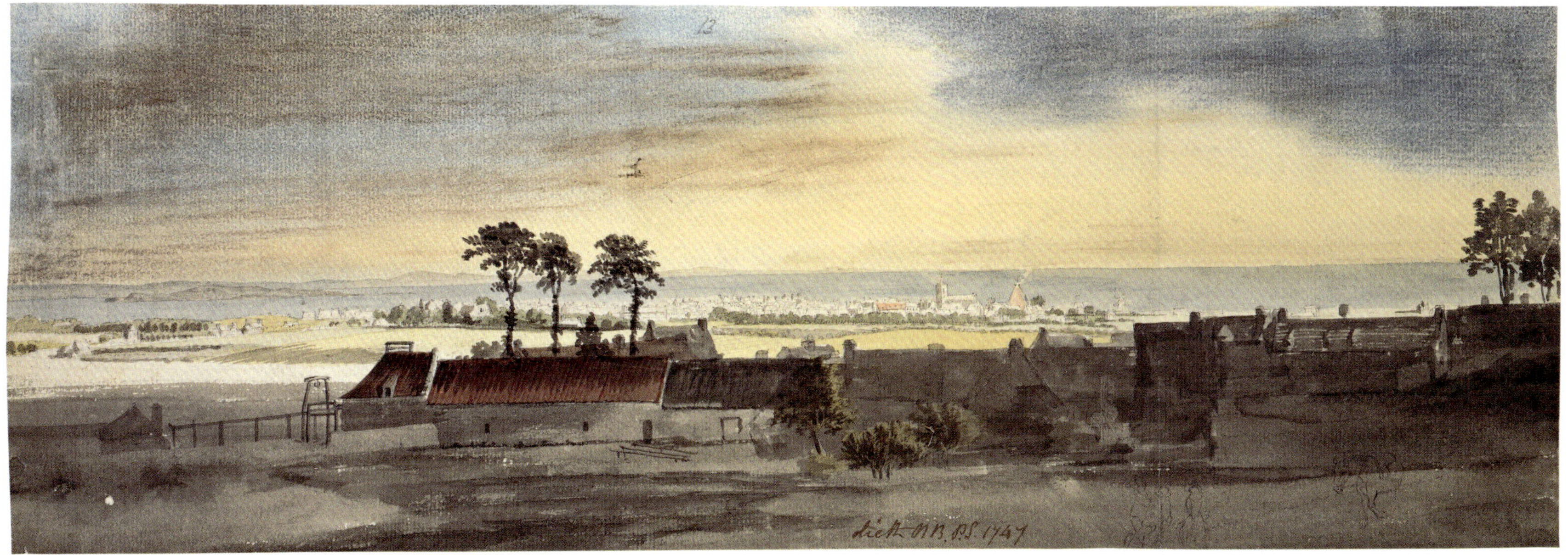

FIG. 21
Paul Sandby, *Leith*, 1747.
Chalk and watercolour over graphite, 162 × 453 mm.
Ashmolean Museum, University of Oxford, WA.B.I.IV.240.131

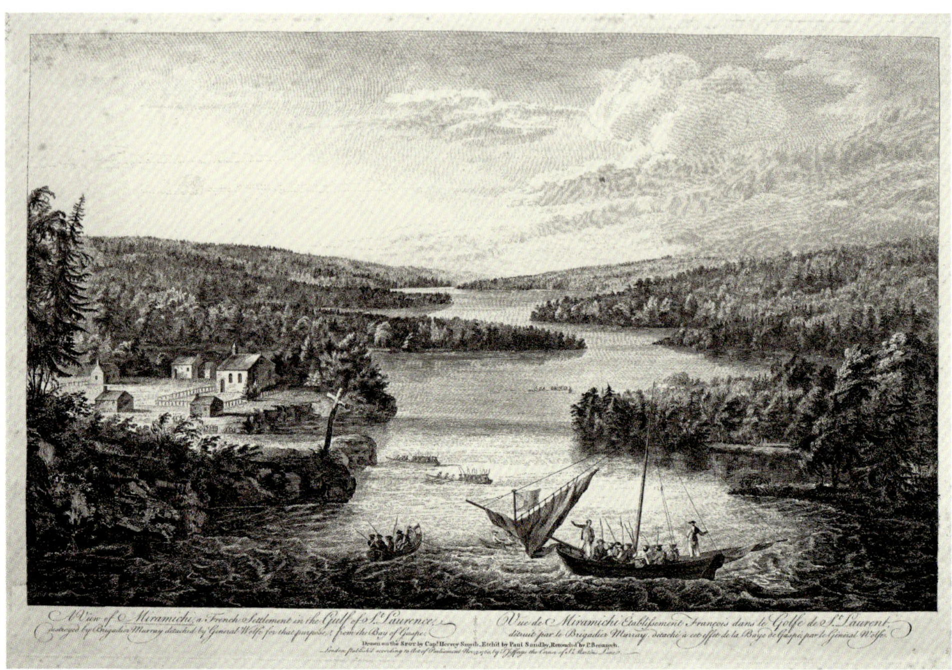

FIG. 22
Paul Sandby and Peter Benezech, after Capt. Hervey Smyth, *A View of Miramichi, a French Settlement in the Gulf of St Lawrence*, published by Thomas Jeffreys, 5 November 1760. Etching and engraving, 363 × 528 mm. British Library, London, Maps K.Top.119.55

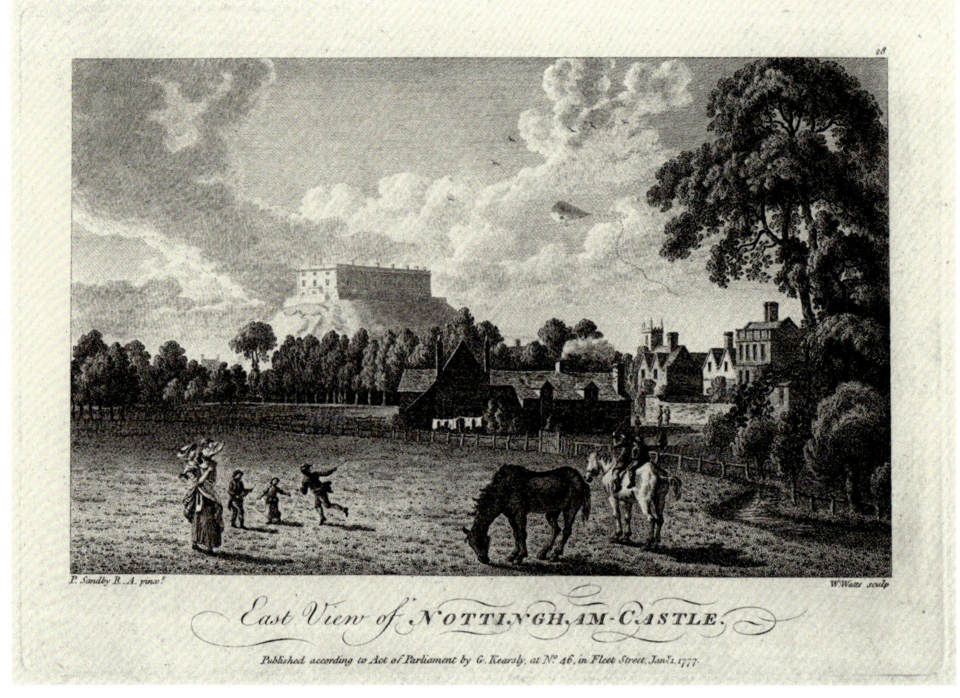

FIG. 23
William Watts after Paul Sandby, *East View of Nottingham Castle*, from *A Collection of Landscapes*, published by George Kearsly, 1 January 1777. Engraving, 165 × 228 mm. Nottingham City Museums and Galleries

London, listed Sandby's engraved and painted views as among the leading sources of 'antiquarian knowledge' in his *Anecdotes of British Topography* (1768).

Sandby published his own topographical prints throughout his career, from etchings of Scotland which were presumably privately issued before being gathered into various publications, to the pioneering large aquatint views of Wales, Shropshire or Warwick. His many depictions of Windsor show a diversity of approach, ranging from highly finished aquatints through to slight etched versions in outline for his pupils to colour and copy. He also worked as a reproductive engraver on topographical prints such as *A View of the Lake and Island at Kew from the Lawn* after William Marlow in William Chambers's lavish *Plans, Elevations, Sections and Perspective Views of the Gardens and Buildings at Kew* (1763), or foreign views by military artists, such as *A View of Miramichi, a French Settlement in the Gulf of St Lawrence* (fig. 22), 'Drawn on the spot by Capt. Hervey Smyth', a set of twenty-four aquatints after Nepalese views by Pietro Fabris which he engraved and published in collaboration with Archibald Robertson between 1777 and 1782, and a set of twelve antiquarian views after ancient monuments in Greece and Asia Minor by William Pars, which the Society of Dilettanti granted him permission to engrave in 1779–80.

As recent work on antiquarianism has suggested, these scholarly expectations should not be entirely separated from commercial values. George Kearsly made use of Sandby's name as a selling point for his publications, even to the extent of making false claims about him being the only contributor of the landscape drawings on which these prints were based.[18] The *Copper-Plate Magazine; or, Monthly treasure, for the admirers of the imitative arts* (1774–78) was popular enough during its print run for the first 32 landscape engravings to be reissued with a significantly new title, as *A Collection of Landscapes, drawn by P. Sandby, Esq. R.A.* (1777), and to warrant the expense of publishing a further 108 views as *The Virtuosi's Museum; containing Select Views, in England, Scotland, and Ireland; drawn by P. Sandby, Esqr. R.A.* (1778–81) (cat. 76, fig. 23). This in turn was reissued with the plates from the *Copper-Plate Magazine* and one additional plate (by Mason after Smith) as *A Collection of One Hundred and Fifty Select Views, in England, Scotland, and Ireland; drawn by P. Sandby*, printed for John Boydell in 1781 and again, with parallel English and French texts by Boydell, in 1782. Bruce Robertson has suggested that at this time engravings and aquatints by and after Sandby had a wider circulation than those of any other artist in England.[19]

Reproduction and collaboration were normal processes for topographical drawings and prints. It was customary for county histories to rely on the submission of plates by the owners of the properties represented,[20] and the *Antiquarian Repertory*'s preface states 'Any Gentlemen possessed of Drawings, Coins or Manuscripts, with which they would choose to oblige the Public may, by sending them to the Publisher, have them, if consistent with the plan, elegantly executed; and if incompatible or improper, immediately returned.' Sandby himself submitted drawings from his collection for publication in this way.[21]

Generally, publishers of antiquarian and topographical material did not see any need to distinguish between when the engraver worked from 'an original' and when from an intermediary study or a print. Sandby's reuse of various images has been looked at elsewhere,[22] but has been explained (even excused) by reference to his training as a military draughtsman.[23] However, replication was simply part of topographical art and publishing: an example of an image by Sandby being reused in different contexts is *Carew Castle, Pembrokeshire*. This is identified in Grose's county index table for the *Antiquities* as by Sandby, but the letterpress accompanying the print (engraved and published by Richard Godfrey on 2 January 1775; fig. 24) states only that 'this view was taken in anno 1772'. The same image is used for *Carey Castle in Pembrokeshire* (fig. 25), plate X of the first set of Sandby's *XII Views in South-Wales*, executed in 1774 and published in 1775,[24] and the *Antiquarian Repertory* (engraved and published by Godfrey, 1 October 1779; fig. 26). A comparison between all three images suggests a common source, but different working practices: the *Antiquities* plate is a simpler image than that used in the *Antiquarian Repertory*, which suggests the use of an intermediary study (a reduction for the engraver by Francis Grose is held by the Society of Antiquaries of London),[25] while Godfrey may have referred either to the 'original' drawing made during Sandby's tour of Wales in 1772 or to the more finished 1775 aquatint for the *Repertory* plate. The date provided for when

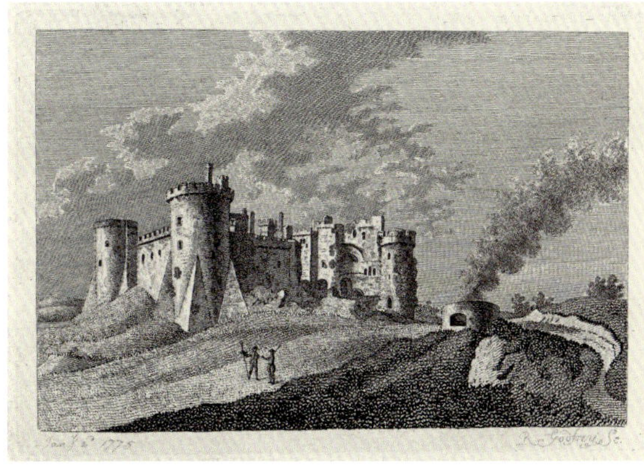

FIG. 24
Richard Godfrey, after Paul Sandby, *Carew Castle, Pembrokeshire*, from Francis Grose, *The Antiquities of England and Wales 1773–1787*, vol. 4, published 2 January 1775. Etching and engraving, 115 × 165 mm. British Library, London, 677.g.4-9

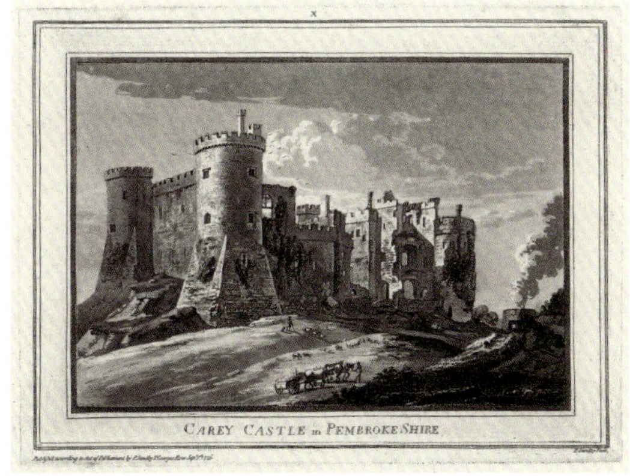

FIG. 25
Paul Sandby, *Carey Castle in Pembrokeshire*, plate X of *XII Views in South-Wales*, published by Paul Sandby, 1 September 1775. Etching and aquatint, 238 × 314 mm. British Library, London, Maps 6.Tab.11

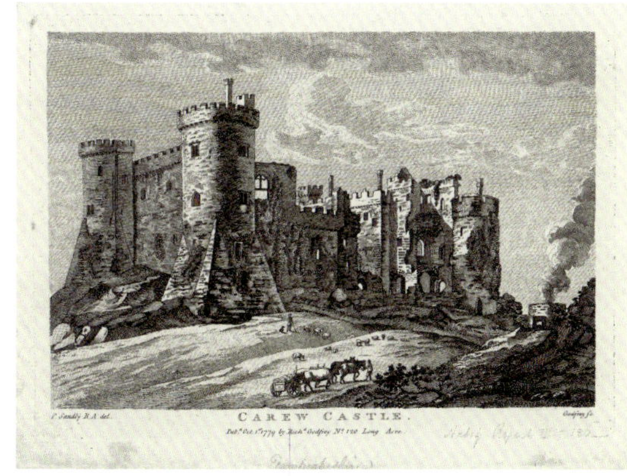

FIG. 26
Richard Godfrey, after Paul Sandby, *Carew Castle*, from the *Antiquarian Repertory, 1775–1784*, vol. 2, published 1 October 1779. Etching and engraving, 171 × 227 mm. British Library, London, 578.i.1,2

the view was taken was seen as important, presumably because the area may have 'mouldered into dust' since.

Popular publications and specialist antiquarian or architectural volumes were all important destinations for Sandby's topographical images, but they had other uses. They were also collected as decorative or artistic objects. Sales catalogues of art collections from the time highlight Sandby's name as a selling point, with those selling his works tending to be respectable figures such as 'a GENTLEMAN of distinguished taste',[26] or 'an artist'.[27] The preface to Kearsly's *Collection of Landscapes* suggests: 'They may be framed with great convenience, as the margins are not diminished by the binding.' They were used as sources of imagery for decoration on porcelain (fig. 27, cat. 73), and there is even evidence that Sandby's prints were used as wallpaper, for a 1785 guidebook to Windsor describes the predecessor of the building now known as Cumberland Lodge as having a room 'neatly hung with plain paper, ornamented with prints, among which are views of the improvements by his royal highness in the park, by Paul Sandby, Esq.'[28]

The important point to take from this evidence is that Sandby's topographical and antiquarian imagery was created for, and circulated between, very different contexts, where it may have served as a form of historical, architectural or landscape documentation, supplementing or replacing texts, as decoration, or as a collectible, an art object. The prevailing over-simplified view of Sandby as a 'fine' landscape artist may partly be explained by the practical difficulty of seeing and classifying eighteenth-century topographical material. This is illustrated by the case of the British Library's outstanding topographical materials. The nature of this collection and the way in which it has come together, been stored and studied suggests both the challenges and rewards of thinking about Sandby in this context.

The Library's topography has been donated, purchased, or acquired by official means. It is not, however, a discrete collection, but scattered across the Library's different departments. It is also extensive, found in thousands of individual collections, ranging from the personal, such as antiquarians' archives of unpublished notes towards the history of a county, to the official, such as those of the East India Company. And it is various in its techniques and media. It covers a wide range of material, printed and manuscript, written and image-based, including maps and views, drawings, prints and oil paintings, as well as photography and, now, digital media.

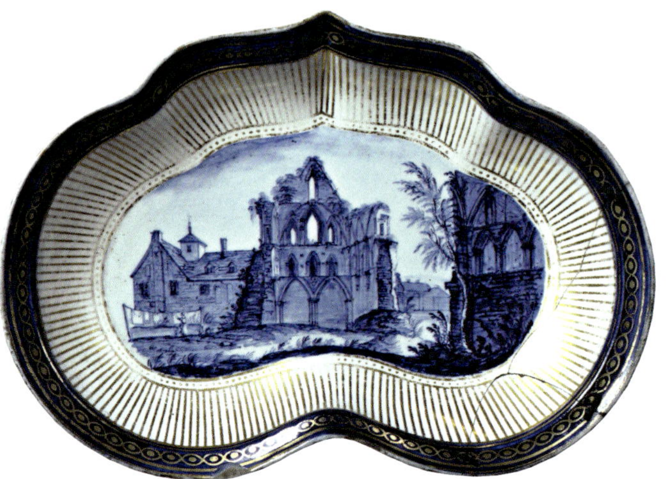

FIG. 27
A Caughley porcelain kidney-shaped dessert dish with *Part of Wenlock Abbey*, after Paul Sandby, hand-painted in underglaze blue, with a richly gilded border, *c.* 1780s. The Ironbridge Gorge Museum Trust, Coalbrookdale, Telford, 1978.86 LB33C

The collections have largely been compiled and stored by their geographical subject-matter, that is according to the place or places that are represented. The vast majority have never had their contents individually itemised by the Library and certainly no attempt has been made to research the separate images, to make artistic attributions, or to trace provenance or original publishing contexts in the case of prints or print studies.

Therefore if researchers now are interested in the work of a single artist like Sandby, they encounter difficulty in locating examples in the Library simply because of the mass of potentially relevant material, its historical dispersal across collections, and the manner in which it has been stored and catalogued. There is a further important factor here: the historical division of materials between the British Library and the British Museum. Topographical materials have been divided between these collections on the basis of perceived artistic merit, informed by the value systems and historiographical traditions outlined above, with the most artistically important material going to the Museum. Topographical imagery which was seen to be of aesthetic value was thus exempted from being 'mere' topography, and reclassified as 'art'. An art-theoretical distinction was given real force in the organisation of the national collections of topographical imagery.[29]

This has had an impact on how Sandby's topographical art has been approached, with even as important a collection as that of George III tending to be overlooked: Paul Oppé writes, 'none of the drawings by the Sandbys in the royal collection can be traced back to George III … The king's collection contained very few English drawings of any kind. With his patronage of West on a large scale, he aimed at encouraging English painters to higher objects, both in his and in the artist's eyes, than topographic landscape.'[30] George III's vast King's Topographical Collection (donated to the nation by George IV and held in the British Library)[31] in fact holds several preparatory watercolours for Sandby's paintings and engravings, and proof copies of his engraved views, aquatints and etchings. More is sure to come to light elsewhere within the Library as cataloguing improves: in 2007, previously unrecorded Sandby drawings were found in his *A Collection of Etchings* (1765; 62.i.17; cat. 17), which also originated in the Royal Collection, and an extra-illustrated life of J. M. W. Turner (Tab.438.a.1).

Topography relies on the matching of word and image, a process that can be difficult because antiquarian and topographical collections often consist of albums of single prints and drawings, brought together as reference material to illustrate an area. Currently museums, galleries and libraries may hold several versions (preparatory studies and different editions) of a topographic image but due to historical divisions between 'art' and library cataloguing, the information necessary to discover them (such as accompanying letter press) is usually not captured by any institution. Preparatory studies for Irish views from *The Virtuosi's Museum* are held by both the British Museum and British Library, for example, but catalogued as by Sandby in the former although the letterpress accompanying the printed versions clearly states that the views were not drawn by him, and only by place depicted in the latter.[32]

As the examples presented here should illustrate, 'topographical' images may require an interpretative framework which neither the British Library's concern with 'place' nor the British Museum's focus on attribution, aesthetic quality and technique may fully provide. The historical reality of topographical production challenges – sometimes dramatically, sometimes more subtly – assumptions made on the one hand about the documentary value of images, and on the other, about their aesthetic significance, authorship and attribution. Arguably, the general narrative of Sandby's career could be rewritten to begin to take account of this shifted perspective. Sandby's career has been presented as a compression, at the level of biography, of the whole history of watercolour in Britain. His employment as a military draughtsman in Scotland tends to be seen as a juvenile period before he became a true artist, and his appointment in 1768 as Chief Drawing Master at the Royal Military Academy at Woolwich is glossed over in favour of his contemporaneous appointment as a foundation member of the Royal Academy. Woolwich and the teaching of private pupils are seen as little more than a necessary evil, providing demeaning work but a stable income. However, as J. T. Smith suggested in *Nollekens and His Times* (1829), teaching enabled Sandby to interact with the 'highest persons in the country', securing commissions and influencing their artistic taste, so that they actively preferred his 'plain', 'topographical' 'highly finished drawings' to the 'mere sketches' of his friend Richard Wilson.[33] Far from being a visual style which needed to be left behind for the artist to progress, or a tedious and distracting activity that debased the painter, 'topography' was here a field of lively social and commercial interaction which actively sustained Sandby and his art.

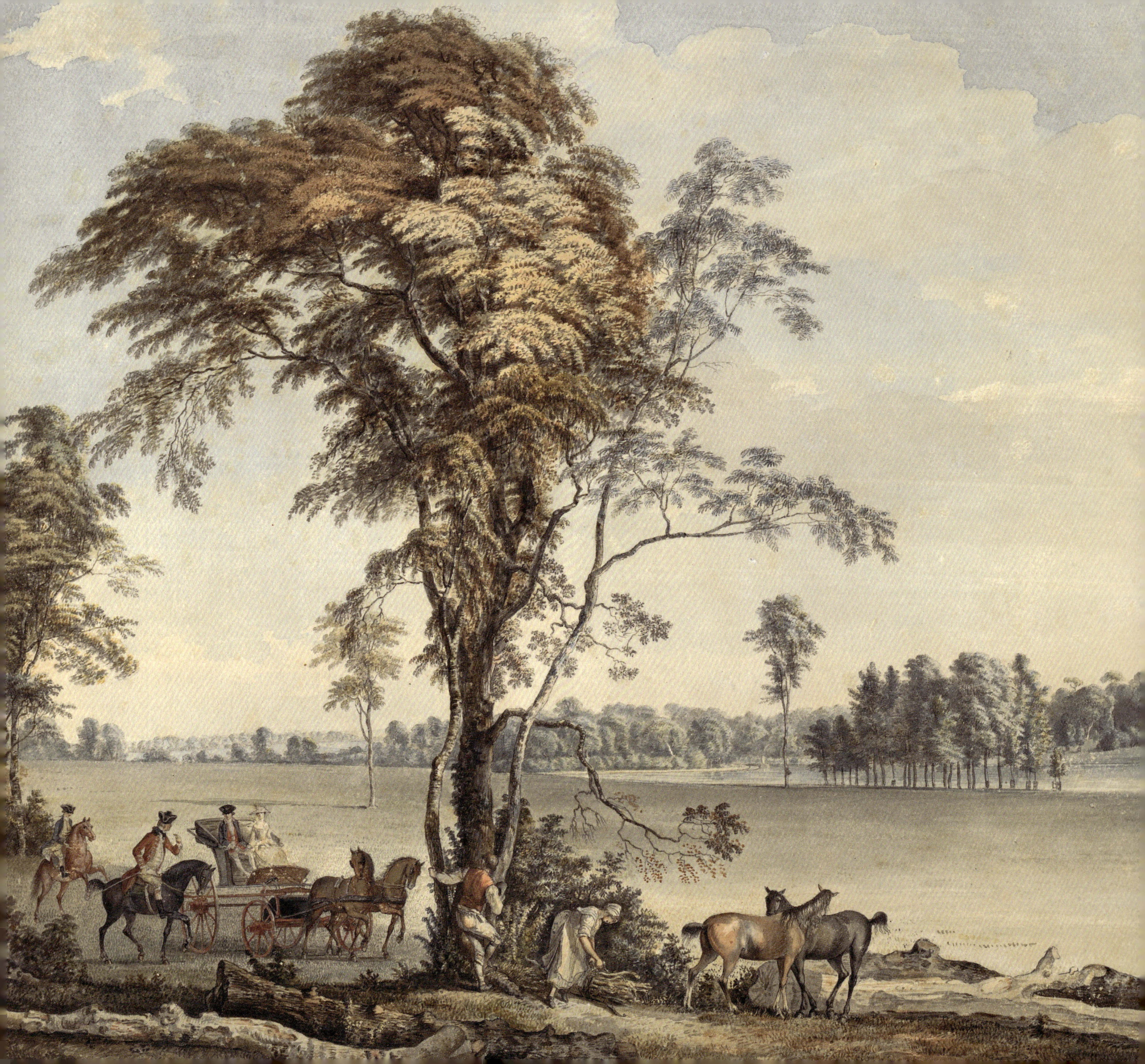

'Grand Secrets': Sandby's Materials and Techniques

JOHN BONEHILL AND SARAH SKINNER

Writing to his close friend and former pupil William Gravatt in a letter dated 9 October 1797, Paul Sandby divulged several art-world 'secrets'. Chief among these disclosures was the key to an enclosed 'Song for 1797'. Set to a popular tune of the day, entitled 'Doodle doo', the verses revelled in a hoax recently played on the art establishment by the little-known miniaturist Ann Jemima Provis. Claiming to be in possession of a copy of an authentic, early Venetian painting manual, Provis – in collusion with her father, the somewhat shadowy Thomas Provis – had persuaded a number of leading Royal Academicians to purchase the lost secrets contained within the manuscript. Credulous artists eager to achieve the luminous colour effects of the Venetian School had paid a ten-guinea subscription fee, 'under a Bond to forfeit two thousand pound if anyone disclosed the secret'.[1] Clearly suspicious of Provis's claims, Sandby mocked those who deemed 'Old Titian's Smutchpan worth Inspection', those who thought the recipes: 'May raise the Letch o satisfaction / And cause in Art a Resurection.'[2]

Other verses took satirical swipes at those of Sandby's fellow Academicians most enthusiastic about the so-called 'Venetian Secret': Joseph Farington, John Opie, James Northcote, John Hoppner, J.-F. Rigaud, Thomas Stothard, Richard Westall and the President, Benjamin West. A month or so after Sandby gave Gravatt this account, James Gillray's epic graphic satire *Titianus Redividus; – or The Seven-Wise-Men consulting the new Venetian Oracle*, published on 2 November 1797, exposed the folly of this group to a wider public (fig. 28).[3]

This was not the first time Sandby had made fun of his contemporaries in verse, art-world politics prompting a number of such squibs over the years.[4] On this occasion, Sandby took evident delight in uncovering Provis's mysteries, claiming that he and William Beechey had put 'our wise heads together and soon found out all the tricks without subscribing a shilling'. Indeed, the veteran artist had good claim to mastery of his profession's materials, having recorded his experiments on numerous sheets or scraps of paper. Passing on some of his discoveries to friends, he would often joke he was relating some '*Grand* Secrets'.[5] In his 1797 letter to Gravatt, he confided 'a *grand* discovery I have just made, and you shall have the *secret*, so here it comes, a few weeks ago I had a French brick for breakfast, the crust was much burnt in the baking, I scraped off the black and ground it with gum water it produced an excellent warm black colour'. Other 'secrets' given away in the letter included guidance on varnishing, dead colouring, and removing stains from prints, as well as how split peas might be prepared to give a 'very dark and warm colour and not opake like Ivory black' that would cause his correspondent to 'throw your Indian Ink a side'.

'Few people had a more varied mode of execution, or possessed more knowledge respecting his art,' remarked the artist's son, Thomas Paul Sandby, before going on to observe that 'there were few persons more perfectly skilled in the theory and practice of painting than himself.'[6] A collection of Sandby's unpublished manuscript notes and recipes recording his experiments with different materials and techniques was passed down the family line, and today survives in the British Library. Drawing on this fascinating documentation, which Sandby's son described as a 'repository of his discoveries and peculiar methods of working',[7] as well as the physical evidence of individual artworks, this essay will explore Sandby's use of materials and novel

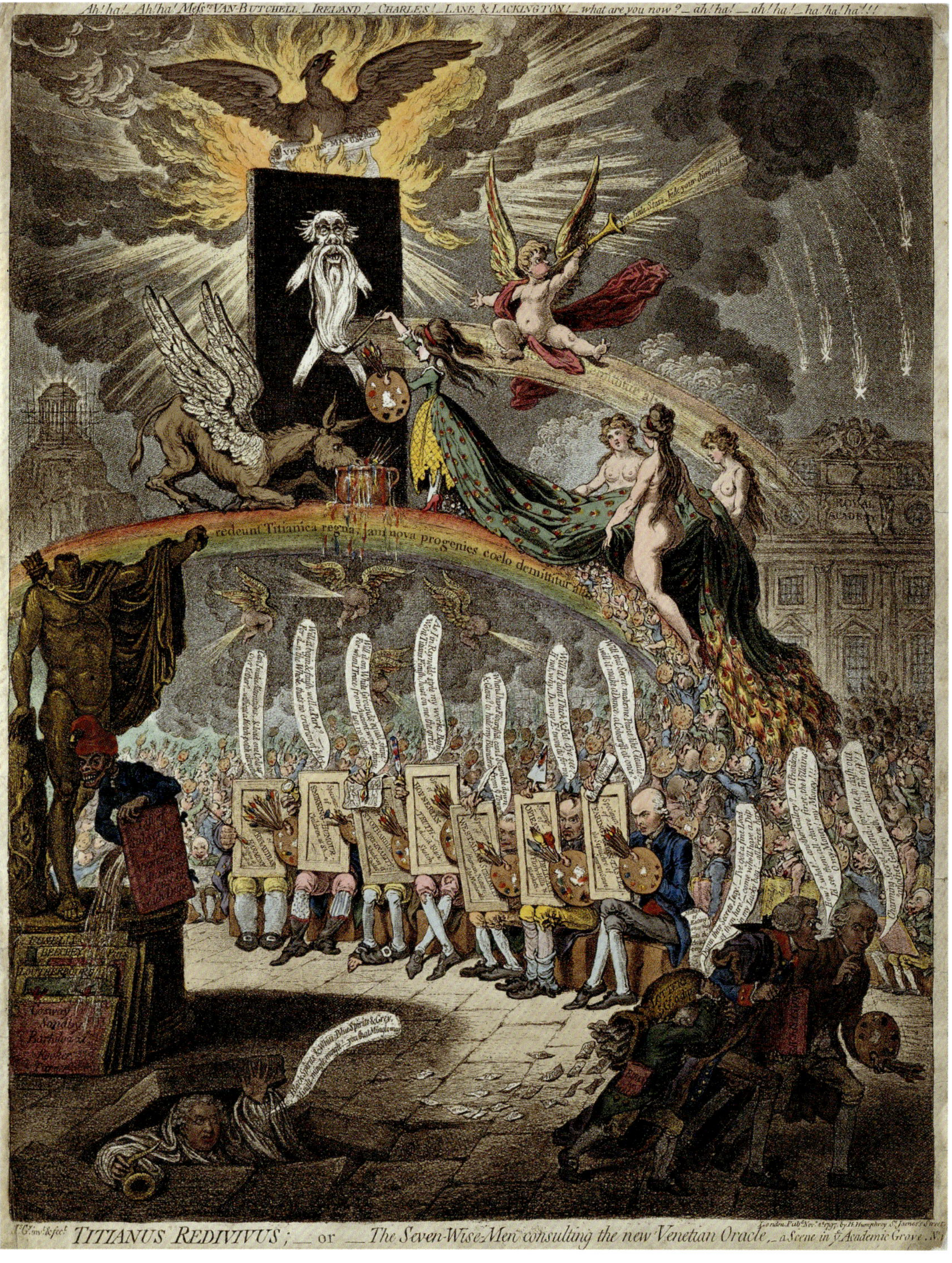

FIG. 28
James Gillray (1757–1815), *Titianus Redivivus; – or The-Seven-Wise-Men consulting the new Venetian Oracle. – A Scene in ye Academic Grove, No. 1*, published by Hannah Humphrey, 2 November 1797. Hand-coloured etching and aquatint, 549 × 420 mm. Royal Academy of Arts, London

techniques in painting and printmaking. More broadly, it will consider how the artist's handling of materials and use of innovative and more conventional techniques were shaped by what was considered suitable to certain themes and Sandby's acute sensitivity to market conditions.

The art of drawing and painting in watercolours

Part of Sandby's enjoyment of Provis's confidence trick must have lain in seeing the reputations of those who practised in oil damaged. A figure long associated with the progress of a 'modern landscape painting in water-colours', a form of practice marginalised by the Academy's genre and media hierarchy, he revelled in the foolishness of those theoretically superior.[8] What was meant by 'watercolour' requires no little qualification, however. Recent scholarship has drawn attention to the rich and diverse scope of the practices associated with the medium over the course of the eighteenth century, with Greg Smith foremost in highlighting the limitations of traditional narratives of the development of watercolour painting into a 'high' art.[9] Smith has shown that little distinction was made in drawing manuals or sales and exhibition catalogues of the period between watercolour used transparently or rendered opaque, for instance. Although it is possible, in broad terms, to determine that a 'drawing', variously described as 'stained', 'tinged' or 'tinted', implied a work predominantly executed in translucent washes, and that a 'picture' denoted something more consistently solid employing bodycolour, or gouache, such definitions by no means cover the range of possibilities. Some of Sandby's works conformed to these categories, but others demonstrated a still more versatile command of materials and techniques, deftly blending ink, graphite and chalks, watercolour, wash and bodycolour.

In an 1806 letter to the architect James Gandon, Sandby observed of himself: 'His Majesty was graciously pleased to say that I am never idle, but can turn my hand to anything: like a fox, I have many shifts, but none will make me independent.'[10] For all an artist's industriousness, resourcefulness and talent, rewards were hard won in an overcrowded London art market. Such was the uncertainty that those concerned to make a living from art were forced to adopt any number of expedients, with Sandby accepting commissions over his long career from a diverse range of institutional bodies and individual patrons, working as a military draughtsman, a drawing master and a theatrical scene-painter as well as a printmaker and publisher. A jobbing artist was required to pursue a range of practices, as opportunities arose, patrons demanded or the market dictated. Choice of materials and techniques was invariably informed by these requirements, as well as by a work's subject and its function.

Bodycolour involved the mixing of colour pigment and opaque white with a binding agent, whether gum arabic, distemper or – as Gravatt noted of Sandby's practice – isinglass, a glue made from fish.[11] Over three days in October 1802, Gravatt watched his former tutor paint *A View inland of Conway Castle* (untraced), recording Sandby's procedures in his diary. His detailed notes shed considerable light on Sandby's working methods in this medium. They record the artist first preparing the paper and ground, then building up a series of transparent washes before adding local colour, using materials probably purchased from apothecaries, dry salters and grocers rather than from the growing specialist colour shops, who catered more to the amateur market. On the final day, Gravatt noted that Sandby 'heightened' his dead colouring, adding highlights and layers of bistre and wash to saturate the darks and give a sense of depth.[12] Close scrutiny of Sandby's bodycolours, such as the striking views of the North Terrace at Windsor Castle now in the collection of the Yale Center for British Art, New Haven, reveals the luminous qualities that could be achieved through this painstaking process (cats 57–58). Here, additional layers of translucent and opaque watercolour scumbled and glazed over the preparatory ground create a lustrous surface effect. Theresa Fairbanks Harris's recent examination of *A View of Vinters at Boxley, Kent, with Mr Whatman's Paper Mills* (cat. 92), a picture first exhibited at the Royal Academy in 1794, has shown that the artist was still making use of similar effects some thirty years later.[13]

Bodycolour seems to have been Sandby's preferred medium for works sent to the London exhibition rooms, its intense hues and weightier presence bearing comparison with the visual heft of the oils dominating the densely hung walls better than drawings executed in transparent washes.[14] Nevertheless, this was far from always being the case, with a number of key exhibits being described by the catalogue as a 'stained drawing'. *North West View of Wakefield Lodge* (cat. 87), exhibited at the Society of Artists in 1767, is a 'stained drawing' that Sandby considered fit for public scrutiny. In places, some of the original underdrawing, outlining central elements of the composition such as the foreground tree, the centrally placed lake and distant building, remains visible. These elements would have been sketched in faint pencil, and later reinforced with pen and ink. Layers of wash were brushed in and overlaid with touches of local colour, producing the 'keeping', or use of colour, rather than black and white, to create the tonal contrast that reviewers admired[15]. This is a technique described in many drawing manuals of the period, such as Carrington Bowles's *Art of Painting in Watercolours* (1783) or Julius Caesar Ibbetson's *Process of Tinted Drawing* (1794).[16] However, the drawing also contains a number of individual touches, for example the artist's use of gold paint in the trees and bodycolour in the figures. These additions give these foreground elements greater visual weight. Such a use of different media on the same sheet was the result of a lengthy period of experimentation, stretching back to the earliest years of Sandby's career. A view of Leith (fig. 21), signed and dated 'P. S. 1747', makes heavy use of coloured chalks over a ground of transparent washes, to convey the impression of an early evening sky. A drawing like this also exploits the chain lines of the laid-paper support for texture.[17] Other examples of Sandby supplementing his basic working methods in such a way include the not entirely successful experiment *Old Welsh Bridge at Shrewsbury* (fig. 29), a picture datable to the early 1770s that was begun in bodycolour but finished in oil, and worked on a coarse piece of canvas.

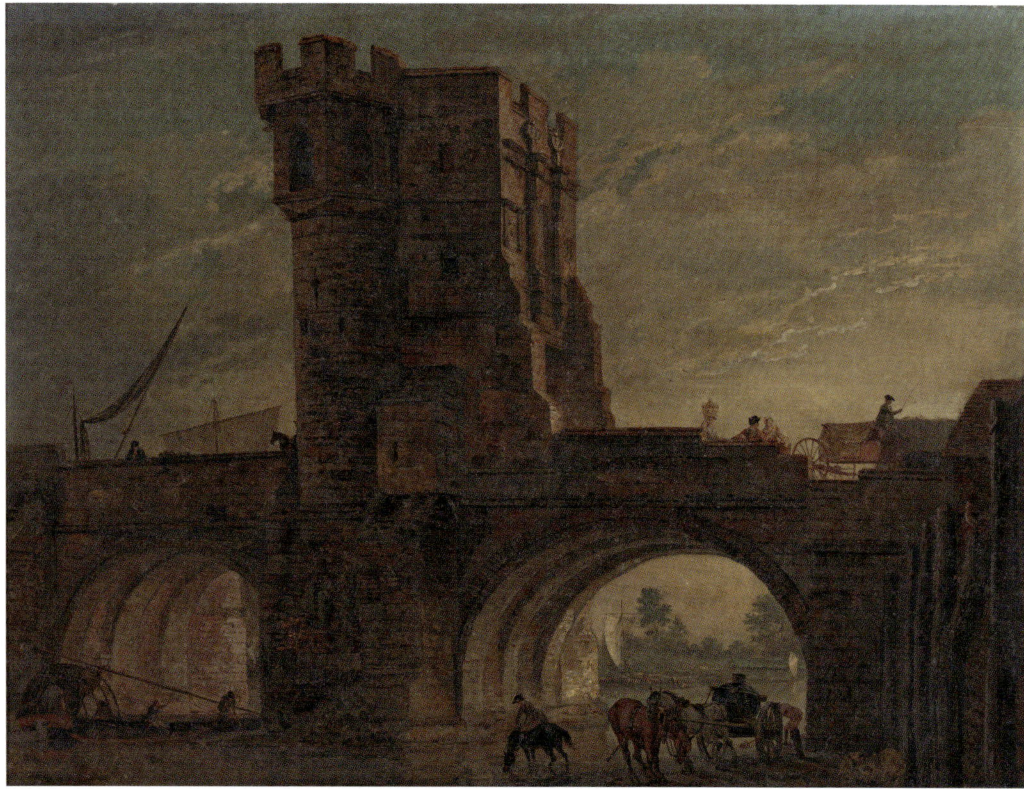

FIG. 29
Paul Sandby, *Old Welsh Bridge at Shrewsbury*, 1772. Bodycolour, gum and oil on canvas, 724 × 929 mm. Yale Center for British Art, New Haven, Paul Mellon Collection, B1976.7.143

Sandby's 'pictures' were often close-framed and glazed, making them suitable for display in modest domestic interiors or the smaller rooms of grand country houses. A majority of watercolours were designed to be handled, however, permitting close scrutiny. Seldom framed, they were kept in library portfolios or albums. Such works were often mounted on a protective secondary support, forming a decorative border. Many of the views in and around Windsor Castle and the Great Park that Sandby executed in the 1760s (cats 57–58, 61–62) are presented in this way, with the artist continuing the practice into the following decade. A view of the ruins of Wenlock Abbey (cat. 73), datable to the 1770s, is edged with ruled ink lines and a band of watercolour wash complementing the tones of the drawing. Traces of blue and brown that have strayed from the drawing suggest that Sandby would on occasion paint on paper already mounted. A title was often inscribed within the border, revealing the value placed on the subject of the drawing. When translated into a print these features would all be reproduced, as is the case with William Walker and William Angus's 1779 engraving after the Wenlock Abbey view for *The Virtuosi's Museum* (fig. 30). Although it is unclear whether this is a case of drawings imitating prints or vice versa, it does indicate the importance of the trade in reproductions to the artist's career.[18]

The art of etching and aquatinting

A print was the published record of a composition, and the form in which it would be most widely encountered. Concerned to carve a place in the contemporary art world, Sandby made printmaking a central feature of his practice from the very earliest years of his career, D. Voisin and T. Butcher publishing at least five sets of the artist's etched landscapes between 1747 and 1749. Our knowledge of Sandby's development as an artist over the course of the next decade is also best traced through his work as a printmaker, from the vicious etchings directed against William Hogarth to the fine engravings made for his brother's *Eight Views of Windsor*, to the *Twelve London Cries* (cats 77–80, 35). These works show him to have been adept in various forms of printmaking, and a variety of manners, with the *Cries* of particular note for their array of skilled and inventive techniques and free handling. These prints show Sandby already acquiring the knowledge that would later enable the development of his principal technical innovation, the '*Grand* Secret' that was aquatint.

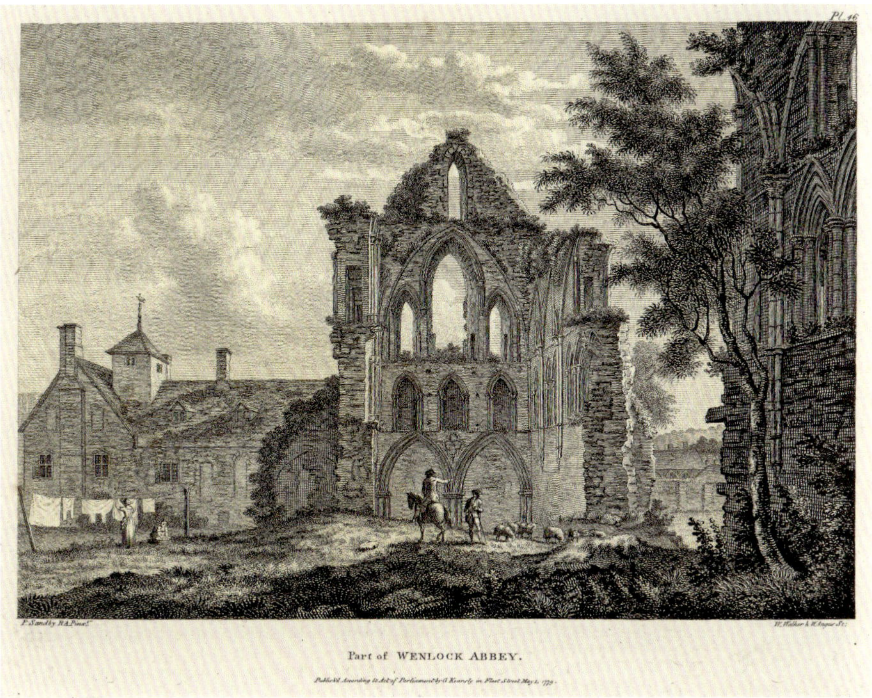

FIG. 30
William Walker and William Angus, after Paul Sandby, *Part of Wenlock Abbey*, from *The Virtuosi's Museum; Containing Select Views in England, Scotland and Ireland*, published by George Kearsly, 1 May 1779. Engraving, 208 × 286 mm. Nottingham City Museums and Galleries

How he came by this method, which allowed for the reproduction of wash-like effects, is uncertain. However, there is good evidence that it was given to him by George and Charles Greville, who probably purchased it from its leading exponent on the continent, Jean-Baptiste Le Prince.[19] Indeed, William Gilpin claimed that he could not obtain the secret from his friend George Greville, because 'his brother Charles, who was equally concerned in it, had given it to P. Sandby with a kind of promise that he should have a monopoly on it'.[20] Although he was not the first artist on this side of the Channel to experiment with the medium, Peter Perez Burdett having exhibited *An Etching in imitation of a wash drawing* at the Society of Artists as early as 1772, Sandby was its principal populariser.[21] He was clearly excited about the new process and discussed it in a letter to the enthusiastic amateur etcher John Clerk of Eldin, dated

8 September 1775, referring to it as 'Le Prince's Secret'.[22] He claimed to have 'already done 24 views in Wales and 4 Large Warwicks' by this date: presumably the sets of prints comprising *XII Views of South-Wales*, published from Sandby's business address at 4 St George's Row, opposite Hyde Park, that same month; four *Views of Warwick Castle* issued by John Boydell in January 1776; and the *XII Views of North Wales* made available at the beginning of September 1776 (cat. 93). The artist's indebtedness to the Grevilles was made explicit by the title pages of the two Welsh sets, which he dedicated to Charles and George respectively, and by the subject of the Warwick views, the castle being their family's ancestral seat (figs 31.1–2).

Among the assorted recipes in the archive of family papers found in the British Library is 'A Mode of Imitating Drawing on Copper Plates discovered by P. Sandby, R.A., in the Year 1775, to which he gave the Name of Aquatinta'. This provides evidence of the nature of the artist's experiments with the new medium, and begins:

> In a bottle that hold a gill or more according to the quantity wanted to flote over a copper plate the size wanted for present operation, put of powdered white Rosin about one third of the depth of the bottle, then nearly fill it with rectified spirits of wines, shake it, let stand an hour or more before you try it on the copper plate, which ought to be well burnished or coated in oil and be free from scratches, it will be necessary before you venture to use this menstrum, to try what grain it will produce on a small plate by pouring a little of the mixture on it holding at the same time the plate in a sloping direction thus \. When its dry which will be in a few seconds, look at it through a magnifying glass the cracks appear very fine and close it will produce a delicate tint but will not last long in printing, if very open like nett work it will be too coarse for a general purpose – a medium is best, the close or open grain depends on the quantity of Rosin dissolved in Spirits of Wine, if very fine add more powderd R. if coarse more spirits till the grain satisfies you.[23]

The process that Sandby had developed, and explains here, employed a resin ground to give the effect of a tonal wash,

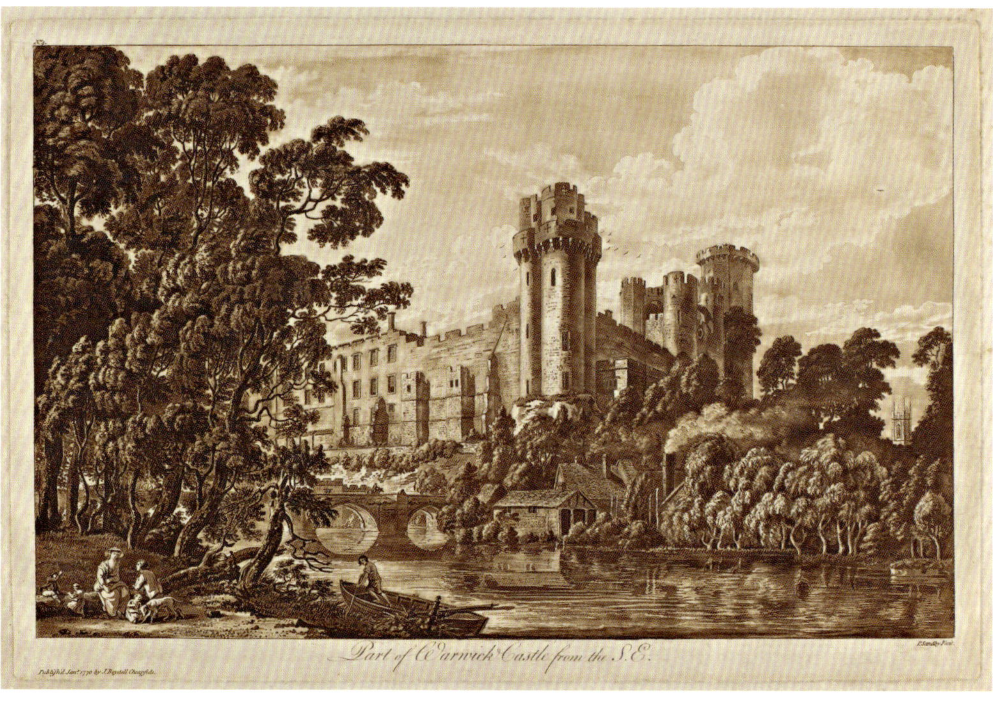

and controlled the biting of the copperplate to different degrees, using stopping-out varnish and varying the length of time the acid lay on the surface to create different densities of 'tint' when the plate was finally inked and printed. Etching remained an integral part of the printmaking process, producing the linear elements, for example trees or buildings, and aquatint creating the effect of tone, conveying an atmospheric quality, perhaps best observed in the artist's experiments with nocturnal effects (cats 93.3–4).

Engraving continued to be a central feature of Sandby's practice, as his work for *The Copper-Plate Magazine* and *The Virtuosi's Museum* illustrates, especially as he attempted to remedy some of the technical problems in the aquatints. However, there was clearly a market for the new product; he produced over 80 aquatints after his own or others' designs, and he was concerned to guard the technique's secrets. In another letter to Clerk, written shortly after the one cited above, Sandby declared: 'I dare not disclose to you any part of the method, being sworn to secrecy.' By way of

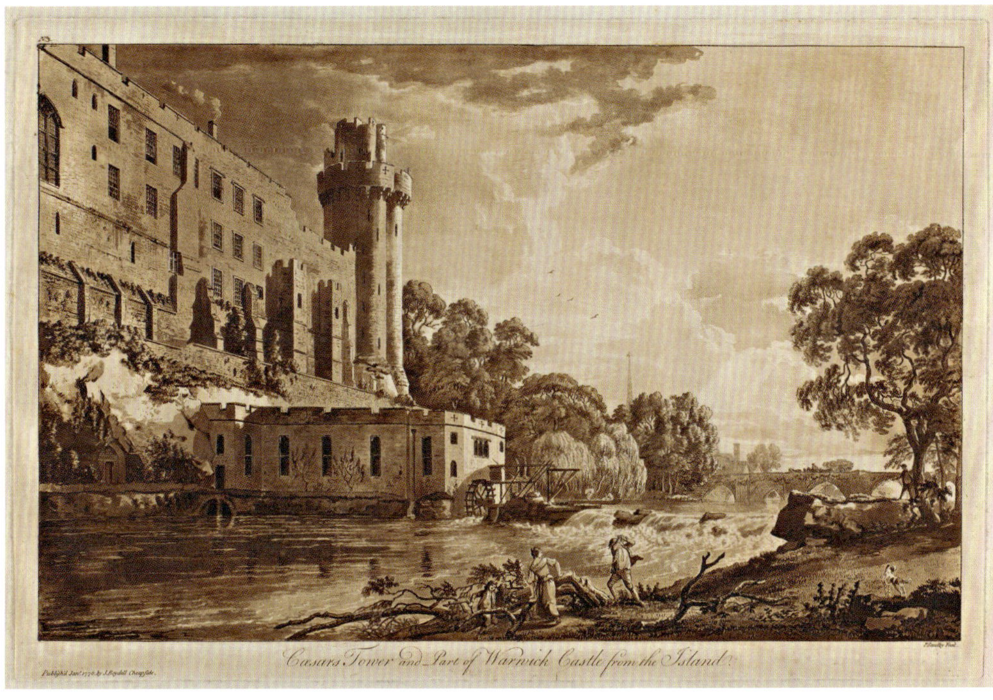

FIG. 31.1–2
Paul Sandby, *Part of Warwick Castle from the S.E* and *Caesar's Tower and Part of Warwick Castle from the Island*, from *Views of Warwick Castle*, published by John Boydell, January, 1776. Aquatint, 331 × 416 mm. Hunterian Museum and Art Gallery, University of Glasgow

consolation, Sandby could only offer some advice on soft-ground etching and other processes.[24] Although he appears to have shared the secret with such friends as Francis Jukes and Richard Cooper, Sandby was clearly reluctant that it should become common knowledge. Artists were generally inclined to keep their hard-earned knowledge secret; one amateur, the author of a treatise entitled *The Art of Etching and Aquatinting* (1794), complaining of 'the extreme secrecy of the artists, and the high price they demand for instruction'.[25]

'The seal of public approbation'

At the moment that Sandby was relating the latest gossip on the scandal of the 'Venetian Secret' to Gravatt, critical opinion on his own art was divided. Reviewers of the 1790s and early 1800s revered him as one of the founding figures of a national school of landscape painting, one 'whose reputation has been long stamped with the seal of public approbation'. His art was indeed held up as a corrective to current tastes, which increasingly favoured 'gaudy hues, glittering effects, and mechanical fopperies'.[26] Critics who responded more positively to such dramatic, spectacular effects, however, found Sandby's art, and especially his continued use of bodycolour, unappealing. A reviewer for *The London-Packet* was not untypical in judging '*opake water colours* … ever cold in effect'.[27] Recipes recording a lifetime's experiment and experience, written down and collected possibly with publication in mind, were of little interest to emerging artists who achieved their brilliant effects in transparent watercolour, and who were developing a whole new repertoire of techniques, including scratching, scraping or rubbing the paper. Such artists as Thomas Girtin or J. M. W. Turner were nevertheless indebted to Sandby, not least for his role in developing the market for views of the national topography, whether intended for the folio or translated into print. Their eagerness to achieve ever more novel and spectacular effects may also be seen as continuing and building upon Sandby's restless experiments in watercolour and print.

I

Picture-making

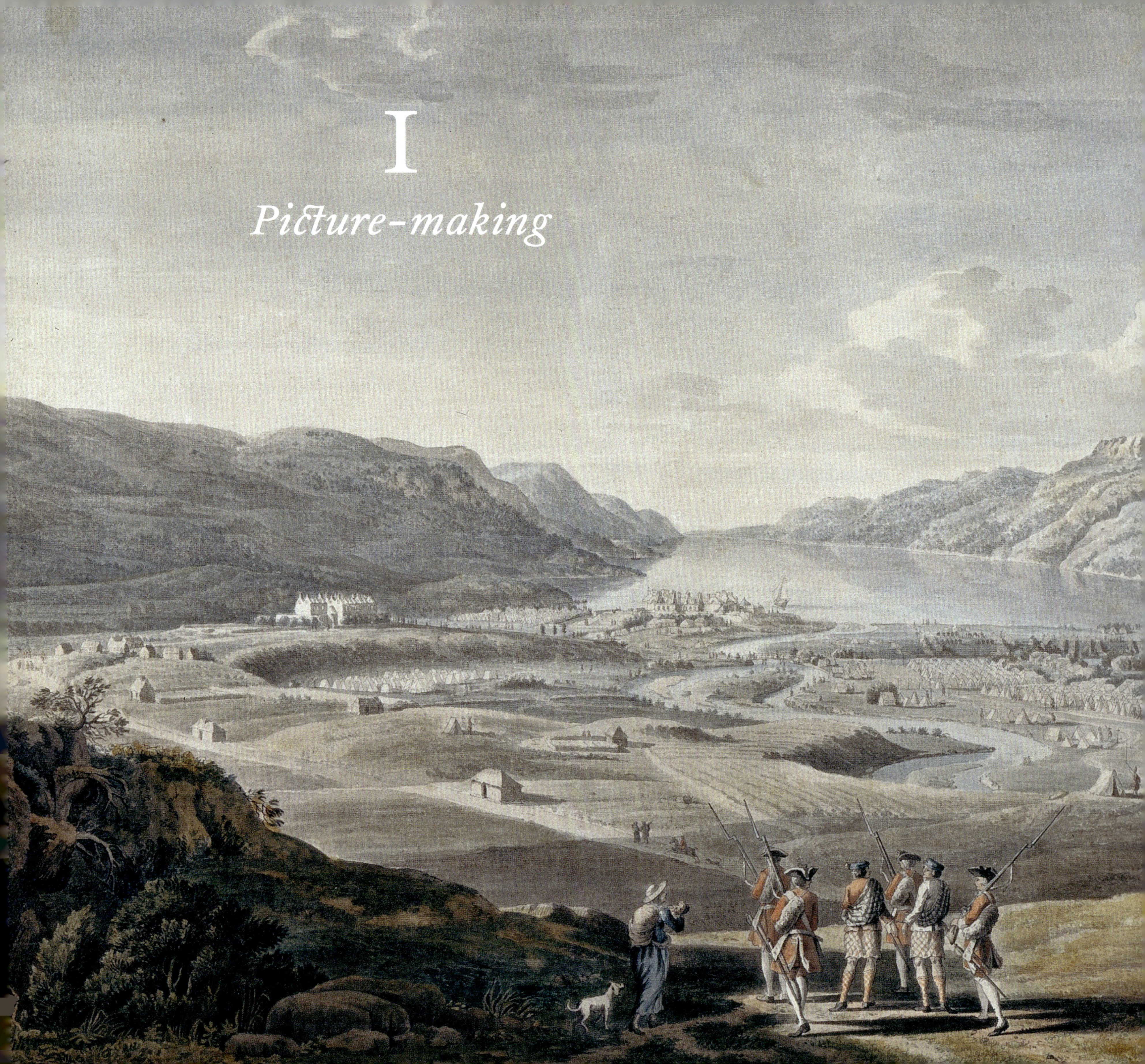

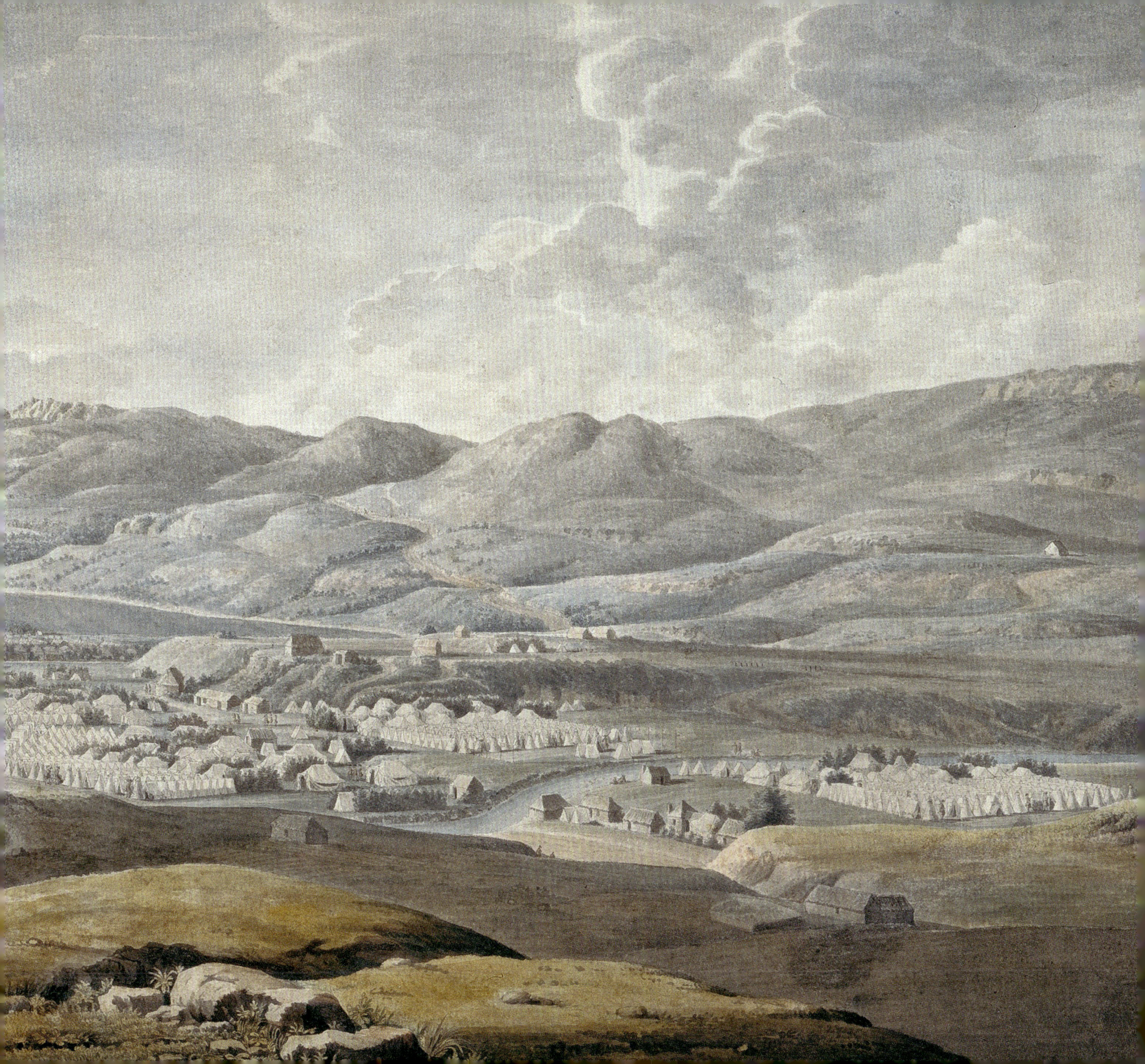

In the course of a lecture to students of the Royal Academy Schools, delivered in his capacity as Professor of Painting, Henry Fuseli railed against the debasement of art by the forces of commerce, finding 'the last branch of uninteresting subjects' to be 'that kind of landscape which is entirely occupied with the tame delineation of a given spot ... what is commonly called Views'. With evident distaste, Fuseli went on to argue that:

> These, if not assisted by nature, dictated by taste, or chosen for character, may delight the owner of the acres they enclose, the inhabitants of the spot, perhaps even the antiquary or the traveller, but to every other eye they are little more than topography. The landscape of Titian, of Mola, of Salvator, of the Poussins, Claude, Rubens, Elzheimer, Rembrandt and Wilson, spurns all relation with this kind of map-work.
> (Fuseli 1831, vol. 2, p. 217)

These remarks may well have been aimed at the Professor's fellow Academician, Paul Sandby, his art having long appealed to antiquarians, tourists and those members of the landed classes who required portraits of 'a given spot'. 'Map-work' was also an appropriate slur on the work of a man who had not only begun his career as a draughtsman for the army but had also tutored officers in drawing for the best part of thirty years. And this was clearly work, not art. Cartography had a cultural significance far beyond that implied by Fuseli, however, not least as a means of translating a local, vernacular sense of place into more sophisticated forms of geographical knowledge (Daniels 1993B). For Sandby, map-making provided a model for expanding the scope of his topographical views, for laying out information about life and land, and displaying a place's connections with regional and national geography. Yet, for all that mapping and a wider culture of observation and description clearly shaped Sandby's later practice as a professional artist, his art was never divorced from the work of Old Masters or contemporaries. His depiction of 'a given spot' would often frame it in terms of Flemish or Italianate taste, incorporate historicising or literary allusions, or be peopled with figures, both observed and drawn from the repertoire of academically sanctioned tradition, in ways which would expand its meaning beyond the local and the particular. Moreover, for all the often minute delineation of objects and topography in Sandby's art, a concern with the accurate rendering of the man-made or natural world is invariably secondary to the demands of picture-making.

Works featured in this section are drawn from the earliest years of the artist's career, covering his tenure as chief draughtsman on the Military Survey of North Britain as well as his first incursions into an increasingly commercialised London art world. They show Sandby familiarising himself with a variety of pictorial traditions, as well as experimenting with the possibilities of various media. This capacity to move between the conventional and novel, or across genres, often blurring distinctions between the observed and the imagined, was to remain a feature of his *oeuvre* throughout his career. Sketches of sites in and around Edinburgh or made in the north and west of Scotland early in his career also sustained his practice over several decades. Indeed, views, motifs and figure groups might be recycled a number of times. This interplay of the observed and the copied, the freshly noted and the traced, was an aspect of his work for the Military Survey that Sandby carried into his later professional practice.

Mapping and topographical description, whether visual or verbal, were of obvious value to the army as tools of surveillance and information gathering. Yet, these endeavours were only part of a more general cultural concern to chart the physical and human geography of the country which was apparent in the activities of antiquarians, naturalists and estate owners, as well as artists, surveyors and travel writers. Off-duty studies made by Sandby while employed on the Survey are consistent with these more general pre-occupations, and they attend closely to the natural history, ancient and modern settlement patterns or recent improvement of the landscape north of the border. Views taken in the highlands place the region's forts, towns and antiquities, especially its ancient baronial manor houses and ruined castles, in the wider landscape, setting these structures against dramatic, mountainous backdrops. Views of the varied scenery surrounding the capital included expansive prospects, taking in the nearby port of Leith, villages and local estates, common land, enclosed fields and gardens, as well as fine, closely observed studies of industry and technology, street life and native custom.

Edward Burt, a member of General Wade's highland road-building expedition in the 1720s, had found the landscapes featured in many of these drawings bleak, observing 'such a seeming *Sameness* in all the rocky Places' (Burt 1754, II, 20). Ironically, it was agents in the improvement process like Burt, or those sympathetic to commerce and trade like the travel writer Thomas Pennant, who helped create the taste for the mountainous scenery north of the border that had developed by the end of the century. Pennant's *Tours* celebrated the contribution that North Britain would make to the nation as a whole, and were illustrated with engravings after some of Sandby's earliest drawings, giving shape to the admiration for such scenery that was then emerging.

Sandby's awareness of the importance of printmaking and publishing to an artist's career was already evident while he was in Edinburgh. While in the city, according to Thomas Paul Sandby's memoir of his father, Sandby made the acquaintance of 'Mr Bell, an engraver', who allowed him 'some insight into his mode of etching' (Sandby 1811). However, early prints, marked by a free handling of the needle, closely akin to his sketching technique, imply that he was largely self-taught. They show the artist sampling a wide range of manners and techniques, shifting between naturalistic landscapes, recalling figures like Abraham Rademaker, and generalised, Claudean compositions. A knowledge of the tradition of the *veduta* (or view), with Sandby moving between its *ideate* and *ideale* forms, is also apparent. In the words of the great populariser of the picturesque, William Gilpin, a capricious landscape was 'formed from a collection of some of the happiest circumstances which belong to all', one in which the 'most pleasing shapes' of nature were 'culled out, and beautifully grouped' (Gilpin 1798, p. 15). Capriccios remained an important part of Sandby's portfolio, with such favoured architectural motifs as Edinburgh Castle or the Old Welsh Bridge in Shrewsbury (cat. 19) being reassembled in imaginary, Italianate scenery or framing views of classicised landscapes. His work as a printmaker provides the best evidence of his activities in the years immediately following his period in North Britain, printmaking being the practice through which he first attempted to make his mark as a professional artist.

Upon his arrival in London in early 1751 Sandby immersed himself in the capital's vibrant artistic community, focused around the St Martin's Lane Academy. During the winter of 1753–54 he made a series of vicious graphic satires targeting William Hogarth, the pre-eminent native-born artist of the previous generation (cats 21–28). Their imagery, both verbal and visual, is, at once, coarse and erudite, scatological yet also learned. References are made to one of the cheapest, most debased forms of street entertainment, the magic lantern, but there are also allusions to literature, mythology and academic doctrines, as well as the work of modern artists and the Old Masters. Considerable technical accomplishment is evident, as Sandby mimics Hogarth's own style or essays plates in emulation of Rembrandt. They announce his ambitions and factional allegiance to his fellow artists as well as his brother's principal patron, William Augustus, Duke of Cumberland. His elder brother's connections at court and Sandby's own work north of the border were to prove an invaluable introduction to a powerful network of patronage. Identification with such prominent patrons as Cumberland or his aide George Simon, 1st Earl of Harcourt, was a significant feature of Sandby's public profile in the years after 1760 and the advent of public art exhibitions.

A leading figure in the London art world for over half a century, Sandby was one of few artists to make the transition from an era dominated by the personalities around St Martin's Lane to the new world of annual shows, public appraisal and picture-making. That he was able to make this shift, when other artists of the previous generation, most notably Hogarth, failed, was due less, perhaps, to his ability to attract attention through eye-catching exhibits than on a careful cultivation of aristocratic patronage and a recognition of the growing market for prints. 'Map-work' of this kind, surveying the private property of the nation's élite or recording sites of historic significance for the perusal of antiquarians and tourists alike, may have held little interest for Academicians like Fuseli, who were committed to a properly public form of artistic practice, but it was highly significant in asserting the value of the national topography and forging a native landscape art.

1

East View of Edinburgh Castle, c. 1746–47

Pen and ink, 192 × 307 mm
Signed and dated: 'Paul Sandby delint. 1746–7' (l.l.)
Department of Prints and Drawings, British Museum, London, 1880-9-11-1779

PROVENANCE
Transferred from the Map Library, British Library, 1880

SELECTED EXHIBITIONS
London 1960, no. 102; Edinburgh 1978A, no. 4.11; Nottingham 1986, n.n.; Nottingham 1990, no. III.12; London 2000, no. 92

SELECTED REFERENCES
Binyon 1898–1907, no. 106, vol. 4, p. 18; Robertson 1987, pp. 129–30; London 2000, no. 92, pp. 130–32

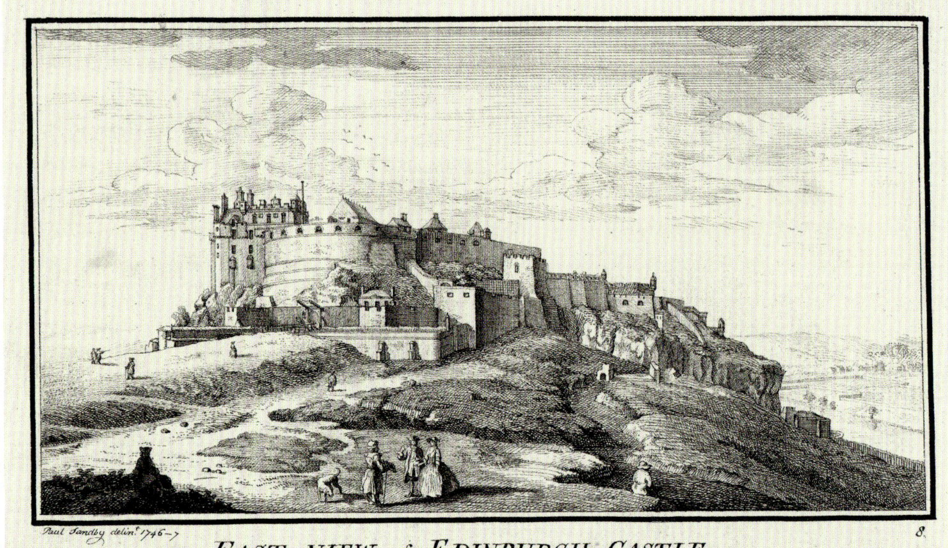

2

Prospect of the Entrance into the Tower taken from the back of the Stone Kitchen, c. 1746–47

Pen, ink and wash, 285 × 412 mm
Signed and dated: 'Paul Sandby delin. 1746–7' (l.l.)
Victoria and Albert Museum, London, E1119-1931

PROVENANCE
Bequeathed by E. C. Ellis, 1931

SELECTED EXHIBITIONS
Hamilton 1981, no. 1; London 1986, no. 1

SELECTED REFERENCES
Hardie 1966, vol. 1, p. 99; Hamilton 1981, no. 1, p. 1; London 1986, no. 1, p. 80; Robertson 1987, pp. 129–30

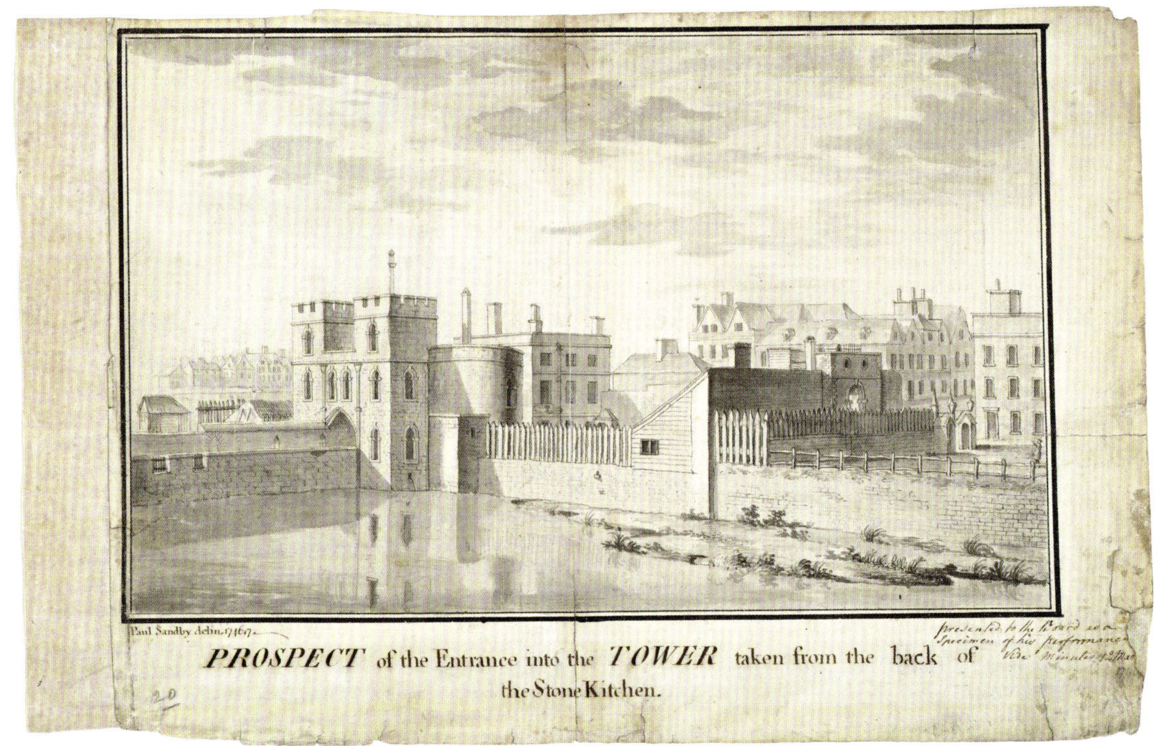

In or about March 1747 Paul Sandby submitted a set of studies to the Drawing Room of the army's Board of Ordnance. Contemporary inscriptions describe these nine works, all but one after an engraving, as specimens of his 'performance'. Most of the drawings submitted were derived from military or *banditti* figures that featured in a popular manual, Abraham Bloemart's *Recueil de Principes pour Designer* (1655). In order better to demonstrate his range, Sandby also included these two topographical views, rather pointedly depicting the buildings housing the Drawing Rooms of the Board of Ordnance in England and Scotland. Although the prospect of the Tower of London's famous Stone Kitchen (cat. 2) appears to have been executed 'on the spot', the view of Edinburgh (cat. 1) was probably copied, with only minor alterations, from a print published before 1745 by the Royal Engineer John Elphinstone (see fig. 32). The area to the east was a well-established vantage point from which to take views of the castle, as Thomas Sandby's 1744 drawing of the Scottish capital's rocky citadel illustrates (National Library of Wales, Aberystwyth). No doubt this set of drawings, as a whole, was compiled to demonstrate Sandby's abilities in transcription and accurate sketching in the field, thus illustrating levels of competence in the kind of work undertaken in the Drawing Room. Recalling his elder brother's remarkable approximation of the incised line in his earlier *Nottingham Market Square from the West*, Sandby even imitates the technique of a copper engraving's cross-hatched lines (fig. 44).

Little if anything is known of Sandby's artistic training, yet these very earliest drawings clearly indicate that much was learnt from prints, and much from Thomas Sandby. Given the status the elder of the brothers had come to assume by the date these drawings were submitted, it can also be assumed that he was instrumental in securing Paul Sandby's place on the Military Survey of North Britain.

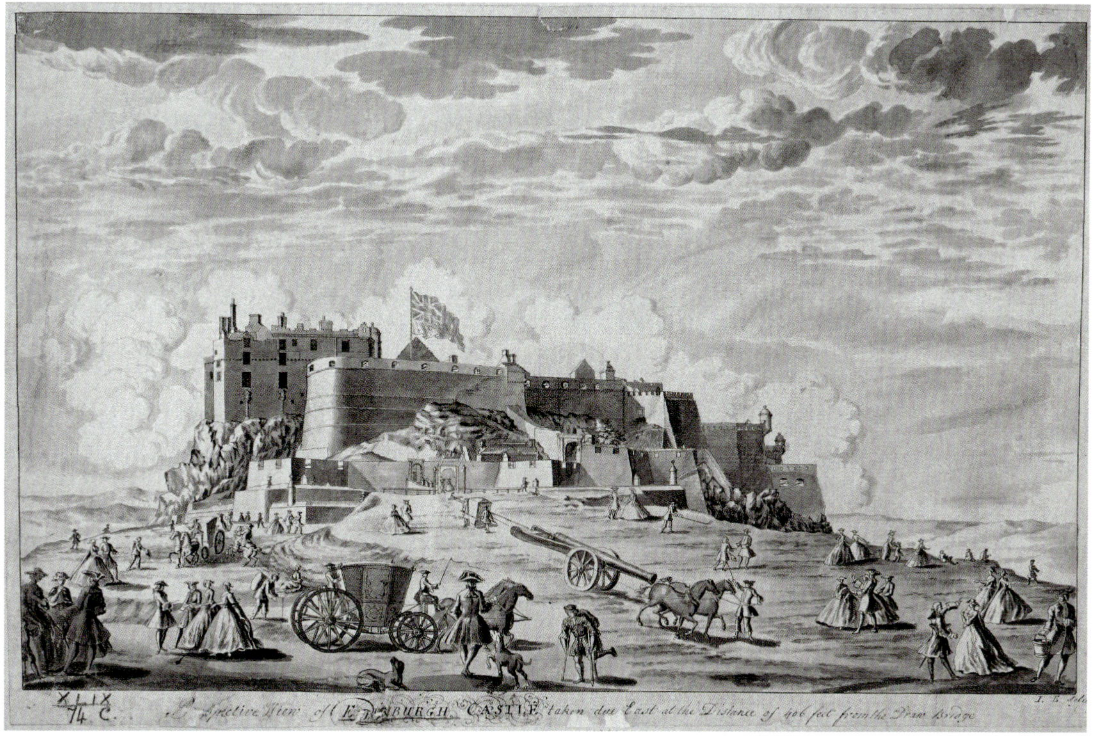

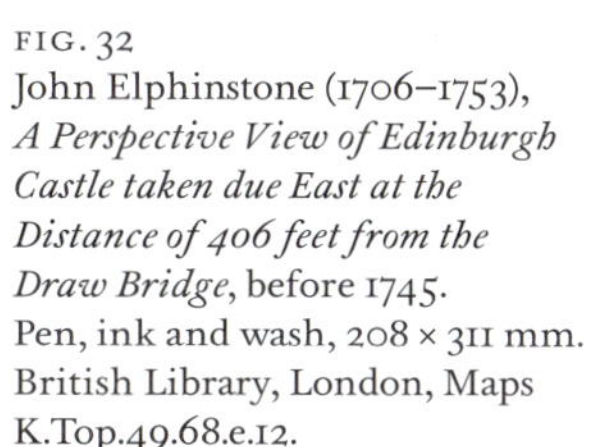

FIG. 32
John Elphinstone (1706–1753), *A Perspective View of Edinburgh Castle taken due East at the Distance of 406 feet from the Draw Bridge*, before 1745.
Pen, ink and wash, 208 × 311 mm.
British Library, London, Maps K.Top.49.68.e.12.

This is the study for the print by Nathaniel Parr, after John Elphinstone, *Prospect of Edinburgh Castle from the South East*, forming part of *Twelve Perspective Views of the Principal Buildings in Edinburgh*, before 1745.

3

THOMAS SANDBY

Fort Augustus, *c.* 1746

Pen, ink and watercolour, 317 × 701 mm
Royal Collection, London, RL 14725

PROVENANCE
Thomas Sandby (sale Leigh & Sotheby, 18 July 1799; bt Colnaghi); Prince of Wales by 20 June 1804

SELECTED EXHIBITIONS
Yale 1985, no. 16; Nottingham 1986, n.n.; Nottingham 1990, no. III.8

SELECTED REFERENCES
Oppé 1947, no. 154, p. 47; Yale 1985, no. 16, p. 22; Charlesworth 1996, p. 255

There is a tradition, first recorded by the critic John Williams, that Thomas Sandby, stationed at Fort William, 'when the Pretender landed', was 'the *first* person who conveyed the intelligence of the event to Government, in the year 1745' (Pasquin 1796, p. 141). Although apocryphal, the anecdote illustrates how closely the artist's career was bound to the events and personalities of the '45 and its aftermath. Having served in the Board of Ordnance Drawing Room in Edinburgh for some three years, Thomas Sandby joined the staff of William Augustus, Duke of Cumberland, second son of George II and Captain-General of land forces at home and in the field. Cumberland's accounts record the elder Sandby as being employed as the Duke's 'Draughtsman & Designer' on £100 a year from around April 1746, thus coinciding with the defeat of the Jacobite cause at Culloden (Cumberland Papers, Royal Collection, Box 68/x.36.5). Presumably, Thomas Sandby's prodigious graphic skills, as exemplified by this striking watercolour recording the fort and encampment that had become the centre of Cumberland's operations, brought him to the Duke's attention.

Whereas earlier draughtsmen attached to the army like Clement Lempriere, the head of the Ordnance Drawing Room until his death in 1746, did little more than delineate objects, Sandby's delicate tonal washes establish a previously unseen atmospheric quality and pictorial breadth. A minuteness of touch and detail is apparent in every inch of the composition, particularly in the fine delineation of the architectural ruins and extensive camp alongside. Michael Charlesworth has seen such drawings as significant for the level of information they provide on the rises and falls of this militarised landscape, picking out areas of refuge, hazard and fields of fire of strategic value (Charlesworth 1996, pp. 255–56). Such a highly wrought drawing is unlikely to have had a field

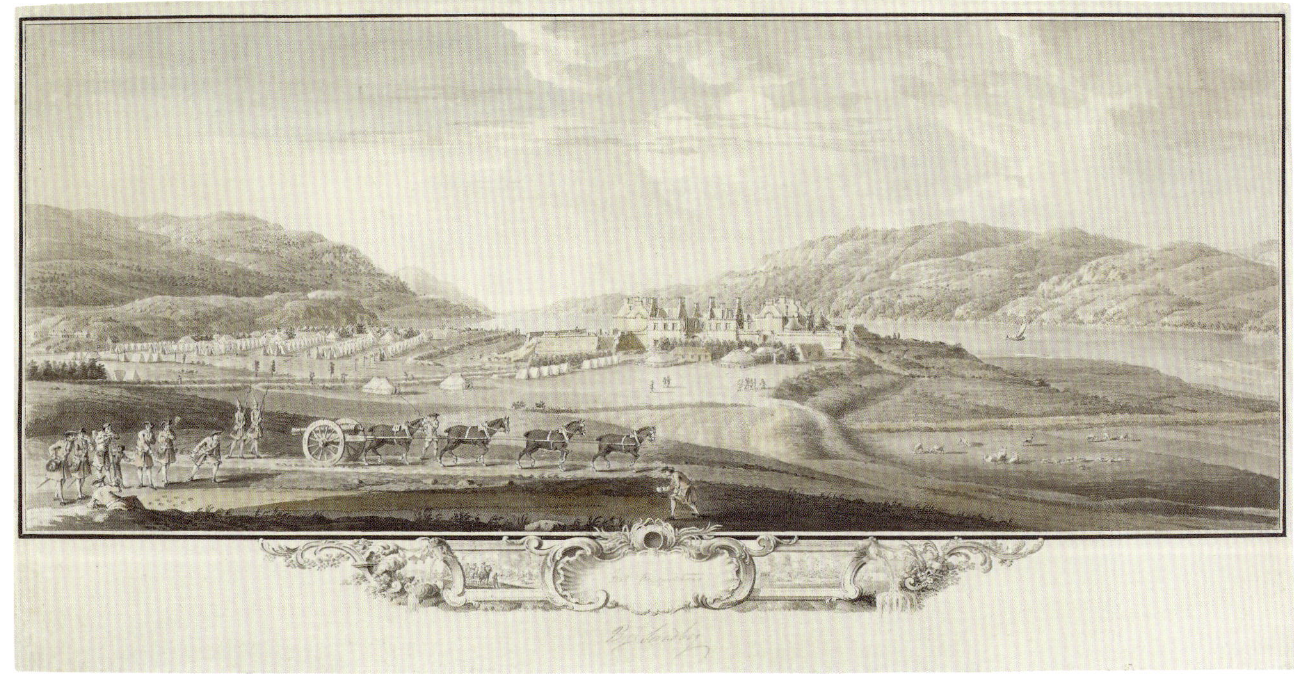

FIG. 33
Thomas Sandby,
Fort Augustus, *c.* 1746.
Pen and wash over graphite, 284 × 700 mm. The Royal Collection, RL 14724

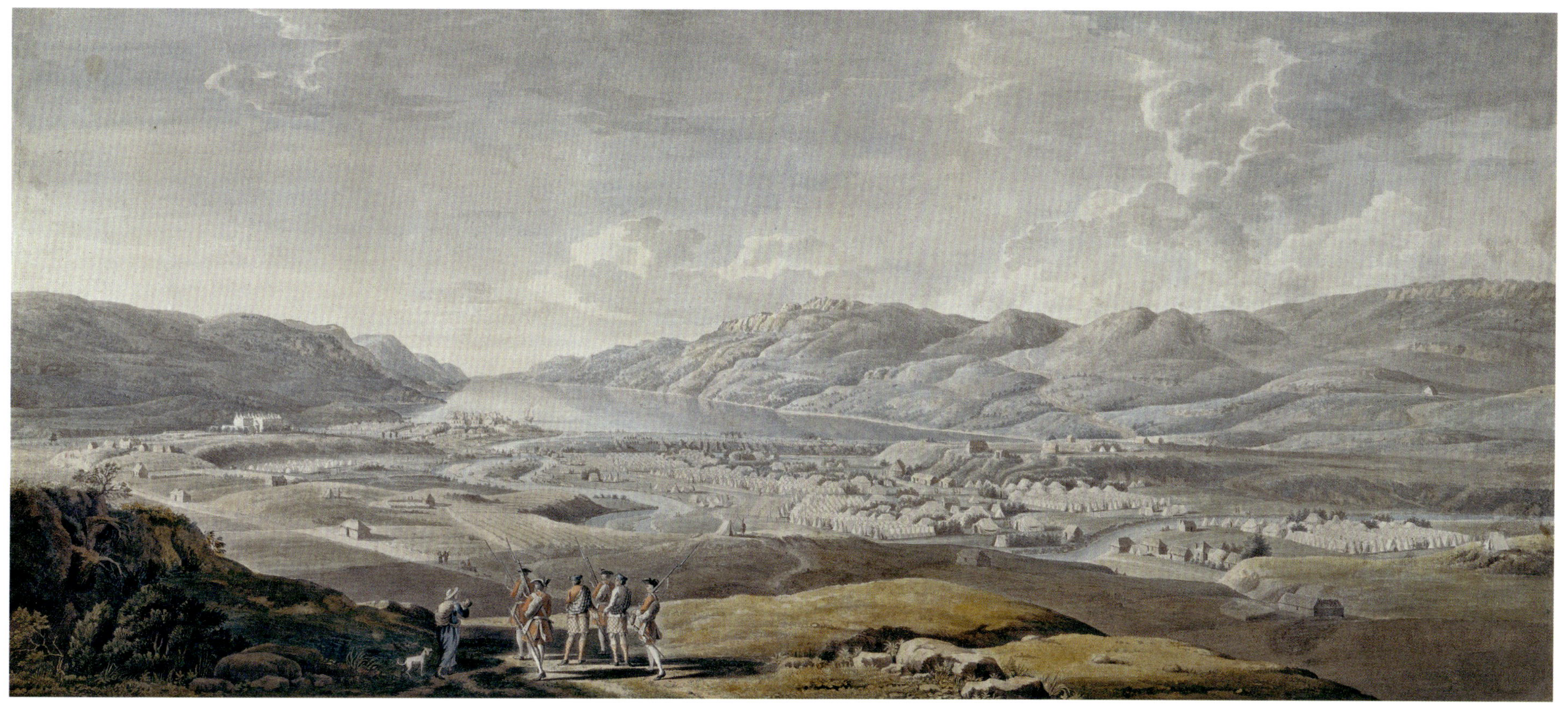

use, however. Rather, its function seems essentially commemorative, not least in celebrating the values of discipline and order that were widely regarded as instrumental to securing victory in the highlands. Indeed, the meticulous qualities of the drawing itself might be taken as demonstrating competence in such matters.

That a wider significance was to be attached to this image is further suggested by the foreground figures. Another highly finished view of this landscape, also in the Royal Collection, looks down on the camp and the adjacent 'sleighted' ruins from further down the valley slope (fig. 33). Its foreground is enlivened by a group of relaxing soldiers playing 'nine holes', explaining the rules of this simple, skittles-like game to a nonplussed-looking highlander. This might be seen as complementing the foreground vignette of the drawing under discussion, which most likely forms a pendant view, in which chained Jacobite prisoners being led off to the fort are delayed by a pleading woman and child. If in the first drawing the highlanders are presented as comically stupid, in the second their pursuit of a futile cause is shown to have led them to renege on their domestic duties. Aside from animating what might otherwise have been a monotonous, if beautifully realised prospect, these crude caricatures of the enemy establish a none-too-subtle justification for the military presence. A decorative cartouche appended to the view featuring the soldiers playing 'nine holes', along with the fact that these drawings remained in the artist's own collection throughout his life, perhaps implies that they were intended for engraving as paired prints, calculated to appeal to the patriotic fervour surrounding Cumberland in the wake of the routing of the Jacobite threat. In addition, the figures provide good reason to consider this drawing one of the earliest products of the brothers' long collaborative enterprise, a study of the foreground figure group being attributable to Paul Sandby (cat. 32.2).

4

THOMAS SANDBY

Plan of the Battle of Culloden, 1746

Pen and watercolour over graphite, 320 × 425 mm
Signed and dated: 'T. Sandby delint: April 23rd, 1746, at Inverness' (l.l.)
Royal Collection, London, RL 17177

PROVENANCE
Transferred from the Cumberland Papers, vol. X, no. 28

SELECTED EXHIBITIONS
Nottingham 1986, n.n.

SELECTED REFERENCES
Oppé 1947, no. 150

5

THOMAS SANDBY

A Sketch of the Field of Battle at Culloden, 1746

Pen and watercolour, 292 × 531 mm
Signed and dated: 'T. Sandby 1746' (l.c.)
Royal Collection, London, RL 14722

PROVENANCE
In the Royal Collection by 1884

SELECTED EXHIBITIONS
Nottingham 1884, no. 5; London 1977, no. 5; Nottingham 1986, n.n.

SELECTED REFERENCES
Oppé 1947, no. 151, p. 46; London 1977, no. 5. pp. 6–7; Charlesworth 1996, p. 255

CATALOGUE NUMBERS 4–5

On 16 April 1746 Cumberland's troops engaged the Jacobite forces on Culloden Moor, southeast of Inverness and a few miles southwest of Nairn. One eyewitness account of the day's events, published as *A Plain Narrative and Authentic Journal of the Late Rebellion*, claimed that Cumberland's troops 'formed in Line of Action … with great Beauty of Discipline and Order'. This restraint and regulation was contrasted with the 'desperate Attack' made by the rebels, who 'like Wildcats … came down in Swarms' and in 'Fury' (Hughes 1746, pp. 37, 39). Comparisons of Cumberland's mastery of the field of battle and the strategic errors of the Jacobite command, which had left troops exhausted, hungry and bogged down, were to become central to the numerous printed accounts, whether written or pictorial, of this final, decisive engagement. Thomas Sandby's plan and sketch of the battle, which may well have been drawn up with an eye to future publication, might also be seen as celebrating the discipline and order that had secured victory for Cumberland's forces.

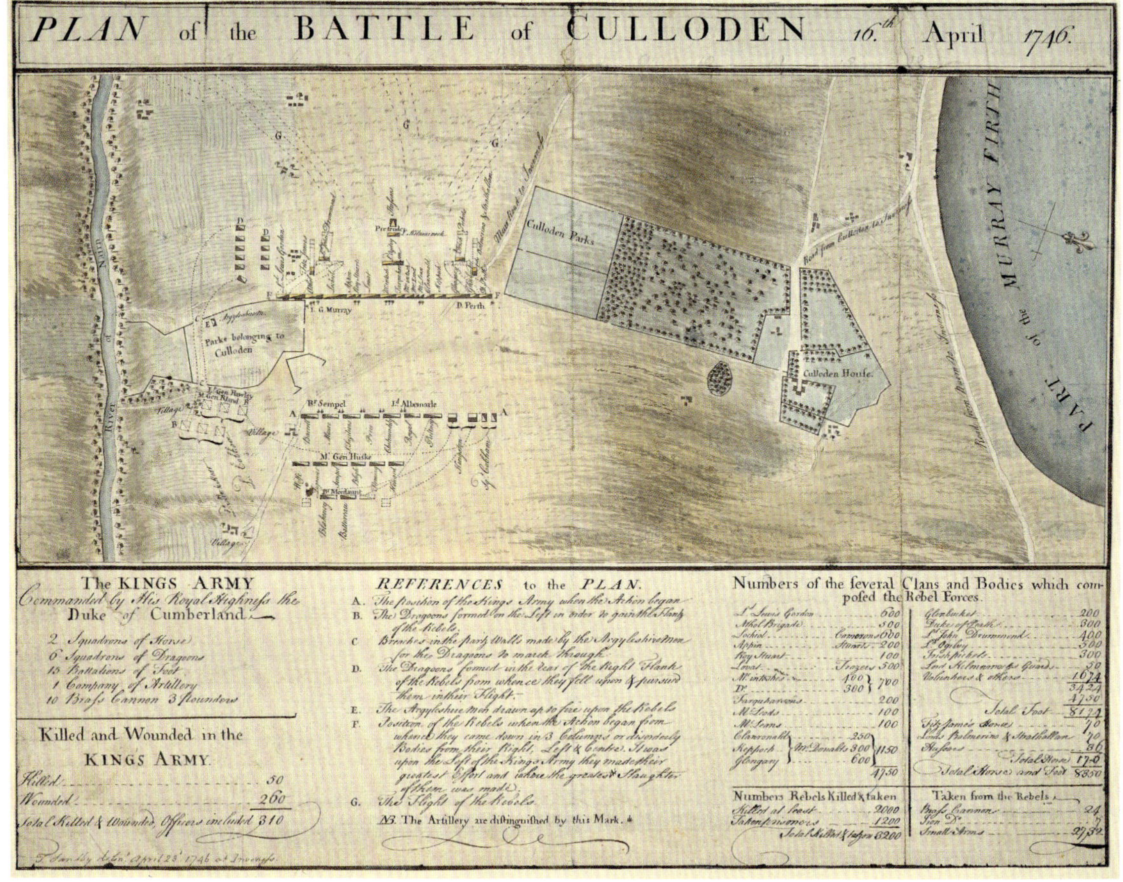

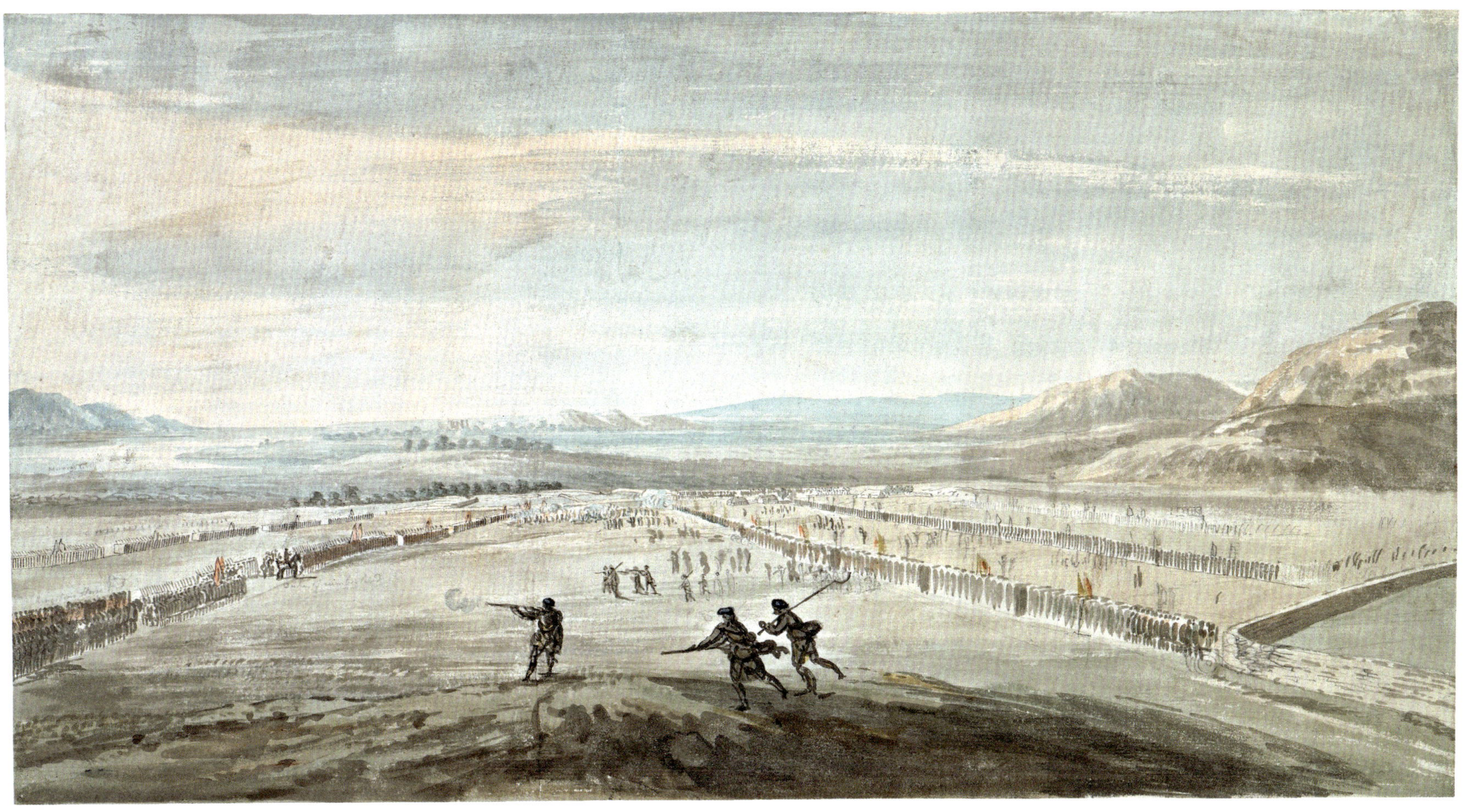

Both works are to be aligned with a tradition of military art established in the 1660s and 1670s in commemoration of the campaigns of Louis XIV. Plans and orders of battle, including a map of the topography of the battlefield and indication of the strategic positioning of military units, overlaid with textual information on the dead, ordnance or chain of command, comprised one strand of this tradition. Other depictions of the battlefield were more naturalistic, invariably placing a commanding general or monarch on horseback surveying the action from a distanced, foreground promontory. Artists like David Morier, who painted several equestrian portraits of Cumberland, had imported this tradition from across the Channel. Authenticity was central to such images, whether it was secured by the accumulation of statistics in the plan or the apparent topographical accuracy offered by the commanding view. Thomas Sandby's familiarity with the conventions of such imagery is well demonstrated by his plans and view of the battlefield at Culloden. Nevertheless, his sketch of the battle also departs from that tradition, as it views the battle from the perspective of the enemy by placing a group of Jacobites advancing down the foreground rise. When faced with the regular, straight lines formed by Cumberland's troops, the enemy ranks appear even more disorderly, however. Celebrated when securing victory in the highlands, Cumberland's Prussian-like military discipline was very shortly to become the target of censure and satire, not least from artists like William Hogarth (cats 21–28).

6

THE BOARD OF ORDNANCE

A sheet of the fair copy of the Military Survey of the North of Scotland (Culloden Moor), *c.* 1750

Pen, wash and watercolour over graphite, 2910 × 755 mm
British Library, London, Maps C.C.5.a441(26)

PROVENANCE
George III's Topographical Collection; transferred to the British Museum (now British Library), 1829

SELECTED REFERENCES
Skelton 1967; London 1977; Christian 1990; Bermingham 2000, pp. 78–83; Great Map 2007

Paper landscapes of the battlefield have a long history in European warfare, enabling military commanders to plan broad outlines of strategy, for example. However, it was only in the second half of the eighteenth century that military reformers began to tout maps and drawings as essential documents of war, such that it became a commonplace that officers should possess a degree of graphic ability. And it was as a result of the Board of Ordnance's undertakings north of the border that the army's need for draughtsmen trained in these skills first began to establish itself. The English army's forays into the highlands in pursuit of Bonnie Prince Charlie, and their subsequent attempts to pacify the country, made the production of adequate maps or topographical descriptions a pressing concern. In response to this need, the mapping of the highlands by the Board of Ordnance began in 1747 under the direction of Colonel David Watson and his assistant William Roy. Reporting to the Royal Society nearly forty years later, Roy explained that the Rebellion 'convinced Government of what infinite importance it would be to the State that a country, so very inaccessible by nature, should be thoroughly explored and laid open' (Roy 1785, p. 386).

Laying open the highlands involved six teams of eight men led by a surveyor. Compiling notes and information in the field over the summer months, they returned to the Ordnance Drawing Room in Edinburgh every winter, where, according to one early account, 'they protracted on royal paper

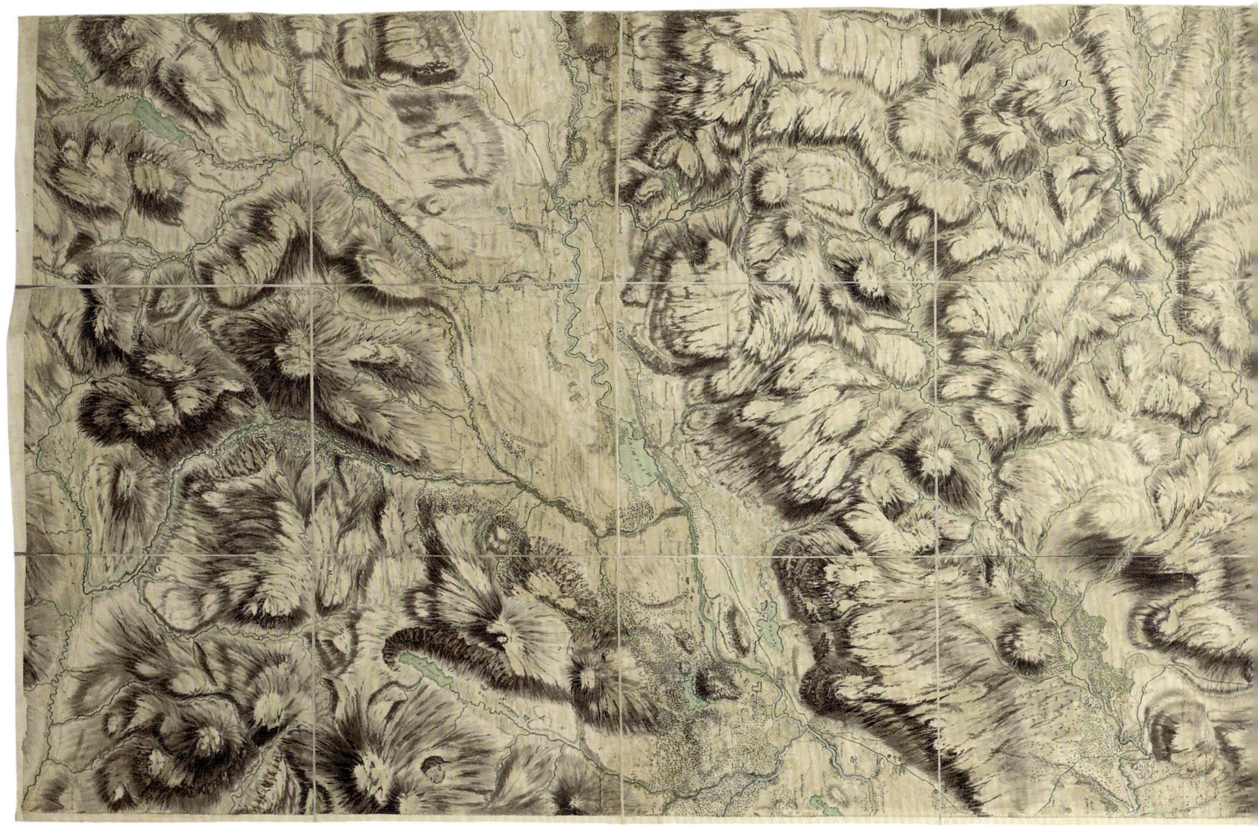

their several surveys' (Chalmers 1807, vol. 2, p. 63). Paul Sandby's role was to draw up some of the original protractions or 'manuscript maps' and collate them into a 'fair copy' or presentation map. Assisted by Charles Tarrant and others, Sandby was chiefly responsible for the 'Mountains and Ground' (Arrowsmith 1809, p. 8). Sections from the so-called 'Great Map', as it was known to contemporaries, illustrate the artist's highly painterly and decorative interpretation of contemporary military cartographic technique, most probably developed in close association with Roy. Aligned brush strokes indicate the direction of slopes, and graduations of tone express increases in steepness and height. In depicting the varied features of the terrain the map followed established conventions, with red indicating architectural structures, brown for roads, yellow for cultivated ground, green for woodland, buff for moorland, and blue-green for water. Tilled land was further distinguished by the use of parallel hatching, while the sands or shoals around rivers or expanses of water were indicated by stipple effects. These features are often minutely described, as in the details showing designed landscapes around larger country houses and estates.

For Roy, the map was rather a 'magnificent military sketch, than a very accurate map of the country'; as he observed: 'no geometrical exactness is to be expected, the sole object in view being, to shew remarkable things, or such as constitute the great outlines of the Country' (Roy 1785, p. 387). With the primary concern being to facilitate the movement of troops, the focus fell on coastlines, rivers or roads, leaving other features less than accurately recorded. There was considerable difficulty in translating the pictorial language of the surveyors' topographical observations into cartographic form, and this is most apparent in the depiction of relief, which appears as a hybrid combination of bird's-eye and perspectival views. These features are all well illustrated by this section of the 'Great Map', centring on the area around Culloden Moor, which forms part of the original twelve rolls of the fair copy of the Military Survey of North Britain, cut up in the nineteenth century and mounted into folding sheet form.

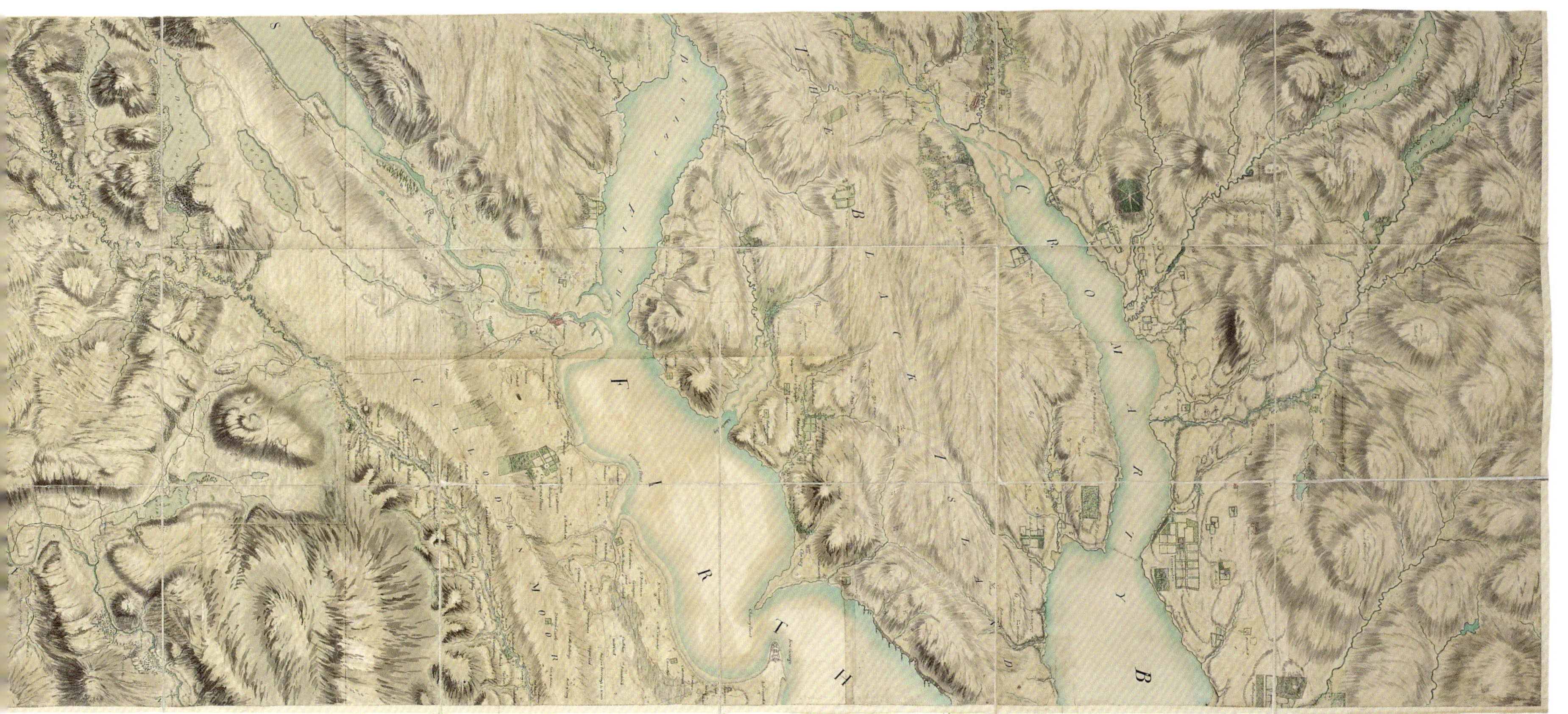

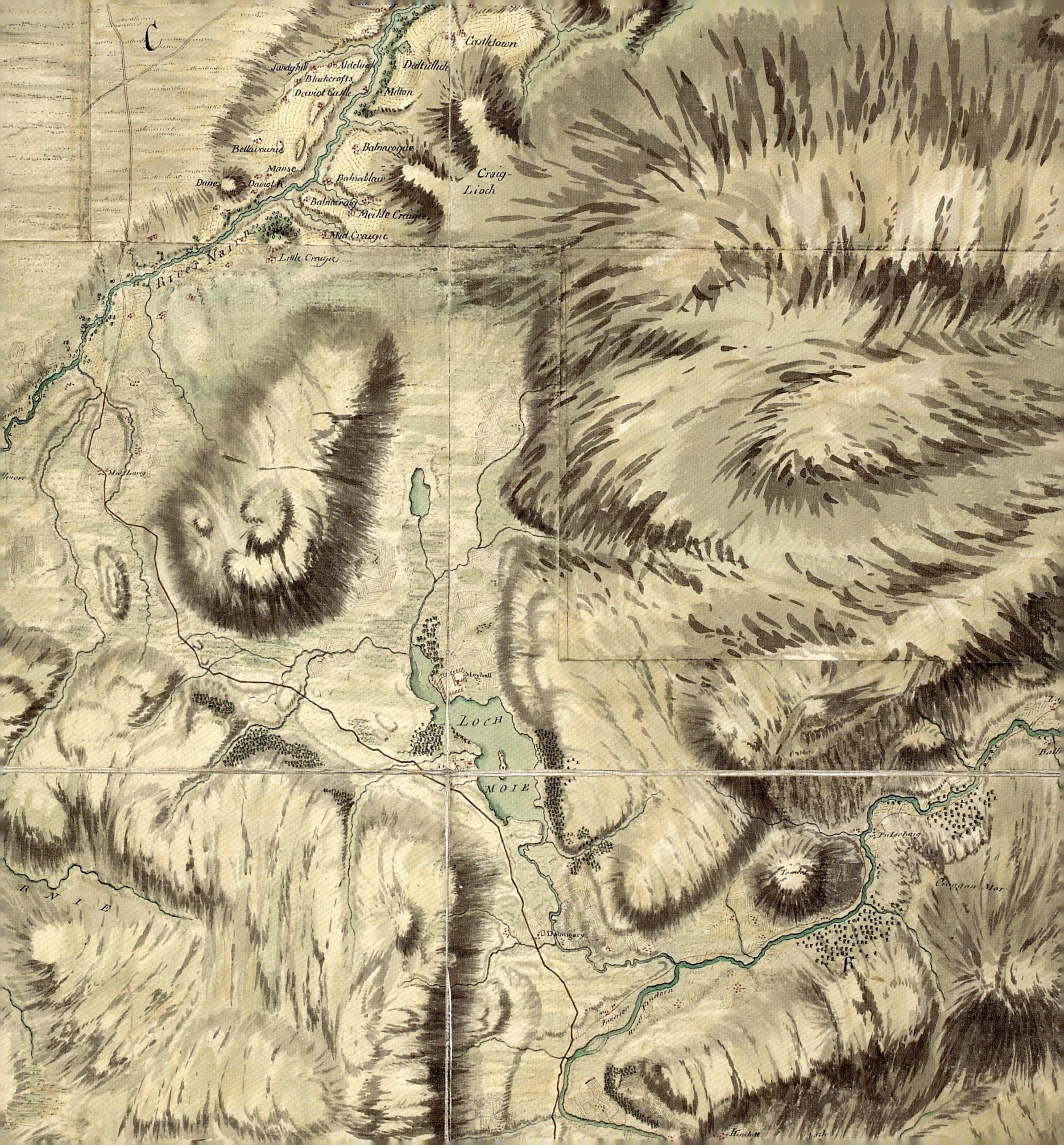
Castletown
Daltullich
Altclunich
Sandyhill
Blackcrofts
Daviot Castle
Milton
Bellairound
Balnarogue
Dune
Manse
Daviot K
Balnablaw
Craig-Lioch
Balnacraig
Meikle Craggie
Mid Craggie
Little Craggie
River Nairn
Loch Moie
Moyhall
Dalmagary
Craggan Mor

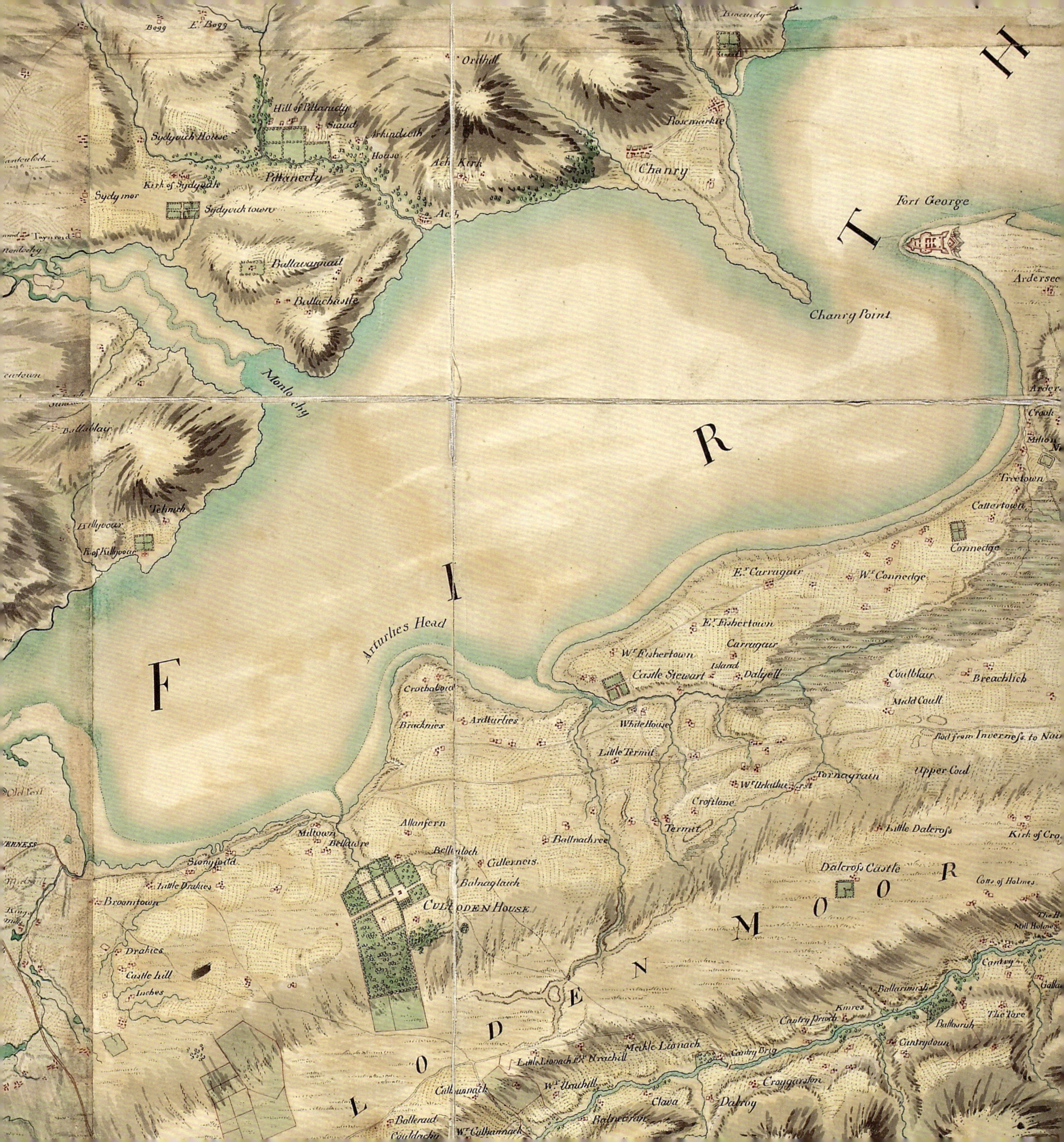

F I R T H
Fort George
Chanry Point
Chanry
Rosmarkie
Monlochy
Arturlies Head
Castle Stewart
White House
Culloden House
Dalcross Castle
Little Dalcross
Upper Coul
Croftlone
Ballnachree
Allanfern
Stonyfeild
Broomtown
Drakies
Castle hill
Inches
Ardersee
Treetown
Connedge
W^t. Connedge
E^t. Carragair
Carragair
Dalyell
Coulblair
Breachlich
Cantrydown
Clava
Dalroy
Ballachastle
Pittancrly
Sydyeich House
Sydyeichtown
Kirk of Sydyeich
Ach Kirk
Orlhill

7

THE BOARD OF ORDNANCE

Part of the Reduction from the Great Map, shewing the Kings Road which is express'd by a Red Line, & the Country Roads by a Brown Line, c. 1753

Pen, wash and watercolour over graphite, 340 × 225 mm
British Library, London, K.Top.48.64

PROVENANCE
George III's Topographical Collection; transferred to the British Museum (now British Library), 1829

SELECTED EXHIBITIONS
London 1977, no. 26b; Nottingham 1990, no. III.28

SELECTED REFERENCES
London 1977, no. 26b, p. 19; Christian 1990

Paul Sandby returned south for most of 1751, sharing lodgings with his elder brother at Windsor and in London, this being the period in which he first became active on the metropolitan art scene. Nevertheless, his commitments to the Board of Ordnance were to continue, leading him to return north once or twice more over the following two years. At least one of these visits was to work on a reduction of the Military Survey of the north of Scotland, to one quarter of the scale of the original protraction. This highly finished map, showing the country along military roads between Stirling and Amulree, probably dates from this later period – the scale given on the inscription corresponds to that of the reduction. With William Roy probably responsible for the fine detail and inscriptions, traces of Sandby's hand are detectable in the painterly flourish of the relief shading. In its most decorative passage, the scalloped edges of an elaborate, rococo cartouche follow the contours of the mountainous ridge leading from Stirling to the coastline of the Firth of Forth. This was, as Roy observed, rather a 'magnificent military sketch, than a very accurate map of the country' (Roy 1785, p. 387).

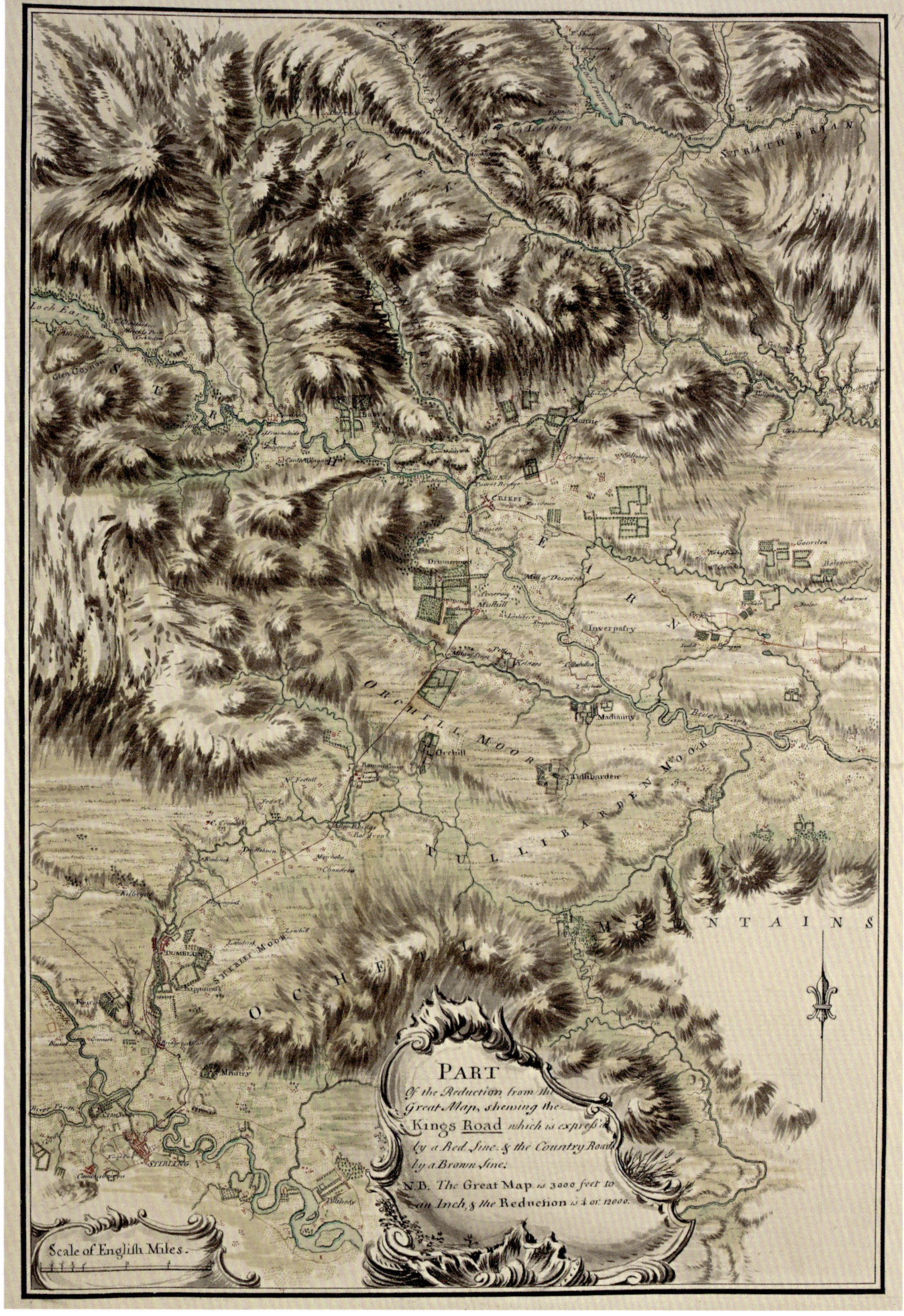

8

Surveying Party by Kinloch Rannoch, 1749

Pen, wash and watercolour over graphite, 173 × 233 mm
British Library, London, K.Top.50.83.2

PROVENANCE
George III's Topographical Collection; transferred to the British Museum (now British Library), 1829

SELECTED EXHIBITIONS
London 1977, no. 9; Edinburgh 1978A, no. 4.1; Nottingham 1990, no. III.15; London 1991, no. 23

SELECTED REFERENCES
Skelton 1967; London 1977, no. 9, p. 10; Christian 1990; London 1991, p. 15; Great Map 2007

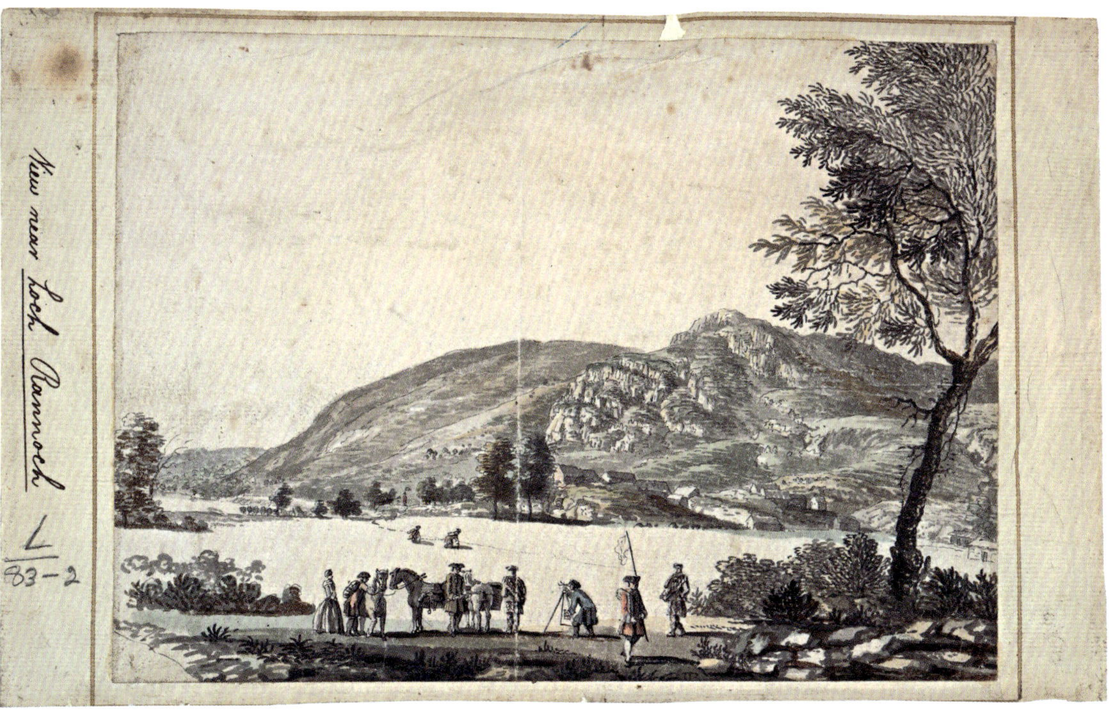

One of the few contemporary accounts of the Military Survey of North Britain, that of the engineer David Dundas, as recorded by the cartographer Aaron Arrowsmith, offers invaluable testimony of the day-to-day operations of the survey parties that traversed the highland landscape during the summer months. According to Dundas, 'Each of the Surveyors … was attended by a Non-Commissioned Officer and Six Soldiers as Assistants; One carried the Theodolite: Two measured with the Chain: Two for the fore and back Stations, and the remaining one acted as Batman, or attended on the party' (Arrowsmith 1809, p. 8). This description accords well with the pictorial record offered by this small, off-duty study of a party at work at the eastern end of Loch Rannoch, which is also known in a second, less finished form (National Library of Wales, Aberystwyth).

Only selected features, roads, rivers and lochs, were surveyed; the rest, towns and settlements, enclosures and woodland, as well as relief, was sketched in by eye or copied from existing maps. 'Each surveyor kept a field-book and a sketch-book,' recalled one survey team member: 'in the first he inserted the angles and measurements of his stations … In the second, which was of sufficient size, he delineated his stations and the face of the country, which was then much less inclosed and woody than at present, and favourably featured for a military sketch' (Arrowsmith 1809, p. 8). While there was a reliance on measuring devices, such as the small open-sighted circumferentor shown here, much was recorded by observation. To survey was, therefore, pictorial as well as mathematical. The present drawing reveals how Sandby's cartographic work informed his topographical views: the hillside, with its hatched shading and rocky, serrated edges etched in pen, is strongly reminiscent of the relief work found in the fair copies of the Military Survey.

9

Ben Lomond. View near Dumbarton, c. 1747

Pen, ink and wash over graphite, 165 × 978 mm
Pasted in Thomas Pennant's own extra-illustrated copy of his *Tour of Scotland 1769–72*, 1772 (vol. 1, part 2, facing p. 249)
National Library of Wales, Aberystwyth

PROVENANCE
John Towneley (sale King's, May 1816, lot 585); David Pennant and by descent

SELECTED EXHIBITIONS
Nottingham 1986, n.n.; Nottingham 1990, no. III.24

SELECTED REFERENCES
Joyner 1983, pp. 9–10

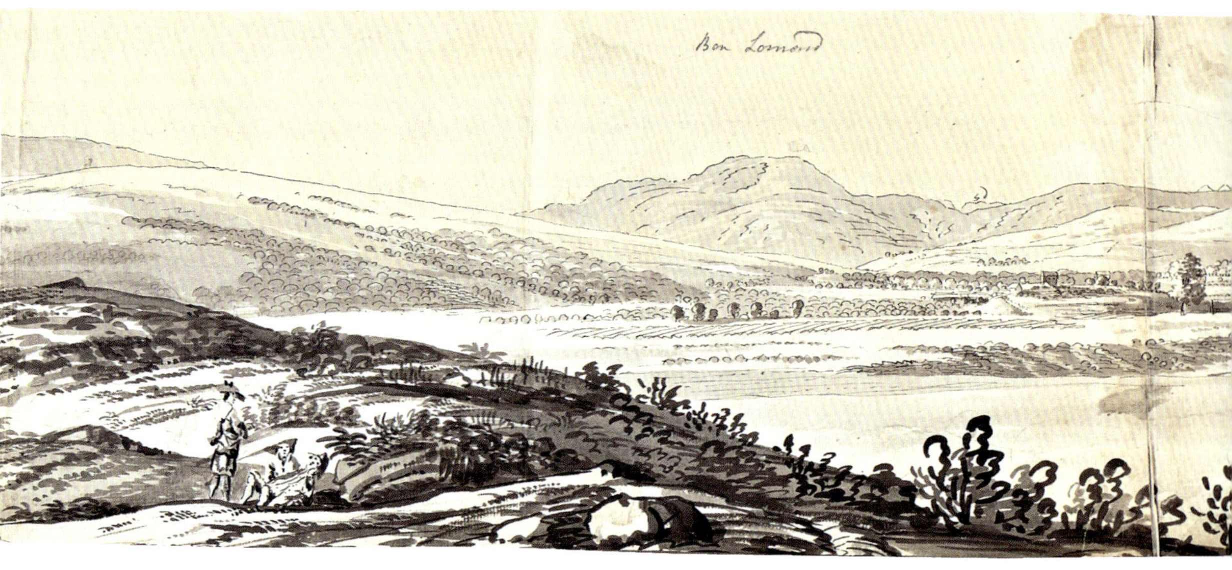

In this remarkable panoramic survey of an area he clearly knew well, Sandby comes close to the kinds of extended drawings his elder brother was executing at this moment for the Duke of Cumberland, who was on campaign on the continent during the War of Austrian Succession (fig. 34). Such drawings, surely made using an optical device such as a *camera obscura*, were formed by joining several pieces of paper end on end. Each sheet appears to have been drawn separately, finished and then joined. The result is the kind of wide-angled view seen here, to be read as if it were a map, closely and across. This is made explicit in this example by the incorporation of now badly faded lettering, picking out features and suggestive of a key. Each drawing was seen as a distinct, finished element, to be cut and pasted together, and their assembly was also map-like. In his work in the Ordnance Drawing Room back in Edinburgh, Sandby would have been required to make accurate copies of drawings or prints made by others; his sketching of the relief was only one part of a collaborative enterprise.

These skills later came to inform the artist's professional practice, as is illustrated by the present drawing, in its eventual translation into a print for *The Virtuosi's Museum* series some thirty years later (fig. 35). This contracted the composition, making Ben Lomond the most distinctive feature. The column of marching soldiers was retained, but the large military encampment in the middle distance was reduced to just the first two tents. 'This delightful and romantic spot', as the accompanying letterpress described it, had in

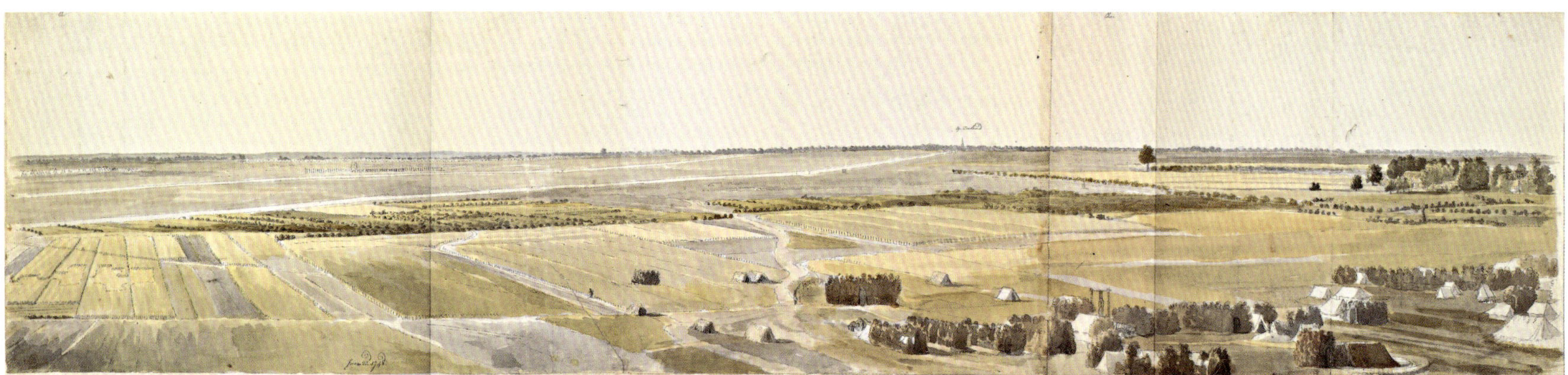

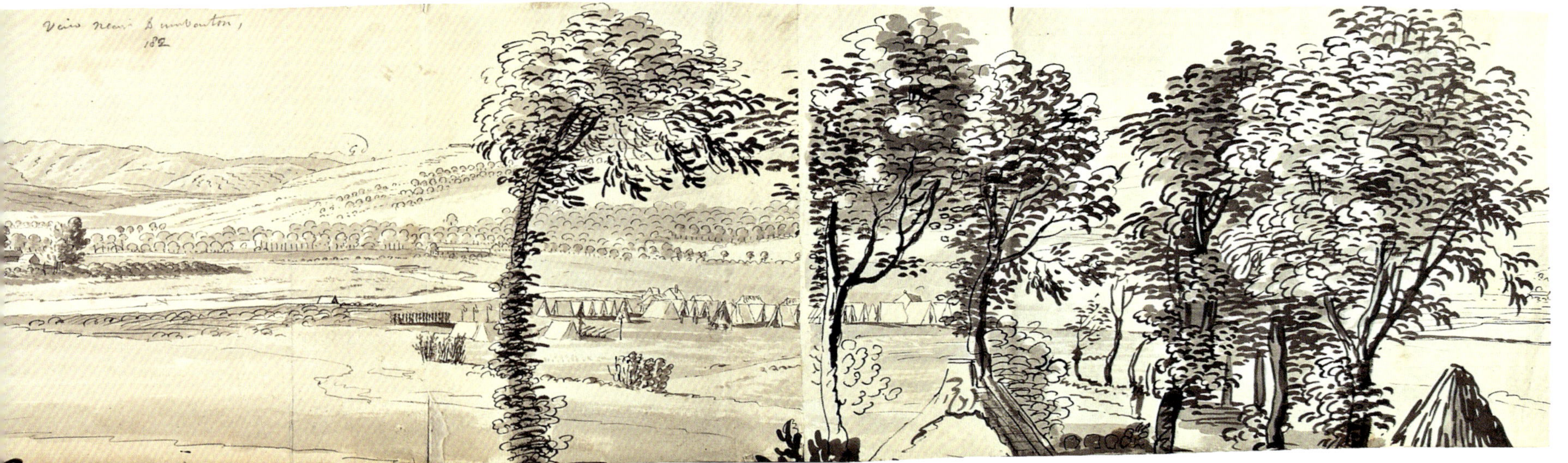

the intervening years become part of the region's touristic itinerary, as is indicated by an extended, accompanying quotation from Thomas Pennant's enormously popular *Tour of Scotland* (1772). However, Pennant makes it clear that this 'unspeakably beautiful' locale was far from untouched, being 'decorated with bleacheries, plantations and villas'. Rather, its appeal lay in its variety, its blend of the natural and the human, the raw and the improved: 'One way is seen part of the magnificent lake, Ben-Lomond and the vast mountains above Glen-Crow. On the other hand appears a fine reach of the Clyde enlivened by shipping, a view of the pretty seats of Roseneth and Ardincapel, and the busy towns of Port-Glasgow and Greenock.'

This drawing is now pasted into an extra-illustrated copy of Pennant's pioneering *Tour*. Often described as 'grangerising', such customising of a published text by cutting and pasting in prints and watercolours related to the thematic concerns of the book was a common practice (see Peltz 1999). This particular volume was Pennant's own, extra-illustrated over a number of years by the author and his son David. It features a number of Sandby's very earliest drawings, along with contemporary etchings by his close friend, the amateur artist John Clerk of Eldin, collected prior to or during Pennant's visits to Scotland in 1769 and 1772. However, the Pennants also include drawings purchased after these excursions, with David still buying at auction long after his father's death in 1798. The contents represent, therefore, the best part of fifty years of collecting – an illustration of the continued currency of Sandby's Scottish views. Paul and Thomas Sandby's popularity with an antiquarian audience is further indicated by the presence of a number of their works in perhaps the most celebrated and opulent example of extra-illustration, John Charles Crowle's fourteen-book edition of a single volume of Pennant's *Some Account of London*. Paired views of the Thames from the garden terrace of old Somerset House (cats 53–54) were once pasted into Crowle's volumes. Antiquarians like Crowle or Pennant valued the fine, careful delineation of objects in the brothers' drawings. Yet this striking field study of a landscape freighted with historical associations, both ancient and more recent, suggests also that a premium was placed on the subject of a drawing and its fidelity to the topography.

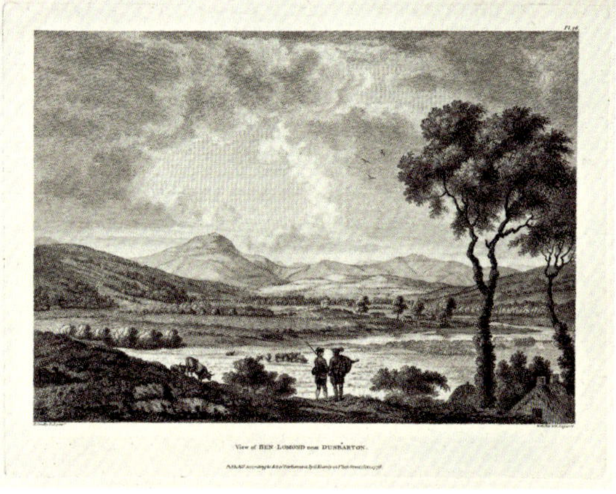

FIG. 34 (OPPOSITE)
Thomas Sandby, *View of a Camp in the Low Countries*, 22 June 1748. Watercolour and wash over graphite, 250 × 1150 mm. British Library, London, Add Mss 15968(a)

FIG. 35 (ABOVE)
Thomas Medland, after Paul Sandby, *View of Ben Lomond*, from *The Virtuosi's Museum*, published by George Kearsly, 1 August 1780. Engraving, 208 × 268 mm. Nottingham City Museums and Galleries

10

Plan of the Castle of Dumbarton, *c.* 1747

Pen and wash over graphite, 708 × 499 mm
National Library of Scotland, Edinburgh, MS 1649 Z.03/57

PROVENANCE
General William Skinner and by descent; presumably passed to the Board of Ordnance after 1872; transferred from the Board of Ordnance, 1934

SELECTED EXHIBITIONS
Nottingham 1990, no. III.22

SELECTED REFERENCES
Christian 1990; Bermingham 2000, pp. 82–83

The fact that mapping and drawing were understood as related practices is clearly indicated by these views of Dumbarton Castle, in which a plan of the rock citadel and two profiles are combined on a single sheet. Placed adjacently, in this way, they provide multiple perspectives on this historic, much rebuilt fortress. In the topographical views at the bottom of the page Sandby describes the distinctive rises and falls of the craggy outcrop in the mouth of the Clyde, highlighting the sheer, jagged cliffs, with their narrow precipitous gullies, and the masses of rock and sandbank rising out of the water below. These provide information on those features less readily intelligible from the cartographic plan above, which is marked by a still imperfect rendering of relief in which the relative heights of the principal landmarks are uncertain. These technical difficulties were allayed somewhat by the provision of profile views, and ensuring that these elements were precisely rendered required fine judgement. Accuracy depended upon careful measurement of the angular distances between features. This presented a particular problem for vertical recording, however, since the breadth of a range was invariably greater than its height. A terrain characterised by high, rising features might therefore produce an unacceptably long drawing. In such a case, areas of the drawing would be slightly compressed or exaggerated in the interests of legibility.

Following the Jacobite Rebellion of 1715 General George Wade, then Commander-in-Chief of the armed forces in North Britain, planned and oversaw the building of a series of new roads, bridges and fortresses, in order to facilitate the movement and barracking of troops in a still largely inaccessible highland landscape. This work was continued after the '45, with engineers extending the construction of roads and forts as well as reporting on the possible repair of damaged or derelict structures. It is possible that the present work formed part of such an appraisal, given that Sandby's drawings fulfilled a similar role in surveys of strategically important but ruined sites in Argyll. Plans for improving the defences of Dumbarton Castle were certainly advanced by the subsequent owner of this sheet, who is referred to in the inscription below the map, General William Skinner, Director of Engineers in Scotland (see National Library of Scotland, Edinburgh, MS.1647 Z 02/74a–b).

REFERENCES

PLAN
of the *CASTLE* of
Dunbarton

Handed over to Lieut.t Monier Skinner Rl Engineer by his father in 1772.

11

Plan of Castle Tyrim in Muydart,
Plan of Castle Duirt in the Island of Mull,
1748

Pen, wash and watercolour, 327 × 526 mm
Signed: 'P. Sandby delin' (l.l.)
National Library of Scotland, Edinburgh,
MS 1648 Z.03/28e

PROVENANCE
Transferred from the Board of Ordnance, 1934

SELECTED EXHIBITIONS
Edinburgh 1978A, no. 4.8; Hamilton 1981, no. 6; Nottingham 1986, n.n.; Nottingham 1990, no. III.20; London 1991, no. 11

SELECTED REFERENCES
Edinburgh 1978A, no. 4.8, p. 43; Hamilton 1981, no. 6, p. 6; Christian 1990; London 1991, no. 11, pp. 10–11

In 1748 Colonel David Watson led a survey party into the more remote areas of Argyll; their itinerary took in visits to the strategically important Duart Castle on Mull, Tioram Castle at the entrance to Loch Moidart, and Castle Stalker, to the south of the Isle of Shuna. This sheet, combining plans and views of Duart and Tioram Castles, was drawn up to accompany Watson's spare written summary of the state of repair of these structures, dated 3 October 1748, which noted of the first fortress, sited on the east side of the Isle of Mull:

> its Situation is very strong but the Entrance of the Sound is too broad to be commanded from the Castle; the Walls are sufficient but the Roof the Barracks where the Party is lodged quite Ruinous. If this Castle was properly repair'd it might accommodate 150 Men, which repairs would Cost 1500£. The repairs necessary for quartering the present Detachment which consists of a subaltern, and 20 Men must Cost 300£. (National Library of Scotland, Edinburgh, MS 1648 Z/28f)

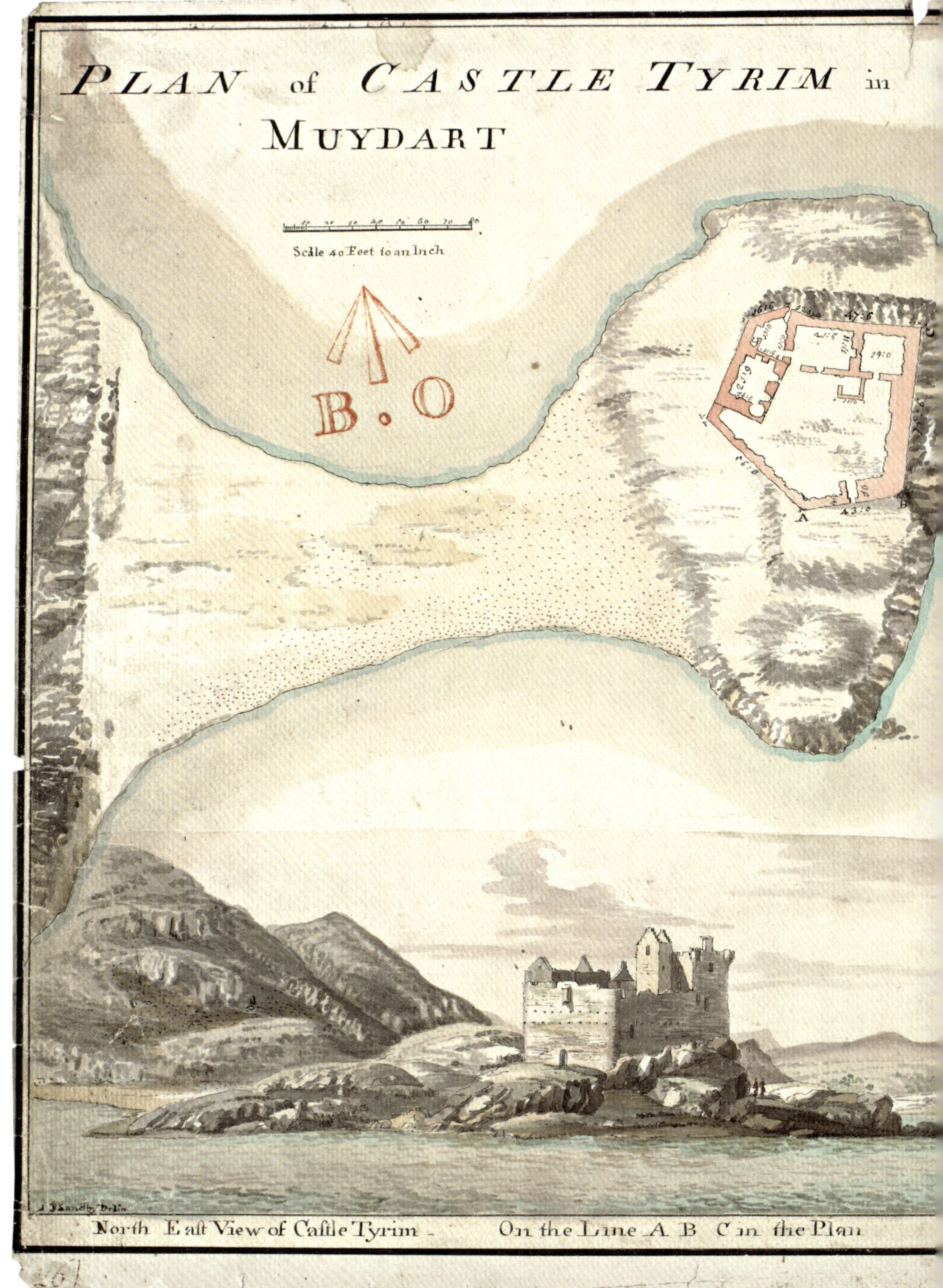

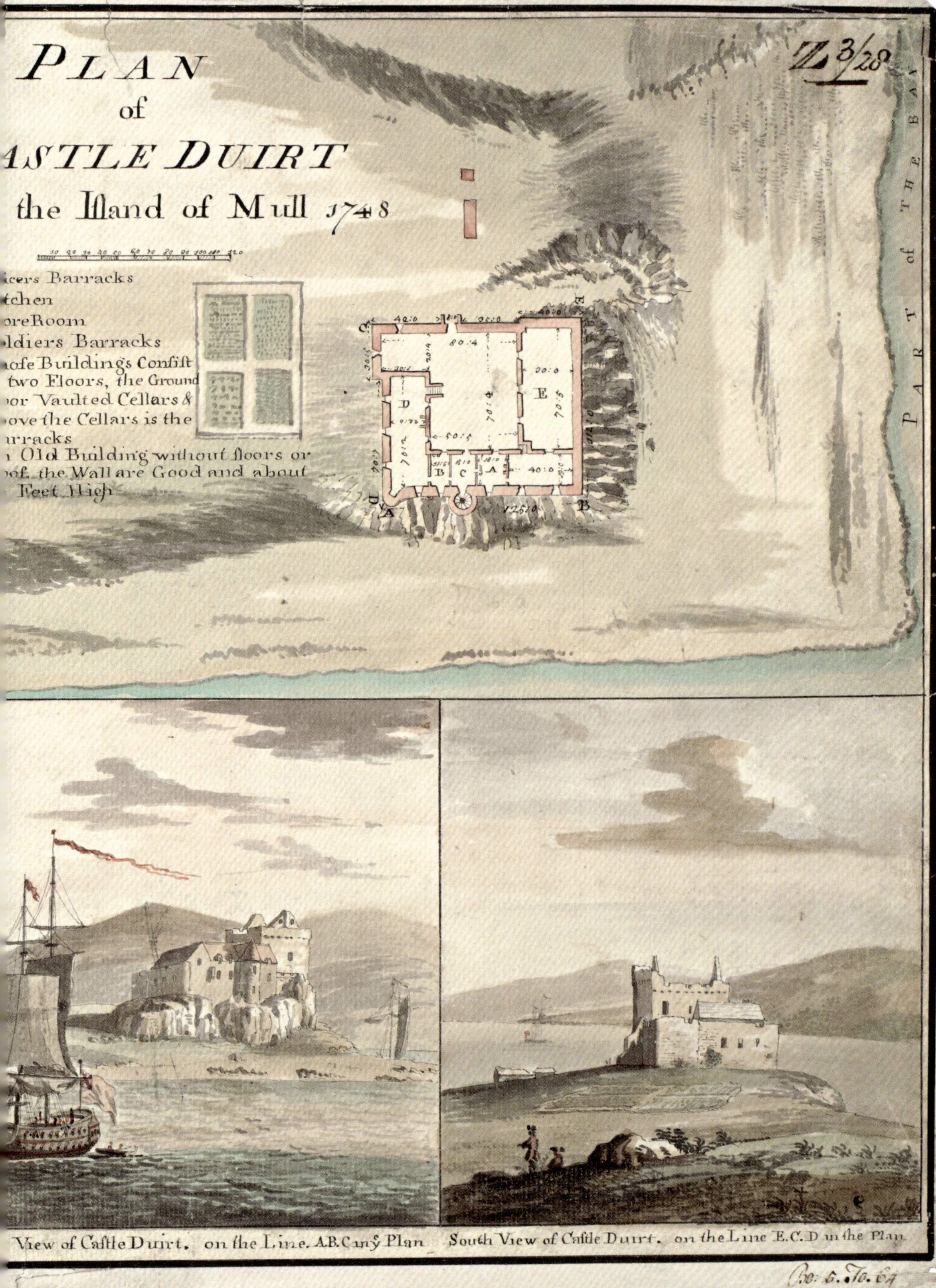

Watson's appraisal was largely concerned with the cost of reconstructing these strongholds, reduced to ruins during earlier conflicts. Observations on their strategic value were communicated primarily through Sandby's richly informative assemblage of plans and views. Such composite images, incorporating different visual modes in the same frame, not only allowed the accommodation of multiple perspectives but also conveyed information less easily reducible to words.

William Roy considered such plans and views as self-sufficient, and not necessarily reliant on any supporting textual exposition, as is indicated by his remarkable study, *The Military Antiquities of the Romans in North Britain*, a text published posthumously by the Society of Antiquaries of London in 1793, but based on field studies undertaken during work on the 'Great Map' and drawn up in 1773. Of its maps, plans and sections of the Antonine Wall, which so obviously benefit from the survey skills Roy had developed when working for the Board of Ordnance, the author argued 'a short description may suffice, since from a general plan of this kind, topographically expressed, a much truer notion may be obtained ... than what, without such assistance, could possibly be conveyed in many words' (Roy 1793, pp. 155–56). This evident faith in the communicative power of images is to be seen in the context of a more general cultural conviction current in the period, which saw visual forms occupy a privileged place in the collation and summary of knowledge (see Smiles 2000). The existence of a close copy of this sheet, very possibly also attributable to Sandby, illustrates the importance of accurate reproduction for military purposes (National Library of Scotland, MS 1648 z.03/28d).

12

Castle Duart, Isle of Mull, 1748

Pen and wash over graphite, 192 × 301 mm
Signed: 'Paul Sandby' (l.l.); and dated '1748' (l.c.)
National Gallery of Scotland, Edinburgh, D.82

PROVENANCE
David Laing; transferred from the Royal Scottish Academy, 1910

SELECTED EXHIBITIONS
Edinburgh 1978A, no. 4.6; Hamilton 1981, no. 5; Nottingham 1990, no. III.21

SELECTED REFERENCES
Edinburgh 1978A, no. 4.6, pp. 40, 43; Hamilton 1981, no. 5, p. 5

This drawing was presumably a preliminary study for the compilation of plans and views of Duart and Tioram Castles, taken during Colonel David Watson's 1748 survey of Argyll (cat. 11). Viewed from the south, and placed at some distance, the castle is established as part of the wider landscape. Sandby notes its position in relation to the shoreline and surrounding mountains, and provides some indication of scale by including various vessels and figures.

A careful copy of this drawing by John Clerk of Eldin, now in the collection of the National Gallery of Scotland, Edinburgh, suggests that this was one of the 30 or so watercolours by Sandby once owned by the antiquarian. Clerk's own drawings and etchings focus largely on the region's antiquities and were much admired by Thomas Pennant, who collected them, along with studies by Sandby (see Edinburgh 1978B). Copies were valued in antiquarian circles as much as original studies, with Pennant lending works from his collection to fellow scholars for tracing, as well as setting his own servant, Moses Griffiths, to reproduce drawings loaned from others. Such practices indicate a concern with the provision of information in visual form that is markedly similar to that required by map-making and surveying.

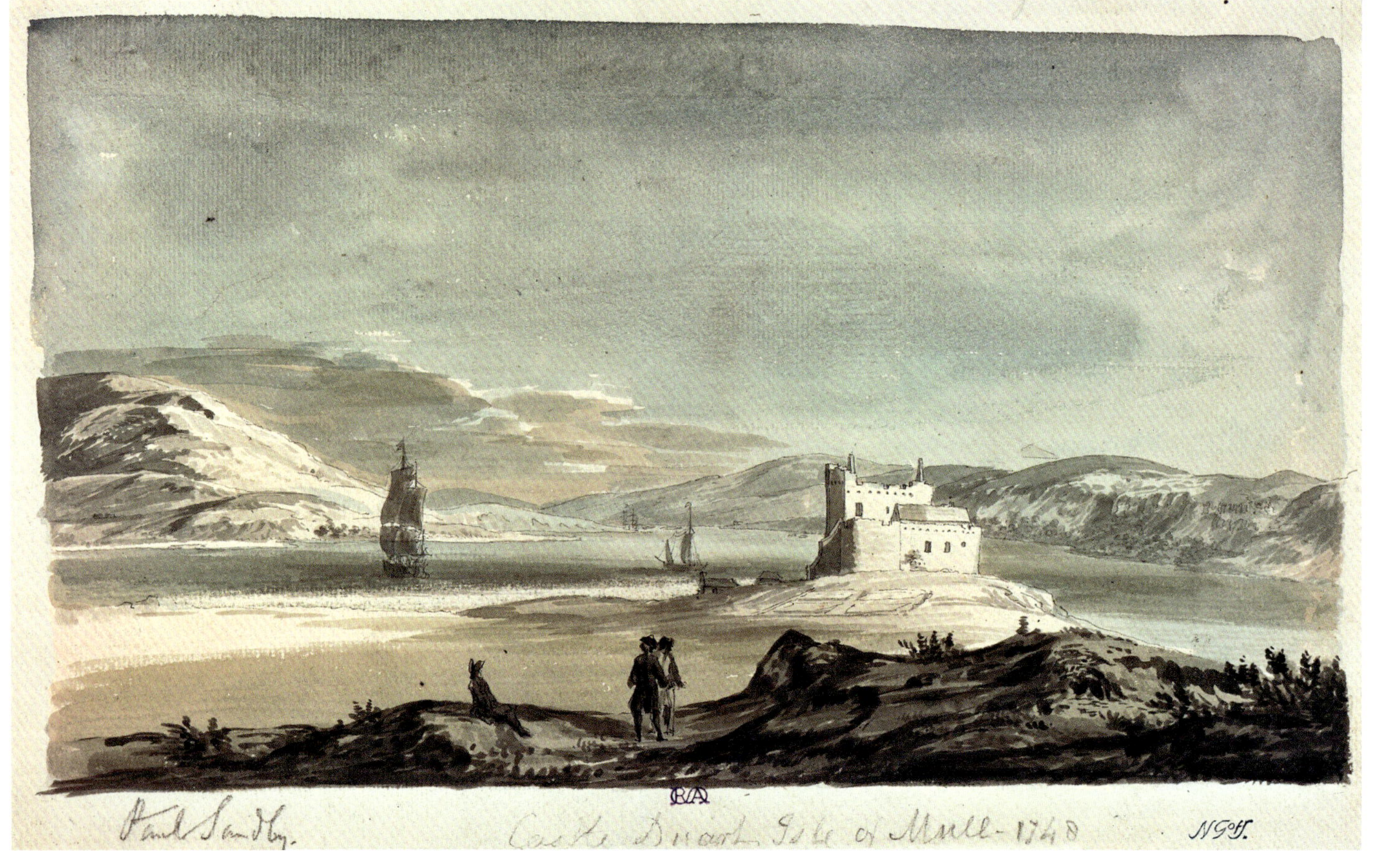

13

Edinburgh panorama looking out to the Firth of Forth from the Castle Bank, with Allan Ramsay's house, c. 1750

Pen, wash and watercolour over graphite, 249 × 541 mm
British Library, London, K.Top.50.96b

PROVENANCE
George III's Topographical Collection; transferred to the British Museum (now British Library), 1829

SELECTED EXHIBITIONS
Edinburgh 1978A, no. 4.13; Nottingham 1990, no. III.42

SELECTED REFERENCES
Edinburgh 1978A, no. 4.13, p. 44

This prospect view looks out from Edinburgh's Castle Bank, across the valley landscape to Broughton and Leith in the middle distance and the Forth and the coast of Fife beyond. Although it is an early work, there is considerable deftness in the handling of such a broad, open expanse. The drawing also shows Sandby to be already equally confident in picking out fine detail, as is most apparent in the scratches of pen delineating the buildings of Leith and its surrounding farmsteads.

Below the tenements of the Old Town, in the centre foreground of the drawing, is the distinctive self-built home of the poet Allan Ramsay. His celebrated Goose Pie house, based on the Aberdonian architect James Gibbs's Octagon at Twickenham, was dedicated to the Horatian sister arts of poetry and painting. During the Rebellion, Jacobite forces had used the building as a vantage point for firing on the castle garrison above. Despite his well-known sympathy for the Stuart cause, Ramsay himself eluded the disturbance by staying with his friend, the fervent pro-Unionist Sir John Clerk of Penicuik. Sandby's relationship to these two figures reveals that political allegiances were far from cut and dried in this period. Clerk was father to the artist's friend, and Robert Adam's brother-in-law, John Clerk of Eldin, as well as being instrumental in securing Sandby's only known private commission of this period (cat. 14). In addition to anecdotal evidence connecting the young artist to the poet, 1758 saw Sandby etch a set of five illustrations to Ramsay's famous poem *The Gentle Shepherd* (Oppé 1947, no. 214; Edinburgh 1978A, pp. 40, 45–46). Eventually published by Ryland and Byer in 1765, these prints set various key scenes of Ramsay's pastoral in and around Edinburgh, recycling compositional studies such as the example illustrated here. That the central protagonist of Ramsay's verse, Sir William Worthy, was widely recognised as a thinly veiled James Stuart, does not appear to have concerned Sandby. Clearly artistic matters might provide common ground on which those of distinct political opinion might meet.

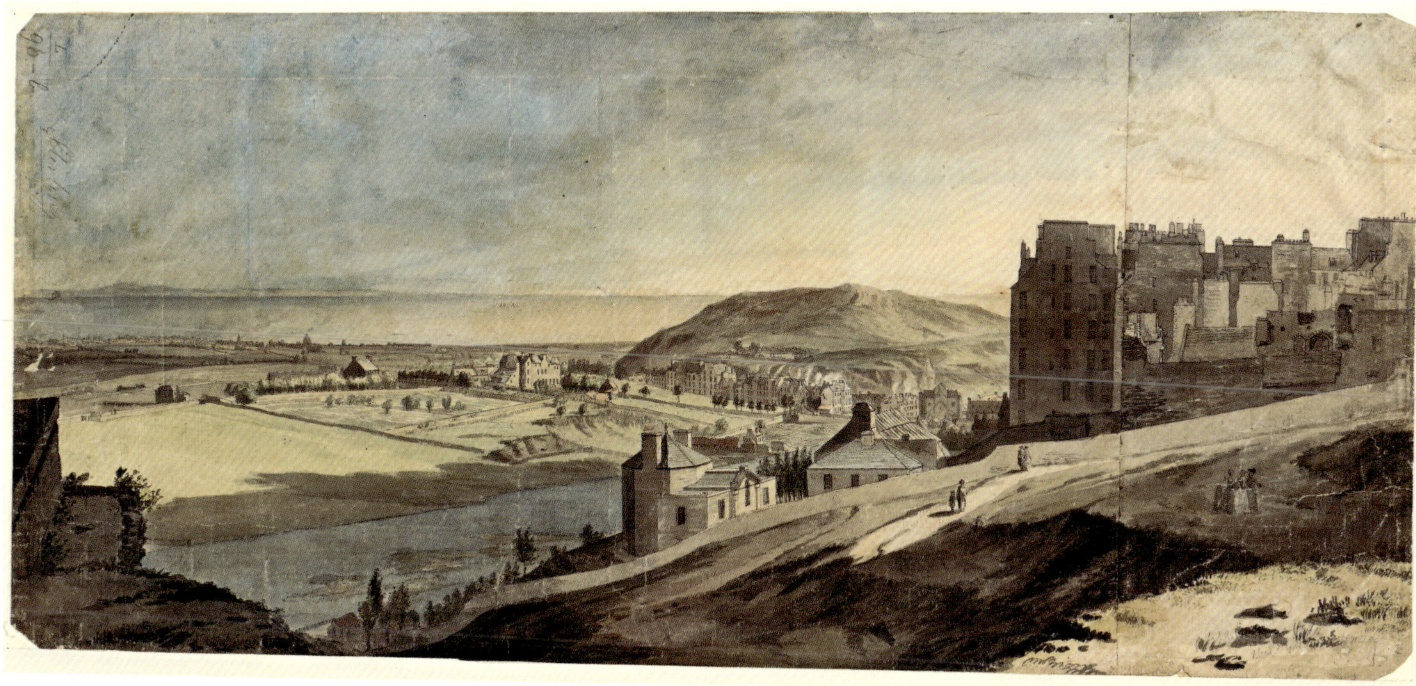

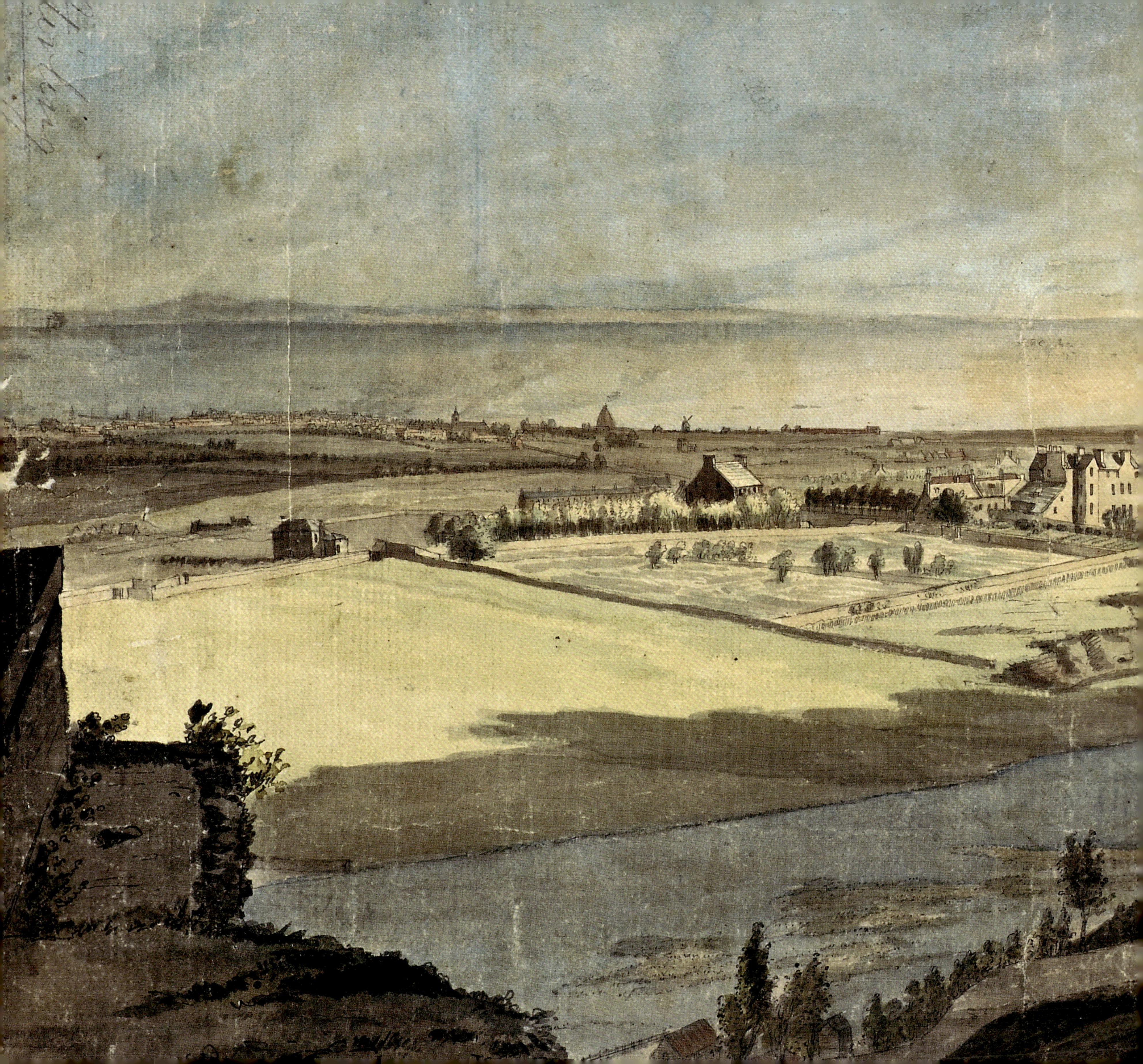

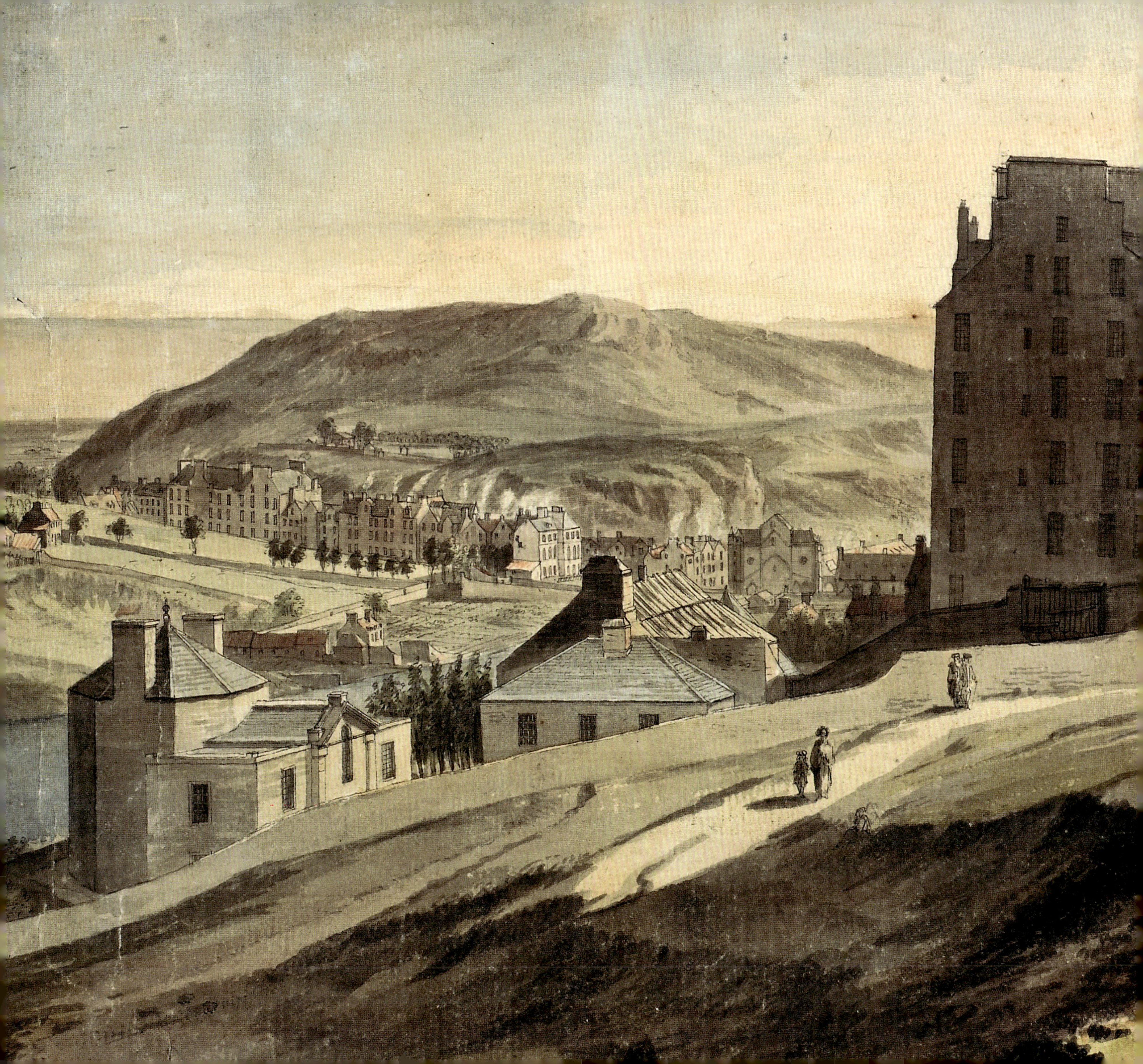

14

Nithsdale, with Drumlanrig, c. 1751

Pen, wash and watercolour over graphite, 250 × 416 mm
British Library, London, K.Top.49.54.1c

PROVENANCE
George III's Topographical Collection; transferred to the British Museum (now British Library), 1829

SELECTED EXHIBITIONS
London 1977, no. 20; Edinburgh 1978A, no. 4.21; Nottingham 1990, no. III.44

SELECTED REFERENCES
London 1977, no. 20, p. 15; Edinburgh 1978A, no. 4.21, pp. 35–37, 44

In March 1751, just prior to returning south, Sandby travelled to the estate of Francis Scott, 2nd Duke of Buccleuch, at Drumlanrig. A letter from the Duke's factor James Fergusson to Sir John Clerk of Penicuik, who had recommended the young artist, survives, relating something of the painter's activities at Drumlanrig:

> My Lord
>
> I have been extremely oblidged to you for the pleasure of Mr Sandby's company here. He has made several drawings of the house and policy which I am persuaded you will be much pleased with. I was with him last week in Dumfries but the weather was so bad it was impossible for him to do anything material there – I dare say the Duke and Duchess will be much pleased with him. I hope we will have the happiness of your company here in April. My wife joins me in our respectfull compliments to my Lady Clerk and all the family
>
> I ever am with the greatest regard My Lord,
> Your most faithful and obdt humble Servant
>
> JA FERGUSON
>
> Drumlangrig
> March 22nd 1751
> (National Archives of Scotland, Edinburgh, GD18/4676)

Of Sandby's 'several drawings of the house and policy', his only recorded private commission of this period, only two are known to survive, this fine panorama of Nithsdale being one of them. Compositionally, the work anticipates the estate portraiture with which Sandby was to make a name for himself in the London exhibition rooms of the 1760s. Indeed, when engraved by Peter Mazell for publication in *The Virtuosi's Museum* some thirty years after Sandby's visit, it conformed readily to the views of country seats to be found elsewhere in the series. The elevated viewpoint and wide-angled prospect format allow Sandby to map the varied features of this productive landscape in the manner of an economic or military survey. Viewed at a distance and set amid an expanse of surrounding gardens, farmland, woods and floodplain, with the mountains of Galloway as backdrop, the house is established in its wider domain.

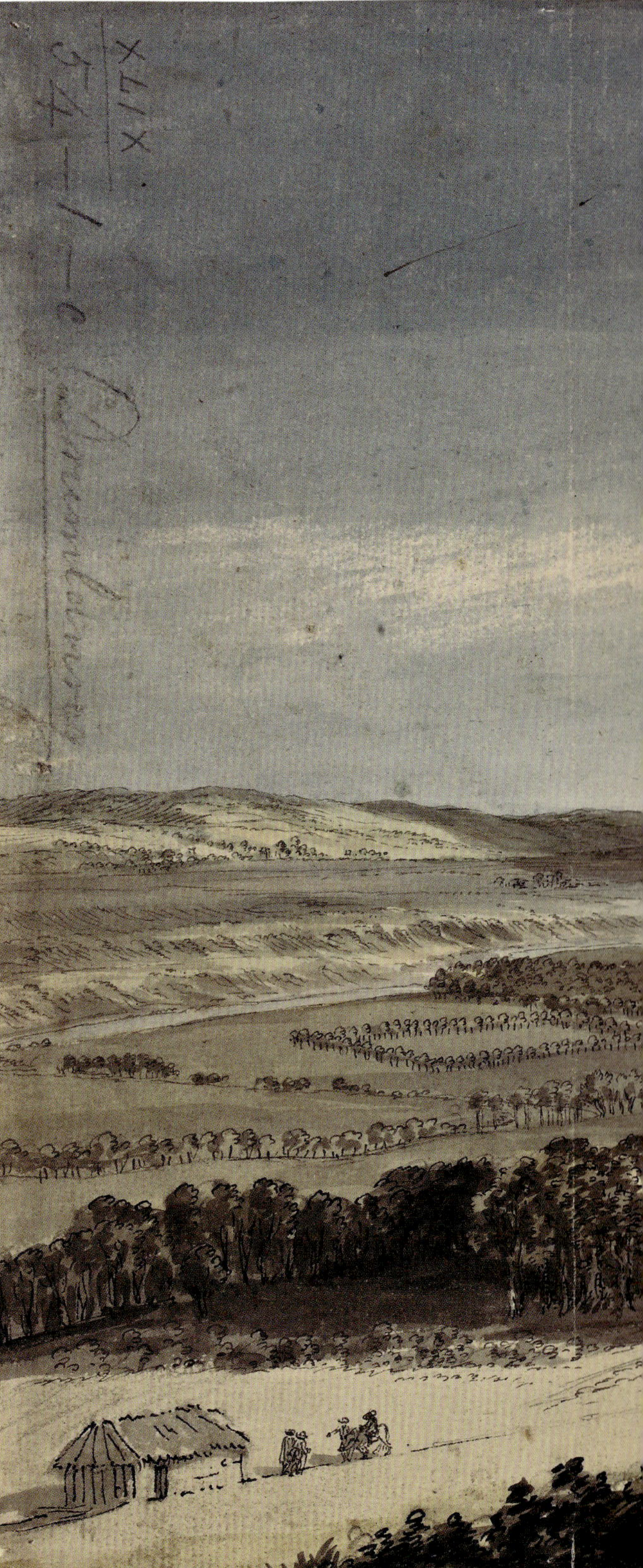

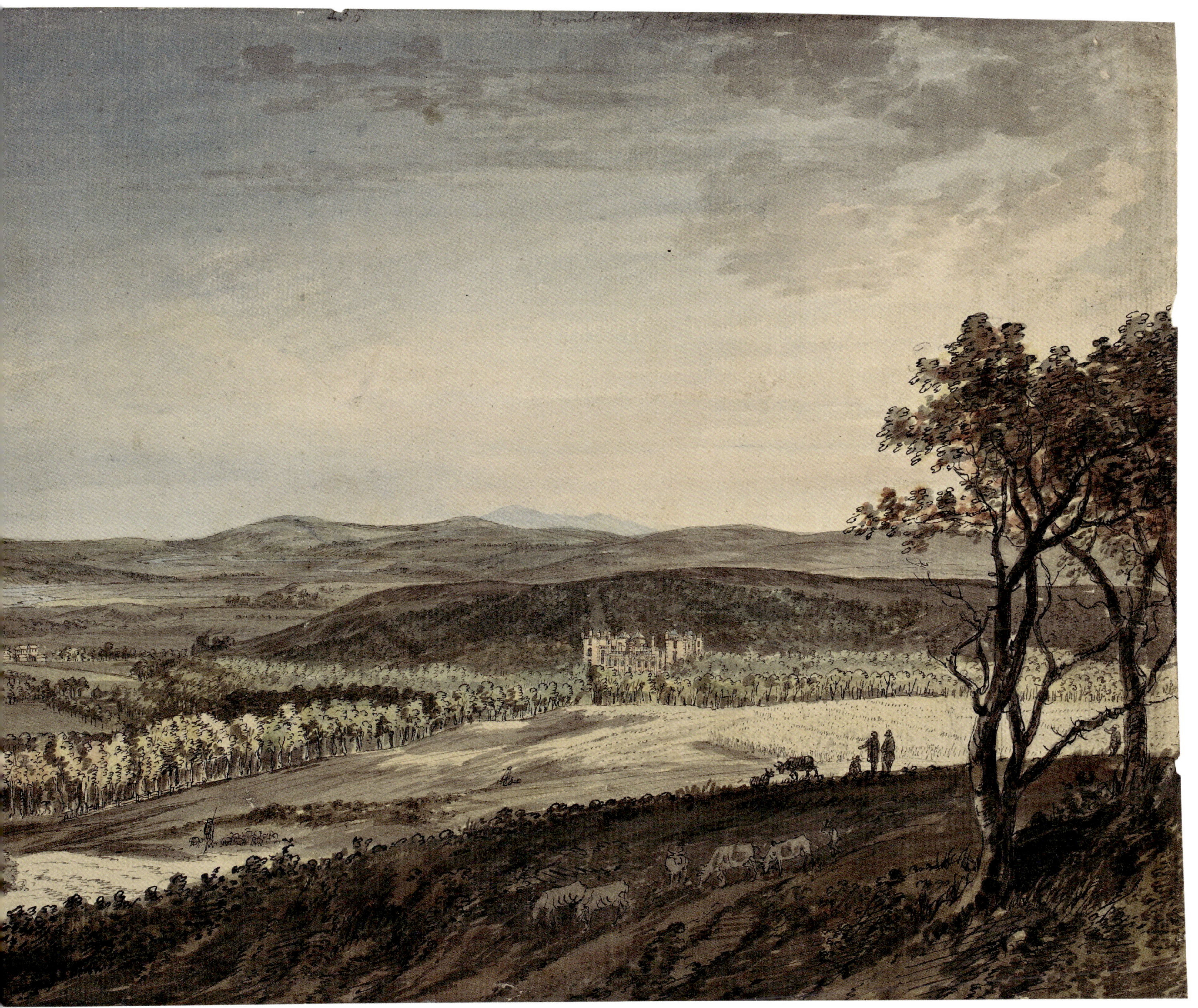

15

A Fulling Mill, Fife, *c.* 1750

Pen and watercolour over graphite, 165 × 305 mm
National Gallery of Scotland, Edinburgh, D.136

PROVENANCE
David Laing; transferred from the Royal Scottish Academy, 1910

SELECTED EXHIBITIONS
Edinburgh 1978A, no. 4.26; Hamilton 1981, no. 7

SELECTED REFERENCES
Edinburgh 1978A, no. 4.26, p. 44; Hamilton 1981, no. 7, p. 7

On reaching the village of South-Ferry on the banks of the Firth, during his 1769 tour of Scotland, Thomas Pennant found himself struck by the beauty of the prospect afforded by its 'fine and extensive bay', observing:

> a rich country, frequently diversified by towns, villages, castles, and gentlemen's seats. There is vast view up and down the Firth, from its extremity, not remote from *Stirling*, to its mouth near *May* isle; in all, about sixty miles. To particularize the objects of this rich view: from the middle of the passage are seen the coasts of *Lothian* and *Fife*; the isles of *Garvie* and *Inch-Colm*; the town of *Dumfermline*; S. and N. *Queen's Ferries*; and *Burrowstoness* smoaking at a distance from its numerous salt-pans and fire-engines. On the south side are *Hopetoun* house, *Dundass* castle, and many other gentlemen's seats; with *Blackness* castle. On the north side, *Rosythe* castle, *Dunibrissel*, and at a distance the castle and town of *Brunt-Island*; with the road of *Leith*, often filled with ships, and a magnificent distant view of the castle of *Edinburgh* on the south.
> (Pennant 1772, p. 77)

Clearly, this prospect was to be admired as much for its industry as for its antiquities. Signs of commerce, manufacturing and trade are much in evidence in Pennant's description, providing evidence of the benefits that to the author's mind flowed from the Union (see page 16).

Sandby knew this landscape well, having sketched many of the sites listed some years before. These drawings demonstrate a similar interest in the variety of scenery afforded by such a landscape, taking in its ancient fortresses, baronial manor houses and its industrial developments. Studies of local industry, such as this fine drawing of an open-air mill used in the cleansing and thickening of wool cloth, show the artist to be keenly attentive to mechanical technology and to attempts to make use of and improve the local geography. In Pennant's judgement, wool production was not much less to be regarded than agriculture. Its historical importance to the export trade made it an important pointer to economic well-being, and he praised its introduction on the Duke of Buccleuch's Dumfriesshire estate at Drumlanrig (Pennant 1774, p. 127). Its benefits are, perhaps, indicated in this drawing by Sandby's inclusion of a respectable rustic family group, whose productivity might be contrasted with the indolence of many of the characters peopling the artist's sketches of Edinburgh and Leith street life (cats 31–32).

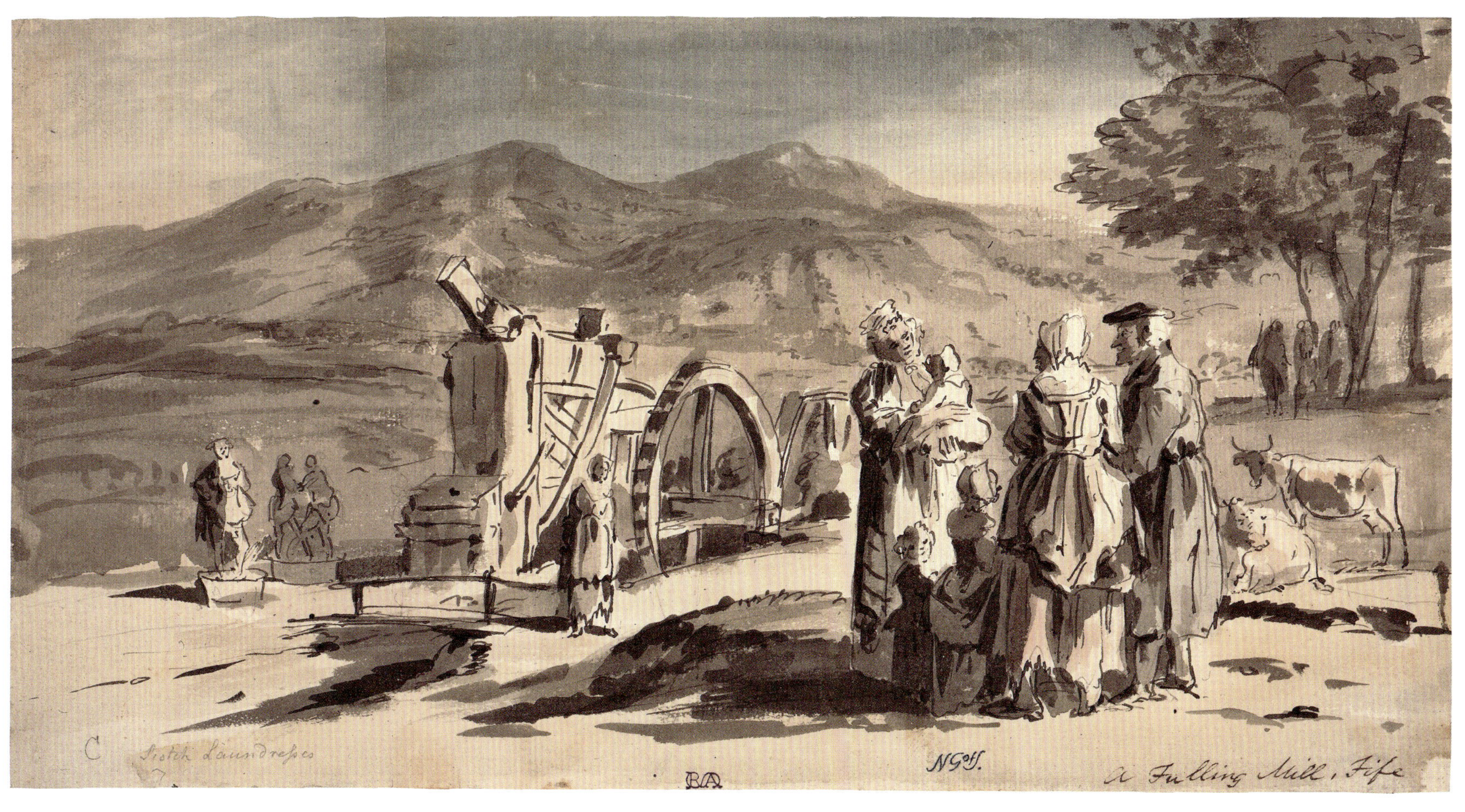
C
Scotch Laundresses
A Fulling Mill, Fife

16

Sketchbooks of drawings made in the Scottish Highlands, late 1740s

National Gallery of Scotland, Edinburgh, D.5339A and D.5339B

PROVENANCE
A. B. L. Munro Ferguson; entered National Gallery of Scotland, 1993

SELECTED REFERENCES
Herrmann 1965

As in the 'Great Map' itself, several hands can be discerned across the pages of these sketchbooks. They contain a wide variety of imagery, incorporating figure studies and caricatures, landscapes and plans of fortifications, all executed in a variety of media. Some sketches are relatively finished, others little more than hesitant pencil lines. Views of Fort William and Inverness, as well as several unidentified houses and estates, suggest that these were made in the field, during the surveys of the summer months. Several images are duplicated, perhaps implying that Sandby was instructing others in the party. But the assured handling apparent in some drawings indicates the artist's own hand. Depictions of soldiers resting, a local market scene or 'A Gillee wet feit or Errand Runner' recall the recording of local characters and custom in Sandby's numerous off-duty drawings of Edinburgh and Leith street life (cats 31–32). A portrait of a young man in military dress sketching, possibly William Roy or Sandby himself, anticipates similar studies of friends and staff at Windsor of a few years later (Oppé 1947, nos 322–54). An amusing caricatured group, depicting a meeting of the Board of Ordnance, also looks forward to the graphic satires Sandby was to publish on returning south (cats 21–28).

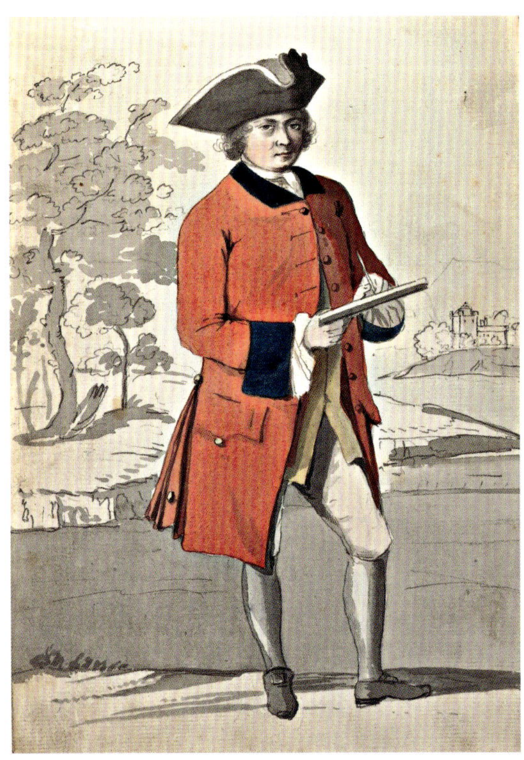

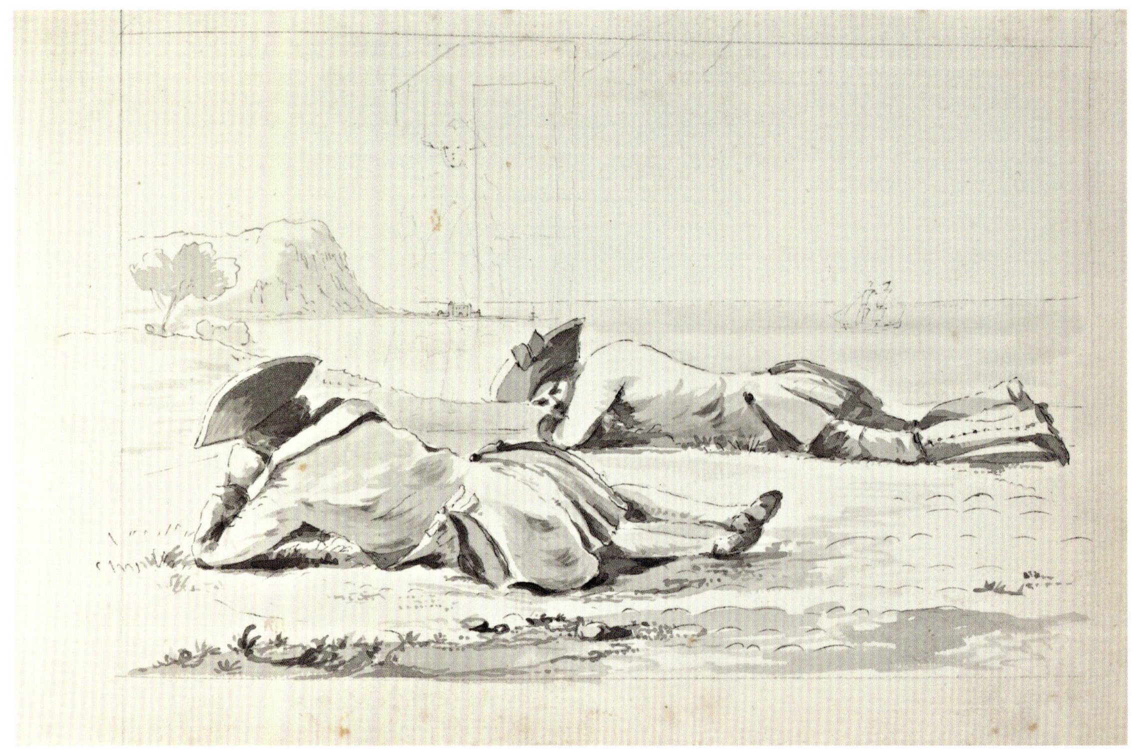

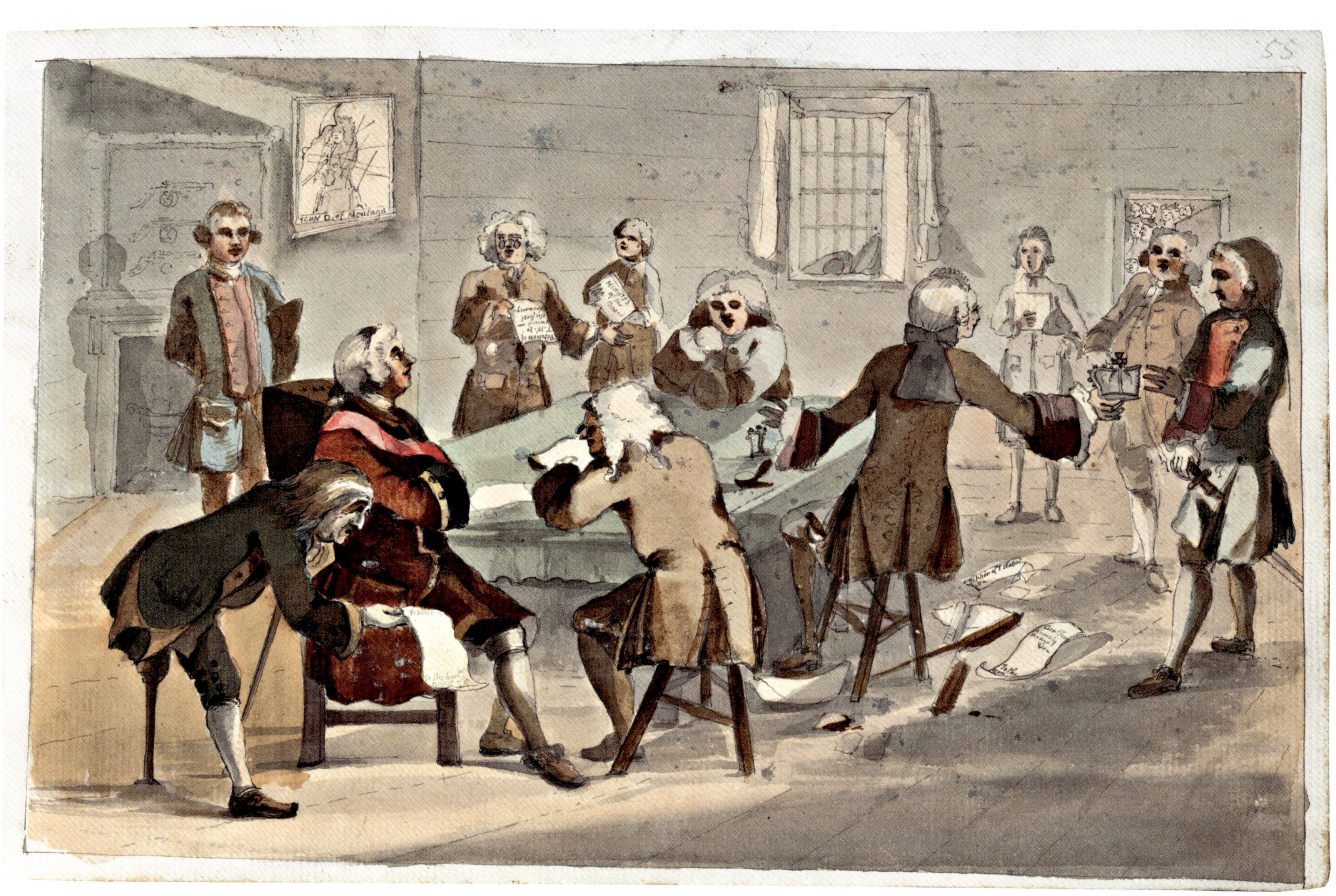
55
JOHN D. of Montagu
MINUTES of the Board

In June 1765 the London printsellers Ryland and Byer announced publication of a collection of 100 of Sandby's etchings printed on 54 half sheets (*Public Advertiser*, 19 June 1765). Largely comprised of plates etched during the artist's period working on the Military Survey of North Britain or shortly afterwards, *A Collection of Etchings* reveals much about Sandby's familiarity with landscape conventions, showing him essaying works in a range of manners, producing Italianate scenes in the Grand Style, after Gaspard Dughet, or in the tradition of the Venetian *capriccio* of Marco Ricci, as well as views imitative of Dutch artists of the previous century, such as Abraham Rademaker. Equally eclectic is the choice of subject-matter, which includes elegant rustic figure groups and crude caricatures, classical ruins and market scenes. A scene of a survey party at work in the highlands appears in some editions of the collection printed alongside views of flourishing local scenery, connecting the mapping of this landscape with its improvement. The stylistic diversity of Sandby's early etched work is apparent in the two rare, single-sheet impressions: although *Scottish Beggars Resting Near a Well*, based on a closely observed study of a decrepit draw-well at Broughton, near Edinburgh (British Museum, London), is consistent with the topographic studies discussed above, *Capriccio with Edinburgh Castle and Arthur's Seat* relocates these local architectural landmarks to a highly theatrical, imaginary landscape. This latter print is strongly reminiscent of Dughet's views of Tivoli, in which a dark tree to the left often frames a distant view of a waterside building placed on an eminence. That Sandby would move between traditions, or blur distinctions between the imagined and the observed, has been little noted by scholars, eager to place the artist firmly in histories of topographical landscape. Yet, as these plates illustrate, his interest in exploring a range of pictorial conventions and their narrative associations was an established feature of his art from the outset.

Reconstructing the history of the publication of Sandby's etched work presents a considerable challenge, as most etchings were issued privately and undated. Plates were also turned over to commercial publishers like James Sayer or John Boydell, who produced volumes of the artist's etchings in several formats. Published on demand, they often had an extended shelf life, with some prints still being issued well into the nineteenth century. No two volumes of the 1765 Ryland and Byer set are the same, differing in layout, pagination, paper and plates, an illustration of the complexity of the history of these Scottish views.

17

A Collection of Etchings

Published by Ryland and Byer, June 1765
Nottingham City Museums and Galleries

SELECTED REFERENCES
Yale 1985, no. 35, pp. 36–38; Robertson 1987, pp. 382–83

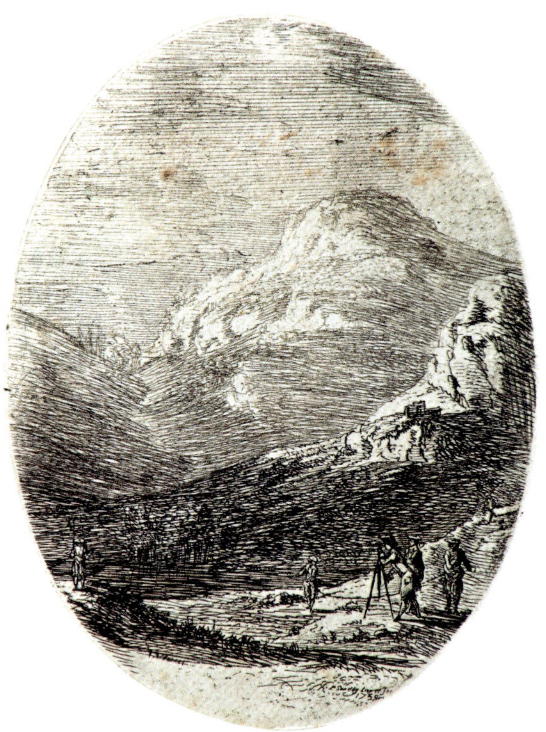

18

Scottish Beggars Resting Near a Well, c. 1750

Etching, 207 × 171 mm
Yale Center for British Art, New Haven,
Paul Mellon Fund, B1983.7.1

SELECTED REFERENCES
Yale 1985, no. 31, p. 36; Robertson 1987, p. 143

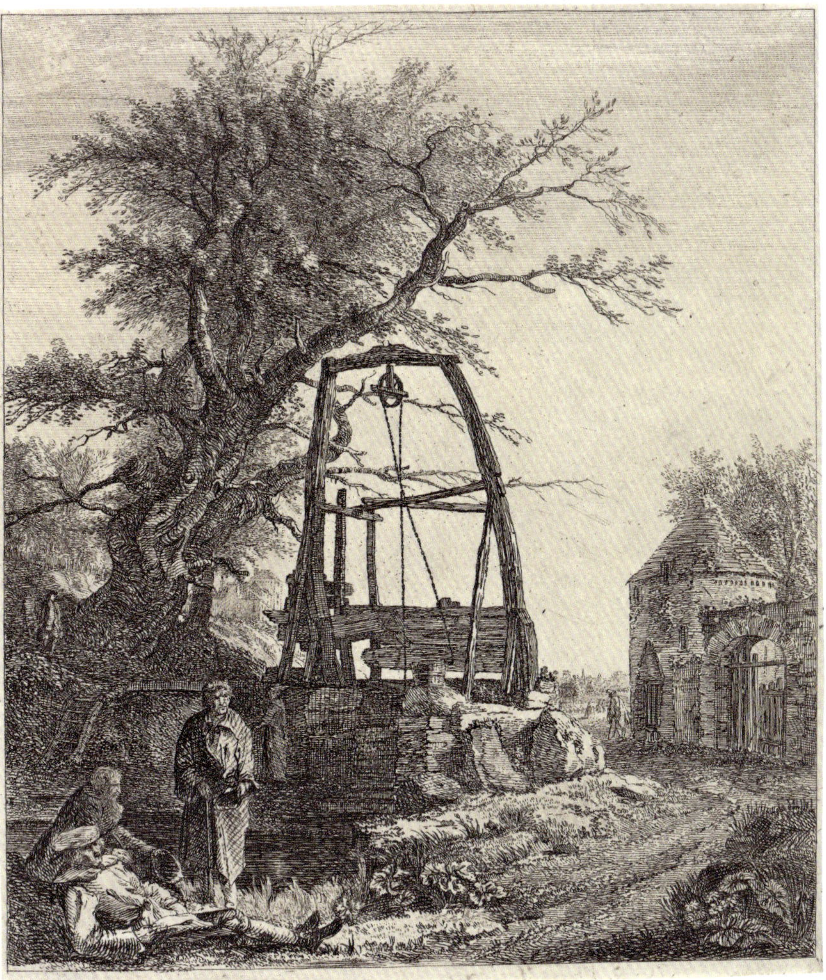

19

Capriccio with Edinburgh Castle and Arthur's Seat, before 1773

Etching, 220 × 175 mm
Yale Center for British Art, New Haven,
Paul Mellon Fund, B1983.7.2

SELECTED REFERENCES
Yale 1985, no. 34, p. 36; Robertson 1987, p. 143

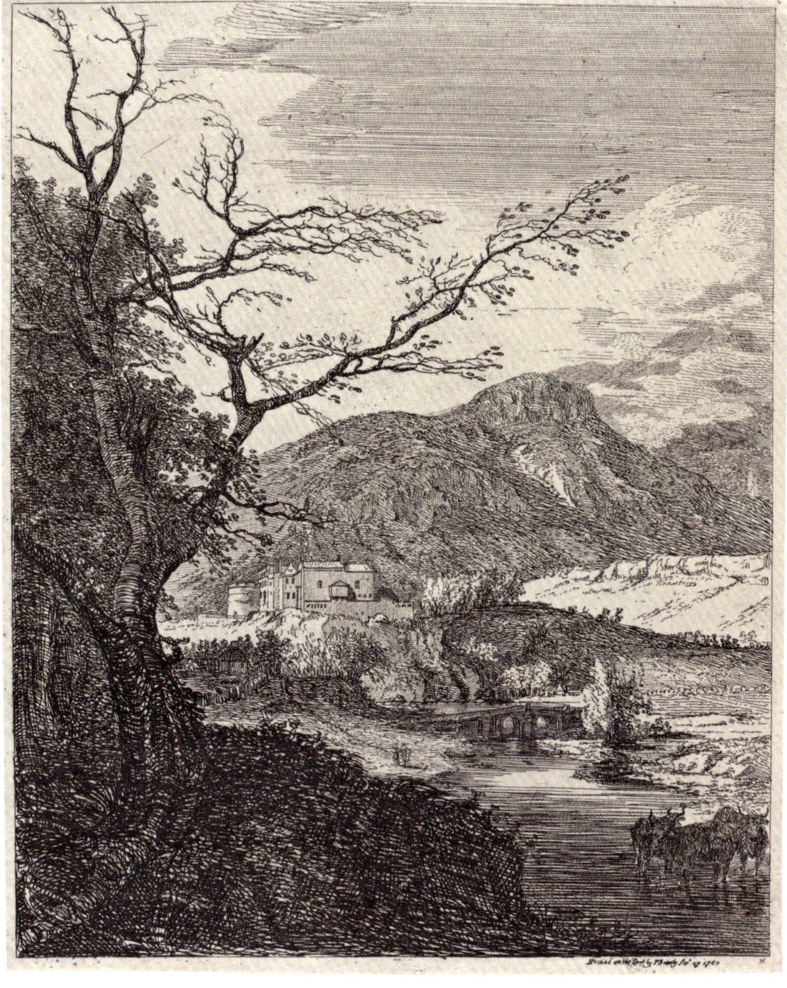

20

The Magic Lantern, 1753

Bodycolour and watercolour, with pen and ink over graphite, 372 × 538 mm
Department of Prints and Drawings, British Museum, London, 1862-10-11-890

PROVENANCE
Purchased from Lady Hawes, 1862

SELECTED EXHIBITIONS
Yale 1985, no. 44; Nottingham 1986, n.n.

SELECTED REFERENCES
Stephens and George 1870–1954, BM 3240; Yale 1985, no. 44, pp. 42–44; Robertson 1987, p. 179

On returning south in early 1751, Sandby stayed with his brother at Sandpit Gate Lodge, Windsor, and produced numerous studies of life on the royal estate (see Oppé 1947, nos 245–56). Aware of the need to maintain a presence in the capital, the brothers also shared lodgings at 36 Poultney Street. This placed them at the centre of the burgeoning metropolitan art world, only streets away from the artists' haunts around the St Martin's Lane Academy. There was little by way of consensus on artistic theory or organisation among the disparate parties consorting in and around St Martin's Lane and the brothers were active participants in these frequently fractious debates. John Gwynn, author of *An Essay on Design* (1749) and a long-time friend of the brothers, had promoted the cause of a formal, consciously professional organisation, arguing that the deficiencies of English artists arose from the want of not having 'been regulated by the same Culture' as the French (Gwynn 1749, p. 16). Long opposed to such imported, authoritarian models of instruction and corporation, William Hogarth propounded a model of artistic training quite out of step with Gwynn's proposals. Following the publication of his *Analysis of Beauty* in late 1753, a text which advocated an idiosyncratic aesthetic at odds with continental academic doctrines, Paul Sandby issued the first of what was to become a series of eight graphic satires directed against the older artist. One of these predicted 'a Public Academy Erecting in Spight of his endeavours to prevent it', making the Sandbys' factional affiliation explicit.

Hanging on the wall of the painter's studio depicted in the first engraving in the ensemble, *Burlesque sur le Burlesque* (cat. 21), is a framed picture depicting Hogarth with, according to the inscription below, 'his Brains taken & and his Soul serving for a Magic lanthorn'. *Paul before Felix*, Hogarth's attempt to correct what he perceived as Rembrandt's failings, 'is reflected from it on ye Wall'. A later print in the series, consciously executed in the manner of Rembrandt's etchings (cat. 24), isolated this element of the composition. Having turned away from the lessons of the Old Masters and transformed himself into a magic lantern, Hogarth projects his own vision of sublime history painting. Such is the artist's conceit that he shuts himself off from tradition, leaving himself literally 'in the dark'. A magic lantern, a form of 'optic Delusion' associated by Daniel Defoe with mountebanks and their tricks (Defoe 1754, p. 331), is a fitting image for an artist with a gift for self-publicity.

Although Hogarth himself does not feature in this drawing of a magic-lantern show, several allusions to the quarrels of the St Martin's Lane Academy relate it to these etched satires. A book carried under the arm of the black servant is entitled 'Dr Taylor on Sight' in reference to Joshua Kirby's forthcoming edition of a study of perspective long known to be illustrated with a frontispiece by Hogarth. Thomas Sandby had developed a new model of perspective, and one of the motivations for his younger brother's attack on the elder statesman of British art may have been Hogarth's role in the promotion of a rival system (see cat. 63). Bruce Robertson has seen a further reference to Hogarth's art in the image projected to this eccentric family group, identifying it as a parody of *Chairing the Member*, the final plate of the artist's *Election* series (Yale 1985, p. 44). Although this procession certainly shares some of that picture's carnival-like quality, Sandby's motley crowd of banner-waving grotesques appears to be led by a Quixotic knight-errant mounted on an emaciated farm horse. Such an allusion is entirely in keeping with the imagery of delusion and hubris observable elsewhere in this drawing and related prints.

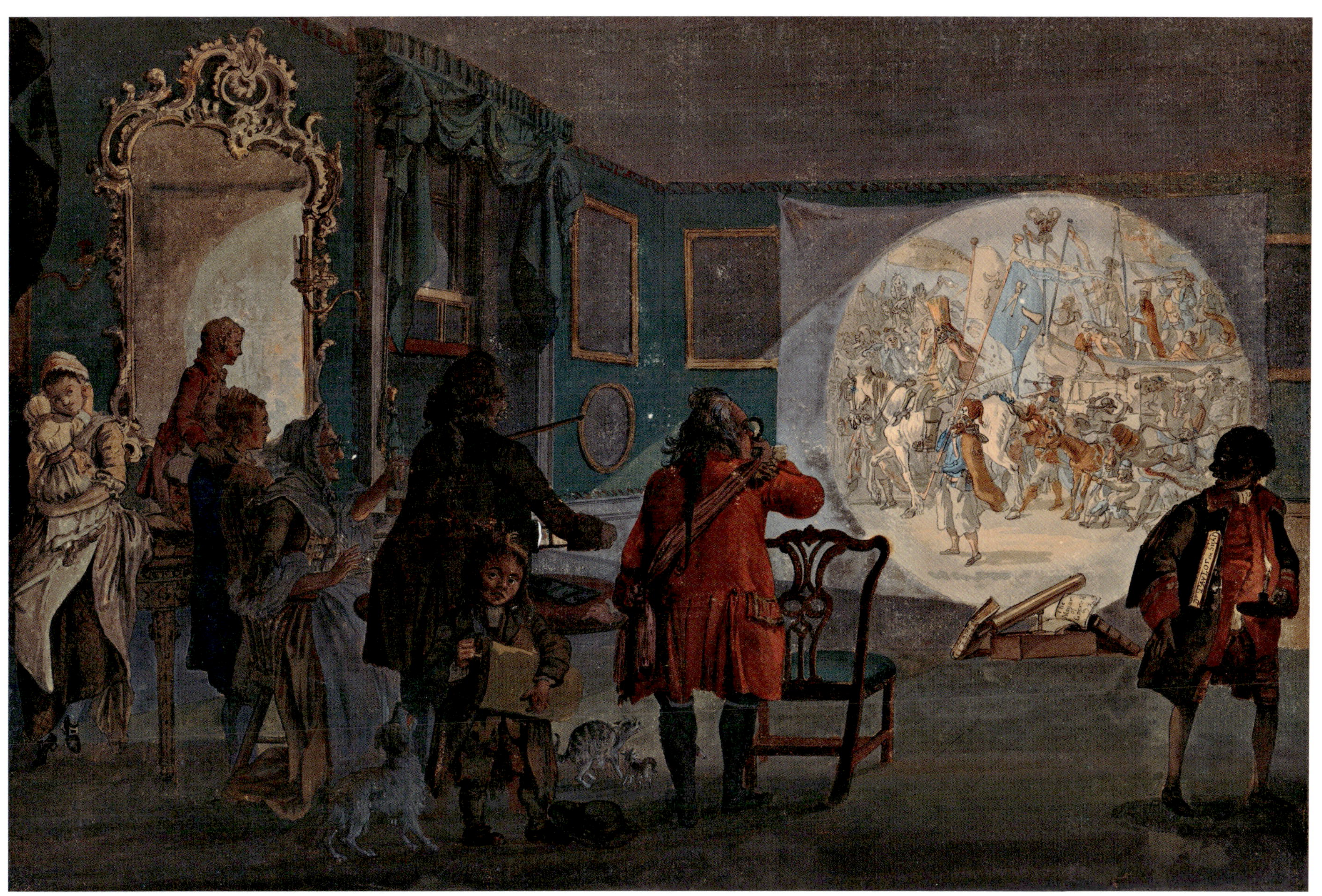

William Hogarth's *The Analysis of Beauty*, 'written with a view of fixing the fluctuating Ideas of Taste', was published in the first week of December 1753, following a sustained advertising campaign in the London dailies. Paul Sandby issued the first plate of what he was later to entitle *The Analysis of Deformity*, 'done to fluctuate the fix'd Ideas of Taste', within days of the appearance of Hogarth's treatise (the series was advertised under this title in the *Daily Advertiser* on 4 March 1754). This witty inversion of Hogarth's aims and ambitions is apparent throughout Sandby's own *Analysis*, which comprised these eight prints plus a title page. Geoff Quilley provides a detailed reading of the scabrous iconography of these prints elsewhere in this catalogue (pp. 38–47). This entry will therefore limit discussion to a brief summary of the circumstances surrounding their publication.

Announcements of the forthcoming publication of Hogarth's volume coincided with a series of acrimonious disputes within the St Martin's Lane Academy. These centred, as noted above, on plans to establish a more structured form of academy. On 23 October 1753 Francis Milner Newton, a minor portrait painter, circulated a letter concerning a 'scheme ... for erecting a public academy, for the improvement of the arts of painting, sculpture, and architecture' (Edwards 1808, p. xxii). He called for a meeting at the Turk's Head Tavern on Gerrard Street on 13 November to discuss the proposals, as well as to elect professors from an enclosed list of candidates. A letter in the *Public Advertiser*, dated 7 November, addressed to the 'Gentlemen of the Academy', enquired why 'several ingenious Artists are omitted ... and others of less Consequence inserted'. Hogarth, who had already attempted to repossess studio props lent to the St Martin's Lane Academy long before, was the probable author of this purposefully divisive missive. Opponents directed their enmity principally towards Hogarth's *Analysis*, orchestrating a sustained campaign aimed at discrediting the author, of which Sandby's prints were only part (see Hargraves 2005, pp. 13–15). A further, more personal source of Sandby's ire was, perhaps, as suggested above, Hogarth's promotion of Joshua Kirby's perspectival system, ahead of his brother's own development. His parody of Hogarth's *The March of the Guards to Finchley* (Foundling Museum, London) also suggests that the attack was, in part at least, a defence of the Sandby brothers' chief patron. Hogarth had dedicated the engraving of his famous subject picture, a chaotic scene of militia troops preparing to meet an advancing Jacobite army, to Frederick II, King of Prussia. This was widely understood as an attack on William Augustus, Duke of Cumberland, whose controversial Militia Bill, intended to introduce Prussian standards of discipline, order and precision into the army, was then being debated by the Commons.

In later life, Sandby attempted to distance himself from these plates, dismissing them as youthful folly. In a memoir of the artist published in the 1790s, almost certainly composed in consultation with Sandby, it is remarked that: 'if he had known Mr Hogarth's merit *then*, as well as he does *now*, he would on no account have drawn a line which might tend to his dispraise' (European Magazine 1796, p. 76). By this stage, Sandby was one of the few survivors of that pioneering generation of native-born artists who had come to prominence in the years around the mid-century. His concern to make amends for his early attacks on Hogarth perhaps indicates Sandby's awareness of his place in debates current in the 1790s over the history and nature of a British school of art.

21

Burlesque sur le Burlesque, first state, published 1 December 1753

Etching, 360 × 260 mm
Department of Prints and Drawings, British Museum, London, BM 3240

SELECTED REFERENCES

Stephens and George 1870–1954, BM 3240; Paulson 1993, vol. 3, pp. 138–41; London 1997, no. 103a, pp. 174–75

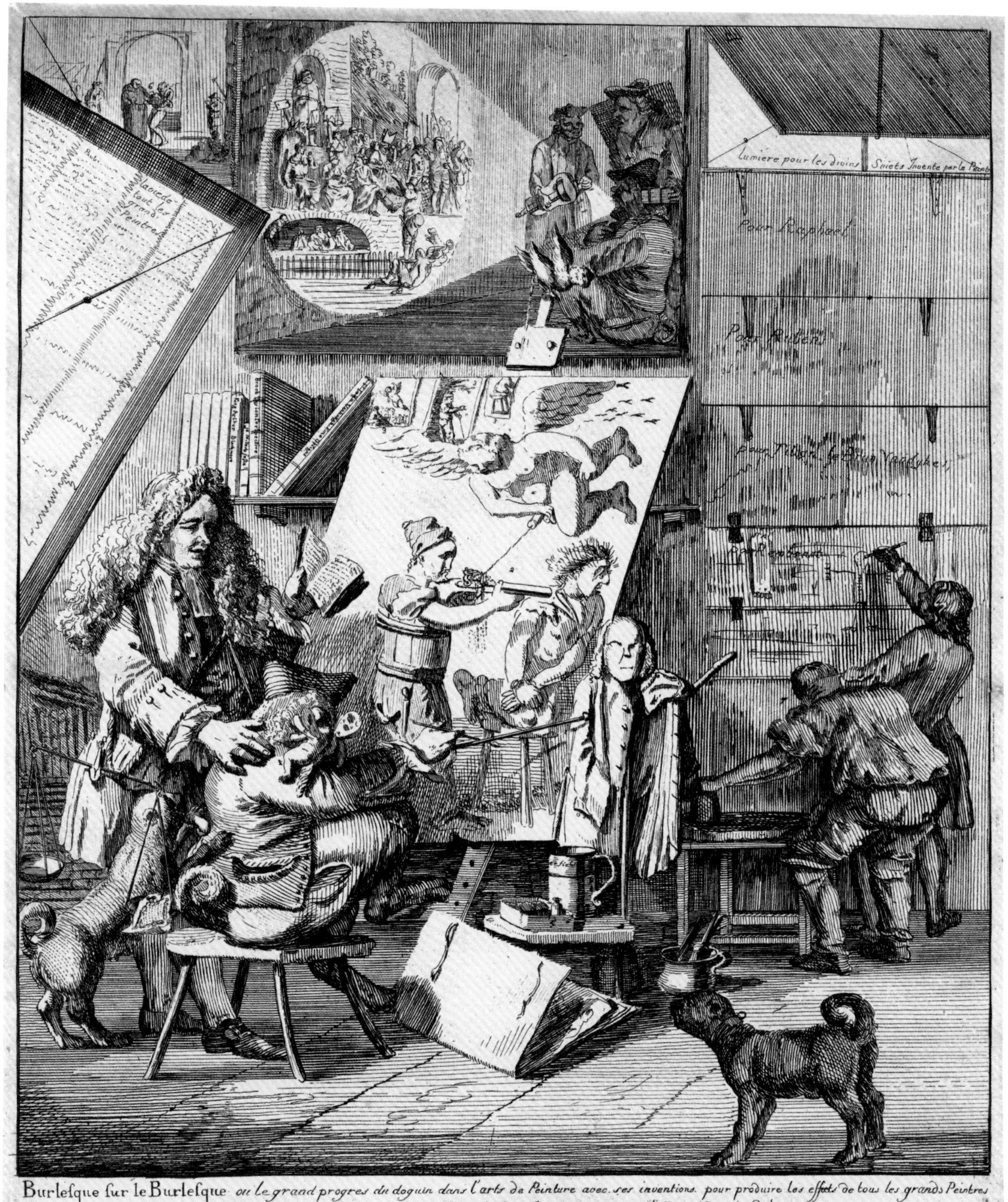

Burlesque sur le Burlesque ou le grand progres du doguin dans l'arts de Peinture avec ses inventions pour produire les effets de tous les grands Peintres depuis Raphael. et sa production pour montrer combien il ont Inveintez et excellez dans la composition dans l'effect et dans le Coloris

1. un Insecte inspirant la vanité au Peintre 2 Isaac et Jacob tiré d'un manuscrit Hollandois, 3. Vielles estempes pour server de Modelle au Doguin 4 La tete du doguin servant de lanterne Magique ainsy quell a apparue dans un reve fait par le Picque auteur de cette Estempe 5 un Manequin 6 un aloyeau rotty 7 Eleves du doguin

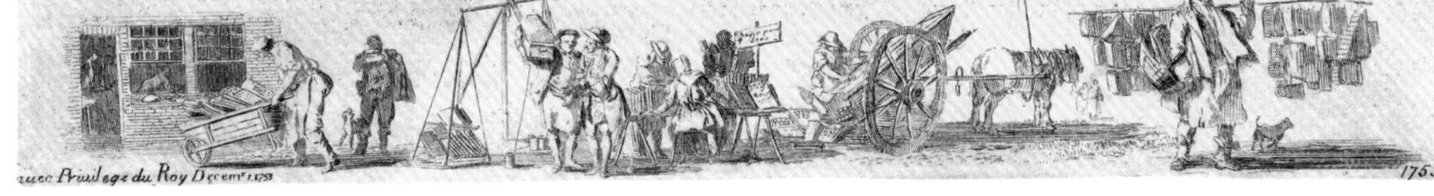

avec Privilege du Roy Decemr. 1.1753

1753

22

Puggs GRACES Etched from his ORIGINAL Daubing, 1753

Etching, 230 × 232 mm
Department of Prints and Drawings, British Museum, London, BM 3242

SELECTED REFERENCES
Stephens and George 1870–1954, BM 3242; Paulson 1993, vol. 3, pp. 137–38; London 1997, no. 104, p. 176

23

The Analyst Besh–n : in his own Taste P^t. 1^s., 1753

Etching, 263 × 185 mm
Department of Prints and Drawings, British Museum, London, BM 3243

SELECTED REFERENCES
Stephens and George 1870–1954, BM 3243; Paulson 1993, vol. 3, pp. 137–39; London 1997, no. 105, p. 176; Hargraves 2005, p. 13

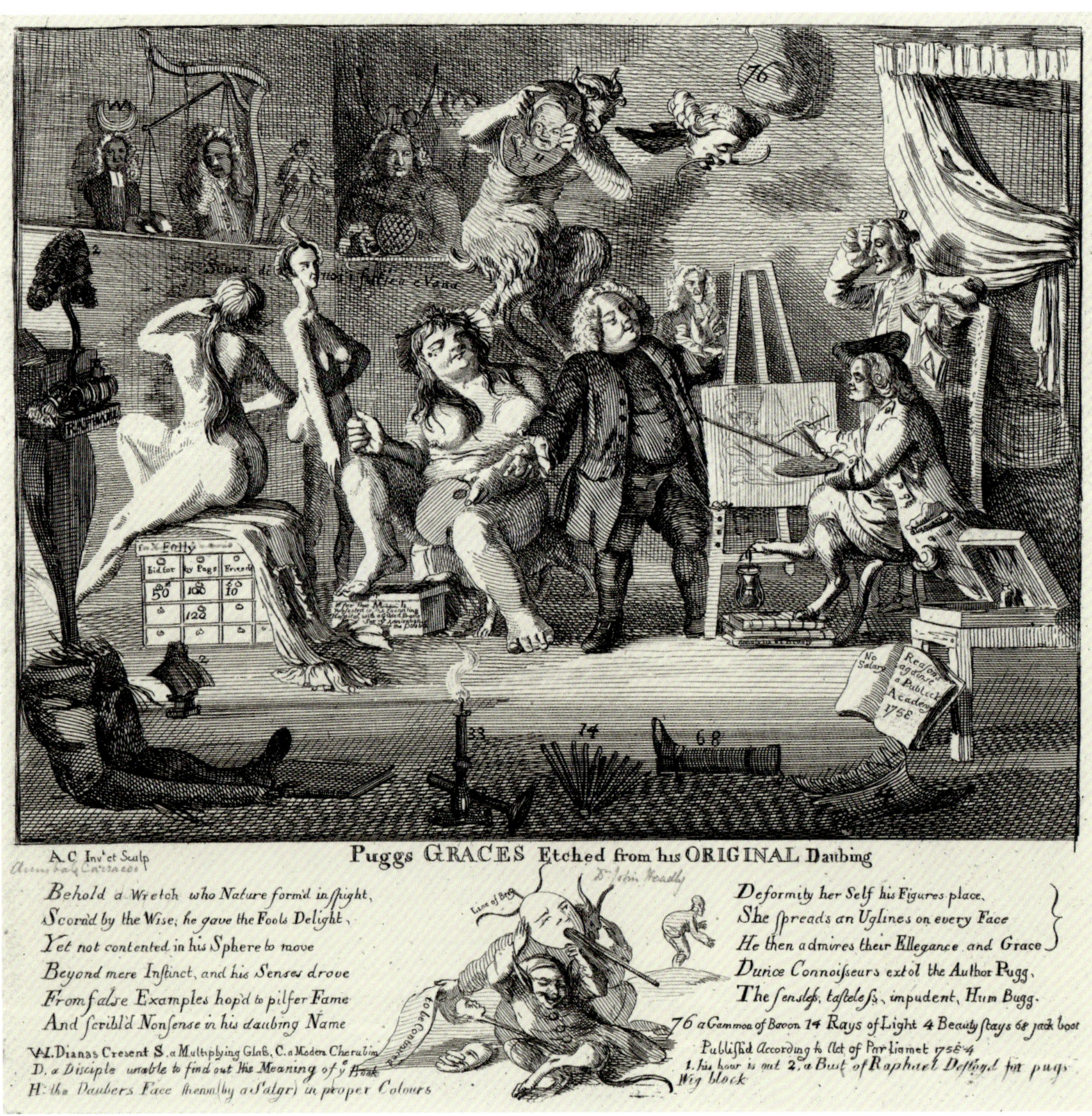

The Analyst Besh—n: in his own Taste Pt. 1st

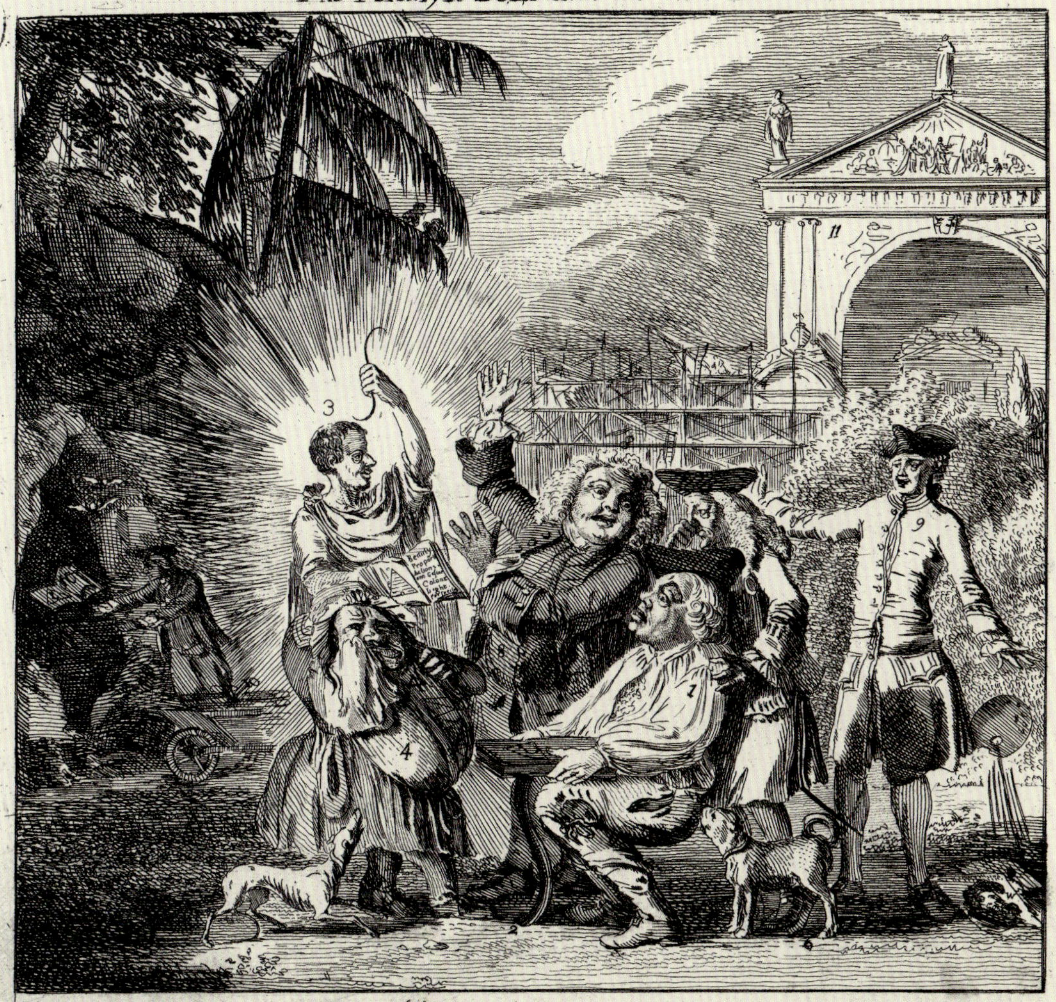

1. an Author Sinking under the weight of his Saturnine Analysis 2 a Strong support bent in the Line of Beauty by the Mighty Load upon it. 3 Lomazzos Ghost detecting the Fraud, bearing the Line of Beauty in one Hand. in the other Hand, his Treatise on Painting. 4 Deformity Weeping at the Condition of her Darling Son. 5 a Friend of the Author endeavouring to prevent his sinking to his Natural Lowness. 6 his Faithful Pugg finding his Master by the Scent. 7 a Greyhound bemoaning his Friends Condition. 8 The Authors Friend and Corrector Astonish'd at the sight of the Ghost and smell of the Author.

9 a Disciple droping the Palate and Brushes thro' Concern for his Masters forlorn state. / 10. Volum's of his Analysis Thrown into the Caves of Dulness and Oblivion. 11 a Public Academy Erecting. in spight of his endeavours to prevent it.

Lomazzo's speach. *Thou Ignorant Contemptable wretch how hast Thou mangled & perverted the Sense of my Book, in thy Nonsensical Analysis.*

From Lomazzos Treatise, speaking of the Line of Beauty, it shoud resemble the form of the Letter S placed right, or else turnd the wrong way, as ∾; because then it hath his beauty. Neither ought he only to observe this form in the whole body, but even in every part: so that in the Leg when a Muscle is rais'd outwards on one side, that which answereth directly on the contrary side, must be drawn in and hid (as may be seen in the Life) — this shews the disingenuty of the Man, in his Quotation from Lomazzo, endeavouring to Insinuate every Painter is Ignorant of this but himself tho' every Person which Learns to Draw, are first tought it, and tho' he Vainly endears to fix what is Beauty and Gra[ce] he Never gave an Instance of it in his own works. — The following is a Quotation From the Modern Analysis. in the Preface.

Rubens does not seem to be acquainted with what we call the precise Lin[e]

Raphael from a streight and stiff manner on a sudden changed his taste at sight of M Angelo's works, & so fond was he of the serpentine Line that he carried it into a Rediculous excess &c.

Correggio's Figur's might be mended by a common sign Painter

Whilst A. Durer never so much as diviated into Grace.

Vandykes picture are void of all Grace & Merit the epithet Simplicity

A picture Copier require no more knowledge than a weaver —

many more Instances of his Vanity & Ignorance might be exposed but as the subject is endless as well as too Low to meddle Further with I shall give him up to the stings of his own Consci[ence]

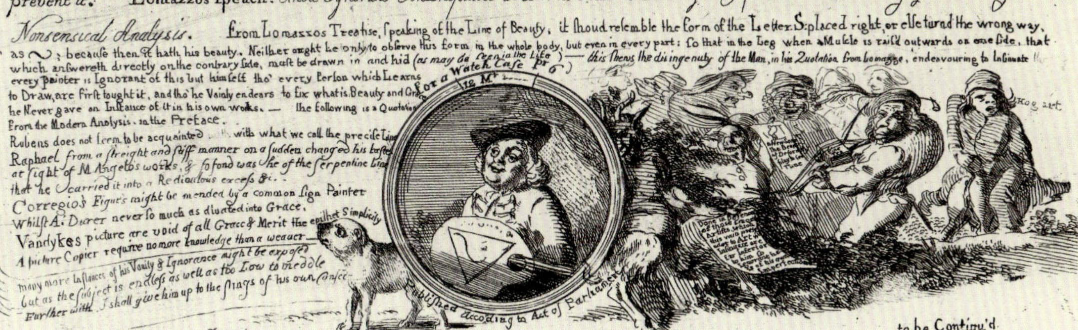

W: Vile Imitations of Rembrant

to be Continu'd

24

The Magic Lantern, 1753

Etching, 166 × 226 mm
Department of Prints and Drawings, British Museum, London, BM 3247

SELECTED REFERENCES
Stephens and George 1870–1954, BM 3247; London 1997, no. 107, p. 178

25

The Vile Ephesian, 1753

Etching, 230 × 191 mm
Department of Prints and Drawings, British Museum, London, BM 3245

SELECTED REFERENCES
Stephens and George 1870–1954, BM 3245; Paulson 1993, vol. 3, p. 137; London 1997, no. 108, p. 179

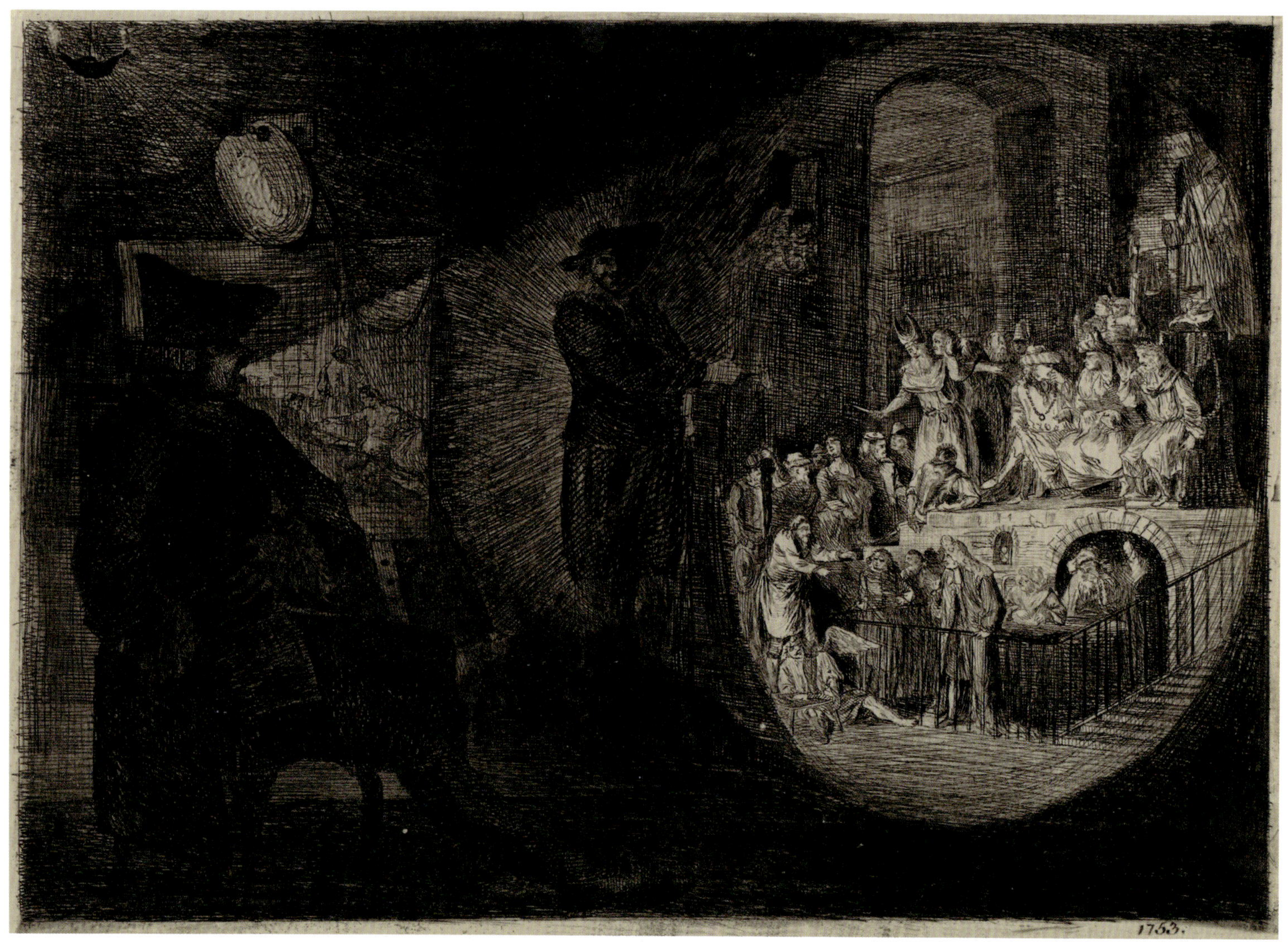

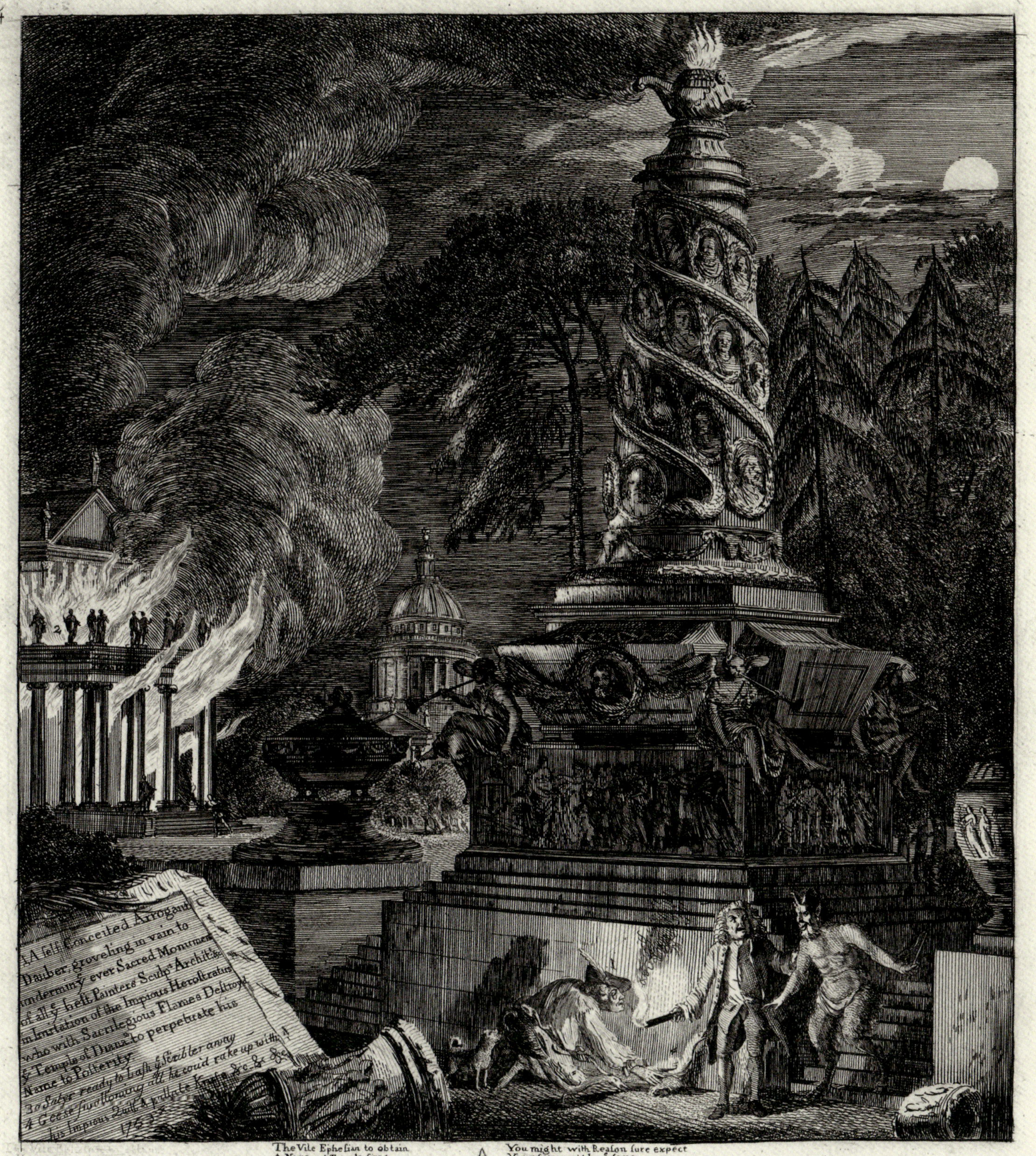

The Vile Ephesian to obtain
A Name — A Temple fires,
Observe friend H—g—th 'twas in Vain
He had not his desires —

You might with Reason sure expect
Your fate would be ye same
Men first thy Labours will neglect
Next quite forget thy Name —

26

The Painters March from Finchly, 1754

Etching, 175 × 172 mm
Department of Prints and Drawings, British Museum, London, BM 3248

SELECTED REFERENCES
Stephens and George 1870–1954, BM 3248

27

A Mountebank Painter, 1754

Etching, 230 × 191 mm
Department of Prints and Drawings, British Museum, London, BM 3249

SELECTED REFERENCES
Stephens and George 1870–1954, BM 3249; Paulson 1993, vol. 3, p. 138; London 1997, no. 109, p. 180

28

The Author run Mad, 1754

Etching, 260 × 180 mm
Department of Prints and Drawings, British Museum, London, BM 3244

SELECTED REFERENCES
Stephens and George 1870–1954, BM 3244; Paulson 1993, vol. 3, p. 135; London 1997, no. 106, p. 178

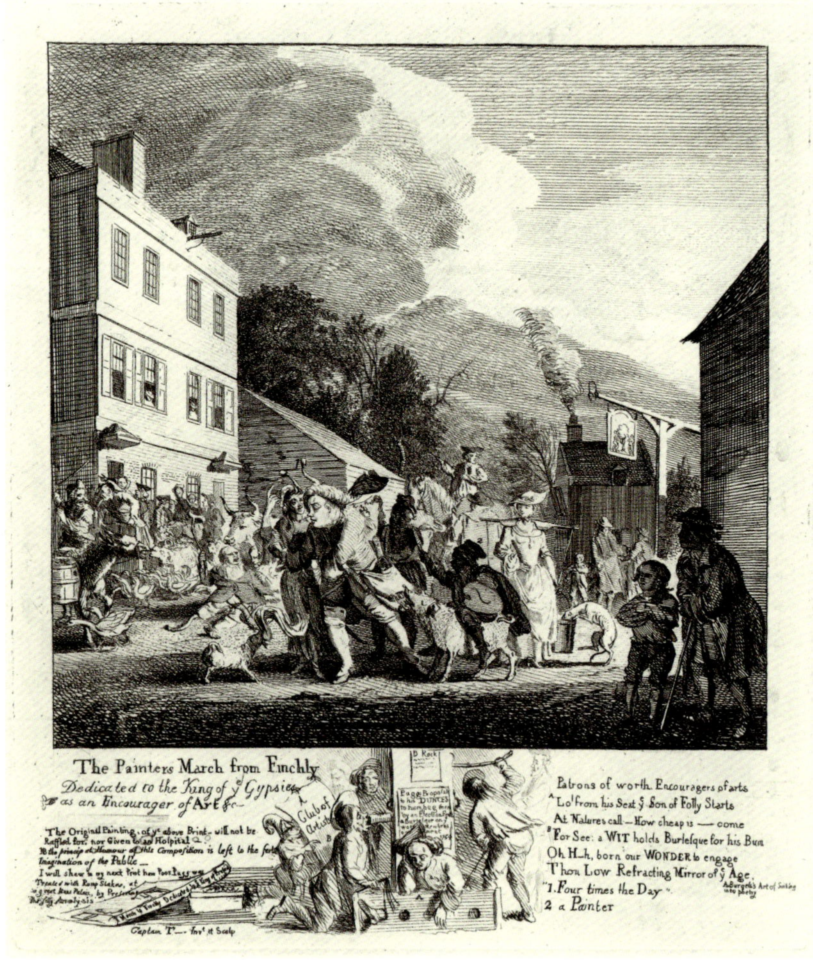

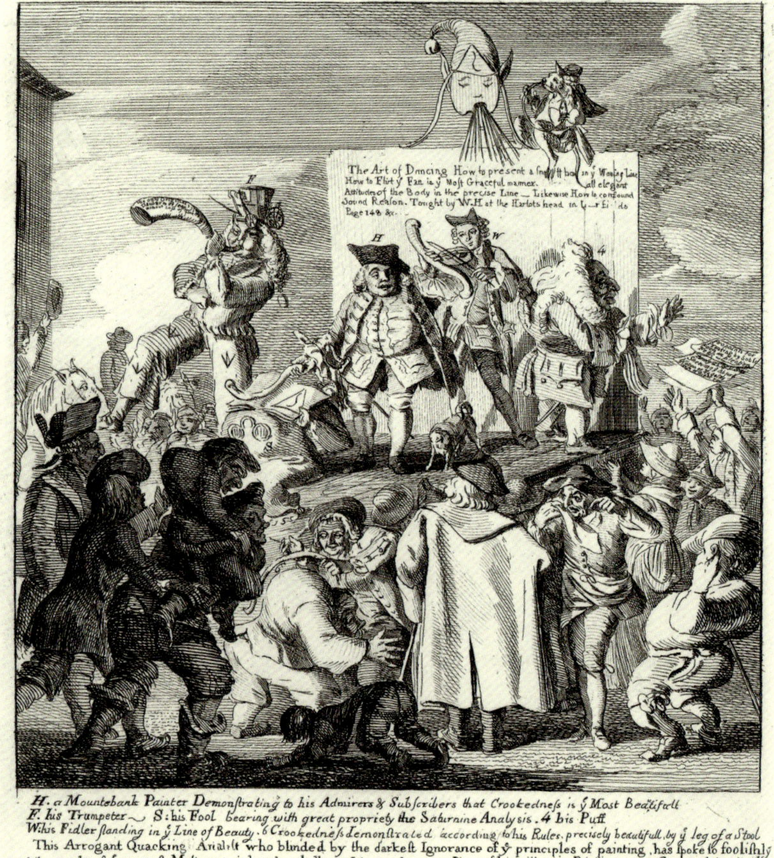

The Author run Mad

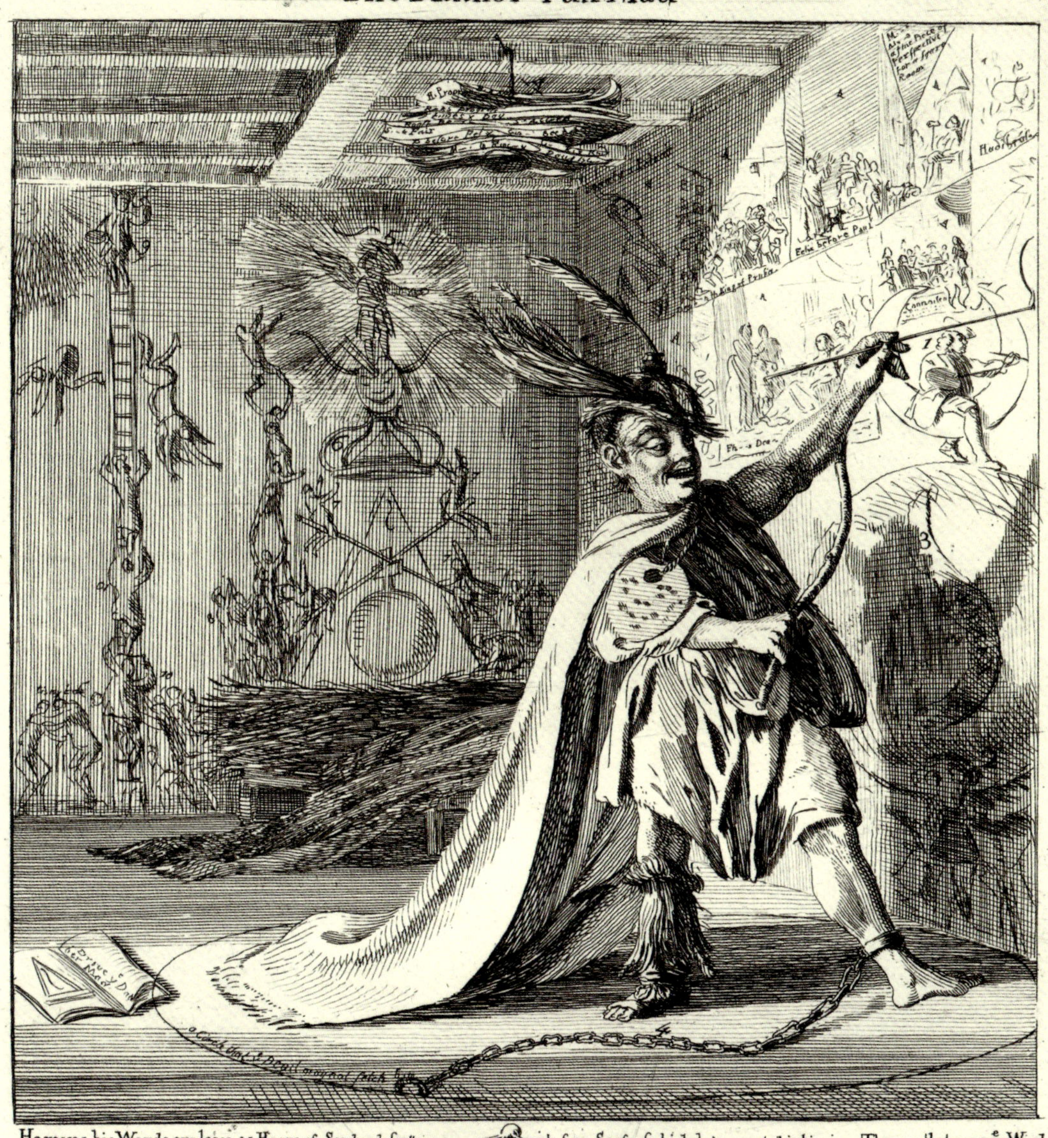

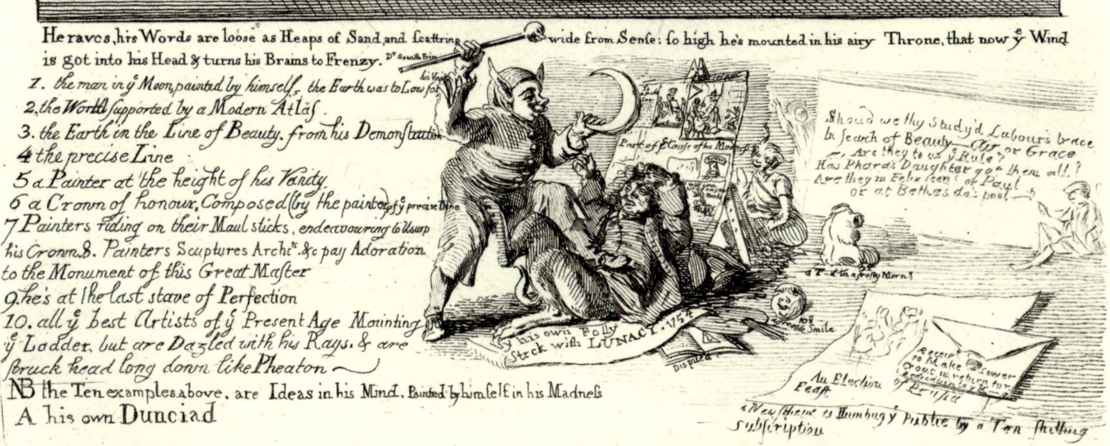

In early September 1762 Hogarth published *The Times, Plate 1*, a political satire in defence of the young George III's chief adviser and former tutor, John Stuart, 3rd Earl of Bute (fig. 18). King and courtier were unpopular among those with commercial interests in the City for their failure to capitalise on recent military victories, their politics of appeasement having resulted in the resignation of the chief architect of the country's new-found empire, William Pitt. Hogarth's print depicts Bute as a fireman, extinguishing the conflagration engulfing the globe, assisted by a united force of sailors, soldiers and plaid-wearing highlanders. His actions are hampered by Pitt, disguised as Henry VIII and supported by a mob of butchers and clerics, whose bellows fan the flames. This was a subject that, according to the artist's *Autobiographical Notes*, 'tended to Peace and Unanimity' (Burke 1955, p. 221). His decision to defend plans to bring an end to the Seven Years War, however, provoked only derision and anger among such erstwhile friends as John Wilkes and old enemies as Paul Sandby.

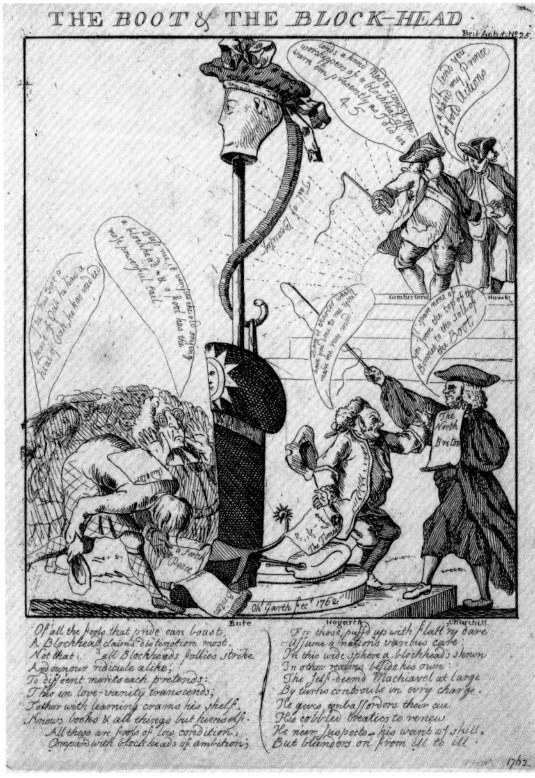

FIG. 36
Paul Sandby, *The Boot and the Blockhead*, published by Edward Sumpter, 1762. Etching, 890 × 700 mm. British Museum, London, BM 3977

Sandby issued *The Butifyer. A Touch upon The Times, Plate 1* before the end of the month. *The Boot and the Blockhead* and the remarkable *Fire of Faction* appeared before the end of the year (figs 36, 37). Plans for a fourth print, the complex, untitled satire shown here, were shelved, presumably because the theme had lost its topicality. Wilkes and his supporters sponsored a number of prints attacking Bute, Sandby's satires trading with their emblematic imagery, reducing the monarch's favourite minister to a jackboot (see Donald 1996, pp. 50–56). However, they also refer back to the engraver's own earlier attacks on Hogarth, including references to the 'Line of Beauty'. Sandby's final, unpublished satire on events, in which Bute is shown attempting to force a peace treaty down the throat of a bull (that is, John Bull), also includes at its centre a portrait of William Augustus, Duke of Cumberland, brandishing a whip. He had also appeared, coming to the defence of constitutional liberties, in *The Boot and the Blockhead.*

It is difficult to identify Sandby's precise motivation for renewing his attack on Hogarth. It may have been prompted by Hogarth's ongoing dispute with the Society of Artists, following the public humiliation he had suffered on exhibiting there the previous year (see Hargraves 2005, pp. 34–41). Alternatively, Hogarth's appointment to the post of Serjeant-Painter to His Majesty in 1758 may have spurred Sandby to etch this second set of satires. He perhaps judged it inappropriate for a holder of that court office to involve himself in factional politics. Artists' relationships with politically influential and powerful patrons are certainly among the issues at stake in this group of prints. Sandby's attack on Hogarth's supposed patron, Bute, appears not to have been a bar to future employment, however; he was commissioned to execute views of Bute's Luton estate within a year of these satires (see cats 89–91).

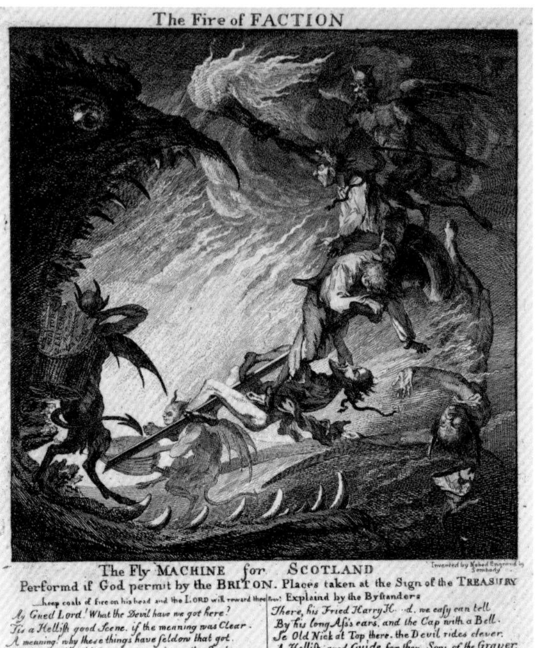

FIG. 37
Paul Sandby, *The Fire of Faction*, 1762. Etching, 265 × 203 mm. British Museum, London, 1904,0819.713

29

The BUTIFYER. A Touch upon The Times Plate 1, September 1762

Etching, 251 × 202 mm
Department of Prints and Drawings, British Museum, London, BM 3971

SELECTED REFERENCES

Stephens and George 1870–1954, BM 3971; Paulson 1993, vol. 3, p. 382; London 1997, no. 114, p. 186

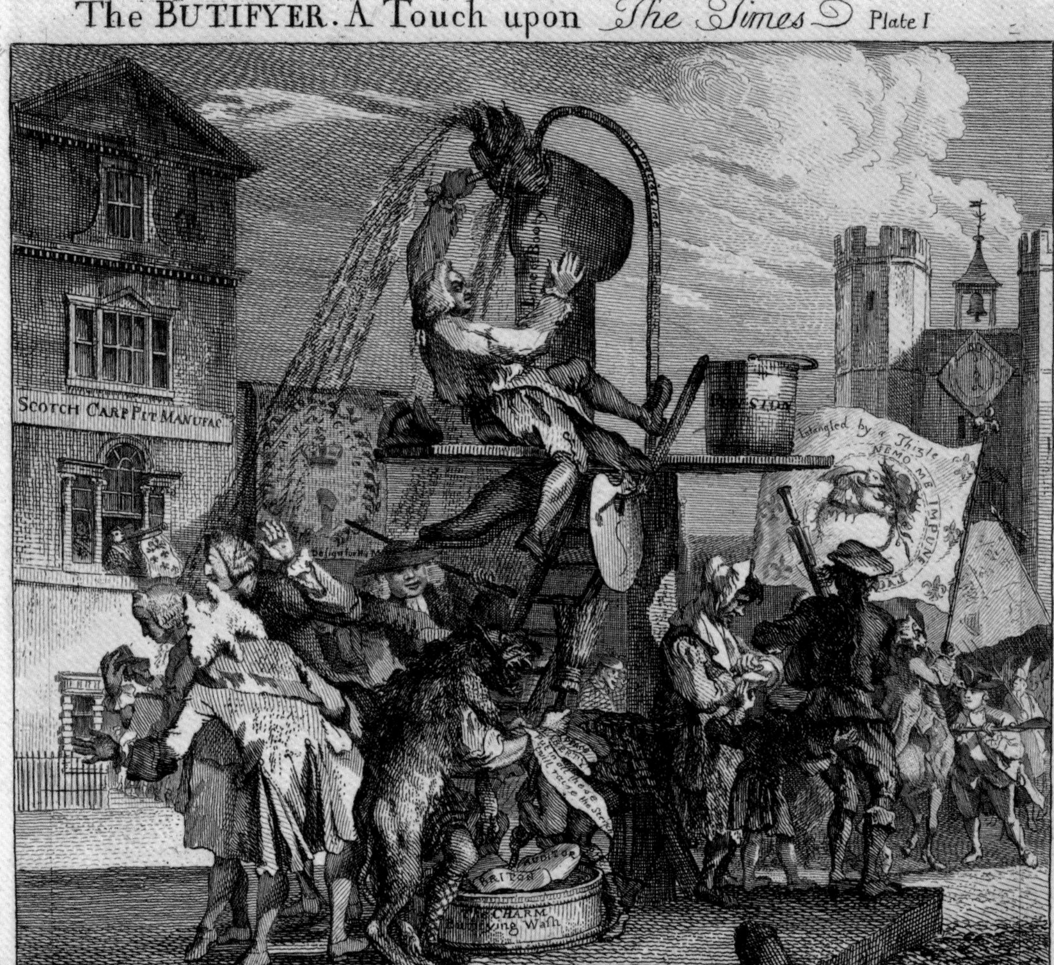

30

Untitled satire on Bute and Hogarth, late 1762

Etching, 257 × 364 mm
Department of Prints and Drawings, British Museum, London, BM 3910

SELECTED REFERENCES

Stephens and George 1870–1954, BM 3240; Paulson 1993, vol. 3, pp. 134–40; London 1997, no. 103a, pp. 174–75

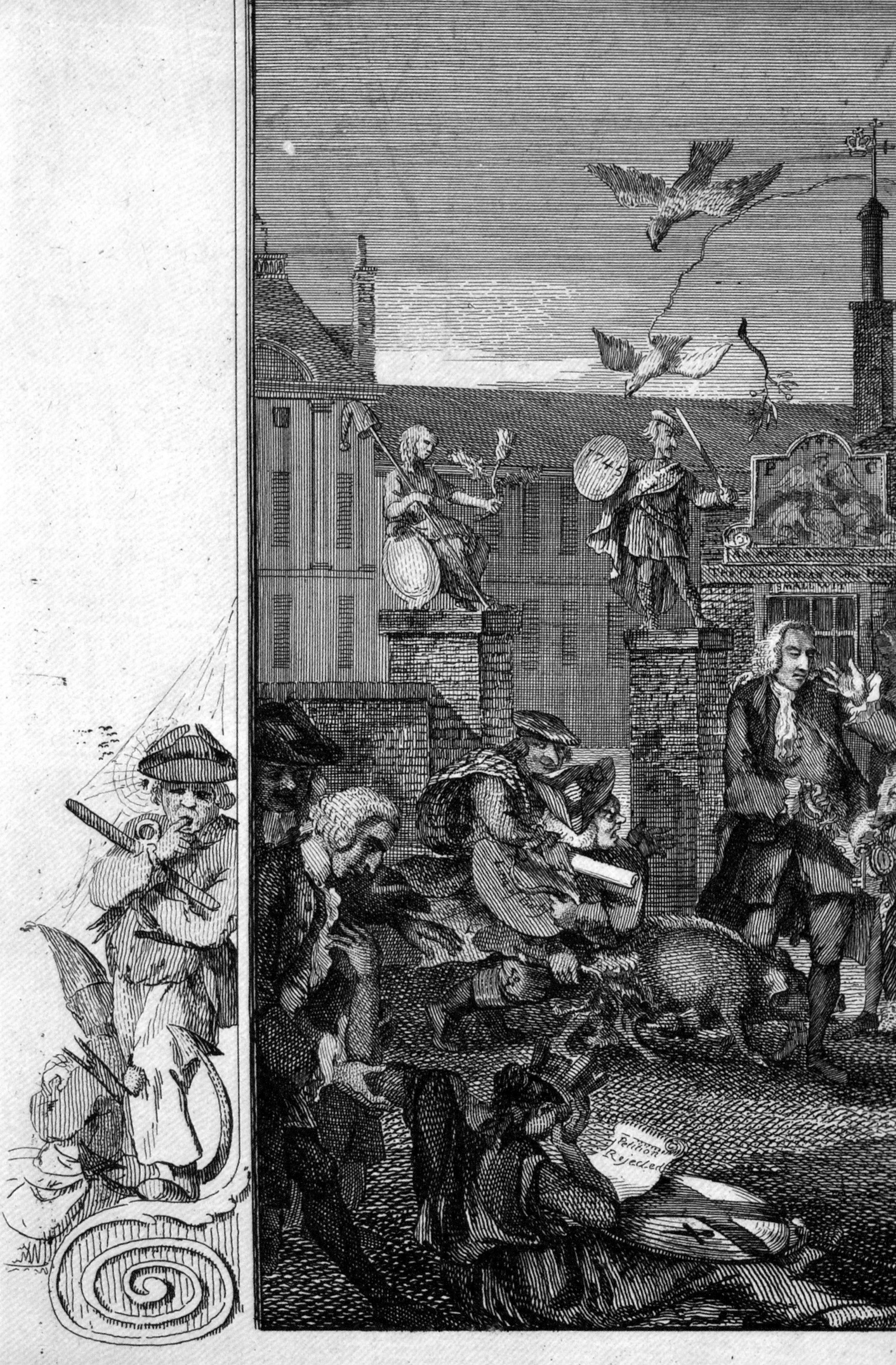

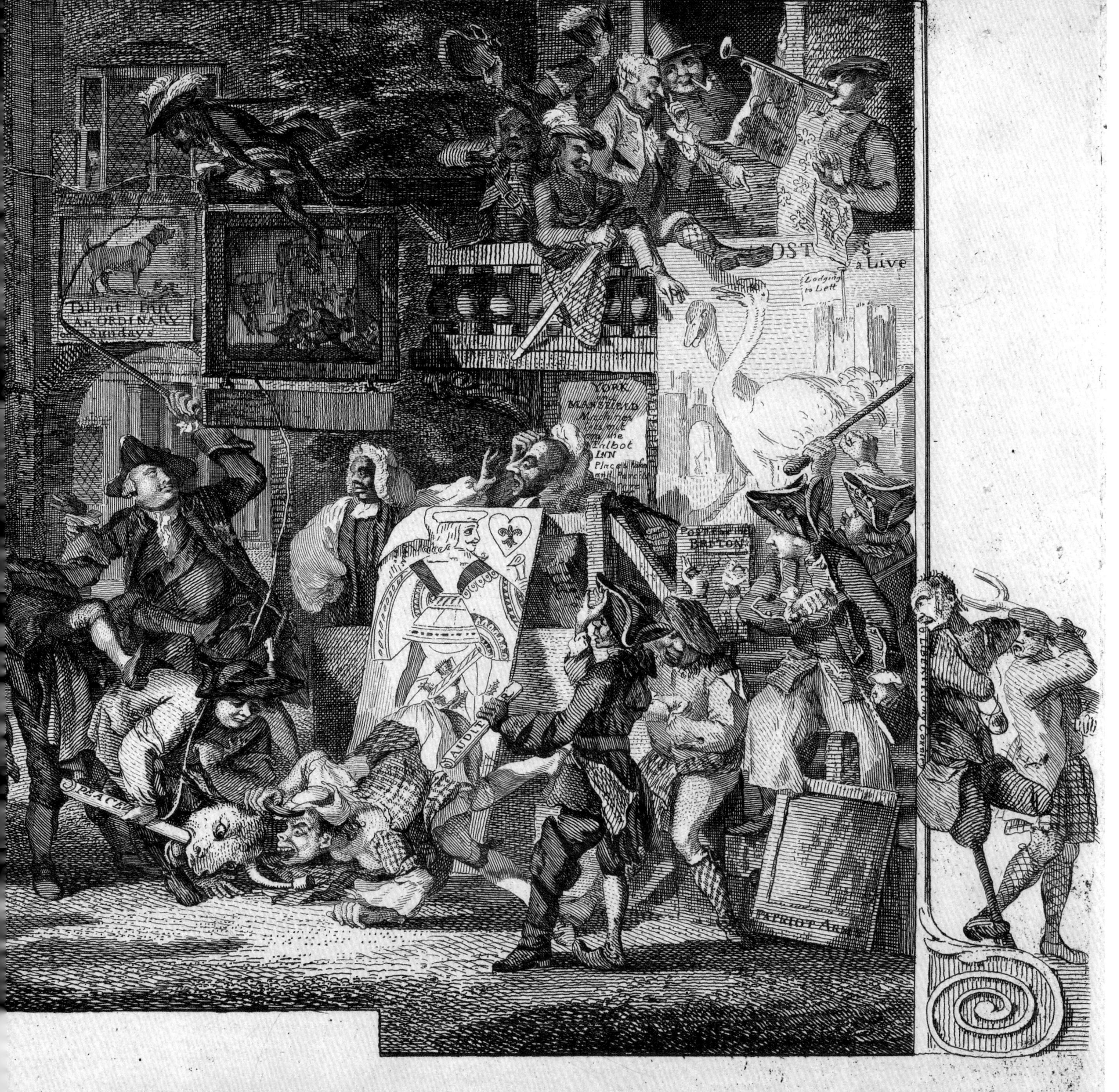

Talbot Inn
An ORDINARY
Sundays
a Live
Lodging to Lett
YORK
MANSFIELD
Talbot
INN
PLACE
AUDITOR
PATRIOT ARMS

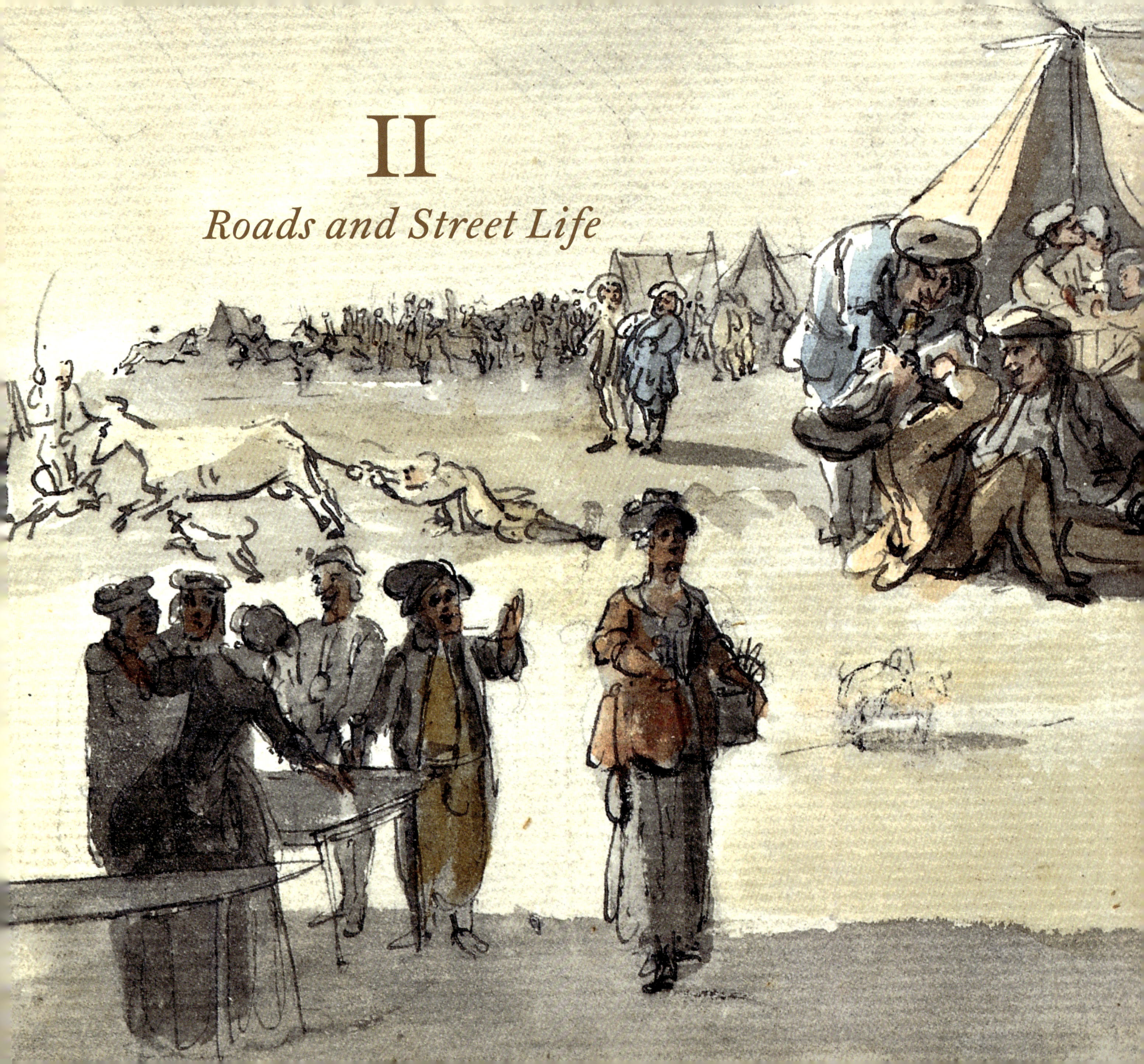

II

Roads and Street Life

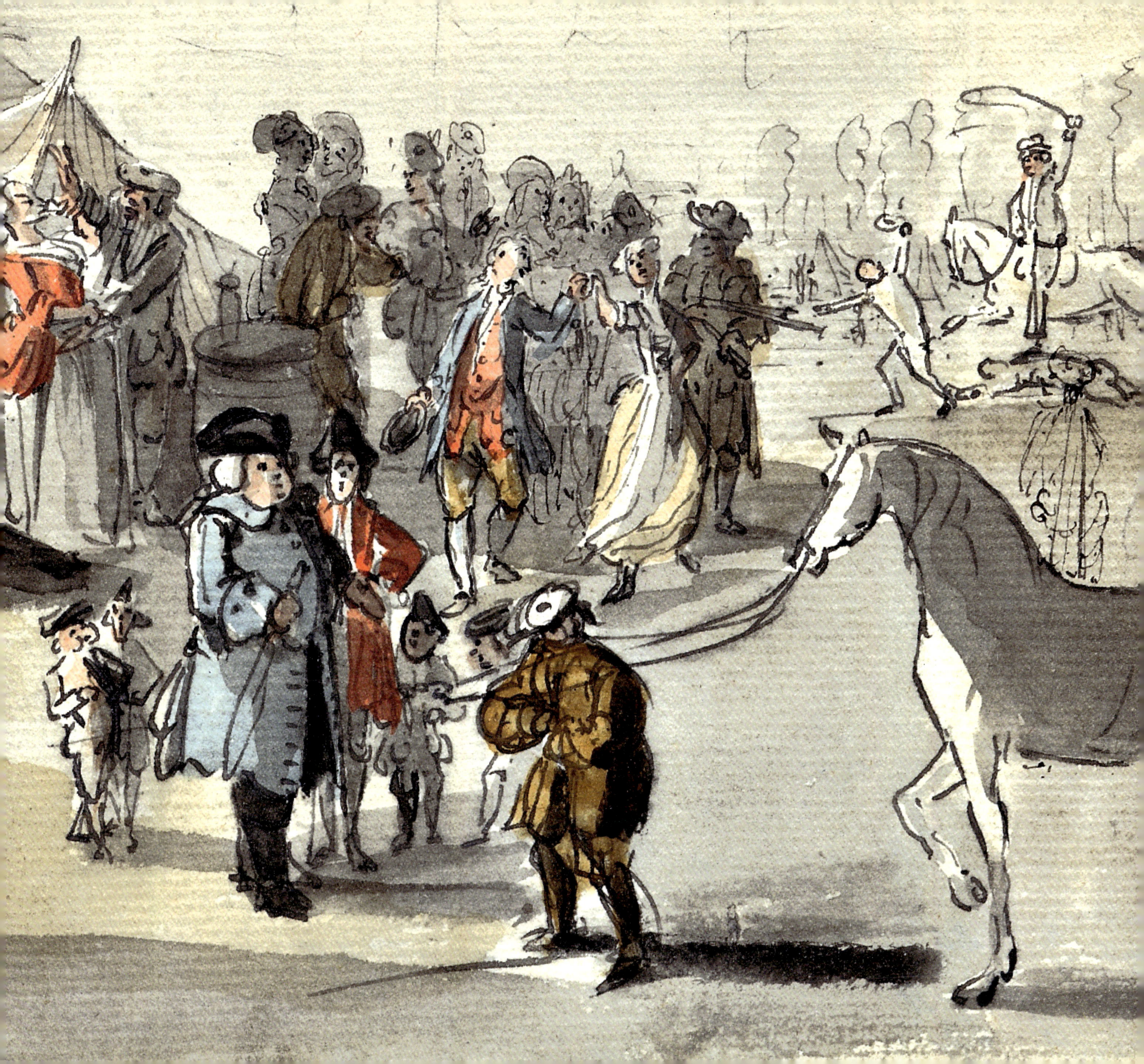

Roads and streets were the subject, as well as the vantage point, of much of Sandby's art, shaping its scenic and social character. A variety of route ways feature in his work, including new turnpike roads and paved streets, the walks and rides of aristocratic parkland, as well as old drove roads and woodland bridleways. He also portrayed a range of passengers, civilian and military vehicles, livestock, gateways, bridges and coaching inns. Eighteenth-century Britain was a society on the move, whether the travel was for business or pleasure, over long or short distances, country-wide or local. In views along country lanes and city streets, across new turnpike gates, urban squares and royal parks, Sandby not only recorded this moving panorama but also commented on its wider significance.

Over the course of a long career, in large part characterised by mobility, Sandby was witness to major changes in travel and transport. A period of 'turnpike mania' in the middle decades of the century led to over 15,000 miles of road being covered by some 500 turnpike trusts, which used revenue from tolls to repair road surfaces (Pawson 1977). 'Flying coaches', also introduced at mid-century, coupled with improvements in road infrastructure, including hard-stone rolled surfaces, meant drastic reductions in journey times. A greater variety of destinations and an increase in the number of routes gradually opened up the whole of the country, as the coaching network became increasingly less centred on the busy routes in and out of London. This acceleration and expansion of the transport system, binding places and people together, was accompanied by a rapid increase in the volume of traffic. Groups of travellers on the road included military personnel, subsistence migrants and vagrants, as well as members of polite society visiting patrons or relatives, on excursions to the country seats of the landed élite or searching out picturesque scenery.

This latter set of road users would have included professional artists like Sandby, making sketching tours or visiting the estates of wealthy patrons. Travelling the roads that took him from location to location had a profound effect on Sandby's practice: the developments outlined above had significant implications not only for the use of the land but for the perception of landscape. They expanded Sandby's field of work and his vision. Roads had long been a central feature of much landscape art, especially within the topographical tradition. Yet, Sandby is attentive to their traffic, construction and management, and to their role in articulating the landscape, in a way that is not apparent in the work of earlier figures in that tradition. In paired views of the Bayswater Turnpike, looking east and west along a receding road at morning and evening, Sandby details the steady streams of people and goods making their way into and out of the capital (cat. 48, fig. 40). These are views of a peripheral urban interchange, a meeting point for day-trippers and the troops barracked nearby, a gateway for those supplying food and produce to the city, a place where the erosion of distinctions between urban and rural cultures was most pronounced.

Life on the city streets provided Sandby with a range of subjects, from the down and out to the fashionable and polite. In post-Rebellion Edinburgh he made comedy out of the city's poorer inhabitants, as well as the pretensions of its more polite residents, as they attended local outdoor entertainments of various kinds, including pleasure gardens, fairs and executions (cats 31–34). His *Twelve London Cries* of a decade later feature a motley assortment of ragged hawkers, prostitutes and vagrants, a monstrous group, some noisy and insolent, others cowed and docile; the artist claimed these were 'done from life' (cat. 35). This might appear to grant Sandby's denizens of the city's thoroughfares a certain authenticity, but they are also part of a well-established literary and visual tradition, addressing the very nature of urban experience, whether the city travelogues of writers like John Gay and Ned Ward or the street theatre produced by artists like Marcellus Laroon and William Hogarth. Such images appear to demonstrate a simultaneous distaste for and a fascination with the chaotic and seamy, as well as the prosaic and everyday side of the modern city.

People from all levels of society frequently took offence at the sight of military personnel, demonstrating a good deal of hostility towards uniformed men. Their rough, violent or dissolute conduct was deemed offensive to polite codes of behaviour, and it pitched them against the lower ranks of society against whom their actions were often directed. Yet, the nation was also dependent on its soldiers' actions and ultimately their lives for the extension of empire, national defence and resolution of domestic disorder. Regiments of regulars and volunteers were a near-permanent presence on the country's roads or at its hostelries, as well as on the city's streets and at its places of promenade, and they appear regularly in Sandby's art. In a series of views of military encampments, established for the safeguarding of various London landmarks during the Gordon Riots of June 1780, Sandby depicts a peaceful grouping of regular and auxiliary troops, little hinting at the violent events that had brought them together (cats 50–52). Set in the capital's royal parks and the common land to the west of the city, the scenes' focus is on the colourful spectacle of military life. They feature a wide range of civilian visitors and military personnel intermingling, a graphic vision of the liberties enjoyed by a free, democratic people. Their embodiment of these freedoms, and the role played by the soldiers in their protection, is made still more explicit by their occupation of the royal landscapes of Hyde and St James's Parks, where they are overlooked by buildings associated with both church and state.

Rising above the terraces at the back of the view of St James's Park is one of the city's grandest historic landmarks, Westminster Abbey. This integral part of the national fabric also features as one of the grand parade of monuments stretching along the city skyline in paired prospects of the Thames from the garden terrace of old Somerset House by the Sandby brothers (cats 53–54). These present a vision of London as at once ancient and modern, historic but at the centre of a still-expanding commercial and maritime empire. Such perspective views, recalling Canaletto's magisterial paintings of the Thames, order the haphazard development of the commercial buildings of the river bank, regularising them as part of a grand, expansive urban vista. They offer further demonstration of Sandby's concern with the circulation of commodities and people, whether along its historic waterways or new fast roads, as well as the ordinary, mundane activities that take place along their routes or the architectural sites encountered along the way. These sites were now not merely local, or even regional, but part of an integrated national landscape.

31.1–3

Edinburgh Street Scenes, *c.* 1747–51

(1) 'Scene at the execution of John Young'
(2) 'Officers questioning a crowd'
(3) 'A street scene'
Pen, ink and wash with watercolour, 66 × 183 mm (1); 106 × 222 mm (2); 81 × 185 mm (3)
Department of Prints and Drawings, British Museum, London, Nn. 6-47-34-37

PROVENANCE
Paul Sandby's studio sales, Christie's, 1811 (lots 12–46) and 1817 (lots 41–42)?; The Revd Charles Sloman (sale Wheatley's, 20 June 1835, lot 113)

SELECTED EXHIBITIONS
Nottingham 1986, n.n.

SELECTED REFERENCES
Binyon 1898–1907, no. 82 a–c, IV, 14

Recalling his father's period of residence in North Britain over 60 years before, Thomas Paul Sandby recorded him taking 'numerous sketches from nature, with surprising accuracy', and making 'many drawings of figures, in the costume, and of the habits and employments, of the inhabitants of Edinburgh, that are peculiarly interesting, and mark a fertility of genius, that had only to select its path in art, to attain excellence' (Sandby 1811). Studies of street life in and around the Scottish capital made in the late 1740s and early 1750s provided Sandby with motifs for the rest of his life, and were still to be found in the artist's studio on his death, hence his son's familiarity with drawings such as those illustrated here. A large number of these sketches, largely housed in the Department of Prints and Drawings at the British Museum, document local customs, peoples and places.

Although the Battle of Culloden had effectively ended the chances of a Stuart being restored to the throne, Jacobite unrest persisted. In depicting the city's rough mix of beggars, hawkers and street traders, sailors, soldiers and Jacobites, Sandby's character studies captured the economic and political tensions of post-Rebellion Scotland at street level. Soldiers questioning a crowd or leading away plaid-covered figures, seen against an everyday backdrop of eateries and taverns, allude to the larger political events that had

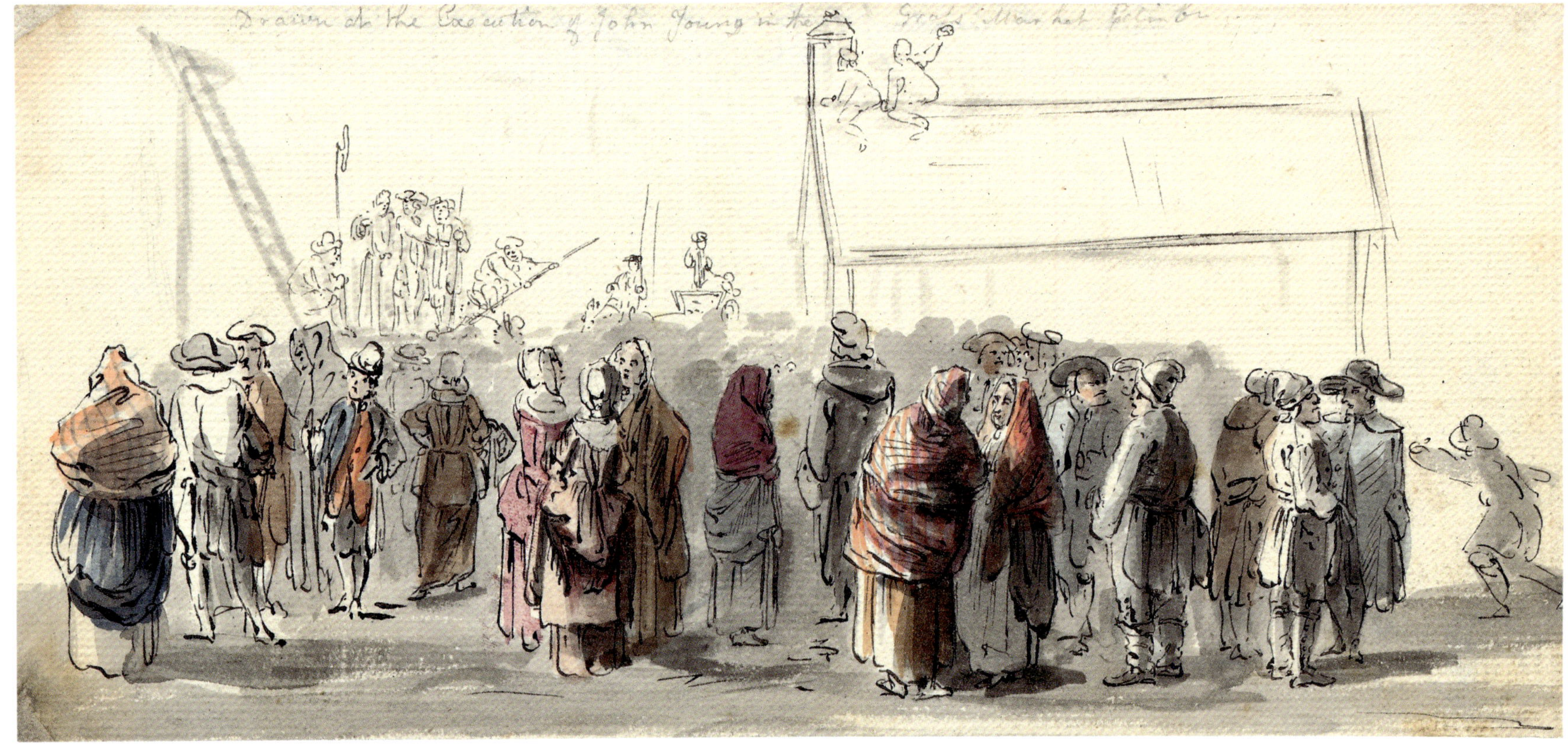

CAT. 31.1

brought the artist to the city. Sandby clearly had an eye for topical events, as is illustrated by the sketch of the hanging of John Young, a soldier convicted of forging banknotes, whose case and execution made the London dailies in the first week of January 1751. Such was the notoriety of the case that *Read's Weekly Journal* (5 January 1751) reported 'an infinite Multitude of Spectators' milling around the gallows. This variously enthusiastic and indifferent crowd is suggested with admirable economy by Sandby's pencil and pen.

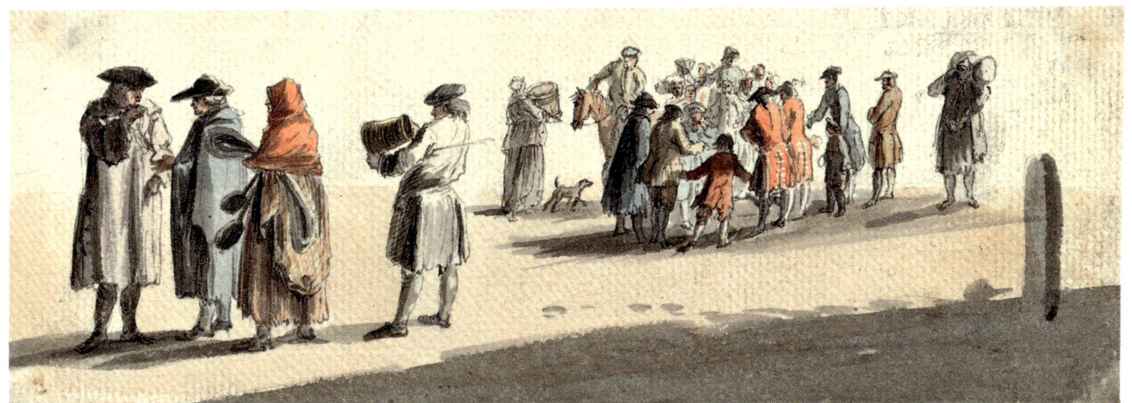

CAT. 31.2

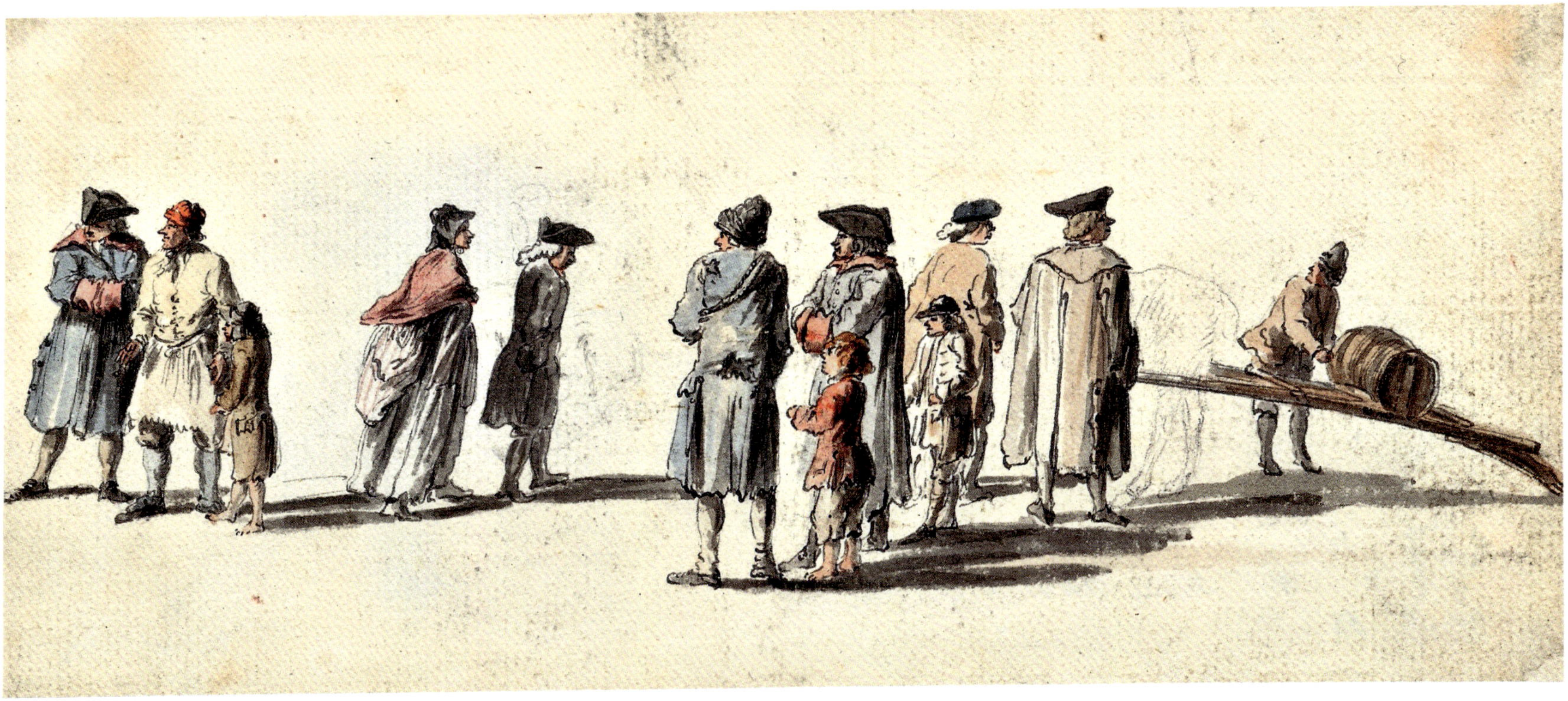

CAT. 31.3

32.1–3

Edinburgh Street Scenes, *c.* 1747–51

(1) 'A horse-fair on Bruntsfield Links'
(2) 'The taking of Jacobite Prisoners'
(3) 'A scene in the High Street'
Pen, ink and watercolour over graphite, 82 × 142 mm (1); 105 × 240 mm (2); 122 × 209 mm (3)
Department of Prints and Drawings, British Museum, London, Nn. 6-45-40-67

PROVENANCE
Paul Sandby's studio sales, Christie's, 1811 (lots 12–46) and 1817 (lots 41–42)?; The Revd Charles Sloman (sale Wheatley's, 20 June 1835, lot 113)

SELECTED EXHIBITIONS
Edinburgh 1978A, no. 4.17; Nottingham 1990, no. III, 33–35

SELECTED REFERENCES
Binyon 1898–1907, no. 80 a–c, IV, 13; Edinburgh 1978A, no. 4.17, p. 44

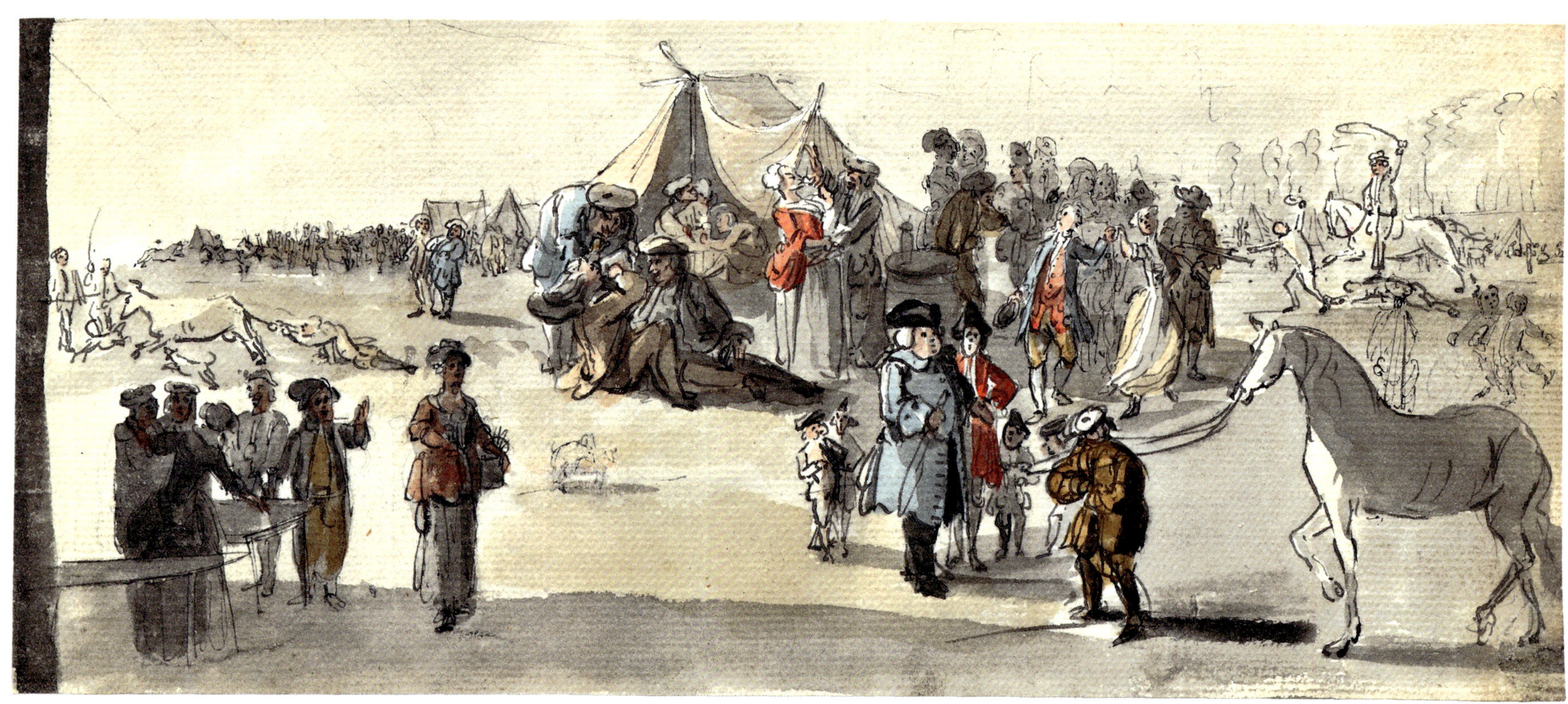

CAT. 32.1

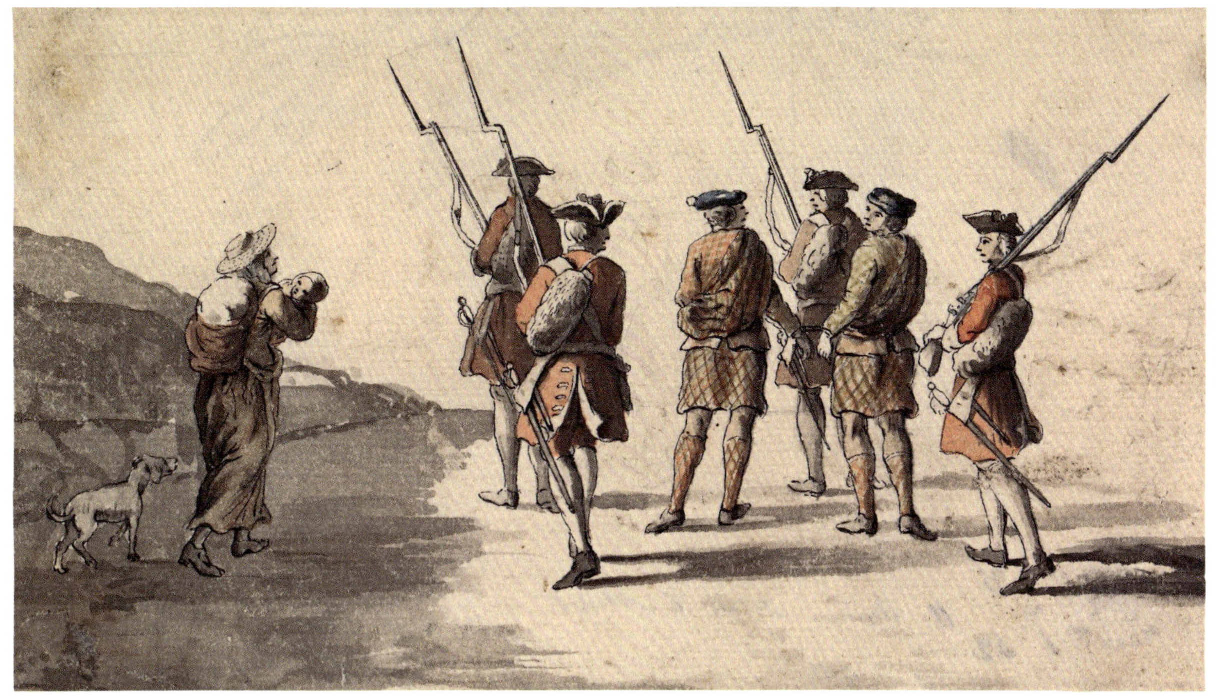

CAT. 32.2

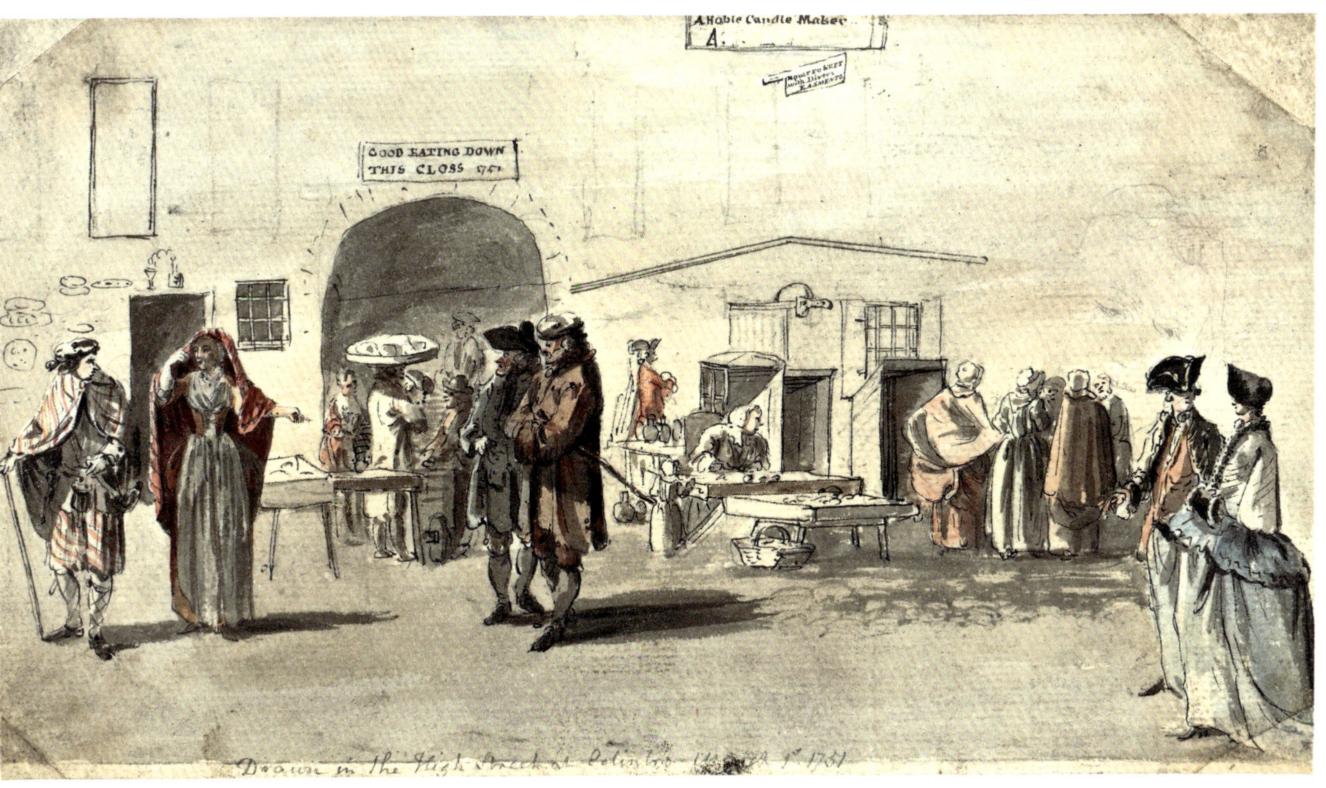

CAT. 32.3

33

Horse Fair on Bruntsfield Links, Edinburgh, 1750

Watercolour over graphite, 244 × 376 mm
Signed and dated: 'P Sandby Delin 1750' (l.r.)
National Galleries of Scotland, Edinburgh, D5184

PROVENANCE
Simmonds family; Mrs R. Hollis; Albemarle Gallery, London; National Galleries of Scotland, 1990

SELECTED EXHIBITIONS
Edinburgh 1978A, no. 4.19; London 1993, no. 249; Edinburgh 1999, no. 62

SELECTED REFERENCES
Robertson 1987

This drawing of a horse fair on Bruntsfield Links on the Boroughmuir, an expanse of common land to the southwest of Edinburgh, is one of very few fully developed figurative compositions datable to Sandby's stay in the city. Such fairs were a traditional aspect of the city's economy, serving as hiring grounds, market-places and social venues. Various forms of entertainment or social activity took place alongside the trading and provided Sandby with rich comic material. This motley crowd of customers and traders, English soldiers and plaid-clothed Jacobites, variously young and old, fat and thin, appear largely fuelled by their appetite for the street food and alcohol on offer, consumed outside makeshift eateries and dram shops. Horse and cattle trading is clearly secondary to the drunken fighting and revelry of the fair-goers. A number of these figures are traced from the artist's sketches of the area's street life, which accounts for the odd disjunctions in scale. Others demonstrate a familiarity with the work of Sandby's London-based contemporaries: an elegant, somewhat incongruous couple, dancing to the accompaniment of a piper and fiddler, appearing in the middle ground, are borrowed from a drawing by the French-born Louis-Philippe Boitard (British Museum, London). Such a quotation suggests that Sandby had an eye on his future career as a professional artist. Some of the thematic concerns of his later work are also anticipated by this drawing. In setting this raucous scene against the magisterial backdrop of the castle rising above and the ancient, baronial mansion of Wrychtishousis to the left, Sandby adopts the conjunction of rough plebeian culture and grand architectural backdrop that was to be such a prominent feature of his art on his return to London (cats 59–60, 62).

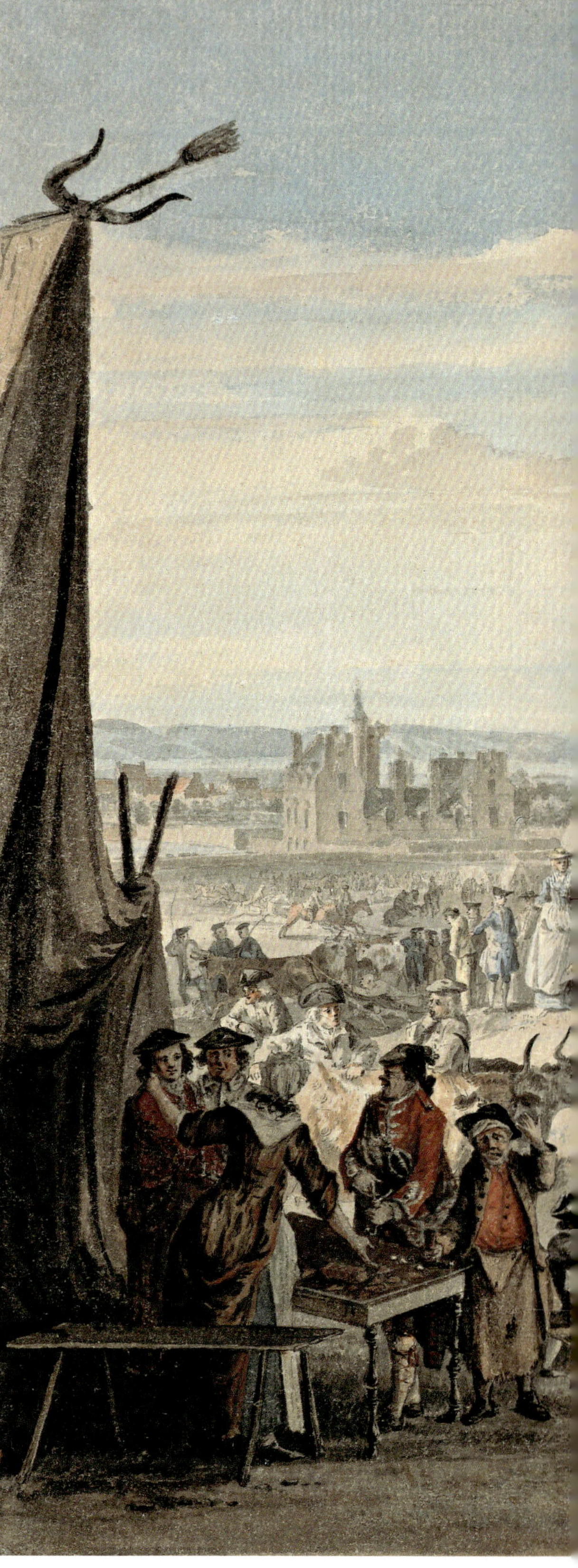

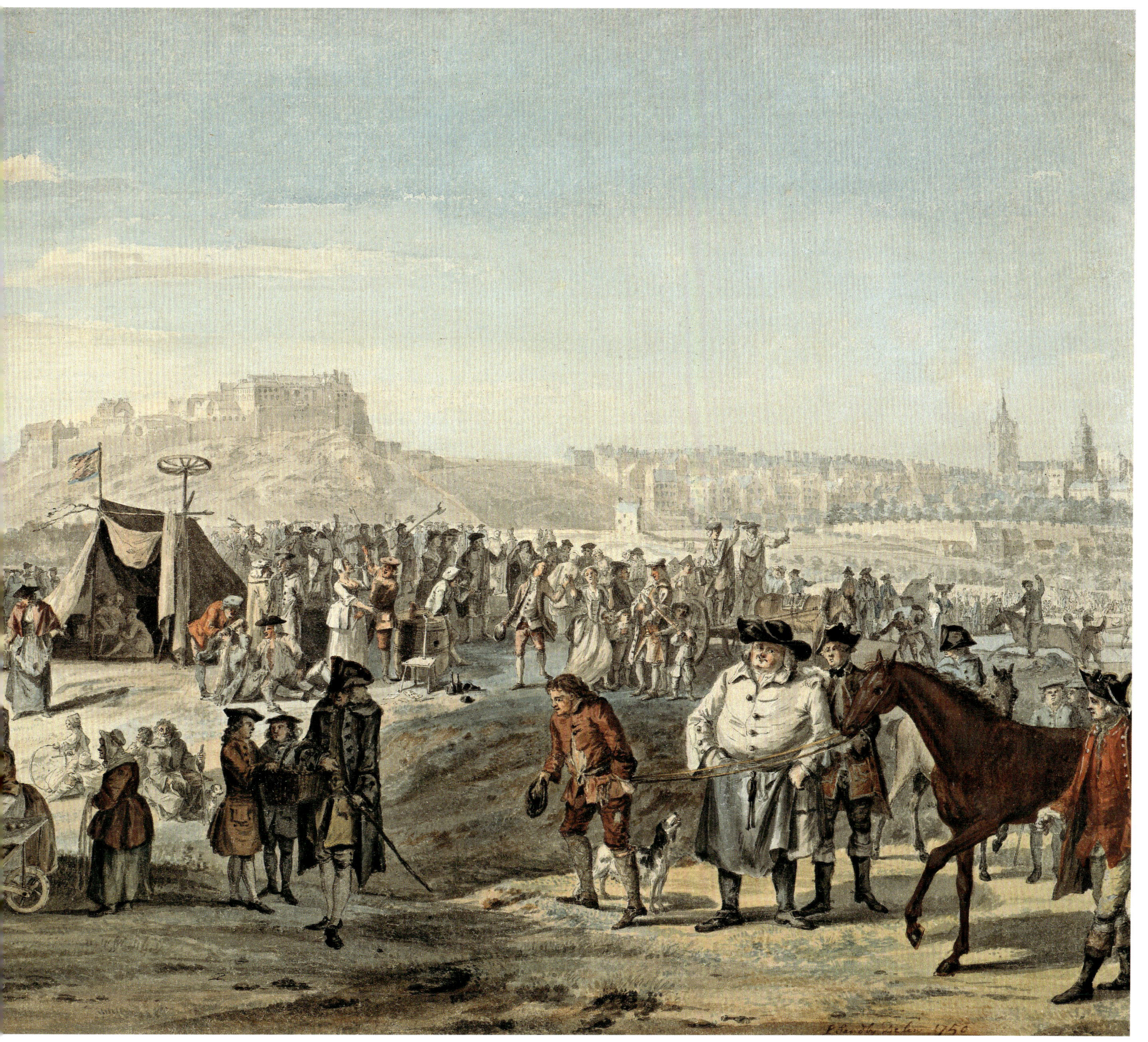

34

A humble imitation of Vauxhall in the Grounds of Heriot's Hospital, Edinburgh, early 1750s

Pen and watercolour over graphite, 117 × 162 mm
Royal Collection, London, RL 14452

PROVENANCE
In the Royal Collection by 1947

SELECTED REFERENCES
Oppé 1947, no. 219, p. 59

Recalling his 1769 visit to Edinburgh, the antiquarian and travel writer Thomas Pennant described Heriot's Hospital, situated on the summit of the southern ridge of Edinburgh, as 'a fine old building', if 'much too magnificent for the end proposed, that of educating poor children'. He went on:

> it was founded by *George Herriot*, jeweler to *James* II, who followed that monarch to *London*, and made a large fortune. There is a fine view of the castle and the sloping part of the city from the front: the gardens were formerly the resort of the gay; and there the *Scotch* Poets often laid, in their comedies, the scenes of intrigue.
> (Pennant 1772, p. 52)

This finely observed, near-miniature depiction of a makeshift pleasure garden, established in the grounds of the hospital, dates from the period when this was 'the resort of the gay'. In the ramshackle pavilion, housing the musicians, Sandby draws a comic contrast between the claims to refined leisure that such activities represented and its model in the largest and most spectacular of London's commercial pleasure-grounds, Vauxhall Gardens, which were being recorded at this moment in fine engravings after views by Antonio Canaletto and Samuel Wale (Solkin 1993, pp. 125–37). Comedy is also to be found in the parody of refined gestures, relaxed poses and congenial groupings of the painted theatre of the *fête galante*, a genre presumably familiar to the artist through prints after Jean-Antoine Watteau. A knowledge of such continental developments is also apparent in the drawing's feathery trees and delicate blue and rose tints.

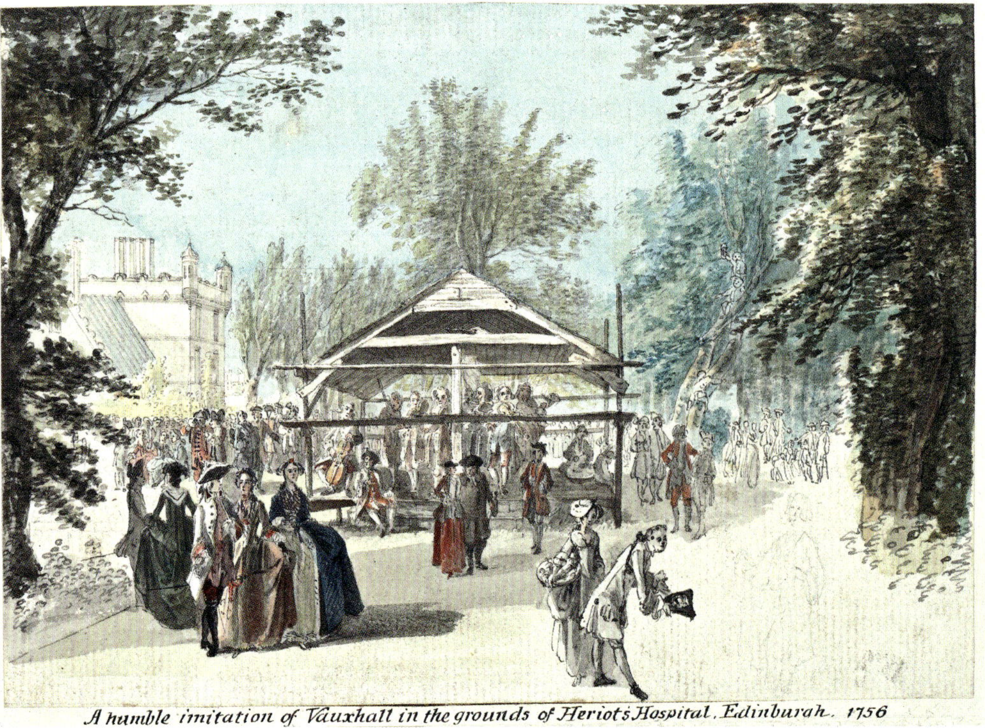

35.1–12

Twelve London Cries done from the Life, Part 1st, 1760

(1) Frontispiece
(2) 'My pretty little Gimy Tarters'
(3) 'Any Tripe'
(4) 'Will your Honour buy a Sweet Nosegay'
(5) 'All Sorts of Earthenware'
(6) The Walking Stationer
(7) 'A pudding a pudding a hot pudding'
(8) 'Rare Mackerel'
(9) 'All Fire and no smoke'
(10) 'Rare Meltin Oysters'
(11) 'Do you want any Spoons'
(12) 'Fun upon Fun'

Published by Paul Sandby
Etchings, average 213 × 156 mm
Guildhall Art Gallery, London, PR.L21.21

SELECTED REFERENCES
Robertson 1987, pp. 179–98; Shesgreen 2002, pp. 123–31; Bills 2003; London 2003A, pp. 77–81

In 1760 Sandby published this set of twelve prints in which he reworked the traditional genre of London street *Cries*. According to the inscription on the title page they were sold through François Vivares's Great Newport Street print shop, off Charing Cross Road, as well as 'by P. Sandby Next door to the Fountain in Broad Street Carnaby Market', priced at 'Three Shill'. Such sets of figures, depicting itinerant performers, hawkers and traders, had been a commonplace in European art since the sixteenth century: Marcellus Laroon's *Cryes of the City of London*, first issued in 1688 and republished throughout the eighteenth century, were the most popular of such series on the market at the time of Sandby's ensemble. The bookseller Robert Sayer had issued a revised six-part edition of Laroon's prints at some point in the 1750s, with what the title page described as 'Improvements' by the Parisian-born Louis-Philippe Boitard. By updating the clothing and smoothing over some of the haggard faces of Laroon's original images, Boitard and Sayer hoped to appeal to developing Francophile taste. Sandby's projected six-part series was clearly a response to this, replacing Boitard's elegant, simpering hawkers and traders with rougher, more confrontational types, 'done from life', as the title page had it. A comparison of Boitard's nosegay vendor (fig. 38), derived not from Laroon but François Boucher, with the corresponding figure in Sandby's set illustrates the nature of this rejoinder. In contrast to Boitard's graceful, retiring innocent, a character transposed from the *faux*-rural idyll of the *fête galante*, Sandby's flower girl is challenging, confident and clearly experienced. That she is trading herself, as well as the contents of her basket, is made explicit in the provocative inscription below: 'Will your Honour buy a Sweet Nosegay or a Memorandum Book'. In the wake of the 'glorious summer' of 1759, with Britain's victories over France in Canada, this parody and rejection of imported French pictorial models was in keeping with the patriotic hubris of the moment. In this light, Sandby's bilingual titling can be seen, perhaps, less with an eye to the lucrative export market and more as a further gibe at the pretensions of the competition.

Sandby's down and outs are anything but genteel. In the frontispiece to the series a milk-maid, conventionally associated with bucolic health, is reduced to entertaining the low and vulgar with the simple trickery of a raree show. Other characters in Sandby's series sell cheap street food, hot puddings, fish and offal, deal in second- or third-hand pottery and scrap metal, or – in the final print – hawk a scurrilous ballad about the actress and courtesan Kitty Fisher. A number of common themes or visual parallels are observable across the prints: the boy fending off a dog while

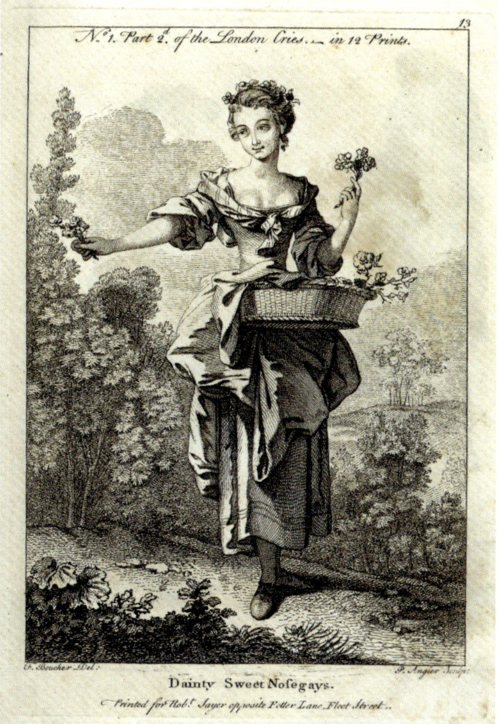

FIG. 38
Louis Philippe Boitard (fl. 1733–1767), Paul Angier (1723–1757) and Ignace Fougeron (fl. 1750–1768), after François Boucher (1703–1770), *Dainty Sweet Nosegays*, from *London Cries*, published by Robert Sayer, *c.* 1750s. Engraving, 250 × 165 mm. Lilly Library, Indiana University

scoffing a pie, who sits seated below the title card, for example, may be a comment on those who have and those who have not, a theme later echoed in the image of the pudding seller. There is a ready visual equivalence to be observed in the third and fourth plates between the sellers and their goods, between a crumpled old man and the offal piled up in his barrow or an attractive young girl and her nosegays. Such imagery took Sandby into territory that had long been dominated by William Hogarth, the artist against whom he had conducted a vicious satirical campaign only a few years earlier. In urban scenes, such as *The Enraged Musician* (1741) or *Beer Street* and *Gin Lane* (both 1751), Hogarth had incorporated figures calculated to draw comparison with Laroon's images of the capital's street commerce (London 2007, p. 60). For all the harshness of some of Hogarth's figures, however, arguably none appear as broken or as vicious as the hawkers and traders of Sandby's *Cries*. In contrast to the customary presentation of these figures as types, Sandby's street people are marked – as Sam Smiles has noted – by a 'physiognomic specificity' (Smiles 2000, p. 87). Unlike Laroon's isolated individuals, Sandby's criers are also placed in dramatic confrontation with customers or identified with specific London sites and locations.

Sandby's point in taking on this conventional subject-matter is inferred by the frontispiece to the series. In the background of a raree show and its customers we see the figure of a porter bringing boxes of images to be viewed inside the magic chamber. Each of these boxes is labelled with the name of a print in the series, suggesting that the fate of the venture was for them to become the exhibits of this cheapest of street entertainments. Much as Sandby's prints reflect a subtle, sophisticated, self-deprecating turn of humour, it is to be assumed that he did not expect his prints would be used in this way. Exhibitions by itinerant magic-lantern men were typically understood by artists of the mid-eighteenth century, for whom they were a popular subject, to appeal to children and the credulous poor who were easily impressed by unsophisticated illusions. Sandby's jocular reference to his prints being used thus is perhaps in anticipation of the ignorant supposition that vulgar subject-matter was destined to appeal to vulgar viewers.

The joke is similar to, and probably influenced by, an episode in Hogarth's famous image of *Beer Street* (fig. 39). Here a porter of waste paper, the kind of tradesman who featured in the *Cries*, pauses to take a swig of beer. His basket is placed in the foreground allowing the viewer to see that it contains books which, from the carefully engraved spines, can be recognised as copies of learned texts on the theory of art. These works were, in Hogarth's opinion, sufficiently over-exalted and arcane to remain surplus to social requirement. It was Hogarth's somewhat pompous assumption that his own print, stressing the stolid worth of common people, was sufficiently accessible to deserve better sales. By introducing the spectre of boxes of his own unsold prints ending their days as disposable fodder for magic-lantern shows Sandby stresses that he could envisage his works becoming waste paper. This was an apposite joke in that the series does not seem to have been a great commercial success; further sets were promised but not produced. Whether this frontispiece was the statement of an artist who could afford to show humorous bravado at the failure of a venture is an open question. Indeed, the inference that large numbers of prints had been made may well have been an in-joke for those friends and admirers who were aware of the limited circulation of many of Sandby's etched works.

In some sense it is reasonable to interpret the whole venture as a satire on the commercialism of artists who made series of prints with a popular touch. Indeed, in the early 1750s, Hogarth had switched to a type of print series – *Gin Lane* and *Beer Street*, *The Four Stages of Cruelty* and *The Idle and Industrious Apprentices* – that was intended to establish his moral identification with the choices made by persons in London's lowest trades. Commercial artists such as Laroon and Hogarth had a pretext for sympathy with London's lowest

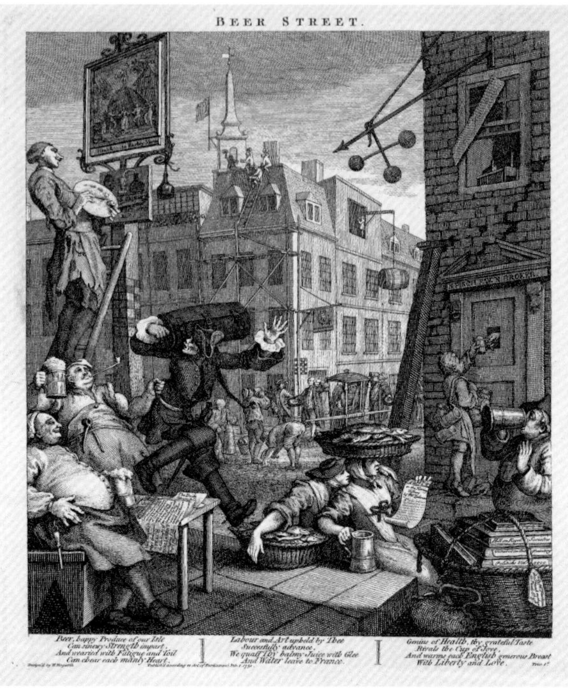

FIG. 39
William Hogarth (1697–1764), *Beer Street*, published 1751.
Etching and engraving, 383 × 325 mm.
British Museum, London, 1868,8,22.1593

form of tradesmen, as they too were obliged to hawk for custom. As such, the *Cries* can be classed with Sandby's earlier satires on Hogarth's hubris and vulgar commercialism. Unlike Hogarth, Sandby shows himself free of the vanity of identifying only other people's printed works with redundancy and the pursuit of irrelevant and arcane ideals. As the content of Sandby's series makes clear, he did not fall for the central assumption of *Beer Street*: that the peripatetic traders of the streets of London were likely to be of the beer-drinking kind; that is, necessarily stolid and admirable in their humble pursuits. He appears to have regarded the ideal of the commonality between commercial people of all classes as a somewhat foolish one in itself.

Sandby's animosity to the fiction of the street hero or heroine is evident in the palpably hostile characterisation of some of his figures in the *Cries*. One of the types who seems most repellent, the female mackerel seller, is, significantly, greeted by Hogarth, in *Beer Street*, as a veritable symbol of the attractive good health of London's street people. Hogarth's *Beer Street* makes a clear case for London being under the influence of a good healthy drink. The viciousness of the city, as the companion piece *Gin Lane* suggests, is determined merely by a choice of beverages. In *Beer Street* Hogarth's fish girls, who brought their healthy wares from country to city, lounge lasciviously beneath a tavern sign. As if to further the comparison between the good city and the country, the urban landmark of the tavern carries an image of fertile rustics dancing around the maypole. Placed directly beneath this emblem of fertility, the fish women of *Beer Street* are overtly provocative. Sandby's mackerel woman could not, by contrast, be more repellent. Indeed, we are encouraged to smell her off the page. A curious device suggests the level of Sandby's humour, for she wears a crested helmet, somewhat reminiscent of the skin of a flayed lion hoisted over her head. This reference suggests the learned tenor of the series, for she appears to combine the attributes of two classical heroes: Minerva and Hercules. The latter was famous for the heroic labour of slaying the Nemean Lion, whose skin he wore thereafter as a sign of his virile conquest. Minerva, the classical goddess of war and wisdom, who was regarded as the prime protector of the fine arts, was known for her high, crested helmet. Her emblem, carried in outstretched arms, was the owl, a symbol of her wisdom. Instead of the owl, the disgusting fishwife carries her tray of mackerel before her. The arts she protects are the raucous shrieks of the streets. So obnoxiously forceful is her screeching temperament that she seems to outdo even the strength of the armed Minerva by assuming the attributes of her ferocious male equivalent, Hercules. As such, the print appears to be a brutal satire of the sentimentalism of *Cries* as made in the tradition of Laroon, from whose example Hogarth's figures were adopted. The sentiment of these prints, as carried to a fine art in Hogarth's famous oil sketch of the *Shrimp Girl* (National Gallery, London), was that the humble girls who pursued trades on the streets of London might exhibit all the physical attributes of the ideal that were usually associated with classical goddesses.

Clearly designed to draw comparison with Hogarth, as much as with Boitard and Laroon, the figures in Sandby's *Cries* are also part of a literary discourse of city street life in which the polite, pedestrian spectator is confronted with, and sometimes jostled threateningly by, a range of importuning low-life figures, including bawds, beggars, performers and thieves. Among the countless hazards likely to be encountered on a morning stroll about the city, the poet John Gay warned prospective urban tourists of 'Trades prejudicial to Walkers'. In his widely read satire *Trivia: Or, The Art of Walking* (1716) Gay recounted:

> Now Industry awakes her busy Sons,
> Full charg'd with News the breathless
> Hawker runs:
> Shops open, Coaches roll, Carts shake
> the Ground,
> And all the Streets with passing Cries resound.
> (Gay 1716, pp. 22–23)

Noise is very much part of Sandby's series, as the inscriptions and the figures caught mid-cry imply. With several characters associated with foodstuffs there is, as noted in *Rare Mackerel*, also a reminder of the pungent aromas of the street.

Sandby's hawkers and traders, in their finely observed hand-me-down, make-do-and-mend clothing, have attracted the attention of latter-day historians of the eighteenth-century lower orders (Hitchcock 2007; Styles 2007). Indeed, Sandby's claim that his *Cries* were 'from life' has led some commentators to see these figures as more naturalistic than the sentimental figures usually to be seen in such series. However, they clearly exhibit Sandby's concern about insolent conduct and moral degradation. Far from being free-spirited, enterprising Britons, these hawkers and vendors should clean up their act or move on to make way for well-regulated commerce and circulation.

JOHN BONEHILL AND MATTHEW CRASKE

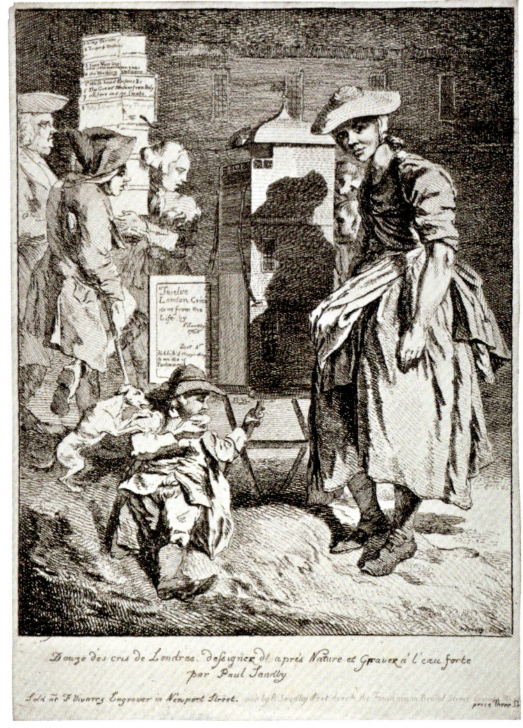

CAT. 35.1

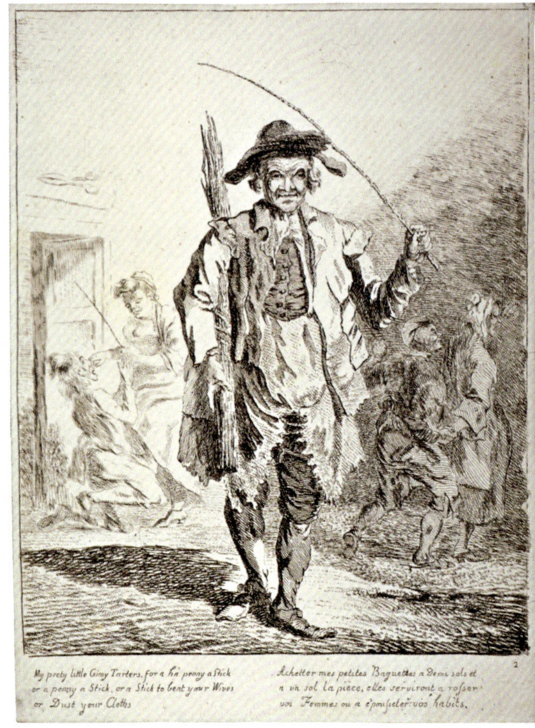

CAT. 35.2

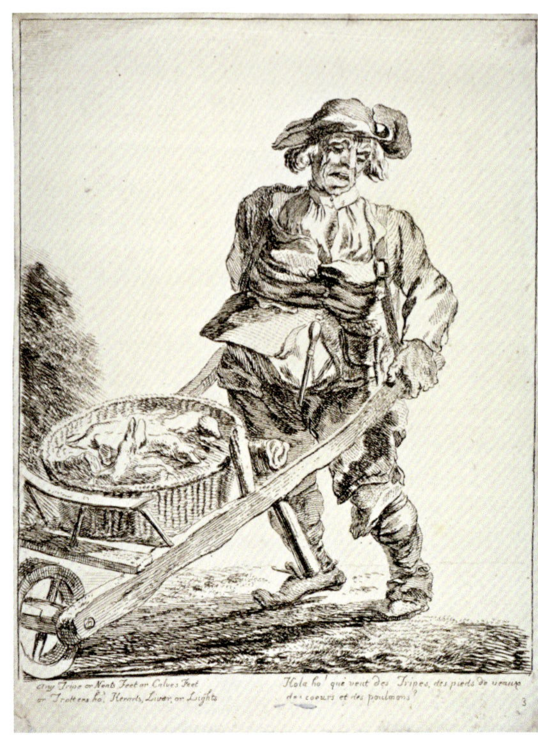

CAT. 35.3

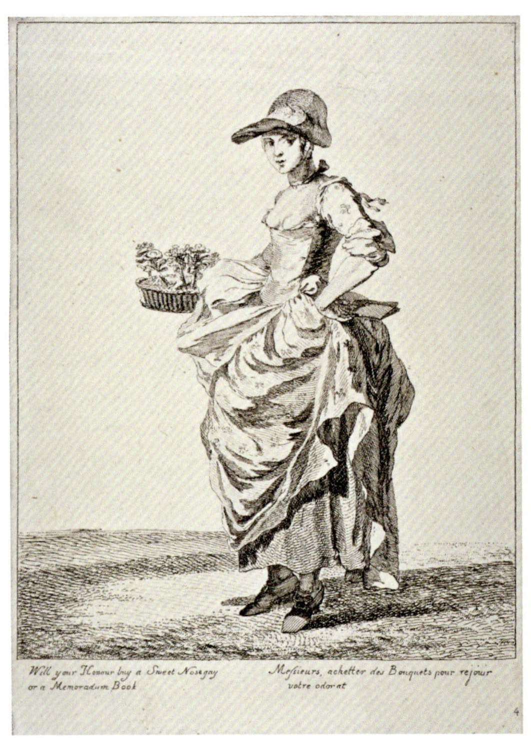

CAT. 35.4

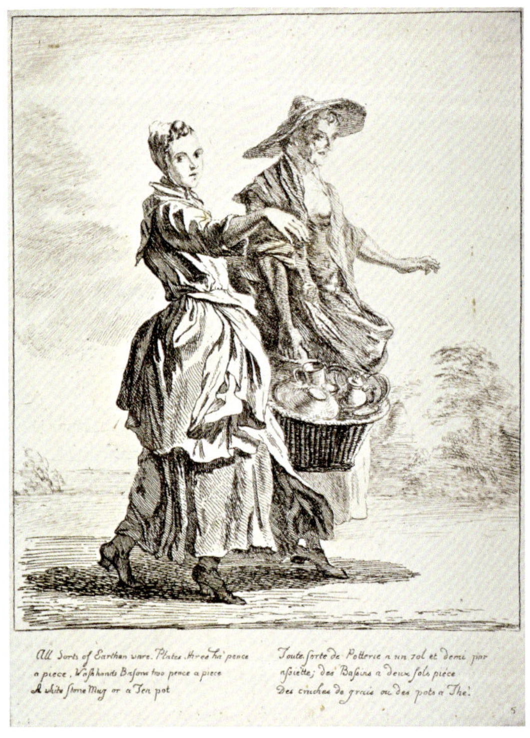

CAT. 35.5

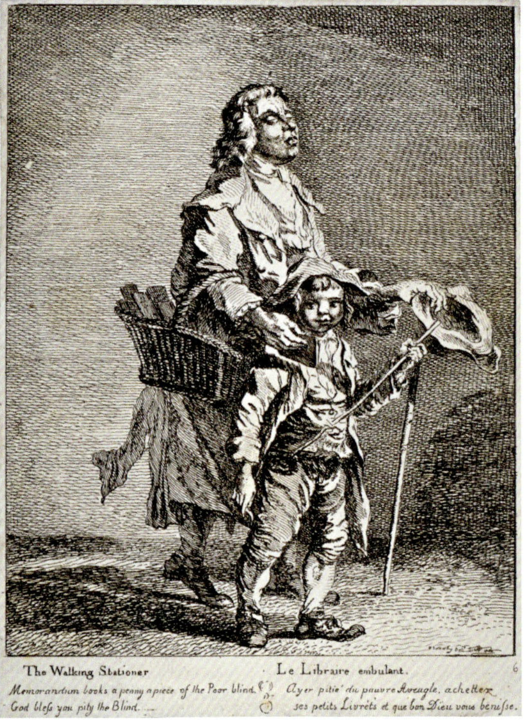

CAT. 35.6

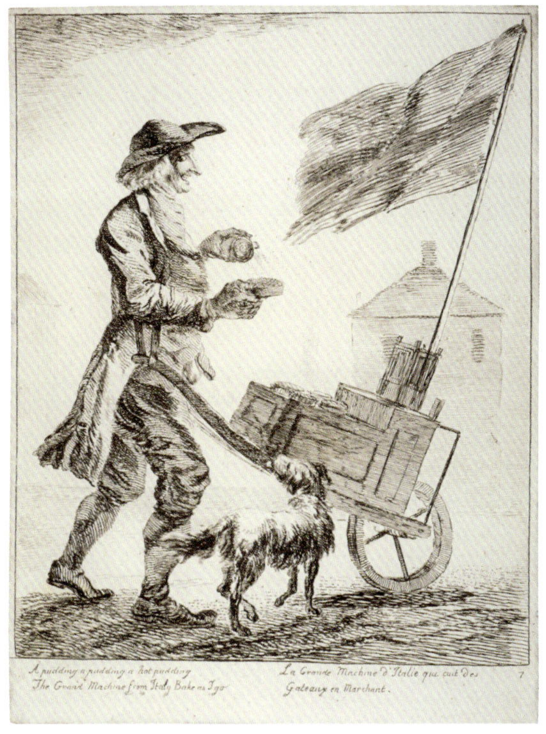

CAT. 35.7

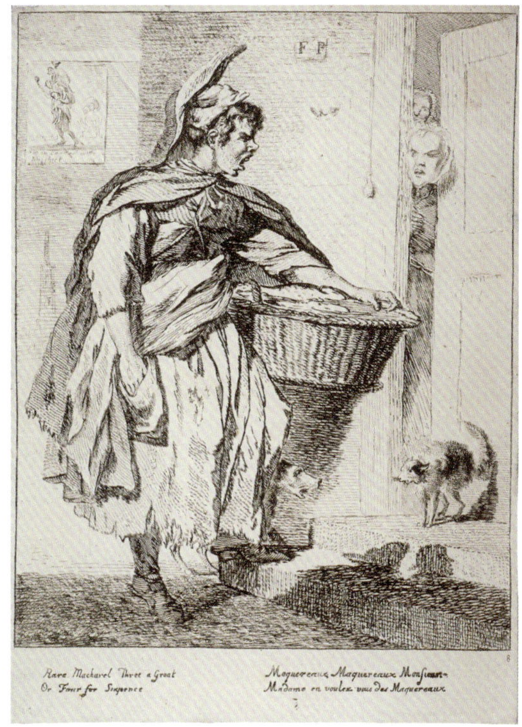

CAT. 35.8

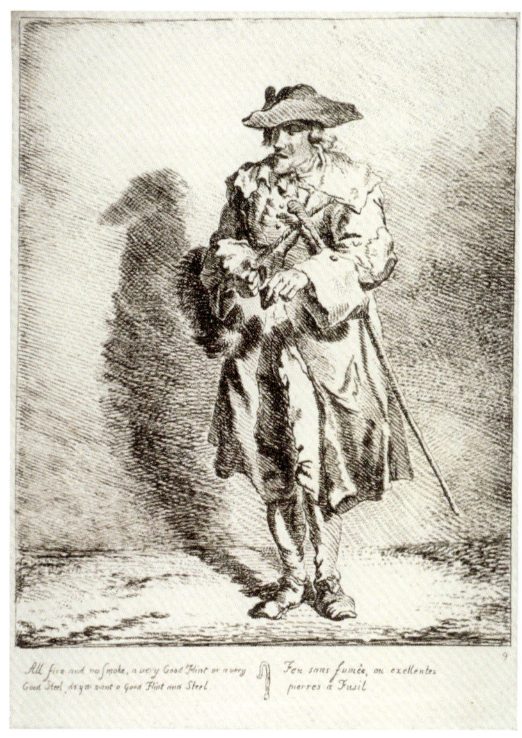

CAT. 35.9

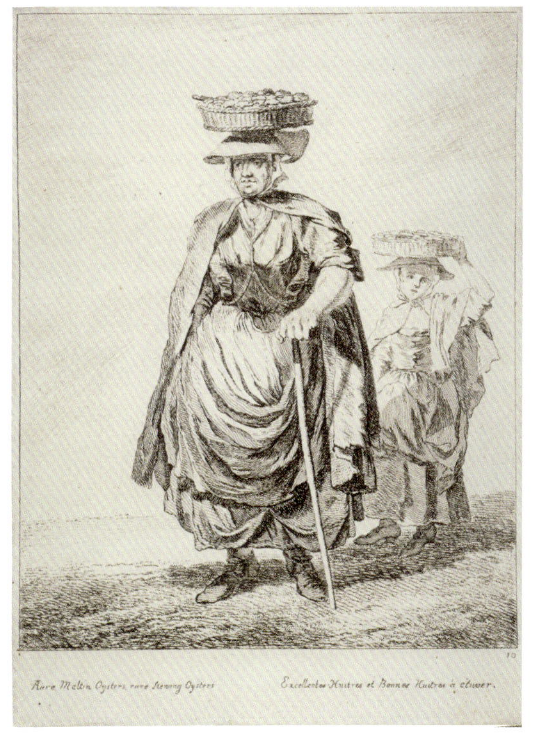

CAT. 35.10

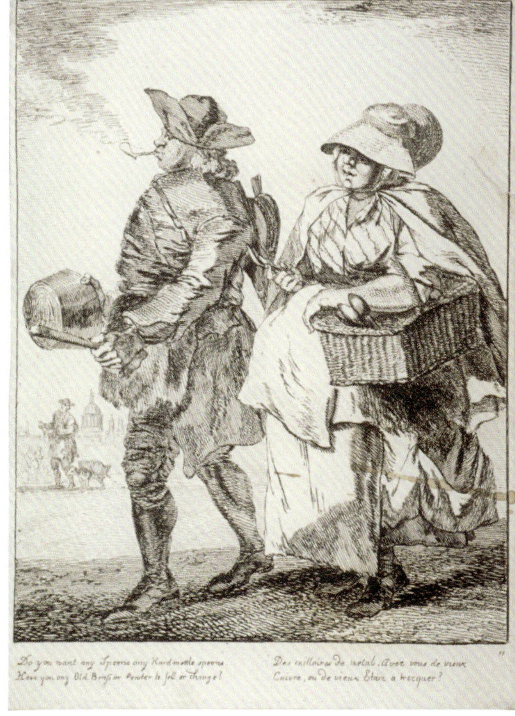

CAT. 35.11

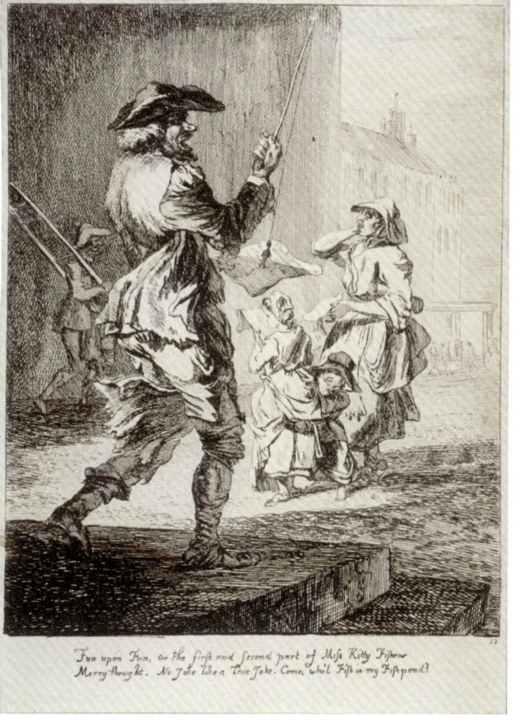

CAT. 35.12

36

'Turn your Copper into Silver now before your Eyes', c. 1759

Pen, ink and watercolour over graphite, 197 × 155 mm
Yale Center for British Art, New Haven, Paul Mellon Collection, B1975.3.202

PROVENANCE
Lord Bruce (sale Christie's, 27 April 1965, lot 59)

SELECTED EXHIBITIONS
Yale 1985, no. 48

SELECTED REFERENCES
Yale 1985, no. 48, p. 46; Shesgreen 2002, p. 131

37

'My pretty little Gimy Tarters', c. 1759

Pen, ink and watercolour over graphite, 197 × 155 mm
Yale Center for British Art, New Haven, Paul Mellon Collection, B1975.3.203

PROVENANCE
Lord Bruce (sale Christie's, 27 April 1965, lot 59)

SELECTED EXHIBITIONS
Yale 1985, no. 54

SELECTED REFERENCES
Yale 1985, no. 54, p. 47; Shesgreen 2002, pp. 123–31

38

Milkmaid, c. 1759

Pen, ink and watercolour over graphite, 196 × 149 mm
Yale Center for British Art, New Haven, Paul Mellon Collection, B1975.3.209

PROVENANCE
Lord Bruce (sale Christie's, 27 April 1965, lot 59)

SELECTED EXHIBITIONS
Yale 1985, no. 51

SELECTED REFERENCES
Yale 1985, no. 51, p. 47; Shesgreen 2002, pp. 123–31

39

Buy My Muffins, c. 1759

Pen, ink and watercolour over graphite, 196 × 138 mm
Yale Center for British Art, New Haven, Paul Mellon Collection, B1975.3.205

PROVENANCE
Lord Bruce (sale Christie's, 27 April 1965, lot 59)

SELECTED EXHIBITIONS
Yale 1985, no. 50

SELECTED REFERENCES
Yale 1985, no. 50, p. 46; Shesgreen 2002, p. 123–31

40

'Any kitchen stuff', c. 1759

Pen, ink and watercolour over graphite, 146 × 191 mm
Yale Center for British Art, New Haven, Paul Mellon Collection, B1975.3.204

PROVENANCE
Lord Bruce (sale Christie's, 27 April 1965, lot 59)

SELECTED EXHIBITIONS
Yale 1985, no. 59

SELECTED REFERENCES
Yale 1985, no. 59, p. 50; Shesgreen 2002, pp. 123–31

41

'The King's most Gracious speech to both House of Parliament', c. 1759

Pen, ink and watercolour over graphite, 191 × 155 mm
Nottingham City Museums and Galleries, NCM 1966-47

PROVENANCE
Lord Bruce (sale Christie's, 27 April 1965, lot 63); bought with the assistance of a grant-in-aid administered by the V&A, 1966

SELECTED EXHIBITIONS
Hamilton 1981, no. 86

SELECTED REFERENCES
Shesgreen 2002, pp. 123–31

CATALOGUE NUMBERS 36–47

Only one set of Sandby's London *Cries* was published, although large numbers of surviving related studies show that several further sets were planned. An album of these original drawings, almost complete, was sold at auction in 1965 (Christie's, 27 April 1965, lots 58–63). Divided into arbitrary lots of twelve, they were bought mainly by the dealers Colnaghi and Frank Sabin. They then found their way into various public collections, including those of Nottingham Castle and the Yale Center for British Art, New Haven. They show how far Sandby was intent on pushing the genre, paying ever-greater attention to location and dramatic incident.

A range of sites feature in the drawings illustrated here, both urban and suburban. They include the waterfront of the Thames, the arcades of Covent Garden, the gallows at Tyburn, residential streets and major thoroughfares. A demobilised sailor, reduced to selling socks, is placed in Charing Cross Road, identifiable by the pillory on the left and the equestrian statue of Charles I, on which someone has climbed. This was the recognised centre of London: the crossroads of the city's various social flows, polite and plebeian, commercial and social. Confrontation between the different social orders or criers and customers plays more of a role in these drawings than in the published designs: an old crone is compared with an attractive milkmaid; a pastry vendor with polite takers of tea; a scrawny hawker of 'kitchen stuff' with a complacent, well-fed cook. The drawings also show that Sandby was still preoccupied with illusion and delusion: a title page for a projected third instalment, *'Turn your Copper into Silver now before your Eyes'*, features an enterprising young woman forging.

There is also a considerable degree of stylistic and technical diversity across these drawings, despite their presumably having been executed within a relatively short space of time. Some are remarkably free and assured, characterised by a rhythmic, flowing line, while others feature a scratched, etching-like mark-making. Although

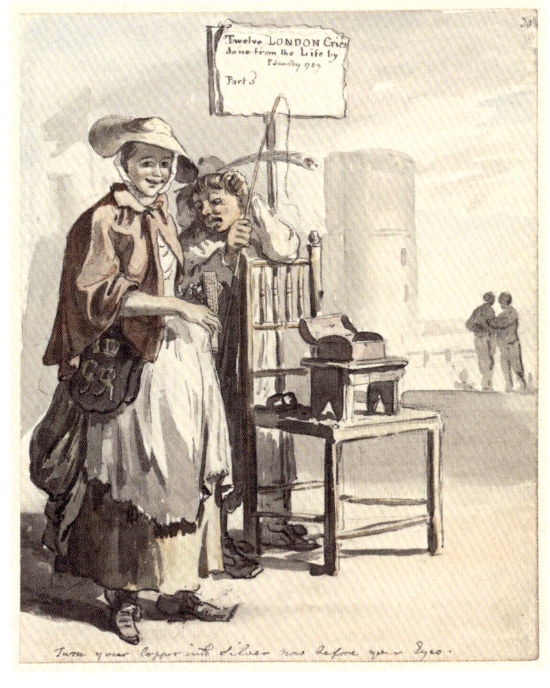

CAT. 36

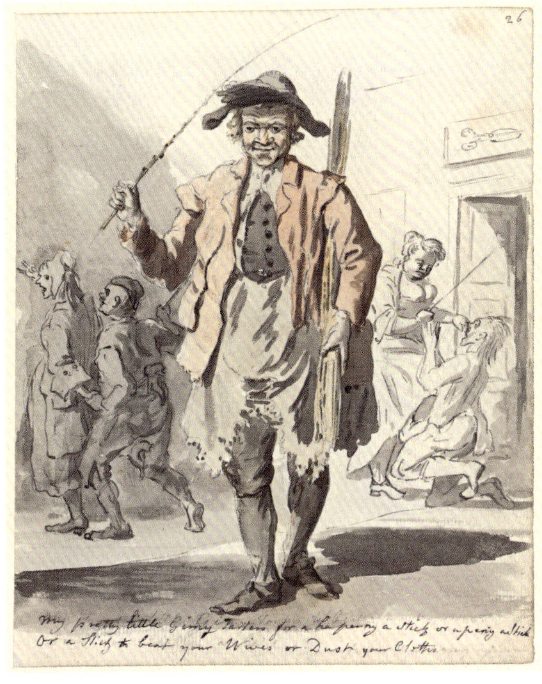

CAT. 37

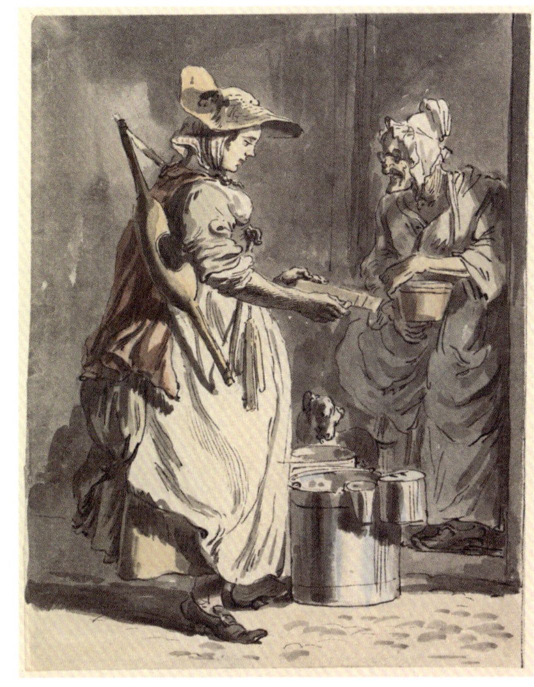

CAT. 38

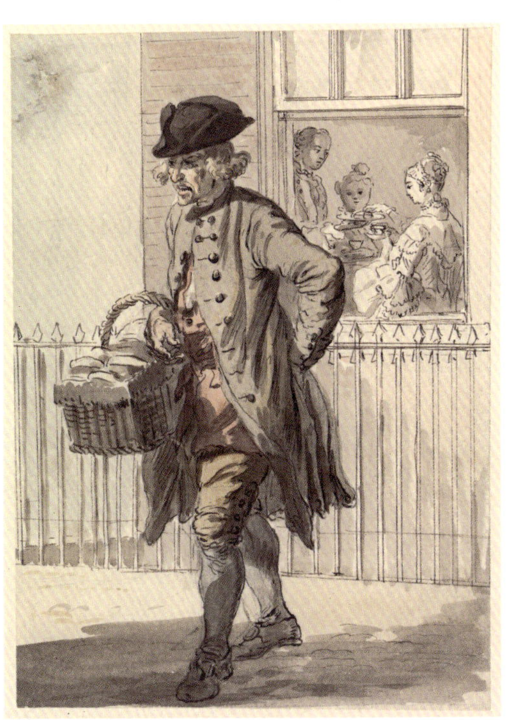

CAT. 39

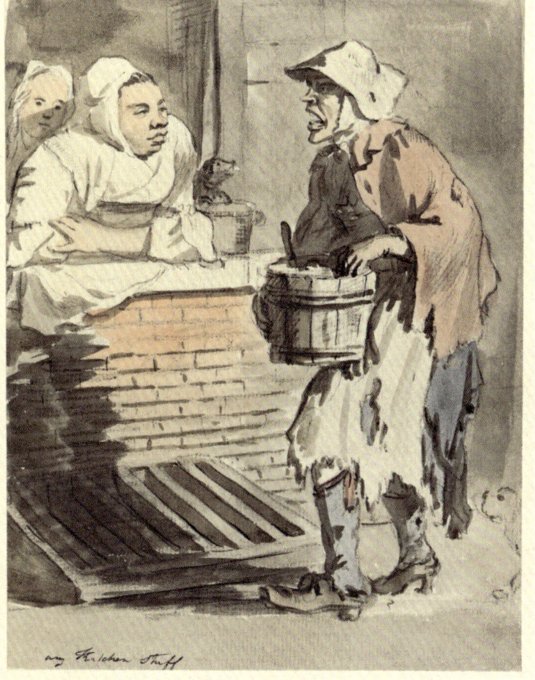

CAT. 40

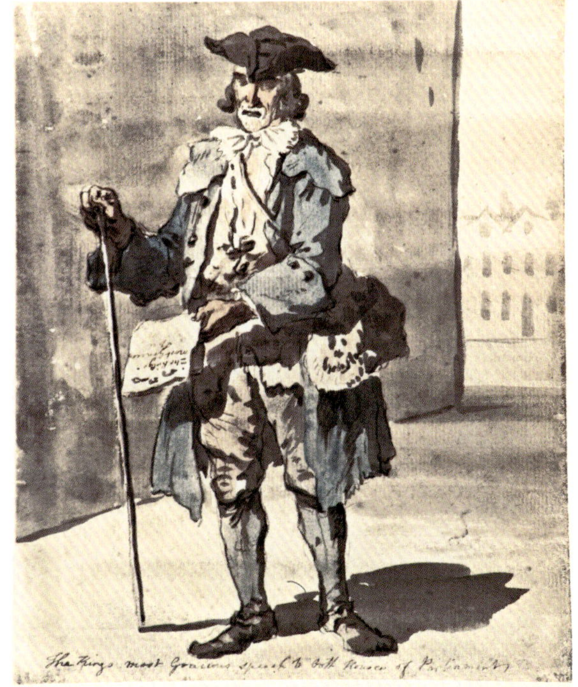

CAT. 41

42

Last Dying Speech and Confession, *c.* 1759

Pen, ink and watercolour over graphite, 171 × 144 mm
Yale Center for British Art, New Haven, Paul Mellon Collection, B1975.3.225

PROVENANCE
Lord Bruce (sale Christie's, 27 April 1965, lot 62); bought with the assistance of a grant-in-aid administered by the V&A, 1966

SELECTED EXHIBITIONS
Yale 1985, no. 55

SELECTED REFERENCES
Yale 1985, no. 55, p. 47; Shesgreen 2002, pp. 123–31, particularly p. 127

43

Fish Vendor, *c.* 1759

Pen, ink and watercolour over graphite, 198 × 138 mm
Nottingham City Museums and Galleries, NCM 1966-43

PROVENANCE
Lord Bruce (sale Christie's, 27 April 1965, lot 63); bought with the assistance of a grant-in-aid administered by the V&A, 1966

SELECTED EXHIBITIONS
Hamilton 1981, no. 82

SELECTED REFERENCES
Hamilton 1981, no. 82, p. 82; Shesgreen 2002, pp. 123–31

44

'Will you buy my Crabs come buy my Crabs', *c.* 1759

Pen, ink and watercolour over graphite, 198 × 160 mm
Nottingham City Museums and Galleries, NCM 1966-42

PROVENANCE
Lord Bruce (sale Christie's, 27 April 1965, lot 63); bought with the assistance of a grant-in-aid administered by the V&A, 1966

SELECTED EXHIBITIONS
Hamilton 1981, no. 81

SELECTED REFERENCES
Hamilton 1981, no. 81, p. 81; Shesgreen 2002, pp. 123–31

45

Stocking Vendor, *c.* 1759

Pen, ink and watercolour over graphite, 198 × 150 mm
Nottingham City Museums and Galleries, NCM 1966-46

PROVENANCE
Lord Bruce (sale Christie's, 27 April 1965, lot 63); bought with the assistance of a grant-in-aid administered by the V&A, 1966

SELECTED EXHIBITIONS
Hamilton 1981, no. 85

SELECTED REFERENCES
Hamilton 1981, no. 85, p. 85; Shesgreen 2002, pp. 123–31

46

'Rare Mackerel, Three a Groat Or Four for Sixpence', *c.* 1759

Pen, ink and watercolour over graphite, 193 × 152 mm
Nottingham City Museums and Galleries, NCM 1966-51

PROVENANCE
Lord Bruce (sale Christie's, 27 April 1965, lot 63); bought with the assistance of a grant-in-aid administered by the V&A, 1966

SELECTED EXHIBITIONS
Hamilton 1981, no. 90; Nottingham 1986, n.n.

SELECTED REFERENCES
Hamilton 1981, no. 90, p. 90; Shesgreen 2002, p. 123–31

47

'Any Tripe or Neats Feet', *c.* 1759

Pen, ink and watercolour over graphite, 219 × 153 mm
Nottingham City Museums and Galleries, NCM 1966-52

PROVENANCE
Lord Bruce (sale Christie's, 27 April 1965, lot 63); bought with the assistance of a grant-in-aid administered by the V&A, 1966

SELECTED EXHIBITIONS
Hamilton 1981, no. 91; Nottingham 1986, n.n.

SELECTED REFERENCES
Hamilton 1981, no. 91, p. 91; Shesgreen 2002, pp. 123–31

the works illustrated here are, by and large, wash drawings, worked over in pen and ink, a number of other designs are heavily worked in chalk. Moreover, as Bruce Robertson has noted with regard to those works in which we can trace the translation of the drawing into printed form, the etching 'preserved the visual effect of the drawings' (Robertson 1987, p. 189). A broken, half-hidden line defines the form of the *Rare Mackerel* seller in both etching and drawing, for example.

Although Sandby issued no further sets of his ground-breaking series, many of the figures from the drawings are featured in compositions executed over the next decade or so, most notably the characters he furnished for his brother's *Six London Views* (1766) and those that people his own views in and around Windsor (cat. 60, fig. 20).

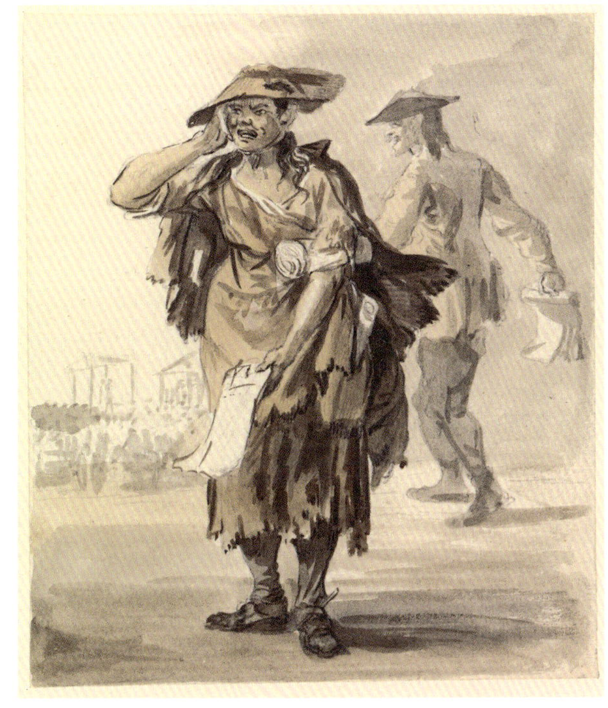

CAT. 42

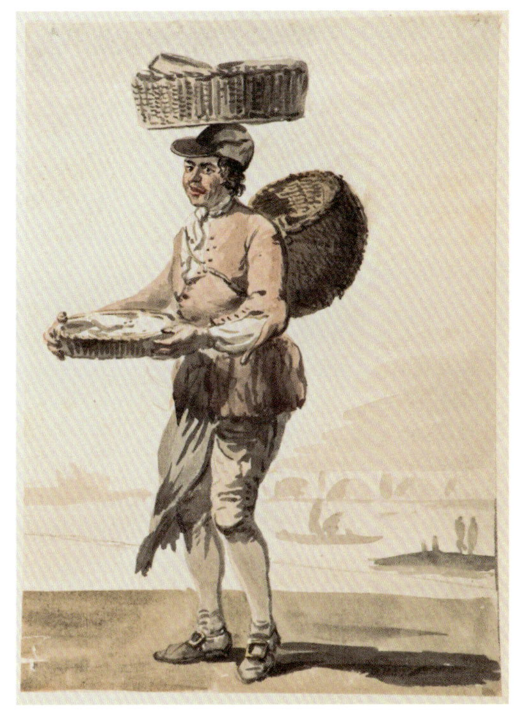

CAT. 43

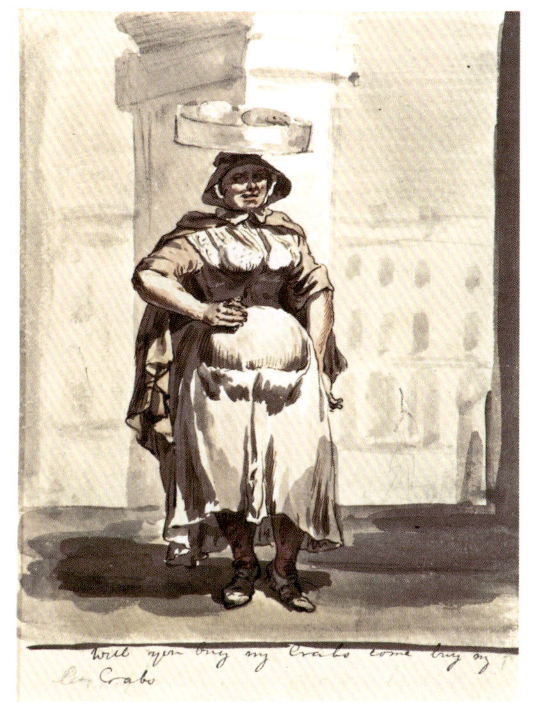

CAT. 44

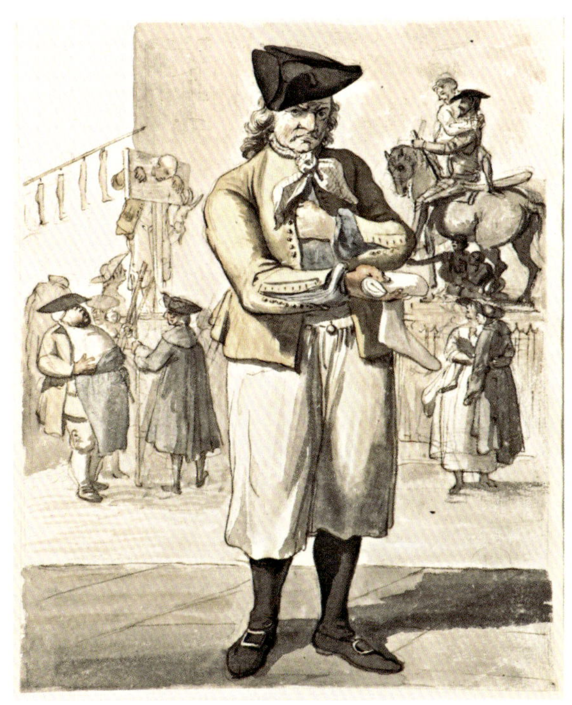

CAT. 45

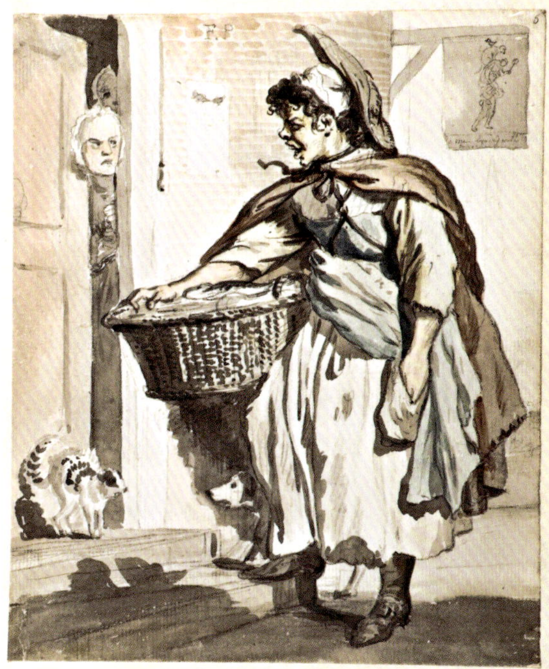

CAT. 46

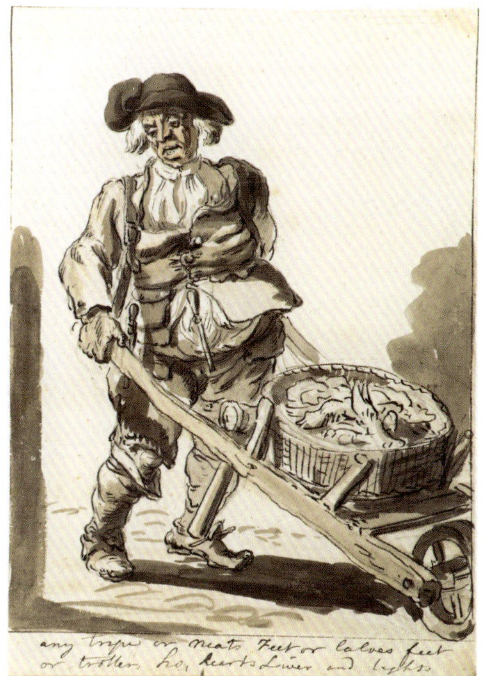

CAT. 47

48

Morning – view on the road near Bayswater turnpike, 1790

Watercolour over graphite, 648 × 890 mm
Signed and dated: 'P. Sandby 1790' (l.r.)
Victoria and Albert Museum, London, D1831-1904

PROVENANCE
Presented by William Sandby, 1904

SELECTED EXHIBITIONS
RA 1791, no. 586; Nottingham 1884, no. 157; London 1960, no. 42; London 1986, no. 24; London 2001, no. 189

SELECTED REFERENCES
London 1986, no. 24, p. 106

In 1772 Sandby moved out of the centre of London and into one of the rapidly developing western suburbs, taking a house at 4 St George's Row overlooking Hyde Park. The location provided the artist with a variety of subjects, with the flow of traffic around the turnpike gate making it a particularly favoured motif.

Large companion views of the turnpike, looking along the road east and west (fig. 40), at the beginning and end of the working day, were exhibited at the Royal Academy in 1791. They demonstrate Sandby's keen interest in the movement of people and things in this rapidly developing London suburb. In the morning view, depicting the gateway from the forecourt of the Swan Inn, which still exists today, no less than 33 figures go about their business. They include a foreground group of builders mixing mortar, in a witty echo of the artist's work, fetching buckets of water from the Westbourne stream, which runs under the road into the Serpentine lake and Kensington Gardens, marked by the profusion of ornamental trees beyond the far wall. On the opposite side of the road, approaching the Bayswater sign, a procession of elegant laundresses heads for the stream. One is distracted by the attention of a passing, mounted officer, perhaps the commander of the troops resting in front of the Swan. Staff serve refreshments to two itinerant agricultural labourers, as well as passing carters. Along the road itself, approaching the tollgate, are two prancing horse riders, and down the hill in the distance comes a stage heading out of London. This range of incident, focused on the passage of goods, people and things through this city conduit, conveys much about the physical and human geography of the place, its situation, settlement and recent development.

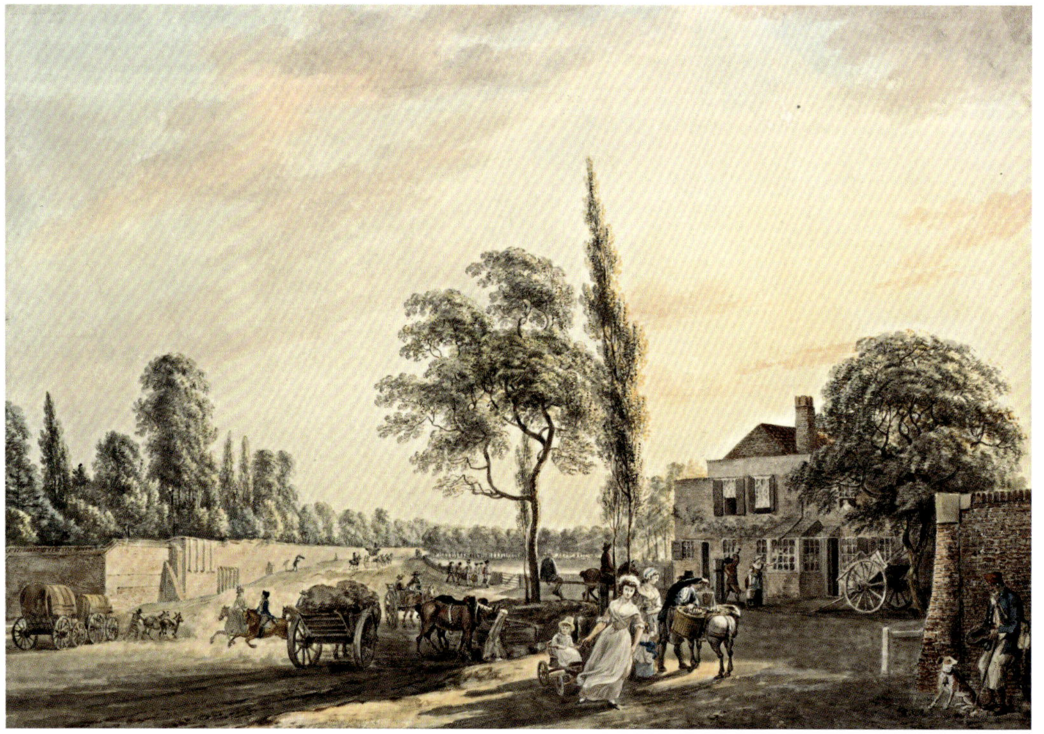

FIG. 40
Paul Sandby, *Evening view near Bayswater*, 1791. Watercolour over graphite, 635 × 885 mm. Private collection, courtesy of Sotheby's

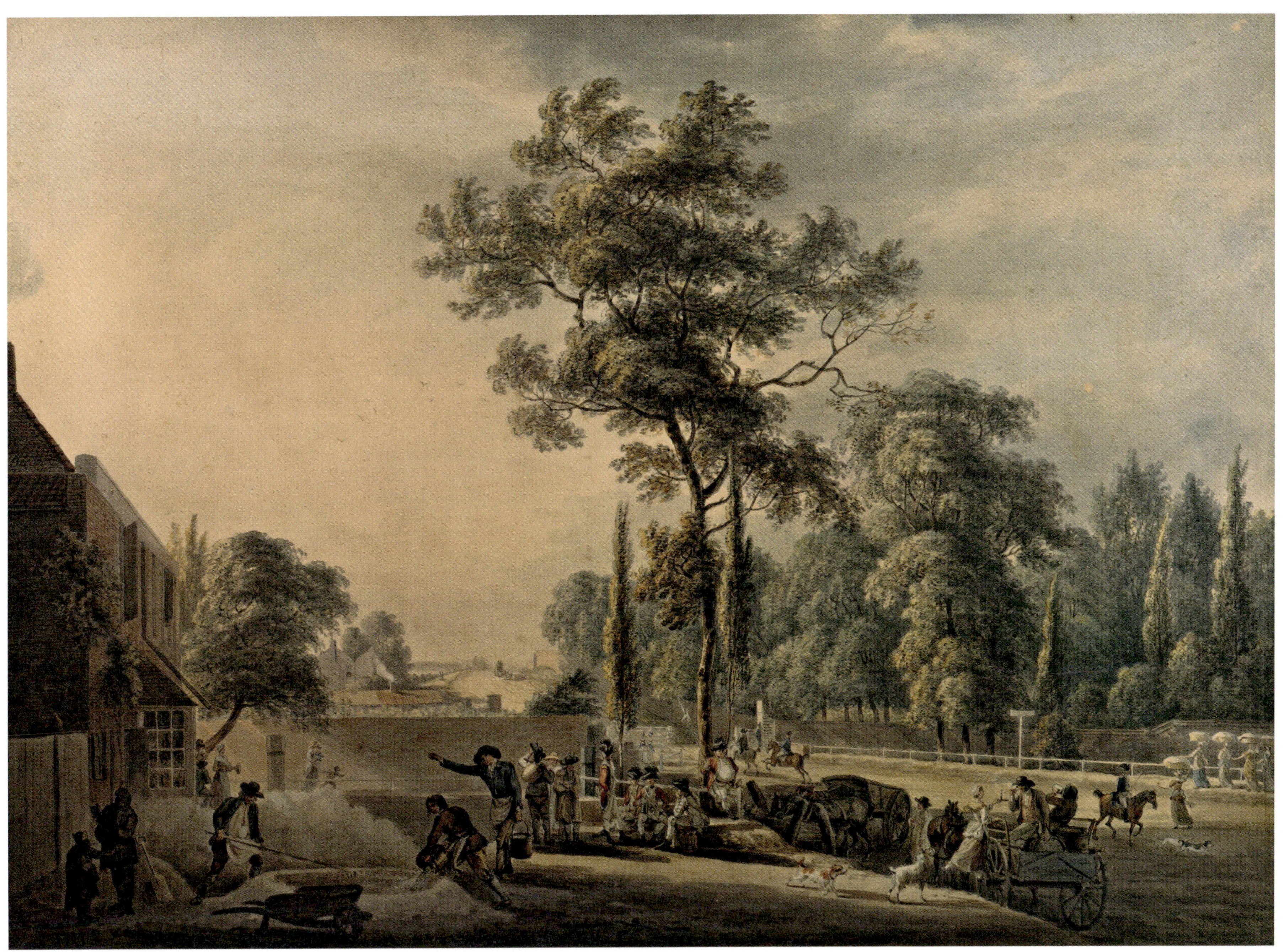

49

PAUL AND THOMAS SANDBY

The Camp on Warley Common, 1778

Pen, ink and watercolour, 491 × 1473 mm
Royal Collection, London, RL 14729

PROVENANCE
Presumably painted for George III

SELECTED EXHIBITIONS
London 2004, no. 193

SELECTED REFERENCES
Oppé 1947, no. 158, pp. 47–8; London 2004, no. 193, pp. 218–19

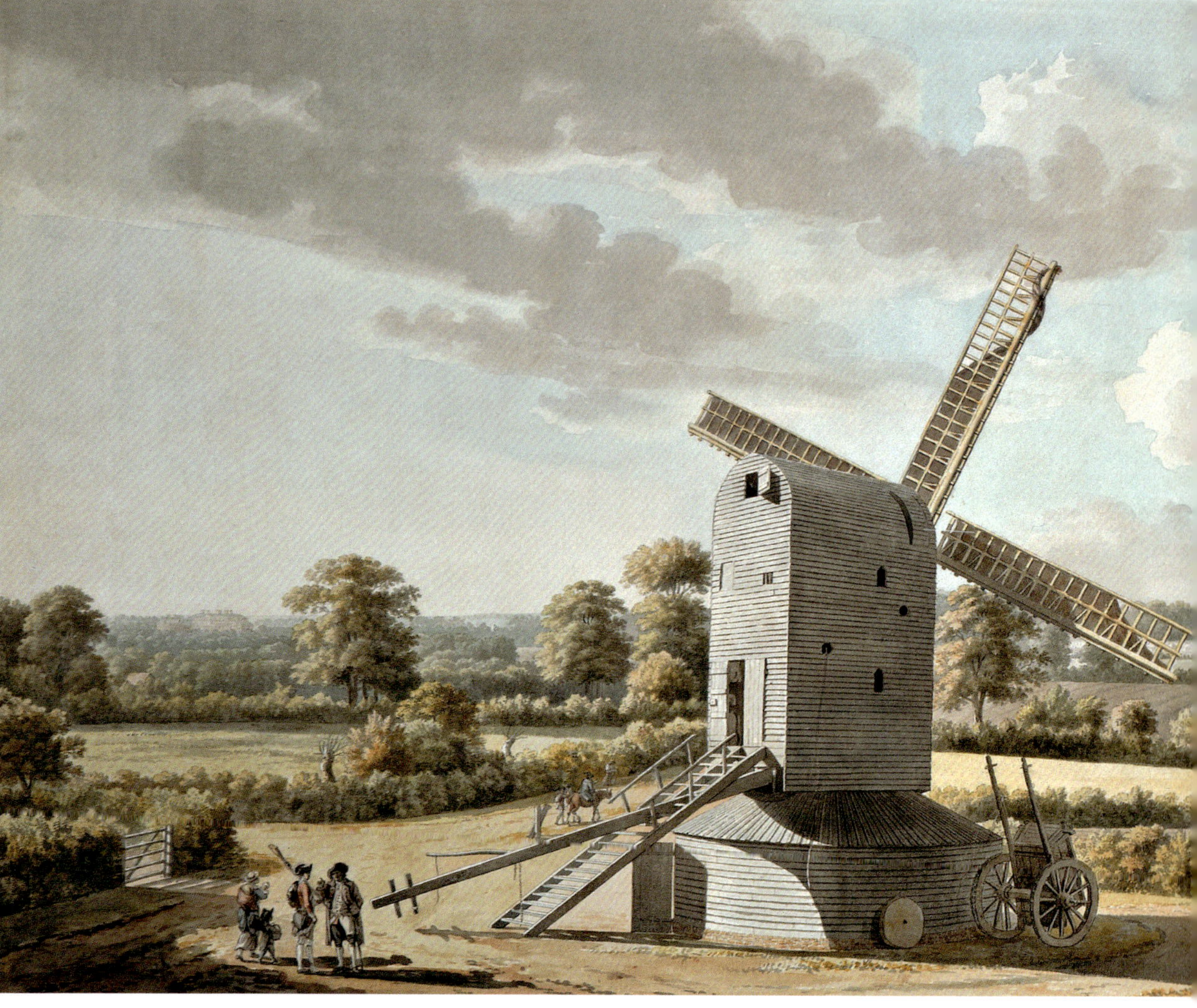

Over the summer of 1778 London's exhibition rooms, pleasure gardens and theatres faced competition from compelling 'shows' in the suburbs, in the form of large military camps at Coxheath, near Maidstone, and Warley Common, near Brentwood. These encampments had a sound practical purpose: to train a combined force of regular militia and newly founded volunteer regiments in the arts of war, necessary for the defence of the realm at a time of national crisis. Overstretched by the war with American colonists across the Atlantic, Britain had left her home shores vulnerable to invasion from the traditional enemy, the French, who had recently allied themselves to the American rebels. Coxheath and Warley Common were the largest of a series of encampments, located at strategic points across the country, that were intended to frustrate the advance of any invading force and give some reassurance to a concerned populace. With reassurance the objective, the public was positively encouraged to visit the camps. Indeed, they were soon to become as much sites of polite assembly and spectacle as strategic defensive measures. The encampments' cacophony of movement, colour and sound – the drills, manoeuvres and sham battles that were an essential part of an army's preparations – quickly caught the public imagination, attracting the height of fashionable London society, the 'middling Cit' and the lowest of the artisan class alike. Reports of the camps and the free exchange between military personnel and the civilian population that they appeared to licence were a constant preoccupation of the metropolitan press for the duration of the invasion crisis. 'Camp intelligence' provided the gossip columns of the day with an apparently endless source of tittle-tattle and scandal, which in turn fed the opportunist productions of countless Grub Street hacks, printmakers and playhouses (Russell 1995, pp. 26–51).

Yet these hastily assembled encampments also encouraged the most fervent of loyalist addresses, inspiring patriotic song and verse. It was widely hoped that the glories of the Seven Years War might be revisited and that, following recent defeats in the American colonies, Britain's military reputation might be restored. The encampments have, therefore, been seen as significant in promoting national belonging (Conway 1997). They were clearly of value in acclimatising a country long suspicious of a monarch at the head of massed armed ranks to such a grand spectacle. On 19–20 October 1778, George III visited Warley, where 'his Majesty on horseback, attended by his suite, and also by general Amherst, reviewed the troops', watching events unfold 'from a stand erected by Lord Petre in the centre of the scene' (*Annual Register*, 1779, p. 237). During their two-

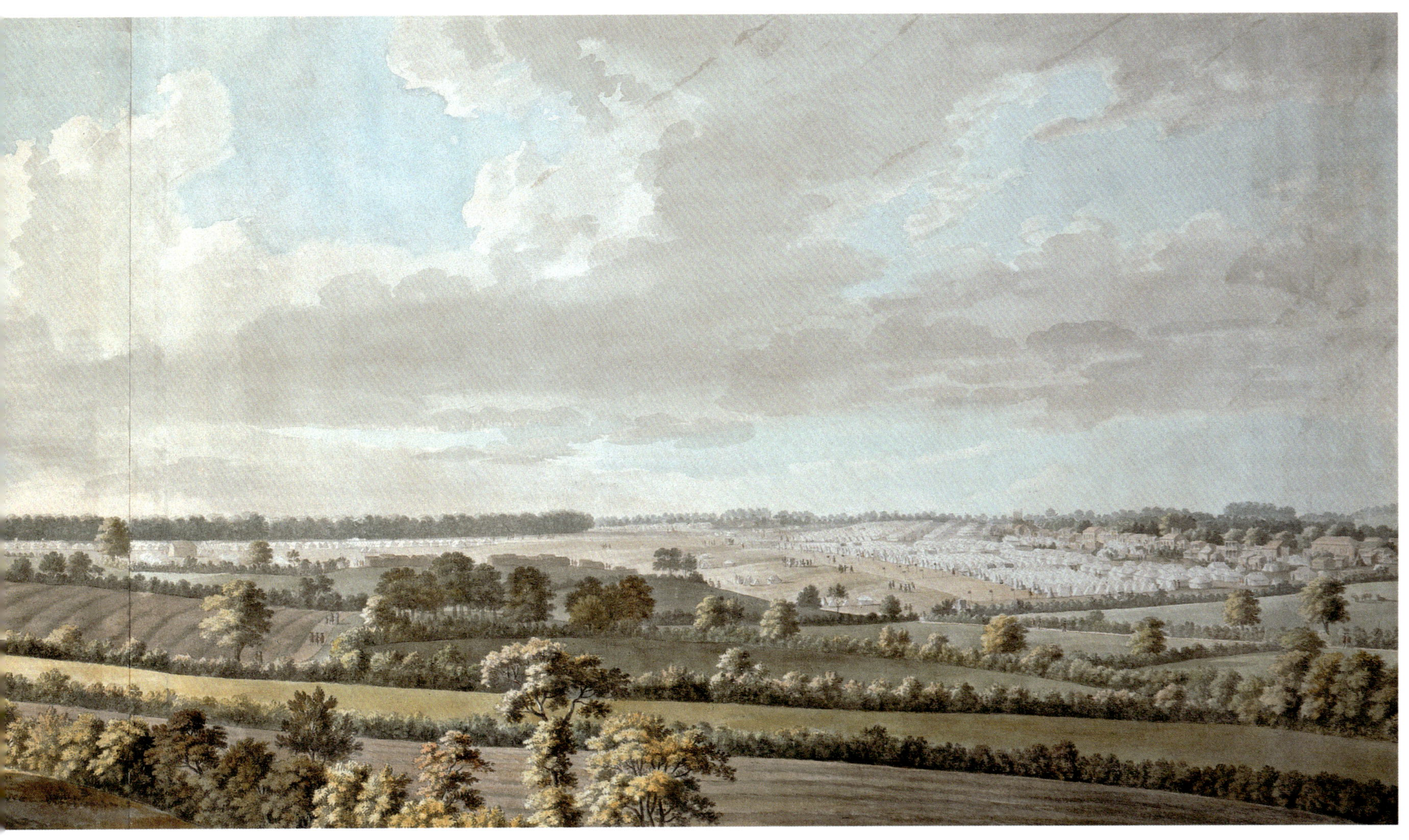

day visit the King and his consort Queen Charlotte also witnessed a carefully choreographed but spectacular mock battle, as was recorded in a pair of major paintings by Philippe Jacques de Loutherbourg that were presented to the King by one of the commanders that day, Captain Pierson (Royal Collection, London). Other commemorative tokens of this regal visitation included elaborate plans of the day's manoeuvres and the Sandbys' magnificent panorama of the camp.

On visiting Warley, Samuel Johnson considered it 'one of the great scenes of human life' (Johnson 1992–94, vol. 3, p. 128). Visiting crowds and the large number of military personnel transformed the local economy and landscape, with makeshift eating and ale houses quickly establishing themselves alongside the camp's tents and parade and artillery grounds. This was a militarised landscape, but also one that presented assorted pleasures. One London newspaper, *The Gazetteer and New Daily Advertiser*, noted that 'formed on the side of a hill', the camp afforded 'a beautiful view of Kent and the River Thames' (29 May 1778). This temporary landscape was spread over a number of acres of common land, adjacent to Lord Petre's Thorndon estate. The Sandbys' survey of this terrain carefully distinguishes pasture from arable land, the common heath occupied by the encampment from the cultivated grounds surrounding Petre's Thorndon Hall to the far left of the composition. This is all depicted with a meticulous, microscopic detail, recalling the pictorial records of encampments in the Low Countries that Thomas Sandby had made for Cumberland in the late 1740s (fig. 34). It also looks back to the Sandby brothers' very earliest collaborations, in reusing foreground figures datable to their period in Edinburgh and the view of Fort Augustus (cats 3 and 32.2).

CATALOGUE NUMBERS 50–52

Over six days in early June 1780 the streets of London and Westminster were overrun by a rioting mob protesting against the limited concessions of the first Catholic Relief Act, passed by Parliament two years earlier. A week of sustained violence in the capital followed an initially peaceful gathering in St George's Fields and a march upon the House of Commons to present a petition against the Act to Parliament. Co-ordinated by the Protestant Association under the presidency of Lord George Gordon, this semi-official protest was soon hijacked by an uncontrollable mob. Enraged by the numerous handbills, broadsheets and pamphlets circulating in the capital, as well as the many meetings of debating societies championing the slogan 'No Popery', the incensed crowd were led to riot. With civil disorder escalating, the army – which could draw on a reserve of some 12,000 men – was used in a determined fashion: 285 rioters were killed, 173 injured and another 25 subsequently hanged.

Encampments were established in St James's Park, Hyde Park and the gardens of Montagu House, with the troops comprising the latter then moving on to the defence of Blackheath Common. Remaining in place for several months, these camps, like Coxheath and Warley before them, quickly became places of fashionable parade and entertainment. The letterpress accompanying the views of the camps that were engraved by James Fittler and Francis Chesham after designs by Sandby for the serial publication *The Virtuosi's Museum* states: 'The novelty of such spectacles in London, together with their excellent bands of music, who performed some of our best compositions morning and evening, naturally captivated the multitude.' Sensing the likely marketability of the theme, Sandby sent several camp views for exhibition at the Royal Academy a matter of months after these prints first appeared. At least one of these three drawings was among that group, probably intended to publicise a related set of aquatints published between early June 1781, the first anniversary of the riots, and 1783.

Their fate, on being displayed in the Royal Academy's Great Room at Somerset House in the summer of 1781, reveals the status of tinted drawings in the exhibition rooms of the period. *The Public*

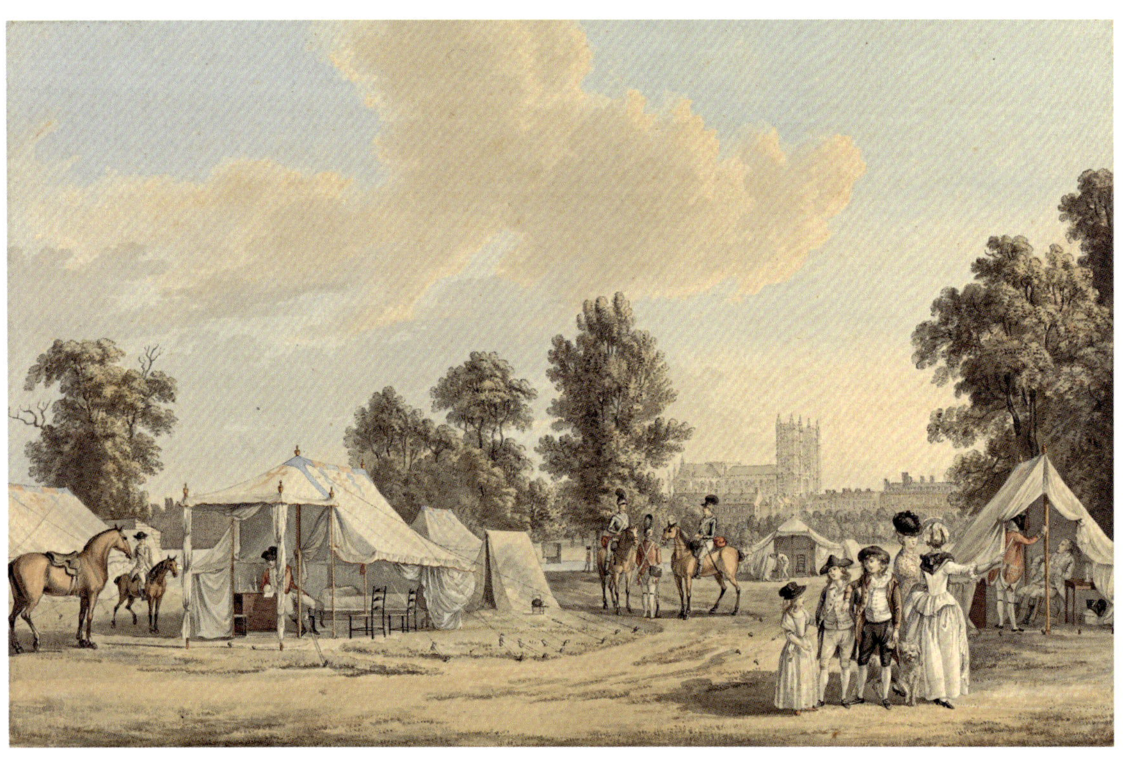

50

View of the encampment in St James's Park, c. 1780

Pen, ink and watercolour over graphite, 305 × 457 mm
Yale Center for British Art, New Haven, Paul Mellon Collection, B1981.25.2690

PROVENANCE
6th Earl of Harewood; 7th Earl of Harewood; Christie's, 13 July 1965

SELECTED EXHIBITIONS
RA 1781, no. 156?; Yale 1985, no. 112; London 2001, no. 182; Yale 2007, no. 6

SELECTED REFERENCES
Yale 1985, no. 112, pp. 84–86; Richmond 2007, pp. 20–22

51
View of the encampment in Hyde Park, c. 1780

Pen, ink and watercolour over graphite, 290 × 471 mm
Birmingham Museum and Art Gallery, 1953P80

PROVENANCE
The Rt Hon. H. O. Garrold Forster; bequeathed by J. Leslie Wright, 1954

SELECTED EXHIBITIONS
London 1960, no. 49; Nottingham 1986, n.n.

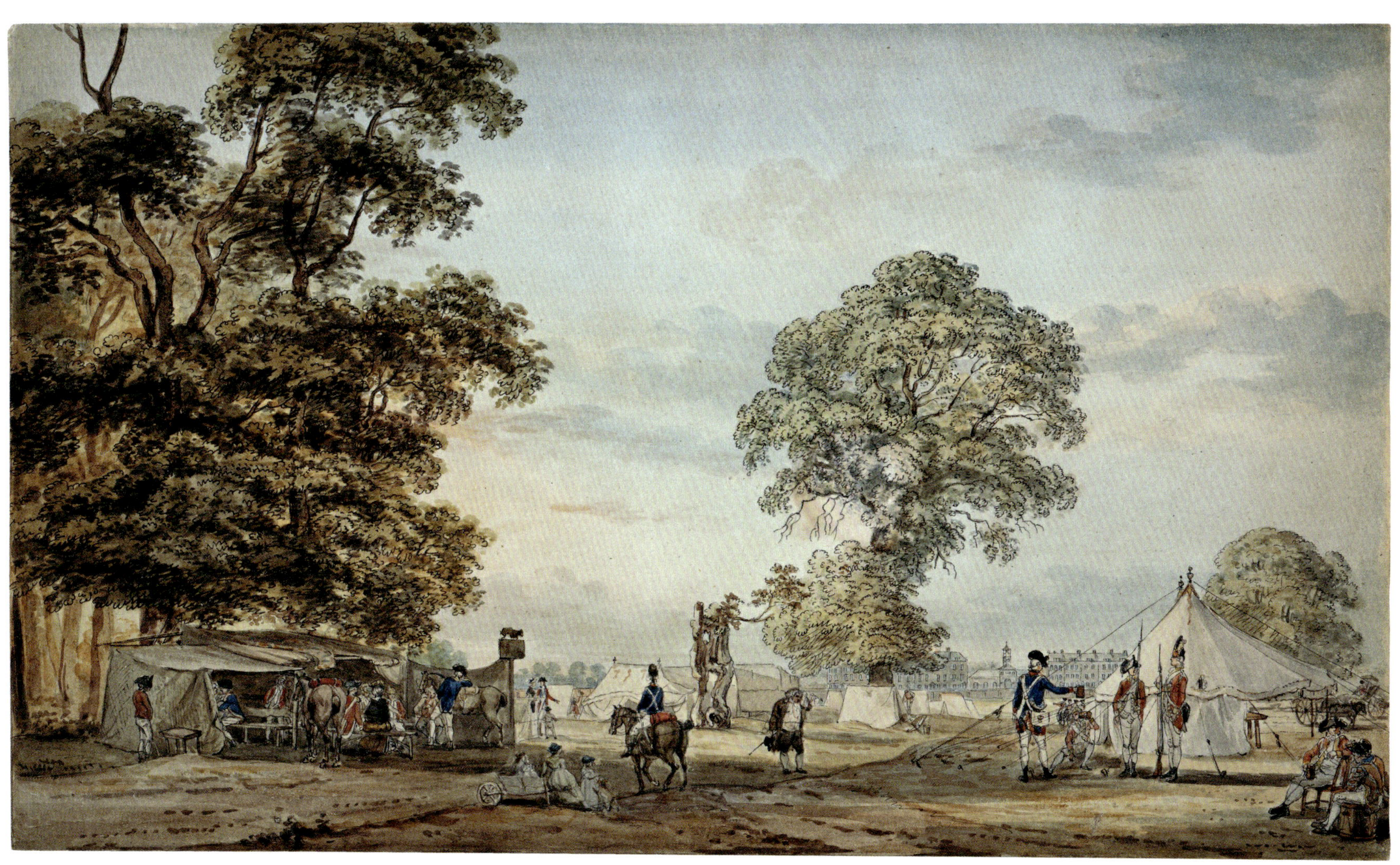

52

View of the encampment on Blackheath, c. 1780

Pen, ink and watercolour over graphite, 305 × 453 mm
Department of Prints and Drawings, British Museum, London, 1850-8-10-524

PROVENANCE
Purchased from A. E. Evans & Sons, 1850

SELECTED EXHIBITIONS
Nottingham 1986, n.n.

SELECTED REFERENCES
Binyon 1898–1907, no. 111, IV, 19

Advertiser (3 May 1781) noted that 'they are *below* the Level of the Spectator's Eye'. Nevertheless, the critic assured his readership 'they are *Sandby*'s, and they will *recompense* any Person for his stooping'. Other reviewers willing to inconvenience themselves were also to consider these works noteworthy, with the *St James's Chronicle* (15–17 May 1781) finding 'The Skies are beautiful, the Trees well touched; and they abound in a Variety of Figures, which make them particularly interesting'. This was not the only commentary to draw attention to the varied staffage of these views, the *London Courant*'s critic describing them (8 May 1781) as 'elegantly grouped, not without humour; nicely drawn and well touched'.

There was also a droll element to the description of the camps accompanying the original prints, as it slyly acknowledged how 'officers of every rank seemed to vie with each other in attention to their numerous visitors, not only inviting them, though strangers, into their markee's, but entertaining them also (the ladies particularly) with variety of refreshments'. Such gentle humour is also very much part of these images, especially in those variously drunk or amorous figures 'guarding' Hyde Park. On one hand, such elements concur with the numerous literary and visual satires of camp life in the period, which would often delight in the comic or erotic frisson afforded by officers' encounters with visitors (see Russell 1995, pp. 26–51). On the other hand, Sandby's figures make reference to the markedly different social character of each of the encampments. Correspondingly, the more elegant figures of the St James's Park scene might be seen to refer to the élite Regulars allotted to this royal landscape and the protection of an array of monarchical residences. In contrast, the encampments in Hyde Park and Blackheath were comprised principally of militia troops drawn, in the main, from the provinces. Having been embedded in military culture for much of his career, Sandby would have been highly attuned to distinctions in the make-up of the troops assigned to each of the camps and the relative strategic significance of their locations. Indeed, many of his Woolwich Academy pupils were active in drawing up plans and maps of these encampments (Royal Collection, London).

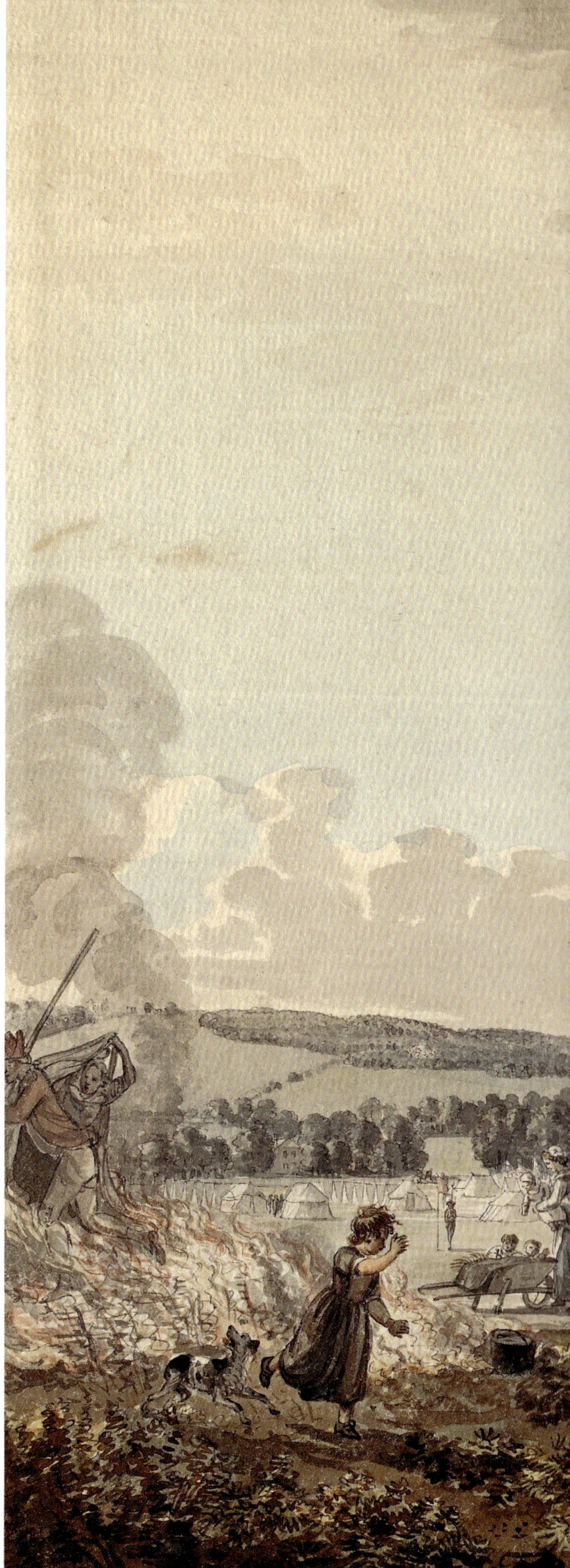

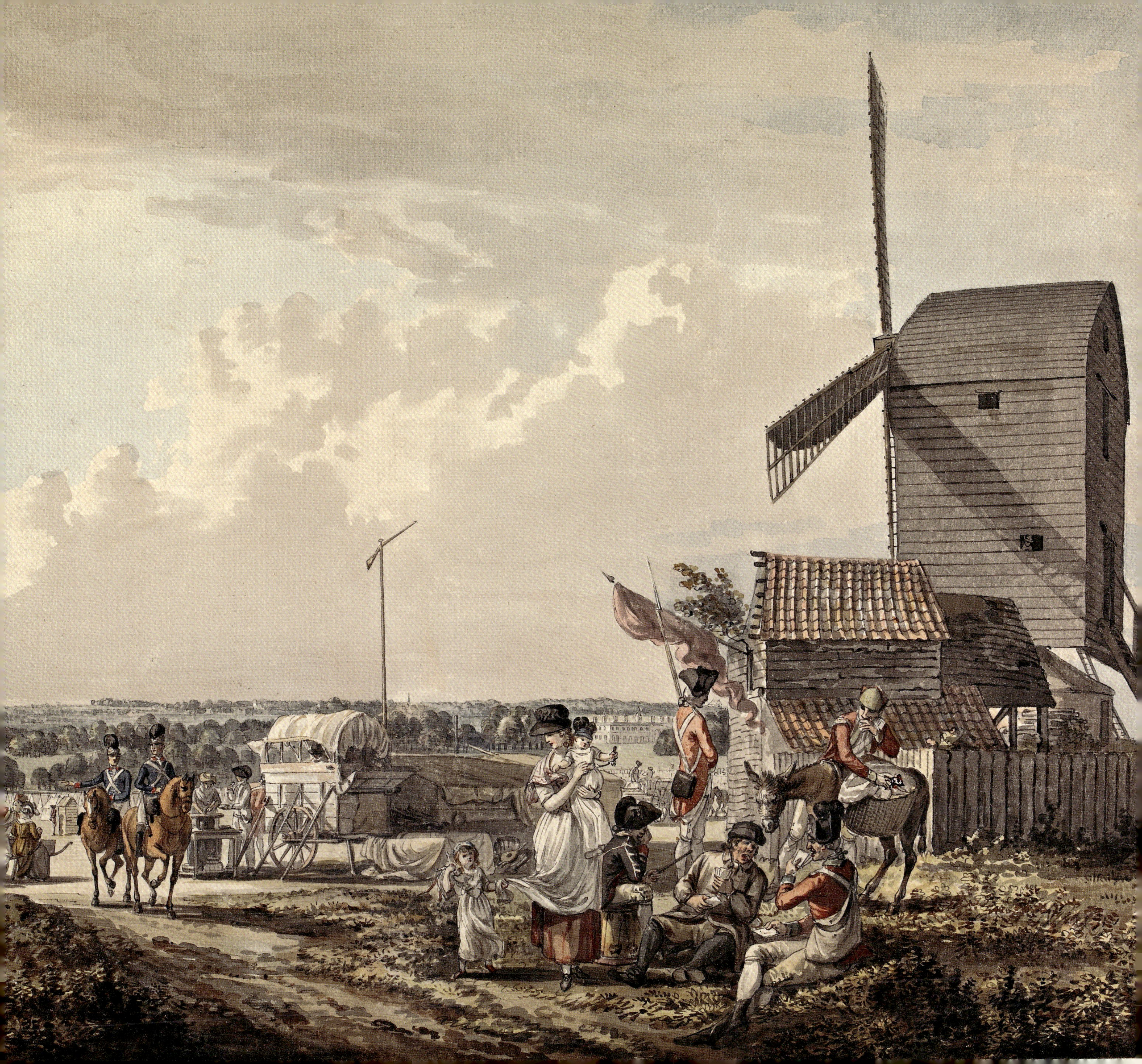

53

PAUL AND THOMAS SANDBY

View to the west from the gardens of Somerset House, before 1776

Pen, ink, wash and watercolour over graphite, 467 × 1924 mm
Department of Prints and Drawings, British Museum, London, G.13-30

PROVENANCE
Bequeathed by John Charles Crowle, 1811

SELECTED EXHIBITIONS
London 1985, no. 21b; London 1990, n.n.; London 2003A, no. 2.34

SELECTED REFERENCES
Robertson 1987, pp. 110–11; London 2003A, no. 2.34, pp. 125–27

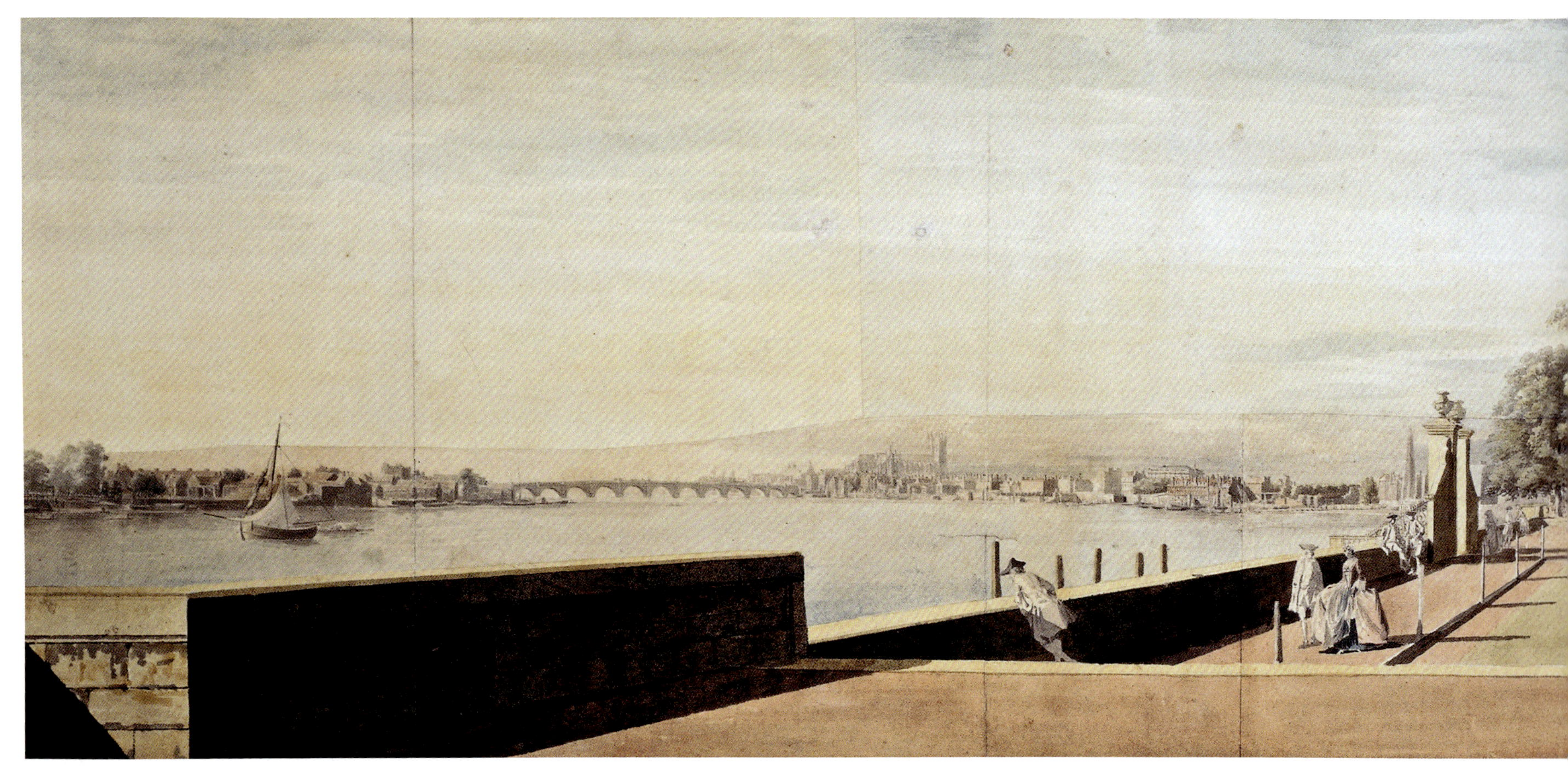

CATALOGUE NUMBERS 53–54

Views from the gardens and river walk of old Somerset House had long been popular with artists and urban tourists alike. Situated on a bend of the River Thames, the terrace afforded expansive prospects upstream, towards the City of Westminster, and downstream, towards the City of London. Pendant views, looking east and west, published in 1751 by Edward Rooker and Johann Sebastian Mueller, after the Italian painter of *vedute*, Canaletto, were perhaps the best-known topographical images of the river from this vantage point. They were almost certainly known to the Sandbys, very probably in the original oils sold to George III by the Venetian consul Joseph Smith in 1762 (Yale 2006A, pp. 62–69). While clearly trafficking with such earlier views, not least in a shared implied parallel with the imagery of another mighty maritime power, Venice, the Sandbys' panoramic survey of this stretch of water is nonetheless distinguished by its accumulation of detail, information and range of association.

Although damaged and unfinished, the pair of works exemplify the elder brother's mastery of minutely calibrated, controlled recession and precise, meticulous observation. In the view east, a succession of microscopically delineated architectural landmarks – St Paul's, the spires and towers of the City's churches and the Monument – rise above the crowded, narrow and irregular warehouses of the waterfront. This contrast of grand public works with haphazard commercial structures is also a notable feature of the pendant view, looking west towards historic Westminster Abbey and the modern, neo-Palladian wonder of Westminster Bridge. Further contrasts are drawn between the manicured, ornamental gardens and the irregular layout of riverside warehouses and wharfs, and between the polite, leisured assembly of Paul Sandby's foreground figures and the busy,

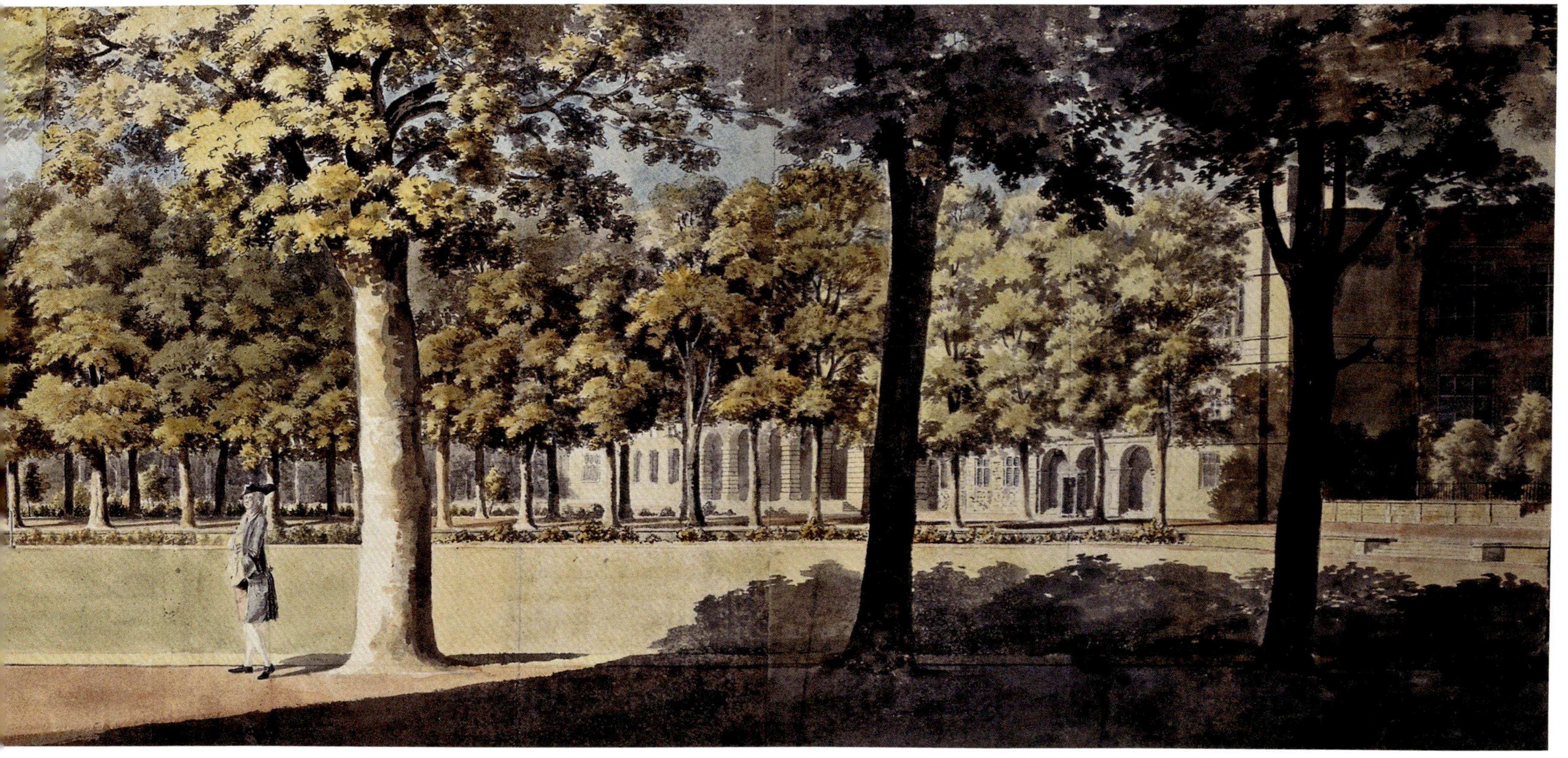

54

PAUL AND THOMAS SANDBY

View to the east from the gardens of Somerset House, before 1776

Pen, ink and watercolour over graphite, 514 × 1893 mm
Department of Prints and Drawings, British Museum, London, G.13-31

PROVENANCE
Bequeathed by John Charles Crowle, 1811

SELECTED EXHIBITIONS
London 1985, no. 21b; Nottingham 1986, n.n.; London 1990, n.n.; London 2003A, no. 2.35

SELECTED REFERENCES
London 2003A, no. 2.35, pp. 125–27

industrious activity of the waterway stretching out a few feet below.

This was a site of no little significance to the elder Sandby, who made a number of drawings of old Somerset House before its demolition in 1776, probably in deference to the building's associations with another royal architect, Inigo Jones, who was responsible for the river stairs and possibly the palace's riverfront gallery. That the design of grand civic buildings such as this, or those that dominated the London skyline from this vantage point, was the noblest task of the architect was central to Thomas Sandby's thought, as is illustrated by the lectures he was to deliver to the architectural students of the Royal Academy Schools within a few years of making these drawings. These were the ideals that informed Sandby's designs for a Bridge of Magnificence, for example, illustrating his sixth and final Academy lecture on matters of 'Taste, Symmetry and Grandeur' (fig. 11). Over 40 elevations, plans and sections for the bridge, which was intended to span the Thames at Sir William Chambers's new Somerset House, the building that replaced the palace depicted here, demonstrated the wedding of art and utilitarian function in a structure serving civic needs. A full

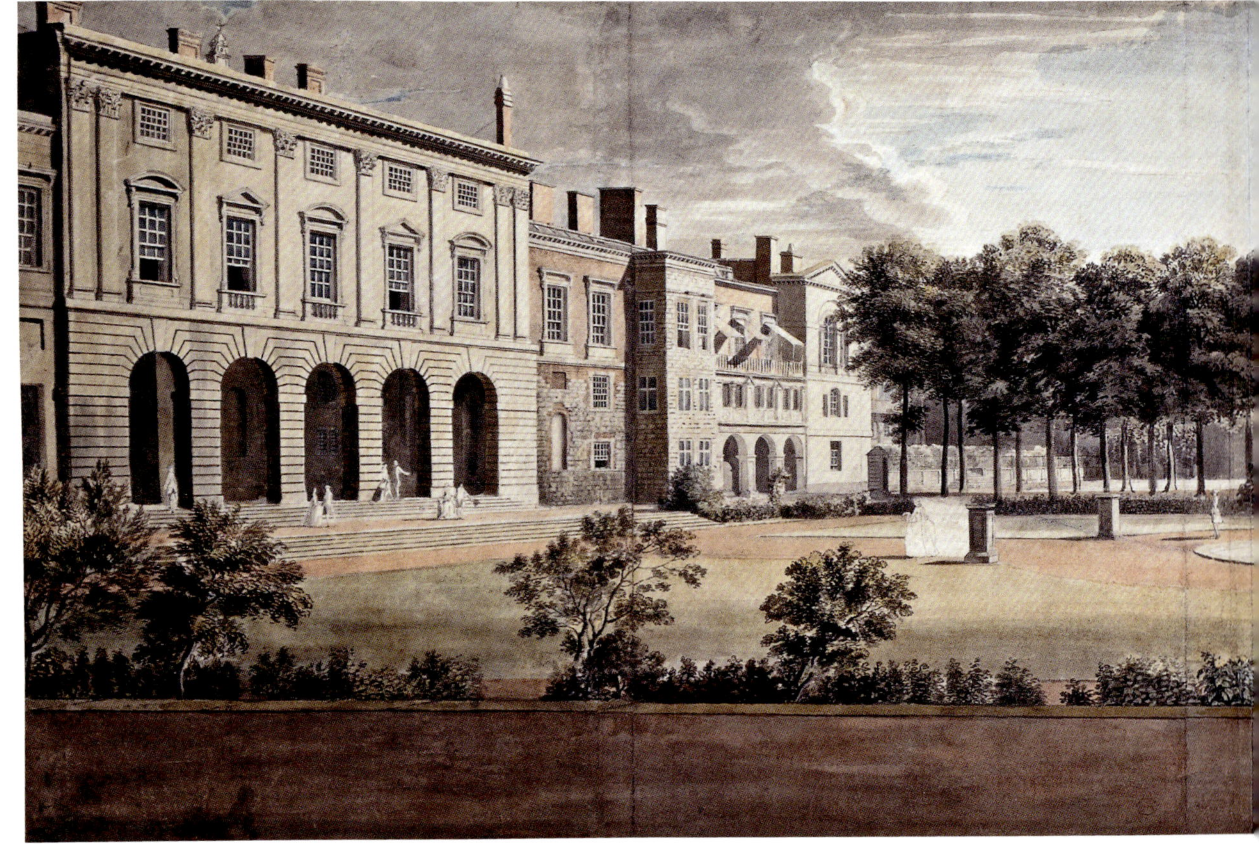

elevation, some sixteen feet in length, was unfurled at the close of the lecture (RIBA, London). Drawings of the bridge exhibited at the Royal Academy in 1781 were much admired by newspaper critics. Expressing a hope of seeing the work actually commissioned, one writer, acknowledging its poetic, sublime quality, observed 'the Motion for it, in the House of Commons, should originate with Mr *Burke*' (*Public Advertiser*, 8 May 1781).

In the course of that final lecture, Sandby made approving reference to his friend John Gwynn's remarkable *London and Westminster Improved* and its advocacy of an architecture of 'Publick Magnificence'. Published in 1766, and therefore probably contemporary with these views from old Somerset House, Gwynn's book had called for a radical series of urban improvements, comprising grand new palaces, streets and squares, affording striking vistas. Such a cityscape was considered by Gwynn justly fitting for the capital of a country which now, in the wake of the dramatic victories of the Seven Years War, rivalled the grandest cultures of the past:

> The English are now what the Romans were of old, distinguished like them by power and opulence, and excelling all other nations in commerce and navigation. Our wisdom is respected, our laws are envied, and our dominions are spread over a large part of the globe.
> (Gwynn 1766, p. xv)

In their record of a thriving cityscape, dominated by architectural landmarks ancient and modern, the Sandbys' views along the Thames can be seen to accord entirely with such a grand, imperial conception of London.

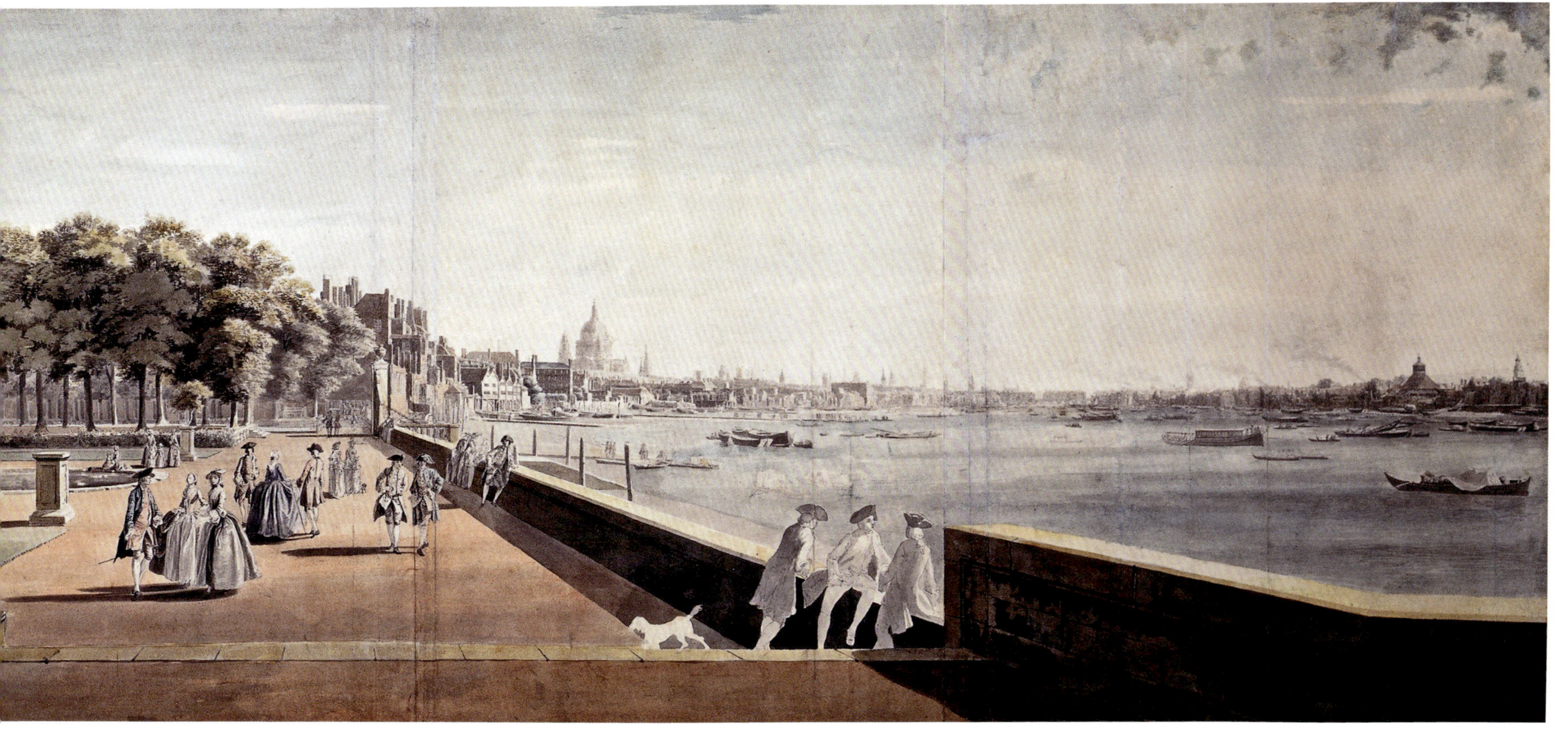

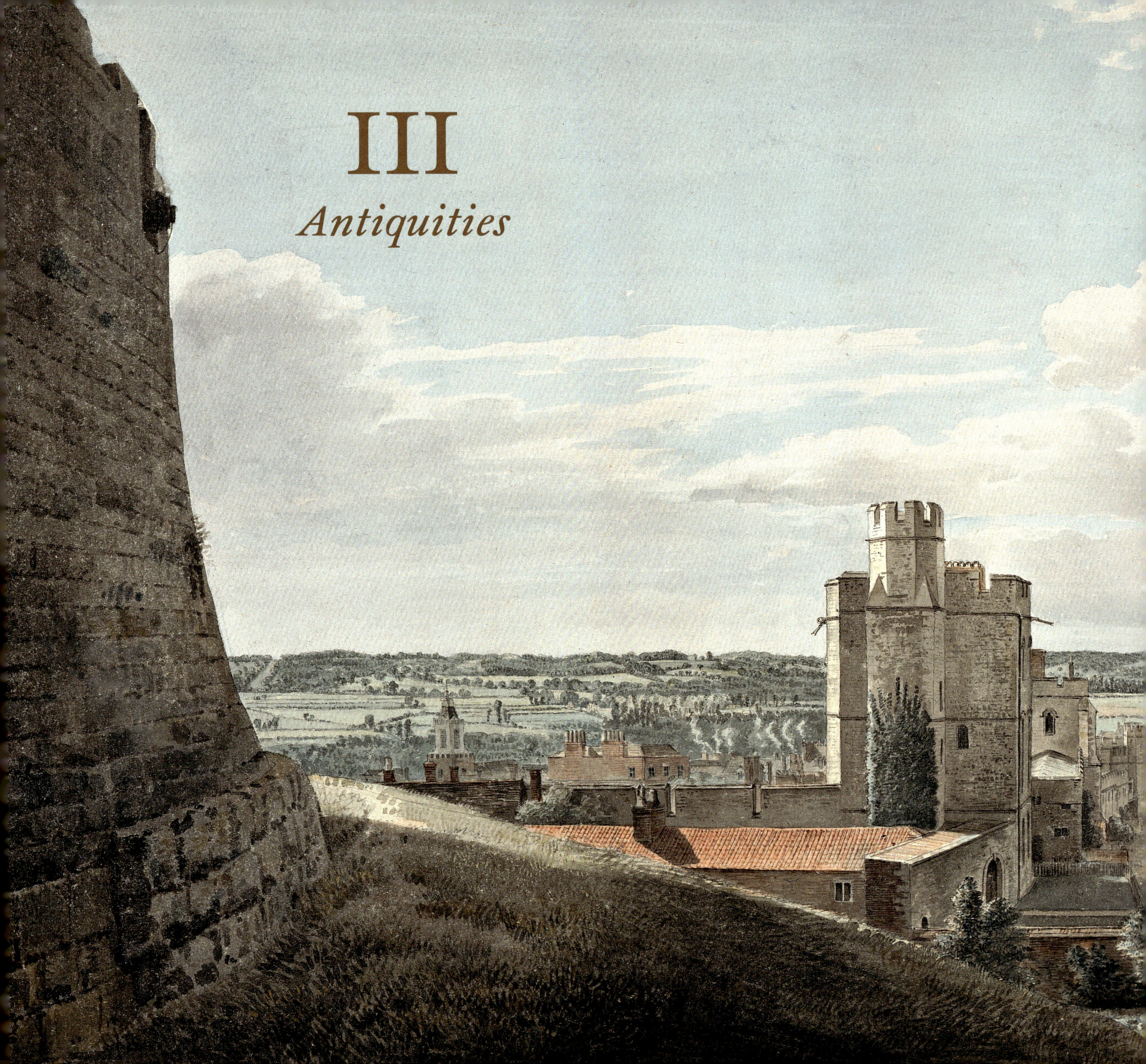

III

Antiquities

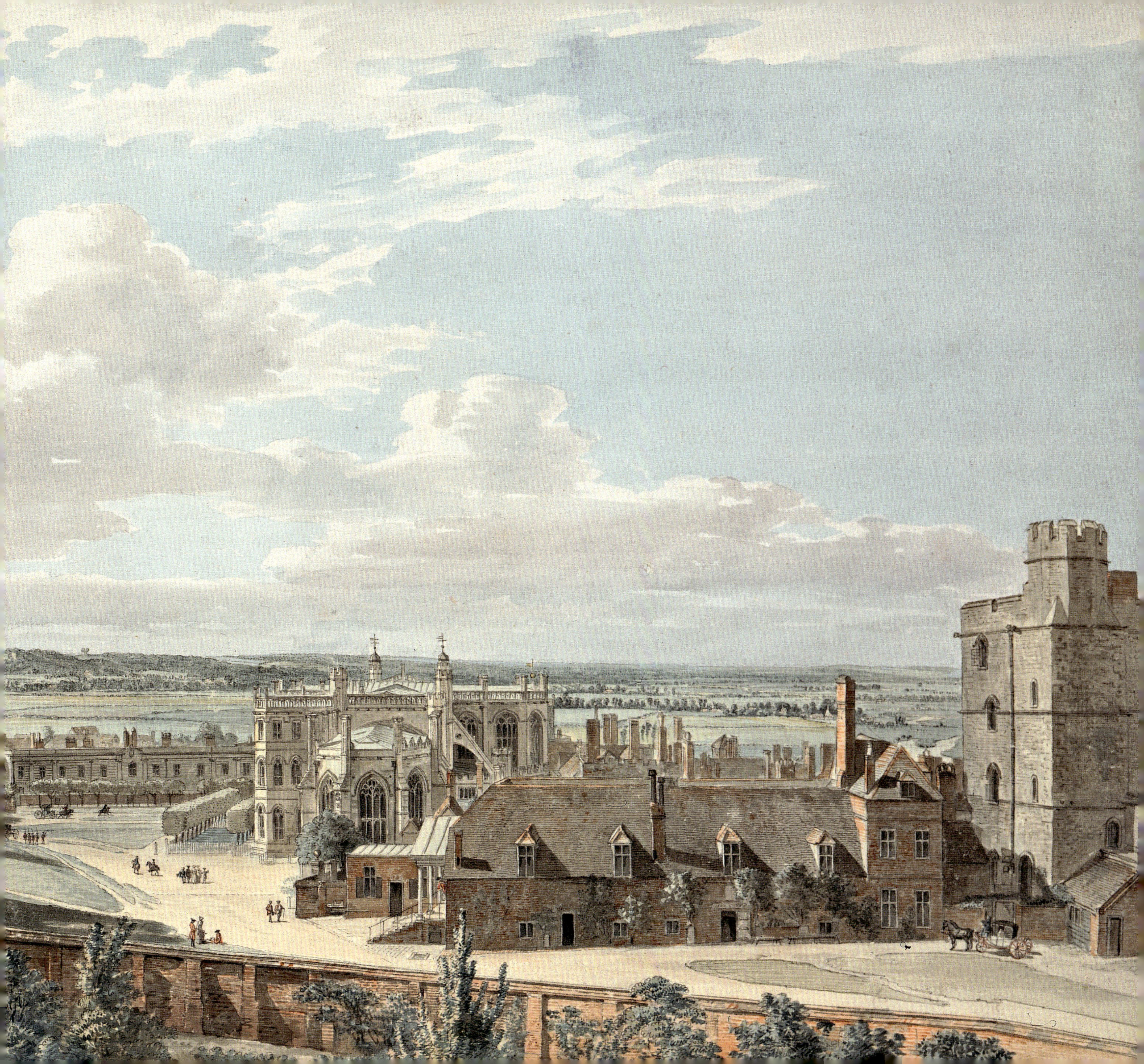

IN AUGUST 1796 a brief account of Paul Sandby's career appeared in the *European Magazine and London Review*. Such biographical vignettes, a prominent feature of this and other periodicals at the time, played an important role in generating publicity and maintaining an artist's public profile. Published at a time when a new generation of artists with ambitions to advance the scope and standing of 'painters in water-colours' had begun to emerge, the article puffed Sandby's pioneering status in the art. His famed depictions of the country's antiquities, just the kind of motifs that were the principal focus of the early exhibits of figures like Thomas Girtin or J. M. W. Turner, were singled out for particular praise:

> For force, clearness, and transparency, it may very truly be said that his Paintings in water colours have not yet been equalled; the Views of Castles, Ruins, Bridges, & c. which are frequently introduced, will remain monuments to the honour of the Arts, the Artists, and the Country, when the originals from which they are designed are mouldering into dust.
> (*European Magazine*, 1796, p. 75)

Early patrons of young artists then making a name for themselves in developing watercolour included a number with antiquarian interests (see London 2002). Girtin and his contemporaries were, however, also responding to a well-developed market for topographical views, buoyed by the popularity of domestic tourism among the leisured and moneyed classes. As the author of the *European Magazine*'s memoir suggested, this was a clientele that Sandby had been instrumental in first exploiting. Views of the nation's ancient monuments, especially its ruined abbeys and castles, established as part of a wider landscape, were by far the most prominent feature of his drawn or printed designs. They held a particular appeal, notably when made available as a print, to those growing numbers who toured the country each summer in search of the picturesque.

Views of historic architectural remains had been a part of Sandby's art from the beginning, with the studies of antiquities that he made while at work on the Military Survey of North Britain holding a particular fascination and value for many leading antiquarians. Their interest in

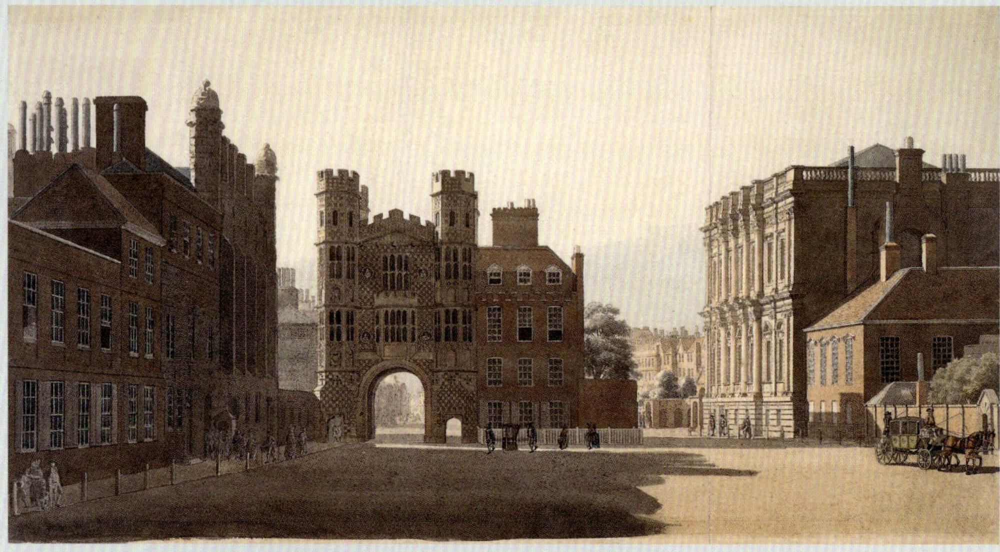

FIG. 41
Paul and Thomas Sandby, *Whitehall with the so-called Holbein Gate*, c. 1750s. Pen, ink and watercolour, 326 × 563 mm. British Museum, London, 1941, 0618.1

Sandby's art was prompted by a growing concern to record, evaluate and preserve the country's architectural heritage. Although neither brother was a member of the Society of Antiquaries of London, both Sandbys were close to prominent figures who were and they sympathised with its concern to document the historical fabric of the country. Their meticulously delineated studies of Whitehall, executed just before the demolition of the so-called Holbein Gate (fig. 41), are to be aligned with the antiquarian impulse to record and thus preserve in paper form a historic heritage that was about to moulder 'into dust' or be swept away by modern improvement. Individual studies by Thomas Sandby of the gateway itself, whose materials had been acquired by the Duke of Cumberland with a view to its reassembly at Windsor, are characterised by precision, scrupulous attention to detail, and lack of picturesque effect or stylistic mannerism that were all attractive to those concerned with the provision of accurate visual information (fig. 42).

Beyond their appeal to specialist antiquarian collectors, Paul Sandby's designs enjoyed wider circulation in printed form through serial publications like *The Virtuosi's Museum* (cat. 76). A collection of prints, marketed as a 'cheap and rational amusement', the ensemble made areas of the country visibly more accessible, conveying a sense that the true spirit of the nation lay in its localities, rather than its metropolis. A perusal of this scenery was in itself an 'improving' experience, a 'rational amusement', whereby the purchaser viewed and – in the accompanying letterpress – read of historic structures as well as improvements being made across the national territories. Such publications offered a vicarious tour through a series of national landscapes, or more particularly a succession of estates. Sites such as Roche Abbey, which was featured in the series and also provided the subject for a separate drawing, were often to be encountered as part of a gentleman's estate, in this case that of the Earls of Scarborough (cat. 74). Views of antiquities were frequently related therefore to studies of nearby seats. This concern to represent the nation's heritage and celebrate property or patronage was invariably made explicit in the titling or letterpress of the engraved view, in which tribute was paid to the beneficence of the estate owner. Architectural remnants of the country's past were often placed in the context of estate improvements, whether agricultural, industrial or cultural. This interest in evaluating the place of the past in a rapidly modernising nation is nowhere more apparent than in Sandby's pioneering aquatint views of south Wales, in which pointed contrasts are drawn between agreeable rural scenes of present-day agricultural labour and the ruins of a violent past (cat. 71).

In introducing tourists to Windsor, subject of an important series of views executed by Sandby in the 1760s, one popular guidebook to the area noted that:

> at present the Strength of this Castle is considerably abated, by the Currency of many Years, and from the Excellency of our national Constitution, whereby Fortresses and strong Holds, are not frequent in this Kingdom, and a happy Union between the Prince and Subject is the great Security of both.
> (Pote 1763, p. 3)

A happy peace and prosperity was now to be observed across the kingdom, guaranteed, and kept in harmonious equilibrium, by the constitutional balance achieved by the Glorious Revolution and settlement of 1688. Liberties won were symbolised by those fortresses, now either rebuilt as residences or lying derelict, which had formerly been the focus of so much division. Such structures could elicit

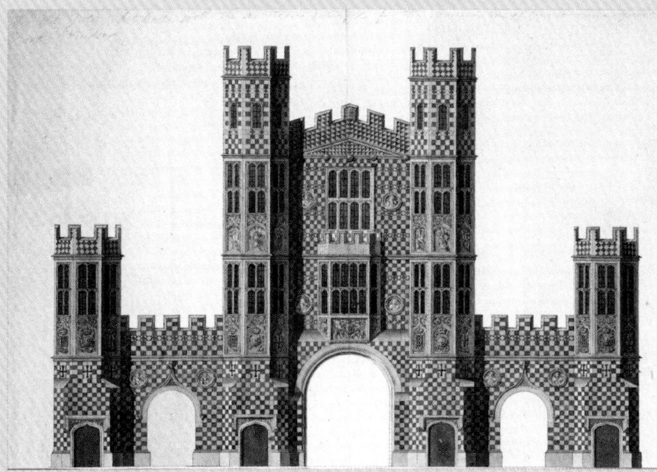

FIG. 42
Thomas Sandby, *The Old Gate, Whitehall, with the additions intended*, *c.* 1760. Pen, ink and watercolour, 484 × 694 mm. Royal Collection, RL 14701

a range of associations, not only moral and sentimental but also political.

Abbeys were similarly rich in association with regard to the nation's history. They were significant as signs of the fragility or transience of human designs, and were thus likely to prompt melancholic thoughts. However, especially when included in scenes of present circumstances, they were also spurs to historical and religious reflection. Abbeys were reminders of a Britain under the tyrannical, ecclesiastical rule of Rome, their now ruined state making them exemplars of the modern nation's triumph over the superstitions of the past. One of Sandby's collaborators, the poet William Mason, made just this point in his influential poem *The English Garden*, where Time's 'gradual touch' had 'moulder'd into beauty' 'many a fane / Monastic, which, when deck'd with all its spires, / Serv'd but to feed some pamper'd Abbot's pride, / And awe th' unletter'd vulgar' (Mason 1783, vol. 1, lines 355–71). Ruins and other antiquities were vehicles for historical reflection on the stages of national social progress, and emblematic of the country's uninterrupted connection with its past. Their depiction in Sandby's art can be seen as part of a broader, ongoing concern with the representation of Britain and Britishness through its historical sites, contemporary architecture and topographies that was also apparent in the enormously influential tours of figures like William Gilpin or the publications of the popularising antiquarian Francis Grose.

According to one early memoir of Paul Sandby's career, the artist's 'many fine drawings, views of the castle and adjacent park' at Windsor were first encouraged by George Brudenell Montagu, Governor of the Castle (Sandby 1811). The views of the fortress and its environs that were executed by Sandby in the 1760s, whether alone or with his elder brother, captured the building and its setting from a range of vantage points. Windsor Castle was not yet what it was to become upon the accession of George III, a permanent, private country residence, segregated from the town, its precincts cleared of shops as well as beggars and street criers. Largely given over to grace-and-favour lodgings, it was in a somewhat shabby, shambolic state. Haphazard modern improvements to the ancient structure, in the form of gravel paths, sash windows or a profusion of chimneys, had diminished its grandeur. Sandby's close-up, fragmentary views, richly attentive to details of masonry, guttering, railings and windows, record these contemporary alterations to the architectural fabric.

There is a parallel to be drawn between Sandby's approach and that of the growing number of guidebooks to the area, such as Joseph Pote's much-reprinted 1755 pocket book *Les Délices de Windsore*. This offered a place-by-place tour, much as Sandby's drawings did, around the precincts of the castle, taking in various forms of spectatorship and a variety of views, including close-ups of gardens and gateways and breathtaking prospects of the Thames valley, such as that from the base of the Round Tower. In Sandby's series, the castle is not seen as an isolated monument but as part of a succession of spaces, including the convivial, commercial areas around the gates that were later cleared away by George III's improvements. Tourists themselves feature prominently, and are depicted idly strolling around the site. Like the traders seen haunting the wards, gateways and adjacent streets, they are as much a part of the spectacle as the royal surroundings.

On exhibition, views of the castle's North Terrace such as those shown here attracted considerable critical approbation, *The Court Miscellany* remarking of a picture on display at the Society of Artists in 1766: 'This drawing is extremely fine, and deserves the highest encomiums.' (*The Court Miscellany*, 1766, p. 239). Such was the popularity of compositions set on this platform, which afforded fine, extensive views out towards Eton, that Sandby continued to exhibit works on the subject as late as 1801. Figures promenading on the terrace are often comic, with some satirical contrast drawn. In the view looking east (cat. 58), an elderly, overdressed couple, whose prancing gait is mimicked by the dogs at their feet, are contrasted with the elegant simplicity of the family group to the right. Comic encounters of social opposites are also a feature of exterior views of the castle, taken from the cramped, 'straggling, and cursed inconvenient' streets of the town (*Sentimental Excursions*, 1781, p. 93). In the view down Castle Hill (cat. 59), figures familiar from the London *Cries*, the chair-mender and peep-show entrepreneur, contrast with the elegant, polite couple in the middle distance. Such a startling conjunction of grand patrician edifice and low plebeian culture is also to be found in the view of the Moat Bridge (cat. 60), where an impoverished, wounded veteran of the Seven Years War and his family are summarily dismissed by a passing parson. In the foreground of the grand, patriotic display of celebratory fireworks depicted in *View of Windsor on a rejoicing night* (cat. 62), a dishevelled drunk, apparently insensible to the pleading of his wife and children, staggers off into the night. As in the London *Cries* that provided many of the figures found in Sandby's Windsor views, there is a notable absence of sentimentality.

Although the comic or mundane and quotidian is often stressed in such pictures, in other instances the castle provided a dramatic, dazzling backdrop. It proves a suitably Gothic setting for the evocation of sublime forces in the startling *The north-east corner of the Castle seen from below, with lightning* (cat. 61), for example. Signs of the sublime, as codified most influentially by Edmund Burke,

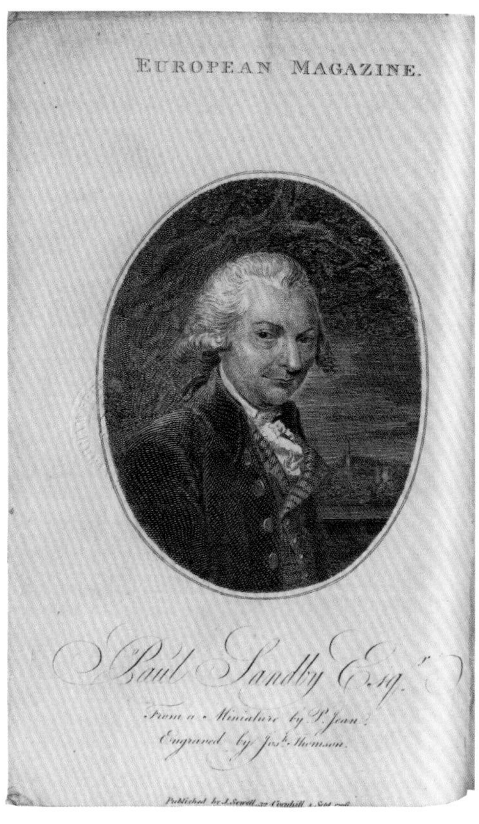

FIG. 43
Joseph Thomson, after Philippe Jean, Portrait of Paul Sandby, from the *European Magazine, and London Review*, August 1796. Birmingham Central Library

dominate the picture. Obscurity, darkness and immensity were all qualities identifiable as sublime, and are summoned here by dramatic contrasts of tone, scale and form. For Burke, sublime terror was peculiarly pleasurable: 'The passions which turn on self-preservation are delightful when we have an idea of pain and danger without actually being in such circumstances' (Burke 1757, p. 51). In Sandby's picture, 'delight' is to be taken in a sympathetic identification with the frightened horse. George Stubbs's recent exhibits, such as the two paintings on the theme of a lion attacking a horse that he sent to the Society of Artists in 1763, had already illustrated the potential for tragic effect in such imagery, as well as its capacity to prompt reflection on the barbaric violence of the wild (Amsterdam 1995, p. 104). However, Sandby's picture may also be connected to the contemporary cultural fascination with the power of atmospheric electricity. A print recording a meteor passing over the castle, illuminating its setting to spectacular effect, and published by Sandby in 1783, similarly showed this historic landscape as a location for the scientific observation of sublime natural phenomena.

Views of Windsor became a mainstay of Sandby's exhibited work, proving popular with critics; paired pictures shown at the Royal Academy in 1775 prompted one reviewer to observe 'what at first may seem a paradox, that the *best* views of Windsor Castle are to be taken from *Pall-mall*' (*London Evening-Post*, 6–9 May 1775). When seen alongside other views of native scenery by artists such as George Barret or William Marlow, pictures like Sandby's *View of Windsor on a rejoicing night*, shown at the Society of Artists in 1768, helped to shape responses to and a taste for the British landscape. They also appealed to such collectors as the noted naturalist Joseph Banks, who purchased upwards of 70 of Sandby's Windsor pictures. A majority of these date from around 1770 and are watercolour replicas of drawings originally executed in bodycolour. One contemporary account of Sandby's career contended that Banks admired them for their 'accuracy, taste, and spirit' (*European Magazine*, 1796, p. 76). An enthusiastic antiquarian, Banks no doubt appreciated the documentary precision with which Sandby recorded the architectural fabric of the castle. Given his prominence in promoting surveys of various kinds, however, he must surely also have valued the artist's careful description of the building's contemporary usage by tourists or by those employed in the industries servicing the castle's residents and visitors, as well as appreciating the rich historic and patriotic associations generated by Sandby's delineation of the castle and its landscape. Such was Sandby's identification with the castle and its environs that a portrait used to illustrate an early account of his life and work featured him beneath the heavy boughs of a Windsor oak with the castle in the background (fig. 43).

55

The Lower Ward seen from the base of the Round Tower, c. 1760

Pen, ink and watercolour over graphite, 281 × 609 mm
Royal Collection, London, RL 14559

PROVENANCE
Sir Joseph Banks; Sir Wyndham Knatchbull (sale Christie's, 23 May 1876, lot 45)

SELECTED EXHIBITIONS
Hamilton 1981, no. 17; Amsterdam 1995, no. 8

SELECTED REFERENCES
Oppé 1947, no. 37, p. 26; Amsterdam 1995, no. 8, p. 44

56

The Quadrangle looking west, c. 1765

Pen, ink, watercolour and bodycolour over graphite, 305 × 522 mm
Royal Collection, London, RL 14560

PROVENANCE
Sir Joseph Banks; Sir Wyndham Knatchbull (sale Christie's, 23 May 1876, lot 49); Lord Stair; Christie's, 19 June 1936, lot 76

SELECTED EXHIBITIONS
Amsterdam 1995, no. 15

SELECTED REFERENCES
Oppé 1947, no. 38, p. 26; Amsterdam 1995, no. 15, p. 62

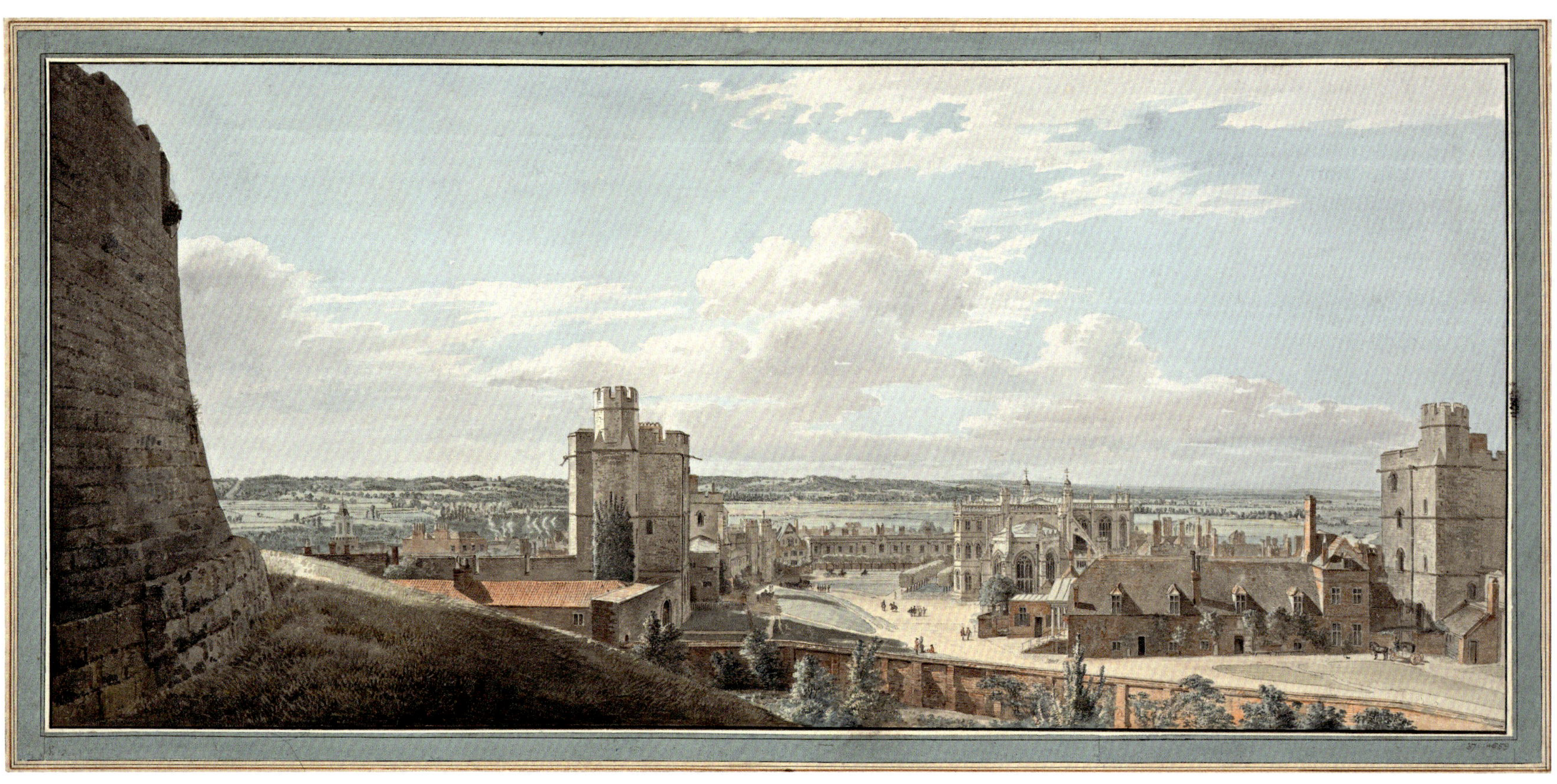

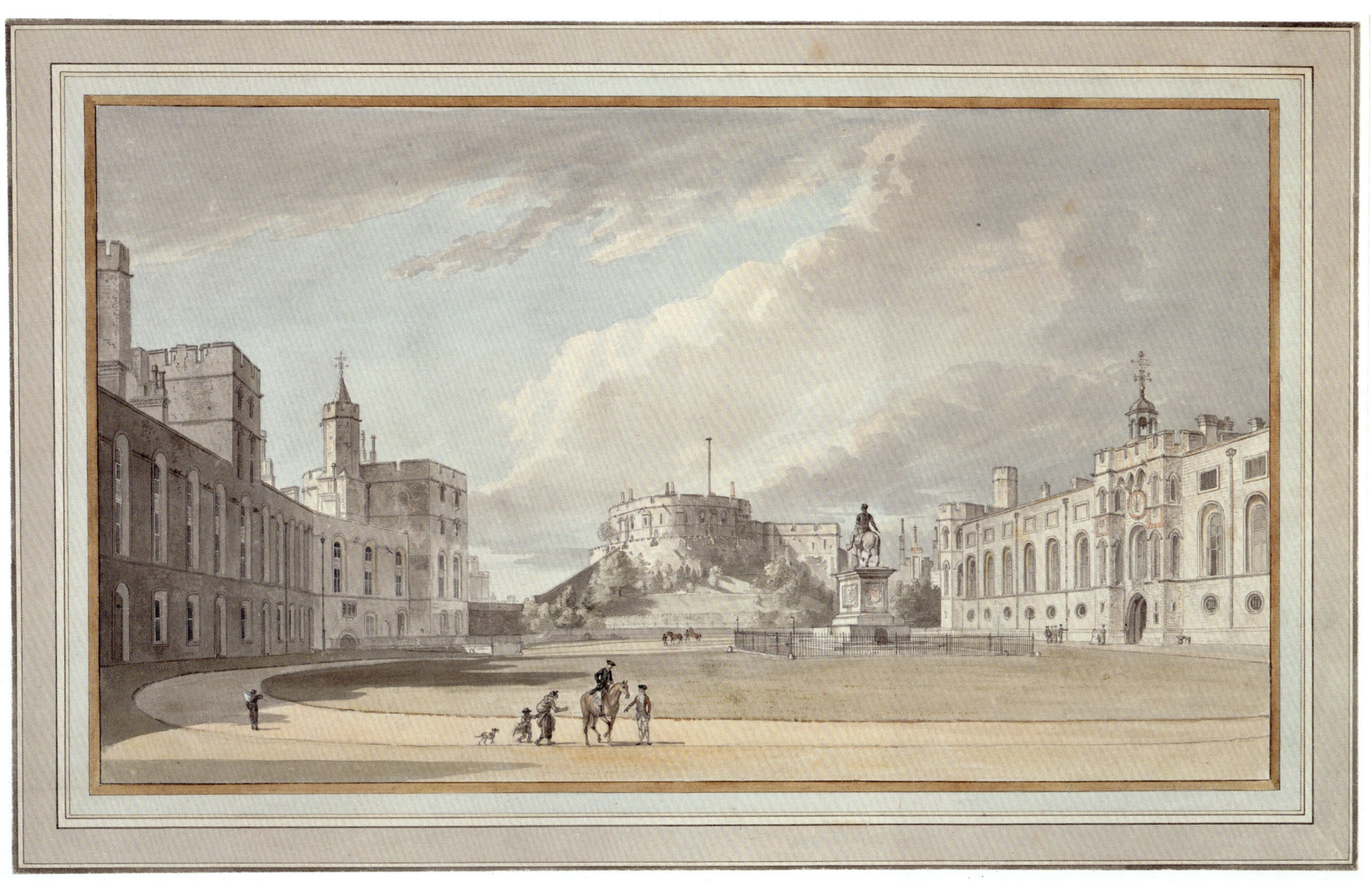

57

The North Terrace, Windsor Castle, Looking West, c. 1765

Bodycolour over graphite, 379 × 545 mm
Yale Center for British Art, New Haven, Paul Mellon Collection, B1981.25.2693

PROVENANCE
Sir Richard Frederick Molyneux, by whom presented to HRH The Princess Royal on her marriage to the Earl of Harewood; Christie's, 13 July 1965, lot 173; bt Colnaghi

SELECTED EXHIBITIONS
Yale 1985, no. 81

SELECTED REFERENCES
Yale 1985, no. 81, pp. 60–62

58

The North Terrace, Windsor Castle, Looking East, c. 1765

Bodycolour over graphite, 380 × 540 mm
Yale Center for British Art, New Haven, Paul Mellon Collection, B1981.25.2689

PROVENANCE
Sir Richard Frederick Molyneux, by whom presented to HRH The Princess Royal on her marriage to the Earl of Harewood; Christie's, 13 July 1965, lot 172; bt Colnaghi

SELECTED EXHIBITIONS
Yale 1985, no. 80; Yale 2001, no. 134

SELECTED REFERENCES
Yale 1985, no. 80, p. 60; Yale 2001, no. 134, pp. 158–59

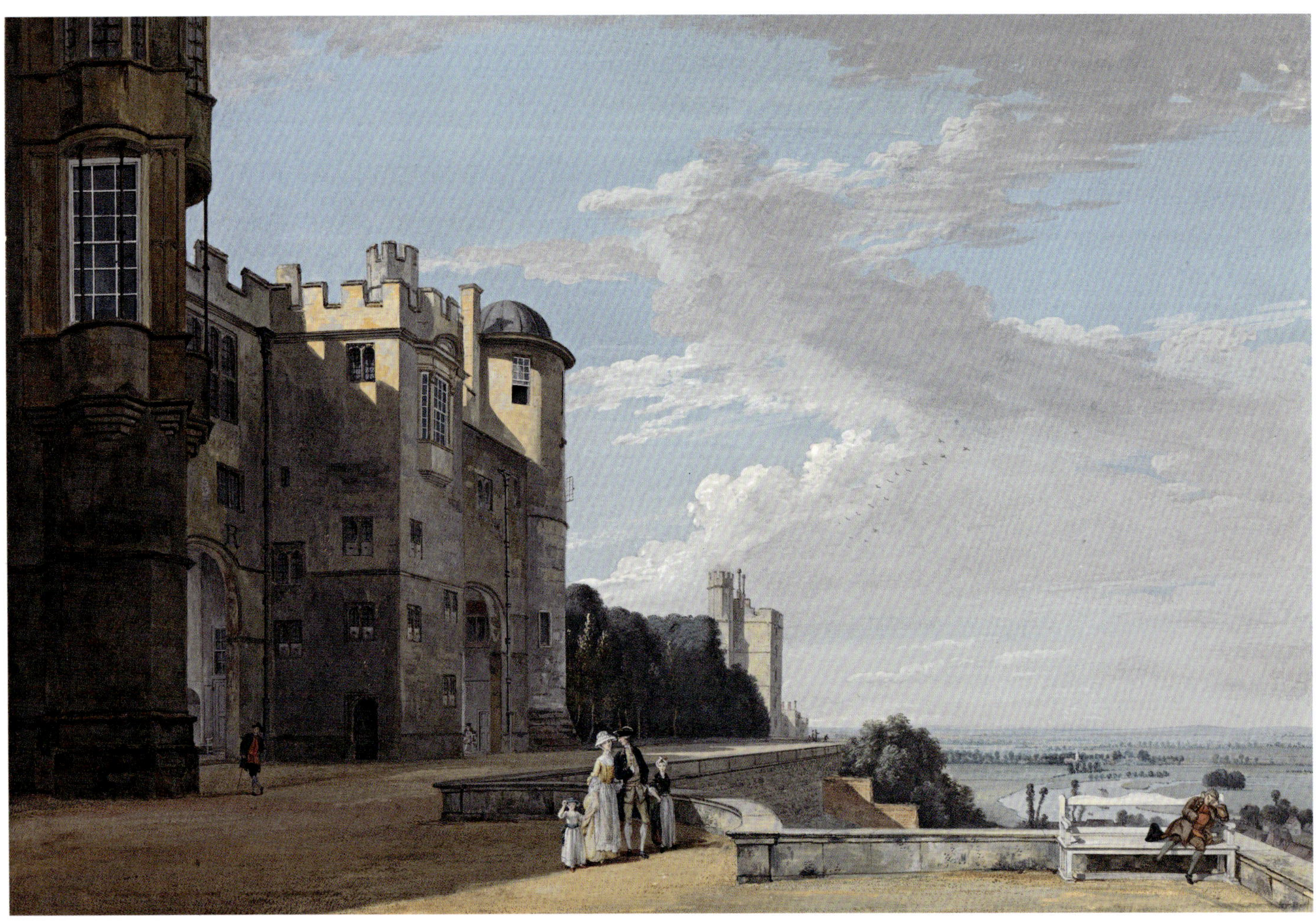

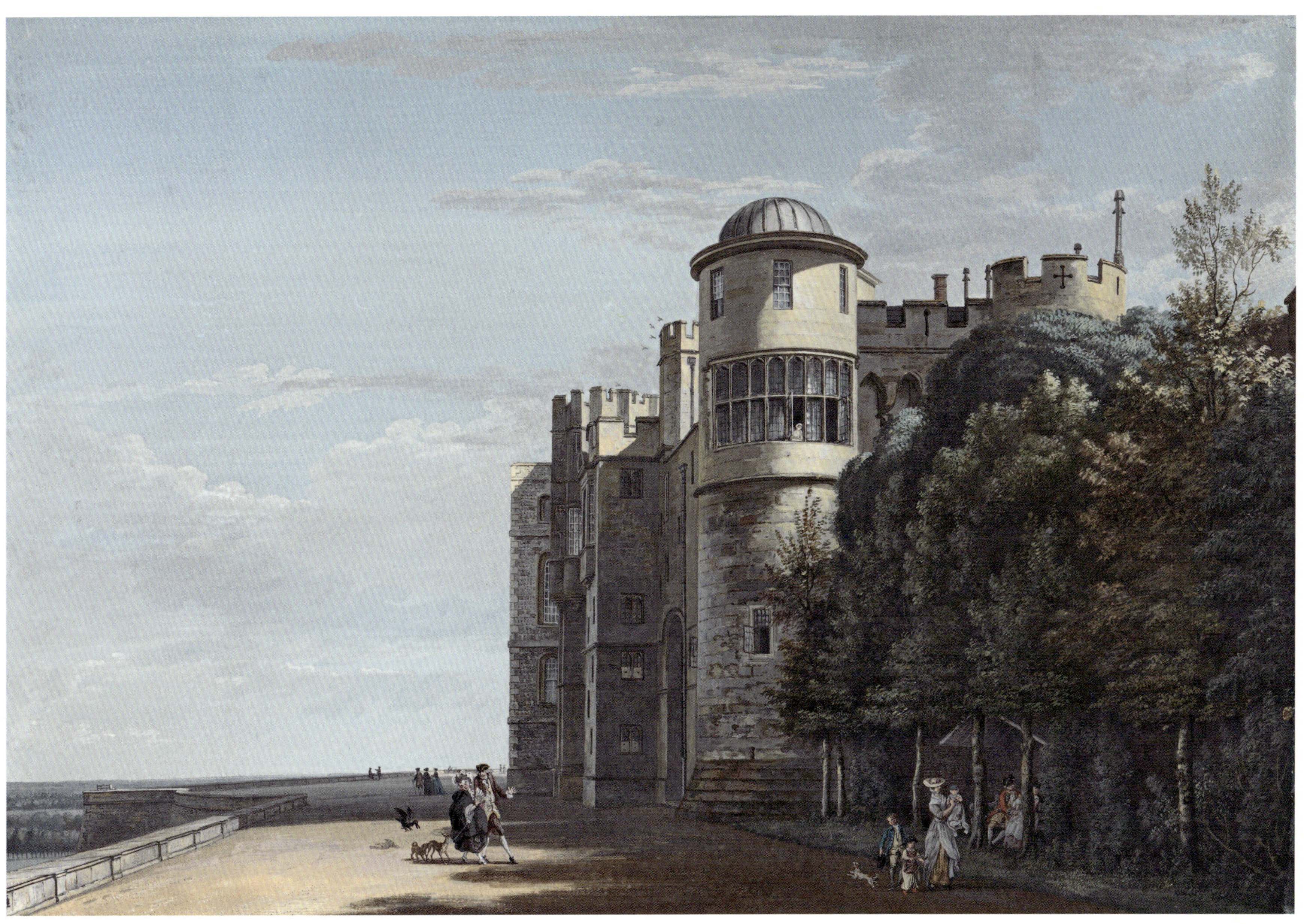

59

Castle Hill with the Henry III Tower and the Mary Tudor Tower seen from the south, c. 1765

Pen, ink, watercolour and bodycolour over graphite, 222 × 361 mm
Royal Collection, London, RL 14561

PROVENANCE
Sir Joseph Banks; Sir Wyndham Knatchbull (sale Christie's, 23 May 1876, lot 6)

SELECTED EXHIBITIONS
Amsterdam 1995, no. 26

SELECTED REFERENCES
Oppé 1947, no. 19, p. 23; Amsterdam 1995, no. 26

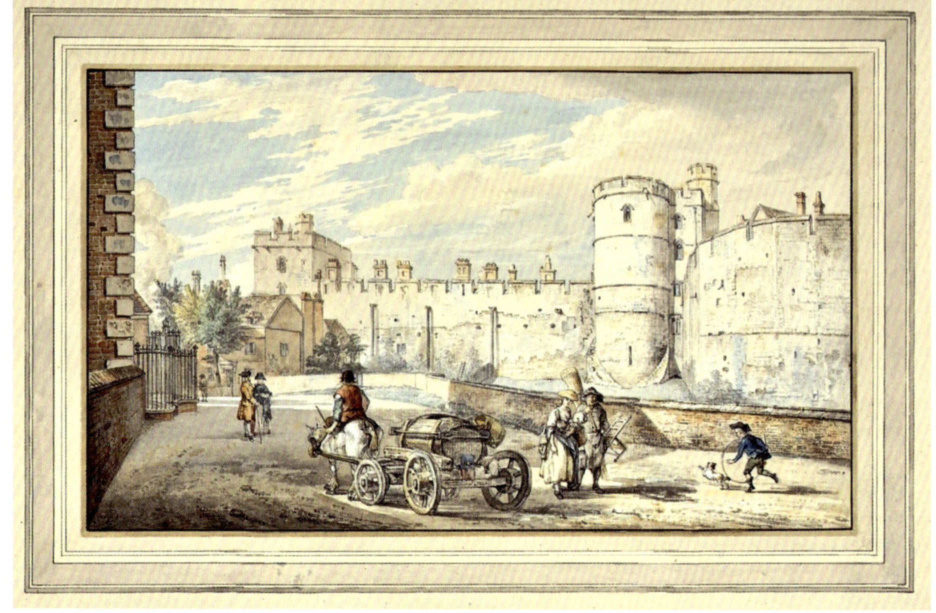

60

The Moat Bridge, the King's Gate and the entrance to the South Terrace, c. 1765

Pen, ink and watercolour over graphite, 195 × 268 mm
Royal Collection, London, RL 14538

PROVENANCE
Sir Joseph Banks; Sir Wyndham Knatchbull (sale Christie's, 23 May 1876, lot 10)

SELECTED EXHIBITIONS
Amsterdam 1995, no. 28

SELECTED REFERENCES

Oppé 1947, no. 16, pp. 22–23; Amsterdam 1995, no. 28, p. 92

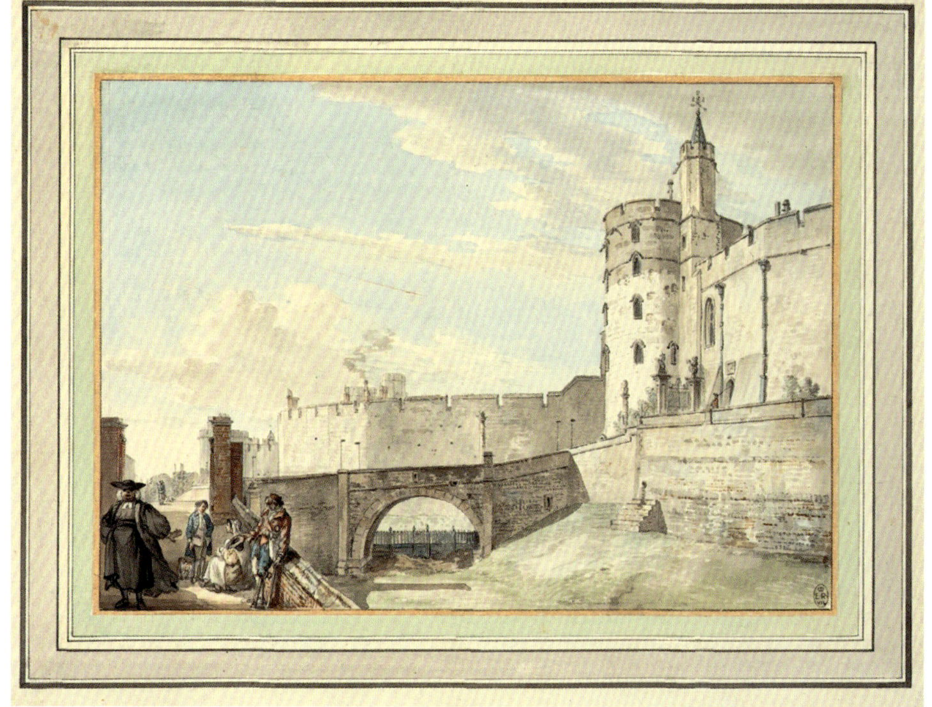

61

The north-east corner of the Castle seen from below, with lightning, c. 1765

Bodycolour with pen and ink, 380 × 485 mm
Royal Collection, London, RL 14581

PROVENANCE
Paul Sandby (sale Christie's, 2 May 1811, lot 91); Prince Regent (later George IV); by descent

SELECTED EXHIBITIONS
Amsterdam 1995, no. 34

SELECTED REFERENCES
Oppé 1947, no. 57, p. 29; Amsterdam 1995, no. 34, pp. 104–06

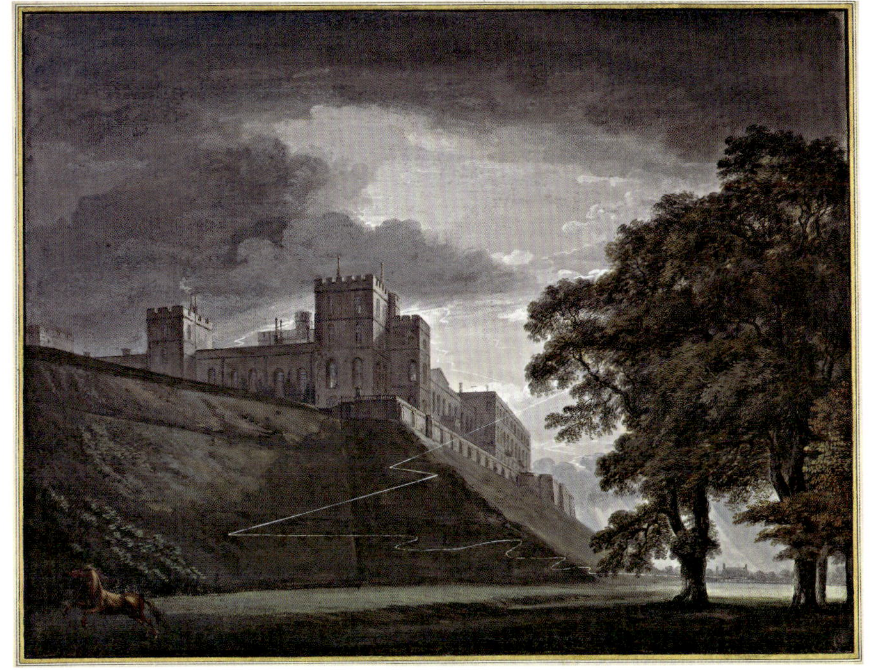

62

View of Windsor on a rejoicing night, 1768

Watercolour and bodycolour, 465 × 725 mm
Signed and dated: 'P. Sandby 1768' (l.l.)
Royal Collection, London, RL 14584

PROVENANCE
in the Royal Collection by 1910

SELECTED EXHIBITIONS
SA 1768, no. 145; Hamilton 1981, no. 20; Amsterdam 1995, no. 19

SELECTED REFERENCES
Oppé 1947, no. 60, p. 29; Hamilton 1981, no. 20, p. 20; Amsterdam 1995, no. 19, p. 72

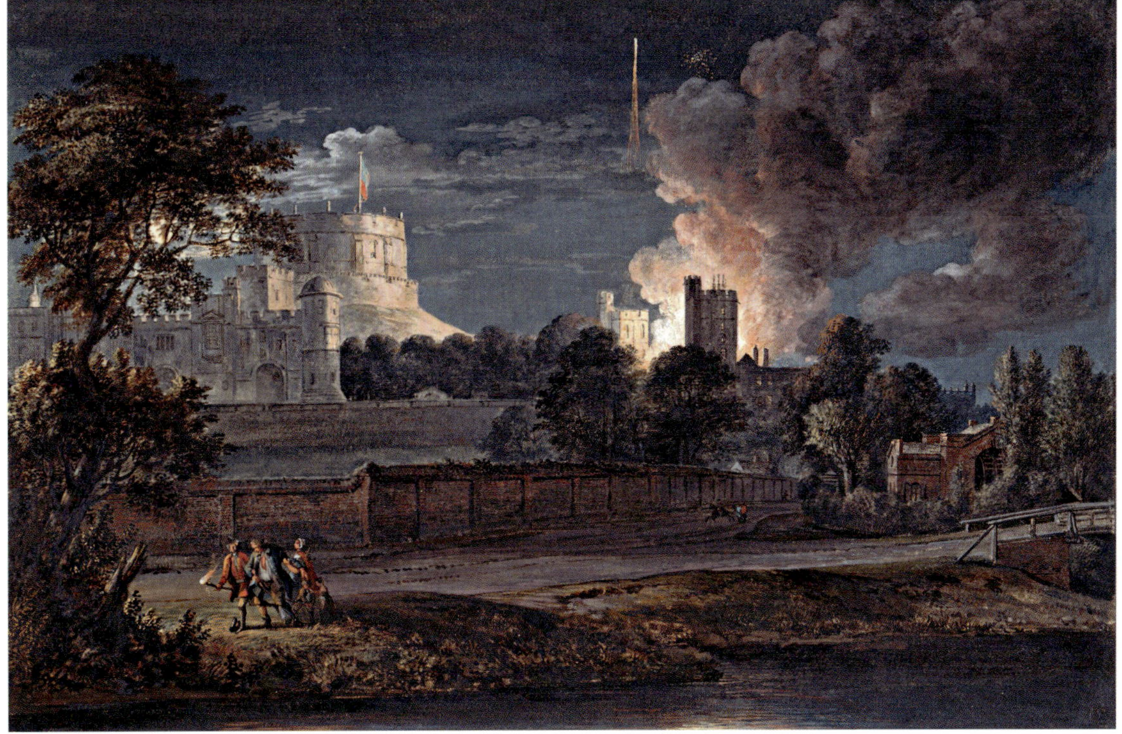

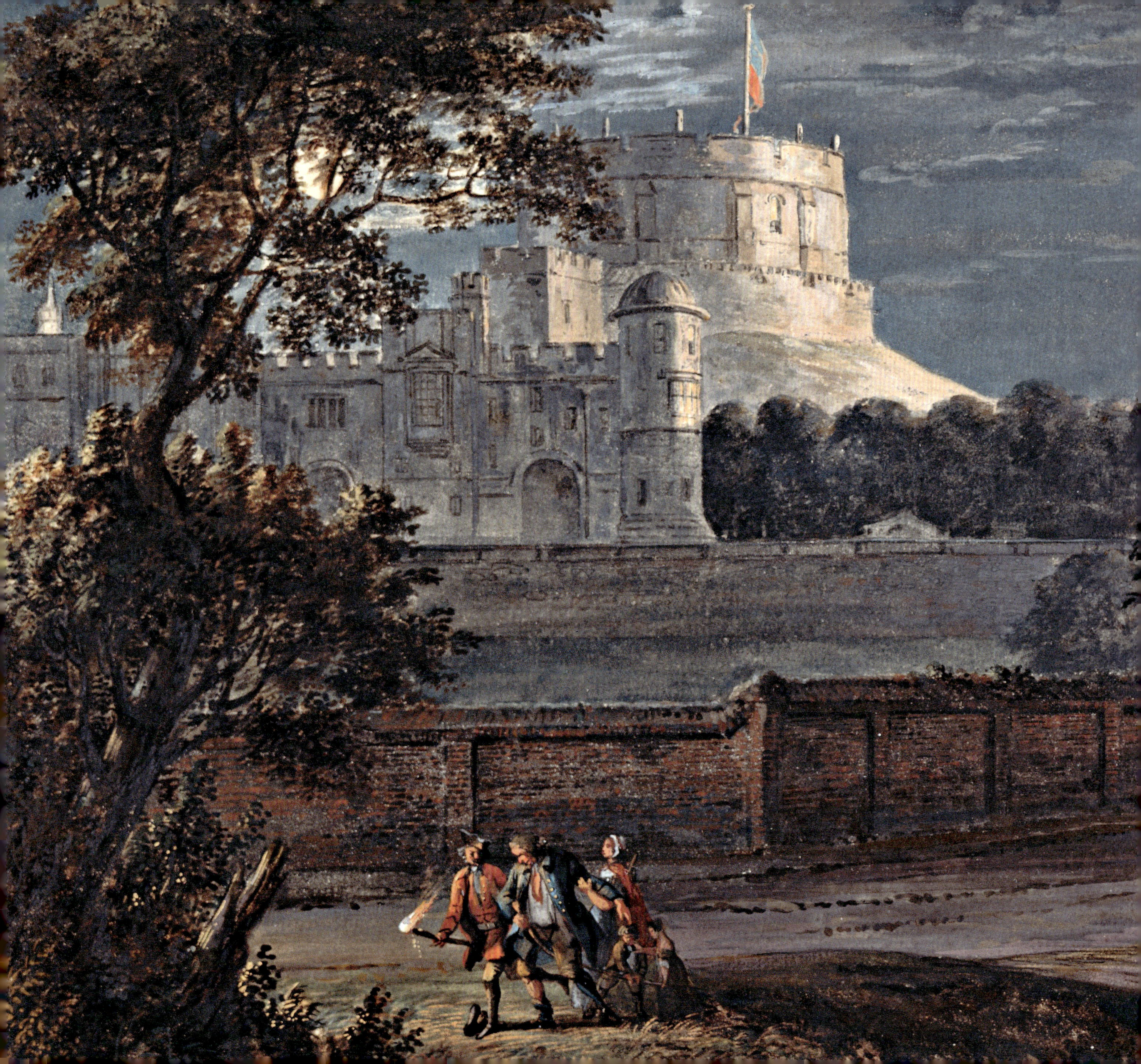

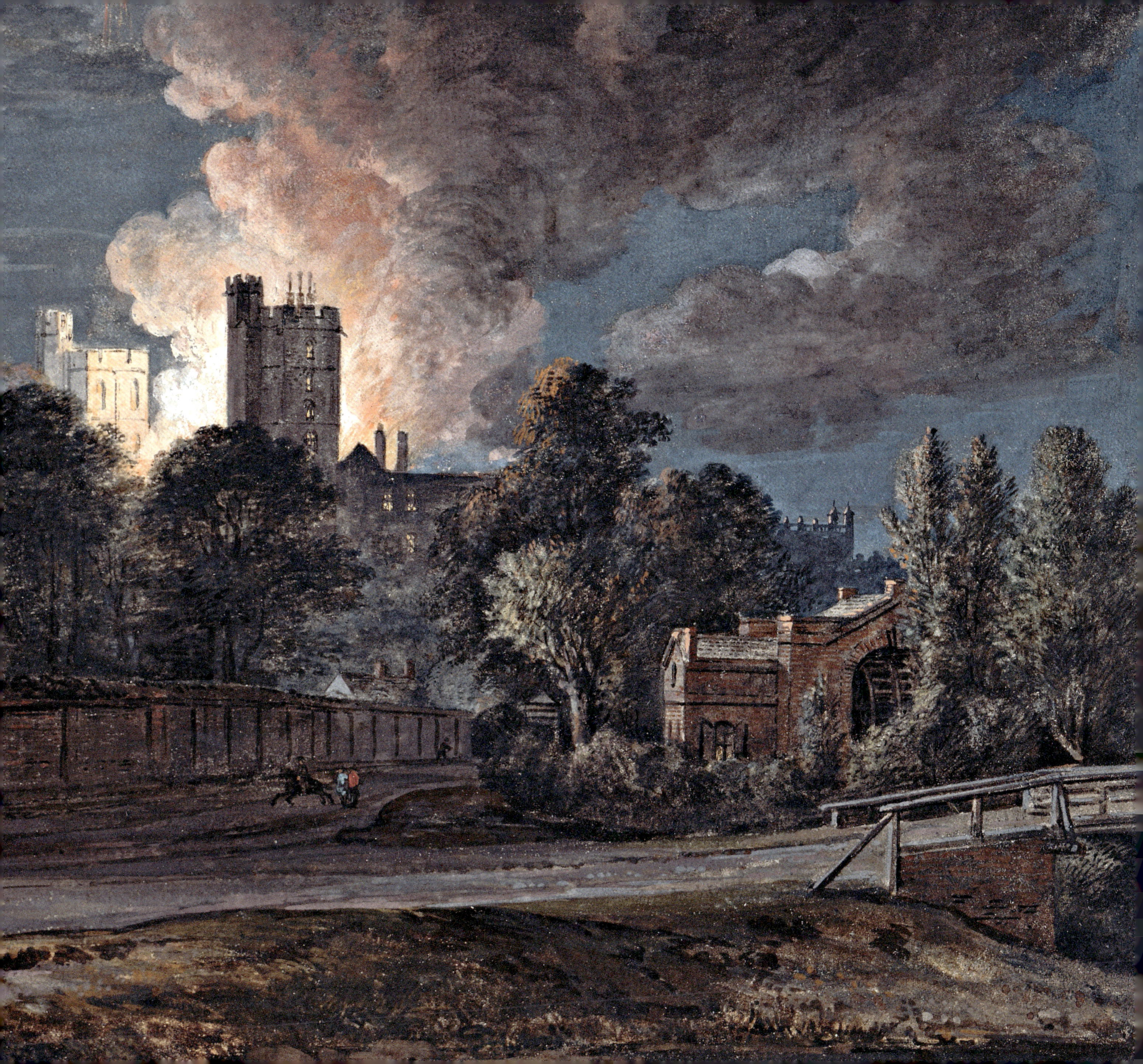

63

THOMAS SANDBY

Nottingham Market Square from the East, c. 1740s

Pen and watercolour over graphite, 435 × 1220 mm
Nottingham City Museums and Galleries, NCM 1939-63

PROVENANCE
Purchased from H. Sotheran, 1939

SELECTED EXHIBITIONS
Reading 1972, no. 4

In his chorographic study of Nottingham (1751) Charles Deering directed the 'Travellers View' towards the city's market-place, a public square 'in spaciousness superior to most; inferior to very few (if any) in the Kingdom' and 'graced with many beautiful Buildings' (Deering 1751, p. 7). A number of these fine structures are illustrated in Deering's volume by engravings after studies by Thomas Sandby. They also feature in this large, unfinished drawing by the artist, looking out across the market-place from the east. Sandby records the square's historic Malt Cross, as well as the more distant, barely visible landmark of Nottingham Castle, but places these markers of the town's past in the context of a number of recent improvements, whereby the commercial and judicial centre of the town was paved, the shambles colonnaded and a new Exchange built. A second drawing of the square (fig. 44), showing the same developments from the west and datable to a similar period, imitates the effects of copper engraving. Although this might suggest that Sandby had thoughts of publishing this view, the drawing may also be an early indication of his architectural ambitions. Renaissance theorists such as Leon Battista Alberti or Sebastiano Serlio had made *disegno*, or design conveyed through line, a central tenet of both painting and architecture. *Nottingham Market Square from the East*, however, with its delicate colour washes and tonal modelling, is more remarkable still for its assured and sophisticated handling of perspective.

Writing of Thomas Sandby's early career, John Williams recorded him:

> absorbed in contemplation upon a new system of perspective, which he progressively pursued, until he brought it to a state of unequalled perfection and readiness of application; and, acting upon these novel rules, he made a drawing of his natal town, which procured him such a reputation, as emboldened him to visit London for the purposes of having it engraved. (Pasquin 1796, p. 141)

This was presumably a reference to Sandby's prospect of his native Nottingham, depicting the town from the River Trent, which was engraved by Isaac Basire and published on 1 May 1742 (fig. 45). This ambitious, remarkably assured townscape certainly demonstrates the elder Sandby's prodigious abilities at this early stage. However, if Williams's account of its conception accorded with the artist's own claim to have been self-taught, other evidence suggests that it was the product of the experimental circles in which the young Sandby moved. His associates at this time included the Hon. Rothwell Willoughby, to whom *A South Prospect of the Town of Nottingham* had been dedicated, a figure with a 'peculiar genius for mechanicks and other parts of the mathematicks', inclined to the study of 'natural and experimental philosophy' (Deering 1751, p. 231). Another mathematician, Thomas Peat, who also had a keen interest in astronomy, had employed Thomas Sandby to supplement his 1744 cartographic survey of Nottingham with views of the town's principal public buildings, and may have played a role in the young draughtsman's tuition.

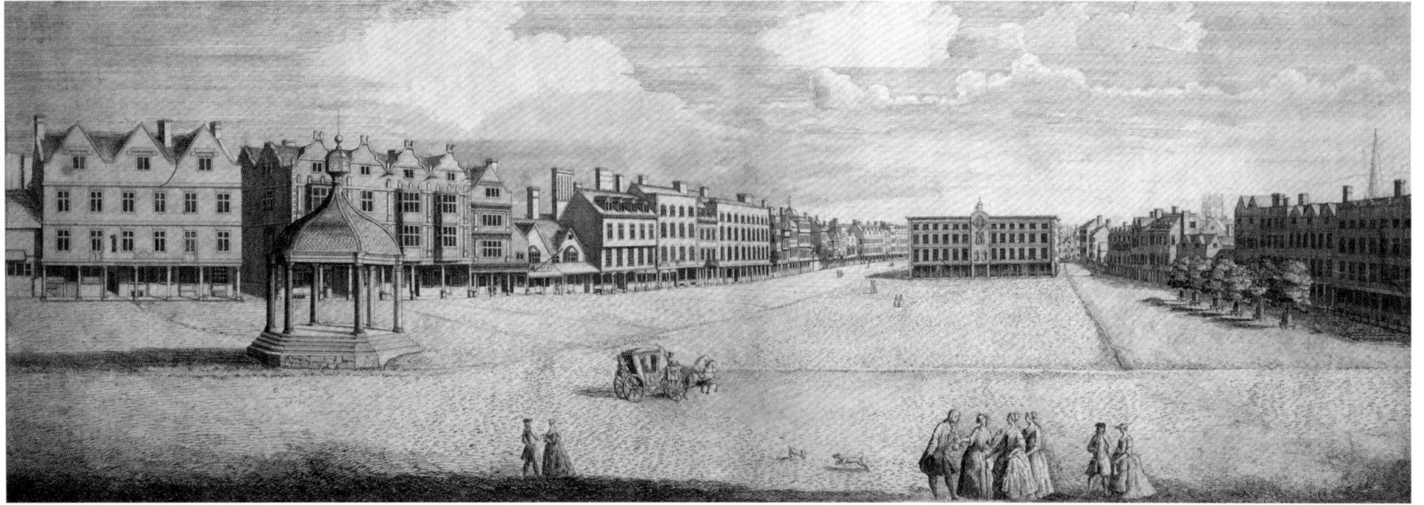

FIG. 44
Thomas Sandby, *Nottingham Market Square from the West, c.* 1740s. Pen and ink over graphite, 267 × 750 mm. Nottingham City Museums and Galleries

FIG. 45 (OPPOSITE)
Isaac Basire, after Thomas Sandby, *The South Prospect of the Town and County of the Town of Nottingham*, published 1 May 1742. Engraving, 500 × 1130 mm. Nottingham City Museums and Galleries

Perspective was to hold a continued fascination for the elder of the Sandby brothers throughout his career. In listing skills necessary 'to form a good Architect', Thomas Sandby advised his students at the Royal Academy Schools, first and foremost, to apply themselves to the study of arithmetic, geometry and perspective. Of the significance of the last, Sandby suggested: 'Perspective will, on many occasions, lend her assistance to the ingenious Artist, that he ought to obtain a competent knowledge there of as it represents & displays those happy forms in Buildings which produce an essential breadth of light and shade, and at the same time enables the Artist to conceive, or know the true effect of his Designs in their various Situations and dispositions' (Sandby Lectures, I, fols 11–12). Among the numerous texts on perspective to be found in Thomas Sandby's library was the most successful of all 'made-easy' guides to the subject, Joshua Kirby's 1754 edition of the mathematician Brook Taylor's famed study. Like Sandby, Kirby was prominent in that mix of artists and writers congregating around St Martin's Lane, where concern to establish and promote a peculiarly English method of perspective was much debated, as distinct from the imported 'Jesuit' principles of Jean Dubreuil's standard *The Practice of Perspective, or, an Easy Method of Representing Natural Objects According to the Rules of Art* (first English edition, 1726), which were so distasteful to the fierce, decidedly Protestant-flavoured patriotism of that decade's art community. A large number of treatises claiming to introduce an alternative orthographic system, like Benjamin Martin's *Principles of Perspective* (1770) or Thomas Malton's *A Royal Road to Geometry* (1774), were published in the years after mid-century, nearly always bearing dedications emphasising their patriotic worth. Sandby was greatly interested in these matters and developed 'Compasses for Drawing perspectively in Architecture, landscapes, and other real objects' to be sold through the St James's shop of the mathematical instrument-maker James Simons. These were 'contrived to answer the purposes of a Theodolite and quadrant', according to the press notice advertising their availability (*Gazetteer and New Daily Advertiser*, 6 June 1775). Although these did not come to market until 1775, they may well have comprised or, at least, been developed from that 'new system' remarked upon by Williams. This remarkable drawing of Nottingham's Market Square, dating from the 1740s, certainly demonstrates Thomas Sandby's assured mastery of spatial recession at this early date.

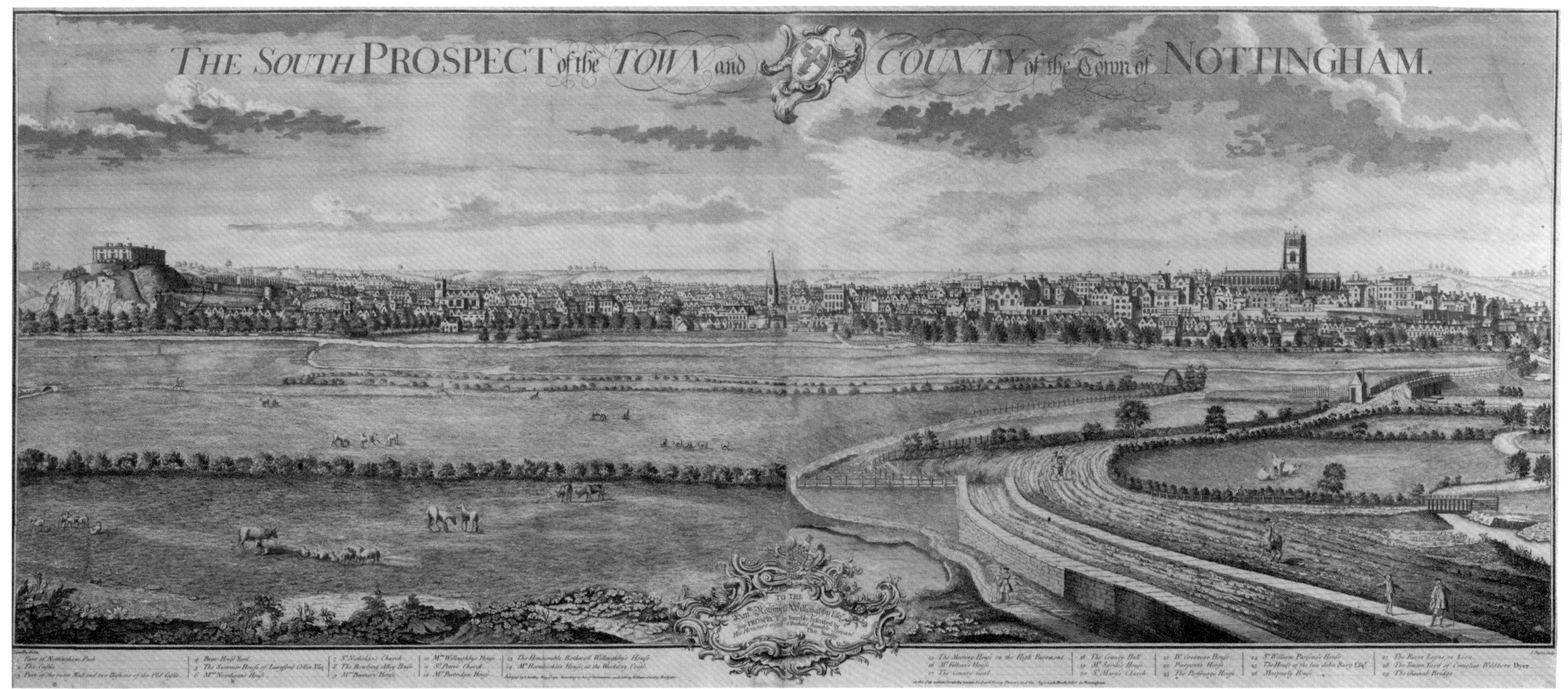

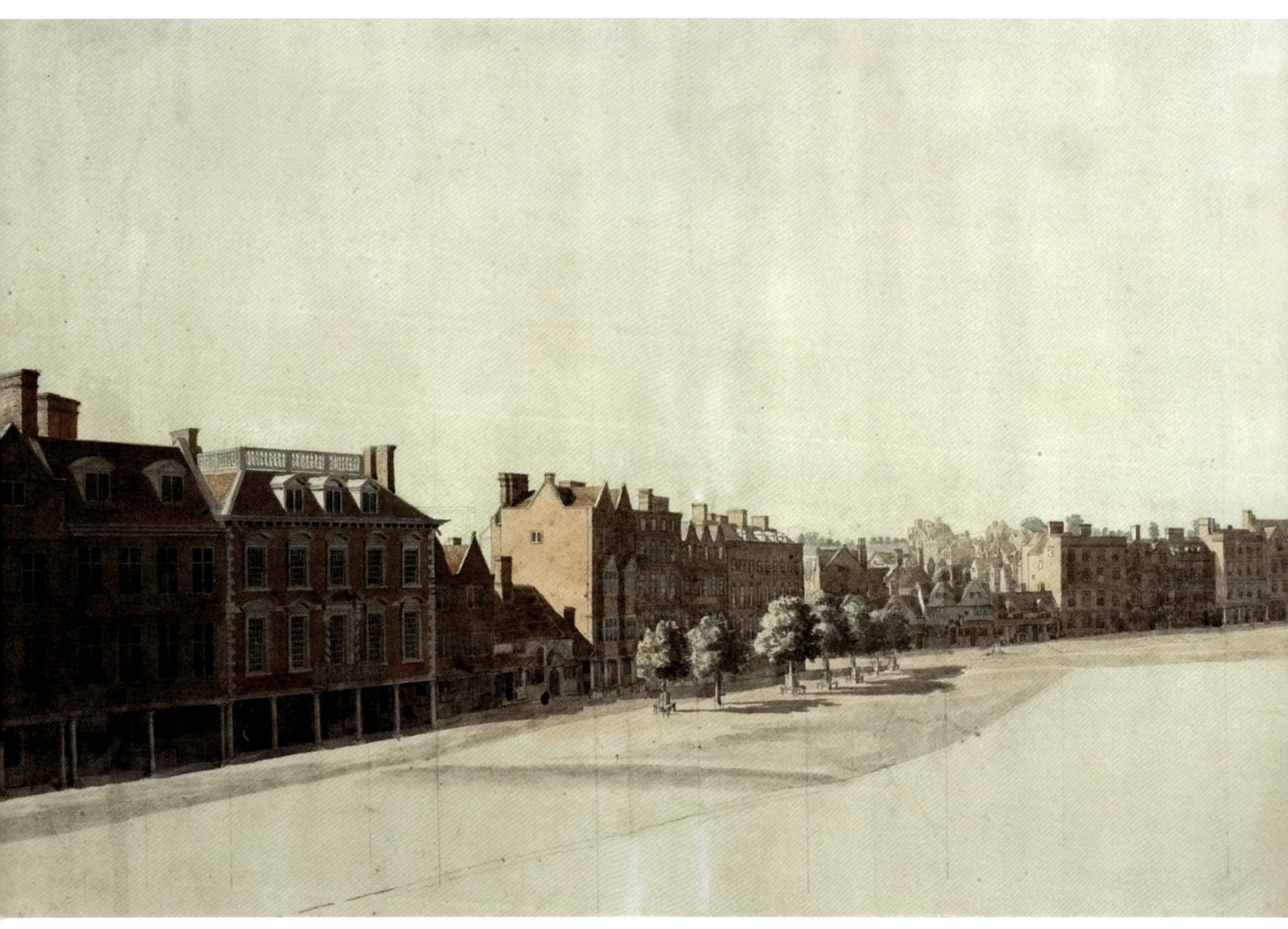

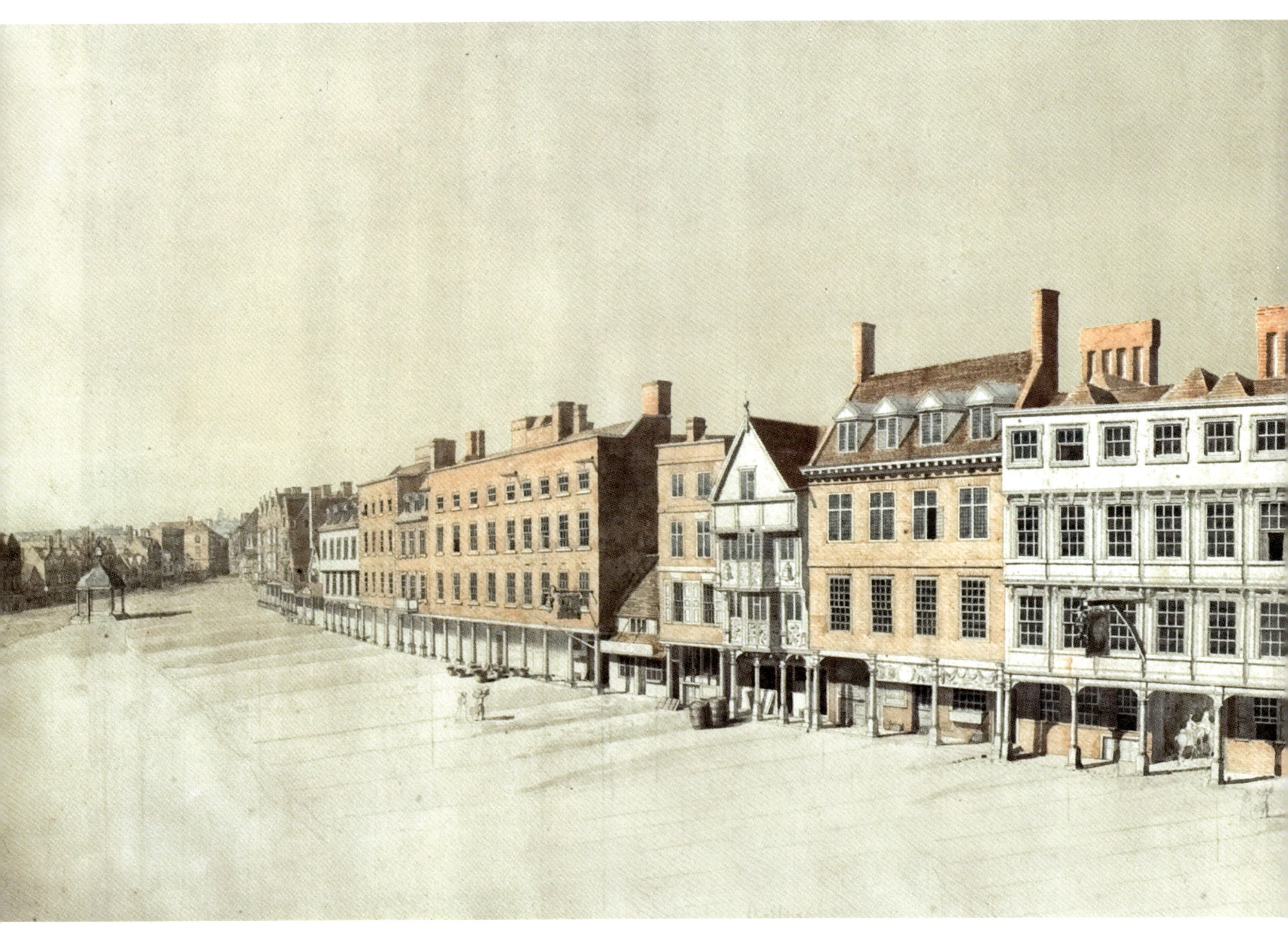

64

Nottingham Castle, *c.* 1774

Pen, ink and wash over graphite, 139 × 364 mm
Yale Center for British Art, New Haven, Paul Mellon Collection, B1977.14.5349

PROVENANCE
Sir Thomas Phillips; J. A. Crabtree, September 1956; L. G. Duke, 1956 to November 1960

SELECTED EXHIBITIONS
Yale 1985, no. 41

SELECTED REFERENCES
Yale 1985, no. 41, p. 42

65

THOMAS SANDBY

Windsor from the Goswells drawn in a Camera, *c.* 1760s

Pen, ink and watercolour over graphite, 124 × 577 mm
Royal Collection, London, RL 14602

PROVENANCE
In the Royal Collection by 1892

SELECTED EXHIBITIONS
Reading 1972, no. 9

SELECTED REFERENCES
Oppé 1947, no. 78, p. 31

Comparison of these two unfinished studies illustrates the considerable difficulty of assigning certain drawings to one or the other Sandby brother. Indeed, the attribution of the view of Nottingham Castle from the east to Paul rests only on what Bruce Robertson has characterised as the younger brother's 'slightly nervous pen line' (Yale 1985, p. 42). Otherwise, whether in terms of subject-matter or composition, the congruencies in the brothers' work are often more striking than the distinctions.

The Sandbys enjoyed a long association with both castles, sketching them or reworking existing studies on numerous occasions. As often as not, the resulting works were collaborative, with Paul's figures animating his brother's landscape or architectural views. Collaboration might take a variety of forms, however. In other instances, the younger brother clearly worked up studies provided by Thomas alone, as was probably the case with this drawing of Nottingham Castle. Replication of views and, indeed, figures was central to the brothers' practice, as they drew on methods perfected during their respective stays in the Ordnance Drawing Rooms. These two drawings illustrate that there were significant continuities across their work as military and professional artists. Pieced together from four separate sheets of paper, the view of Windsor is assembled much like the earlier, long panoramic studies of camps in Scotland and the Low Countries. Likewise, there is a similar reliance on optical devices, in this case a *camera obscura*, which admitted light through a small aperture, focusing an image on the back of a dark chamber, which was reflected by an angled mirror onto a glass surface where it could be traced. The process enabled ready replication, with a study like this example representing the earliest stage. This study of Nottingham Castle also shows evidence of having been produced mechanically. The work was subsequently engraved by William Watts for publication in *The Copper-Plate Magazine* in January 1777, where it was enlivened by a foreground family scene (fig. 23).

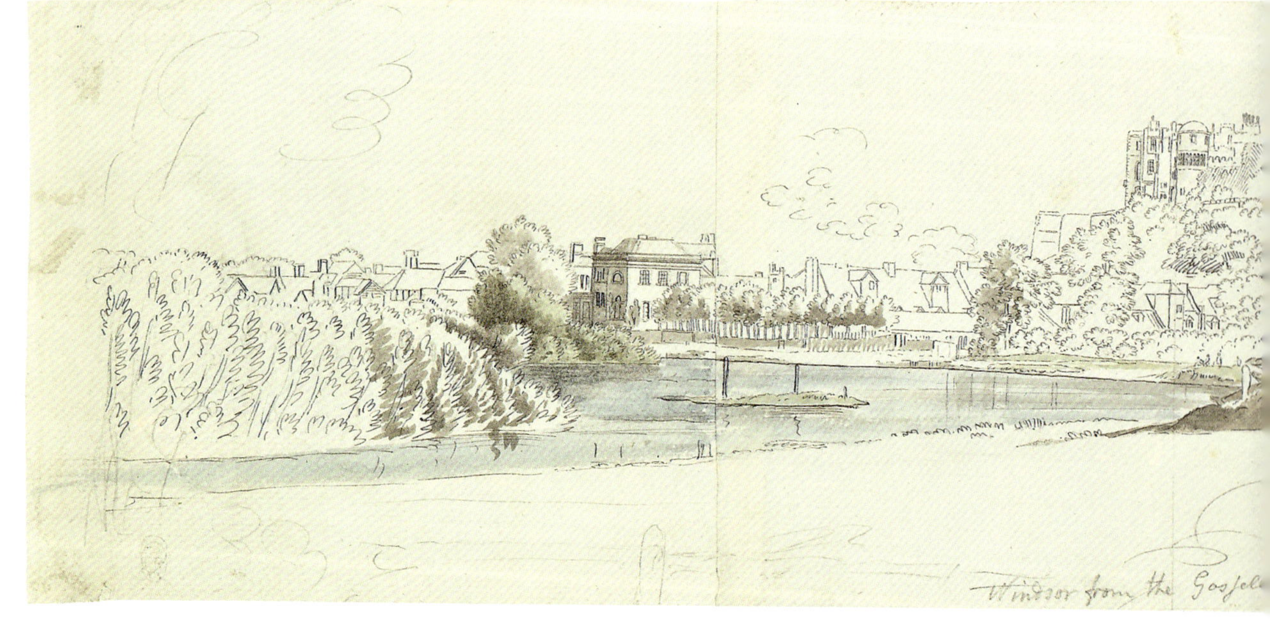

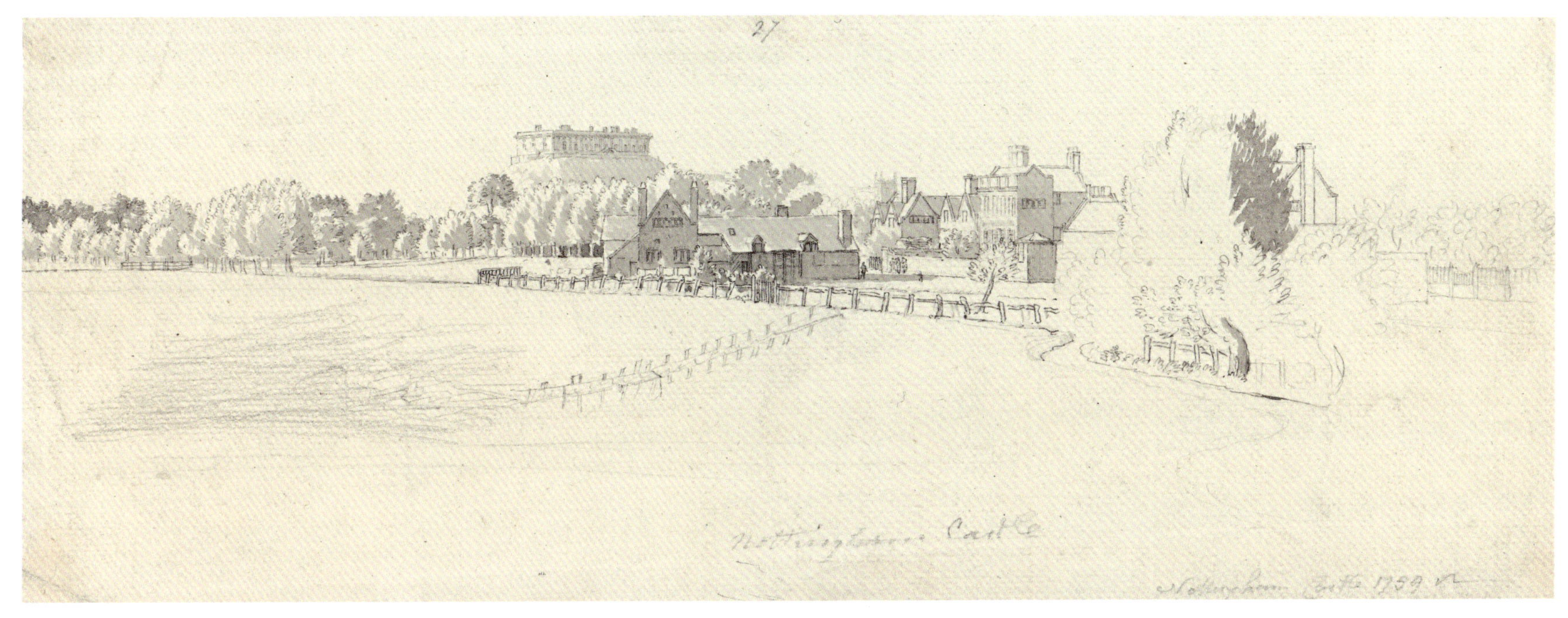

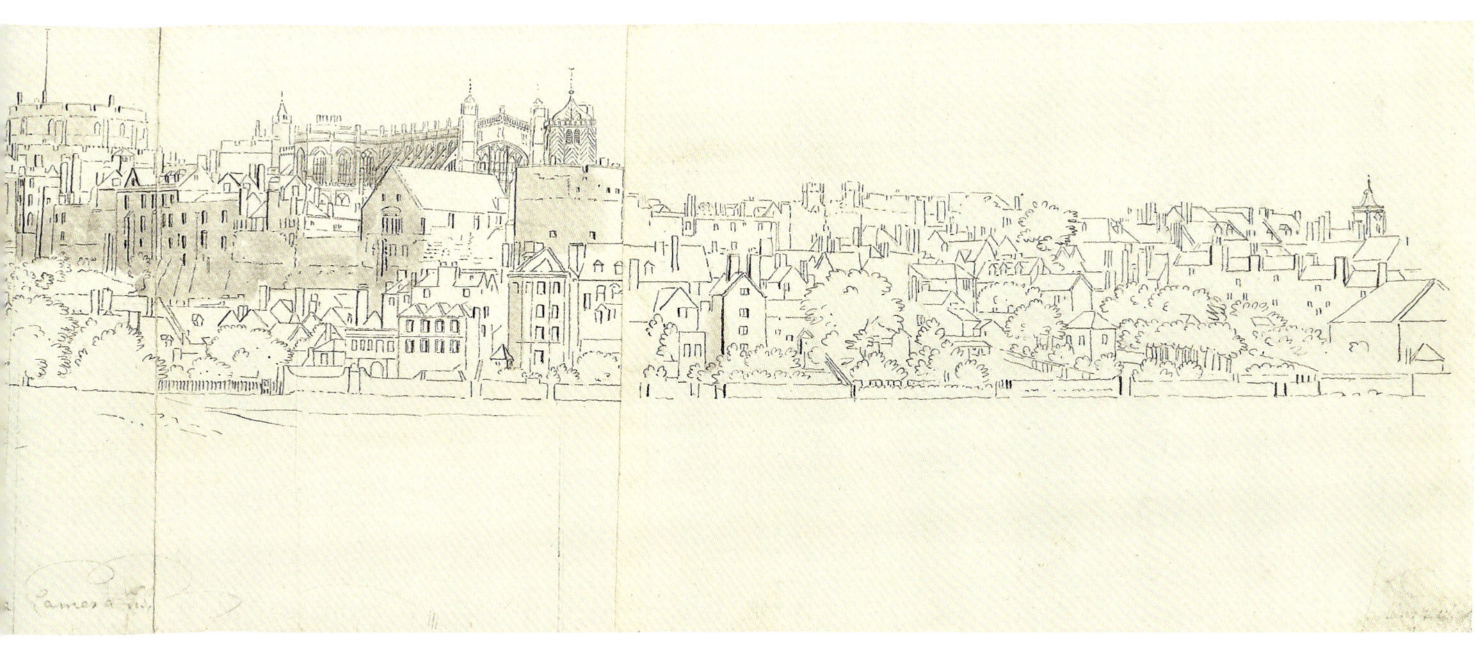

66

A Lady Drawing, *c.* 1760s

Watercolour over graphite, 195 × 152 mm
Royal Collection, London, RL 14377

PROVENANCE
In the Royal Collection by 1934

SELECTED EXHIBITIONS
Hamilton 1981, no. 77; London 2000, no. 170

SELECTED REFERENCES
Oppé 1947, no. 259, p. 65; London 2000, no. 170, pp. 232–33

67

Lady Elizabeth Harcourt, 1759

Watercolour over graphite, 175 × 137 mm
Private collection

PROVENANCE
Simon, 1st Earl of Harcourt, and by descent

CATALOGUE NUMBERS 66–67

From the seventeenth century onwards, an interest in drawing and painting came to be recognised as one of the defining features of a gentleman. 'Every Gentleman ... will find some Skill in Drawing, if he has it, of great Use to him,' observed one proponent of the art (Gwynn 1749, p. 62). Learning to draw, as recent scholarship on amateur practice in the period has shown, was considered useful and beneficial, a means of exchanging and circulating knowledge as well as a form of pleasurable, improving leisure activity (London 2000; Bermingham 2000). Students of the art not only developed their rational faculties but their moral sensibility. John Locke had advocated drawing as a universal form of writing, a means to communicate visually, in his *Thoughts on Education* (1693), and his acolyte Joseph Addison had promoted its moral worth in his *Spectator* essays on 'the pleasures of the fancy and imagination' (1712).

Paul Sandby was one of the most sought-after drawing masters of the period, counting members of the royal family, the Grevilles, the Harcourts and individuals like Sir Watkin Williams Wynn and Therese Robinson among his many pupils (see London 2000, pp. 107, 117–18, 129–45, 232–33). He may also have given additional tuition to officers studying at the Royal Military Academy in Woolwich, supplementing the lessons he gave as part of the curriculum (see pp. 17–18). This instruction focused largely on students making copies after his designs, rather than making studies from nature. A drawing closely related to the study of the young woman painting shown here, now in the collection of the Yale Center for British Art, New Haven, shows her copying from a portrait sketch. The unidentified sitter, shown seated before a window, making a watercolour, was presumably one of Sandby's students. For young women of the period, drawing represented a form of polite 'accomplishment', an important social attribute, like the ability to play a musical instrument or skill at embroidery. Lady Elizabeth Harcourt was an accomplished amateur artist, who studied under Alexander Cozens and Joshua Kirby, as well as Sandby, who depicted her several times (Oppé 1947, no. 268, 315; London 2000, p. 157). She is shown here sewing.

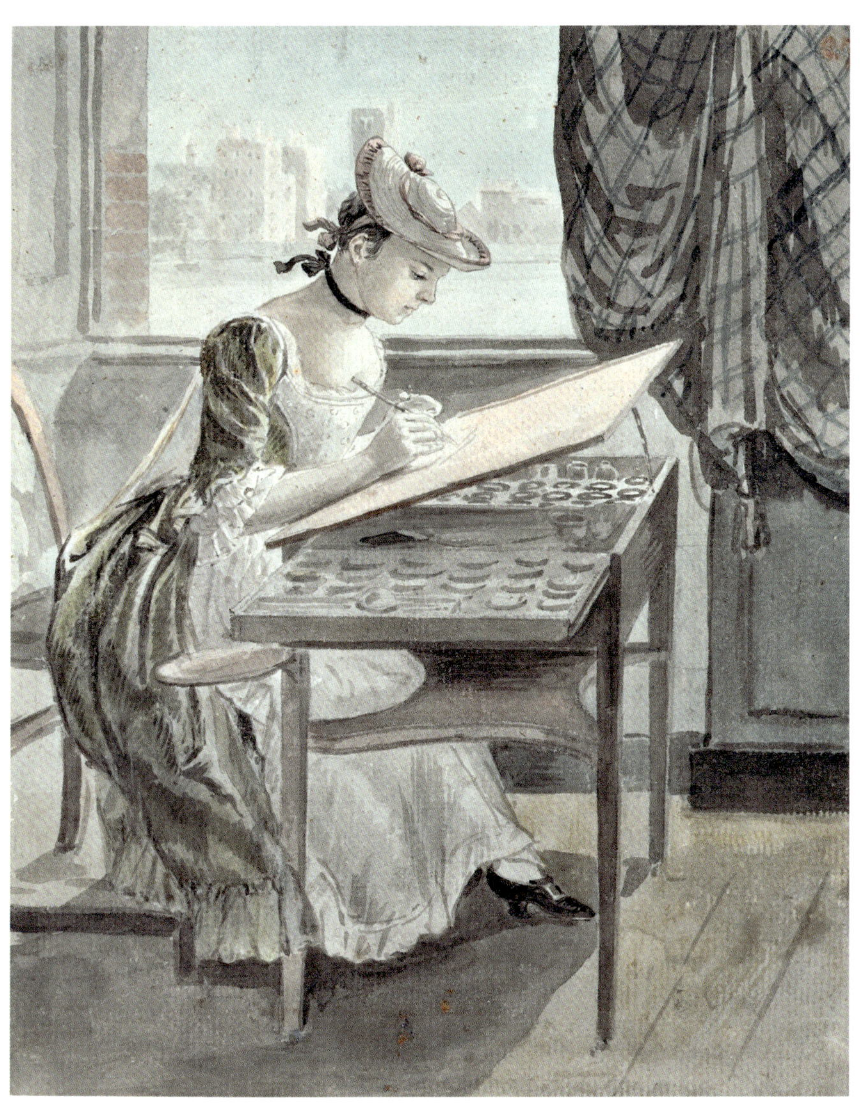

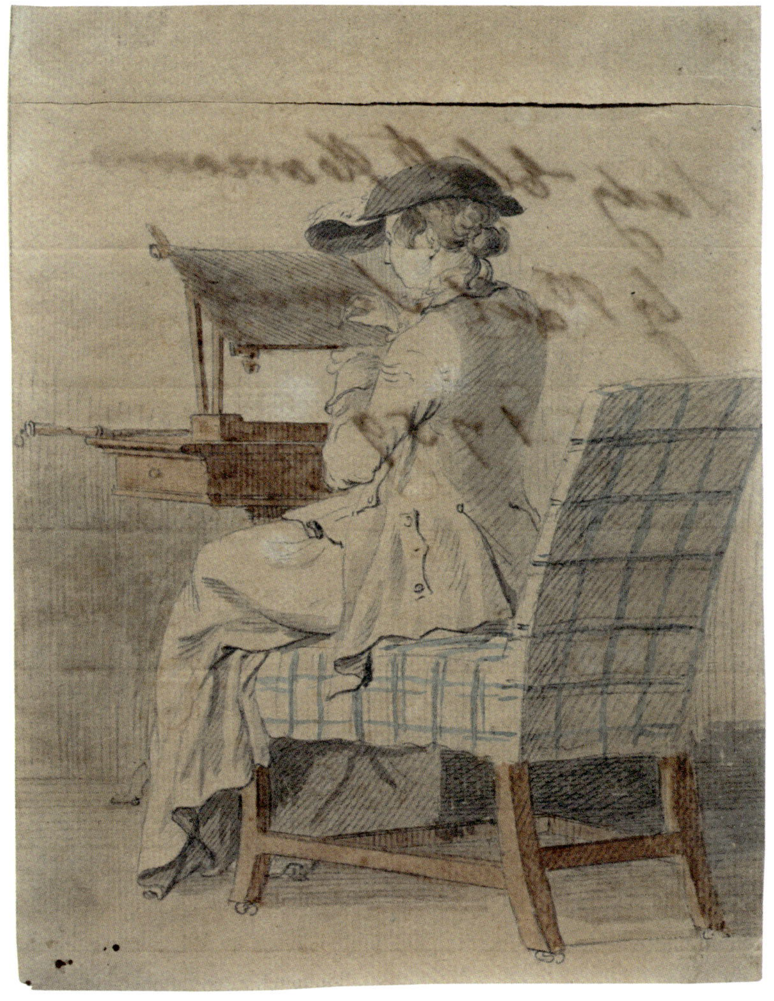

68

GEORGE SIMON, VISCOUNT NUNEHAM

A View of the Ruins of the Chappel at Stanton-Harcourt, 1763

Published by the Society of Antiquaries of London, 1785
Etching, 430 × 522 mm
The Society of Antiquaries of London

SELECTED REFERENCES

Robertson 1987, pp. 248–49; Salway 1996; Hannah 1998; London 2000, no. 96a, pp. 135–37

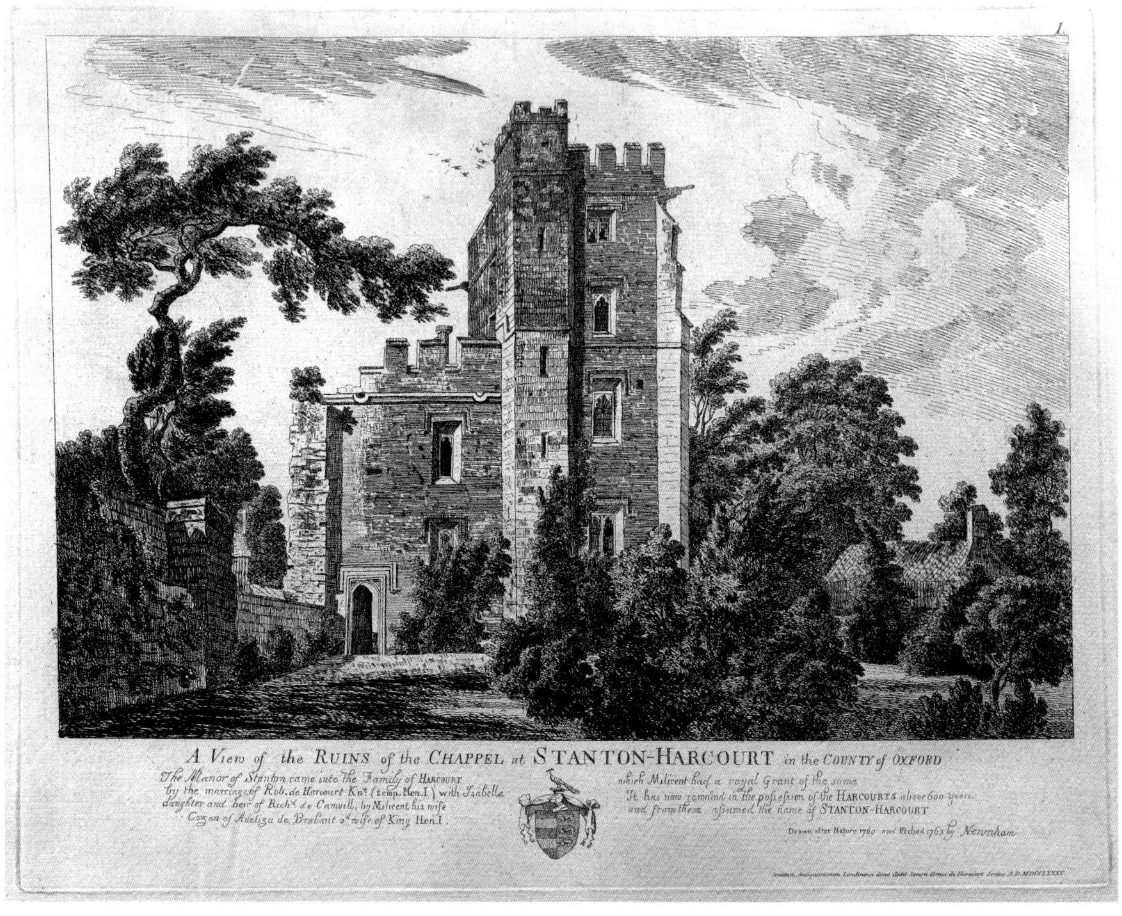

CATALOGUE NUMBERS 68–69

During the late 1750s Paul Sandby appears to have acted effectively as painter-in-residence to the Harcourt family, tutoring Simon, 1st Earl of Harcourt, his sons George and William and their sisters Mary and Elizabeth. Family papers record a series of regular payments over an extended period, placing him in their Oxfordshire villa, Nuneham Courtney, for a number of months over several years (Bodleian Library, University of Oxford, Mss Harcourt Papers). Sandby's connection with the family, which presumably had come about through Cumberland, Harcourt having served as the Duke's aid, was advertised publicly in March 1760 with the display at the country's very first public art exhibition of a large oil depicting the newly built Nuneham Courtney (cats 84–85). His instruction of various family members centred on their making copies after his designs, whether capriccios or studies of the family estate, in watercolour and etched form.

These included views of the ruins of the ancient manor house on the family's ancestral lands at Stanton Harcourt. Only the chapel and kitchen remained standing, but they were much

69

GEORGE SIMON, VISCOUNT NUNEHAM
after PAUL SANDBY
View of the Ruins of the Kitchen at Stanton-Harcourt, 1763

Published by the Society of Antiquaries of London, 1785
Etching, 390 × 525 mm
The Society of Antiquaries of London

SELECTED REFERENCES
Robertson 1987, pp. 248–49; Salway 1996; Hannah 1998; London 2000, no. 96b, pp. 135–37

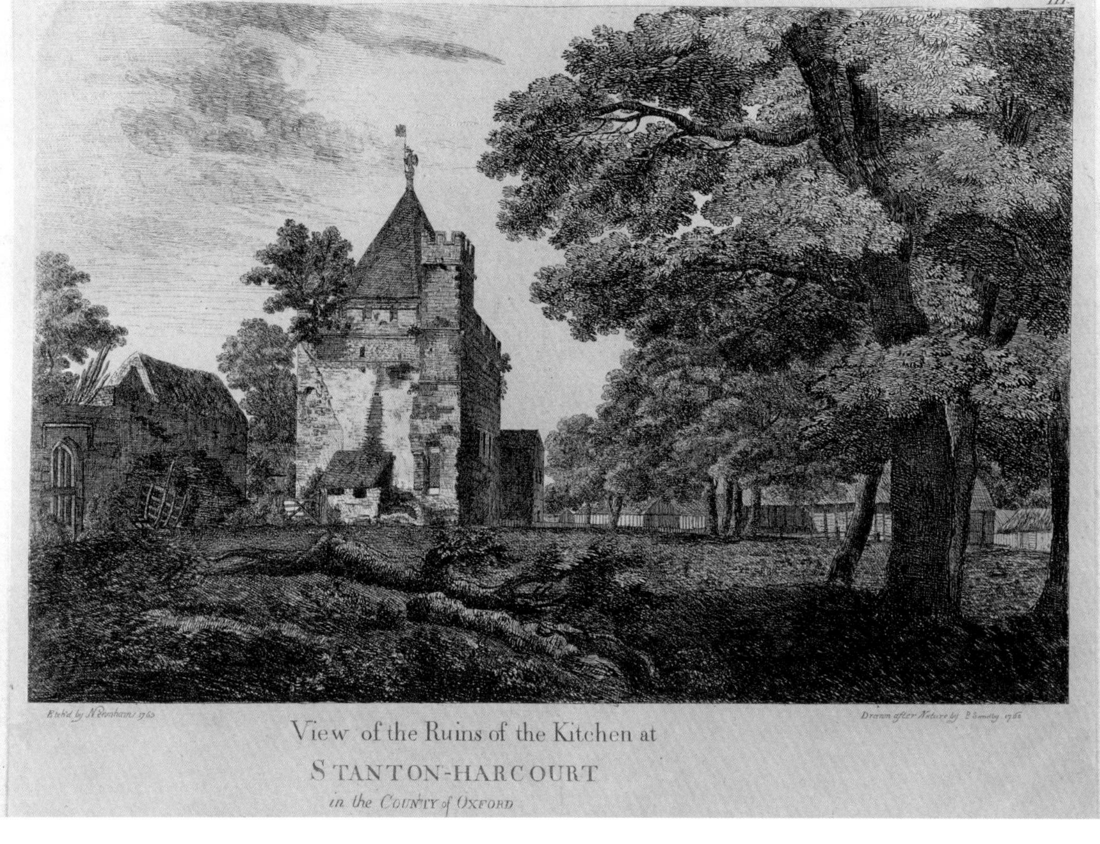

admired by both antiquarian scholars and picturesque tourists for their literary and historical associations. Alexander Pope had stayed in the chapel's tower earlier in the century, and the family could trace their occupancy of the land back to the Norman Conquest. These ancestral roots are recorded in the heraldry and legend etched below the view of the chapel ruins illustrated here, 'Drawn after Nature 1760 and Etched 1762 by Newnham'. *View of the Ruins of the Kitchen at Stanton-Harcourt* is inscribed 'Etched by Newnham 1763 Drawn after Nature by P Sandby 1760'. Surviving drawings, now in a private collection, certainly suggest that Sandby guided the artist, George Simon, Viscount Nuneham, through the execution of both compositions, if not their translation into print. He also oversaw two further views of this site, again later etched by the gentleman amateur. On becoming a Fellow of the Society of Antiquaries of London, Viscount Nuneham presented the plates of these etchings to the Society, which published them shortly afterwards.

Remarkably accomplished, whether in terms of their composition, perspective or the free handling of the needle, the etchings were much admired by contemporaries. In an essay 'On Modern Gardening', Horace Walpole was to observe of such prints: 'Lord Nuneham's etchings are superior in boldness and freedom of stroke to any things we have seen from established artists' (Walpole 1765–71, vol. 4, p. 150). Other etchings by Nuneham after drawings by Sandby include a number of Italianate capriccios in the manner of Salvator Rosa, as well as copies after paintings by Claude. These were circulated privately, inscribed to friends such as Georgiana, Duchess of Devonshire, Mary, Lady Hervey and 'To the Author of Elfrida & Caractacus', William Mason.

70

Roslin Castle, Midlothian, c. 1780

Bodycolour, 457 × 629 mm
Yale Center for British Art, New Haven,
Paul Mellon Collection, B1975.4.1877

PROVENANCE
William Sandby; Herbert Peake; Mrs Mew; Christie's, 7 July 1959; Agnew, 1960; bt Paul Mellon, 1960

SELECTED EXHIBITIONS
Yale 1985, no. 109; Yale 1989, no. 147; Yale 2001, no. 138; Yale 2007, no. 34

SELECTED REFERENCES
Yale 1985, no. 109, p. 82; Andrews 1989, p. 208; Yale 2001, no. 138, p. 162; Yale 2007, no. 34, p. 256

These ruins, located about eight miles southwest of Edinburgh, were described by the antiquarian Francis Grose as 'inconceivably romantic and pleasant', their situation, on a rocky promontory high above the River Esk, recommending them to artists, poets and tourists alike (Grose 1789–91, vol. 2, p. 49). Paul Sandby had published views of Roslin Castle as early as the 1750s, having probably encountered its remnants first on a visit to the nearby estate of John Clerk of Penicuik. However, given the freedom of handling and the figures' costumes, this picture must date from a later period, the artist reworking an earlier composition. A related sketch, inscribed with the names Lady Frances Scott and Lady Elliott, dated 1780 and now part of the Paul Mellon Collection, confirms this and reveals the identities of the women in the foreground. Lady Scott, who is here depicted sketching with the aid of a portable *camera obscura*, was a much-admired amateur artist and poet, who may well have studied under Sandby at one time. The present, highly finished painting might, therefore, have been a commission from one of these sitters' families. Beyond these specific circumstances, the work is particularly revealing of a more general growth of interest in the less familiar sites of the national landscape, prompted in large part by the popularity of picturesque tourism, and a related surge in the number of women wishing to learn to draw.

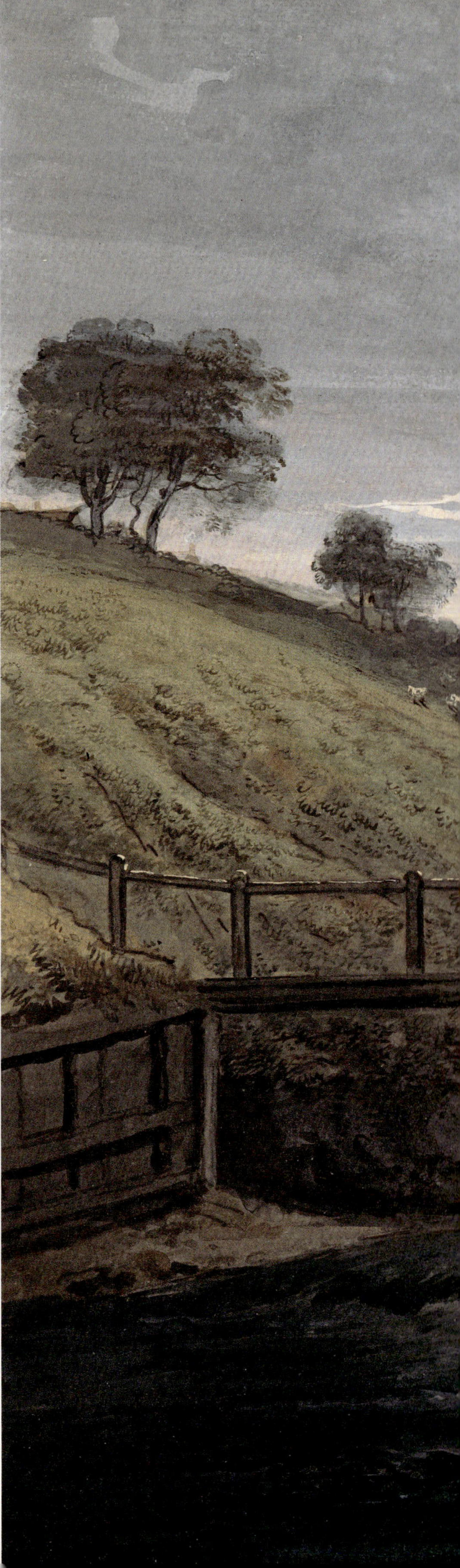

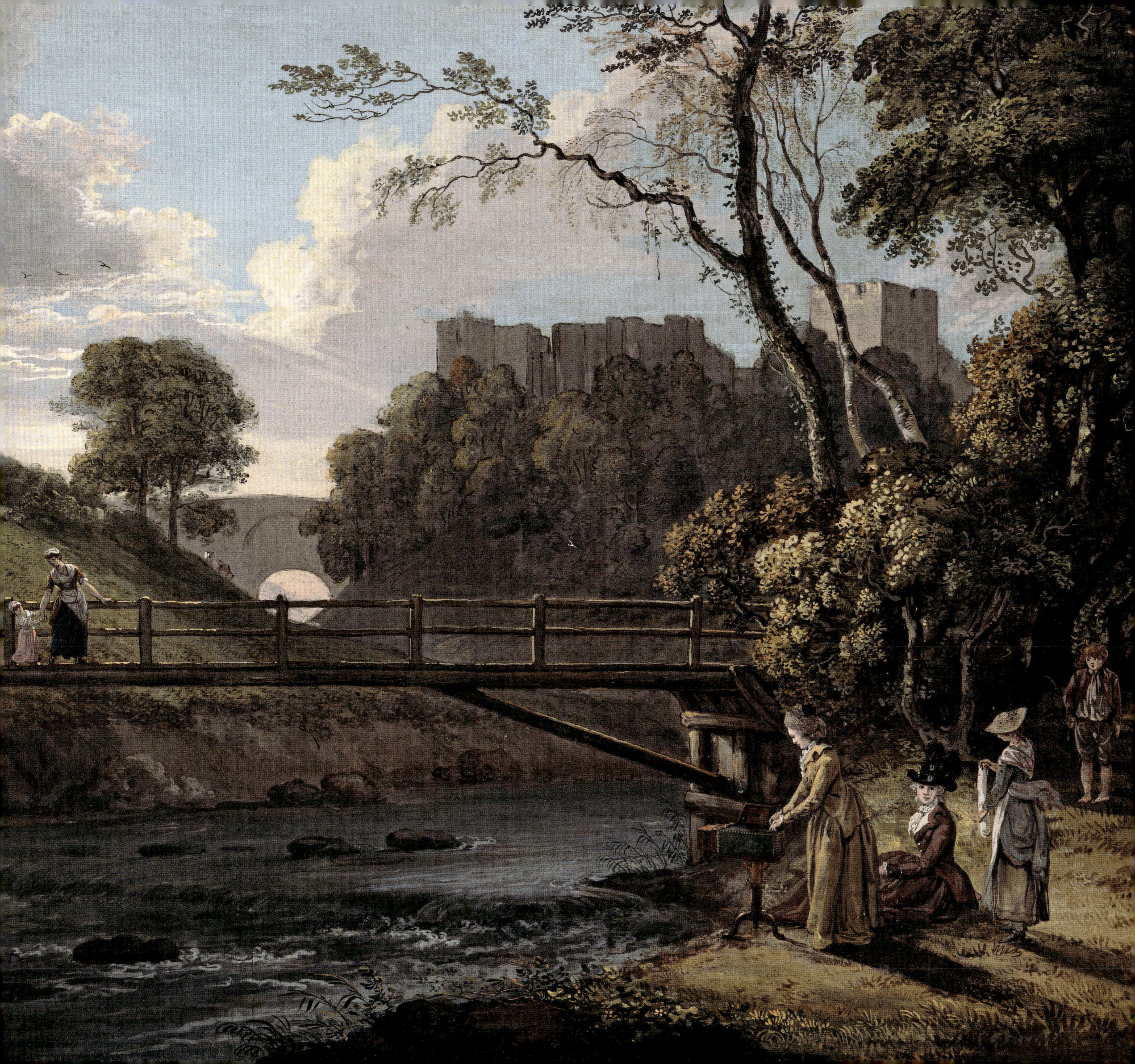

71.1–4

XII Views in South-Wales, published September 1775

(1) Plate I: 'Chepstow Castle in Monmouthshire'
(2) Plate VI: 'Pembroke Castle'
(3) Plate VII: 'Part of the Remains of Llanphor, near Pembroke'
(4) Plate IX: 'Manerbawr Castle From the Inward Court'

Etching and aquatint, average 233 × 312 mm
Hunterian Museum and Art Gallery, University of Glasgow

SELECTED REFERENCES
Hughes 1975; Yale 1985, nos 89–90, pp. 68–72; Robertson 1987, pp. 324–30

Henry Penruddocke Wyndham's *A Tour through Monmouthshire and Wales*, published in 1781, suggested the novelty of the author's travels by comparing 'crowded' English roads with those of the Welsh principality, 'so rarely visited, that the author did not meet with a single party of pleasure, during his six-week journey'. This neglect was occasioned by a mistaken belief that Welsh country roads were coarse and irregular and the people 'insolent and brutish', Wyndham observed. In an effort to dispel such prejudices he wrote to reassure the reader that the introduction of modern turn-pike roads had made the landscape open and accessible, and that contrary to rumour, the Welsh were 'universally civil and obliging'. Descriptions of the 'spirit of industry … in all parts of the Neath river, and neighbourhood', with its copper works and iron forges, tin works and coal mines, offered further assurance that the many antiquities to be viewed along the route taken were to be encountered as part of a modern, commercialised landscape. Wyndham's *Tour* was illustrated with 'views taken on the spot' by Samuel Hieronymous Grimm. Concerned to answer criticisms that these engravings omitted 'many of the most romantic ruins', such as those of Chepstow, Pembroke or Conway, Wyndham pointed out that these were 'too well known to be again repeated', having been the subject of 'late numerous publications' (Wyndham 1781, pp. i, ii, viii). This defence of the book's plates was almost certainly in deference to the 36 aquatint *Views of Wales* published by Paul Sandby between 1775 and 1777. Although Richard Wilson had distributed a much-admired set of six prints of Welsh mountain peaks and ruined castles in the late 1760s, and his pupil Thomas Jones *Six Views in South Wales, Drawn after Nature* in the mid-1770s, these were engraved and arguably lacked the visual appeal of Sandby's novel approximations of wash drawings. Like Wyndham's written account of tours through this still largely unfamiliar landscape, Sandby's views addressed not only its ancient architectural sites but their place in present circumstances.

In a letter to Thomas Pennant, dated 23 June 1777, Sandby praised the beauties of the Welsh landscape, but lamented 'it was to me great mortification not to have time to make sketches of all the fine scenes I saw' (National Library of Wales, Aberystwyth, Ms. 14005E). Indeed, Sandby is only known to have made three visits to Wales. In 1770 he was at Wynnstay, the seat of Sir Watkin Williams Wynn, to whom he taught drawing, returning the following summer to tour his patron's north Wales estates and, in 1773, he toured south Wales with a group of naturalists led by Joseph Banks (see cat. 93). Sketches made on these journeys were used to produce the three sets of aquatints clearly known to Wyndham: *XII Views in South-Wales*, dedicated to Banks and Charles Greville, were published in September 1775; *XII Views in North Wales* (cat. 93), dedicated to Wynn, were published in September 1776; and *XII Views in Wales* were published in September 1777. A fourth set of *XII Views in North and South Wales* was published in 1786, with plates for a further series rejected at some point as unsuitable for publication.

Although the result of his final tour of the principality, *XII Views in South-Wales* was published first. With one exception, a view along the shoreline of the River Neath, the views focus on ancient strongholds like the castles of Chepstow and Pembroke and ecclesiastical ruins like those of Llanphor Abbey or the episcopal palace of St David's. Nevertheless, these archaic structures, recalling the country's medieval or even Roman past, are also firmly established within the course of everyday agricultural and commercial activity, with harvesting to the fore in the view of Llanphor and restoration of the ruins of Manebawr Castle the subject of another print. Attention is also paid to the circulation of people and goods around these sites, whether in the form of gentlemen on horseback, a harvest wagon or the river traffic along the Wye at Chepstow. Such features of the landscape would have been of particular interest to one of the dedicatees of the series, Joseph Banks, a passionate advocate and sponsor of improvement as well as an enthusiastic antiquarian and naturalist. His 1773 tour of Wales in the company of the artist and his fellow naturalists Daniel Solander and John Lightfoot took in sites of personal, familial interest as well as of botanical, historical and com mercial curiosity. Travelling to the Carmarthenshire estate of Edwinsford, near Tally on the River Cothy, belonging to Banks' uncle, Robert Banks-Hodgkinson, the party ranged west into Pembrokeshire, making excursions to coastal sites, and afterwards toured the shores and hills of the north via Hereford and Shropshire. In depicting a selection of these locations, Sandby's sequence attends to their historic and modern, personal and patriotic, local and national associations.

In a letter to Banks, dated a few months after the tour of Wales, Sandby described himself as in a 'fit of castle building' (Osborn Collection, Beinecke Library, Yale University). In a later letter to his old friend John Clerk of Eldin, dated 8 September 1775, Sandby claimed to have produced '24 Views in Wales and 4 Large Warwicks' in the new aquatint method (National Art Library, V&A, London, MSL/1932/1563). A set of views of Warwick Castle was published in January 1776, with *XII Views in North Wales* appearing a few months later (see pp. 69–70).

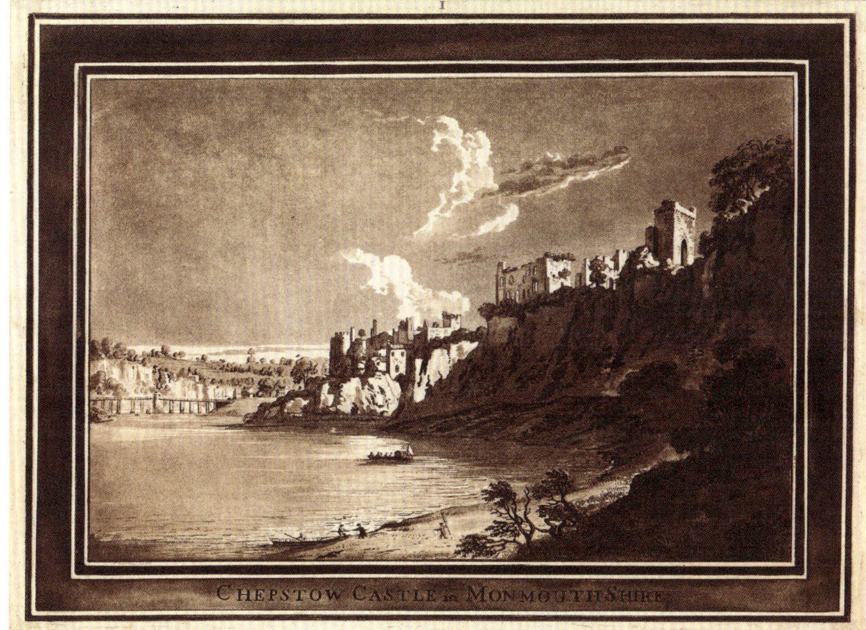

CAT. 71.1

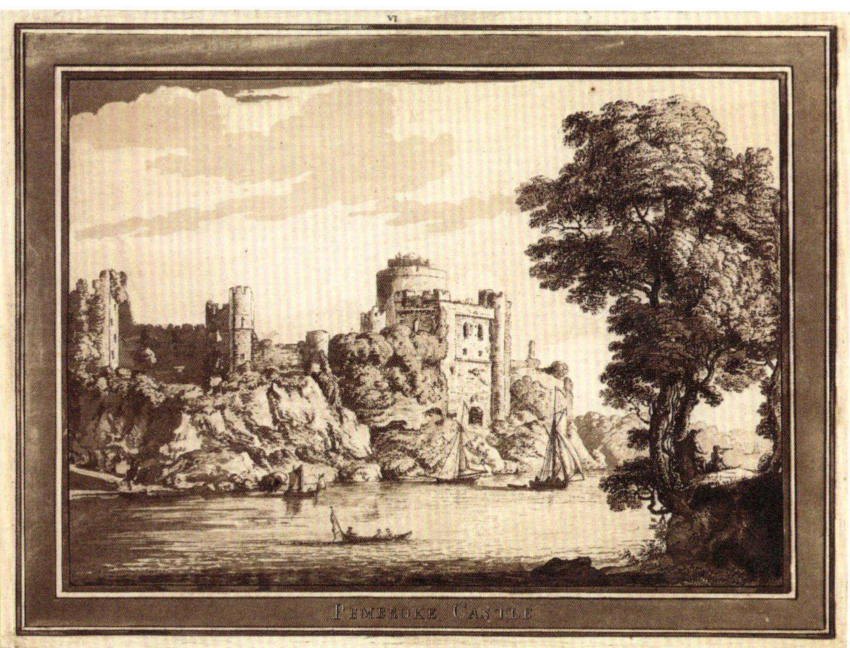

CAT. 71.2

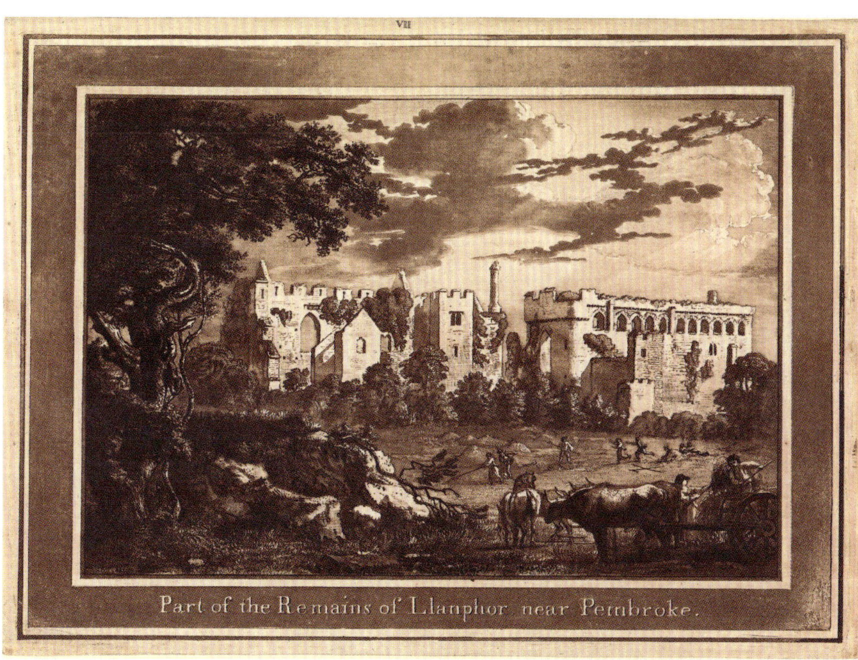

CAT. 71.3

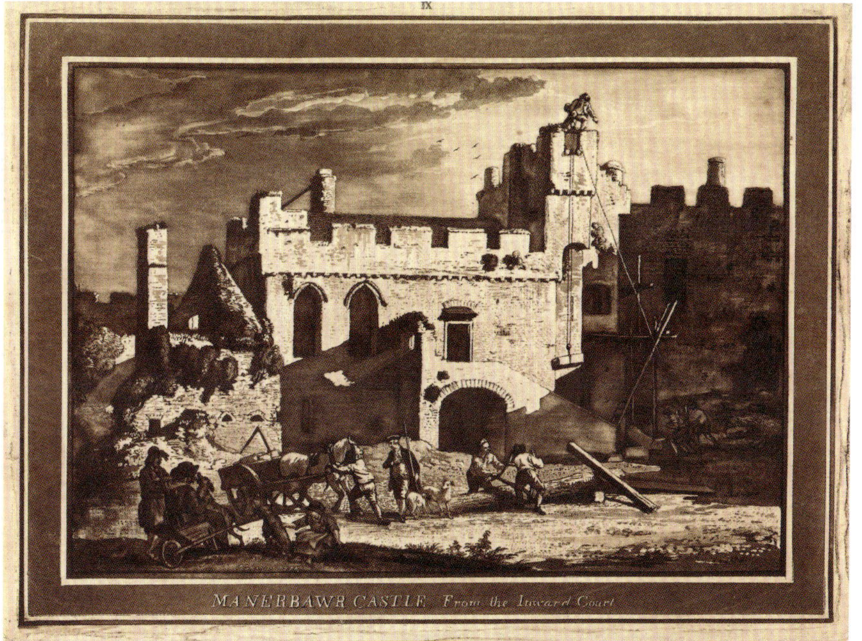

CAT. 71.4

72

The west gate of Cardiff, Glamorganshire, 1777

Bodycolour, 324 × 471 mm
Signed: 'P Sandby RA' (l.r.)
Private collection

PROVENANCE
Purchased from Francis Hervey, *c.* 1910s, and by descent

SELECTED EXHIBITIONS
RA 1777, no. 313?

In 1777 Sandby sent companion views of the south (now lost) and west gates of Cardiff to the annual Royal Academy exhibition. He had shown his first Welsh scene at the Academy four years earlier, and views of the principality were to remain central to his exhibition entries for the remainder of his career.

Although Cardiff and its castle were of considerable antiquarian interest, being strongly associated with the history of Roman as well as Norman Britain, Sandby gives at least equal prominence to signs of modern progress. In the picture of what is actually the north gate of the town shown here, he depicts an early morning scene along a road, eroded by vehicles and livestock and framed by the town's walls. The twelfth-century parish church of St John the Baptist towers above the developing, smoking townscape below. A number of bucolic figures make their way into and out of the town, including most prominently an elegant young female farmworker and a couple accompanying an empty ox-drawn cart who have presumably already delivered their produce to market.

Letterpress accompanying a view of the grounds of the interior of Cardiff Castle by Peter Mazell, after a design by Sandby, published the following year for *The Virtuosi's Museum*, highlighted the town's scenic pleasures and its ancient walls and stronghold, as well as the benefits flowing from recent modernisation:

> It is a pretty large well-built town, esteemed the handsomest in all South Wales. It is seated in a rich and fertile soil, proper for corn and pasture; the ground about it is level; but at the distance of three or four miles, it is surrounded with pleasant hills, that yield a delightful prospect. There is a handsome bridge over the river Taff, to which vessels of small burthen may come up; and a commodious harbour, by which the inhabitants carry on a good trade to Bristol, and other places. The houses are well built, and streets clean and in good order … It is enclosed by a wall, which has four gates, and has a castle, which is a large strong, and stately edifice (*The Virtuosi's Museum*, 1778–81, plate XIII).

Sandby's views of Cardiff, whether sent for public exhibition or translated into print, addressed the implications of improvement for the locality and the country at large, placing emphasis on the productivity of the town and adjacent country, and its commercial links to other places. They are alert to the particular claims of the place, its situation and aspect, as well as its wider significance within the country at large.

In 1776 John Stuart, the future 4th Earl of Bute, had been elevated to the peerage as Baron Cardiff, the Windsor estates in south Wales having passed to him by marriage. He was elected a Fellow of the Society of Antiquaries of London that same year, and Sandby's decision to display views of the town adjoining the peer's property a year later may have been informed by knowledge of the commercial and scholarly interests of the son of one of his most prominent patrons, the 3rd Earl of Bute (see cats 89–91). These pictures were also, no doubt, intended to promote the forthcoming publication of Sandby's third set of Welsh views, issued in September 1777 and featuring a view of the road into Cardiff as its title page.

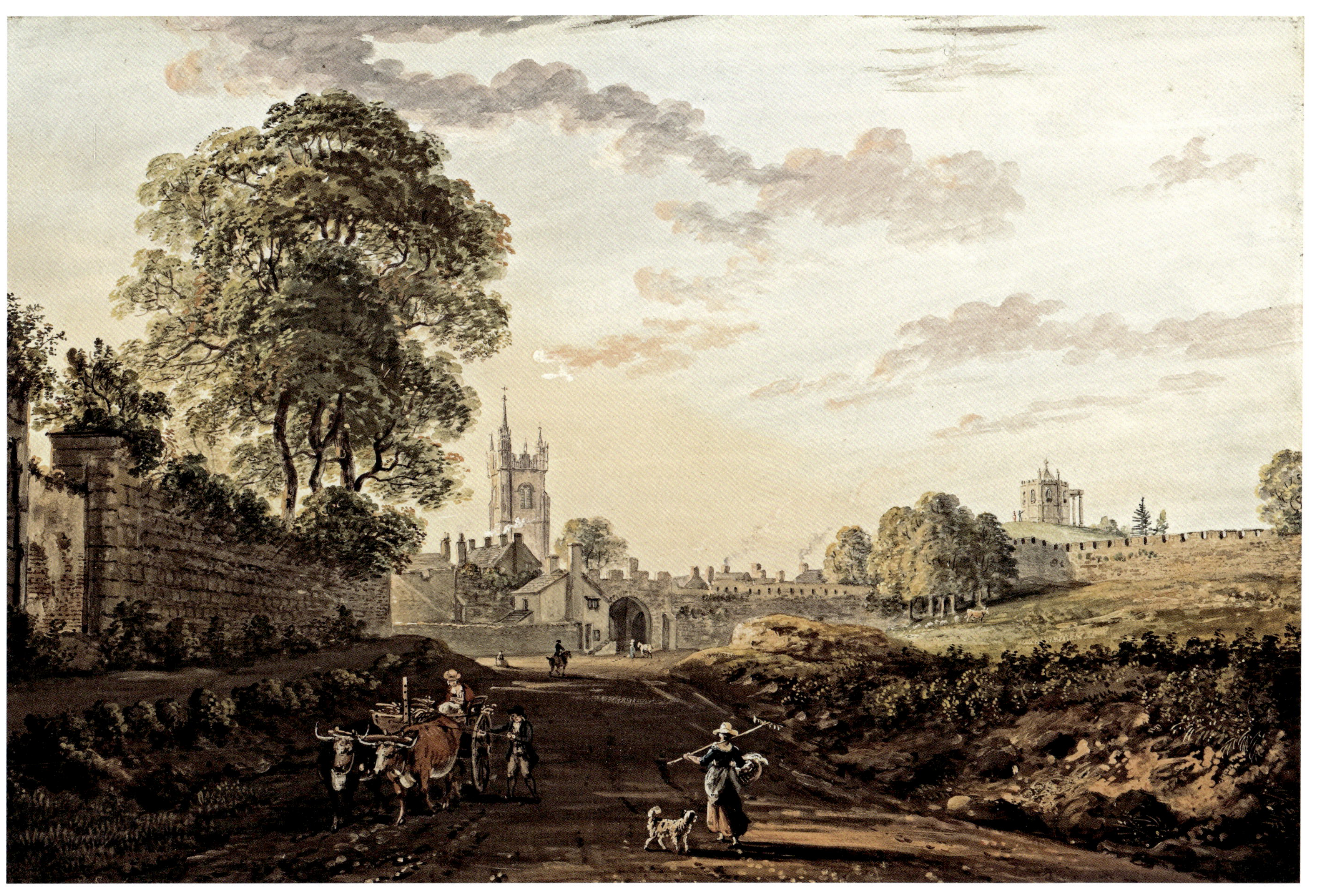

73

Part of Wenlock Abbey in Shropshire, c. 1770s

Watercolour over graphite, 352 × 547 mm
Signed: 'P Sandby RA' (l.r.)
Royal Academy of Arts, London

PROVENANCE
John Yenn; bequeathed by Mrs Augusta Thackeray, 1865

SELECTED EXHIBITIONS
London 1963, no. 69; Hamilton 1981, no. 39

SELECTED REFERENCES
Hamilton 1981, no. 39, p. 39; Smith 1998, p. 33

Situated about eleven miles southeast of Shrewsbury, on the road to north Wales, the ruins of Wenlock Abbey stood on land that enjoyed the patronage of one of Sandby's most important clients of the early 1770s, Sir Watkin Williams Wynn. Accounts of the abbey's remains invariably credit the Wynn family with arresting further decay of a structure that had provided the stone for many local buildings. A prominent member of the Honourable Society of the Cymmrodorion, which continues to further interests in Welsh antiquity, literature and customs, as well as natural philosophy and manufacturing, to this day, Wynn had a vested interest in the antiquities of a region with close associations to 'the ancient princes of Powis land' (*The Virtuosi's Museum*, 1778, plate 1). He also served as Vice-President of the Most Honourable and Loyal Society of Ancient Britons, claiming a lineage as far back as the ninth-century Welsh king, Rhodri Mawr.

Views of the historic town of Shrewsbury, especially its castle and Old Welsh Bridge, were to become a recurring feature of Sandby's art following his first visit to Wales in 1770, when he stayed at Wynn's Denbighshire home. Views of Wenlock Abbey were also to become a perennial motif following this initial trip, when he executed *A view of Wenlock Abbey in Watercolours* for his patron (fig. 48). A description of the abbey's state of repair at this time is provided by Francis Grose's *Antiquities of England and Wales*:

> Of the buildings there still remains what is now made a good dwelling-house, with proper offices for a farm: adjoining to this house is a range of cloisters. The church itself was built in the form of a cross; part of its walls are standing; those particularly of the southern end of the transept are pretty entire. At the extremity of it are seen the remains of a chapel, into which the entrance lies under three circular arches adorned with undulating zigzags; the pillars are so far buried, that the architraves appear but just above the ground. On the inside of the walls are razed figures of painted and circular arches mutually intersecting. Other broken and detached parts of the body of the church, and the bottom of the south aisle is converted into stabling. (Grose 1773–87, vol. 5, pp. 18–19)

This account highlights the irregular outlines and fragmentary forms that made such ruins appealing to picturesque taste. In Sandby's drawing, which shows the south transept and converted Prior's Lodge, these features are further accentuated by the foliage and vegetation that threaten to engulf the remains, reminding the viewer of the long-term processes by which nature wears away even the grandest of man's designs. A further melancholic note is struck, perhaps, by the simple toil of the occupants of the farm buildings described by Grose's account and Sandby's drawing, the labour of those of a lowly station often prompting reflection on man's lot, especially when observed against a backdrop of grandiose ruins.

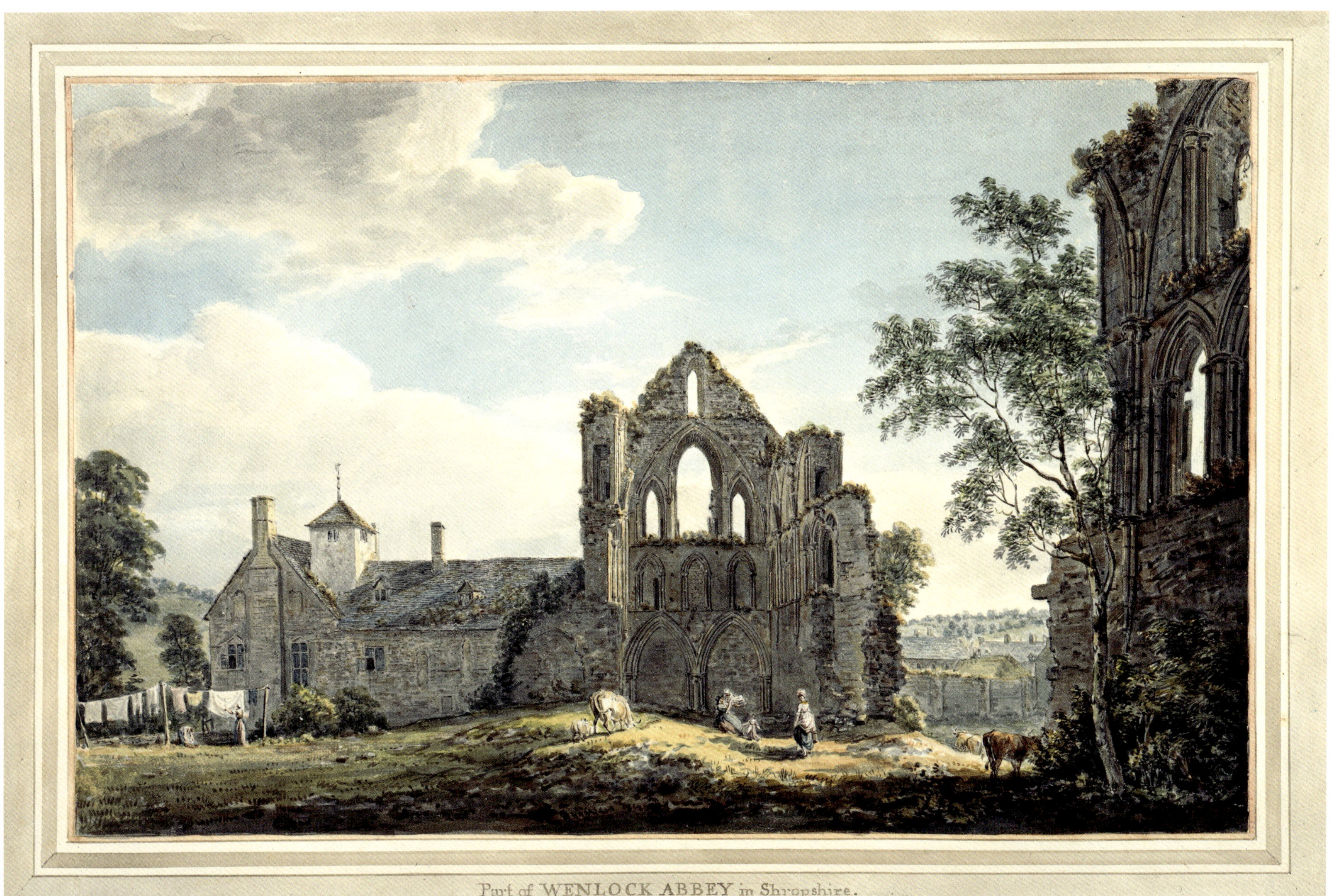

Part of WENLOCK ABBEY in Shropshire.

74

Roche Abbey, Yorkshire, c. 1770s

Watercolour over graphite, 300 × 588 mm
Signed: 'P Sandby RA' (l.l.)
Royal Academy of Arts, London

PROVENANCE
John Yenn; bequeathed by Mrs Augusta Thackeray, 1865

SELECTED EXHIBITIONS
London 1963, no. 74; Reading 1972, no. 41; Hamilton 1981, no. 38

SELECTED REFERENCES
Hamilton 1981, no. 41, p. 41; Smith 1998, p. 32

Views of Roche Abbey were a mainstay of Sandby's exhibited and printed works from as early as 1763, when he showed a drawing of the site at the Society of Artists. His introduction to these ruins of a Cistercian abbey church located in Sandbeck Park, on what was then the estate of Richard Lumley-Saunderson, 4th Earl of Scarborough, may well have been through the local poet William Mason. Artist and poet had recently collaborated on *The Bard*, one of Sandby's few exercises in historical landscape, and both were enjoying the patronage of the Harcourt family (see cats 68–69). In a letter of the period to George Simon, Viscount Nuneham, Mason remarked: 'In a word Sandby improves as much in painting as your Lordship does in caprice … and in short time will be that Claude Lorraine, that Brown assured him he was at Lord Scarbro's in my hearing' (Harcourt 1880–1905, vol. 7, p. 15). In September 1774 Lancelot 'Capability' Brown was employed to improve the grounds surrounding a new house at Sandbeck, built to a design by James Paine, the contract specifying that these modifications also 'finish all the valley of Roach Abbey in all its Parts, according to the Ideas fixed on with Lord Scarborough (with Poet's feeling and with Painter's eye)' (cited in Coffin 1994, p. 54). This was a reference to the first book of Mason's *The English Garden*, published in 1772 (vol. 1, line 21), a verse in imitation of Virgil's *Georgics*, advocating a synthesis of the poetic and painterly.

For Mason, historic ruins such as those of the abbey at Sandbeck were far more suited to the English landscape than the classical structures of much recent garden and park design:

> But Time's rude mace has here all Roman piles
> Levell'd so low, that who, on British ground
> Attempts the task, builds but a splendid lye
> Which mocks historical credence. Hence
> the cause
> Why Saxon piles or Norman here prevail:
> Form they a rude, 'tis yet an English whole.
> (Mason 1783, vol. 3, lines 406–12)

While ruins like Roche Abbey might prompt contemplation of the nation's past in this way, they might also of course inspire melancholic musings on the depreciations of time. When Sandby's distant prospect of the abbey, engraved by Francis Chesham for *The Virtuosi's Museum*, was published in October 1780, the accompanying letterpress accentuated the meditative mood formed by the abbey and its setting, observing that:

> these ruins, among which large trees are now grown up, with the objects around them, form a picture inexpressibly charming, especially when viewed with the lights and shadows they receive from a western sun; and its reclusive situation, free from every noise, except the singing of the birds and the murmur of the brook, together with the fragments of sepulchral monuments, and the gloomy shades of ivy and yew, which creep up, and luxuriantly branch out and mix with the whiteness of the rocks, give such solemnity to the scene, as fills the mind with a pleasing melancholy.
> (*The Virtuosi's Museum*, 1778, plate 97)

Concerned to place emphasis on the pictorial aspect of his improvements, in the manner recommended by Mason's verse, Brown raised the ground level around the remnants of the abbey, covering the foundations and leaving visible only the tall, ruinous transept walls. For William Gilpin, however, visiting in 1776, Brown's modifications were profoundly damaging, with the most famous of writers on the picturesque finding: 'There is certainly little judgment shewn in this mode of improvement … in a ruin the reigning ideas are *solitude*, *neglect*, and *desolation* … a ruin should be left in a state of wildness, and negligence' (Gilpin 1789, vol. 1, pp. 23–24). No doubt Gilpin would have admired Sandby's watercolour, datable to some time around the early 1770s, in that it appears to record, and thus also preserve on paper, the structure just prior to Brown's intervention. This tranquil, sequestered scene, lit by brilliant sunlight, also makes for what Gilpin described elsewhere as a 'habitation of chearful solitude', 'tending to smooth and amuse', rather than 'rouse and transport; like the great scenes of nature' (Gilpin 1789, vol. 2, p. 180).

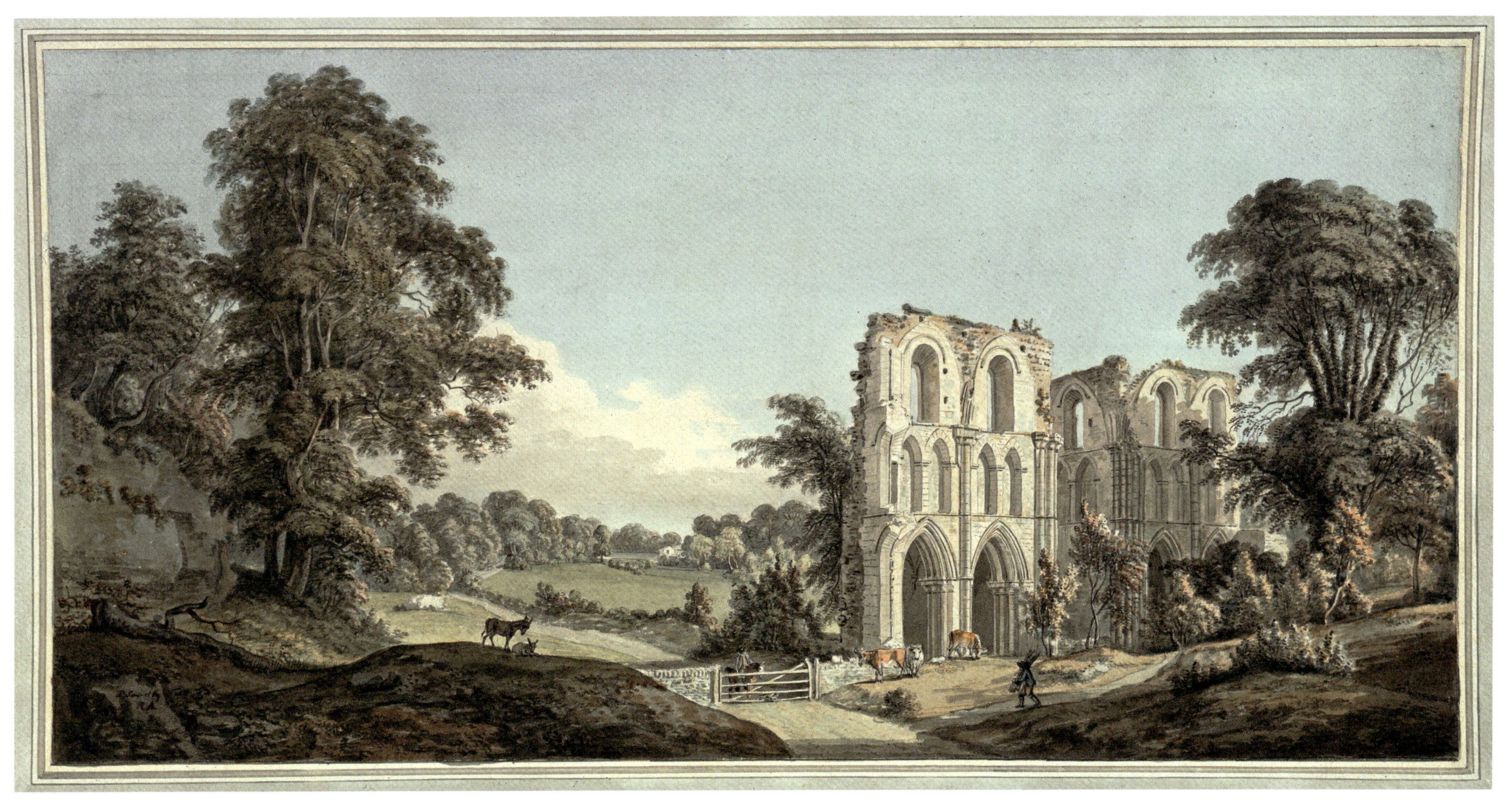

75

THOMAS SANDBY

The Devil's Peak Cave, Castleton, Derbyshire, page from *A Tour Through Part of Yorkshire and Derbyshire*, August 1774

Pen, ink and watercolour over graphite, 319 × 211 mm
Department of Prints and Drawings, British Museum, London, 1904-8-19-406

PROVENANCE
Bequeathed by William Sandby, 1904

Castleton.

Here is one of the Seven Wonders of the Peak, called the Devils, or Peak Cave. It is a large Subterraneous Cavern, running under the Hill at Castleton. The entrance into it is thro' a a great Natural Arch, on the perpendicular side of a Rocky Mountain, and immediately expands into a very Capacious and irregular Vault. On our first approach to this Stupendou Cave we were struck with the singular appearance of Several small and Miserable huts, the habitations of some poor people, who have been permitted their wretched dwellings therein, and where, we were told these miserable objects constantly reside, to raise contributions from such as visit the place.

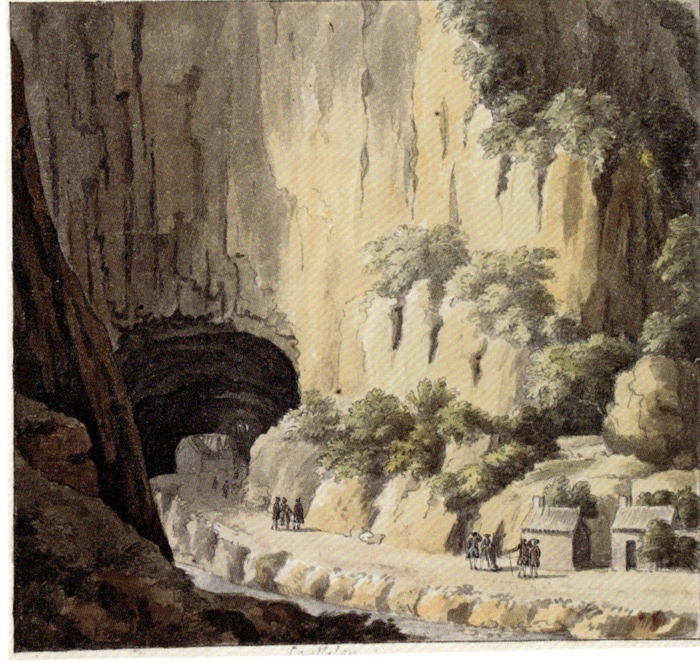

In the summer of 1774, Thomas Sandby embarked on a sketching tour of 'Gentlemen's Seats and Beautiful Landscapes' in the company of his London art-world friends and associates Samuel Cotes, William Elves, Theodosius Forrest and William Tyler. Their excursion led them through the Midlands, and up into the West Riding of Yorkshire, taking in the houses and grounds of the Duke of Norfolk (Worksop Manor), Edwin Lascelles (Harewood House) and the Marquess of Rockingham (Wentworth Woodhouse), along with several other notable estates, towns and scenic sights. A journal detailing Sandby's response to these buildings and landscapes provides evidence of a keen, informed interest not only in contemporary architecture and improvements but the structural remnants of earlier times.

On reaching Derbyshire Sandby visited 'one of the Seven Wonders of the Peak, call'd the Devils or Peaks Cave'. Several pages of the journal were given over to an elaborate description of 'this Gloomy Cave', accompanied by a detailed ground plan and this fine watercolour. A series of small ramshackle buildings, such as those described in the fragment of the journal entry on this detached leaf, are seen along a narrow path, leading into the mouth of the cavern. Its scale is made much more dramatic and imposing by the diminutive figures of the tourists shown visiting the site. In the passages that follow this introduction to the cave, recorded in a contemporary copy of the journal housed in the British Library, Sandby describes a boat journey along a Stygian tributary below the surface that accentuates the Gothic quality of these subterranean spaces. This fascination with underground spaces is also apparent in his accounts of man-made hollows and fissures encountered elsewhere. For the tourists' itinerary encompassed not only aristocratic parkland and places of natural wonder but also sites of industry, such as the lead mines of Matlock. These were of great contemporary significance, and played a key role in both the development of domestic scenic tourism and scientific inquiry, close observation of the caverns, mine shafts and quarries of the region shaping John Whitehurst's famous *Inquiry into the Original State and Formation of the Earth* (1778), as well as featuring in William Gilpin's influential *Observations relative to Picturesque Beauty* (1786). Some of Sandby's architectural designs for the embellishment of Virginia Water in Windsor Great Park (cats 77–80) were also to demonstrate an interest in the range of associations generated by such subterranean structures.

76

The Virtuosi's Museum; containing Select Views, in England, Scotland and Ireland, London, 1778–82

Nottingham City Museums and Galleries, NCM 1987-1032

SELECTED REFERENCES
Kennedy 2003

Published by George Kearsly between February 1778 and January 1781, *The Virtuosi's Museum* was the first series of topographical prints to cover the whole country. Issued in monthly instalments, typically featuring an English and an Irish scene, accompanied by either a view of Scotland or Wales, the series was eventually to comprise some 108 plates. With the exception of the views of Ireland, which were adapted by the artist from sketches made by the Hon. John Dawson, later Viscount Carlow, Sandby was solely responsible for the compositions, using studies made several decades earlier in the case of the Scottish scenes, and drawings made on more recent tours. A large team of talented engravers, including Daniel Lerpinière, Peter Mazell, James Walker and William Watts, sealed the success of the venture. With each plate available for 'the very moderate price of One Shilling', the appeal of the series was broader than the title implied, with its connotations of élite, connoisseurial collecting. According to the publisher's preface, the views offered 'a cheap and rational amusement … for less than the value of a masquerade ticket!' This was a patriotic enterprise, directed by a growing 'national taste' for 'innocent and refined amusements', surveying a remarkable range of native scenery: ports, towns and hamlets, mountains, rivers and spectacular waterfalls, historic structures, including abbeys, cathedrals and castles, and modern improvements, in the form of bridges, roads and factories.

War with France and the ongoing threat of invasion throughout the period of publication gave the project added poignancy. A notable feature of the plates is the emphasis on the healthy, productive state of the landscapes depicted. They present a view of British territories united by both their history and recent improvement. The accompanying letterpress often relates the historic significance of the sites featured, partly to throw the modern progress flowing from the political stability ensured by the union of the three kingdoms into still more stark relief. Extracts from Thomas Pennant's *Tours* note the benefits of agricultural improvement and modernising estate management on the Scottish landscape. Landowners such as Sir Watkin Williams Wynn are praised for their enlightened patronage. Among the scenes 'Sketched on the Spot' in Ireland by the Hon. John Dawson, a prominent member of the Anglo-Irish Protestant ascendancy, is a view along the River Boyne. Framing the broad expanse of water is a monument erected, according to the letterpress, 'in memory of the glorious and important victory obtain'd here, on the 1st of July, 1690, by king William the III over James the II by which the revolution was finally establish'd, and the happy constitution of the three kingdoms in church and state preserv'd from impending ruin'.

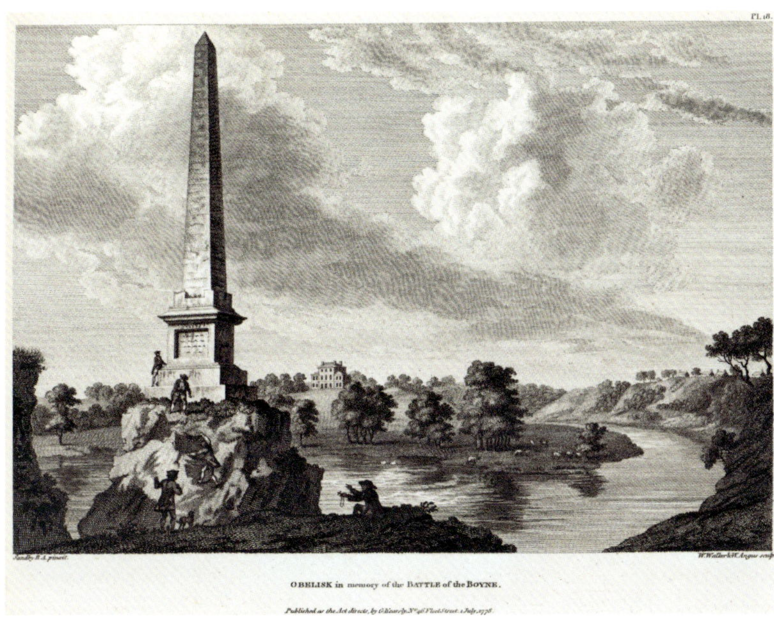

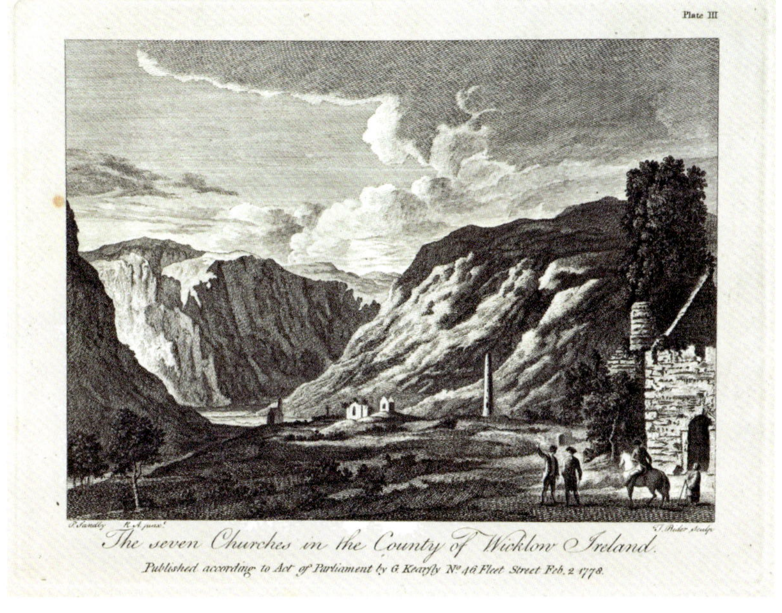

IV

Estates

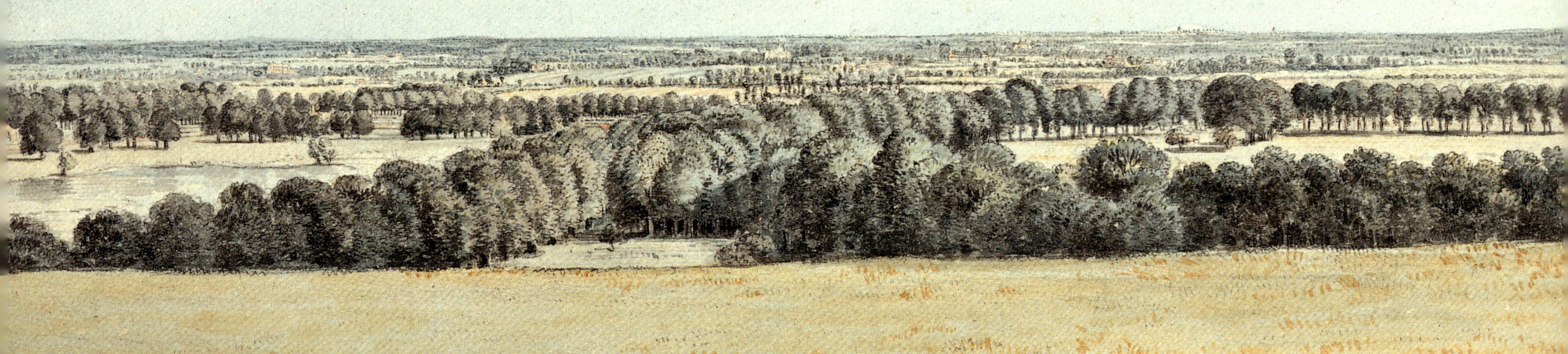

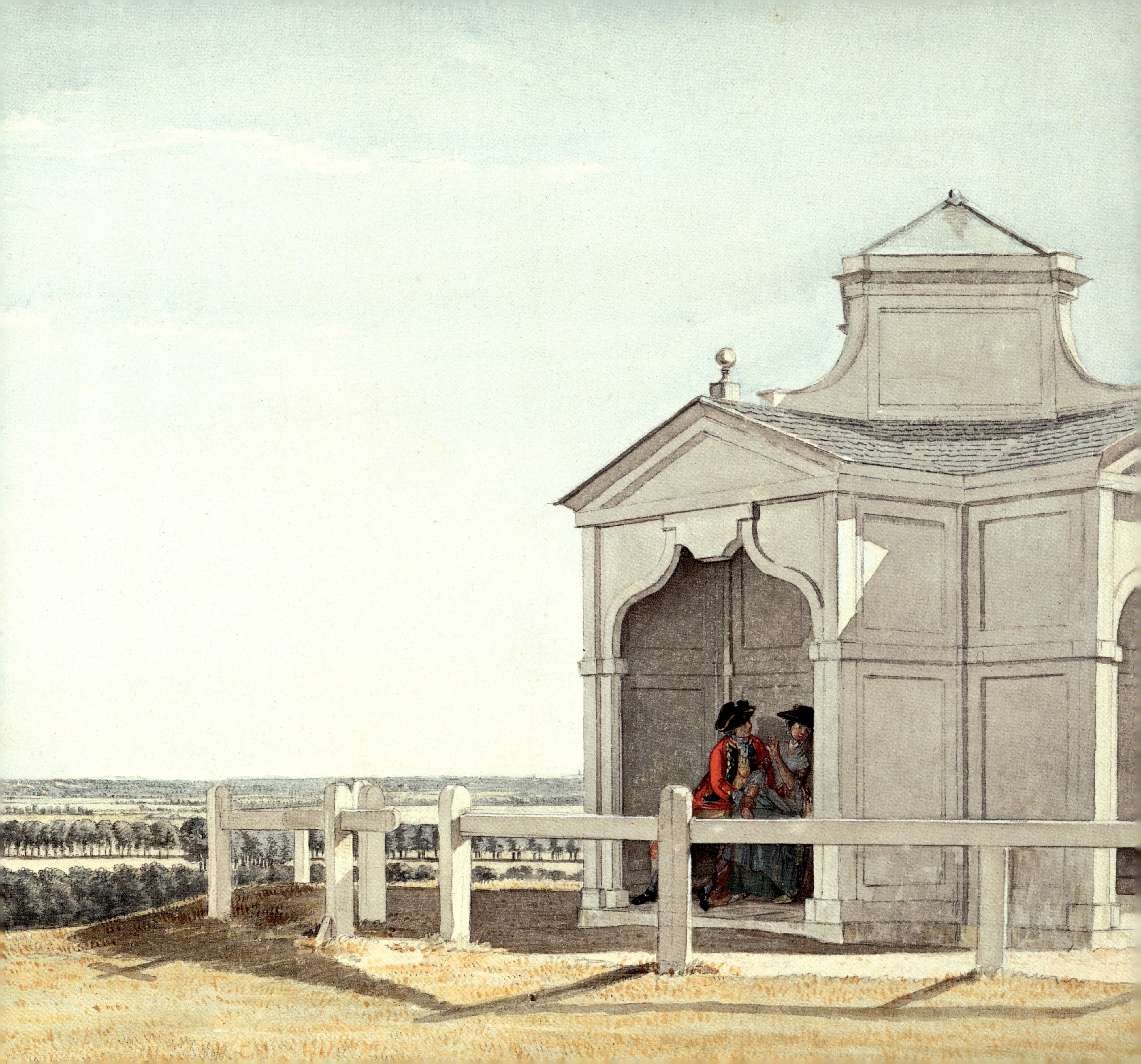

In early 1764 Thomas Gainsborough had occasion to decline an invitation from Philip Yorke, 2nd Earl of Hardwicke, to paint on his newly acquired estates, remarking that 'with regard to *real Views* from Nature in this Country, he had never seen any Place that affords a Subject equal to the poorest imitations of Gaspar or Claude'. He went on to recommend Paul Sandby as 'the only Man of Genius … who has employ'd his Pencil that Way'. Clearly Gainsborough considered the taking of '*real Views*' as incompatible with his own professional ambitions, arguing that 'to have anything tolerable of the name of G. the Subject altogether, as well [as] figures & c must be of his own Brain' (Hayes 2001, p. 30). Yet, despite this disdain for estate portraiture among artists with academic aspirations, commissioned views of aristocratic seats featured prominently in London's earliest public art exhibitions. Views of the private property of the nation's political and cultural élite sent to these new fashionable spectacles had already confirmed Sandby's 'genius' for such pictures, while the titles of his exhibits also identified him firmly with 'Nature in this Country'.

Country-house and estate portraits of the kind exhibited by Sandby in the 1760s, great oils like that of Nuneham Courtney, the seat of Simon, 1st Earl of Harcourt, not only recorded recent improvements to these houses but also offered extensive views of their estates, whether parkland or farmland, rides or woodland, roads or waterways, as well as natural or man-made features that lay beyond their boundaries, in the form of surrounding hillsides or the landmarks of nearby towns (cats 84–85). These were leisured landscapes, comprised of attractive walks and rides, designed with such noble sporting pursuits as hunting or racing in mind, as well as sites of agricultural and industrial production. These features are often framed by, or viewed through, trees, connecting them to, or integrating them with, the surrounding fields and woods, hedges and lanes, villages and farmsteads. Conservative political theorists, alarmed by the fragmentation of a society increasingly driven by commerce, saw connection as an important means of reconciling the moral welfare of a community with the pursuit of profit through improvement (Everett 1994). Estate portraiture celebrated prudent management and ownership, social harmony and productivity, in which the resources of the land were employed to stimulate morality as much as prosperity. Good estate management, as many an essayist, novelist or poet noted, offered a metaphor for effective government. Supervision of such a wide extent of variegated land endowed the owner with the independence of means and capacity for generalising thought that were considered essential to participation in government.

Land ownership was the foundation of economic wealth, social status and political authority. In the wake of the constitutional settlement of 1688, which secured a new political dispensation for parliament, landed property and its improvement became the basis of power and influence. Large, consolidated estates enabled landowners to concentrate their political influence over the surrounding countryside and permitted them to exploit more fully its resources and gain greater control over the appearance of the landscape. Estates might proclaim an owner's taste and knowledge or express political ideals, as well as assert his wealth and power.

Estates, in all their variety, from large royal and aristocratic parks to domestic and commercial gardens and agricultural and industrial sites, remained a central theme of Sandby's art beyond the estate portraits of the 1760s. The antiquities depicted in the previous section were often encountered by the artist on a tour of a gentleman's property, where they might not only contrast with improvements recently made but also symbolise ancestral connections with the landscape. Ancient forts and strongholds dating from the reigns of Edward I and Edward II feature prominently alongside images of improvement and industry in Sandby's *XII Views of North Wales*, recording the extensive properties of Sir Watkin Williams Wynn, and include newly built houses, roads and bridges, mills, forges and towns, raw, mountainous scenery and landscaped parks (cat. 93).

Thomas Sandby had a long-standing interest in the landscaping of pleasure grounds, as his work as Deputy Ranger of Windsor Great Park and his lectures to Royal Academy students delivered in his capacity as that institution's first Professor of Architecture attest. In these discourses, he argued that:

To me the talents of ingenious Landskip Painters has always appeared the most congenial with the Art of Ornamental Gardening; their studies being chiefly directed to such objects as are noble, grand and Picturesque: such they endeavour to select, arrange & combine, so as to display, on their canvas, the most beautiful forms and effects of nature; and would therefore be more likely to succeed in that department of Gardening which should produce the most varied and agreeable Scenery. (Sandby Lectures, I, fol. 36)

Such a picturesque approach to landscaping had been promoted by several theorists, not least William Mason. A close friend of Paul Sandby, the poet-gardener had recently laid out the famous flower garden at Nuneham 'with Poet's Feeling and with Painter's eye' (Mason 1783, vol. 1, line 21). In drawings showing Mason's design, Sandby details the innovative planting of garden and wild flowers, the classical temples and natural bowers sheltering verse-inscribed monuments, and animating the scenes with gardeners and visitors (fig. 46). This was a garden that its patron, William, 2nd Earl of Harcourt, described in a letter to the artist as one that must be 'perceived and felt' (Bodleian Library, University of Oxford, Bodleian MS Eng. Letters d310 f15; Batey 1994). When engraved by William Watts for *The Copper-Plate Magazine* in 1778 these views of Harcourt's planted tribute to the philosophy of Jean-Jacques Rousseau made this sequestered spot visually accessible to those subscribers of the 'middling sort' principally targeted by the publication.

Thomas Sandby observed a peculiar pleasure in viewing someone else's acreage, arguing: 'All the surrounding Country within our View, may be looked on as our own property, when considered with regard to pleasure ... as if placed there by our own expence' (Sandby Lectures, IV, fol. 6). Such 'pleasure' was surely to be found in the brothers' views of Windsor's parkland and forest, where labourers, grounds-men and gardeners, as well as members of the royal family, attendants and polite visitors, enjoy 'All the surrounding Country'. Excursionists to this historic royal domain were briefly allowed to wander and view the landscape like kings.

Advising his students on matters of situating a property, Thomas recommended that 'there should be a proper quantity of Trees, grown near at hand for shelter and fuel' (Sandby Lectures, IV, fol. 5). Trees and woodland were far more than a material resource, however. They were symbolic of the social order, playing a key role in the political iconography of landscape improvement. A great family's occupancy of a landscape was often symbolised by hard-wood trees like beech, elm or oak. Their historic connection with a place through successive generations was naturalised by an imagery of roots and branches. In an island defended by the 'wooden walls' of its navy, timber had long been freighted with patriotic associations. During the long years of war with revolutionary and then Napoleonic France, views of the forests and timber yards of Windsor Great Park had become a favourite Sandby motif, as he exploited patriotic enthusiasm for imagery of the national territory (cats 98–100). One of the first British artists to attend to individual species, growth patterns and the roles of trees in the countryside, Sandby produced several spectacular portraits of individual oaks or ancient beeches, as well as wooded landscapes, in his final years, including atmospheric forest scenes. In such pictures he addressed not only an imagery readily associated with loyalism, but also a growing alarm at the scale of national improvements and the threat posed to tradition when the British landscape and the values it was held to represent were so greatly endangered.

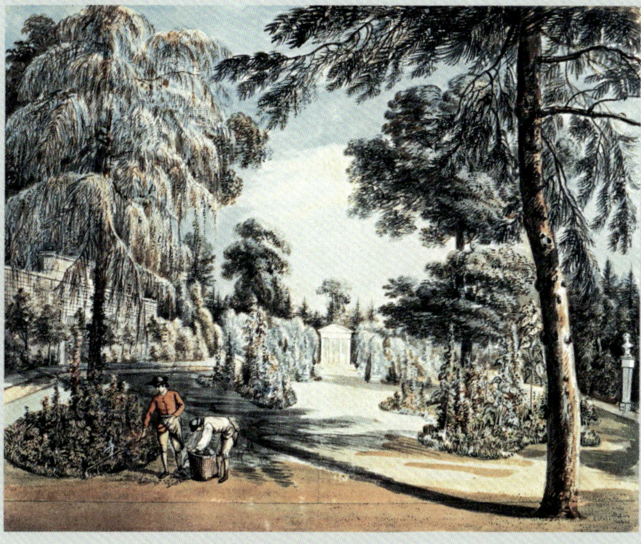

FIG. 46
Paul Sandby, *The Flower Garden at Nuneham Courtney, Oxfordshire*, 1777. Watercolour over graphite, 228 × 381 mm. Private collection

CATALOGUE NUMBERS 77–80

One of the most lavish print series of the eighteenth century, *Eight Views of Windsor Great Park* was first made available by private subscription in December 1754 and presumably published the following year. The set was to reach a wider market when advertised for sale in the *London Chronicle* on 27 April 1758 and on being re-published as hand-coloured engravings by John Boydell on 2 March 1772. However, it is to be assumed that the commentary that the views provided on the political fortunes of the Sandby brothers' patron, William Augustus, Duke of Cumberland, was by this latter date largely lost on purchasers.

Cumberland had been appointed Ranger of Windsor Great Park in July 1746, less than three months after his victory at Culloden. This was one of a number of honours and awards bestowed upon him in recognition of his services to the country in its hour of need. By the time he was granted the Wardenship of Windsor Forest in 1751, giving him direct responsibility for vast tracts of historically important and commercially attractive woodland, Cumberland had already begun to remodel the southern area of the Great Park. The scale of the Duke's programme of building, hydraulics, planting and earthworks was immense, with the work continuing throughout his lifetime and beyond. *A General Plan of the Park, Gardens and Plantations of Windsor Great Park*, drawn up by the architect John Vardy and published in 1750, records and celebrates the early stages of these massive works, as well as prospective future improvements (fig. 47). Vardy's wide-ranging survey of the park includes details of the layout and situation of new and existing buildings, gardens and plantations, new roads and spacious canals, as well as plans and elevations of a series of as yet unrealised structures, including a boat house, a Doric temple and some stables, all illustrated in a series of vignettes decorating the lower edge of the map. A decorative cartouche, festooned with flowers, gardening tools and cornucopias, underlines this as a vision of order and plenty.

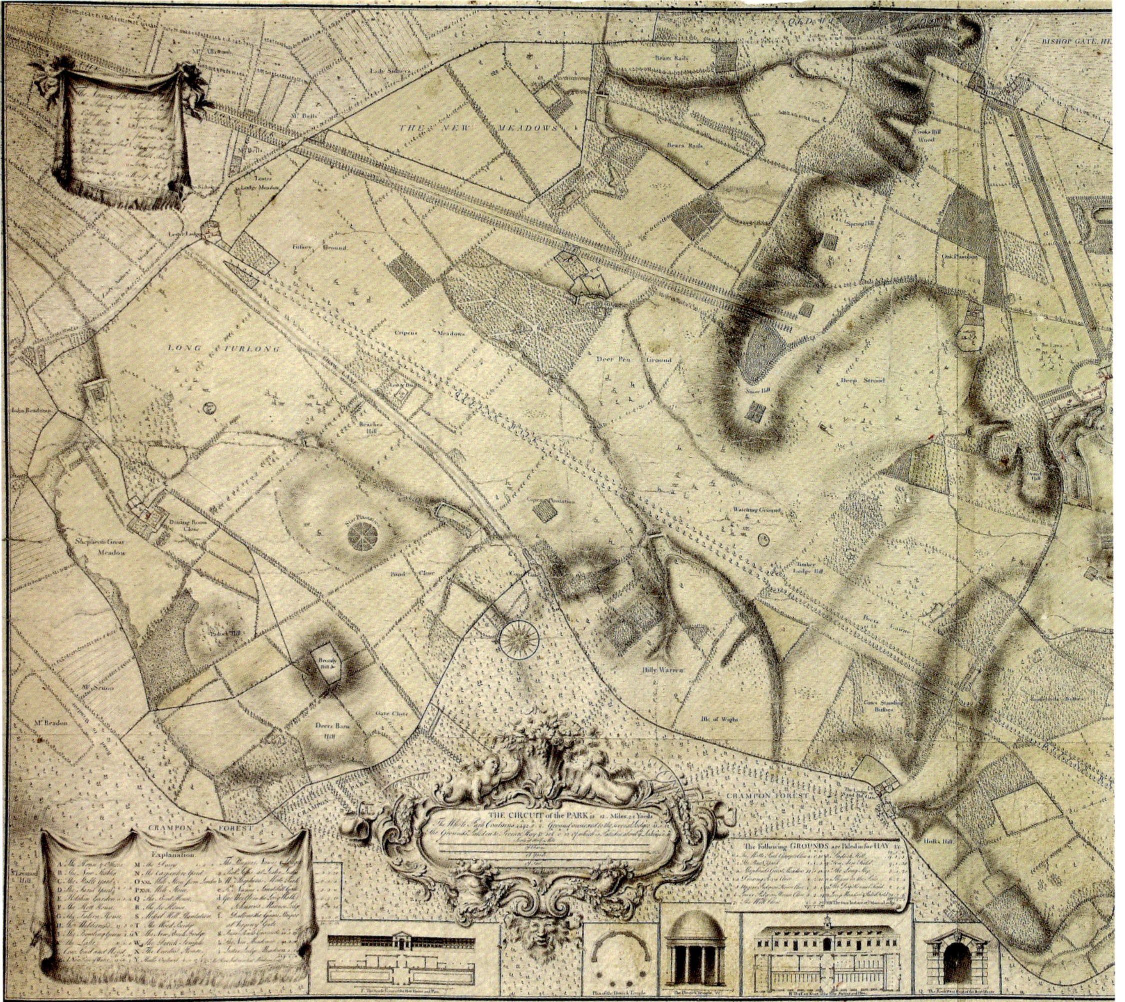

FIG. 47
John Vardy (1717/18–1765), *A General Plan of the Park, Gardens and Plantations of Windsor Great Park, the Seat of His Royal Highness the Duke of Cumberland*, 1750 (detail). Engraving, 870 × 1625 mm. Public Record Office/National Archives, MR1/280

77.1–3

THOMAS SANDBY

Eight Views of Windsor Great Park, *c.* 1754–55

(1) Proposals for Engraving and Title Page
(2) Paul Sandby, after Thomas Sandby, View from the North side of the Virginia River, near the Manour Lodge
(3) Paul Sandby and Edward Rooker, after Thomas Sandby, The Cascade and Grotto

Etching and engraving, average 347 × 583 mm
Royal Collection, London, 814382, 814384, 814378

SELECTED REFERENCES

Yale 1985, p. 54; Robertson 1987, pp. 209–26; Roberts 1997, pp. 39–44

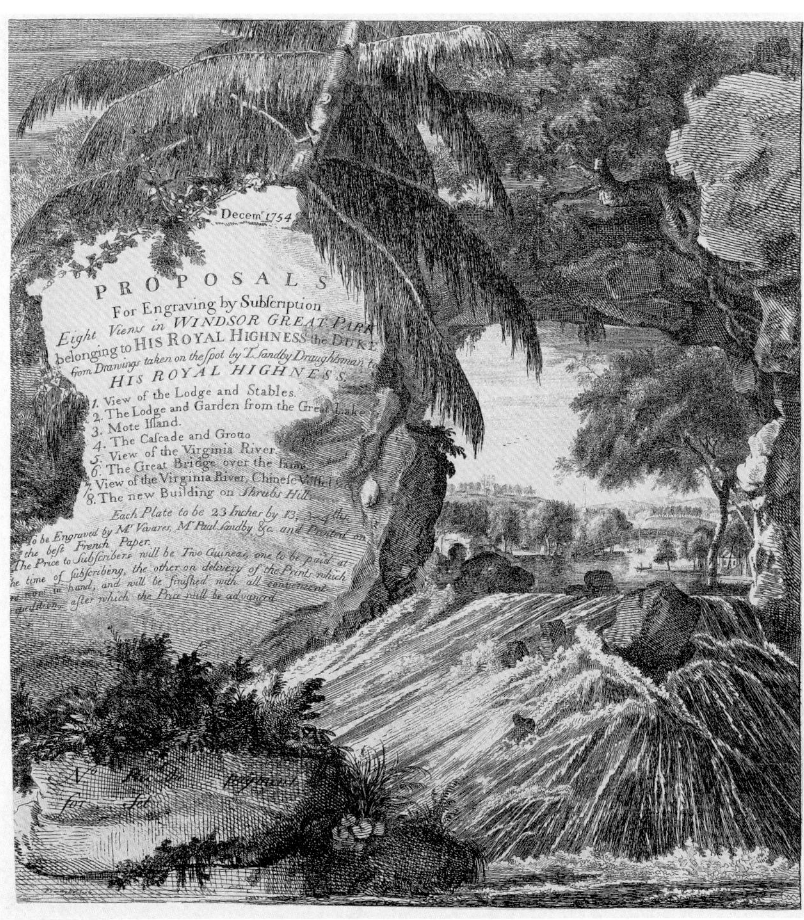

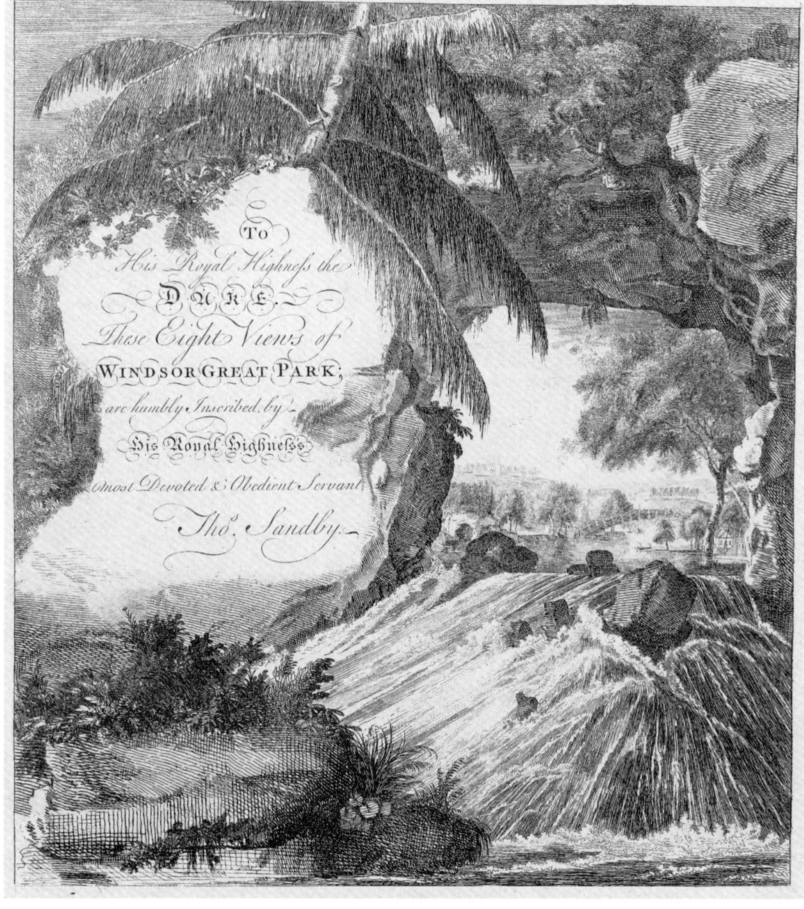

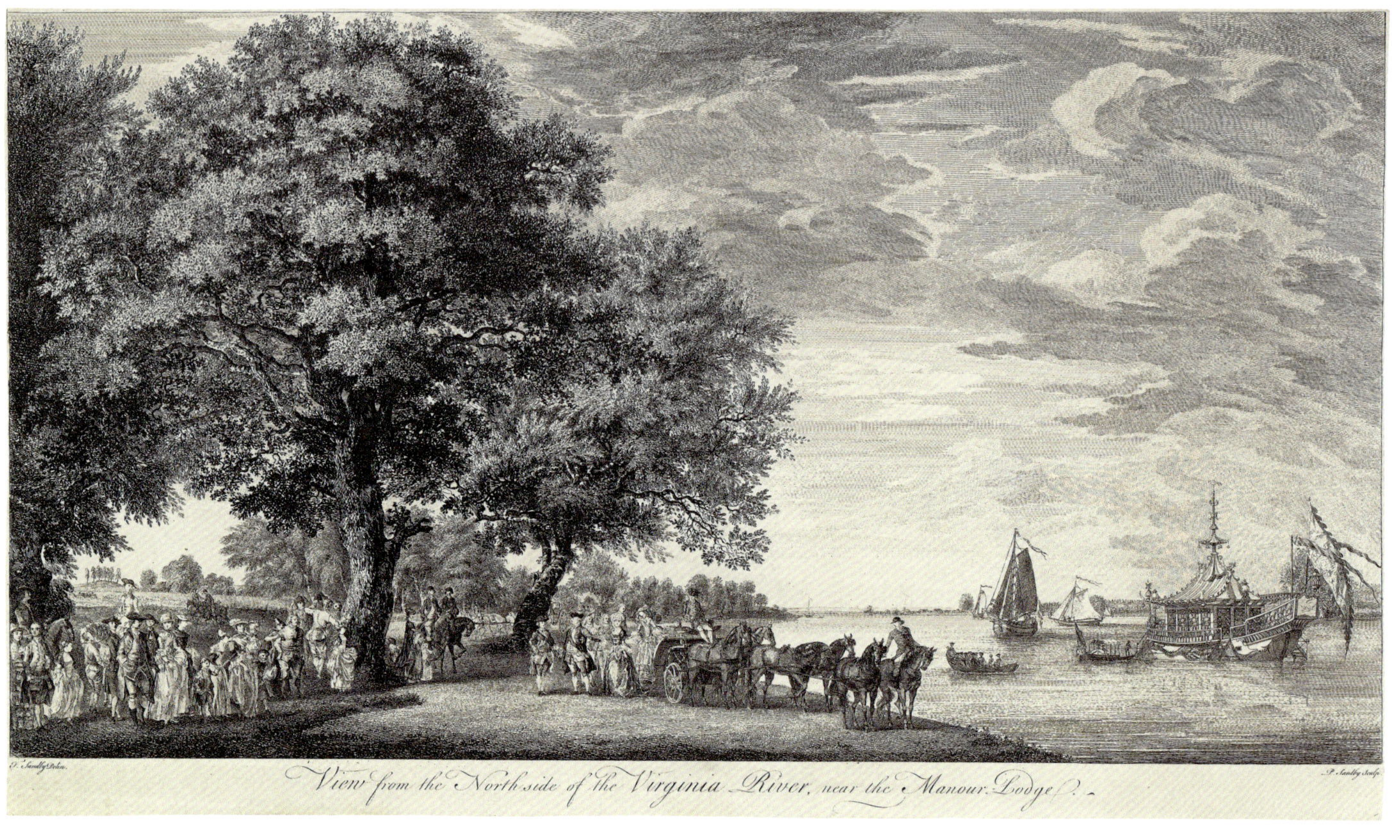

CAT. 77.2

Good management, order and peace are also central to the Sandbys' topographical survey of the Duke's grand works, which complemented Vardy's earlier publication.

A list of the prints is given on the decorative title page and subscription plate, carved into a rock, worn by a gushing torrent of water and enclosed by larch and pine. These features form an archway, framing a prospect of the landscape to be encountered in the plates that follow, dotted with the principal landmarks. The first plate features a carriage leaving Cranborne Lodge, the Duke's main residence, and shows its ostriches and deer, part of a menagerie that ranged 'from the lion to the lowest quadruped, and from the eagle to the meanest reptile' (Henderson 1766, pp. 337–38). Subsequent prints take in the grounds surrounding the Lodge, the Great Lake and its Mote Island, the cascade and grotto at Virginia Water, as well as its Great Bridge and Chinese Junk, concluding with a view of the New Tower or Belvedere on Shrubs Hill, which afforded fine views over these improvements and out towards Windsor Castle. Although there is no plate dedicated solely to the Obelisk, which commemorated Cumberland's role in the defeat of the Jacobite Rebellion, it is a presence in the background. Various figures inspect or work these landscapes, including the Duke himself, who is depicted as guide to members of the royal family, as well as improver and philanthropist, overseeing a gang of military veterans excavating a bank adjacent to one of the park's principal landmarks, Henry Flitcroft's Great Bridge.

The *Eight Views of Windsor Great Park* relate to and adapt a well-established tradition of court art (see pp. 49–55). However, they also engage with the conventions of estate portraiture and mapping, as well as other recent print series focusing on the leisurely inspection of newly improved grounds, such as Jean Rigaud's views of Viscount Cobham's Stowe (*c.* 1739). They are testament to the brothers' extraordinary command of a range of skills and pictorial conventions at this still early date, as well as their ambitions for their art. Surviving compositional studies, such as the *Great Bridge over Virginia Water*, reveal the series to have been very much a collaborative project, with Paul Sandby responsible for the figures that animate his elder brother's exacting studies of Cumberland's improvements. A number of highly regarded

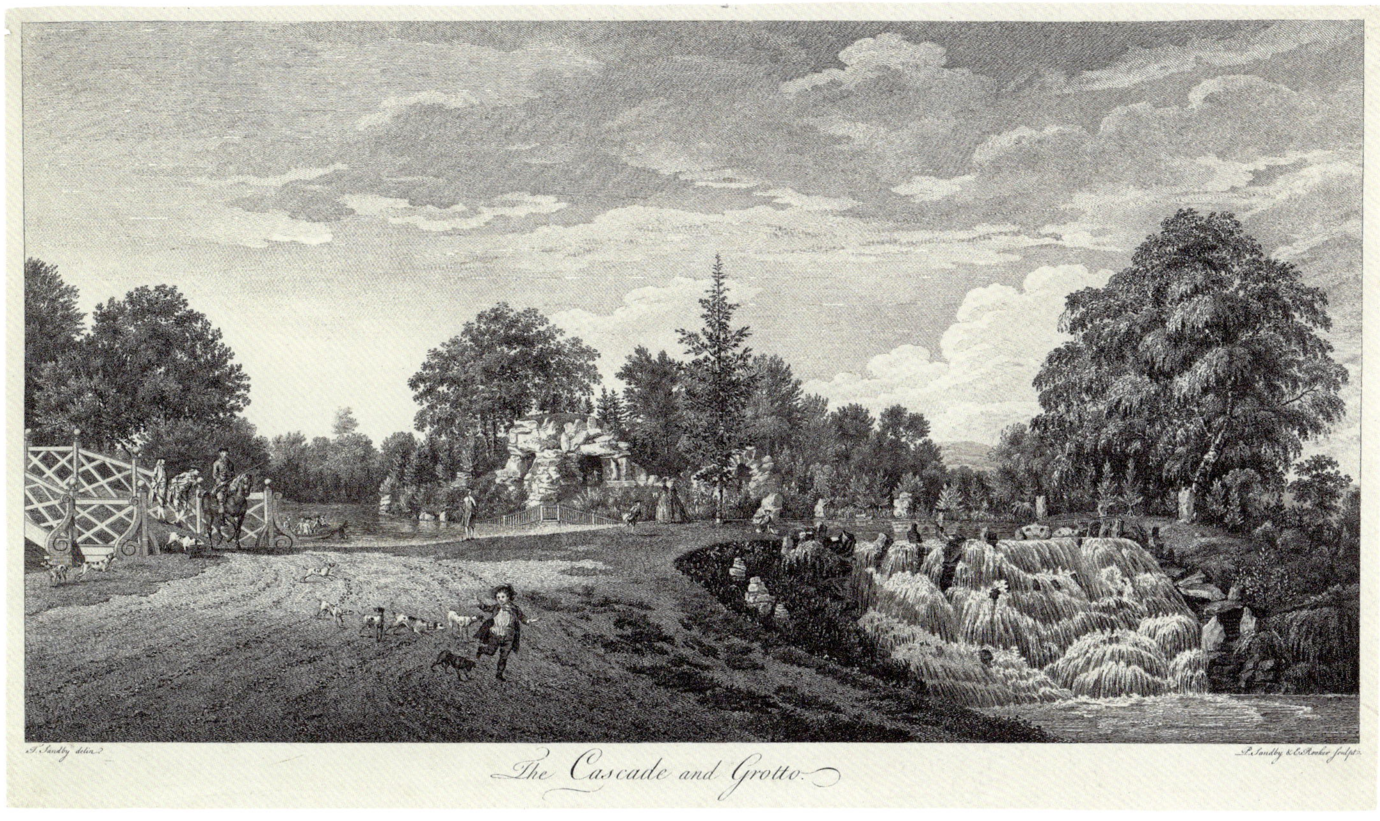

CAT. 77.3

engravers were employed to work up the plates, including Edward Rooker and the French-trained François Vivares and Pierre-Charles Canot, with Paul Sandby etching three plates. He was also responsible for the unpublished plate showing the cascade and grotto (cat. 77.3), which the artist brushed over with wash. The grotto, which may have been a design of the eccentric Thomas Wright of Durham, appears to have held a particular fascination for Thomas Sandby, whose original study is illustrated here. He was to produce a number of similar designs himself some twenty years later, when overseeing further improvements at Virginia Water. Grottoes, hermitages and roothouses were popular additions to gardens in the period, not least as places of entertainment. However, they were also to be associated with the country's ancient past, with the earliest forms of habitation, and thus the elder Sandby's interest in the origins of architecture, one of the central themes of his Royal Academy lectures. Other structures erected in or planned for Windsor Great Park included unrealised plans to relocate the Holbein Gate from Whitehall to the end of the estate's Long Walk (fig. 42), and to build Gothic bridges and classical temples, all no doubt intended to prompt a range of historic or poetic associations.

Visitors were suitably overwhelmed by the scale of the Duke's improvements, with Lady Jane Coke, writing in 1753, describing them as 'magnificent beyond description' (Coke 1899, vol. 2, p. 461). Richard Pococke was struck by the planting, and the rich array of exotic and native trees that frame many of the Sandbys' views (see Pococke 1888, pp. 60–64). These improvements, and their depiction in the Sandbys' views or Vardy's estate plan, were shaped by the politics of the age, as has been suggested elsewhere in this catalogue (see pp. 16–17 and 50–1). Published during a period of great political uncertainty, occasioned by the early death of Frederick, Prince of Wales, the Sandbys' prints were part of a wider campaign to alleviate fears concerning the Duke's designs on the throne. Accordingly, they portray Cumberland as retired from public life, distanced from the machinations of the political world, electing to cultivate his estate.

78

PAUL AND THOMAS SANDBY

The Cascade and the Grotto (Unpublished engraving, touched by hand), *c.* 1754–55

Etching, engraving and wash, 347 × 583 mm
Royal Collection, London, RL 17947

SELECTED REFERENCES
Oppé 1947, p. 41

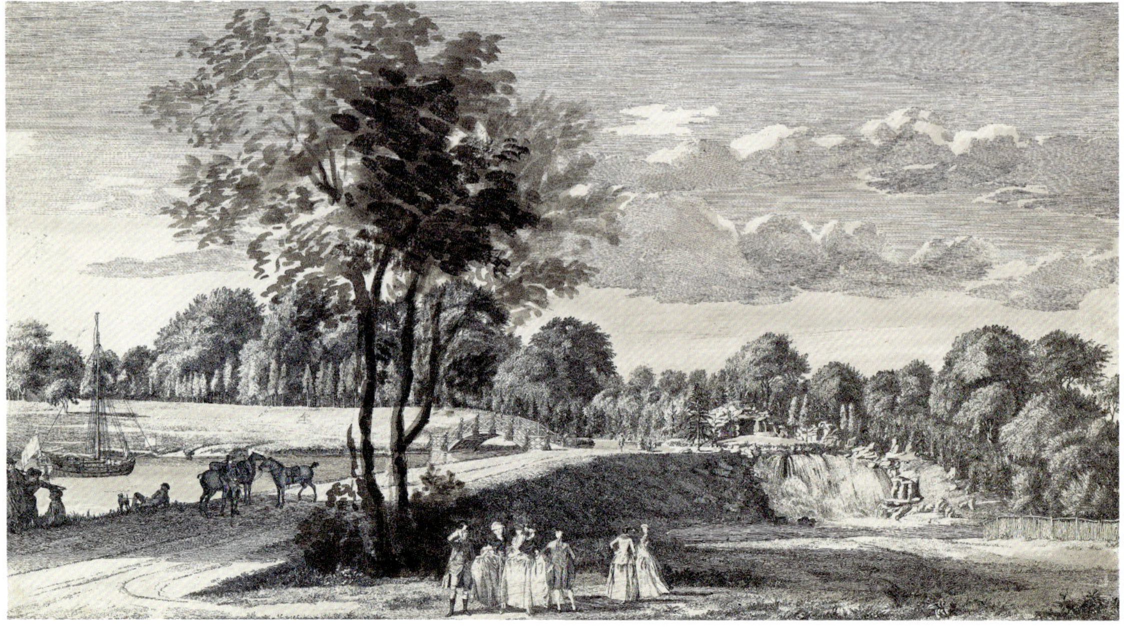

79

THOMAS SANDBY

The Grotto, Virginia Water, *c.* 1754

Watercolour over ink and graphite, 207 × 275 mm
Yale Center for British Art, New Haven, Paul Mellon Collection, B1975.4.1390

PROVENANCE
Colnaghi, to 1964

SELECTED EXHIBITIONS
Yale 1985, no. 21

SELECTED REFERENCES
Yale 1985, no. 21, p. 26; Smiles 1994, pp. 202–03

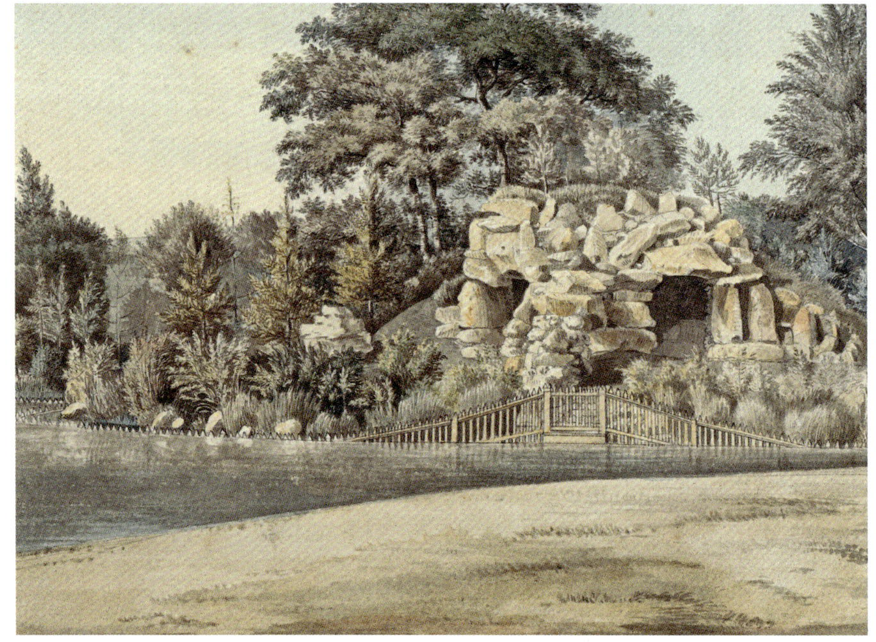

80

PAUL AND THOMAS SANDBY

The Great Bridge over Virginia Water, c. 1754

Pen, ink, watercolour and bodycolour over graphite,
313 × 577 mm
Royal Collection, London, RL 14647

PROVENANCE

Paul Sandby; in the Royal Collection by 1884

SELECTED EXHIBITIONS

Nottingham 1884, no. 21; Amsterdam 1995, no. 44

SELECTED REFERENCES

Oppé 1947, no. 120; Amsterdam 1995, no. 44, pp. 128–29

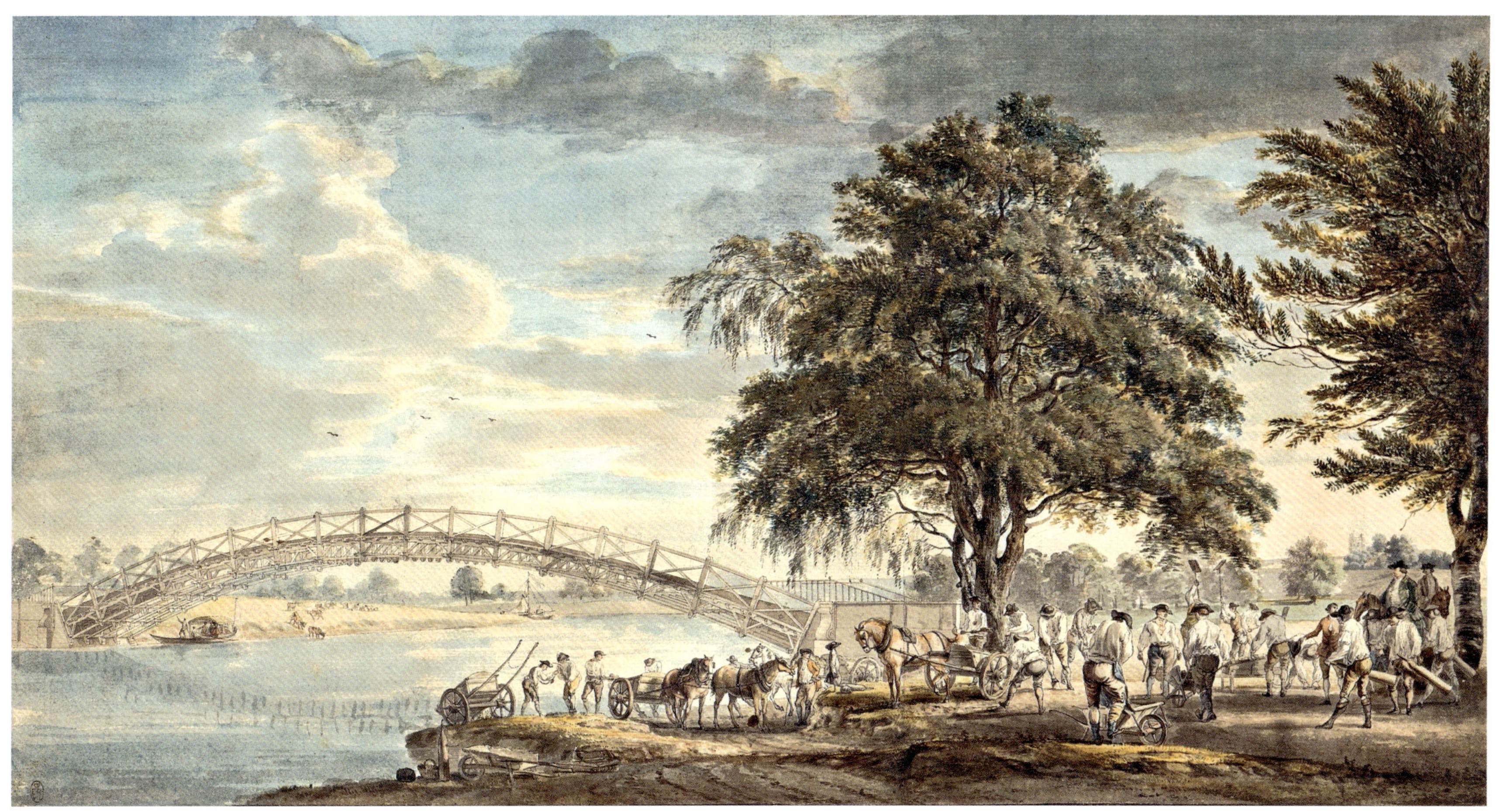

81

PAUL AND THOMAS SANDBY

Ascot Heath races, *c.* 1765

Pen, ink and watercolour over graphite, 495 × 914 mm
Royal Collection, London, RL 14675

PROVENANCE
Thomas Sandby (sale Leigh & Sotheby, 18 July 1799, lot 11); Colnaghi; George, Prince of Wales (1 August 1799); by descent

SELECTED EXHIBITIONS
Reading 1972, no. 25; Nottingham 1986, n.n.; Amsterdam 1995, no. 47

SELECTED REFERENCES
Oppé 1947, no. 147, p. 43–44; Robertson 1987, p. 106; Amsterdam 1995, no. 47, p. 134

This Hogarthian, carnival-like panorama of a crowd gathered at an Ascot race meeting was part of an uncompleted series of drawings documenting the Duke of Cumberland's equestrian pursuits (Royal Collection, London). These depicted the Sandbys' most important patron across a range of settings, from the stables of Cumberland Lodge to the racetrack itself, inspecting his stud and mares, watching over the training of his horses, and surveying the field as his horse comes in to win. Cumberland was both breeder and owner, taking a keen interest in the 'science' of the sport (see Deuchar 1988, p. 67; Roberts 1997, pp. 44–46). These pursuits were recorded in paintings by George Stubbs, William Marlow and Sawrey Gilpin (who may have assisted the Sandbys in this drawing), complementing the equestrian, military portraits of the Duke executed by David Morier.

Race meetings had long been celebrated by the sporting fraternity as arenas of friendly competition, convivial socialising and political bargaining. During the middle decades of the eighteenth century what had once been an exclusively aristocratic pastime was being transformed into a major industry, with the Jockey Club introducing a system of colours and handicaps, as well as overseeing the conduct of races, wagers and attendant crowds. The sport was widely promoted as reflecting the mutual interests of all in society, and the participation of the wider populace was invited. Cumberland's revival of race meets on Ascot Heath, first staged during the reign of Queen Anne, is to be seen in the context of these broader developments, as well as his recent plans to open up his Windsor estates to leisured inspection.

Paul Sandby supplied a wide cast of characters to his elder brother's meticulously delineated view of the Heath, an area of flat, open land to the west of Windsor Great Park. These include portrait studies of Cumberland's employees, an array of polite men and women, as well as people of more modest social station, gamblers, jockeys, owners, soldiers and vendors. With the race in its closing stages, they climb fences and carriages for a better view, cheer from the stands, or else remain in the makeshift taverns at the far right. There is considerable humour in this energetic and diverse group, a quality widely associated with ideals of liberty and patriotic fervour in many a portrayal of an English crowd in the period (Donald 1996, pp. 109–41).

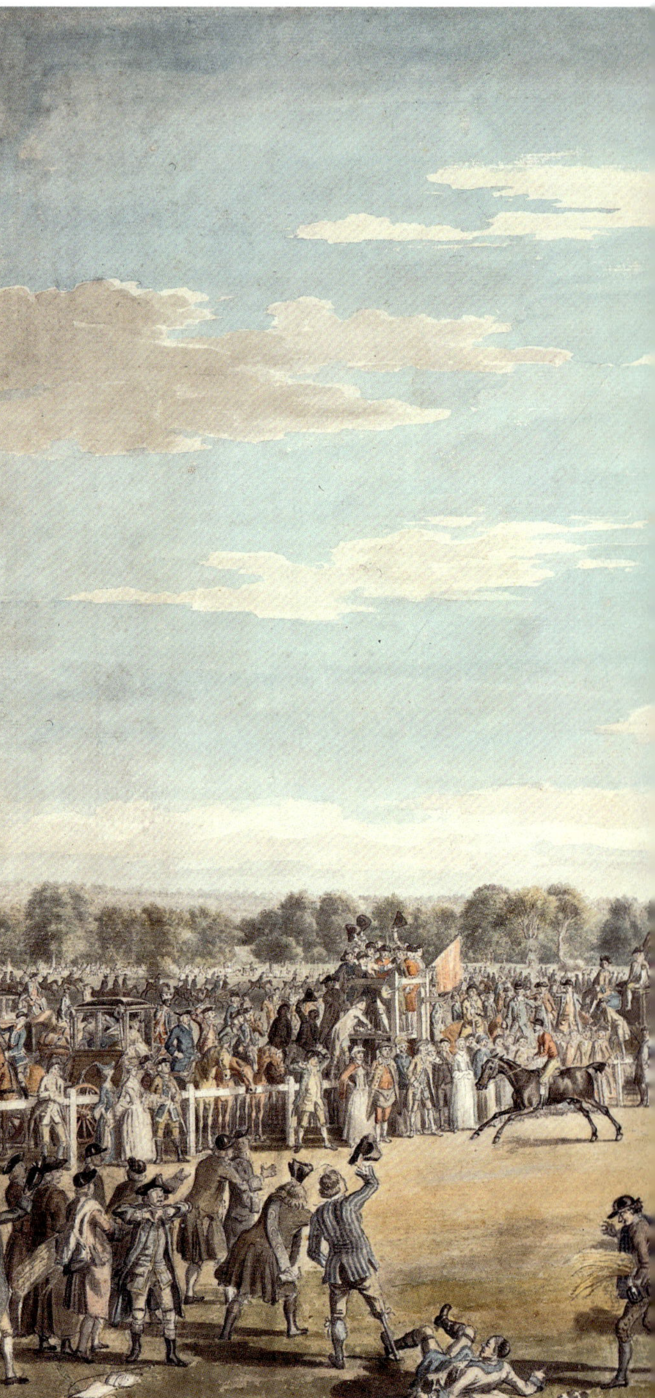

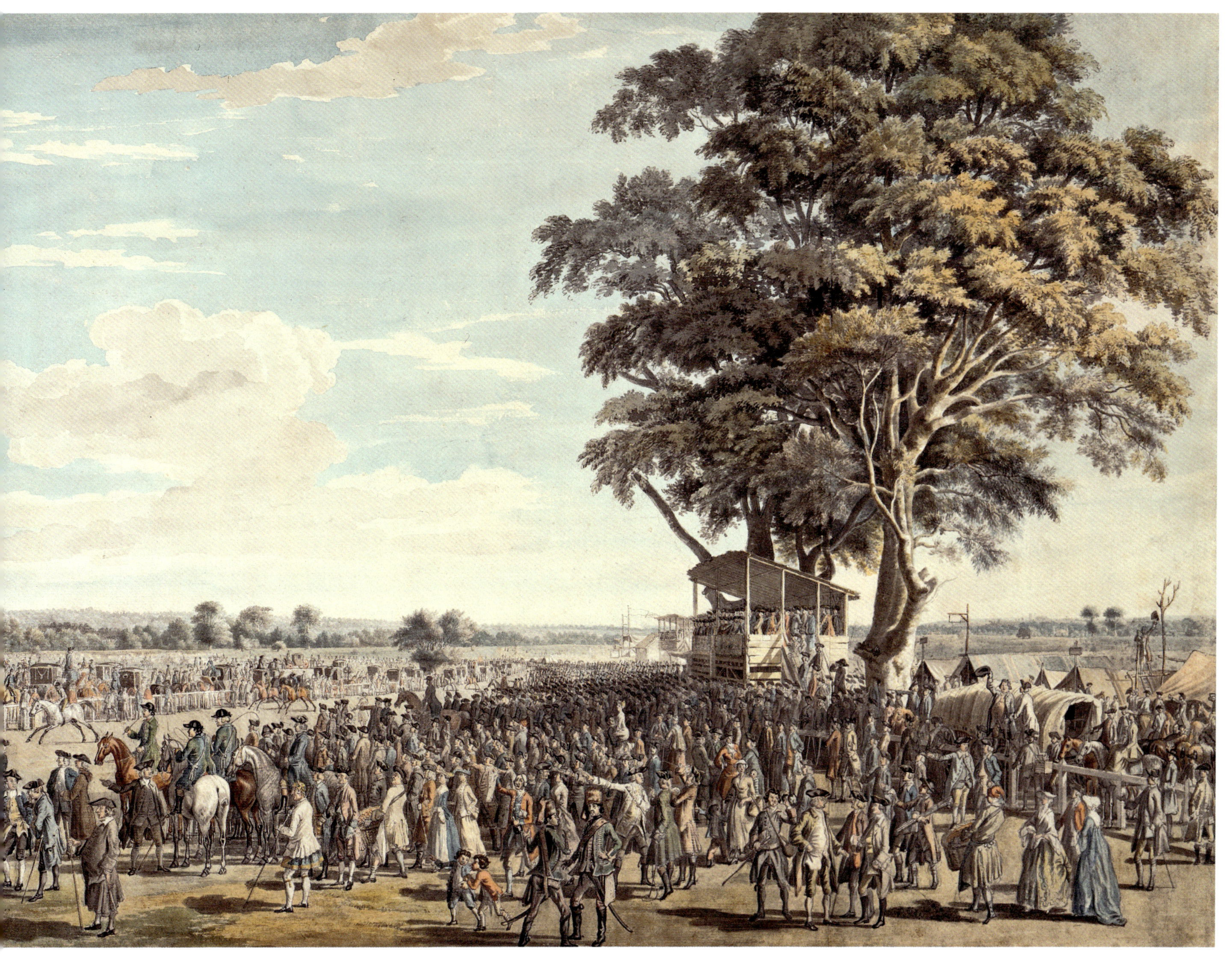

82

PAUL AND THOMAS SANDBY

View to the east over the Little Park, c. 1765

Watercolour with pen and ink over graphite, 286 × 575 mm
Royal Collection, London, RL 14567

PROVENANCE
Sir Joseph Banks; Sir Wyndham Knatchbull (sale Christie's, 23 May 1876, lot 54); Lord Stair; Christie's, 19 June 1936, no. 76

SELECTED EXHIBITIONS
Hamilton 1981, no. 16; Amsterdam 1995, no. 32

SELECTED REFERENCES
Oppé 1947, no. 52, p. 28; Amsterdam 1995, no. 32, p. 100

83

PAUL AND THOMAS SANDBY

The seat near the Terrace with a view of the adjacent country to the north-east, c. 1765

Watercolour and bodycolour over graphite, 276 × 568 mm
Royal Collection, London, RL 14575

PROVENANCE
Sir Joseph Banks; Sir Wyndham Knatchbull (sale Christie's, 23 May 1876, lot 56); Richard Holmes

SELECTED EXHIBITIONS
Yale 1985, no. 85; Amsterdam 1995, no. 33

SELECTED REFERENCES
Oppé 1947, no. 51, p. 28; Yale 1985, no. 85, p. 64; Amsterdam 1995, no. 33, pp. 102–04

Chief among the many attractions featured in guidebooks to Windsor Castle were its extensive views, which Joseph Pote promised 'from the Terrace Walk and the Apartments, over *Windsor* even to *London*, on the *East*, and the whole Country many miles round on the *West*, form the most delightful Prospects' (Pote 1764, p. 20). These two views, looking out from the castle to the east and northeast, detail these 'most delightful Prospects' with great precision, attending closely to the richly varied form and use of the surrounding topography. *View to the east over the Little Park* looks across a landscape which, according to Pote's guide, was 'well stocked with Deer and all sorts of Game, and has most pleasant Ridings and shady Walks regularly planted with Trees; and tho' Art has not been wanting to adorn and make pleasant this royal Park, the whole is so decorated and embellished by Nature, that it surpasses all the Gardens of Art' (Pote 1764, p. 20). In the view from the garden seat, looking out over the park's avenues of trees, it is possible to discern several distant landmarks, including – as Jane Roberts has noted – the King's Engine House, over the park wall at Datchet Lane, to the far left, the flooded Maestricht Pond, and the Thames, just visible through the clearings of the treeline (Amsterdam 1985, p. 102).

Such open, expansive views were laden with patriotic associations, the early eighteenth-century periodicalist Joseph Addison having long before identified landscapes of this kind with political ideals of liberty. In *The Spectator* (23 June 1712), Addison had argued:

> The Mind of Man naturally hates every thing that looks like a Restraint upon it, and is apt to fancy itself under a sort of Confinement, when the Sight is pent up in a narrow Compass, and shortned on every side by the Neighbourhood of Walls or Mountains. On the contrary, a spacious Horison is an Image of Liberty, where the Eye has Room to range abroad, to expatiate at large on the Immensity of its Views, and to lose itself amidst the Variety of Objects that offer themselves to its Observation. Such wide and undetermined Prospects are as pleasing to the Fancy, as the Speculations of Eternity or Infinitude are to the Understanding.
> (Addison 1965, vol. 3, p. 541)

This conception of the pleasures afforded by a varied, unconfined prospect was much indebted to the writings of John Locke, and was to inform Thomas Sandby's lectures to the architectural students of the Royal Academy Schools a few years after his collaboration on these views. On the question of establishing an appropriate situation for a house in a rural setting, Sandby was to observe that 'The great articles in a prospect, are variety and extent', arguing that 'it will generally be found that the Mind of Man, ever on the search for new matter, either of speculation or Amusement, will naturally tire by the reflection of the same object' (Sandby Lectures, IV, fol. 7). Although such a conception of landscape owed much to Addison, this was also a response to the estate he managed and oversaw.

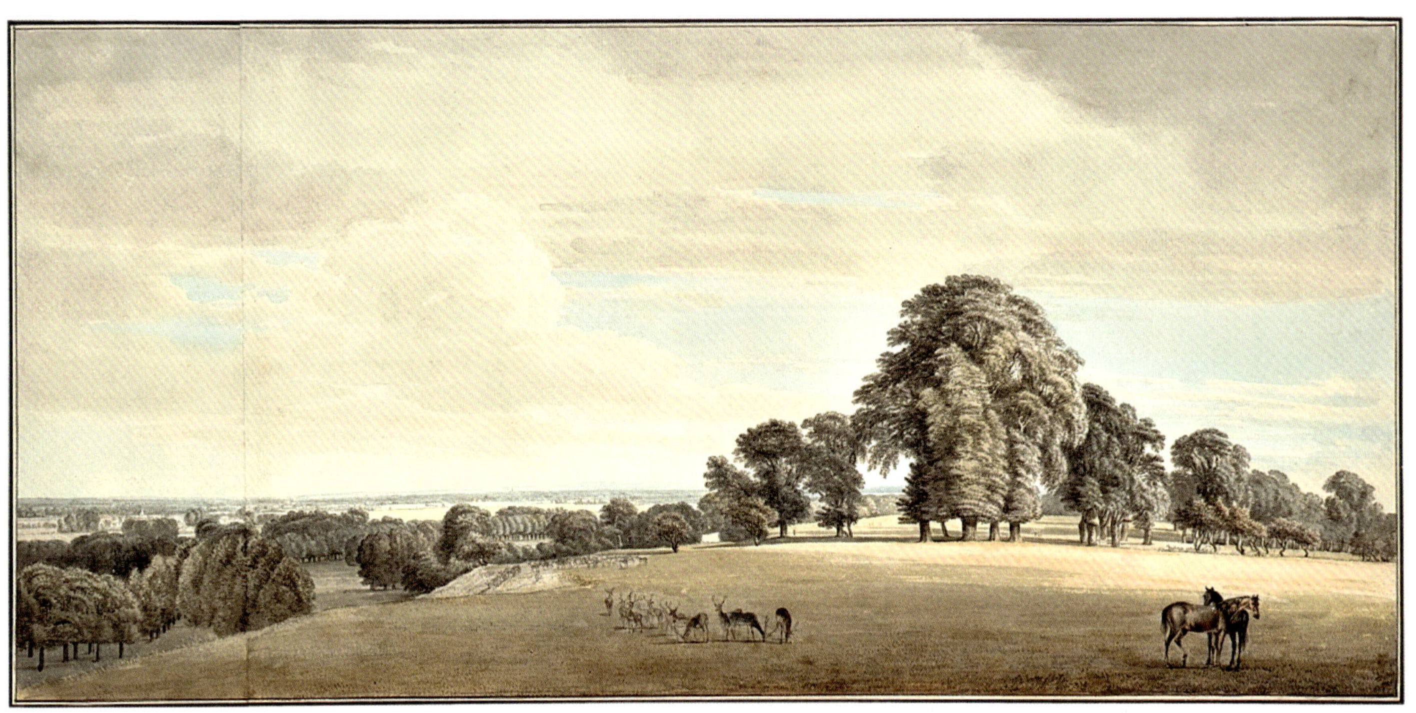

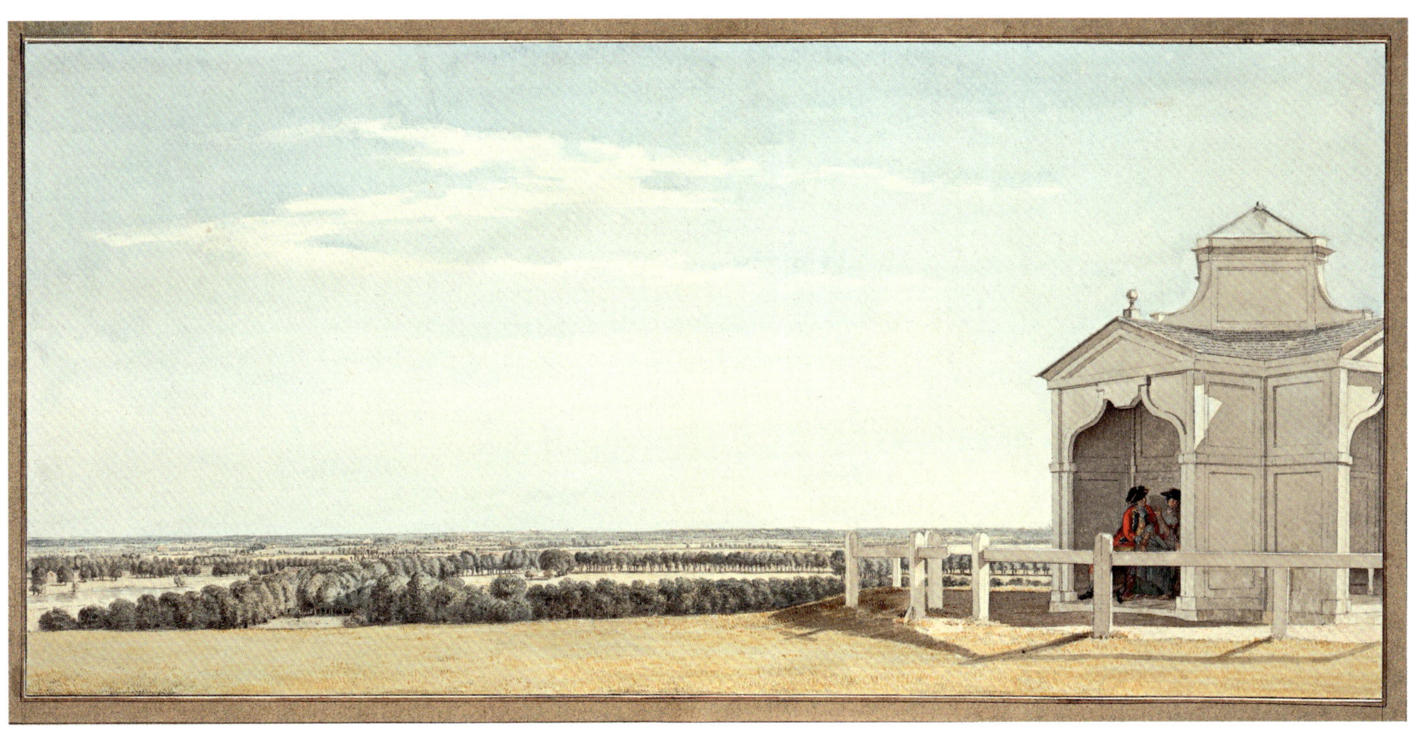

84

Nuneham from the Lock Cottages – Morning, *c.* 1760

Oil on canvas, 900 × 1250 mm
Private collection

PROVENANCE
Simon, 1st Earl of Harcourt, and by descent

SELECTED EXHIBITIONS
SA 1760, no. 54

SELECTED REFERENCES
London 1986, p. 23; Robertson 1987, pp. 283–87

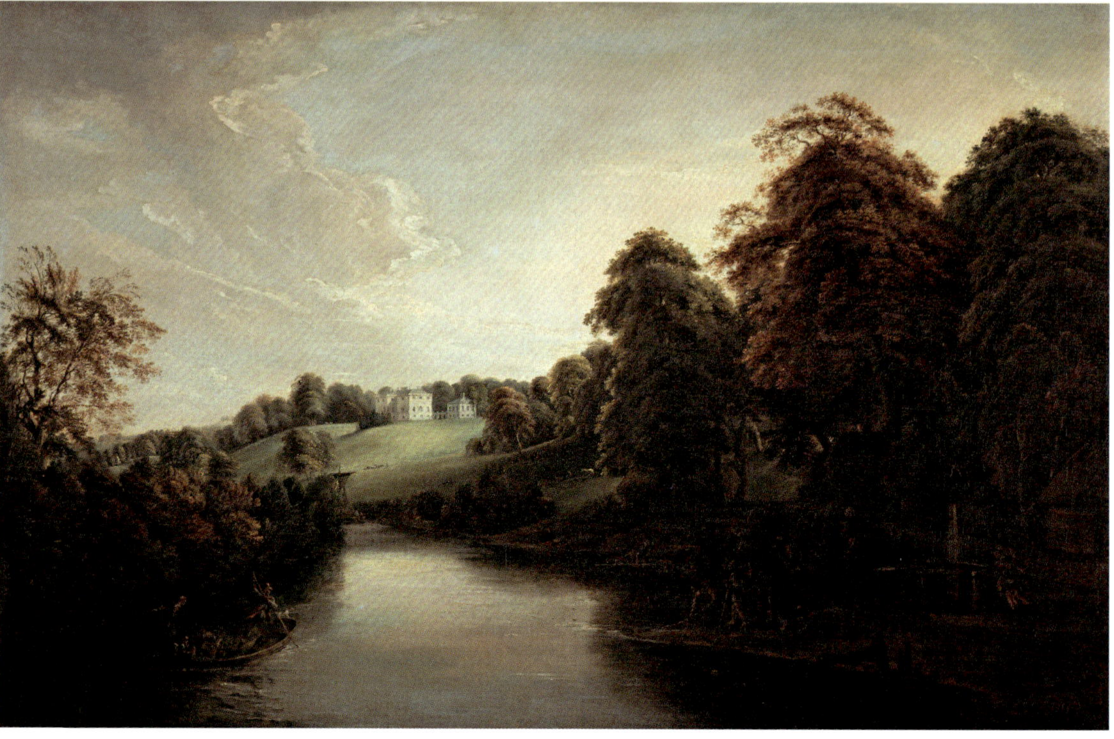

In a letter to his long-term friend Thomas Wharton, dated 21 October 1760, in which he related news of their circle in London, Thomas Gray told of a novel spectacle that he had witnessed the previous April, recalling: 'the last spring (for the first time) there was an Exhibition in a publick-room of pictures, sculptures, engravings, &c: sent in by all the Artists in imitation of what has been long practiced at Paris.' Gray went on to observe that 'among the rest there is a Mr Sandby, who excels in Landscape with figures, Views of Buildings, Ruins, &c: & has been much employ'd by the Duke, Ld Harcourt, Ld Scarborough, & others. hitherto he has dealt in wash'd Drawings & Water-Colours, but has of late only practiced in oil' (Gray 1935, vol. 2, pp. 704–05). One of the paintings admired by the poet at the country's very first art exhibition was an oil, listed in the catalogue as *A view of Lord Harcourt's Seat at Newnham*, showing the newly built villa of one of Sandby's most important and influential patrons. Demonstrating the full power and scope of the painter's art, the large and ambitious picture clearly made an impression on the crowded walls of this new and prestigious showcase. It was one of a commissioned pair of views of this property, remarkable for their range of association and erudite reference.

Simon Harcourt had served with Cumberland in Scotland and on the continent, and was created 1st Earl of Harcourt on his return home in 1749. He was made governor to the new Prince of Wales on Frederick's death in early 1751, only to resign from the royal household the following year, having disagreed publicly with the direction of the future king's education. In 1755 Harcourt began building Nuneham Courtney, on land a few miles from the family's ancestral seat at Stanton Harcourt (cats 68–69). Work on the new villa, designed by Stiff Leadbetter, was complete by 1759. James 'Athenian' Stuart designed the interiors, with Sandby contributing a marble chimney-piece to the Great Drawing Room. Stuart also

85

View of Oxford from Nuneham Courtney – Evening, *c.* 1760

Oil on canvas, 900 × 1250 mm
Private collection

PROVENANCE
Simon, 1st Earl of Harcourt, and by descent

SELECTED REFERENCES
Robertson 1987, pp. 283–87

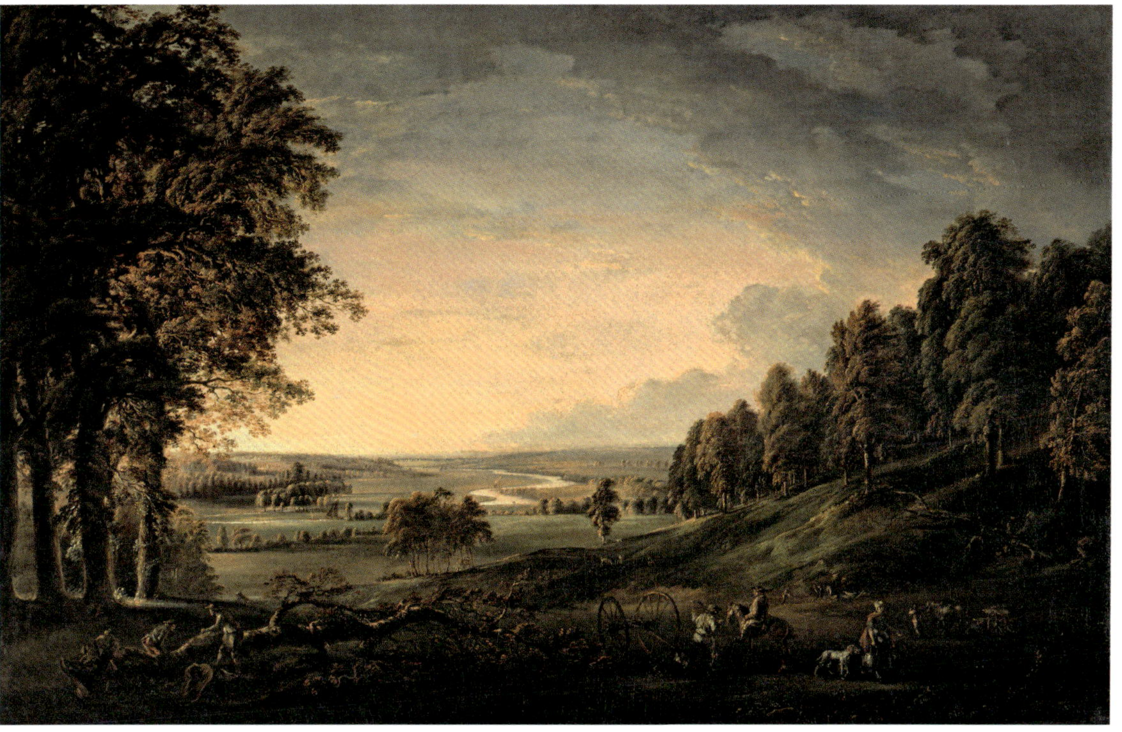

oversaw the construction of a family church, executed to a design by the 1st Earl, which was to be a prominent feature of the parkland surrounding the house, freshly laid out by Lancelot 'Capability' Brown. Sandby's great oils were presumably intended to commemorate these extensive, ongoing improvements.

Nuneham from the Lock Cottages – Morning shows the recently completed villa, rising above the Thames, framed by a great mass of trees to the right and the vegetation of the facing river bank. The house is situated amid an open expanse of rolling parkland, encircled by a belt of trees, but Sandby does not depict an entirely leisured, unproductive landscape: the foreground is filled with men and women trawling the river for fish, casting their nets from the shore and winching in their morning haul. This scene of bucolic, well-ordered plenty and productivity, accentuated by Sandby's rhythmic composition, is complemented by the equally active landscape depicted in the pendant. *View of Oxford from Nuneham Courtney – Evening* looks out beyond the estate, into the surrounding Oxfordshire countryside. A hilltop vantage, just within the borders of Nuneham Courtney, affords a commanding prospect over this valley landscape, the meandering course of the river leading the eye off towards the distant spires of Oxford. A range of figures labour to improve this landscape, shovelling earth, felling, hewing and carting trees, widening the prospect, and they are fed and watered by a serving girl, their work directed by a mounted overseer.

On visiting Nuneham Courtney, Horace Walpole found 'scenes worthy of the bold pencil of Rubens', as well as 'subjects for the tranquil sunshines of Claude le Lorrain' (Nuneham 1806, p. 4). These artists were both represented in Lord Harcourt's extensive collection of old and contemporary masters, which included, Walpole noted, 'A Landscape with a cart overturning, by moonlight' by Rubens (Nuneham 1806, p. 21). Although this picture was the source for neither of Sandby's compositions, they are in the manner of the great Flemish master, and it is likely that Sandby would have been shown the work while he was there. For all the artist's concern to chart the economic and physical connections of the estate with the surrounding countryside, such a reference reveals that his art was seldom entirely removed from the tradition of the Old Masters. Here, the allusion to the art of Rubens casts his patron's property in an historic light, affiliating it with a venerable pictorial ideal. Such an allusion is also indicative of the extent of Sandby's aspirations at this time, his decision to show the picture in public indicating an ambition to elevate the status of the taking of views, complementing (or rivalling) Richard Wilson's attempts to raise the standing of landscape painting by reference to continental tradition.

86

Hackwood Park, *c.* 1764

Oil on canvas, 1021 × 1276 mm
Signed: 'P. Sandby' (l.r.)
Yale Center for British Art, New Haven,
Paul Mellon Fund, B1981.6

PROVENANCE
Charles, 5th Duke of Bolton, and by descent;
Lord Bolton (sale Christie's, 21 November 1980, lot 120)

SELECTED EXHIBITIONS
SA 1764, no. 101; Yale 1985, no. 76; Sydney 1998, no. 25

SELECTED REFERENCES
Yale 1985, no. 76, pp. 56–58; Sydney 1998, no. 25, p. 76

This large, ambitious estate portrait was shown at the Society of Artists in 1764 as *South-East view of Hackwood, the seat of His Grace, the Duke of Bolton*, where it was to be seen alongside two other exhibits advertising Sandby's exalted aristocratic connections: *South-west view of Chatsworth, the Seat of His Grace the Duke of Devonshire* and *View in the menagerie at Worksop Manor, as design'd by Her Grace the Duchess of Norfolk*. Although it is often assumed that the walls of the London exhibition rooms of the period were given over to speculative works, these were clearly all commissioned views, demonstrating not only the painter's skills but also his patrons' taste in their promotion of the fine arts. This view of Hackwood Park, near Basingstoke in Hampshire, was presumably intended to commemorate recent improvements made to the house by Charles Paulet, 5th Duke of Bolton, who had engaged the architect John Vardy to make alterations to the south front in the early 1760s. A still larger prospect, depicting Bolton Hall on the Duke's Wensleydale estate, was also painted at this time, the two pictures probably being hung together at 37 Grosvenor Square, the Duke's London residence.

In looking down on Hackwood Park from the southeast, Sandby's painting offers only a glimpse of the celebrated formal garden created by the first three Dukes of Bolton, famed for its elaborate water features and classical pavilions designed by James Gibbs. Only the parterres to the south of the house and the avenue of trees leading away to the east are visible. Rather, Sandby surveys a mixed landscape of glades, groves, lawns and woodland, as well as working agricultural land, in which the house represents just one element of his patron's extensive holdings. His benevolent stewardship is made apparent not only in the evident productivity of the estate but also in the contentment of its workforce, who are featured in the foreground enjoying a mid-day break, resting and taking ale, having stacked half a field of hay. The work is an image of georgic plenty, of abundance and good order.

The varied features of this landscape were also recorded in the letterpress accompanying a view of the estate engraved for George Kearsly's *A Collection of Landscapes* by Michael 'Angelo' Rooker:

> This elegant mansion is situated in a fine extensive park, about eight miles in circumference; and before each front a fine sheet of water agreeably strikes the beholder. The park is well wooded and watered; particularly in one part, a walk is seen of a mile long, planted on each side with chesnut-trees; and, in another quarter, a walk of almost the same extent, inclosed within two rows of limes. These walks, or alleys, have a pleasing and noble effect; and the connoisseur has frequent opportunities of gratifying his taste in this delightful park, and the adjacent gardens; there being many very fine statues, urns, obelisks, & c. agreeably dispersed; among which a fine Equestrian statue of George the First particularly claims our attention.
>
> The park abounds with game of every kind, and may, with some propriety, be said to be overstocked. We have heard it positively asserted, that, from an hill in the park, near Springfield wood, it is no uncommon thing to see upwards of an hundred hares at a time.
>
> There is also a farm in the park, well stocked with cattle, and domestic poultry of all kinds. (*A Collection of Landscapes*, 1777, plate 13, pp. 17–18)

Richard Michell's poem 'Hackwood Park' was published the year after Sandby's painting was exhibited at the Society of Artists. Dedicated to the 4th Duke, Harry Paulet, this identified the estate as an English Arcadia, and celebrated its sponsorship of agriculture and horticulture, the sport it afforded as well as its forest walks, a place where 'sweet Retirement BOLTON might enjoy, / And quietly a thoughtful Hour employ' (Michell 1765, p. 23).

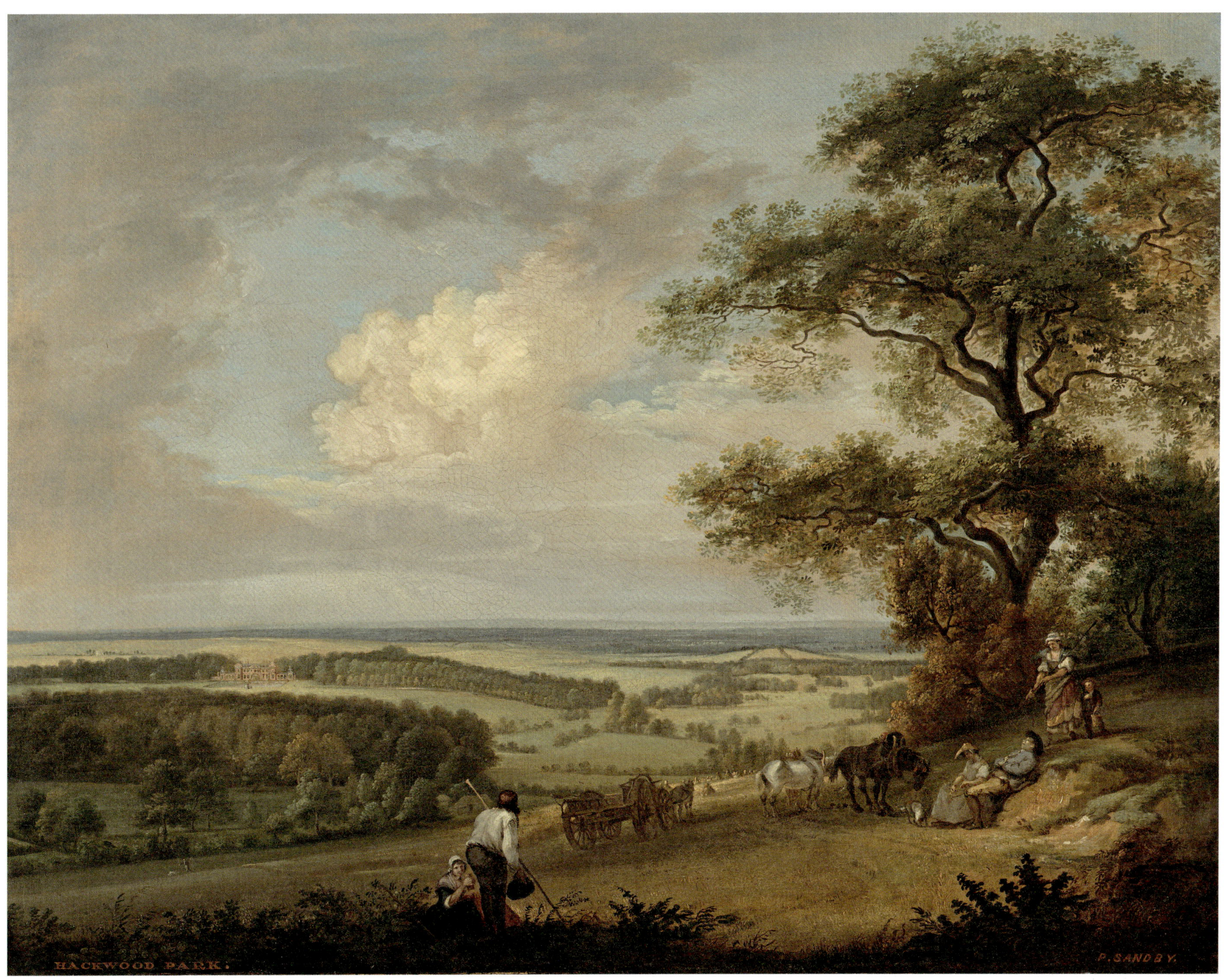
HACKWOOD PARK.
P. SANDBY.

87

North West View of Wakefield Lodge in Whittlebury Forest, 1767

Pen, ink, watercolour and bodycolour over graphite, 425 × 851 mm. Signed: 'P. Sandby 1767' (l.l.)
Yale Center for British Art, New Haven, Paul Mellon Collection, B1977.14-4648

PROVENANCE
The Dowager Lady Hillingdon; Agnews, 1967; bt Paul Mellon, 1967

SELECTED EXHIBITIONS
SA 1767, no. 272; Yale 1985, no. 77; Yale 2001, no. 136; Yale 2007, no. 33

SELECTED REFERENCES
Yale 1985, no. 77, p. 58; Yale 2001, pp. 160–61; Yale 2007, no. 33, p. 256

Wakefield Lodge, in Whittlebury Forest, Northamptonshire, was designed by William Kent for Charles FitzRoy, 2nd Duke of Grafton, and completed by his successor, Augustus Henry FitzRoy. One of Sandby's most important and influential patrons, the 3rd Duke of Grafton was not only instrumental in the artist's appointment to the staff of the Royal Military Academy at Woolwich but also promised to secure him the post of Surveyor and Keeper of the King's Pictures. He was to be disappointed, however, on the death of the erstwhile incumbent, George Knapton, as Horace Walpole reported to William Mason in January 1778: 'the promise to Sandby is superseded, *de par le roi*, because it dates from the Duke of Grafton' (Walpole 1937–83, vol. 28, p. 342). A politically controversial figure, Grafton was by this time out of favour with George III.

In addition to overseeing the completion of the lodge, Grafton initiated an extensive and profitable programme of improvement, enclosing common land, integrating farms, reforming tenancies and introducing new methods of agriculture and silviculture. The estate had been acquired from the Crown in 1712, thereby extending an existing grant that came with the rangership of the royal forests of Whittlebury and nearby Salcey. However, the making of this modern landscape from the customary forest economy was a complex and contentious process, involving protracted disputes with local people, notably over game and timber. Conflicts with the Crown over Grafton's claims on timber trees brought his estate to national attention in the late 1760s, as they featured in a series of letters to the press, written by the self-styled patriot 'Junius', as examples of tyrannical and corrupt governance.

In Sandby's view of the estate, made in the midst of these local and national controversies, Kent's Lodge is set amid a broad expanse of lawn, belted by trees and shrubs. A lawn was an enclosure for deer, which are depicted grazing peacefully to the right, with the inclusion of horses – which echo a group of *Mares and Foals by a stream* that Grafton had purchased from George Stubbs a couple of years previously (private collection; reproduced in Egerton 2007, no. 42) – a further allusion to the sport widely associated with the estate, serving as reminders of the famed Wakefield Lawn Races. That this is essentially a leisured landscape is further indicated by the riders and phaeton entering to the extreme left. In one of the artist's characteristic vignettes of comic encounter, in which the polite and the vulgar or the leisured and the labouring collide, the landowner or some well-connected visitors appear to have disturbed a ragged, rustic couple bundling firewood, gathered either from the dead lower branches of the tree or from fallen boughs nearby. If the richly coloured foliage of this ash-like tree recalls the decorative sidescreens of Claude, heightening pastoral associations of the scene, it also refers, perhaps, to the ornamental planting of the parkland edges that were part of Kent's designs.

Engravings of the house by Michael 'Angelo' Rooker, after two further Sandby drawings, were subsequently issued as part of *A Collection of Landscapes*, published in 1777. Accompanying letterpress, giving 'a description of the place and the adjacent country', celebrated Grafton's improvements, 'where art and nature combine to form a kind of terrestrial Paradise', but also noted the local cost of his enlargement of the estate: 'Many of the neighbouring villages were formerly allowed the use of common in this forest, but they have lately been deprived of that privilege; which has greatly contributed to the depopulating of the adjacent country' (*A Collection of Landscapes*, 1777, plate 1, p. 1). Any anxiety about the social implications of Grafton's improvements was allayed, however, by the prints themselves, with one depicting the lawn as a place of georgic industriousness, complementing the pastoral pleasure of this scene.

On exhibition at the Society of Artists in 1767, Sandby's *North West View of Wakefield Lodge*, along with a now untraced companion drawing of the property, joined a number of other pictures depicting named places on noble estates. They ranged widely, geographically as well as in composition and style, and addressed an assortment of sites and estate activities. They included Richard Wilson's *View from Moor park*, picturing the landscape surrounding the house of Lawrence Dundas, and two paintings set on the property of the Dukes of Portland: George Barret's *A View in Creswell crags* and George Stubbs's *Two gentlemen going a shooting, with a view of Creswell crags*. If Wilson's panoramic prospect, looking out towards a neighbouring seat, ranged over a flourishing, improved prospect, Barret's now-untraced picture in contrast showed an elemental landscape, with a rainbow forming above the spray thrown up by a cascade. Stubbs depicted a near-comic scene of sporting activity, but one admired by a rhyming critic as providing 'A perfect Portrait of the copy'd place / Just heighten'd here and there, by taste and grace' (*Le Pour et le Contre*, 1767, p. 15). If these pictures illustrate the scope and power of the expanded conceptions of estate portraiture and topographic art that emerged in the period, they also indicate an emergent taste for the scenic delights of native British territory. One critic considered Wilson's painting 'one that may convince the World that the simple Grandeur of an extensive, richly-cultivated, wooded Plain, and the Verdure, almost peculiar to our Island, so much admired in Nature, and so much decried in Imitation, may have extraordinary Beauties in a Picture' (*Public Advertiser*, 1 May 1767).

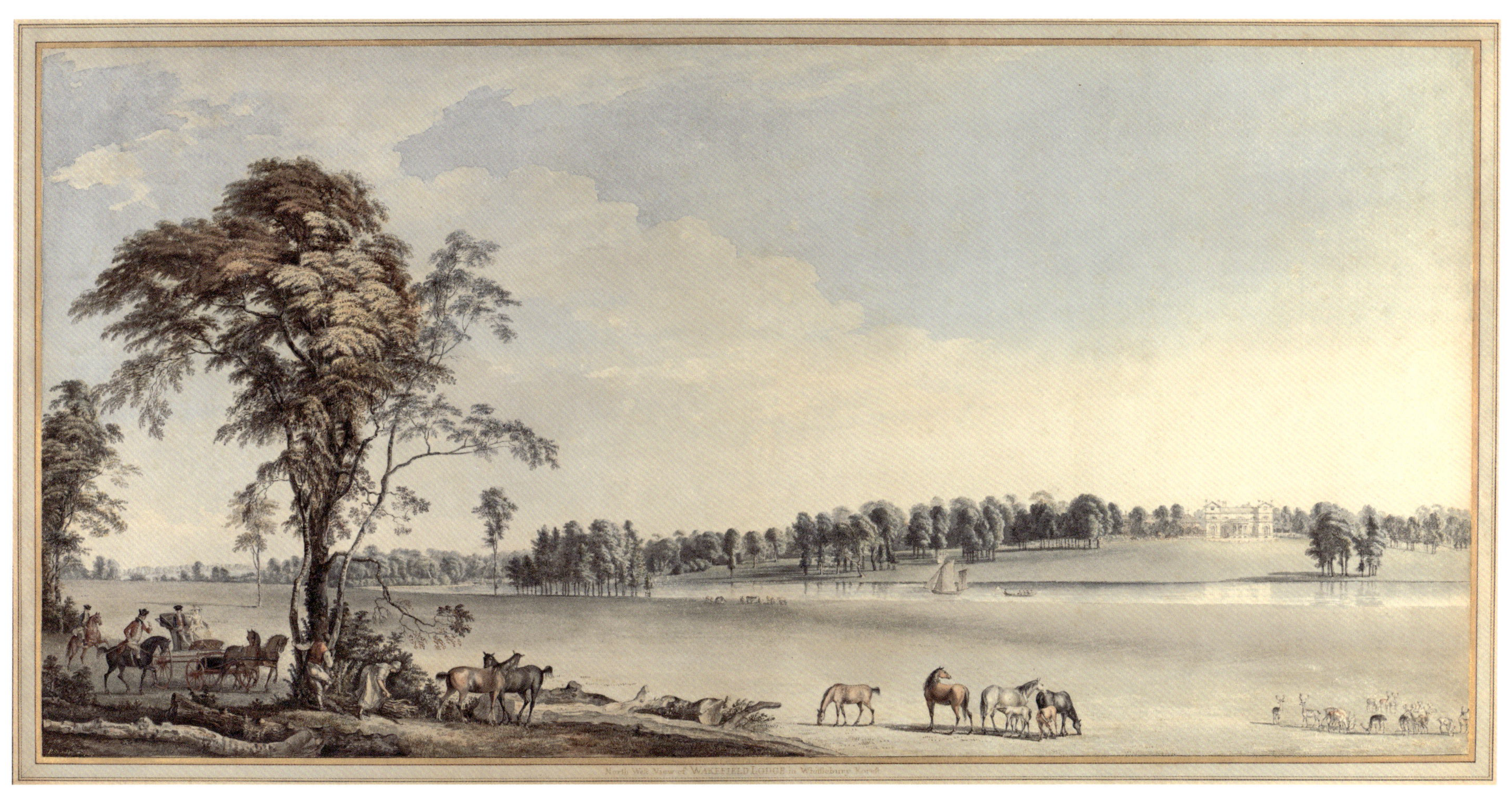
North West View of WAKEFIELD LODGE in Whittlebury Forest

88

THOMAS SANDBY

View of Boxhill from Norbury Park, Surrey, c. 1775

Pen, ink and watercolour over graphite, 309 × 998 mm
Yale Center for British Art, New Haven, Paul Mellon Fund, B1982.17

PROVENANCE
Sir Edward John Poynter; Sotheran, 1930; Alfred Drayson, by descent to Mrs A. Brown; Sotheby's, 16 July 1981, lot 79; bt John Morton Morris, from whom purchased, 1982

SELECTED EXHIBITIONS
Yale 1985, no. 23; Yale 2001, no. 137

SELECTED REFERENCES
Yale 1985, no. 23, p. 28; Yale 2001, no. 137, pp. 160–61

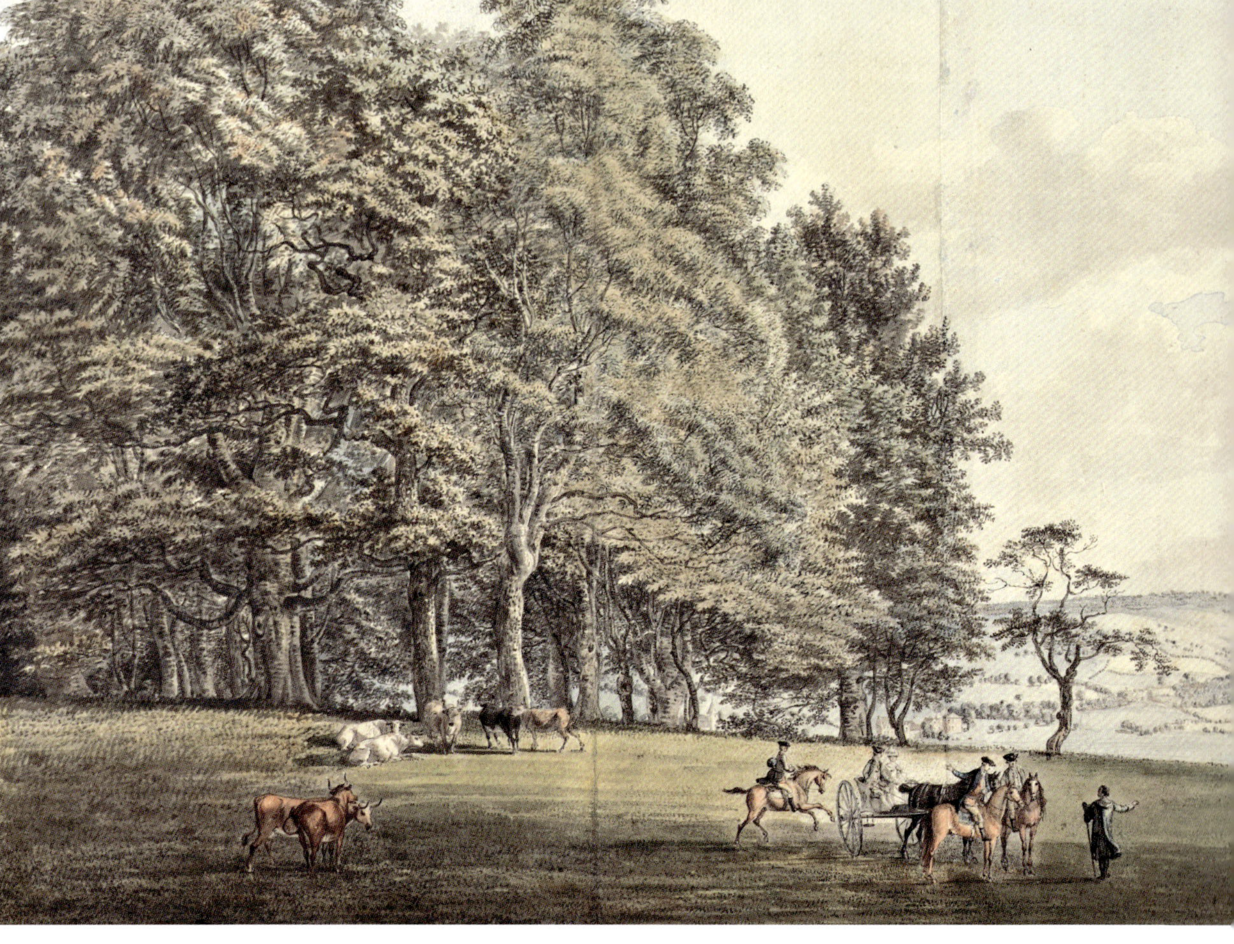

Owned by the noted art collector and connoisseur William Lock, Norbury Park, near Mickleham, Surrey, was famed for its views towards the local landmark of Boxhill. In his *Observations on the Western Parts of England* (1798), recalling a tour of the mid-1770s, William Gilpin wrote appreciatively of this prospect 'as you survey it from the windows of the house'. Of Boxhill, which closed the view down a sloping vale, richly planted 'with ancient oak and beech', Gilpin remarked 'it fills its station with great beauty'. He went on to qualify his praise of this vista, however:

> This view over the vale, (beautiful as it is), is subject, however, to inconvenience. Every house should, if possible, overlook its *own domains*, as far at least as to remote distance. All the intermediate space, in which objects are seen more distinctly, may suffer great injury from the caprice of different proprietors: and, in fact, this view has, in two or three instances, suffered injury from the interference of neighbours. This is indeed one reason, among others, why noble palaces, with extensive property on every side, are most adapted to these commanding situations. (Gilpin 1798, pp. 9, 11, 14)

These concerns were likely to have been shared by Thomas Sandby, who, as Lady Eleanor Butler was to recall, had been invited by Lock, then in Rome, 'to build him a house in a particular part of his ground'. According to Lady Butler, Sandby sent the absent owner 'a ground plan, elevation, and drawings of views from several windows' (Bell 1930, p. 109). This is presumably one of these window views, looking out across the vale so admired by Gilpin.

Questions of 'situation', or the relation of a house like Norbury Park to the surrounding natural scenery, featured prominently in Sandby's architectural theory. In a lecture devoted to the

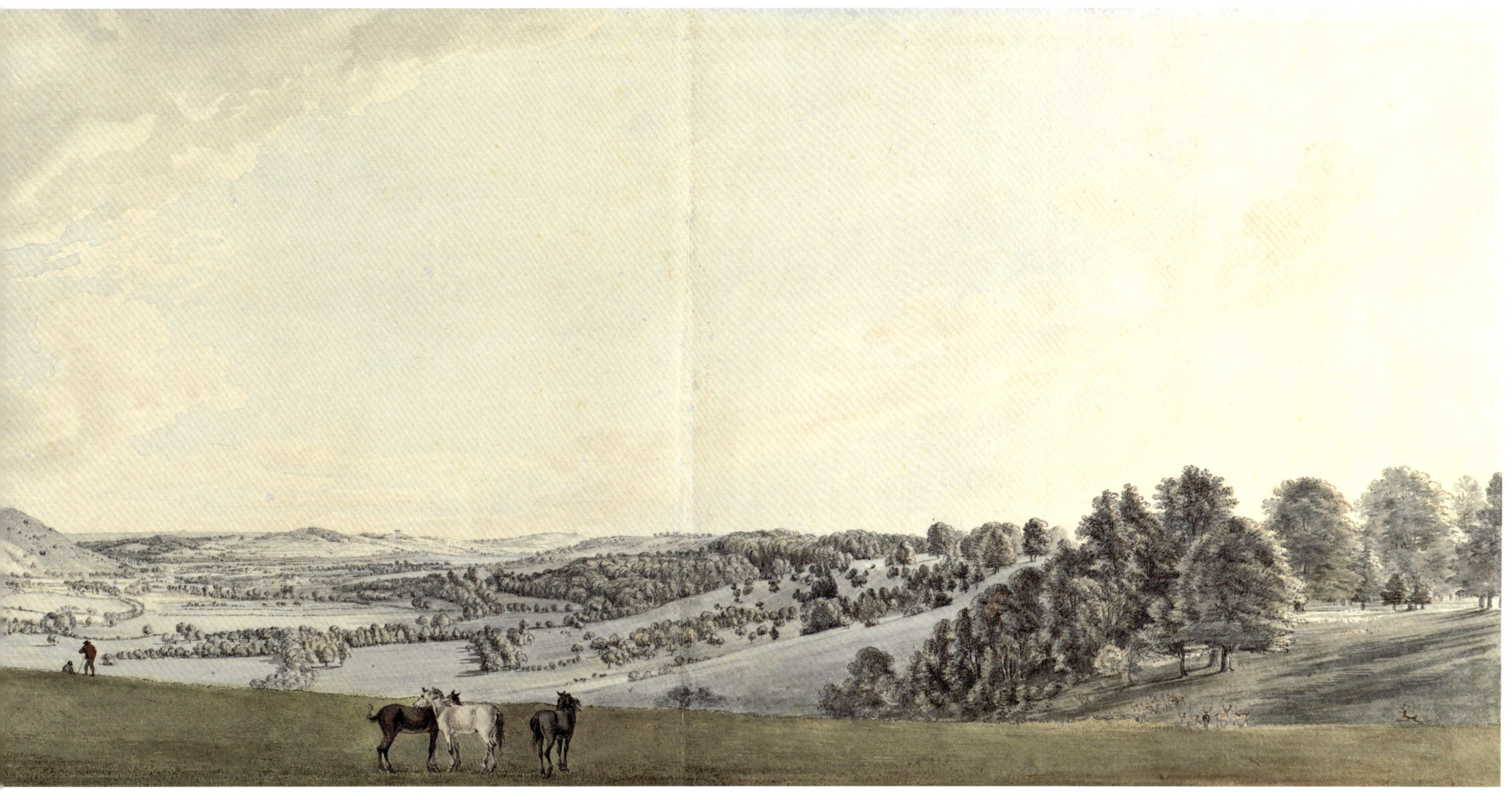

subject, addressed to students of the Royal Academy Schools, he advised that 'objects around us afford a more pleasing relief to the Eye, and set off the Building to the greatest advantage' (Sandby Lectures, IV, fol. 3). This awareness of the scenic possibilities of the natural setting is readily apparent in this expansive yet finely delineated prospect of the landscape surrounding Lock's house, not least in the detailing of the mixed woodland framing the view to the left. Open, richly varied views such as this were, as noted above, particularly favoured by the architect.

It was not only the windows that afforded fine views out across the North Downs at Norbury. On purchasing the house in 1774, Lock commissioned a series of decorative autumnal landscapes from George Barret the Elder, who worked in collaboration with G.-B. Cipriani and B. Pastorini. These comprised, according to Gilpin, 'a bower or arbour, admitting a *fictitious* sky through a large oval at the top, and covered at the angles with trellis-work, inter-woven with honey-suckles, vines, clustering grapes, and flowering creepers of various kinds'. Of the four views on the walls, Gilpin noted that the one 'towards the *south* is *real*, consisting of the vale inclosed by Box-hill, and the hills of Norbury' (Gilpin 1798, p. 15). This remarkable scheme anticipates Paul Sandby's decoration of the dining room at Drakelow Hall, Derbyshire, a few years later (fig. 4). Such *trompe-l'oeil* effects were a means of making interiors more expansive, linking them with the landscape outside both spatially and by association.

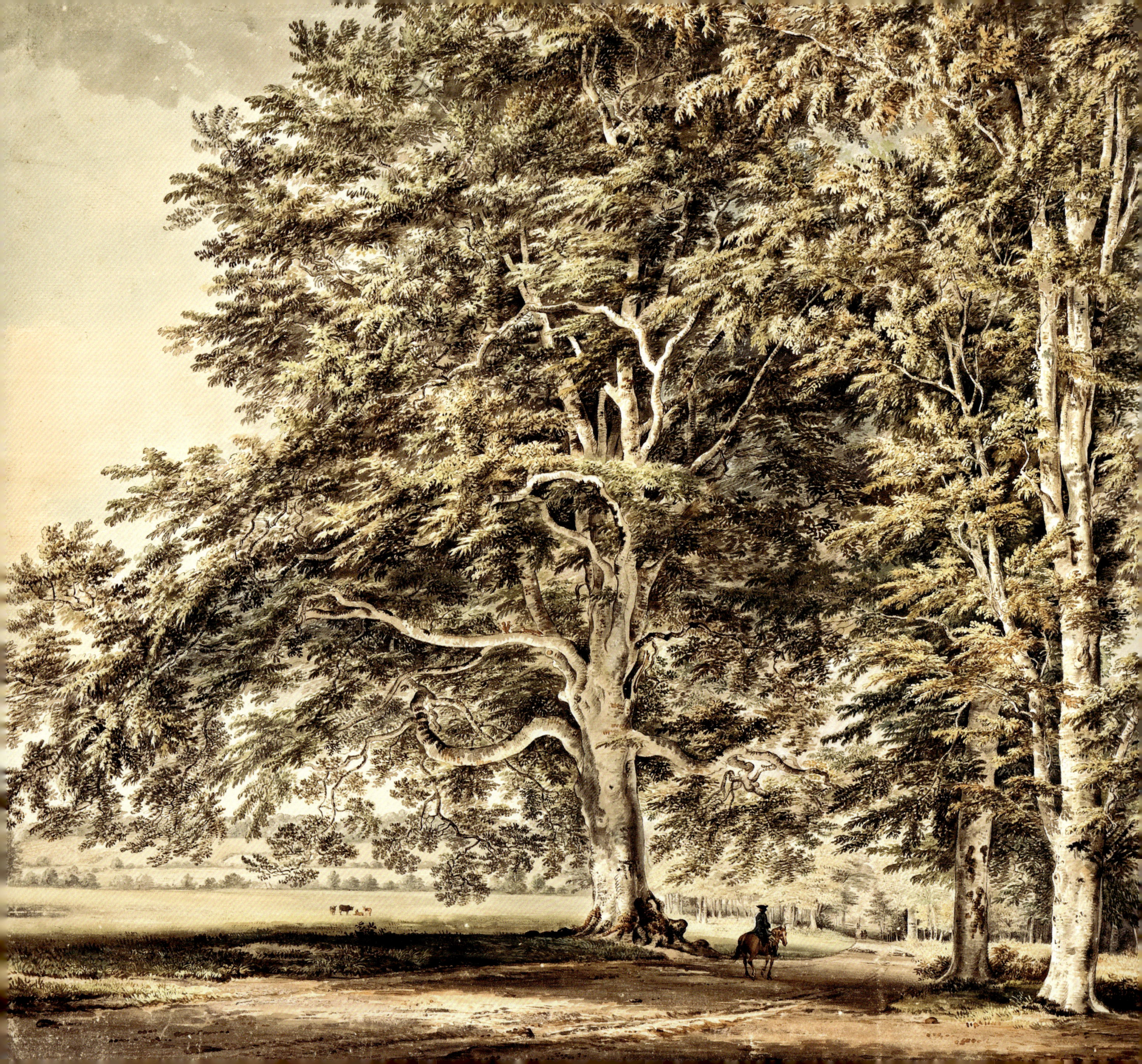

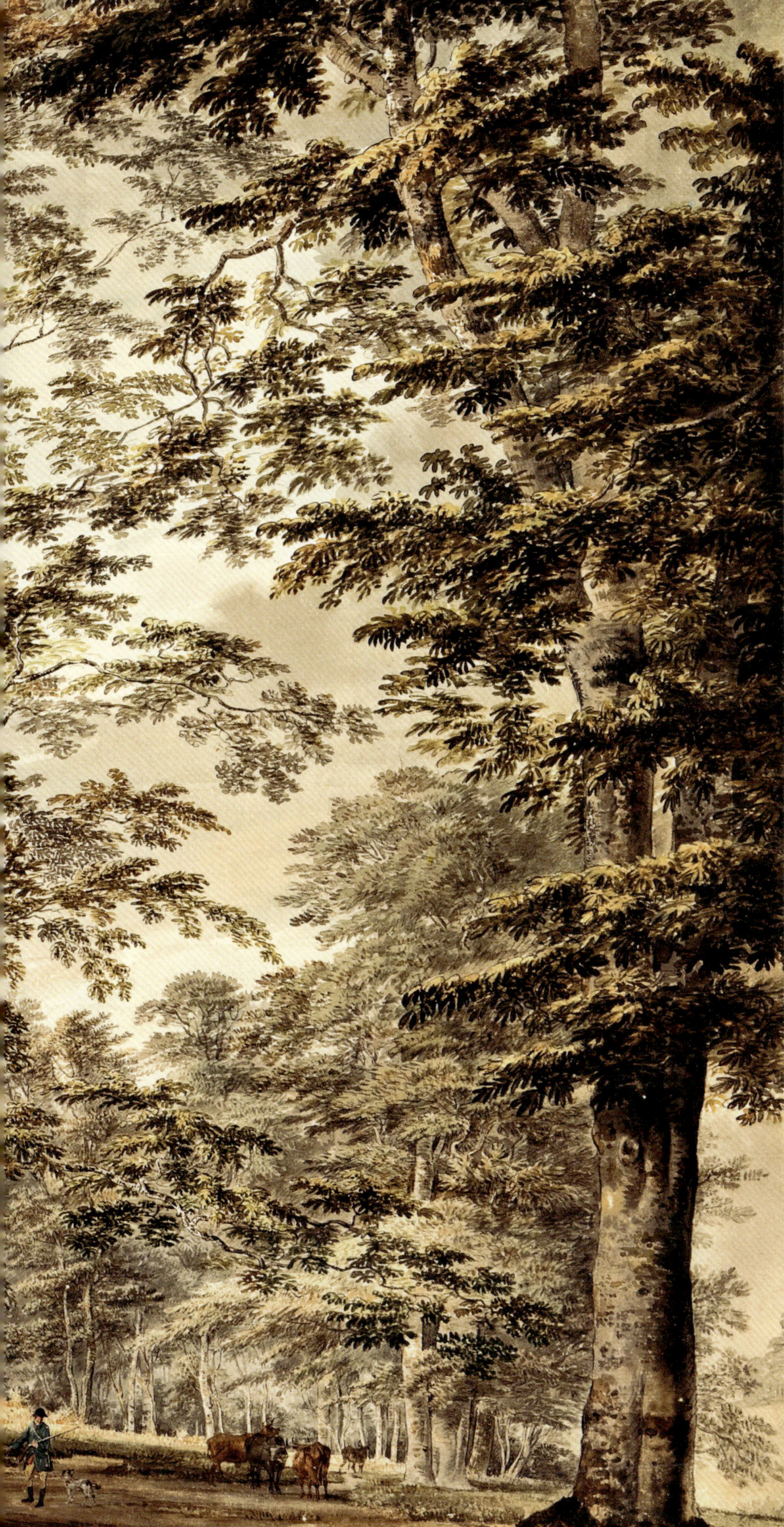

89

View in Luton Park, c. 1765

Pen, bodycolour and watercolour over graphite, 610 × 990 mm
Private collection

PROVENANCE
John Stuart, 3rd Earl of Bute, and by descent

CATALOGUE NUMBERS 89–91

On 8 April 1763 John Stuart, 3rd Earl of Bute, resigned as First Lord of the Treasury, having been vilified in parliament and in print for his part in ending the Seven Years War (see cats 29–30). On retiring from public life he invested heavily in the improvement of Luton Park, a Bedfordshire estate that he had purchased from Francis Hearne MP the previous year. Robert Adam was engaged to redesign the house and Lancelot 'Capability' Brown employed, at considerable expense, to landscape the parkland of an estate covering over 4,000 acres. Adam's work on the house was delayed some years, but Brown's schemes were quickly implemented. His designs included expanses of undulating lawns rolling out from the house down to the River Lea that traversed the estate, and the damming of the waterway to form a lake, which he dotted with wooded islands, thickly planting the far bank. A letter from Brown to his patron dated 11 March 1767 suggests that his work at Luton had advanced apace, and that trees had been obtained 'from the Princess of Wales's garden' (British Library, London, Add MS 5726, fol. 86). Despite Brown's reputation for erasing ancient landscapes (Everett 1994), his plans brought aged coppice as well as large tracts of adjacent farmland into the new park, appropriating, if not conserving, older regimes of estate and woodland management, bringing the old and the new, the established and freshly laid out, into conjunction.

90

View in Luton Park, 1765

Pen, bodycolour and watercolour over graphite,
510 × 740 mm
Signed: 'P. Sandby Pinxt 1765' (l.l.)
Private collection

PROVENANCE
John Stuart, 3rd Earl of Bute, and by descent

Visiting the estate in 1768, with Brown's work still in its early stages, Arthur Young pronounced it 'prettily diversified with scattered trees' and a 'spot wonderfully capable':

> We entered through the Lodge from the town of Luton, and drove along the banks of the river, which was naturally a trifling stream, but is now forming … the road winds among some scattered trees towards the right appearing through them in an elegant manner; there are many fine beeches as you advance up to the house, from the dark side of which the water is seen at a distance in a very picturesque manner (Young 1769, vol. 1, pp. 8, 9).

Paul Sandby's little-known views of Bute's Luton Park property were presumably also commissioned at around this time, with some signed and dated 1765. Twelve or so drawings are known, recording the landscape and its most notable features, including an ivy-coloured lodge, a commemorative column then dedicated to Frances Napier, and the nearby ruins of Someries Castle, prior to and during its redesign. Collected in a large album, bearing the Bute family's arms and inscribed 'Sandby Drawings of Luton', these elaborate, highly finished drawings were presumably intended to form an ensemble which, given the shared dimensions and forms of the hand-painted mounts, comprised a series of companion scenes, as with the two smaller views shown here.

Sandby's series of public prospects and private views on Bute's Bedfordshire property record a landscape of old native trees and woodland, and summon an array of cultural associations. They demonstrate the varied nature, scope and power of estate portraiture as the artist developed the genre in the 1760s. Lawns, farmland and woodland, including coppiced hardwoods and spectacular ancient pollarded trees, are depicted. Avenues lined with massive, aged beech, as well as scattered clumps, screens and belts of trees, including birch and ash, feature prominently. They also allude to the role of timber in the economy of the estate, depicting trees of use and beauty, of commercial as well as scenic value, and showing the transportation of lumber or the sheltering of the fallow deer, cattle and horses that roam the landscape. Gentlemen on horseback, sportsmen and their dogs, polite visitors and estate workers rove the park, moving between and reappearing across the various sites depicted. In recording the ancient hardwoods of this parkland, and placing them in the flow of the day-to-day running of the estate and Brown's improvements, Sandby's views document and preserve this historic sylvan landscape and evaluate its place in the scheme of modern developments in a way that parallels the artist's views of the nation's antiquities, its ruined castles and abbeys.

They are remarkable, as a group, for their attentiveness to the overall structure, foliage and branching of individual tree species, and they

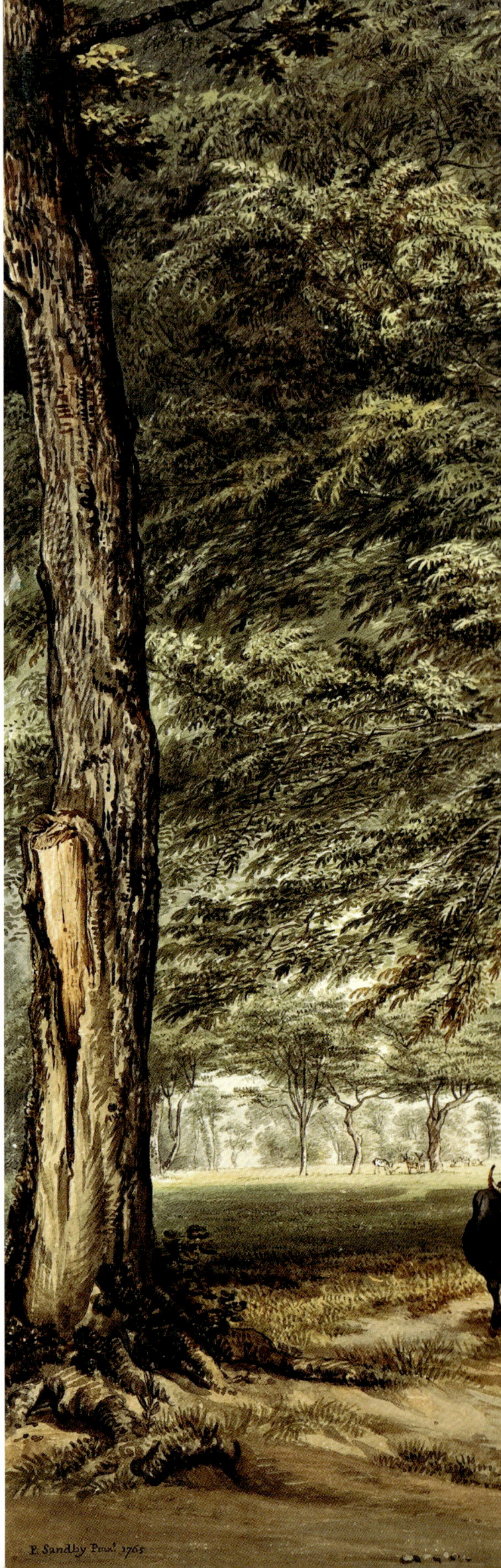

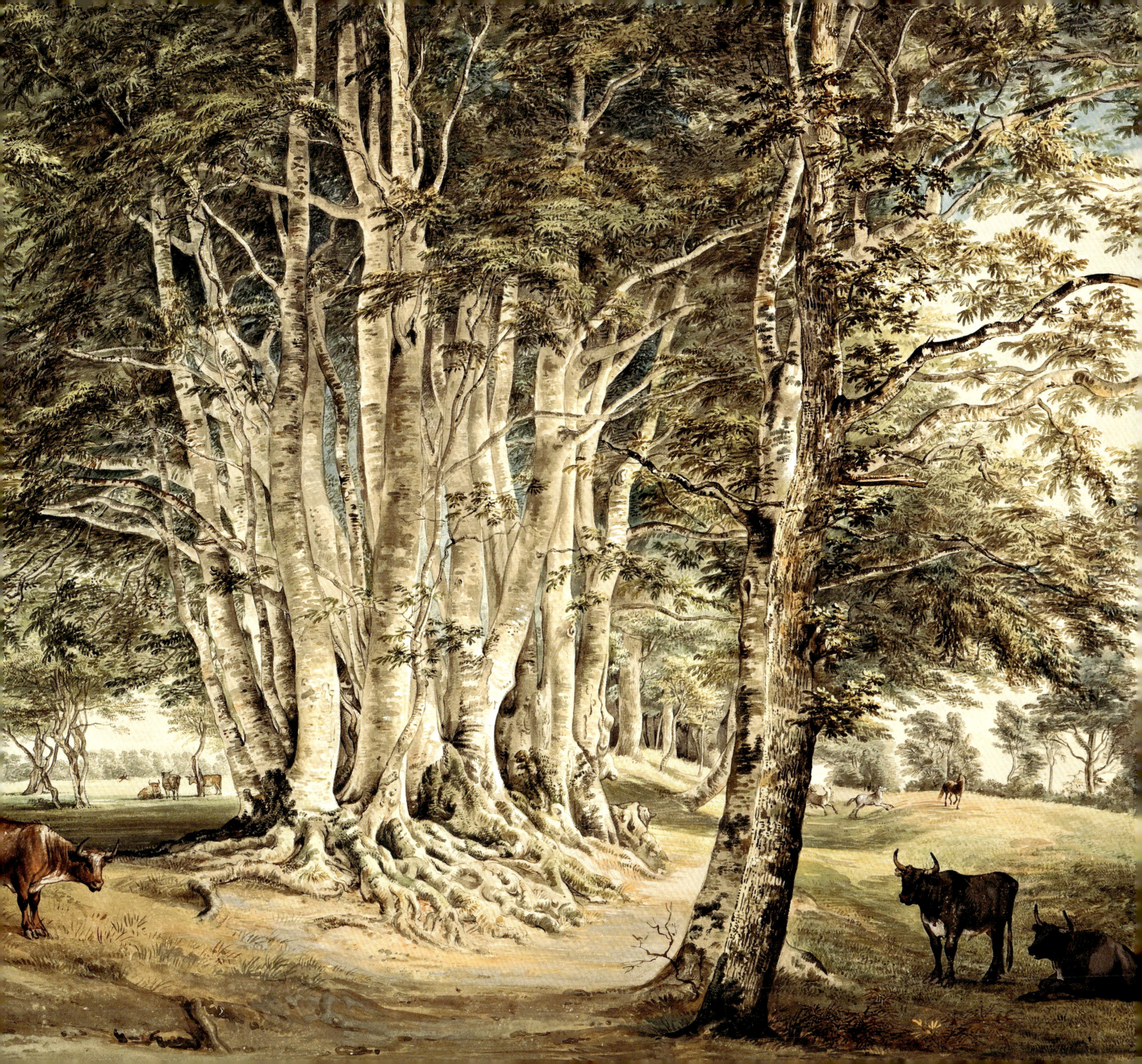

91

View in Luton Park, *c.* 1765

Pen, bodycolour and watercolour over graphite,
535 × 740 mm
Private collection

PROVENANCE
John Stuart, 3rd Earl of Bute, and by descent

anticipate the studies of beech and oak that Sandby was to essay in the 1790s (cat. 101) (Hartley 1996). Although some of these finely observed trees frame broad, sweeping vistas, in other drawings these often massive and complex structures allow only glimpses of the surrounding parkland. Such drawings address what Joshua Reynolds dismissed as the 'Accidents of Nature', or the untypical, focusing on branches, trunks, bark and rooting (Reynolds 1975, p. 70). In the extraordinary drawing of cattle sheltering in a shaded dell beneath an ancient coppiced beech (cat. 90), tree forms shoot through or are cut off abruptly by the frame. A low, sunken viewpoint further accentuates the massiveness of the central tree.

These occluded views are marked by abrupt contrasts of near and far and light and dark, and they effectively communicate the optical confusion and spatial uncertainty that characterise woodland areas. These observations on patterns of growth or the wider cultural significance of trees accorded with some of the scientific enquiries that were promoted by Sandby's patron. The 3rd Earl had a long-standing interest in natural history and philosophy, and encouraged the study of floriculture and horticulture as well as minerals and zoology (Miller 1988). He sponsored the careers and publications of the naturalists John Strange and the notoriously querulous John Hill, who produced a study of *The Construction of Timber* (1770) and catalogued Bute's botanical specimens in 26 volumes entitled *The Vegetable System* (1759–75). Artists like George Ehret and Johann Sebastian Mueller were also engaged in illustrating aspects of Bute's vast collections. Bute's interest in silviculture, as well as agriculture and architecture, shaped improvements at his ancestral Mount Stuart estate, but also informed his supervision of the planting and ornamentation of Kew Gardens. He was instrumental in the appointments of William Chambers as architect and William Aiton as head gardener at Kew, charging the latter with establishing a herbaceous plant garden based on the Linnaean system of classification.

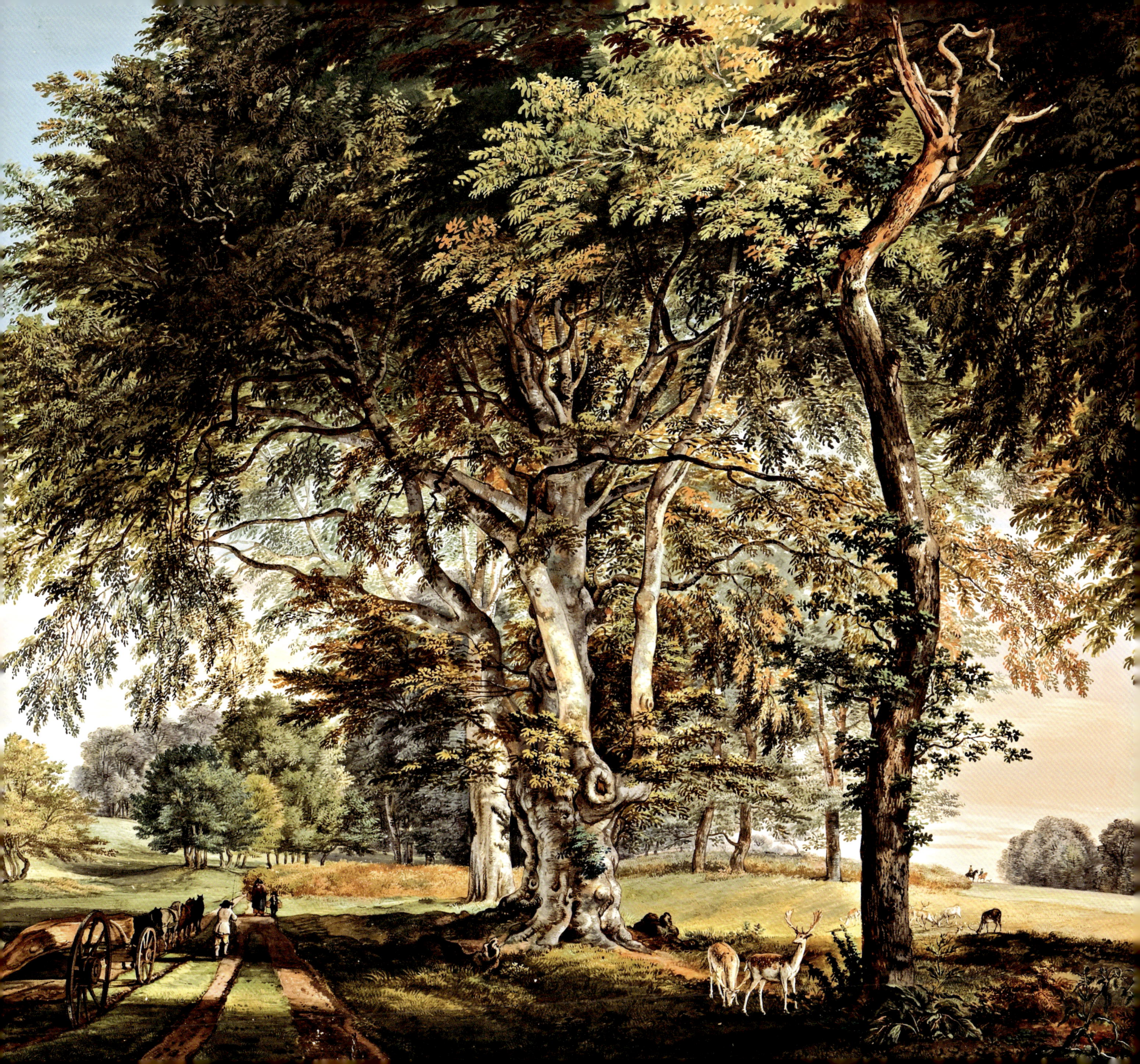

92

A View of Vintners at Boxley, Kent, with Mr Whatman's Turkey Paper Mills, 1794

Bodycolour and watercolour, 673 × 1016 mm.
Signed and dated: 'P. Sandby 1794' (l.l.)
Yale Center for British Art, New Haven, Paul Mellon Fund, B2002.29

PROVENANCE
James Whatman II, and by descent

SELECTED EXHIBITIONS
RA 1794, no. 328; Yale 2006B

SELECTED REFERENCES
Yale 2006B

This prospect of the house and mill of a well-known papermaker was produced at a point in Sandby's career when, according to conventional scholarly wisdom, he was finding himself increasingly marginalised by the rise to prominence of a younger generation of 'painters in watercolour'. In comparison with the work of young contemporaries like Girtin or Turner, a finely delineated, topographical prospect such as this would have appeared 'old-fashioned', perhaps, or lacking in dignity. Yet, as Stephen Daniels has noted in his extended consideration of this picture (Daniels 2006), such views did still command considerable cultural esteem. Critics of the period were, by and large, respectful of Sandby's achievements. His work also remained popular with purchasers of prints of British scenery, as well as private patrons requiring portraits of their property.

A View of Vintners at Boxley was commissioned from the artist by the celebrated papermaker James Whatman II, and depicts his house, park and famed Turkey Mill in the Len valley, near Maidstone in Kent. The work recalls views of country estates made earlier in Sandby's career, not least in the way that Whatman's property is established in the wider landscape. The painting is similarly far from being a straightforward topographical record, documenting a particular time and place. Rather, Sandby is concerned to connect this scenery, and the agricultural and industrial activities depicted, with the geography of the wider countryside, both regional and national. The ties that bind people to the places where they live and work, whether in terms of the physical features of the terrain or their imaginative identification with the place, are featured prominently. Accordingly, routes through this valley landscape play an important part in structuring the scene, beginning with the sharp bend in the road in the foreground, travelled by a horseman in one direction and a milkmaid in the other. Indeed, the picture presents the viewer with a range of vistas, extending to its very margins. Another road, with a speeding stagecoach, runs in front of the mill, parallel to the picture frame. Numerous vignettes detailing the varied, productive uses of the landscape appear, from the recently harvested hop gardens, with their conical stacks of poles, most obvious to the right of the composition, to the finely rendered details of Whatman's house and the paper mill itself, with its water mill and drying lofts. These buildings and structures are depicted with an almost hallucinatory, microscopic exactness. Indeed, such is the attention to observable detail, the remorseless lucidity of everything, that the picture can be seen as not so much a faithful reproduction as an idealised imitation. On one hand, this level of assertion assures the viewer of the work's fidelity to the scene depicted. On the other hand, its level of insistence is quite unnatural: no one view could provide so much information. The work is documentary, but – as Daniels has argued – also emblematic: it records this industrial landscape for its owner, replete with details of the papermaking process, but it is also a patriotic landscape carrying a rich range of associations for a nation at war, as Britain was in 1794. This is a landscape of georgic plenitude, of reassuring industry and productivity, set amid 'the garden of England'.

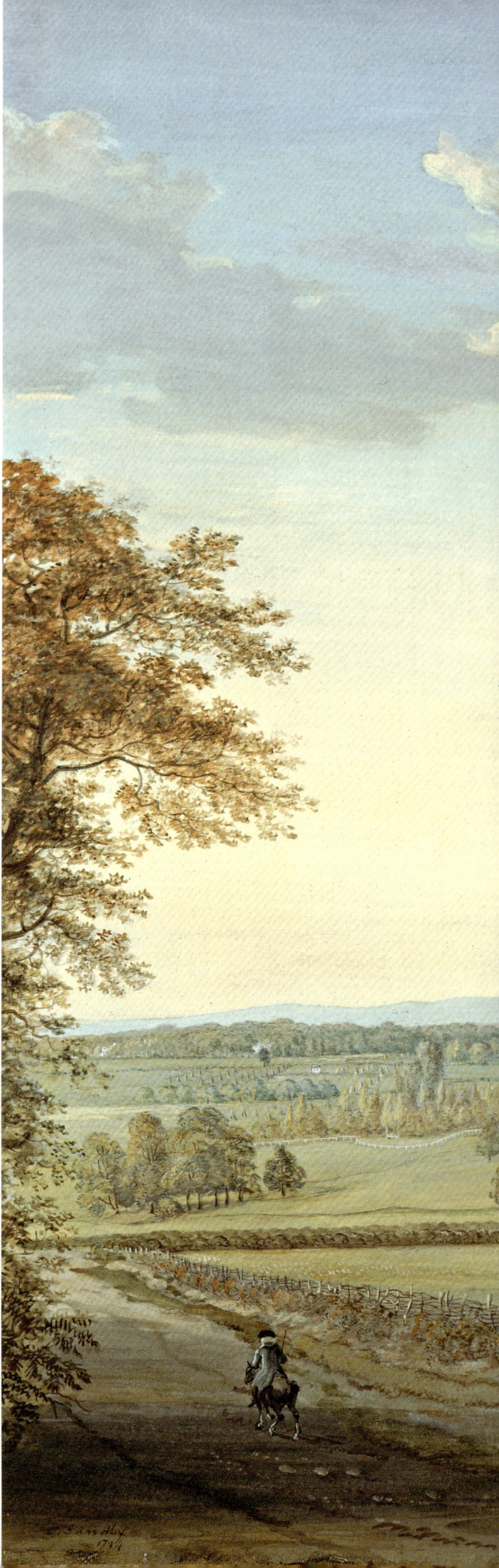

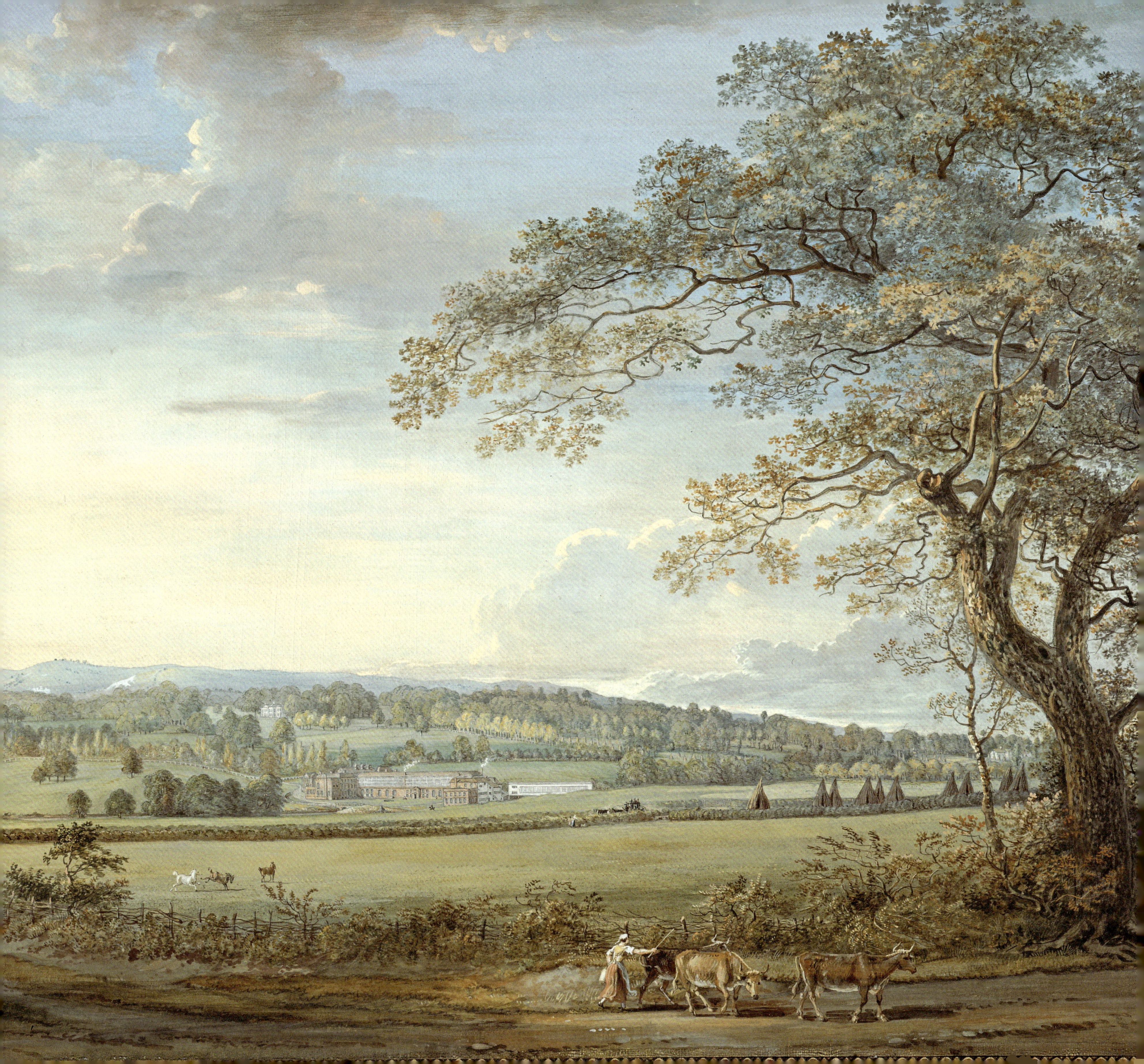

93.1–4

XII Views in North Wales, published September 1776

(1) Plate III: 'Chirk Castle from Wynnstay Park'
(2) Plate IV: 'Llangollen in the County of Denbigh from the Turnpike Road above the River Dee'
(3) Plate VI: 'The Iron Forge between Dolgelli and Barmouth in Merioneth Shire'
(4) Plate VIII: 'Caernarvon Castle'

Etching and aquatint, average 239 × 314 mm
National Museum of Wales, Cardiff

SELECTED REFERENCES
Hughes 1972; Yale 1985, nos 91–98, pp. 68–75; Robertson 1987, pp. 330–37

In 1770 Paul Sandby made his first recorded journey to Wales, staying at Wynnstay, the Denbighshire family seat of Sir Watkin Williams Wynn. A receipt documenting Sandby's various duties, dated June 1771 (fig. 48.1), shows him to have instructed Wynn in drawing, and to have produced several studies of local landmarks. This account of expenditure also lists several errands performed for Wynn on Sandby's return to London. These include a visit to a 'Mr Brown at Hampton Court Palace', which is presumably a reference to Lancelot 'Capability' Brown, who served as Master Gardener there and in which capacity he occupied its Wilderness House. This may suggest that Sandby, who probably knew the gardener through his connections with the poet William Mason, helped to negotiate Brown's subsequent remodelling of the park and gardens at Wynnstay. These were only part of Wynn's extravagant and costly improvements, however, which also saw him employ Robert Adam and commission works of art from William Parry and Richard Wilson. On reaching his majority in May 1770, Wynn invited some 15,000 of his tenants to celebrate at Wynnstay. This grand act of theatre, whereby Wynn affirmed his status as one of the largest landowners in the country, was followed the next year by a ritual tour of his property. Over six weeks in the summer of 1771, Sandby accompanied Wynn on this extended tour of his estate during which they made a circuit from Wynnstay, largely on good roads, in a party of five gentlemen, nine servants and thirteen horses (fig. 48.2). *XII Views in North Wales*, published in September 1776, records the party's passage, surveying the varied antiquities, residences, modern improvements, commercial holdings and natural wonders to be encountered on Wynn's estates, taking in ancient fortresses, country seats, landscape parks, turnpike roads, bridges, mills, forges and mountain scenery.

Overton Bridge, which links England and Wales over the River Dee, features in the first plate, followed by a view overlooking Wynnstay from above this recently built river crossing. This view of expansive landscaped parkland is contrasted with the partial vista afforded by the third plate, showing nearby *Chirk Castle from Wynnstay Park* glimpsed through a screen of trees. Sandby's series

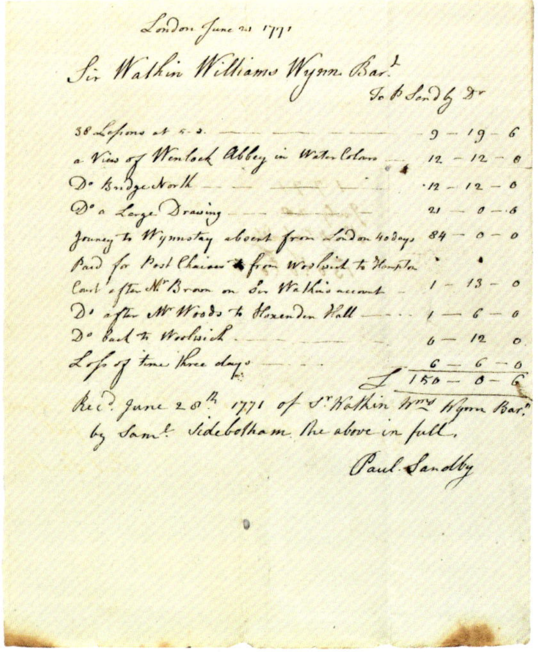

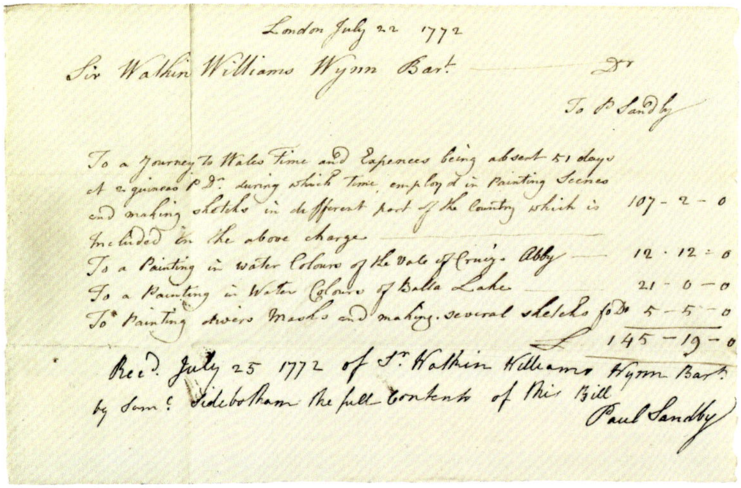

FIGS 48.1–2
Wynnstay bills, June 1771 and July 1772.
Llyfrgell Genedlaethol Cymru (National Library of Wales), Aberystwyth

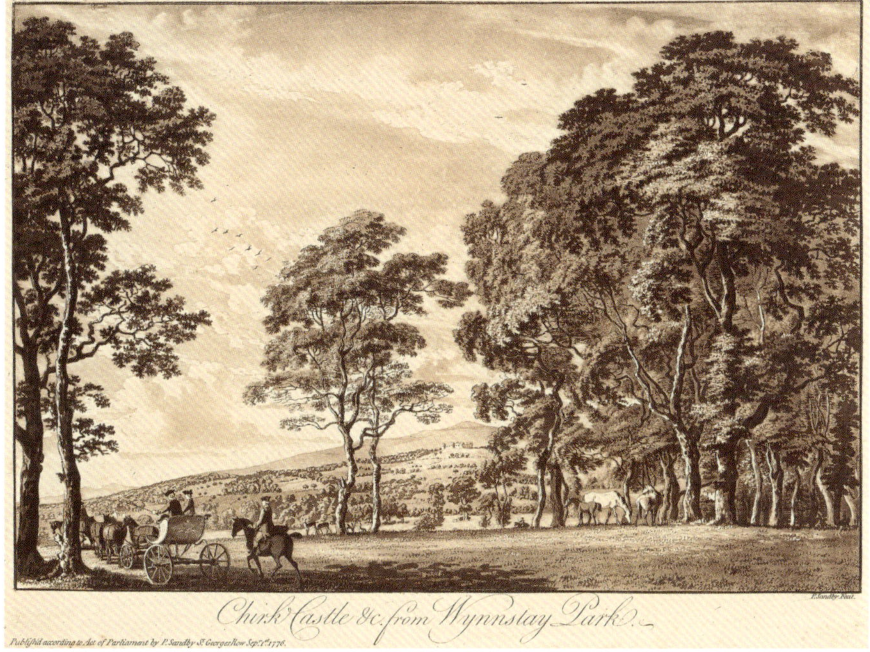

CAT. 93.1

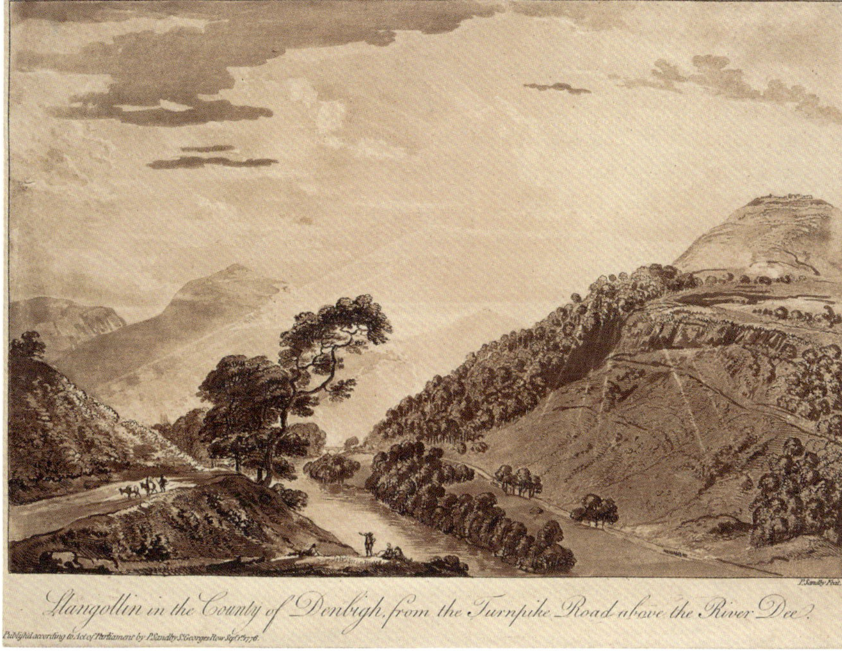

CAT. 93.2

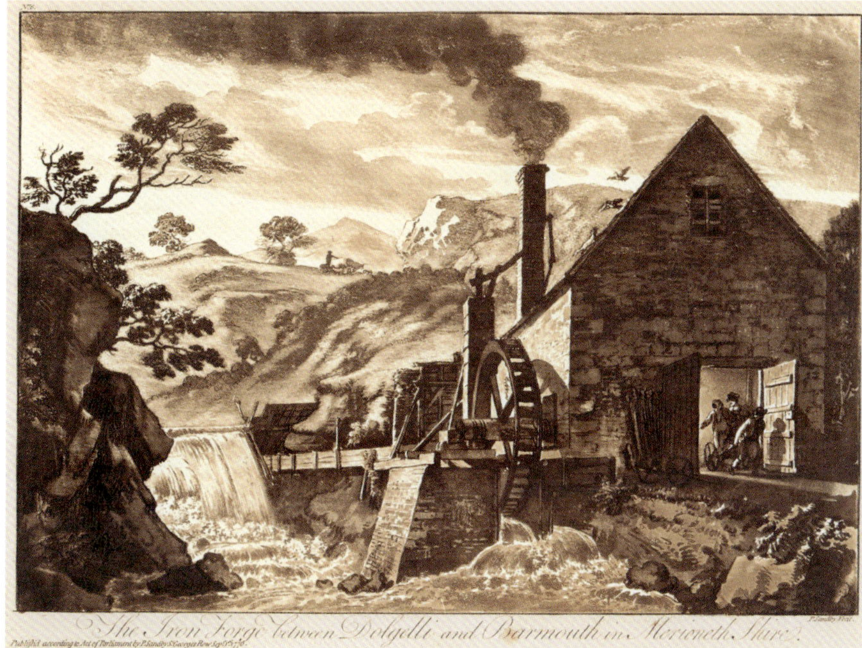

CAT. 93.3

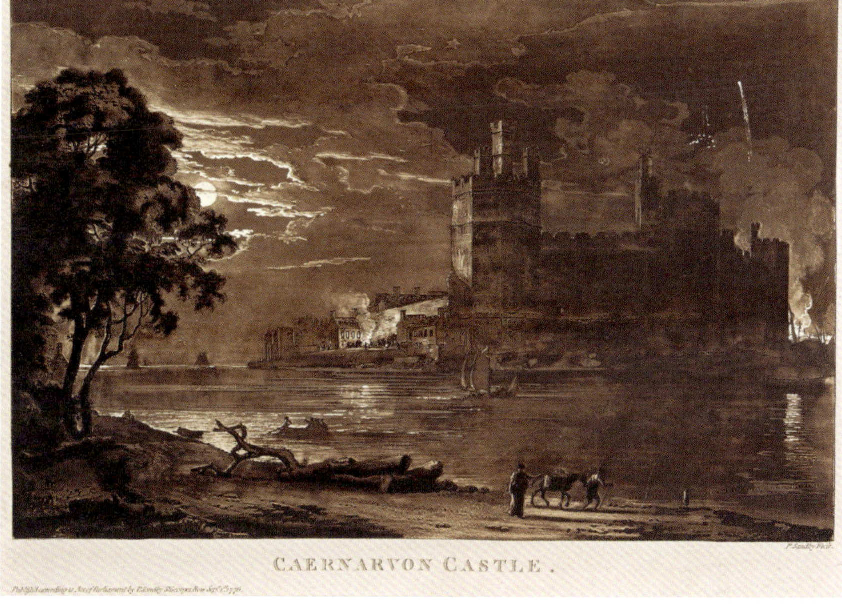

CAT. 93.4

makes full and forceful use of the varied vantage points of the road, as is illustrated by a comparison of the artist's view of the Vale of Llangollen with those painted for Wynn in 1769 by Richard Wilson (figs 49, 50). In Wilson's timeless, classicising scenes, exercises in the manner of Gaspard Dughet and Claude, we look down on or along the River Dee, with the vista closed in each instance by the hilltop fortress of Dinas Bran, an emblem of Wynn's personal and ancestral dominion. In Sandby's temporal, topographical scene, we look, as the print's title says, 'from the Turnpike Road above the River Dee', and are presented with the limited vistas and steep mountains experienced by the traveller in north Wales. This is followed by plates depicting working sites, Conwyd Mill, on the road between Llangollen and Bala, and *The Iron Forge Near Dolgelli and Barmouth in Merionshire*. Here, a millstream powers a wheel turning a tilt hammer inside. This is just visible by the light from the open door in the darkened gable, which also silhouettes the smiths inside. A low viewpoint further exaggerates the drama of this scene of nocturnal industry, set against a steeply rising, mountainous backdrop. Like Joseph Wright of Derby's forge scenes of the same period, the view offers a form of spectatorship that valorised manly, mechanical work as a model for philosophical contemplation through an evocation of the sublime, elemental forces of earth, air, fire and water. Their dependence on water-power meant that mills, furnaces and forges were often located in spectacular surroundings, attractive to those touring the landscape. In *Observations on the River Wye*, made on a tour of the region in 1770, William Gilpin observed of the local waterside industry: 'Many of the furnaces, on the banks of the river, consume charcoal, which is manufactured on the spot; and the smoke, which is frequently seen issuing from the sides of the hills and spreading its thin veil over a part of them, beautifully breaks their lines, and unites them with the sky' (Gilpin 1782, p. 12). This experimentation with nocturnal effects in Sandby's view of smoking industry is continued in the eighth plate, *Caernarvon Castle*, depicting Edward I's stronghold. Other antiquities featured in the series include the coastal fortress of Harlech, another castle datable to Edward's reign, as well as the ancient citadels of Dinas Bran and Dolbadern. These were important sites for Wynn, who was aware of the place of his ancestors in the region's history (see cat. 73). They represented ancient Welsh liberty, as well as Wynn's dynastic authority over this landscape. The fruits of Wynn's ownership are made apparent in later prints in Sandby's series, most notably *Bangor in the County of Caernarvon*, which depicts that thriving town.

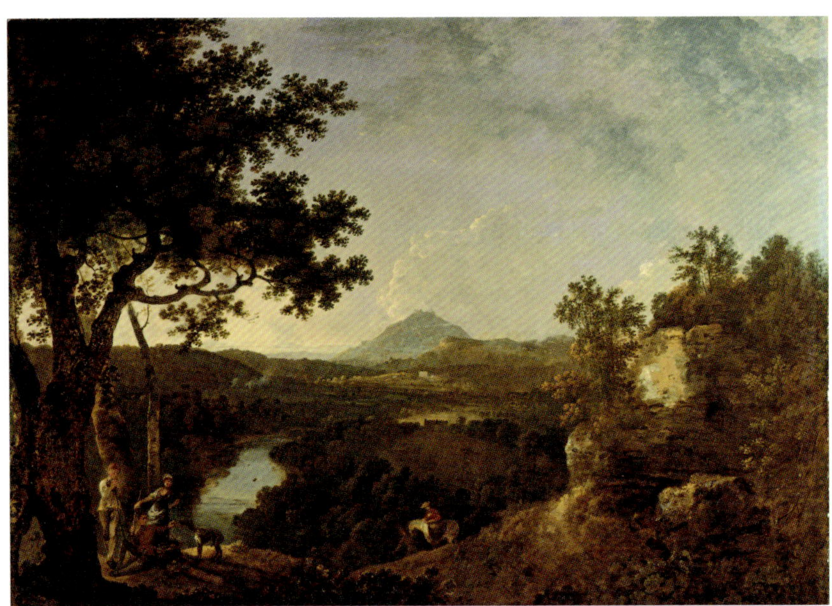

FIG. 49
Richard Wilson (1714–1782), *View near Wynnstay, the Seat of Sir Watkin Williams Wynn Bt*, 1770–71. Oil on canvas, 1803 × 2448 mm. Yale Center for British Art, New Haven, Paul Mellon Collection, B1976.7.84

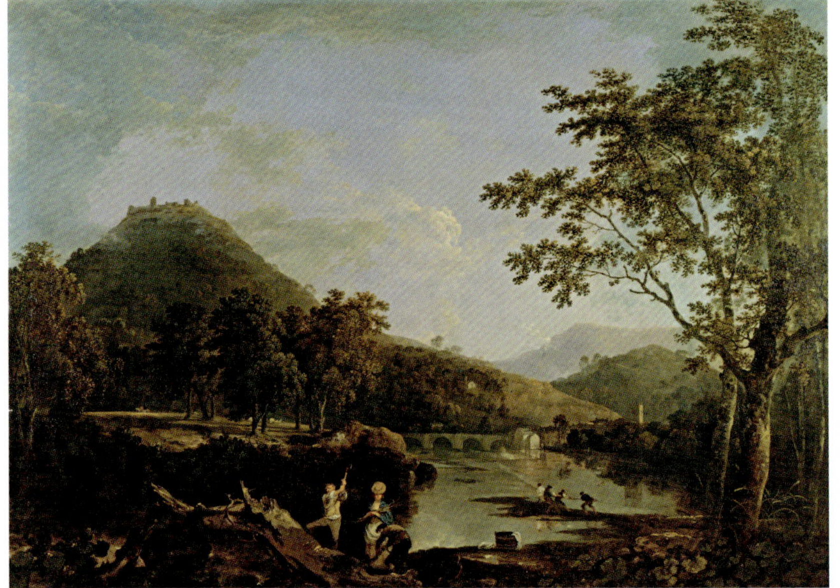

FIG. 50
Richard Wilson (1714–1782), *Dinas Bran from Llangollen*, 1770–71. Oil on canvas, 1803 × 2448 mm. Yale Center for British Art, New Haven, Paul Mellon Collection, B1876.7.83

94

The Studio of Paul Sandby, St George's Row, c. 1772

Bodycolour and watercolour, 173 × 233 mm
Nottingham City Museums and Galleries, NCM 1945-159

PROVENANCE
T. P. Sandby; Mrs Stuart Sullivan; bequeathed by Lady E. J. Rich, 1945

SELECTED EXHIBITIONS
London 1960, no. 155; Hamilton 1981, no. 29; Nottingham 1986, n.n.; London 2003B, no. 41

SELECTED REFERENCES
Hamilton 1981, no. 29, p. 29; London 1986, pp. 42–44; Longstaffe-Gowan 2001, pp. 53–58; London 2003B, no. 41, p. 100; Daniels 2004, pp. 25

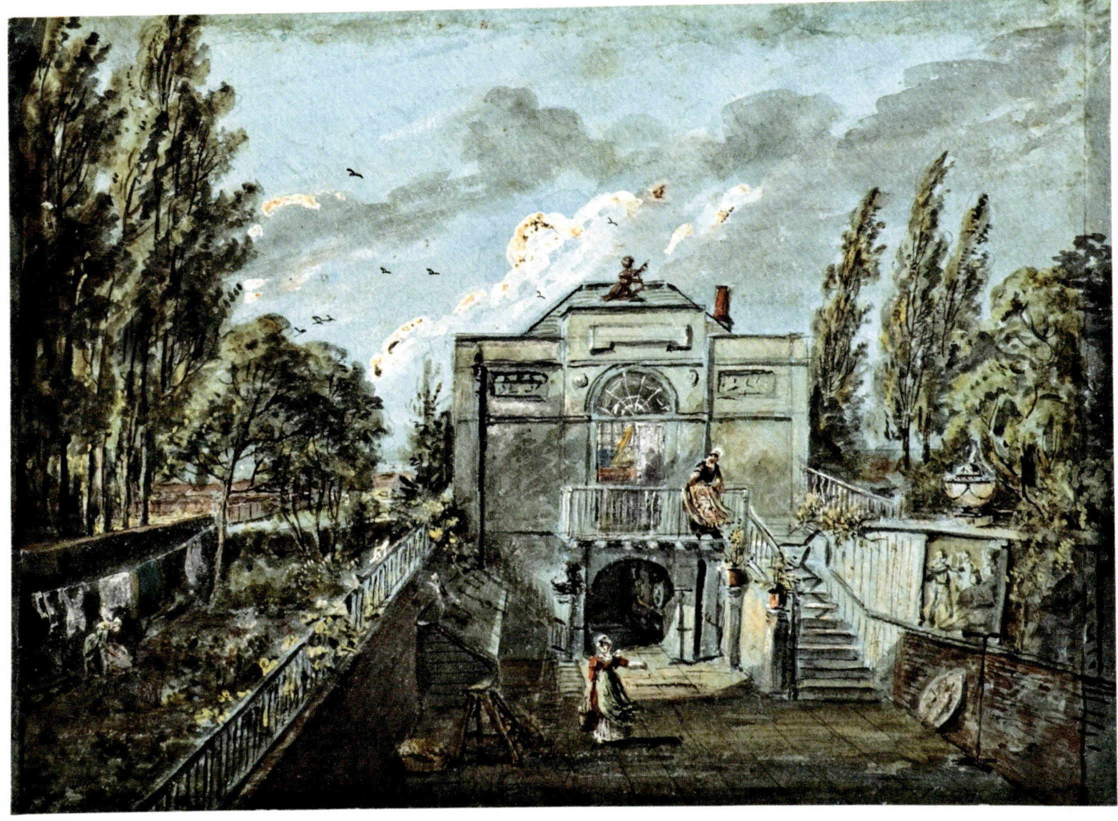

This informal study of a garden studio appears to have been taken from a back window of Sandby's house at 4 St George's Row, off the Bayswater Road. It is unclear, however, whether this is a record or a projection of the set-up of Sandby's painting room. Such an elegant courtyard garden, paved with slabs, filled with potted flowers, urns and sculptural reliefs, would certainly have been fitting for an artist of Sandby's stature, conveying an image of learning, refinement and taste. This elegance is also extended to the studio itself, a decidedly French-looking pavilion resembling garden buildings designed by the artist's elder brother Thomas Sandby, who was well versed in continental architectural theory and practice. The austerity of this design is in marked, and perhaps even humorous, contrast to the adjacent, walled plot, which is filled with an array of flowering shrubs and young trees. That the painting is, perhaps, best seen as an imagined prospect, rather than as a document of Sandby's garden, is further suggested by the inclusion of knowing references to the sort of art he admired: figures animate the scene, servants hang out washing and beat a rug, all recalling depictions of villa life found in the art of Marco Ricci. A second, more finished version of this composition varies these activities (fig. 8).

95

The Garden of the Deputy Ranger's House, c. 1798

Bodycolour, 399 × 592 mm
Royal Collection, London, RL 17596

PROVENANCE
Princess Helena Victoria and Princess Marie Louise (sale Robinson and Foster Ltd, 24–25 March 1947, lot 274); Sabin; purchased 1948

SELECTED EXHIBITIONS
Amsterdam 1995, no. 40

SELECTED REFERENCES
Oppé 1950, no. 429; Amsterdam 1995, no. 40, p. 118

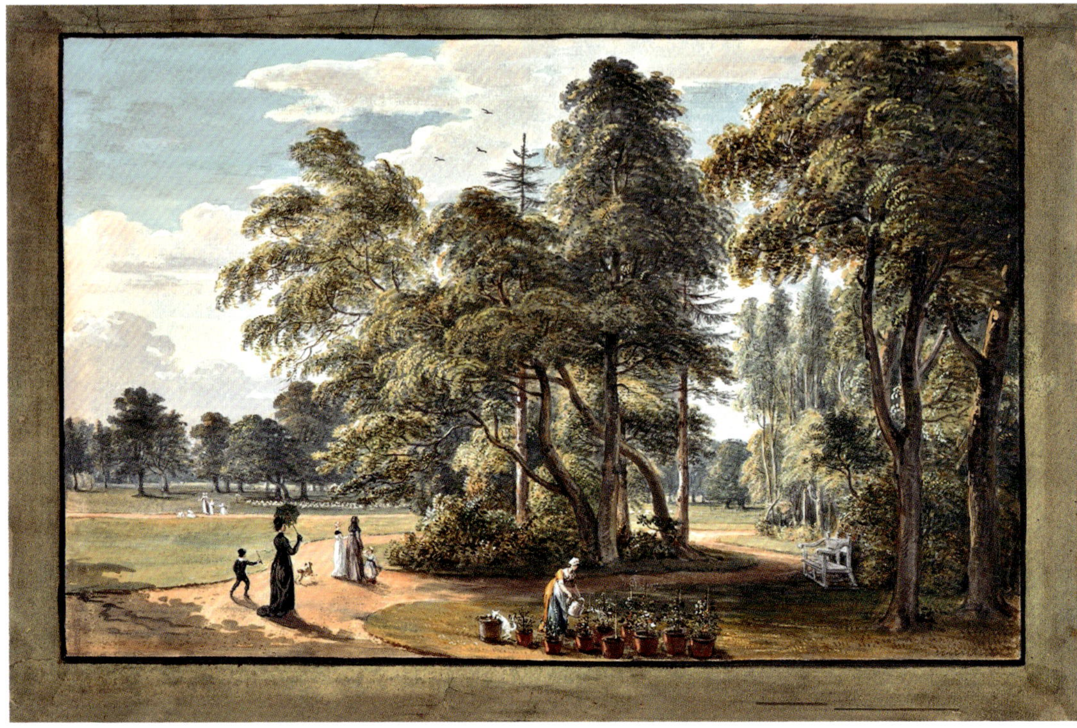

In or about 1770 Thomas Sandby took up residence in a former dairy, situated within easy reach of most of Windsor Great Park's central features. He converted and extended the building considerably, presumably to his own designs. His younger brother made a number of careful studies of the house and gardens in the 1790s, including this finely observed bodycolour, which records the garden plot adjoining the south of the building, a secluded, well-maintained arrangement of potted and bedded flowers, shrubs and trees, bordered by a meandering, rolled gravel path, opening out into the surrounding parkland. This attentiveness to details of design, planting and situation is also apparent in the artist's views of his son's house at Englefield Green (cats 96–97), a further instance of a private garden set amid an expanse of common ground. These pictures of family life, whether set in and around the Deputy's Ranger's Lodge or at Englefield Green, also include a number of comparisons between rest and labour, leisure and work, one of Sandby's favourite motifs.

In 1786 Paul Sandby's son Thomas Paul had married his cousin, Thomas's daughter Harriet, the couple settling at the Deputy Ranger's Lodge. Paul and Thomas Paul Sandby remained resident at their place of business, 4 St George's Row, for much of the time, leaving Harriet with her father. That the Sandby family relied a good deal on the elder brother for their financial security is apparent from a notice that appeared on his death, which entreated: 'He has left a large family, heirs alone to his humble hopes that the known generosity and goodness of the Crown (which he has served faithfully for above 57 years) may beneficently supply, by its spontaneous bounty, that provision which his scrupulous probity would not permit him to amass out of the perquisites and opportunities of his employment' (*The Gentleman's Magazine*, July 1798, p. 631). Jane Roberts has suggested that the inclusion of figures wearing mourning in this drawing may suggest a date around June 1798, when Thomas Sandby passed away (Amsterdam 1995, p. 118). The family were to vacate the house shortly afterwards.

CATALOGUE NUMBERS 96–97

A view of the house of Sir John Elvil at Englefield Green, just to the east of Windsor Great Park, was included by Sandby in *A Collection of Landscapes* in 1777. The accompanying letterpress drew attention to the many charms of its situation, noting that:

> this enchanting spot is celebrated for the salubrity of its air, and that in its environs there are a greater number of elegant seats, and delightful prospects, than in any part of England within the same extent. Its vicinity to the Thames and Windsor Park renders it still more eligible. In a word, the country for several miles round is more agreeable than can be imagined.
> (*A Collection of Landscapes*, 1777, plate 6, pp. 6–7)

This semi-rural landscape was one to be admired, not least because it afforded all the delights of the countryside, good clean air and fine vistas, but also because its proximity to major routes placed the city within easy reach. These qualities were also celebrated in a series of drawings of Englefield Green executed around the turn of the century, by which time the Sandbys had themselves come to occupy one of these 'elegant seats'.

On Thomas Sandby's death in 1798, Thomas Paul and his family moved out of the Deputy Ranger's Lodge and took a house in Englefield Green. Father and son presumably spent most of the week at 4 St George's Row, visiting the house in Surrey at weekends. Drawings made during these visits, such as the highly finished bodycolours shown here, portray their family engaged in various leisured pursuits, across a range of social spaces. These pictures include a number of portraits of family members, friends and servants congregating in the garden of the house, taking tea, conversing or sketching, playing, strolling in the grounds or tending the flowerbeds. They also offer glimpses of the wider landscape and its uses. Views towards adjacent properties are included, across a busy green. Traffic of various kinds makes its way past the fence, including drovers and polite couples out walking, mounted riders and speeding carriages. The works convey an ideal of modest villa life, portraying a small, restricted circle enjoying an informal, leisured existence, a paradigm that had gained considerable currency by the century's end.

96

Englefield Green, near Egham, c. 1800

Bodycolour, 310 × 464 mm
Nottingham City Museums and Galleries, NCM 1945-142

PROVENANCE
Bequeathed by Lady E. J. Rich, 1945

SELECTED EXHIBITIONS
Hamilton 1981, no. 26

SELECTED REFERENCES
Hamilton 1981, no. 26, p. 26

97

Tea at Englefield Green, c. 1800

Bodycolour, 317 × 461 mm
Nottingham City Museums and Galleries, NCM 1945-146

PROVENANCE
Bequeathed by Lady E. J. Rich, 1945

SELECTED EXHIBITIONS
Hamilton 1981, no. 28

SELECTED REFERENCES
Hamilton 1981, no. 28, p. 28

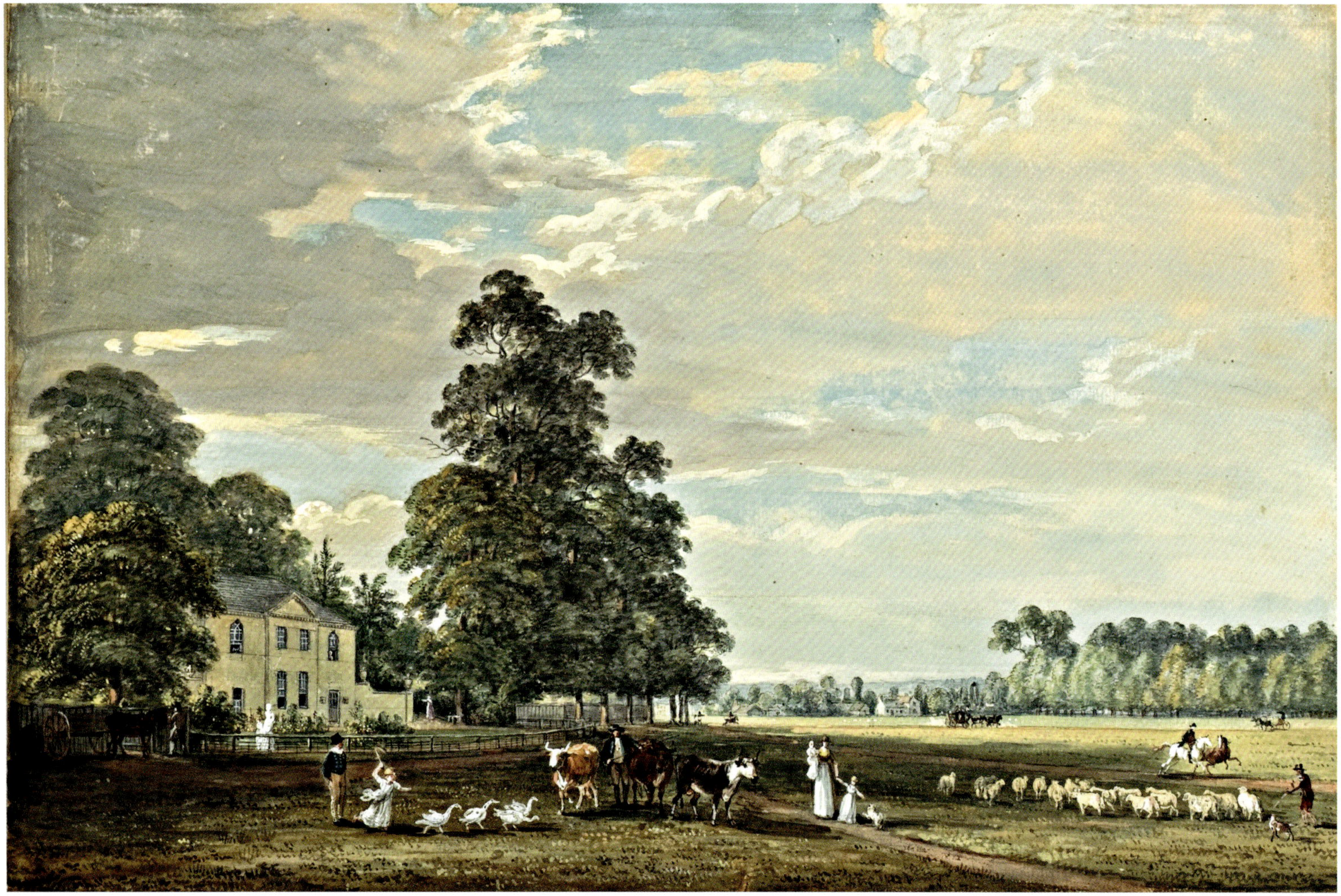

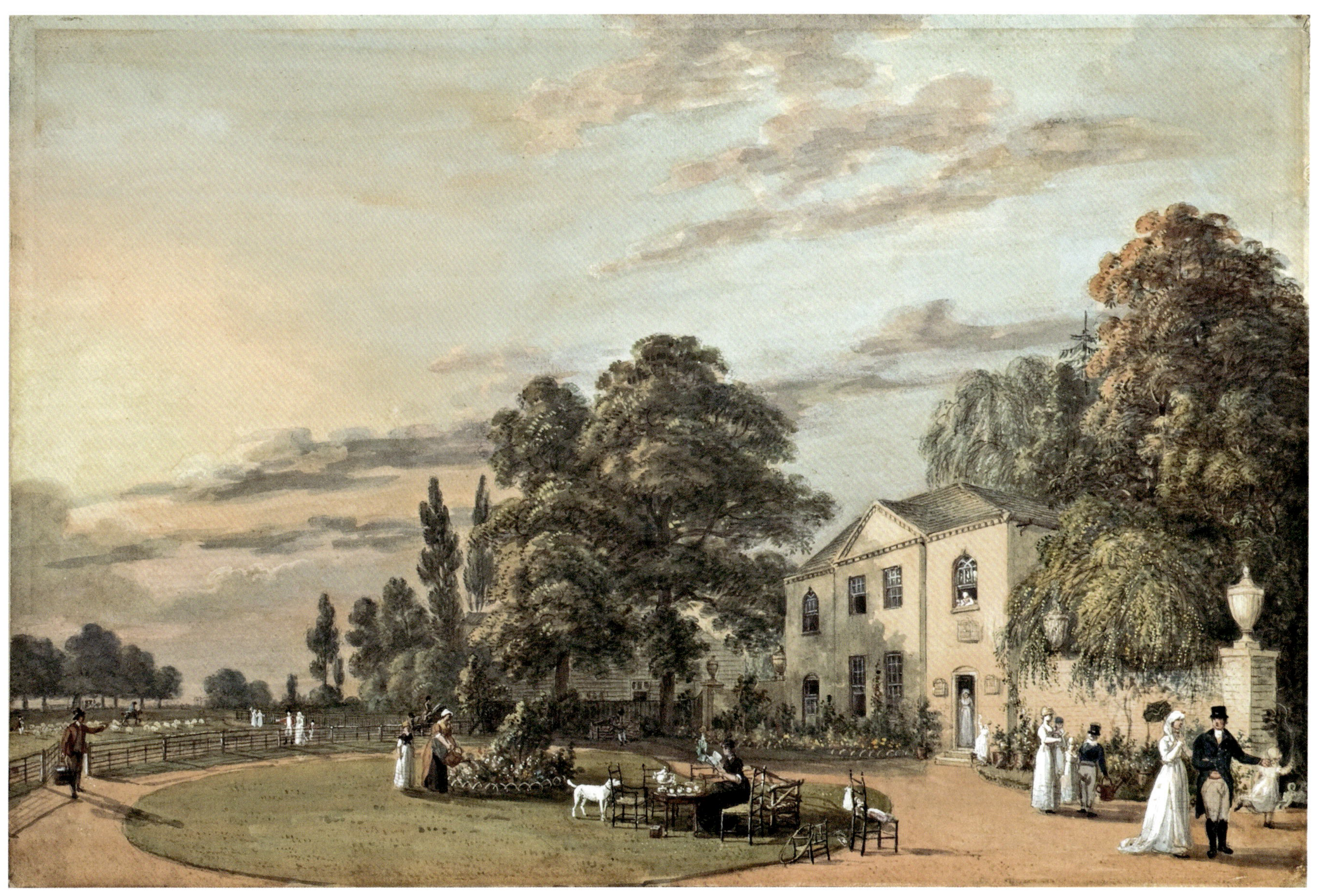

98

The Wood Yard, Windsor Great Park, *c.* 1792

Watercolour, pen and ink over graphite, 252 × 375 mm
Yale Center for British Art, New Haven, Paul Mellon Collection, B1975.4.1383

PROVENANCE
Col. William Gravatt, 1867; William Sandby; G. J. A. Peake; Hubert Peake (sale Christie's, 24 March 1959, lot 63)

SELECTED EXHIBITIONS
Yale 1985, no. 126

SELECTED REFERENCES
Yale 1985, no. 126, p. 94

CATALOGUE NUMBERS 98–100

In 1792 Sandby produced a group of views of the wood yard or 'Carpenters Yard' in Windsor Great Park. Their broad handling and immediacy suggest that they were possibly made *en plein air*. The views survey the yard from a number of different points, and feature a variety of work, machinery and transportation. Sandby's interest in the working of raw materials provided by the countryside is also apparent in the late bodycolour illustrated here, a Thames-side view, presumably taken around Woolwich, showing the felling of massive, ancient oaks, the hard, physical labour of the team uprooting the trees, the carriage and oxen used to transport the timber, and its use in constructing the nation's 'wooden walls', indicated by the ships anchored offshore in the distance. These local, everyday scenes are thus connected with a larger national enterprise, indeed with the very security of the country. The artist's interest in the significance of these landscapes to the defence of the nation is also apparent in his concern over shortfalls in naval timber, which was a cause of considerable contemporary anxiety. In a letter to James Gandon, written towards the end of his long life, Sandby was to lament that 'the majestic forests of Windsor have long since lowly bowed their heads to the adze of keen necessity, and lust of lucre', leaving 'the humble elm' to lend its 'feeble aid to battle with our enemies at sea' (Gandon 1846, p. 184).

Views of the wood yard were included by Sandby in the list of works sent for exhibition at the Royal Academy in 1793, a few months into the war with revolutionary France. The patriotic significance of such scenes was likely to have been heightened further by their association with George III's recent remodelling of Windsor Castle, which transformed it from a 'rough jewel' into a model estate (see Kent 1798). Farmer George's agrarian improvements, largely overseen by William, 3rd Earl of Harcourt, and Nathaniel Kent, reaffirmed and elaborated the dense weave of cultural, historic and political associations that were prompted by Windsor Castle and its surrounding grounds. That the peace, plenty and productivity in this landscape were secured by a benevolent constitution and a virtuous sovereign was a view repeated by many a writer, poet and artist during the 1790s.

Critics of the period greatly admired Sandby's portrayal of these grounds and the artist himself cultivated the association, having himself depicted sheltering in Windsor Great Park (fig. 43). Other artists exhibited pictures of this wooded landscape and its famous trees in the 1790s, including Benjamin West, President of the Royal Academy. No other painter was as firmly associated with the portrayal of this royal domain as Sandby, however.

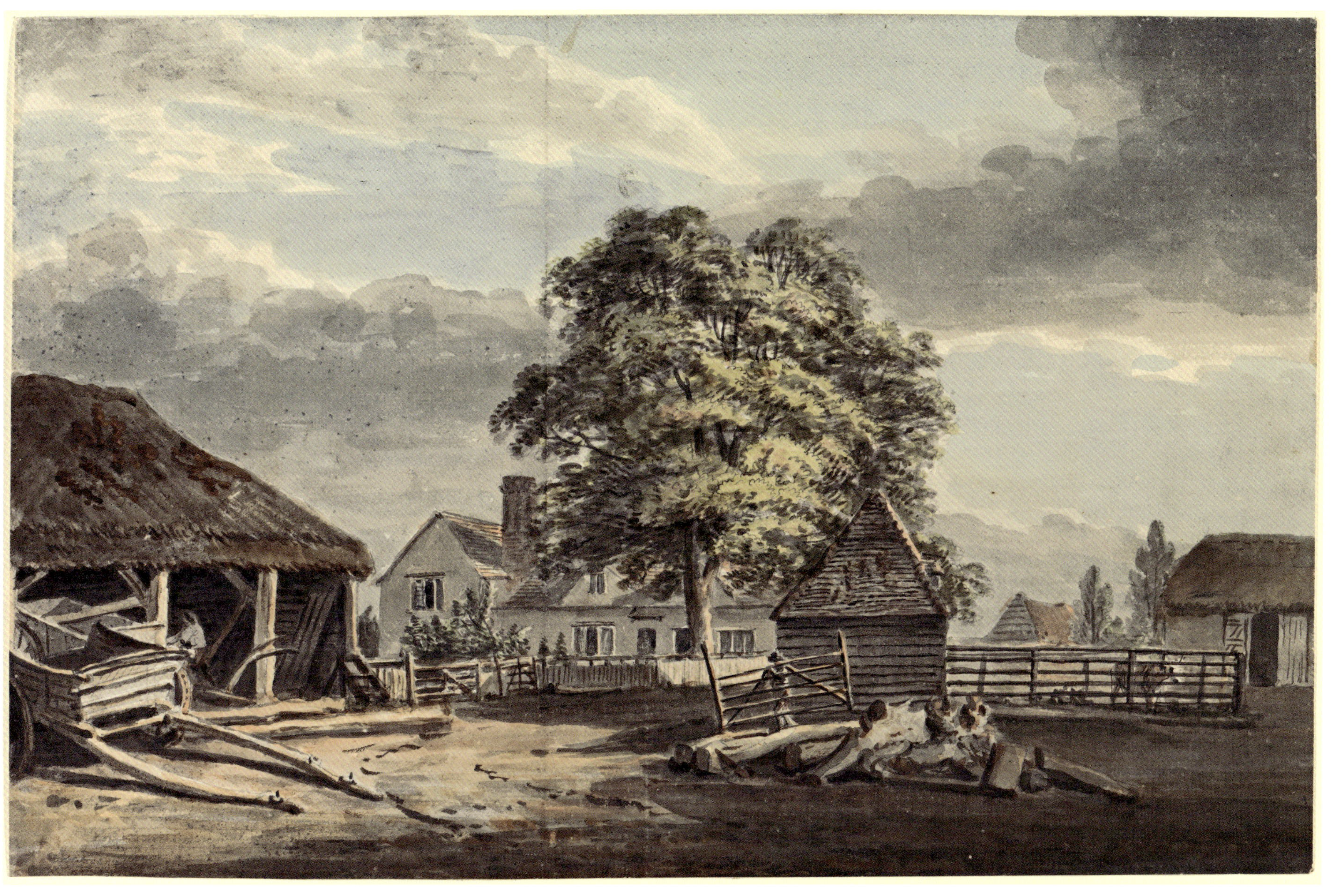

99

The Wood Yard, Windsor Great Park, 1792

Watercolour and bodycolour over graphite, 180 × 297 mm
Royal Library, London, RL 14619

PROVENANCE
Paul Sandby (sale Christie's, 3 May 1811, lot 12); Prince Regent (later George IV), and by descent

SELECTED REFERENCES
Oppé 1947, no. 93, p. 34; Amsterdam 1995, p. 120

100

Tree Felling, *c.* 1800

Bodycolour, 225 × 280 mm
Nottingham City Museums and Galleries, NCM 1945-152

PROVENANCE
T. P. Sandby; Mrs Stuart Sullivan; bequeathed by Lady E. J. Rich, 1945

SELECTED EXHIBITIONS
London 1960, no. 153; Hamilton 1981, no. 69; Nottingham 1986, n.n.

SELECTED REFERENCES
Hamilton 1981, no. 69, p. 69

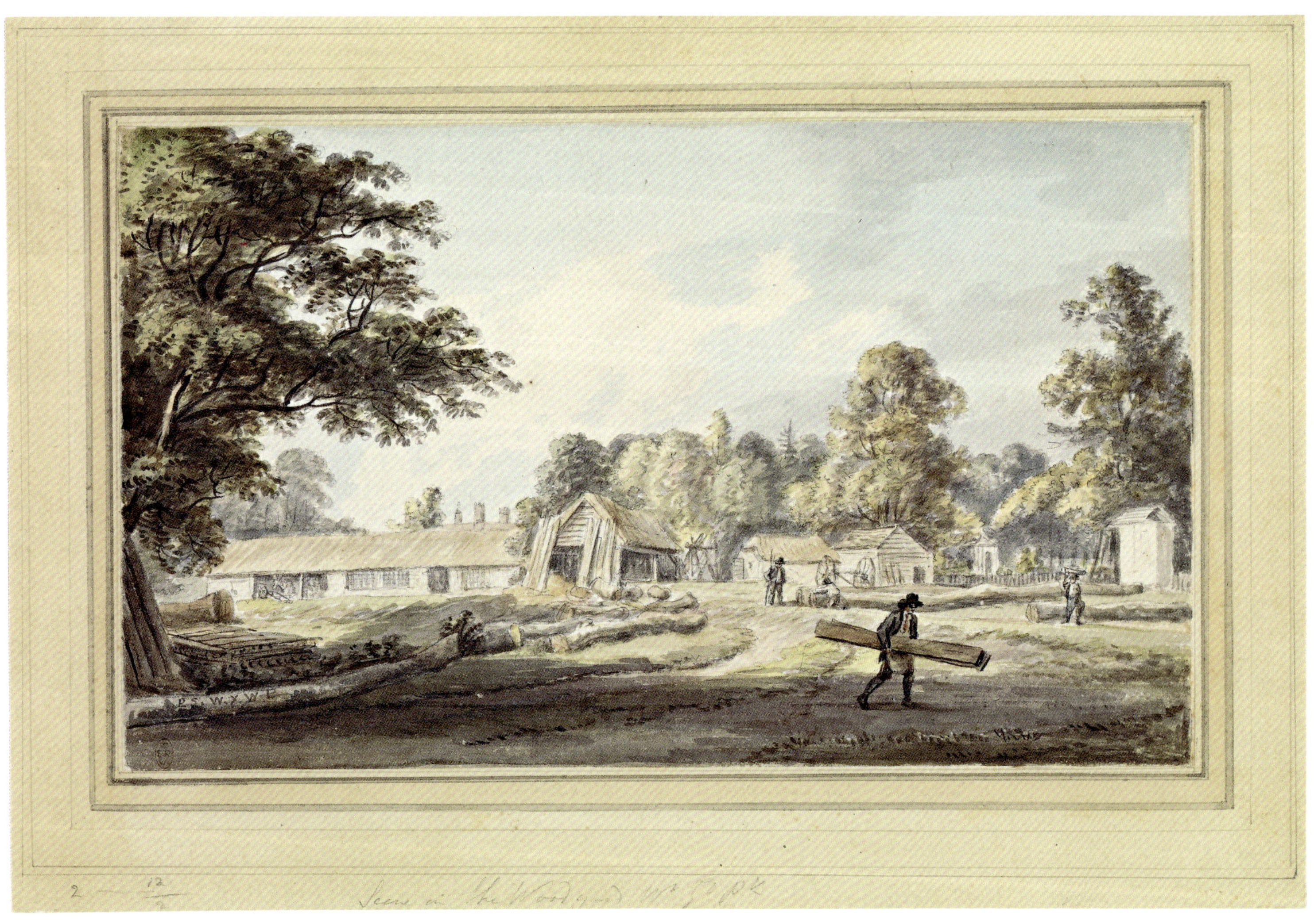

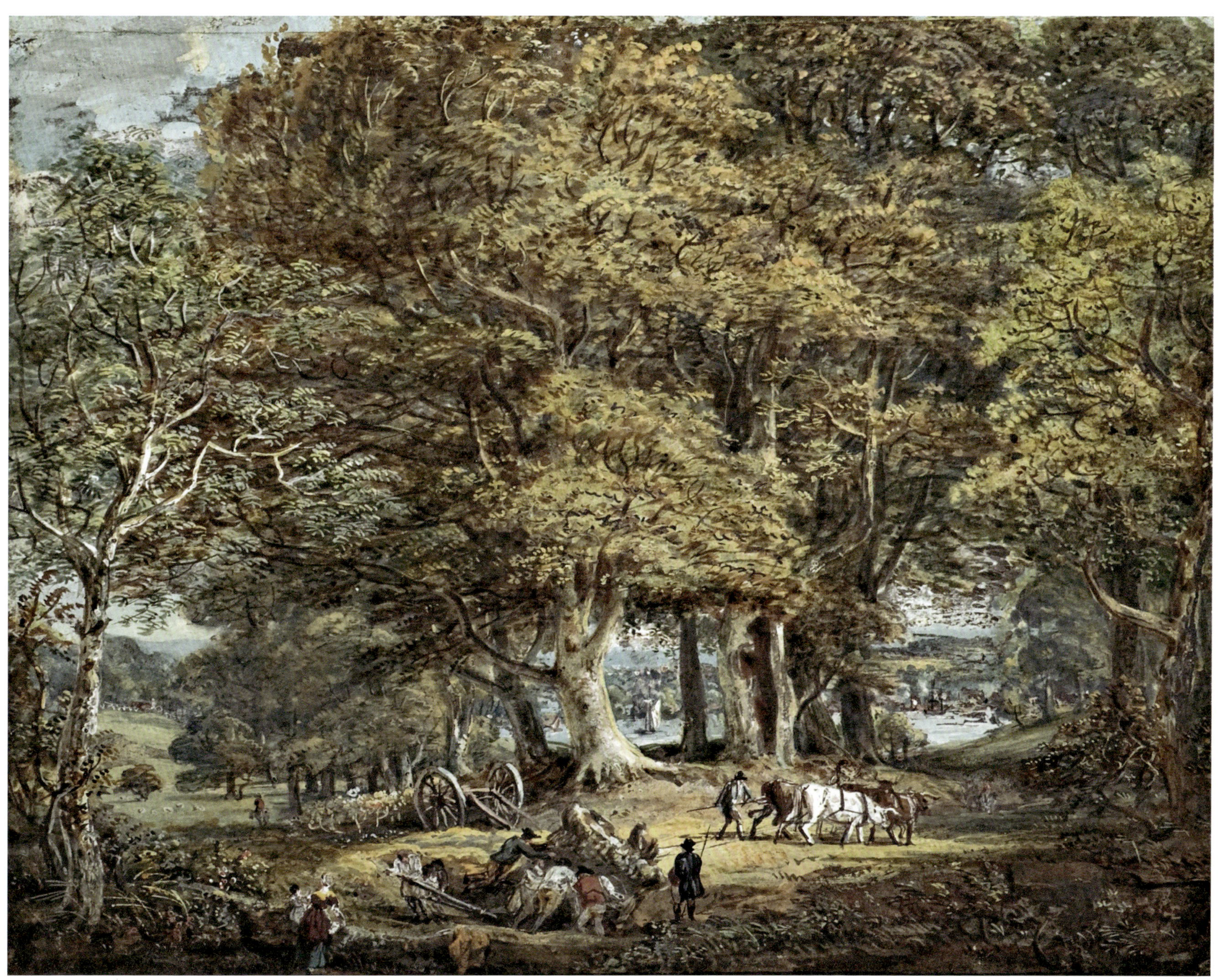

101

Morning, 1794

Bodycolour, 673 × 1016 mm
Signed and dated: 'P. Sandby 1794' (l.r.)
Victoria and Albert Museum, London, FA 383

PROVENANCE
Purchased before 1860

SELECTED EXHIBITIONS
RA 1795, no. 579; London 1986, no. 25; London 2002, no. 13

SELECTED REFERENCES
London 1986, no. 25, p. 108; London 2002, no. 13, p. 31

This portrait of an ancient beech, entitled *Morning* when exhibited at the Royal Academy in 1795, is one of a number of studies of massive, gnarled trees that Sandby essayed in the years around the turn of the century. These are mainly records of much-admired trees in and around Windsor, venerable old oaks and majestic ancient beeches. This fine example places one of these trees in a provincial landscape, setting it against a distant prospect of a thriving river port. On the evidence of a markedly similar picture, now in the Yale Center for British Art, New Haven, this is almost certainly the Shropshire town of Bridgnorth, on the River Severn. Sandby also includes an amusing figure group, locked in some dispute. However, the finely observed beech tree dominates the picture. The artist's delineation of the tree is remarkable for its close attention to the habits of growth peculiar to this species: the sculptural qualities of the trunk and branches, the characteristic hollow and dead lower limbs, the dense foliage of the canopy, as well as the lichens and moss attaching themselves to the smooth, olive-grey bark.

Such subjects had become increasingly popular from the 1780s onwards, finding favour with theorists of the picturesque. In his *Essay on Landscape* (1782) Joseph Holden Pott had recommended certain species as particularly suited to the composition of pleasing scenery, praising 'the silvery colour ... and the graceful sweep' of the beech as 'very beautiful circumstances' (Pott 1782, p. 89). Uvedale Price had observed 'something wonderfully picturesque' in the roots of such trees, admiring how they 'fasten on the earth with their dragon claws', in his influential *Essay on the Picturesque* (Price 1794, p. 30). Price's *Essay* celebrated localism and diversity, 'intricacy and variety', over the uniformity of modern, improved terrain, woodland playing a central role in his promotion of a 'connected' landscape. His writings, and those of a fellow Herefordshire landowner, Richard Payne Knight, had attracted a good deal of controversy in the year before Sandby exhibited this picture (see Daniels 1999, pp. 103–47). Sandby's decision to show a painting locating this ancient beech in the border country that had formed Price and Knight's conception of the picturesque was therefore timely.

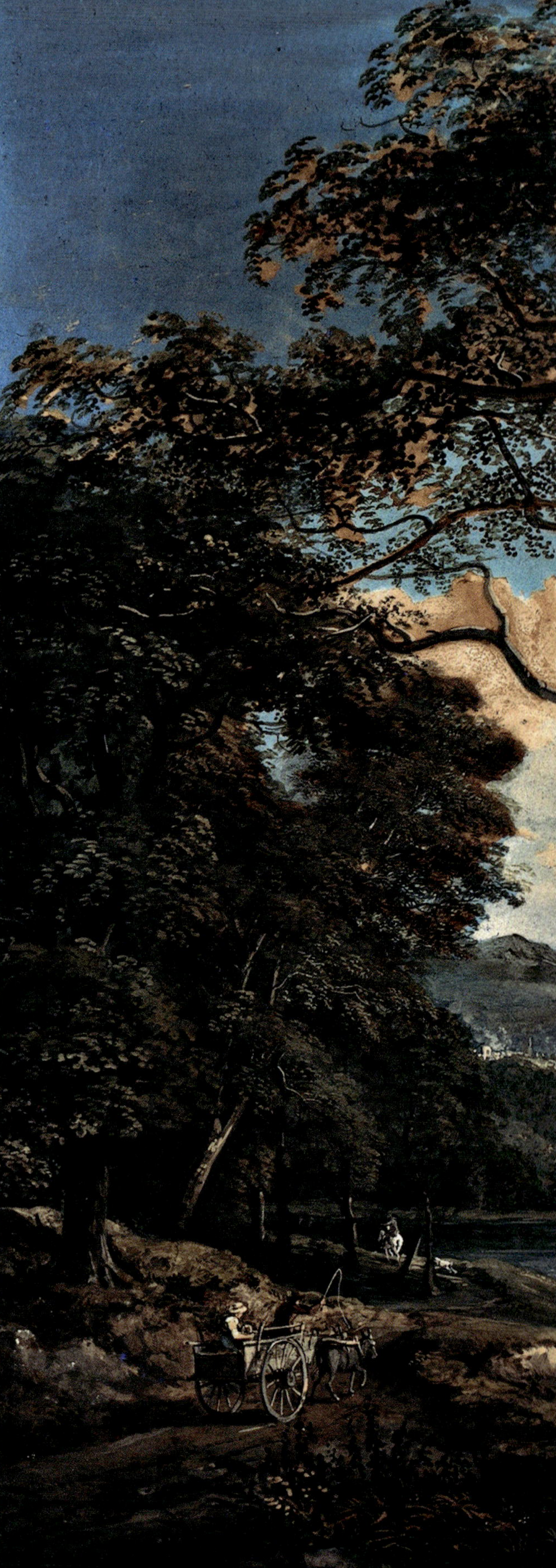

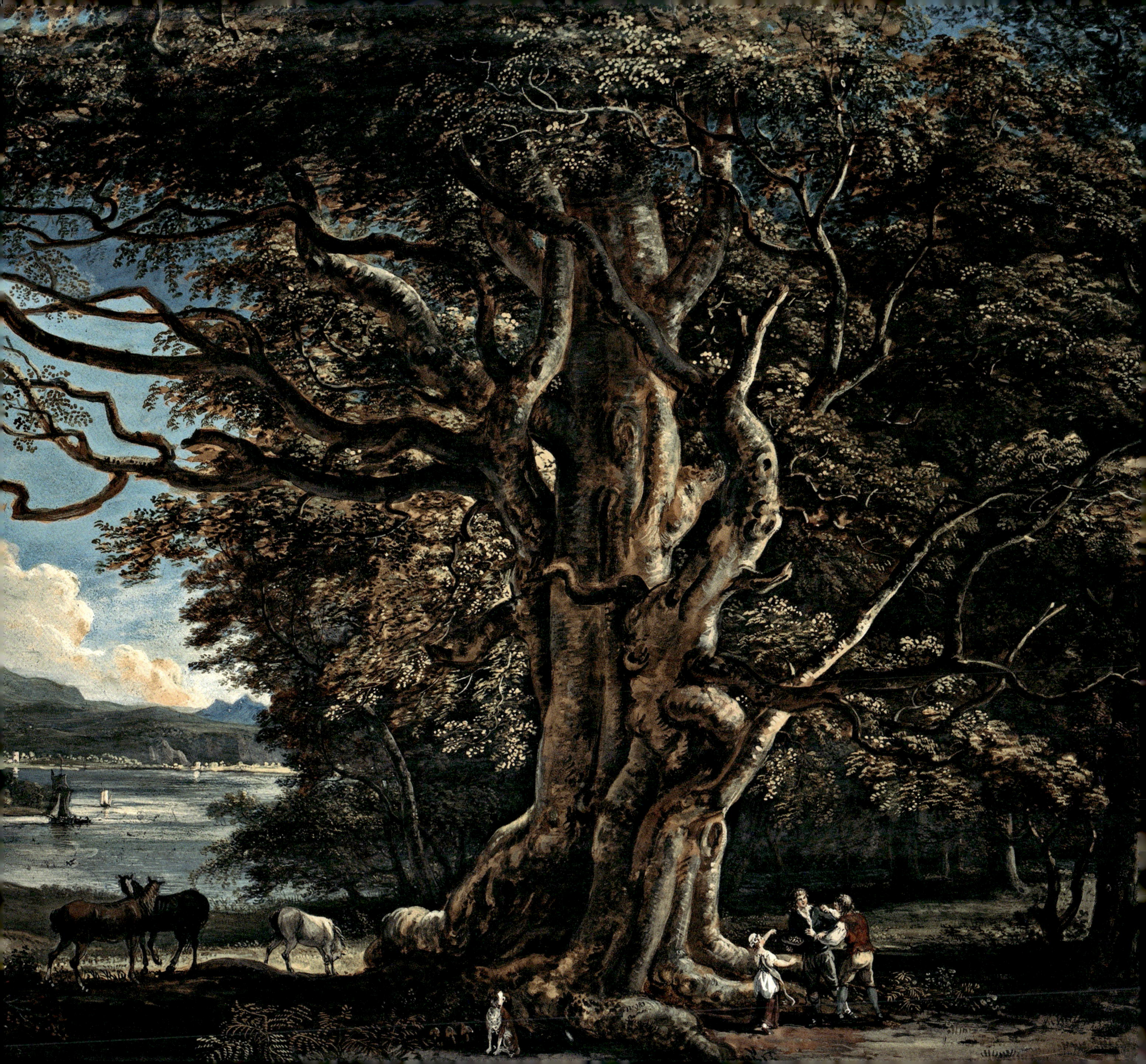

102

The Rainbow, *c.* 1800

Bodycolour, 552 × 762 mm
Nottingham City Museums and Galleries, NCM 1945-96

PROVENANCE
T. P. Sandby; Mrs Stuart Sullivan; bequeathed by Lady E. J. Rich, 1945

SELECTED EXHIBITIONS
London 1960, no. 11; Reading 1972, no. 78; London 1973, no. 72; Hamilton 1981, no. 70

SELECTED REFERENCES
Hamilton 1981, no. 70, p. 70

In his *Remarks on Forest Scenery* (1791) William Gilpin wrote approvingly of the picturesque qualities of native woodland, admiring the '*grandeur*' and '*dignity*' of a landscape that disdained 'all human culture'. He argued that their unimproved, aboriginal state, especially when 'intermixed with patches of pasturage', served 'to *rouse the imagination*' (Gilpin 1791, vol. 1, pp. 209–10). For Gilpin, this 'woody-landscape', growing free and unconstrained, also summoned thoughts of national liberty and the country's historic resistance to tyrannical rule. Written while their author was occupying the New Forest parsonage of Boldre, Gilpin's *Remarks* were shaped by his habitat and his disapproval of the improving tendencies of local landowners. His taste for such scenery, indeed the more general enthusiasm for the country's trees and woodland in the late eighteenth century, was largely formed by the laying out of parkland or commercial exploitation of the native countryside. His concerns were, of course, only part of a much broader contemporary debate over the scenic and commercial value of forests, woods or copses that were of interest to planters, painters and poets, as well as to landowners and politicians. Indeed, native greenwood stirred a range of contradictory and conflicting associations in the wider culture of the period, often around what 'the social order was or ought to have been' (Daniels 1988, p. 43). Those pictures of ancient beech and historic woodland, as well as the studies recording logging in and about Windsor in the 1790s, show Sandby to have been keenly aware of the economic and symbolic significance of timber in the period.

His sensitivity to the wide range of meanings associated with such imagery is also apparent in one of his best-known late works. *The Rainbow* is a view along an aged, well-worn path at the edge of mature woodland, neighbouring a small village, out into a rolling landscape, dramatically lit by a rainbow and a passing storm. On one hand, this large bodycolour, remarkable for its clarity and profusion of detail, looks to the past, to Peter-Paul Rubens's great rainbow landscape, lately arrived in London and now in the Wallace Collection. On the other hand, in its attention to atmospheric effects and phenomena, the work accords well with the observational naturalism of a younger generation of landscape painters then rising to prominence, even though its opaque medium made it appear increasingly out of step with those developments. Yet, in its extensive use of zinc white, a pigment not often employed in the period, the picture shows that Sandby is still experimenting, still striving for novel effects. He also remained alert to the significance of his subject-matter to the imaginative geography of Britain. Indeed, it is possible to see the inclusion of a rainbow in allegorical terms, as a conventional symbol of divine deliverance, promising relief to a landscape long threatened with invasion and insurrection. Accordingly, the picture celebrates community and local attachment, portraying various activities and freedoms associated with a simple country life, placing a milkmaid and a rustic couple, one a musician, amid common woodland, with a village and its church nearby. The picture takes its place among other work of the years around 1800 in which the ancient woodland and localities of the national topography were celebrated, addressing wider cultural concerns over the representation of Britain and Britishness.

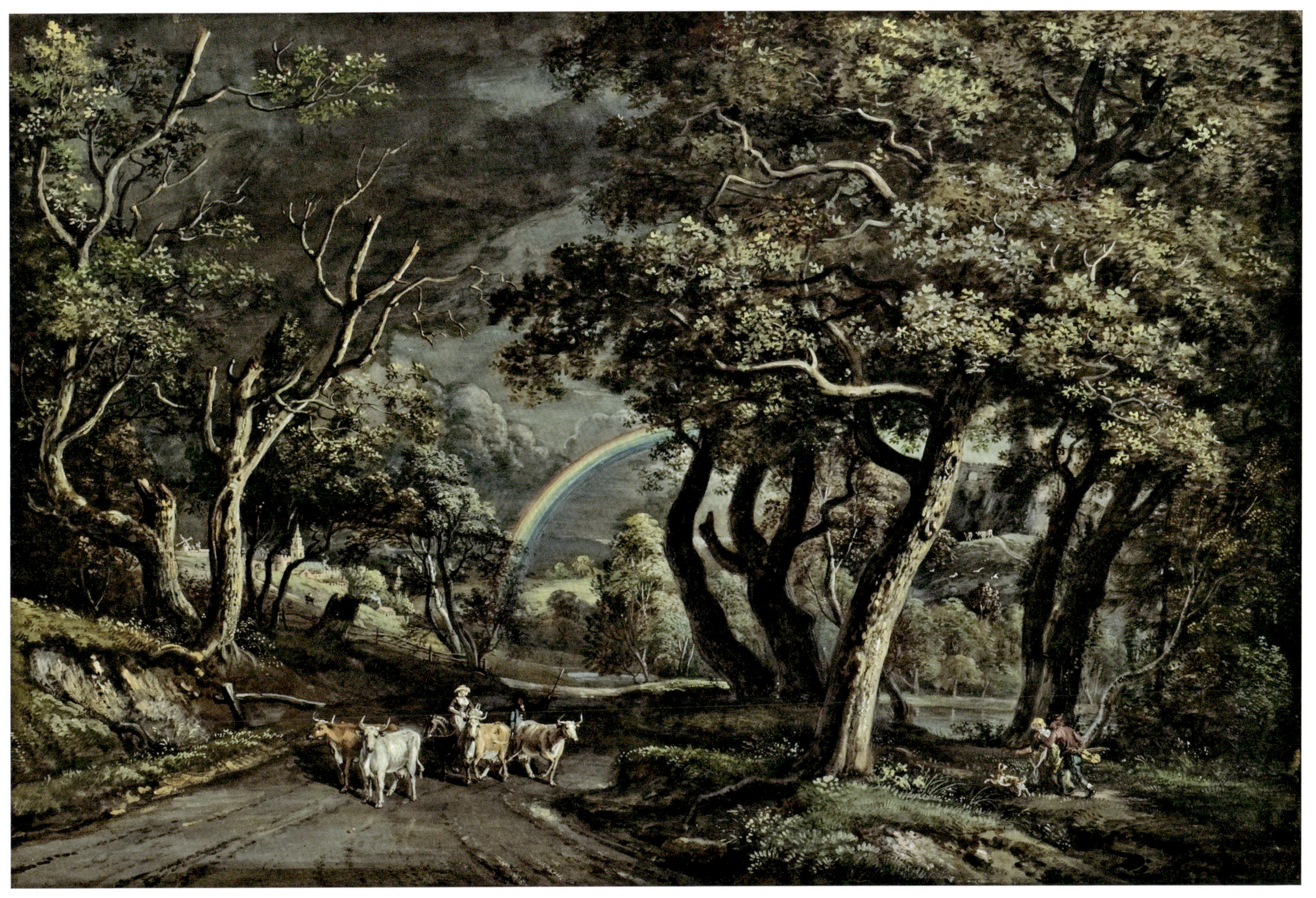

Chronology

JOHN BONEHILL

1731 12 January: Paul Sandby is baptised in St Peter's Church, Nottingham.

1747 Appointed draughtsman to the Military Survey of North Britain, working in the Drawing Room at Edinburgh Castle.

1751 Moves south, staying with his brother Thomas at Sandpit Gate Lodge, Windsor, and Poultney Street, Soho. Becomes associated with the St Martin's Lane Academy.

1753–54 Prints appear satirising William Hogarth's *The Analysis of Beauty*.

1757 Marries Anne Stogden and lives at Mr Pow's in Dufours Court, Broad Street, near Carnaby Market, from around this time.

1760 *Twelve London Cries* published. Exhibits two oils and three drawings at the first exhibition of the Society of Artists.

1765 Thomas Sandby appointed Deputy Ranger of Windsor Great Park. His younger brother shows views of Windsor at the Society of Artists.

1766 Settles in Poland Street.

1768 Appointed Chief Drawing Master at the Royal Military Academy, Woolwich. Paul and Thomas Sandby are foundation members of the Royal Academy, Paul as a member of the Council and his brother as Professor of Architecture.

1770 First recorded journey to Wales, where he stays at Wynnstay, the Denbighshire estate of Sir Watkin Williams Wynn.

1771 Tours north Wales with Wynn.

1772 Moves to 4 St George's Row, Bayswater, opposite Hyde Park.

1773 Tours south Wales with Joseph Banks.

1775 Publishes *XII Views in South-Wales.*

1776 Publishes three further sets of aquatints: *Views of Warwick Castle*, *Views of Windsor* and *XII Views in North Wales.*

1778 Publication of *The Virtuosi's Museum* begins, running until 1781.

1786 Thomas Paul Sandby, Paul's second son, marries Thomas's daughter, Harriet. Paul and Thomas Paul Sandby live at 4 St George's Row, while the latter's wife and children reside at the Deputy Ranger's Lodge, Windsor.

1793 Decorates the dining room at Drakelow Hall, Derbyshire, for Sir Nigel Gresley. Lieutenant Paul Sandby, Paul's eldest son, dies at Barbados.

1796 Resigns as Chief Drawing Master at Woolwich, and is replaced by his son, Thomas Paul.

1797 6 November: death of Paul's wife, Anne Sandby.

1798 25 June: death of Thomas Sandby, who is buried at Windsor. Thomas Paul and his family move to a house at Englefield Green, near Egham, Surrey.

1799 18 July: start of sale of Thomas Sandby's drawings and books at Leigh & Sotheby.

1808 The Royal Academy of Arts grants Paul Sandby a pension of £60 a year in response to an appeal for assistance.

1809 7 November: death of Paul Sandby, who is buried at St George's burial ground.

1811 2–4 May: sale of paintings and drawings at Christie's.

1812 17–19 March: sale of paintings and drawings at Christie's.

1817 16–18 April: sale of paintings and drawings at Christie's.

Endnotes

Paul Sandby: Picturing Britain

JOHN BONEHILL, STEPHEN DANIELS AND NICHOLAS ALFREY

Pages 12–27

1 *Morning Chronicle*, 17 May 1792, p. 3.
2 Public Characters 1801, p. 462.
3 Sandby 1811.
4 What is known or can be surmised of Paul Sandby's early training is discussed in Martin Postle's essay on pages 28–37 and in the section introduction and catalogue entries to section 1: 'Picture-making'.
5 This description is drawn from a memorial to Colonel David Watson, Deputy Quarter-Master General in North Britain and director of the Military Survey, written by his brother John Watson, *c.* 1761: see National Archives of Scotland, Edinburgh, RH1/2/511.
6 Roy 1785, p. 387.
7 Unlike that of his older brother, who remained employed by the Board of Ordnance for the rest of his life, Paul Sandby's name does not appear on any record of those employed in the Drawing Room, suggesting his appointment to the survey was on an *ad hoc* basis. A list of draughtsmen employed in the Drawing Room is given in Marshall 1980. A record of payment relating to plans and views of Castle Duart and Castle Tyrim is the only document to record Sandby's employment by the Board: see Register of Drafts, f.26, entry 26, PRO WO55/2281. The description of Sandby's duties is drawn from the recollections of David Dundas, as recorded by the map-maker Aaron Arrowsmith: see Arrowsmith 1809, p. 8. For recent discussions of Sandby's work in Scotland, see Christian 1990 and Bermingham 2000, pp. 78–84. For the most recent account of the survey, see Great Map 2007.
8 On the politics of 'improvement' in the period, see the Editors' Preface, on pages 8–9.
9 Quoted in Langford 1989, pp. 216–17.
10 Elliot 1752, pp. 6, 7, 8, 24. For a detailed discussion of Elliot's proposals, which owed much to the Lord Provost of Edinburgh, George Drummond, see Youngson 1988, pp. 1–17.
11 *The Virtuosi's Museum*, 1778–82, plate 20.
12 Klonk 1996, pp. 70–74.
13 Mayhew 2000, pp. 143–51.
14 Pennant 1774, pp. 151, 75.
15 Roberts 1997, pp. 47–61.
16 Pococke 1888, p. 63.
17 For fuller consideration of these pictures, see Matthew Craske's essay on pp. 48–55.
18 Further details are given in the entries for cats 68–69. Our thanks to Julian Gascoigne for communicating to us his findings on Sandby's employment by the Harcourt family.
19 On his retirement, Sandby's position was taken by his son, Thomas Paul Sandby, who received £100 per annum, his father being in receipt of the balance of the salary.
20 He succeeded Gamaliel Massiot, who was made Sandby's junior on his appointment and was later replaced by Felix Huguenine.
21 Townshend 1776, p. 19.
22 Smith 1779, p. i.
23 For examples of the kind of drawings they produced, see Robertson 1986 and London 2000, pp. 139–40, 142–45.
24 Gray 1935, vol. 2, p. 705.
25 Harcourt 1880–1905, vol. 7, p. 15. For further discussion of this painting, see Robertson 1984.
26 This fascination with Britain's historic legacy is discussed most fully in Smiles 1994.
27 Farington 1978–98, vol. 1, p. 113.
28 Further details of the tour are given in Hughes 1975. For Lightfoot's journal, see Riddelsdell 1905.
29 For further details relating to this commission, see Hughes 1972.
30 National Library of Wales, Aberystwyth, Mss Wynnstay, Box 115, 22/17.
31 Sandby 1811.
32 Sandby Lectures, IV, fols 6–7.
33 Pennant 1778, vol. 1, p. v. A letter from Paul Sandby to Thomas Pennant, dated 23 June 1777, in which the author is billed for copies of the *Views*, suggests that he consulted them in compiling his own tour: see National Library of Wales, Aberystwyth, Ms.14005E (180).
34 Seward 1811, vol. 3, pp. 380–81.
35 London 2003A.
36 Ramsden 1947.
37 Cf. Geoff Quilley's essay on pp. 38–47.
38 Robertson 1987, pp. 161–89; Ogborn 1998, pp. 75–103; Shesgreen 2002, pp. 123–31; Hitchcock 2004, pp. 219–23.
39 Ogborn 1998, pp. 98–102.
40 Sandby Lectures, IV, fol. 1.
41 Thomas Sandby's drawing of Jones's scheme is reproduced in Oppé 1950, p. 116.
42 *Public Advertiser*, 16 May 1774; Moore 1883, pp. 9–11; *A History of the County of Middlesex*, 1989, vol. 10, pp. 204–06.
43 Phillips 1964, pp. 259–62.
44 Gandon 1846, pp. 39–41.
45 Angelo 1828, p. 229.
46 Sandby 1811.
47 Gandon 1846, p. 40.
48 See Christie's sale catalogues, 2 May 1811, 17 March 1812, 16 April 1817.
49 Paul Sandby, 'To D. Serres on his birthday', British Library, London, Add Ms 36994, fols 54–64.
50 Longstaffe-Gowan 2001, pp. 53–58.
51 Farington 1978–98, vol. 3, p. 1067.
52 McKeller 1999.
53 Pasmore 1979; Woodward 1796, p. 18; Thornbury 1873–78, vol. 5, pp. 77–188; 'Admirable Landscape', *Country Life*, 3 November 1988.
54 Searle 1930.
55 *London Review and Literary Journal*, 8 November 1809, p. 400.
56 Robertson 1987, p. 3.
57 Farington 1978–98, 2 May 1811.
58 Wilton 2006, p. 17 and p. 147, n. 14.
59 See for example the reviews cited at the beginning of this essay; also the review in the *Morning Post and Fashionable World*, 4 June 1795, of Sandby's Royal Academy exhibit that year, *View of Eagle Tower at Caernarvon.*
60 Oppé 1947, p. 147.
61 For the fullest account of Pyne and debates around watercolour, see Smith 2002.
62 Oppé 1947, p. 1.
63 For the provenance of the Sandby drawings in the Royal Collection, see Amsterdam 1995, pp. 136–38.
64 *John Piper*, exh. cat., Tate Gallery, London, 1984, p. 99.
65 Amsterdam 1995. See also Roberts 1997.
66 British Library, London, Add Ms 42232.
67 Nottingham 1884.
68 See for example Ramsden 1947, p. 15, and London 1986, p. 7.
69 Sandby 1892, p. 5.
70 Binyon 1898–1907, vol. 4.
71 A foldout pamphlet was produced to accompany the exhibition. The catalogues of earlier Sandby exhibitions at the Guildhall (1960) and Reading Art Gallery (1972) did not add anything significant to the literature on the artist.
72 Manchester 1993.

The Sandbys and the Royal Academy

MARTIN POSTLE

Pages 28–37

1 The letter, dated 13 December 1768, was sent to Gilpin's address in Sheet Street, Windsor, which neighboured Thomas Sandby's residence in Windsor Great Park: see Bolton 1927, p. 8.
2 See Gandon 1846, pp. 186–87.
3 London 2000, pp. 140–41.
4 Ramsden 1947, pp. 15–18.
5 For Hogarth's own reminiscences on the St Martin's Lane Academy, see Kitson 1968, pp. 46–111. See also Postle 1991.
6 Kitson 1968, p. 94.
7 The circular was printed in the *London Daily Advertiser*, 23 October 1753.
8 Edwards 1808, pp. xxii–xxiii, publishes Sandby's copy of the letter.
9 Bindman 1981, pp. 151–53. For an extended discussion of *The Analyis,* see Paulson 1993, vol. 3, pp. 56–151.
10 Cf. Geoff Quilley's essay on pp. 38–47.
11 London 1986, p. 25.
12 I am grateful to Dr Peter Thwaites, Curator of the Sandhurst Collection, Royal Military Academy, Sandhurst, who has confirmed that the coat worn by Sandby appears to be similar to the uniform of the Gentleman Cadets at Woolwich of the 2nd Academy of 1783, although there is no evidence to suggest that the Masters of the Royal Military Academy, Woolwich, were required to wear uniforms.
13 Farington 1978–98, vol. 3, p. 1029.
14 London 2000, pp. 140–41.
15 Millar 1969, vol. 1, pp. 21–22, vol. 2, pls 13–15.
16 Hoock 2003, p. 20.
17 Hoock 2003, p. 13.
18 It is not known which of the many versions of *A Bridge of Magnificence* Thomas Sandby exhibited at the Royal Academy in 1781. Nicholas Savage notes that the large, five-metre-long version unfurled at the close of the final lecture 'seems unlikely to have been allowed the space necessary for its display in the Life Academy', where architectural drawings were then shown: Savage 2001, p. 267, n. 19.
19 Worsley 1991, pp. 23–24.
20 Savage 2001, pp. 211–12.
21 Thomas Sandby to William Chambers, 4 September 1769, Rare Books and Manuscripts, Yale Center for British Art, New Haven.
22 Harris 1970, p.129.
23 The original manuscript drafts of Sandby's lectures, and a transcription made in 1849 by William Sandby, are in the library of the Royal Institute of British Architects, London (Mss. SaT/1/1-2). A copy made by John Soane and his pupils in 1807 is in Sir John Soane's Museum, London (Ms. AL 31B).
24 Sandby Lectures, IV, fols 158–59.
25 Sandby Lectures, IV, fol. 164. Cf. Matthew Craske's essay on pp. 48–55.
26 Shanes 2008.
27 For the discussion and dissent at the Royal Academy regarding Edwards's role as Sandby's surrogate, see Farington 1978–98, vol. 3, pp. 602, 706, 776, 812, 836–37, 943.
28 Farington 1978–98, vol . 3, p. 1036.
29 Farington 1978–98, vol. 4, pp. 1323, 1325. In the event the incumbent Edward Burch outlived Sandby and was succeeded by Thomas Stothard.
30 Farington 1978–98, vol. 4, p. 1576.
31 On 29 April 1794, Sandby wrote to Boswell stating that, although he was 'totally un-acquainted with Mr Milford [*sic*]' (Boswell's candidate), he would vote for him to succeed Gibbon (Beinecke Library, Yale University, Boswell Collection Gen MSS89, Box 31, C2427). In the event, William Mitford (1744–1827),

a friend of Gibbon, did not become Professor of Ancient History at the Royal Academy until 1818.
32 Farington 1978–98, vol. 3, p. 1067.
33 Farington 1978–98, vol. 8, p. 2964.
34 Sandby 1892, p. 85.
35 Hoock 2003, p. 183.
36 Farington 1978–98, vol. 6, p. 2122.
37 Farington 1978–98, vol. 8, p. 3162.
38 Farington 1978–98, vol. 8, p. 2960.
39 Farington 1978–98, vol. 1, p. 220.
40 Royal Academy of Arts, London, Council Minutes, Ms. CIV, fols 39–40, 46.
41 Ball 1985, p. 268.

The Analysis of Deceit: Sandby's Satires against Hogarth

GEOFF QUILLEY

Pages 38–47

1 Sandby 1892, p. 32.
2 For accounts of these prints and Hogarth's artistic and aesthetic theory against which they were directed, see especially Paulson 1993, pp. 132–51, and London 1997, pp. 168–81.
3 Ireland describes Sandby's prints collectively as 'most vile and vulgar', and individual plates as containing 'naked and most filthy female figures' (*Puggs GRACES*) and a 'nauseous delineation' (*The Analyst Besh_n in his own Taste*): Ireland 1791, vol. 3, pp. 117–18, 123. William Sandby is very careful to play down the vulgarity of his ancestor's satires by avoiding any mention of their impolite character and attempting to distance himself from them: Sandby 1892, p. 39.
4 This is how they have generally been regarded, when considered at all, by historians of British art, although Bindman notes that Sandby only issued the title page once the prints had been completed, by April 1754: see London 1997, p. 174.
5 Kitson 1968, p. 65. For further background on the proposals for an academy at this date, see Hargraves 2005, pp. 10–14.
6 On the visual and iconographic tradition of the satirical print in this period, see especially Donald 1996.
7 On the visual language of political prints in the period, see Donald 1996, pp. 44–74; the standard text remains Atherton 1973.
8 On the distinction between 'high' art and 'low' art in the satirical tradition, and Hogarth's reputation in relation to it, see Donald 1996, pp. 27–35.
9 Hogarth's plates are discussed at length in Paulson 1993, pp. 362–412.
10 Sandby's prints were part of a much wider production of visual lampoons against Bute at this time: this context is discussed by Donald 1996, pp. 50–56.

Court Art Reviewed: The Sandbys' Vision of Windsor and Its Environs

MATTHEW CRASKE

Pages 48–55

1 Weiser 2003, pp. 37–43.
2 Girouard 1993.
3 Pote 1751 (1762 edition), p. 3.
4 Cumberland 1767, p. 461.
5 Pote dedicated the first, twelve-shilling (1749) volume of his Windsor guide to Frederick, Prince of Wales, who had a hunting estate at Taplow. It was after Frederick's death in 1751 that the dedication to Cumberland was inserted.
6 The guides generally refer to this wooden structure as a Palladian Bridge. The structure resembles that described in Palladio's *Quattro Libri*. It was, according to *Windsor and its Environs*, 1774, p. 78, the Duke's pride that it had been built five feet wider than the Rialto Bridge in Venice.
7 *The Whitehall Evening Post*, 1 July 1766.
8 Pote 1751, p. 83, described the opening out of 'a small stream or current of water' to form the basin in which barge displays took place.
9 *Windsor and its Environs*, 1774, p. 77.
10 Sandby 1811
11 Pote 1751, pp. 76–78.
12 For a full description of the paintings that decorated Charles II's Windsor Palace, consult *The London Chronicle*, 17 August 1775.
13 Pote 1751, p. 10.
14 Pye 1775.
15 For an example of the protracted interest in Denham, see *Windsor and its Environs*, 1774, p. 8.
16 Described in political terms in Pote 1751, p. 83.
17 Kramnick 1968; Everett 1994.
18 The property rights of the town are probably relevant here, for it had been a Crown property since the reign of William the Conqueror. Despite this, it was left to residents, outside the gates, to fashion their own town.
19 Eulogies of these civic buildings prevailed before Pote. See, for instance, *New Description of Bedfordshire*, 1749, p. 27.

'The Monarch of the Plain': Paul Sandby and Topography

FELICITY MYRONE

Pages 56–63

1 Anthony Pasquin [John Williams], *Morning Post and Fashionable World*, 4 June 1795.
2 Public Characters 1801.
3 Fuseli 1831, vol. 2, p. 217.
4 Farington 1978–98, vol. 11, p. 3926 [2 May 1811].
5 Hoare 1822, p. 83.
6 Hardcastle 1824.
7 'Sandby Brothers Limited', *National Observer*, 8, 189, July 1892, pp. 175–76.
8 Redgrave 1866, pp. 147, 151.
9 Paris 1947, p. 78.
10 Finberg 1919, p. 22.
11 Ayrton 1947, p. 35.
12 Hardie 1966, pp. 73–74.
13 Hardie 1966, pp. 109–10.
14 Herrmann 1964.
15 Fuller 1987.
16 Edinburgh 1978A; Robertson 1987; Christian 1990; Charlesworth 1996; Kennedy 1998; London 2000; Smith 2002; and Kennedy 2003.
17 Public Characters 1801, p. 364. Sandbys are included in Crowle's extra-illustrated Pennant and the Crace collection at the British Museum and in Percival's extra-illustrated Manning and Bray's *History and Topography of the County of Surrey* (Crach.1.Tab.1.b.1.) and in the King's Topographical Collection in the British Library.
18 Advertisements made such claims as 'Paul Sandby, Esq. R.A. furnishes an original drawing for every number', *London Chronicle*, 17 May 1777.
19 Yale 1985, p. 11.
20 Clayton 1998.
21 *Windsor Castle*, engraved by Godfrey after a drawing said to be by Peter Lely and published by F. Blyth, 1 October 1775 (present whereabouts unknown); and *View of old London from Blackheath*, engraved by Richard Godfrey after a drawing by Thomas Wyck, published 1 July 1776 by F. Blyth (British Museum, London, P&D 1897.0831.1).
22 For example, although the Old Welsh Bridge at Shrewsbury was destroyed in 1782, Sandby continued to paint and exhibit views of it until 1806 (Yale 1985, p. 68).
23 Robertson 1987, p. 111; Smith 2002, p. 59.
24 The aquatint is signed and dated in the image lower left 'P. Sandby 1774' and lettered 'P. Sandby Fecit / Published According to Act of Parliament by P. Sandby St George's Row Sept 1st 1775'.
25 Farrant 2001, p. 114, and Raeburn, Voronikhina and Nurnberg 1995.
26 *True Briton*, 2 February 1799.
27 *World*, 9 February 1789.
28 Pote 1785, p. 87; Raeburn, Voronikhina and Numberg 1995; and Holloway and Marno 2003.
29 This division has never been clear cut, but has been compounded by the institutions' physical split. Parts of the King's Topographical Collection which were deemed to be of high artistic value, such as drawings for etchings after Canaletto, were removed to Prints and Drawings even in the 1950s, while the etchings themselves remain in the Library. The Crace Collection of maps and views of London is divided between the two institutions.
30 Oppé 1947, p. 4.
31 Barber 2004.
32 Binyon 136 (18b), P&D 1904.0819.94; British Library, Maps K.Top.55.5.a.
33 Smith 1829, pp. 89–90.

'Grand Secrets': Sandby's Materials and Techniques

JOHN BONEHILL AND SARAH SKINNER

Pages 64–71

1 Paul Sandby to William Gravatt, 9 October 1797, British Library, London, Add Ms 36994, fol. 23.
2 Paul Sandby, 'Song for 1797', Literary and Historical Manuscripts, The Pierpont Morgan Library, New York. The authors are grateful to Mark Aronson of the Yale Center for British Art, New Haven, for bringing this copy of the verse to their attention. It is scored through and illegible in the letter to Gravatt referred to above. This second version of the song suggests it enjoyed wider circulation.
3 For a full account of the scandal, see Gage 1964.
4 The artist also issued a number of graphic satires ridiculing art-world figures, including the drawing master William Austin in *Fox's Fool* (British Museum, London, BM 6604), the art-dealer Dr Robert Bragge in *The Vertù Scavenger & Duper* (British Museum, London, BM 3647), and most obviously William Hogarth (see cats 21–30).
5 This phrase appears throughout correspondence relating to his recipes, an example being a letter dated 14 November 1791 to the minor Lancashire-based miniaturist Patrick John McMorland: see Manchester Central Library Archives, M84/3/5/3, and Hopkinson 2003.
6 Sandby 1811.
7 Sandby 1811.
8 On the reaction of painters in watercolour to the scandal in general, see Smith 2002, pp. 37–38.
9 See Smith 2001, Smith 2002 and the introduction to this catalogue, pp. 26–7
10 Gandon 1846, p. 186.
11 Sandby 1892, p. 121.
12 Sandby 1892, pp. 121–2.
13 Harris 2006.
14 Although Sandby executed a small number of large oils in the 1760s, he appears to have abandoned the practice by the end of that decade. He only reverted to oils at the very end of his life, in a move largely dictated by growing financial hardship; the diarist Joseph Farington recorded that Sandby had had to abandon his favoured methods because of the high 'price of *glass*': Farington 1978–98, vol. 8, p. 2944.
15 One critic noted of the drawings of Wakefield Lodge, exhibited at the Society of Artists in 1767: 'These are excellent drawings. They have keeping and effect, and the tints are remarkably clear' (*Critical Examination*, 1767, p. 27)
16 For a comprehensive list of contemporary artists' handbooks and pattern guides, as well as drawing and painting manuals, see Bermingham 2000, pp. 286–93.
17 For analysis of Sandby's use of papers, see Donnithorne 1995 and Harris 2006.
18 Smith 1998, p. 7.
19 The best account remains Griffiths 1987.
20 Quoted in Barbier 1963, p. 68.
21 There is some suggestion that the Grevilles purchased the secret from Burdett, although the two artists' prints bear little resemblance to one another technically. It is interesting to note Burdett's attempts to interest Joseph Banks in the method, however, given his patronage of Sandby at this date: see the correspondence published in Hopkinson 2007A. For an excellent discussion of Burdett's work, see Hopkinson 2007B.
22 Paul Sandby to John Clerk of Eldin, 8 September 1775, National Art Library, V&A, London, MSL/1932/1563.
23 British Library, London, Add Ms 36994.
24 Paul Sandby to John Clerk of Eldin, late 1775, National Art Library, V&A, London, MSL/1913/2321.
25 Yrubslips 1794, p. 5.
26 These remarks were made in response to Sandby's *View of Eagle Tower at Caernarvon*, exhibited at the RA in 1795, by the critic of the *Morning Post and Fashionable World*, 4 June 1795.
27 *The London-Packet; Or, New Lloyd's Evening-Post*, 12–14 May 1794.

Bibliography

ADDISON 1965
Joseph Addison, *The Spectator: by Joseph Addison, Richard Steele, et al.*, D. F. Bond (ed.), Oxford, 1965

AMSTERDAM 1995
Jane Roberts, *Views of Windsor: Watercolours by Thomas and Paul Sandby from the Collection of Her Majesty Queen Elizabeth II*, exh. cat., Rijksmuseum, Amsterdam, Portland Art Museum, Oregon, Dixon Gallery and Gardens, Memphis, Dallas Museum of Art and Whitworth Art Gallery, Manchester, 1995–97

ANDREWS 1989
Malcolm Andrews, *The Search for the Picturesque: Landscape Aesthetics and Tourism in Britain, 1760–1800*, Aldershot, 1989

ANGELO 1828
Henry William Angelo, *Reminiscences of Henry Angelo, with Memoirs of his Late Father and Friends*, 2 vols, London, 1828

ANNUAL REGISTER 1779
The Annual Register, Or a View of the History, Politics, and Literature, For the Year 1778, London, 1779

ARNOLD 1998
Dana Arnold (ed.), *The Georgian Country House: Architecture, Landscape and Society*, Stroud, 1998

ARROWSMITH 1809
Aaron Arrowsmith, *Memoir relative to the construction of a Map of Scotland*, London, 1809

ATHERTON 1973
Herbert M. Atherton, *Political Prints in the Age of Hogarth*, Oxford and New York, 1973

AYRTON 1947
Michael Ayrton, *British Drawings*, London, 1947

BALL 1985
Johnson Ball, *Paul and Thomas Sandby, Royal Academicians: An Anglo-Danish Saga of Art, Love and War in Georgian England*, Cheddar, 1985

BARBER 2004
Peter Barber, 'George III and His Geographical Collection', an electronic offprint from Jonathan Marsden (ed.), *The Wisdom of George the Third: Papers from a Symposium at The Queen's Gallery, Buckingham Palace*, June 2004 (Royal Collection Publications, online at http://sherpa.bl.uk/97/01/Barber2.pdf)

BARBIER 1963
Carl Paul Barbier, *William Gilpin: His Drawings, Teachings and Theory of the Picturesque*, Oxford, 1963

BATEY 1995
Mavis Batey, 'Two Romantic Picturesque Flower Gardens', *Garden History*, 22, 2, 1995, pp. 197–203

BEDFORDSHIRE 1749
A New Description of Bedfordshire, London, 1749

BELL 1930
G. H. Bell (ed.), *The Hamwood Papers of the Ladies of Llangollen and Caroline Hamilton*, London, 1930

BERMINGHAM 2000
Ann Bermingham, *Learning to Draw: Studies in the Cultural History of a Polite and Useful Art*, New Haven and London, 2000

BILLS 2003
Mark Bills, 'The *Cries* of London by Paul Sandby and Thomas Rowlandson', *Print Quarterly*, 20, 1, 2003, pp. 34–61

BINDMAN 1981
David Bindman, *Hogarth*, London, 1981

BINYON 1898–1907
Laurence Binyon, *Catalogue of Drawings by British Artists and Artists of Foreign Origin working in Great Britain in the Department of Prints and Drawings of the British Museum*, 4 vols, London, 1898–1907

BOLTON 1927
Arthur T. Bolton (ed.), *The Portrait of Sir John Soane, R.A. 1753–1837, Set forth in Letters from his Friends*, London, 1927

BURKE 1757
Edmund Burke, *A Philosophical Inquiry into the Origin of our Ideas of the Sublime and the Beautiful*, 1757; J. T. Boulton (ed.), London, 1958

BURKE 1955
Joseph Burke (ed.), *William Hogarth, The Analysis of Beauty, with the rejected passages from the manuscript drafts and autobiographical notes*, Oxford, 1955

BURT 1754
Edward Burt, *Letters from a Gentleman in the North of Scotland to his Friend in London*, 2 vols, London, 1754

CHALMERS 1807
George Chalmers, *Caledonia: Or, An Account, Historical and Topographic, of North Britain*, 4 vols, London, 1807

CHARLESWORTH 1996
Michael Charlesworth, 'Thomas Sandby Climbs the Hoober Stand: The Politics of Panoramic Drawing in Eighteenth-century Britain', *Art History*, 19, 2, 1996, pp. 247–66

CHRISTIAN 1990
Jessica Christian, 'Paul Sandby and the Military Survey', in Nottingham 1990, pp. 18–22

CLAYTON 1998
Tim Clayton, 'Publishing Houses: Prints of Country Seats', in Arnold 1998, pp. 45–49

COFFIN 1994
David Coffin, *The English Garden: Meditation and Memorial*, Princeton, 1994

COKE 1899
Letters from Lady Jane Coke to Her Friend Mrs Eyre at Derby, 1747–58, Mrs Ambrose Rathbone (ed.), London, 1899

COLLECTION OF LANDSCAPES 1777
A Collection of Landscapes, Drawn by P. Sandby, Esq., R.A. and Engraved by Mr Rooker, and Mr Watts, with Descriptions, London, 1777

COLLEY 1992
Linda Colley, *Britons: Forging the Nation, 1707–1837*, New Haven and London, 1992

CONWAY 1997
Stephen Conway, 'Locality, Metropolis and Nation: The Impact of Military Camps in England During the American Revolution', *History*, 82, 267, 1997, pp. 547–62

COURT MISCELLANY 1766
The Court Miscellany, London, 1766

CRITICAL EXAMINATION 1767
A Critical Examination of the Pictures, Sculptures, Designs in Architecture, Models, Drawings, Prints, &c. Exhibited at the Great Room in Spring-Gardens, Charing-Cross, April 22, 1767, London, 1767

CUMBERLAND 1767
Historical Memoirs of His Late Royal Highness William-Augustus, Duke of Cumberland, including the Military and Political History of Great-Britain, during that Period, London, 1767

DANIELS 1988
Stephen Daniels, 'The Political Iconography of Woodland in Later Georgian England', in Denis Cosgrove and Stephen Daniels (eds), *The Iconography of Landscape*, Cambridge, 1988, pp. 43–82

DANIELS 1993A
Stephen Daniels, *Fields of Vision: Landscape Imagery and National Identity in England and the United States*, Cambridge, 1993

DANIELS 1993B
Stephen Daniels, 'Re-visioning Britain: Mapping and Landscape Painting, 1750–1820', in Katherine Baetjer (ed.), *Glorious Nature: British Landscape Painting 1750–1850*, exh. cat., Denver Art Museum, 1993, pp. 61–72

DANIELS 1999
Stephen Daniels, *Humphrey Repton: Landscape Gardening and the Geography of Georgian England*, New Haven and London, 1999

DANIELS 2004
Stephen Daniels, 'Suburban Prospects', in Nicholas Alfrey, Stephen Daniels and Martin Postle (eds), *Art of the Garden: The Garden in British Art, 1800 to the Present Day*, exh. cat., Tate, London, 2004, pp. 22–30

DANIELS 2006
Stephen Daniels, 'A Prospect for the Nation', in Yale 2006B, pp. 23–59

DEERING 1751
Charles Deering, *Nottinghamia Vetus et Nova, or An Historical Account of the Ancient and Present State of Nottingham*, Nottingham, 1751

DEFOE 1754
Daniel Defoe, *The Political History of the Devil*, fifth edition, London, 1754

DEUCHAR 1988
Stephen Deuchar, *Sporting Art in Eighteenth-century England: A Social and Political History*, New Haven and London, 1988

DONALD 1996
Diana Donald, *The Age of Caricature: Satirical Prints in the Reign of George III*, New Haven and London, 1996

DONNITHORNE 1995
Alan Donnithorne, 'Media, Paper, Watermarks and Mounts', in Amsterdam 1995, pp. 138–43

EDINBURGH 1978A
James Holloway and Lindsay Errington, *The Discovery of Scotland: The Appreciation of Scottish Scenery through Two Centuries of Painting*, exh. cat., National Gallery of Scotland, Edinburgh, 1798

EDINBURGH 1978B
Geoffrey Bertram, *John Clerk of Eldin, 1728–1812*, exh. cat., 6 North West Circus Place, Edinburgh, 1978

EDINBURGH 1999
The Draughtsman's Art: Master Drawings from the National Gallery of Scotland, exh. cat., National Gallery of Art, Edinburgh, 1999

EDWARDS 1808
Edward Edwards, *Anecdotes of Painters who have resided or been born in England*, London, 1808

EGERTON 2007
Judy Egerton, *George Stubbs, Painter: Catalogue Raisonne*, New Haven and London, 2007

ELLIOT 1752
Gilbert Elliot, Lord Minto, *Proposals for carrying on certain Public Works in the City of Edinburgh*, Edinburgh, 1752

EUROPEAN MAGAZINE 1796
'Paul Sandby, Esq., R.A.', *The European Magazine, and London Review*, August 1796, pp. 75–76

EVERETT 1994
Nigel Everett, *The Tory View of Landscape*, New Haven and London, 1994

FARINGTON 1978–98
The Diary of Joseph Farington, Kenneth Garlick and Angus Macintyre (eds), 17 vols, New Haven and London, 1978–98

FARRANT 2001
John Farrant, *Sussex Depicted: Views and Descriptions, 1600–1800*, Lewes, 2001

FINBERG 1919
Alexander Joseph Finberg, *Early English Water-Colour Drawings by the Great Masters*, London, 1919

FULLER 1987
Peter Fuller, 'The Art of Watercolour' (exhibition review), *Burlington Magazine*, 129, June 1987, p. 413

FUSELI 1831
Henry Fuseli, *The Life and Writings of H. Fuseli*, John Knowles (ed.), 3 vols, London, 1831

GAGE 1964
John Gage, 'Magilphs and Mysteries', *Apollo*, 80, July 1964, pp. 38–41

GANDON 1846
James Gandon, *The Life of James Gandon, Esq.*, Thomas J. Mulvaney (ed.), Dublin, 1846

GAY 1716
John Gay, *Trivia: Or, The Art of Walking*, London, 1716

GILPIN 1782
William Gilpin, *Observations on the River Wye, and Several Parts of South Wales, &c., Relative Chiefly to Picturesque Beauty*, London, 1782

GILPIN 1789
William Gilpin, *Observations on Several Parts of Great Britain, Particularly the High-lands of Scotland, Relative Chiefly to Picturesque Beauty, Made in the Year 1776*, 2 vols, London, 1789

GILPIN 1791
William Gilpin, *Remarks on Forest Scenery, and Other Woodland Views*, 2 vols, London, 1791

GILPIN 1798
William Gilpin, *Observations on the Western Parts of England, Relative Chiefly to Picturesque Beauty*, London, 1798

GILPIN 1799
William Gilpin, *Observations, Relative Chiefly to Picturesque Beauty, Made in the Year 1772, on Several Parts of England*, 2 vols, London, 1799

GIROUARD 1993
Mark Girouard, *Windsor: The Most Romantic Castle*, London, 1993

GRAY 1935
Correspondence of Thomas Gray, Paget Toynbee and Leonard Whibley (eds), 3 vols, Oxford, 1935

GREAT MAP 2007
The Great Map: The Military Survey of Scotland, 1747–55, with introductory essays by Yolande Hodson, Chris Tabraham and Charles Withers, Edinburgh, 2007

GRIFFITHS 1987
Anthony Griffiths, 'Notes on Early Aquatint in Britain and France', *Print Quarterly*, 4, 3, 1987, pp. 255–70

GROSE 1773–87
Francis Grose, *Antiquities of England and Wales*, 4 vols, London, 1773–87

GROSE 1789–91
Francis Grose, *Antiquities of Scotland*, 2 vols, London, 1789–91

GWYNN 1749
John Gwynn, *An Essay on Design; including proposals for Erecting a Public Academy to be supported by Voluntary Subscription (Till a Royal Foundation can be obtain'd) for Educating the British Youth in Drawing and Several Arts thereon*, London, 1749

GWYNN 1766
John Gwynn, *London and Westminster Improved*, London, 1766

HAMILTON 1981
Julian Faigan, *Paul Sandby Drawings*, exh. cat., City of Hamilton Art Gallery, Art Gallery of South Australia, Adelaide, National Gallery of Victoria, Melbourne, and Art Gallery of New South Wales, Sydney, 1981–82

HANNAH 1998
Gavin Hannah, 'Lord Harcourt, the Bodleian Library and the Prints of Stanton Harcourt, Oxfordshire', *The Antiquaries Journal*, 68, 1998, pp. 457–63

HARCOURT 1880–1905
Edward William Harcourt, *The Harcourt Papers*, 14 vols, Oxford, 1880–1905

HARDCASTLE 1824
Ephraim Hardcastle [William Henry Pyne], 'The Rise and Progress of Water-Colour Painting in England', *Somerset House Gazette, and Literary Museum, or Weekly Miscellany of Fine Arts, Antiquities and Literary Chit-Chat I*, 1824, pp. 65–67, 81–84, 97–99, 113–14, 129–33, 145–46, 161–63, 177–79, 193–95

HARDIE 1966
Martin Hardie, *Water-Colour Painting in Britain*, vol. I: *The Eighteenth Century*, London, 1966

HARGRAVES 2005
Matthew Hargraves, *Candidates for Fame: The Society of Artists of Great Britain, 1760–1791*, New Haven and London, 2005

HARRIS 1970
Eileen Harris, 'The Treatise on Civil Architecture', in John Harris, *Sir William Chambers, Knight of the Polar Star*, London, 1970, pp. 128–44

HARRIS 2006
Theresa Fairbanks Harris, 'Paul Sandby's Creation of the Watercolour *A View of Vinters at Boxley, Kent, with Mr Whatman's Turkey Paper Mills*', in Yale 2006B, pp. 121–31

HARTLEY 1996
Beryl Hartley, 'The Living Academies of Nature: Scientific Experiment in Learning and Communicating the New Skills of Early Nineteenth-Century Landscape Painting', *Studies in the History and Philosophy of Science*, 27, 2, 1996, pp. 149–80

HAYES 2001
John Hayes (ed.), *The Letters of Thomas Gainsborough*, New Haven and London, 2001

HELSINGER 1997
Elizabeth Helsinger, *Rural Scenes and National Representation: Britain, 1815–1850*, Princeton, 1997

HEMINGWAY 1992
Andrew Hemingway, *Landscape Imagery and Urban Culture in Early Nineteenth-century Britain*, Cambridge, 1992

HENDERSON 1766
Andrew Henderson, *The Life of William Augustus, Duke of Cumberland*, London, 1766

HERRMANN 1964
Luke Herrmann, 'Paul Sandby in Scotland', *Burlington Magazine*, 106, 736, 1964, pp. 339–43

HERRMANN 1965
Luke Herrmann, 'Paul Sandby in Scotland: A Sketchbook', *Burlington Magazine*, 107, 750, 1965, pp. 467–68

HERRMANN 1973
Luke Herrmann, *British Landscape Painting of the Eighteenth Century*, London, 1973

HITCHCOCK 2004
Timothy Hitchcock, *Down and Out in Eighteenth-century London*, London, 2004

HITCHCOCK 2007
Timothy Hitchcock, *Down and Out in Eighteenth-century London*, London, 2007

HOARE 1822
Richard Colt Hoare, *The History of Modern Wiltshire*, London, 1822

HOLLOWAY AND MARNO 2003
Chris Holloway and Felicity Marno, 'Paul Sandby and Related Influences on Caughley Porcelain', *Monographs on Caughey Porcelain*, 2, April 2003

HOOCK 2003
Holger Hoock, *The King's Artists: The Royal Academy of Arts and the Politics of British Culture, 1760–1840*, Oxford, 2003

HOPKINSON 2003
Martin Hopkinson, 'Paul Sandby and the Secrets of Aquatint', *Print Quarterly*, 20, 2003, pp. 380–82

HOPKINSON 2007A
Martin Hopkinson, 'The Correspondence of Peter Perez Burdett and Sir Joseph Banks', *Print Quarterly*, 24, 2007, pp. 269–73

HOPKINSON 2007B
Martin Hopkinson, 'Printmaking and Print Collectors in the North West 1760–1800', in Elizabeth Barker and Alex Kidson (eds), *Joseph Wright of Derby in Liverpool*, exh. cat., Yale Center for British Art, New Haven, 2007, pp. 85–103

HUGHES 1746
Michael Hughes, *A Plain Narrative and Authentic of the Late Rebellion, Begun in 1745*, London, 1746

HUGHES 1972
Peter Hughes, 'Paul Sandby and Sir Watkin Williams-Wynn', *Burlington Magazine*, 114, July 1972, pp. 459–67

HUGHES 1975
Peter Hughes, 'Paul Sandby's Tour of Wales with Joseph Banks', *Burlington Magazine*, 117, July 1975, pp. 452–57

IRELAND 1791
John Ireland, *Hogarth Illustrated from his own Manuscripts*, 3 vols, London, 1791

JOHNSON 1992–94
The Letters of Samuel Johnson, Bruce Redford (ed.), 5 vols, Oxford, 1992–94

JOYNER 1983
Paul Joyner, 'Some Sandby Drawings of Scotland', *National Library of Wales Journal*, 23, 1983, pp. 1–16

KENNEDY 1998
Andrew Kennedy, 'British Topographical Print Series in Their Social and Economic Context, *c.* 1720 – *c.* 1840', unpublished PhD thesis, University of London, 1998

KENNEDY 2003
Andrew Kennedy, 'Representing the Three Kingdoms: Hanoverianism and the *Virtuosi's Museum*', in Mark Dorrian and Gillian Rose (eds), *Deterritorialisations: Revisioning Landscape and Politics*, London and New York, 2003, pp. 272–83

KENT 1798
Nathaniel Kent, *Some Particulars of the King's Farm at Windsor*, Oxford, 1798

KITSON 1968
Michael Kitson (ed.), 'Hogarth's "Apology for Painters"', *The Walpole Society*, 41, 1968

KLONK 1996
Charlotte Klonk, *Science and the Perception of Nature: British Landscape Art in the Late Eighteenth and Early Nineteenth Centuries*, New Haven and London, 1996

KRAMNICK 1968
Isaac Kramnick, *Bolingbroke and His Circle: The Politics of Nostalgia in the Age of Walpole*, Oxford, 1968

KRIZ 1997
K. Dian Kriz, *The Idea of the English Landscape Painter: Genius as Alibi in the Early Nineteenth Century*, New Haven and London, 1997

LAIRD 1999
Mark Laird, *The Flowering of the Landscape Garden: English Pleasure Grounds 1720–1800*, Philadelphia, 1999

LANGFORD 1989
Paul Langford, *A Polite and Commercial People: England, 1727–1783*, Oxford, 1989

LE POUR ET LE CONTRE 1767
Le Pour et le Contre, Being a Poetical Display of the Merit and Demerit of the Capital Paintings Exhibited at Spring Gardens, London, 1767

LONDON 1960
John L. Howgego, *Paul Sandby, 1725–1809*, exh. cat., Guildhall Art Gallery, London, 1960

LONDON 1963
Treasures of the Royal Academy, exh. cat., Royal Academy of Arts, London, 1963

LONDON 1973
Leslie Parris, *Landscape in Britain, c. 1750–1850*, exh. cat., Tate, London, 1973

LONDON 1977
Yolande O'Donoghue, *William Roy 1726–1790: Pioneer of the Ordnance Survey*, exh. cat., British Museum, London, 1977

LONDON 1982
David Solkin, *Richard Wilson: The Landscape of Reaction*, exh. cat., Tate, London, 1982

LONDON 1985
Lindsay Stainton, *British Landscape Watercolours, 1600–1860*, exh. cat., British Museum, London, 1985

LONDON 1986
Luke Herrmann, *Paul and Thomas Sandby*, exh. cat., Victoria and Albert Museum, London, 1986

LONDON 1990
Treasures of Prints and Drawings, exh. cat., British Museum, London, 1990

LONDON 1991
Yolande Hodson, *Map Making in the Tower of London: Ordnance Survey's Early Years*, exh. cat., Tower of London, 1991

LONDON 1993
Andrew Wilton and Anne Lyles, *The Great Age of British Watercolours, 1750–1880*, exh. cat., Royal Academy of Arts, London, and National Gallery of Art, Washington DC, 1993

LONDON 1997
David Bindman, *Hogarth and His Times: Serious Comedy*, exh. cat., British Museum, London, 1997

LONDON 2000
Kim Sloan, *'A Noble Art': Amateur Artists and Drawing Masters, c. 1600–1800*, exh. cat., British Museum, London, 2000

LONDON 2001
David Solkin (ed.), *Art on the Line: The Royal Academy Exhibitions at Somerset House, 1780–1836*, exh. cat., Courtauld Institute Gallery, London, 2001–02

LONDON 2002
Greg Smith, *Thomas Girtin: The Art of Watercolour*, exh. cat., Tate, London, 2002

LONDON 2003A
Sheila O'Connell, Roy Porter, Celina Fox and Ralph Hyde, *London 1753*, exh. cat., British Museum, London, 2003

LONDON 2003B
David Dewing, *Home and Garden: Paintings and Drawings of English Middle-class Urban Domestic Spaces, 1675 to 1914*, exh. cat., Geffrye Museum, London, 2003

LONDON 2004
Jane Roberts and Christopher Lloyd, *George III and Queen Charlotte: Patronage, Collecting and Court Taste*, exh. cat., Queen's Gallery, London, 2004

LONDON 2007
Mark Hallett, Christine Riding et al., *Hogarth*, exh. cat., Tate, London, 2007

LONGSTAFFE-GOWAN 2001
Todd Longstaffe-Gowan, *The London Town Garden, 1740–1840*, New Haven and London, 2001

MCKELLER 1999
Elizabeth McKeller, 'Peripheral Visions: Alternative Aspects and Rural Presences in Mid-Eighteenth-century London', in Dana Arnold (ed.), *The Metropolis and Its Image, 1750–1950*, Oxford, 1999, pp. 29–47

MANCHESTER 1993
Charles Nugent, *View to Vision: British Watercolours from Sandby to Turner at the Whitworth Art Gallery*, exh. cat., Whitworth Art Gallery and Museum, Manchester, 1993

MARSHALL 1980
Douglas Marshall, 'Military Maps of the Eighteenth Century and the Tower of London Drawing Room', *Imago Mundi*, 32, 1980, pp. 21–44

MASON 1783
William Mason, *The English Garden: A Poem*, London, 1783

MAYHEW 2000
Robert J. Mayhew, *Enlightenment Geography: The Political Languages of British Geography, 1650–1850*, Basingstoke, 2000

MICHELL 1765
Richard Michell, *Hackwood Park: A Poem*, Portsmouth, 1765

MILLAR 1969
Oliver Millar, *Later Georgian Pictures in the Collection of Her Majesty The Queen*, 2 vols, London, 1969

MILLER 1988
David P. Miller, '"My favourite studdys": Lord Bute as Naturalist', in Karl W. Schweizer (ed.), *Lord Bute: Essays in Reinterpretation, Leicester*, 1988, pp. 213–39

MOORE 1883
Cecil Moore, *A Brief History of St George's Chapel*, London, 1883

NEW DESCRIPTION 1749
A New Description of Bedfordshire, London, 1749

NOTTINGHAM 1884
G. Harry Wallis, *Catalogue of the Special Exhibition in the Water Colour Gallery of Drawings and Pictures by Thomas Sandby, R.A., and Paul Sandby, R.A.*, exh. cat., Nottingham Castle, 1884

NOTTINGHAM 1986
The Painters' Progress: The Life and Times of Thomas and Paul Sandby, exh. cat., Nottingham Castle Museum, 1986

NOTTINGHAM 1990
Nicholas Alfrey and Stephen Daniels (eds), *Mapping the Landscape*, exh. cat., University Art Gallery, Nottingham Castle Museum, 1990

NUNEHAM 1806
Description of Nuneham-Courtenay, in the Country of Oxford, London, 1806

OGBORN 1998
Miles Ogborn, *Spaces of Modernity: London's Geographies 1680–1780*, London, 1998

OPPÉ 1947
A. P. Oppé, *The Drawings of Paul and Thomas Sandby in the Collection of His Majesty The King at Windsor Castle*, London, 1947

OPPÉ 1950
A. P. Oppé, 'Supplement', *English Drawings, Stuart and Georgian Periods, in the Collection of His Majesty The King*, London, 1950

PARIS 1947
H. J. Paris, 'English Watercolour Painters', in W. J. Turner (ed.), *Aspects of British Art*, London, 1947

PASMORE 1979
Stephen Pasmore, 'Rural Scenes of Bayswater: The London of Paul Sandby, 1725–1809', *Country Life*, 1 March 1979, pp. 586–87

PASQUIN 1796
Anthony Pasquin [John Williams], *Memoirs of the Royal Academicians; Being an Attempt to Improve the National Taste*, London, 1796

PAULSON 1993
Ronald Paulson, *Hogarth*, vol. 3: *Art and Politics, 1750–1764*, New Brunswick and London, 1993

PAWSON 1977
Eric Pawson, *Transport and Economy: The Turnpike Roads of Eighteenth-century Britain*, London, 1977

PELTZ 1999
Lucy Peltz, 'The Extra-illustration of London: The Gendered Spaces and Practices of Antiquarianism in the Late Eighteenth Century', in Lucy Peltz and Martin Myrone (eds), *Producing the Past: Aspects of Antiquarian Culture and Practice, 1700–1850*, Aldershot, 1999, pp. 115–34

PENNANT 1772
Thomas Pennant, *A Tour in Scotland*, London, 1772

PENNANT 1774
Thomas Pennant, *A Tour of Scotland and Voyage to the Hebrides*, Chester, 1774

PENNANT 1778
Thomas Pennant, *A Tour in Wales*, 2 vols, Chester, 1778

PHILLIPS 1964
Hugh Phillips, *Mid-Georgian London*, London, 1964

POCOCKE 1888
The Travels through England of Dr Richard Pococke, James Joel Cartwright (ed.), 2 vols, London, 1888

POSTLE 1991
Martin Postle, 'The St Martin's Lane Academy: True and False Records', *Apollo*, 134, July 1991, pp. 33–38

POTE 1751, 1763, 1764, 1785
[Joseph Pote], *Les Délices de Windsore: or, a pocket companion to Windsor Castle; and the country adjacent*, London, various editions: 1751, 1763, 1764, 1785

POTT 1782
Joseph Holden Pott, *An Essay on Landscape*, London, 1782

PRICE 1794
Uvedale Price, *An Essay on the Picturesque*, London, 1794

PUBLIC CHARACTERS 1801
'Mr Paul Sandby', *Public Characters of 1800–1801*, Dublin, 1801, pp. 461–67

PYE 1775
J. Henrietta Pye, *A Peep into the Principal Seats and Gardens at and about Twickenham*, London, 1775

RAEBURN, VORONIKHINA AND NURNBERG 1995
Michael Raeburn, Ludmila Voronikhina and Andrew Nurnberg (eds), *The Green Frog Service*, London, 1995

RAMSDEN 1947
E. H. Ramsden, 'The Sandby Brothers in London', *Burlington Magazine*, 89, January 1947, pp. 15–19

READING 1972
Eric J. Stanford, *Paintings and Drawings by Thomas and Paul Sandby*, exh. cat., Reading Museum and Art Gallery and Bolton Museum and Art Gallery, 1972

REDGRAVE 1866
Richard Redgrave, *A Century of Painters of the English School*, 2 vols, London, 1866

REYNOLDS 1975
Joshua Reynolds, *Discourses on Art*, Robert R. Wark (ed.), New Haven and London, 1975

RICHMOND 2007
Matthew Hargraves, *Great British Watercolours from the Paul Mellon Collection*, exh. cat., Virginia Museum of Fine Arts, Richmond, State Hermitage Museum, St Petersburg, Yale Center for British Art, New Haven, 2007–08

RIDDELSDELL 1905
H. J. Riddelsdell, 'Journal of a Botanical Tour to Wales', *The Journal of Botany*, 43, 1905, pp. 290–370

ROBERTS 1997
Jane Roberts, *Royal Landscape: The Gardens and Parks of Windsor*, New Haven and London, 1997

ROBERTSON 1984
Bruce Robertson, 'In at the Birth of British Historical Landscape Painting', *Turner Studies*, 4, 1, 1984, pp. 44–46

ROBERTSON 1986
Bruce Robertson, 'Venit, vidit, depinxit: The Military Artist in America', in Edward Nygren (ed.), *Views and Visions: American Landscape before 1830*, exh. cat., Wadsworth Atheneum, Hartford, 1986, pp. 83–104

ROBERTSON 1987
Bruce Robertson, 'Paul Sandby and the Early Development of English Watercolor', unpublished PhD thesis, Yale University, 1987

ROY 1785
William Roy, 'An Account of the Measurement of a Base on Hounslow-Heath', *Philosophical Transactions of the Royal Society of London*, 75, 1785, pp. 385–480

ROY 1793
William Roy, *The Military Antiquities of the Romans in North Britain*, London, 1793

RUSSELL 1995
Gillian Russell, *The Theatres of War: Performance, Politics, and Society 1793–1815*, Oxford, 1995

SALWAY 1996
Peter Salway, 'The Society of Antiquaries Prints of Stanton Harcourt, Oxfordshire', *The Antiquaries Journal*, 76, 1996, pp. 269–75

SANDBY LECTURES
Thomas Sandby, 'Six Lectures on Architecture. Delivered to the Royal Academy', Royal Institute of British Architects, London, written and first delivered *c.* 1769–70

SANDBY 1811
[Thomas Paul Sandby], 'Memoirs of the Late Paul Sandby Esqre, R.A.', *The Monthly Magazine*, 213, June 1811, p. 437

SANDBY 1892
William Sandby, *Thomas and Paul Sandby: Royal Academicians*, London, 1892

SAVAGE 2001
Nicholas Savage, 'Exhibiting Architecture: Strategies of Representation in English Architectural Exhibition Drawings, 1760–1836', in London 2001, pp. 201–16

SEARLE 1930
Mark Searle, *Turnpikes and Toll-Bars*, 2 vols, London, 1930

SENTIMENTAL EXCURSIONS 1781
Sentimental Excursions to Windsor and Other Places, London, 1781

SEWARD 1811
Anna Seward, *The Letters of Anna Seward: Written between the Years 1784 and 1807*, Archibald Constantine (ed.), 6 vols, Edinburgh, 1811

SHANES 2008
Eric Shanes, 'More Art on the Line: The Royal Academy's Antique Room in the Exhibition of 1792', *Burlington Magazine*, 110, April 2008, pp. 224–31

SHESGREEN 2002
Sean Shesgreen, *The Image of the Outcast: The Urban Poor in the Cries of London*, Manchester, 2002

SKELTON 1967
R. A. Skelton, *The Military Survey of Scotland, 1747–1755*, Edinburgh, 1967

SMILES 1994
Sam Smiles, *The Image of Antiquity: Ancient Britain and the Romantic Imagination*, New Haven and London, 1994

SMILES 2000
Sam Smiles, *Eye Witness: Artists and Visual Documentation in Britain, 1770–1830*, Aldershot, 2000

SMITH 1779
George Smith, *An Universal Military Dictionary*, London, 1779

SMITH 1829
John Thomas Smith, *Nollekens and His Times*, London, 1829

SMITH 1998
Greg Smith, *The Thackeray Gift: Eighteenth-Century Watercolours in the Royal Academy of Arts Library*, London, 1998

SMITH 2001
Greg Smith, 'Watercolourists and Watercolours at the Royal Academy, 1780–1836', in London 2001, pp. 189–200

SMITH 2002
Greg Smith, *The Emergence of the Professional Watercolourist: Contentions and Alliances in the Artistic Domain, 1760–1824*, Aldershot, 2002

SNOWDON 1770
Letters from Snowdon, London, 1770

SOLKIN 1993
David Solkin, *Painting for Money: The Visual Arts and the Public Sphere in Eighteenth-century England*, New Haven and London, 1993

STEPHENS AND GEORGE 1870–1954
F. G. Stephens and M. D. George, *Catalogue of Political and Personal Satires ... in the British Museum to 1832*, 12 vols, London, 1870–1954

STYLES 2007
John Styles, *The Dress of the People: Everyday Fashion in Eighteenth-century England*, New Haven and London, 2007

SYDNEY 1998
Malcolm Warner and Julia Marciari Alexander, *This Other Eden: Paintings from the Yale Center for British Art*, exh. cat., Art Gallery of New South Wales, Sydney, Queensland Art Gallery, Brisbane, and Art Gallery of South Australia, Adelaide, 1998

THORNBURY 1873–78
George Walter Thornbury, *Old and New London: Illustrated. A Narrative of Its History, People and Places*, 6 vols, London, 1873–78; vol. 5, Edward Walford (ed.), pp. 11–188

TOWNSHEND 1776
[George Townshend], *Rules and Orders of the Royal Military Academy*, London, 1776

VAUGHAN 1990
William Vaughan, 'The Englishness of British Art', *Oxford Art Journal*, 13, 2, 1990, pp. 11–23

VIRTUOSI'S MUSEUM 1778
The Virtuosi's Museum; Containing Select Views, in England, Scotland, and Ireland, London, 1778

WALPOLE 1765–71
Horace Walpole, *Anecdotes of Painting in England, with some account of the principal artists, London*, 4 vols, London, 1765–71

WALPOLE 1937–83
The Yale Edition of Horace Walpole's Correspondence, W. S. Lewis (ed.), 48 vols, New Haven and London, 1937–83

WEISER 2003
Brian Weiser, *Charles II and the Politics of Access*, Woodbridge, 2003

WILTON 2006
Andrew Wilton, *Turner as Draughtsman*, Aldershot, 2006

WINDSOR AND ITS ENVIRONS 1778
Windsor and its Environs, London, 1778

WOODWARD 1796
George Mouton Woodward, *Eccentric Excursions or, Literary & Pictorial Sketches of Countenance, Character & Country, in different parts of England & South Wales*, London, 1796

WORSLEY 1991
Giles Worsley, *Architectural Drawings of the Regency Period 1790–1837. From the Drawings Collection of the Royal Institute of British Architects*, London, 1991

WRIGHT 1824
T. Wright, *Some Account of the Life of Richard Wilson, Esq., R.A.*, London, 1824

WYNDHAM 1781
Henry Penruddocke Wyndham, *A Tour through Monmouthshire and Wales*, Salisbury, 1781

YALE 1985
Bruce Robertson, *The Art of Paul Sandby*, exh. cat., Yale Center for British Art, New Haven, 1985

YALE 1989
Fairest Isle: The Appreciation of British Scenery, 1750–1850, New Haven, 1989

YALE 2001
Scott Wilcox, Gillian Forrester, Morna O'Neill and Kim Sloan, *The Line of Beauty: British Drawings and Watercolours of the Eighteenth Century*, exh. cat., Yale Center for British Art, New Haven, 2001

YALE 2006A
Charles Beddington, *Canaletto in England*, exh. cat., Yale Center for British Art, New Haven, 2006

YALE 2006B
Theresa Fairbanks Harris, Scott Wilcox et al., *Papermaking and the Art of Watercolour in Eighteenth-century Britain: Paul Sandby and the Whatman Paper Mill*, exh. cat., Yale Center for British Art, New Haven, 2006

YALE 2007
John Baskett et al., *Paul Mellon's Legacy: A Passion for British Art*, exh. cat., Yale Center for British Art, New Haven, and Royal Academy of Arts, London, 2007–08

YOUNG 1770
Arthur Young, *A Six Month Tour through the North of England*, 3 vols, Dublin, 1770

YOUNGSON 1988
A. J. Youngson, *The Making of Classical Edinburgh, 1750–1840*, Edinburgh, 1966 (1988)

YRUBSLIPS 1794
Francis Yrubslips [Francis Spilsbury], *The Art of Etching and Aquatinting*, London, 1794

Selected Exhibitions

2007

Matthew Hargraves, *Great British Watercolours from the Paul Mellon Collection*, Virginia Museum of Fine Arts, Richmond, State Hermitage Museum, St Petersburg, Yale Center for British Art, New Haven, 2007–08

John Baskett et al., *Paul Mellon's Legacy: A Passion for British Art*, Yale Center for British Art, New Haven, and Royal Academy of Arts, London, 2007–08

2006

Theresa Fairbanks Harris and Scott Wilcox et al., *Papermaking and the Art of Watercolour in Eighteenth-century Britain: Paul Sandby and the Whatman Paper Mill*, Yale Center for British Art, New Haven, 2006

2004

Jane Roberts and Christopher Lloyd, *George III and Queen Charlotte: Patronage, Collecting and Court Taste*, Queen's Gallery, London, 2004

2003

David Dewing (ed.), *Home and Garden: Paintings and Drawings of English Middle-class Urban Domestic Spaces, 1675 to 1914*, Geffrye Museum, London, 2003

Sheila O'Connell, Roy Porter, Celina Fox and Ralph Hyde, *London 1753*, British Museum, London, 2003

2002

Greg Smith, *Thomas Girtin: The Art of Watercolour*, Tate, London, 2002

2001

Scott Wilcox et al., *The Line of Beauty: British Drawings and Watercolours of the Eighteenth Century*, Yale Center for British Art, New Haven, 2001

David Solkin, *Art on the Line: The Royal Academy Exhibitions at Somerset House, 1780–1836*, Courtauld Institute Gallery, London, 2001–02

2000

Kim Sloan, *'A Noble Art': Amateur Artists and Drawing Masters, c. 1600–1800*, British Museum, London, 2000

1999

The Draughtsman's Art: Master Drawings from the National Gallery of Scotland, National Gallery of Art, Edinburgh, 1999

1998

Malcolm Warner and Julia Marciari Alexander, *This Other Eden: Paintings from the Yale Center for British Art*, Art Gallery of New South Wales, Sydney, Queensland Art Gallery, Brisbane, and Art Gallery of South Australia, Adelaide, 1998

1995

Jane Roberts, *Views of Windsor: Watercolours by Thomas and Paul Sandby*, Rijksmuseum, Amsterdam, Portland Art Museum, Oregon, Dixon Gallery and Gardens, Memphis, Dallas Museum of Art and Whitworth Art Gallery, Manchester, 1995–97

1993

Andrew Wilton and Anne Lyles, *The Great Age of British Watercolours, 1750–1880*, Royal Academy of Arts, London, and National Gallery of Art, Washington DC, 1993

1991

Yolande Hodson, *Map Making in the Tower of London: Ordnance Survey's Early Years*, Tower of London, 1991

1990

Nicholas Alfrey and Stephen Daniels, *Mapping the Landscape*, University Art Gallery, Nottingham Castle Museum, 1990

Treasures of Prints and Drawings, British Museum, London, 1990

Fairest Isle: The Appreciation of British Scenery, 1750–1870, Yale Center for British Art, New Haven, 1989

1986

The Painters' Progress: The Life and Times of Thomas and Paul Sandby, Nottingham Castle Museum, 1986

Luke Herrmann, *Paul and Thomas Sandby*, Victoria and Albert Museum, London, 1986

1985

Lindsay Stainton, *British Landscape Watercolours, 1600–1860*, British Museum, London, 1985

Bruce Robertson, *The Art of Paul Sandby*, Yale Center for British Art, New Haven, 1985

1981

Julian Faigan, *Paul Sandby Drawings*, City of Hamilton Art Gallery, Art Gallery of South Australia, Adelaide, National Gallery of Victoria, Melbourne, and Art Gallery of New South Wales, Sydney, 1981–82

1978

James Holloway and Lindsay Errington, *The Discovery of Scotland: The Appreciation of Scottish Scenery through Two Centuries of Painting*, National Gallery of Scotland, Edinburgh, 1798

1977

Yolande O'Donoghue, *William Roy 1726–1790: Pioneer of the Ordnance Survey*, British Museum, London, 1977

1973

Leslie Parris, *Landscape in Britain, c. 1750–1850*, Tate, London, 1973

1972

Eric Stanford, *Paintings and Drawings by Thomas and Paul Sandby*, Reading Museum and Art Gallery and Bolton Museum and Art Gallery, 1972

1963

Treasures of the Royal Academy, Royal Academy of Arts, London, 1963

1960

J. L. Howgego, *Paul Sandby, 1725–1809*, Guildhall Art Gallery, London, 1960

1884

G. Harry Wallis, *Drawings and Pictures by Thomas Sandby, R.A., and Paul Sandby, R.A.*, Nottingham Castle, 1884

Lenders to the Exhibition

Her Majesty The Queen

Aberystwyth, National Library of Wales
Birmingham Museum and Art Gallery
Cardiff, National Museum of Wales
Edinburgh, National Galleries of Scotland
Edinburgh, National Library of Scotland
Glasgow, Hunterian Museum and Art Gallery
London, British Library
London, British Museum
London, Guildhall
London, Royal Academy of Arts
London, Royal Collection
London, Royal Library
London, Tate
London, Victoria and Albert Museum
New Haven, Yale Center for British Art
Nottingham City Museums and Galleries

and others who wish to remain anonymous

Photographic Acknowledgements

All works of art are reproduced by kind permission of the owners. Specific acknowledgements are as follows:

Aberystwyth, by permission of the Llyfrgell Genadlaethol Cymru/National Library of Wales: cat. 9, fig. 48
Birmingham, reproduced with the permission of Birmingham Libraries and Archives: fig. 43
Bloomington, courtesy the Lilly Library, Indiana University: fig. 38
© The Bridgeman Art Library: fig. 46
Roy Fox: cats 67, 84, 85
Keith Hunter: cats 72, 89–91, front cover
London, © The British Library Board: cats 6–8, 13, 14, figs 22, 24–26, 32, 34, pp. 96–7
London, © The Trustees of the British Museum: cats 1, 20–32, 52–54, 75, figs 6, 8, 14, 15, 17, 18, 28, 36, 37, 39, 41, pp. 38, 120–1, back flap
London, © Museum of London: fig. 9
London, National Archives UK: fig. 47
London, © Royal Academy of Arts: cat. 76 (left); photo Prudence Cuming Associates Ltd: figs 12, 28; photo J. Hammond: fig. 13, p. 28; photo M. Slingsby: cats 73, 74, pp. 10–11, 56
London, The Royal Collection © Her Majesty Queen Elizabeth II: cats 3–5, 34, 49, 55, 56, 59–62, 65, 66, 77, 78, 80–83, 95, 99, figs 10, 19, 20, 33, 42, pp. 72–3, 152–3, 164–5, 188–9
London, Society of Antiquaries of London/photo Roy Fox: cats 68, 69
London, © Tate 2009: p. 9
London, V&A Images/Victoria and Albert Museum: cats 2, 48, 101
Courtesy of Sotheby's Picture Library: fig. 40

Index

All references are to page numbers; those in **bold** type indicate catalogue plates, and those in *italic* type indicate essay illustrations.

Benefactors of the Royal Academy of Arts

ROYAL ACADEMY TRUST

Major benefactors

The Trustees of the Royal Academy Trust are grateful to all its donors for their continued loyalty and generosity. They would like to extend their thanks to all those who have made a significant commitment, past and present, to the galleries, the exhibitions, the conservation of the Permanent Collection, the Library collections, the Royal Academy Schools, the education programme and other specific appeals.

HM The Queen
Her Majesty's Government
The 29th May 1961 Charitable Trust
Barclays Bank
BAT Industries plc
The late Tom Bendhem
The late Brenda M Benwell-Lejeune
British Telecom
John and Susan Burns
Mr Raymond M Burton CBE
Sir Trevor Chinn CVO and Lady Chinn
The Trustees of the Clore Foundation
The John S Cohen Foundation
Sir Harry and Lady Djangoly
The Dulverton Trust
Alfred Dunhill Limited
The John Ellerman Foundation
The Eranda Foundation
Ernst & Young
Esso UK plc
The Foundation for Sports and the Arts
Friends of the Royal Academy
John Frye Bourne
Jacqueline and Michael Gee
Glaxo Holdings plc
Diane and Guilford Glazer
Mr and Mrs Jack Goldhill
Maurice and Laurence Goldman
Mr and Mrs Jocelin Harris
The Philip and Pauline Harris Charitable Trust
The Charles Hayward Foundation
Robin Heller Moss
Heritage Lottery Fund
The Malcolm Hewitt Wiener Foundation
IBM United Kingdom Limited
The Idlewild Trust
The JP Jacobs Charitable Trust
Lord and Lady Jacobs
The Japan Foundation
Gabrielle Jungels-Winkler Foundation
Mr and Mrs Donald Kahn
The Lillian Jean Kaplan Foundation
The Kresge Foundation
The Samuel H Kress Foundation
The Kirby Laing Foundation
The Lankelly Foundation
The late Mr John S Latsis
The Leverhulme Trust
Lex Service plc
The Linbury Trust
Sir Sydney Lipworth QC and Lady Lipworth
John Lyons Charity
Ronald and Rita McAulay
McKinsey and Company Inc
John Madejski OBE DL
The Manifold Trust
Marks and Spencer
The Mercers' Company
The Monument Trust
The Henry Moore Foundation
The Moorgate Trust Fund
Mr and Mrs Minoru Mori
Museums and Galleries Improvement Fund
National Westminster Bank
Stavros S Niarchos
The Peacock Charitable Trust
The Pennycress Trust
PF Charitable Trust
The Pidem Fund
The Pilgrim Trust
The Edith and Ferdinand Porjes Trust
The Porter Foundation
John Porter Charitable Trust
Rio Tinto
John A Roberts FRIBA
Simon and Virginia Robertson
The Ronson Foundation
The Rose Foundation
Rothmans International plc
Dame Jillian Sackler DBE
Jillian and Arthur M Sackler
Mrs Jean Sainsbury
The Saison Foundation
The Basil Samuel Charitable Trust
Mrs Coral Samuel CBE
Sea Containers Ltd
Shell UK Limited
Miss Dasha Shenkman
William and Maureen Shenkman
The Archie Sherman Charitable Trust
Sir Hugh Sykes DL
Sir Anthony and Lady Tennant
Ware and Edythe Travelstead
The Trusthouse Charitable Foundation
The Douglas Turner Trust
Unilever plc
The Weldon UK Charitable Trust
The Welton Foundation
The Weston Family
The Maurice Wohl Charitable Foundation
The Wolfson Foundation
and others who wish to remain anonymous

PATRONS

The Royal Academy is delighted to thank all its Patrons for generously supporting the following areas over the past year: exhibitions, education, the Royal Academy Schools, the Permanent Collection and Library, and Anglo-American initiatives; and for assisting in the general upkeep of the Academy.

Platinum
Mrs Allen
Mr and Mrs John Coombe
Mr and Mrs Patrick Doherty
Mrs Helena Frost
Lady Getty
Janicke and Leif Höegh
Mr Frederik Paulsen
Mr and Mrs David Shalit

Gold
Sir Ronald Cohen
The Cowley Foundation
Michael and Morven Heller
Anya Hindmarch
Mr and Mrs Ronald Lubner
Prof and Mrs Anthony Mellows
Lady Jane Rayne
Inna Vainshtock
Mr and Dr Winkler

Silver
Mrs Leslie Bacon
Mrs Gary Brass
Mrs Elie Brihi
Mrs Debbie Burks
Sir Charles and Lady Chadwyck-Healey
Sir Trevor Chinn CVO and Lady Chinn
John C L Cox CBE
Miss Ellison
Benita and Gerald Fogel
Mr and Mrs Eric Franck
Jaqueline and Jonathan Gestetner
Patricia and John Glasswell
Lady Gosling
Margarita Hernandez
Mr and Mrs Alan Hobart
Mr and Mrs Jon Hunt
S Isern-Feliu
Mrs Raymonde Jay
Mr Nand Khemka and Princess Jeet Nabha Khemka
Mrs Aboudi Kosta
Lady Lever of Manchester
Mark and Liza Loveday
Mr and Mrs Richard Martin
The Mulberry Trust
Mr and Mrs D J Peacock
The Lady Henrietta St George
Mr and Mrs Schneer
Mr and Mrs Kevin Senior
The Countess of Shaftesbury
Mrs Stella Shawzin
Richard and Veronica Simmons
Sir James and Lady Spooner
Mrs Elyane Stilling
John and Sheila Stoller
Sir Hugh Sykes DL

Bronze
Agnew's
Mr Peter Allinson
Mrs Marina Atwater
Jane Barker
Stephen Barry Charitable Settlement
James M Bartos
The Duke of Beaufort
Mrs J K M Bentley/Summers Art Gallery
Mr Michael Bradfield
Mr Charles Brett
Miss Deborah Brett
Mr Edward Brett
Mr Ernest Brett
Mr James Brett
Mr Paul Brett
Mrs Charles Brocklebank
Jeremy Brown
Lord Browne of Madingley
Mrs Alan Campbell-Johnson
Mr F A A Carnwath CBE
Jean and Eric Cass
Mrs Vivien Chappell
Mr and Mrs George Coelho
Denise Cohen Charitable Trust
Mrs Cathy Corbett
Mr and Mrs Sidney Corob
Julian Darley and Helga Sands
The Countess of Dartmouth
Mr Davis and Ms Roboz
Peter and Andrea de Haan
The de Laszlo Foundation
Mrs Norah de Vigier
Ms Davina Dickson
Mrs Dobell-Wood
Dr Anne Dornhorst
Lord Douro
Sir Philip Dowson CBE PPRA and Lady Dowson
Mr and Mrs Maurice Dwek
Mr Eddis
Lord and Lady Egremont
Mary Fedden RA
Bryan Ferry
Mrs Donatella Flick
Mrs George Fokschaner
Lord and Lady Foley
Mrs Jocelyn Fox
Mr Monty Freedman
Arnold Fulton
Mark Glatman
Mrs Godwin
Mrs Val Gooding
Nicholas and Judith Goodison
Piers and Rosie Gough
David and Lesley Haynes
Mr Mark Hendriksen
Mr and Mrs Christoph Henkel
Ms Joanna Hewitt
Mrs Jasmine Horowitz
Mrs Pauline Hyde
Mrs Sabine Israel
Sir Martin and Lady Jacomb
Harold and Valerie Joels
Fiona Johnstone
Mrs Joseph
Dr Elisabeth Kehoe
Mr and Mrs James Kirkman
Mr Leon Krayer
Norman A Kurland and Deborah A David
Joan H Lavender
Mr George Lengvari and Mrs Inez Lengvari
Miss R Lomax-Simpson
The Marquess of Lothian
Mr and Mrs Henry Lumley
Miss Jane McAusland
Gillian McIntosh
Andrew and Judith McKinna
Mr and Mrs Magan
Sally and Donald Main
Mr and Mrs Eskandar Maleki
Mr Michael Manser RA and Mrs Jose Manser
Mr Marcus Margulies
Zvi and Ofra Meitar Family Fund
Mrs Carole Meyers
Mrs Diana Mocatta
Mrs Alan Morgan
Dr Ann Naylor
Ann Norman-Butler
North Street Trust
Mr Michael Palin
John H Pattisson
Mr Philip Perry
Mrs Eve Pilkington
Mr and Mrs Anthony Pitt-Rivers
John and Anne Raisman
Mrs Jenifer Rosenberg
Lord Rothschild
Mrs Sirkka Sanderson
H M Sassoon Charitable Trust
Carol Sellars
Dr Lewis Sevitt
Major General and Mrs Shaw
Mr James B Sherwood
Mr David Shovel
Mrs Lesley Silver
Mrs Silverton
Alan and Marianna Simpson
Mr and Mrs Mark Franklin Slaughter
Mr Smith
Brian D Smith
Mr and Mrs David T Smith
Lord Sterling of Plaistow
Mrs D Susman
Lord and Lady Taylor
Miss M L Ulfane
Mr Georg von Opel
John and Carol Wates
Mrs Weinstock
Edna and Willard Weiss
Anthony and Rachel Williams
and others who wish to remain anonymous

BENEFACTOR PATRONS

The Peter Boizot Foundation
Mr and Mrs William Brake
Mrs Mary Graves
Mrs Sue Hammerson
Mr D H Killick
The Lord Marks of Broughton
Sir Anthony and Lady Tennant

BENJAMIN WEST GROUP PATRONS

Chairman
Lady Judge

Gold
Lady J Lloyd Adamson

Silver
Wendy Becker Payton
Mrs Adrian Bowden
Mr and Mrs Paul Collins
Kim Dunn
Charles and Kaaren Hale
Lady Judge
Scott and Christine Morrissey
Mr and Mrs John R Olsen
Frank and Anne Sixt

Bronze
Ms Ruth Anderson
Mrs Alan Artus
Tom and Diane Berger
Wendy Brooks and Tim Medland
Debra Cajrati Crivelli
Mr and Mrs Gunnar L Engstrom
Mrs Clare Flanagan
Cyril and Christine Freedman
Mr Andrew Hawkins
Suzanne and Michael Johnson
Charles G Lubar
Mr and Mrs Patrick Mahon
Neil Osborn and Holly Smith
Ms Theresa A Parker
Lady Purves
Mr and Mrs K M Rubie
Sylvia Scheuer
Mr and Mrs Thomas Schoch
Carole Turner Record
Frederick and Kathryn Uhde
Mr and Mrs Ullmo
Mr John D Winter
Mary Wolridge
and others who wish to remain anonymous

SCHOOLS PATRONS GROUP

Chairman
John Entwistle OBE

Platinum
Campbell Rigg
Matthew and Sian Westerman

Gold
Mr and Mrs Paul Myners

Silver
Lord and Lady Aldington
John Entwistle OBE
Philip Marsden

Bronze
Mrs Inge Borg Scott
Ian and Tessa Ferguson
Prof Ken Howard RA and Mrs Howard
Julia Fuller
Peter Rice
Anthony and Sally Salz
Mr Ray Treen
and others who wish to remain anonymous

CONTEMPORARY PATRONS GROUP

Chairman
Susie Allen

Patrons
Tarek Aguizy
Viscountess Bridgeman
Alla Broeksmit
Dr Elaine C Buck
Jenny Christensson
Helen and Colin David
Belinda de Gaudemar
Chris and Angie Drake
Lissa Engle
Ms Soma Ghosh
Caroline Hansberry
Mrs Susan Hayden
Penelope Mather
Barbara Pansadoro
Mr Andres Recoder and Mrs Isabelle Schiavi
Richard and Susan Shoylekov
John Tackaberry
Inna Vainshtock
Dr Yvonne von Egidy-Winkler
Cathy Wills
Mary Wolridge
and others who wish to remain anonymous

TRUSTS AND FOUNDATIONS

The Atlas Fund
The Ove Arup Foundation
Aurelius Charitable Trust
The Peter Boizot Foundation
The Bomonty Charitable Trust
The Charlotte Bonham-Carter Charitable Trust
William Brake Charitable Trust
The Britten-Pears Foundation
R M Burton 1998 Charitable Trust
C H K Charities Limited
P H G Cadbury Charitable Trust
The Carew Pole Charitable Trust
The Carlton House Charitable Trust
The Clore Duffield Foundation
The Coexist Foundation
John S Cohen Foundation
The Ernest Cook Trust
The Sidney and Elizabeth Corob Charitable Trust
The Coutts Charitable Trust
Alan Cristea Gallery
The de Laszlo Foundation
The D'Oyly Carte Charitable Trust
The Dovehouse Trust
The Gilbert and Eileen Edgar Foundation
The Eranda Foundation
Lucy Mary Ewing Charitable Trust
The Fenton Arts Trust
The Margery Fish Charity
The Flow Foundation
Gatsby Charitable Foundation
Goethe Institut London
The Golden Bottle Trust
The Great Britain Sasakawa Foundation
Sue Hammerson Charitable Trust
The Charles Hayward Foundation
The Hellenic Foundation
Heritage Lottery Fund
A D Hill 1985 Discretionary Settlement
The Harold Hyam Wingate Foundation
Institut fuer Auslandsbeziehungen e.V.

The Japan Foundation
Stanley Thomas Johnson Foundation
The Emmanuel Kaye Foundation
The Kindersley Foundation
The Kobler Trust
Lapada Association of Art & Antique Dealers
Lark Trust
The David Lean Foundation
The Leche Trust
A G Leventis Foundation
The Leverhulme Trust
The Lynn Foundation
The Maccabaeans
The McCorquodale Charitable Trust
Mactaggart Third Fund
The Simon Marks Charitable Trust
The Marsh Christian Trust
Martineau Family Charity
The Paul Mellon Centre
The Paul Mellon Estate
The Mercers' Company
Margaret and Richard Merrell Foundation
The Millichope Foundation
The Henry Moore Foundation
The Mulberry Trust
The National Manuscripts Conservation Trust
The J Y Nelson Charitable Trust
Newby Trust Limited
OAK Foundation Denmark
The Old Broad Street Charity Trust
The Peacock Charitable Trust
The Pennycress Trust
PF Charitable Trust
The Stanley Picker Charitable Trust
The Pidem Fund
The Edith and Ferdinand Porjes Charitable Trust
The Fletcher Priest Trust
The Privy Purse Charitable Trust
Pro Helvetia
Mr and Mrs J A Pye's Charitable Settlement
The Radcliffe Trust
Rayne Foundation
T Rippon & Sons (Holdings) Ltd
The Rose Foundation
Schroder Charity Trust
The Sellars Charitable Trust
The Archie Sherman Charitable Trust
The South Square Trust
Spencer Charitable Trust
Stanley Foundation Limited
Oliver Stanley Charitable Trust
The Steel Charitable Trust
Peter Storrs Trust
Strand Parishes Trust
The Joseph Strong Frazer Trust
The Swan Trust
Swiss Cultural Fund in Britain
Thaw Charitable Trust
Sir Jules Thorn Charitable Trust
Tiffany & Co
Tillotson Bradbery Charitable Trust
The Albert Van den Bergh Charitable Trust
The Bruce Wake Charity
Celia Walker Art Foundation
Warburg Pincus International LLC
Weinstock Fund
Wilkinson Eyre Architects
The Spencer Wills Trust
The Maurice Wohl Charitable Foundation
The Wolfson Foundation
The Hazel M Wood Charitable Trust
The Worshipful Company of Painter-Stainers

AMERICAN ASSOCIATES OF THE ROYAL ACADEMY TRUST

Burlington House Trust
Mr and Mrs James C Slaughter

Benjamin West Society
Mr Francis Finlay
Mrs Deborah Loeb Brice
Mrs Nancy B Negley

Benefactors
Mrs Edmond J Safra
Mr and Mrs Albert H Small
The Hon John C Whitehead
Mr and Mrs Frederick B Whittemore

Sponsors
Mrs Drue Heinz HON DBE
David Hockney CH RA
Mr Arthur L Loeb
Mrs Lucy F McGrath
Mr and Mrs Hamish Maxwell
Diane A Nixon
Mr Arthur O Sulzberger and Ms Allison S Cowles
Mr Vernon Taylor Jr

Patrons
Mr and Mrs Steven Ausnit
Mr Donald A Best
Mrs Mildred C Brinn
Mrs Benjamin Coates
Anne S Davidson
Ms Zita Davisson
Mr and Mrs Stanley De Forest Scott
Mrs June Dyson
Mr and Mrs Lawrence S Friedland
Mr and Mrs Leslie Garfield
Ms Helen Harting Abell
Dr Bruce C Horten
The Hon W Eugene Johnston and Mrs Johnston
Mr William W Karatz
Mr and Mrs Wilson Nolen
Lady Renwick
Congressman Frederick W Richmond
Mr and Mrs Peter M Sacerdote
Mrs Mary Sharp Cronson
Mrs Frederick M Stafford
Ms Louisa Stude Sarofim
Ms Joan Stern
Martin J Sullivan OBE
Dr and Mrs Robert D Wickham
Mr Robert W Wilson

Donors
Mr James C Armstrong
Mr Constantin R Boden
Dr and Mrs Robert Bookchin
Mrs Edgar H Brenner
Mr and Mrs Philip Carroll
Laura Christman and William Rothacker
Mr Richard C Colyear
Mr and Mrs Howard Davis
Mrs Beverley C Duer
Mr Robert H Enslow
Mr Ralph A Fields
Mrs Katherine D Findlay
Mr and Mrs Christopher Forbes
Mr and Mrs Gordon P Getty
Mr O D Harrison Jr
Mr and Mrs Gustave M Hauser
Mrs Judith Heath
Ms Elaine Kend
Mr and Mrs Nicholas L S Kirkbride
Mr and Mrs Gary Kraut
The Hon Samuel K Lessey Jr
Mr Henry S Lynn Jr
Ms Clare E McKeon
Ms Christine Mainwaring-Samwell
Ms Barbara T Missett
The Hon William Nitze and Mrs Nitze
Mrs Charles W Olson III
Cynthia Hazen Polsky and Leon B Polsky
Mrs Patsy Preston
Mrs Nanette Ross
Mrs Martin Slifka
Mrs Judith Villard
Mr and Mrs William B Warren

Corporate And Foundation Support
American International Group, Inc.
Annenberg Foundation
Bechtel Foundation
The Blackstone Charitable Foundation
The Brown Foundation
Fortnum & Mason
Gibson, Dunn & Crutcher
The Horace W Goldsmith Foundation
Hauser Foundation
Leon Levy Foundation
Loeb Foundation
Henry Luce Foundation
Lynberg & Watkins
Sony Corporation of America
Starr Foundation
Thaw Charitable Trust

CORPORATE MEMBERS OF THE ROYAL ACADEMY

Launched in 1988, the Royal Academy's Corporate Membership Scheme has proved highly successful. Corporate membership offers benefits for staff, clients and community partners and access to the Academy's facilities and resources. The outstanding support we receive from companies via the scheme is vital to the continuing success of the Academy and we thank all members for their valuable support and continued enthusiasm.

Premier Level Members
A T Kearney
Accenture
The Arts Club
The Bank of New York Mellon
Booz & Company
CB Richard Ellis
Deutsche Bank AG
Ernst & Young LLP
GlaxoSmithKline plc
Goldman Sachs International
Hay Group
HSBC plc
JTI
Kleinwort Benson Private Bank
LECG Ltd
Lombard Odier Darier Hentsch
Northern Trust
Schroders plc
Smith and Williamson
Standard Chartered

Corporate Members
All Nippon Airways
Apax Partners
BGC Brokers L P
BNP Paribas
The Boston Consulting Group
Bovis Lend Lease Limited
British American Business Inc.
British American Tobacco
Calyon
Canon
Capital International Limited
Christie's
Citi
Clifford Chance
Concateno Plc
Control Risk Group
Curzon Partnership LLP
F & C Asset Management plc
GAM
Heidrick & Struggles
Insight Investment
ITV plc
John Lewis Partnership
JP Morgan
KPMG
Lazard
London College of Fashion
Man Group plc
Mizuho International plc
Momart Limited
Morgan Stanley
Navigant Consulting
Nedrailways
Novo Nordisk
Pentland Group plc
Rio Tinto
The Royal Society of Chemistry
Skadden, Arps, Slate, Meagher & Flom
Slaughter and May
Société Générale
Timothy Sammons Ltd
Trowers & Hamlins
Veredus Executive Resourcing
Weil, Gotshal & Manges

SPONSORS OF PAST EXHIBITIONS

The President and Council of the Royal Academy would like to thank the following sponsors and benefactors for their generous support of major exhibitions in the last ten years:

2009
J. W. Waterhouse: The Modern Pre-Raphaelite
Champagne Perrier-Jouët
GasTerra
Gasunie
241st Summer Exhibition
Insight Investment
Kuniyoshi. From the Arthur R. Miller Collection
Canon
Travel partner: Cox & Kings
Premiums and RA Schools Show
Mizuho International plc
RA Outreach Programme
Deutsche Bank AG
Sackler Wing of Galleries 2009–2013 Season supported by JTI

2008
GSK Contemporary
GlaxoSmithKline
Byzantium 330–1453
J. F. Costopoulos Foundation
A. G. Leventis Foundation
Stavros Niarchos Foundation
Travel Partner: Cox & Kings
Miró, Calder, Giacometti, Braque: Aimé Maeght and His Artists
BNP Paribas
Vilhelm Hammershøi: The Poetry of Silence
OAK Foundation Denmark
Novo Nordisk
240th Summer Exhibition
Insight Investment
Premiums and RA Schools Show
Mizuho International plc
RA Outreach Programme
Deutsche Bank AG
From Russia: French and Russian Master Paintings 1870–1925 from Moscow and St Petersburg
E.ON
2008 Season supported by Sotheby's

2007
Paul Mellon's Legacy: A Passion for British Art
The Bank of New York Mellon
Georg Baselitz
Eurohypo AG
239th Summer Exhibition
Insight Investment
Impressionists by the Sea
Farrow & Ball
Premiums and RA Schools Show
Mizuho International plc
RA Outreach Programme
Deutsche Bank AG
The Unknown Monet
Bank of America

2006
238th Summer Exhibition
Insight Investment
Chola: Sacred Bronzes of Southern India
Travel Partner: Cox & Kings
Premiums and RA Schools Show
Mizuho International plc
RA Outreach Programme
Deutsche Bank AG
Rodin
Ernst & Young

2005
China: The Three Emperors, 1662–1795
Goldman Sachs International
Impressionism Abroad: Boston and French Painting
Fidelity Foundation
Matisse, His Art and His Textiles: The Fabric of Dreams
Farrow & Ball
Premiums and RA Schools Show
The Guardian
Mizuho International plc
Turks: A Journey of a Thousand Years, 600–1600
Akkök Group of Companies
Aygaz
Corus
Garanti Bank
Lassa Tyres

2004
236th Summer Exhibition
A. T. Kearney
Ancient Art to Post-Impressionism: Masterpieces from the Ny Carlsberg Glyptotek, Copenhagen
Carlsberg UK Ltd
Danske Bank
Novo Nordisk
The Art of Philip Guston (1913–1980)
American Associates of the Royal Academy Trust
The Art of William Nicholson
RA Exhibition Patrons Group
Vuillard: From Post-Impressionist to Modern Master
RA Exhibition Patrons Group

2003
235th Summer Exhibition
A. T. Kearney
Ernst Ludwig Kirchner: The Dresden and Berlin Years
RA Exhibition Patrons Group
Giorgio Armani: A Retrospective
American Express
Mercedes-Benz
Illuminating the Renaissance: The Triumph of Flemish Manuscript Painting in Europe
American Associates of the Royal Academy Trust
Virginia and Simon Robertson
Masterpieces from Dresden
ABN AMRO
Classic FM
Premiums and RA Schools Show
Walker Morris
Pre-Raphaelite and Other Masters: The Andrew Lloyd Webber Collection
Christie's
Classic FM
UBS Wealth Management

2002
234th Summer Exhibition
A. T. Kearney
Aztecs
British American Tobacco
Mexico Tourism Board
Pemex
Virginia and Simon Robertson
Masters of Colour: Derain to Kandinsky. Masterpieces from The Merzbacher Collection
Classic FM
Premiums and RA Schools Show
Debenhams Retail plc
*RA Outreach Programme**
Yakult UK Ltd
Return of the Buddha: The Qingzhou Discoveries
RA Exhibition Patrons Group

2001
233rd Summer Exhibition
A. T. Kearney
Botticelli's Dante: The Drawings for Dante's Divine Comedy
RA Exhibition Patrons Group
The Dawn of the Floating World (1650–1765). Early Ukiyo-e Treasures from the Museum of Fine Arts, Boston
Fidelity Foundation
Forty Years in Print: The Curwen Studio and Royal Academicians
Game International Limited
Frank Auerbach, Paintings and Drawings 1954–2001
International Asset Management
Ingres to Matisse: Masterpieces of French Painting
Barclays
Paris: Capital of the Arts 1900–1968
BBC Radio 3
Merrill Lynch
Premiums and RA Schools Show
Debenhams Retail plc
*RA Outreach Programme**
Yakult UK Ltd
Rembrandt's Women
Reed Elsevier plc

2000
1900: Art at the Crossroads
Cantor Fitzgerald
The Daily Telegraph
232nd Summer Exhibition
A. T. Kearney
Apocalypse: Beauty and Horror in Contemporary Art
Eyestorm
The Independent
Time Out
Chardin 1699–1779
RA Exhibition Patrons Group
The Genius of Rome 1592–1623
Credit Suisse First Boston
Premiums and RA Schools Show
Debenhams Retail plc
*RA Outreach Programme**
Yakult UK Ltd
The Scottish Colourists 1900–1930
Chase Fleming Asset Management

*Recipients of a Pairing Scheme Award, managed by Arts + Business. Arts + Business is funded by the Arts Council of England and the Department for Culture, Media and Sport

OTHER SPONSORS

Sponsors of events, publications and other items in the past five years:

Carlisle Group plc
Castello di Reschio
Country Life
Guy Dawson
Derwent Valley Holdings plc
Dresdner Kleinwort Wasserstein
Lucy Flemming McGrath
Fosters and Partners
Goldman Sachs International
Gome International
Gucci Group
Hines
IBJ International plc
John Doyle Construction
Harvey and Allison McGrath
Martin Krajewski
Marks & Spencer
Michael Hopkins & Partners
Morgan Stanley Dean Witter
Prada
Radisson Edwardian Hotels
Richard and Ruth Rogers
Rob van Helden
Warburg Pincus
The Wine Studio